ISBN: 9781407772073

Published by:
HardPress Publishing
8345 NW 66TH ST #2561
MIAMI FL 33166-2626

Email: info@hardpress.net
Web: http://www.hardpress.net

THE
BRITISH NATURE BOOK

BOOKS BY S. N. SEDGWICK

NATURE BOOKS.

The Young People's Nature Study Book.
The Young People's Microscope Book.
The Holiday Nature Book.
In Nature's Nursery.
Nature's Nursery Tales.

The "How to Identify" Series:—
Birds' Eggs and Nests.
Butterflies.
Moths of the Months.
Seaside Wonders.
Beetles and Spiders.
(*Charles Kelly, 25-35 City Road, E.C.*)

NOVELS.

The Last Persecution. (*Grant Richards.*)
The Master of the Commandery. (*Books, Ltd.*)
Caliban Island. " "
Petronilla. (*Geo. Newnes, Ltd.*)

RELIGIOUS BOOKS.

The Romance of Precious Bibles. (*Bagster.*)
The Story of the Apocrypha. (*S.P.C.K.*)
The Catechism with Blackboard and Chart. (*Mowbray.*) Etc., etc.

THE BRITISH NATURE BOOK

A COMPLETE HANDBOOK AND GUIDE TO BRITISH NATURE STUDY, EMBRACING THE MAMMALS, BIRDS, REPTILES, FISH, INSECTS, PLANTS, ETC., IN THE UNITED KINGDOM

By S. N. SEDGWICK

FULLY ILLUSTRATED

London: T. C. & E. C. JACK, Ltd.
35 PATERNOSTER ROW, E.C.
AND EDINBURGH
1922

GH137
84

CONTENTS.

INTRODUCTORY.

"In the Beginning" 1
Some Necessary Apparatus for the Naturalist 6

Part I.—THE ANIMAL WORLD.

Section I.—VERTEBRATES.

I. BRITISH MAMMALS 21
   Cetacea—Whales and Porpoises 22
   Insectivora ("Insect-eaters") 26
   Cheiroptera ("Hand-winged")—Bats 30
   Carnivora ("Flesh-eaters") 32
   Rodentia ("Gnawing Mammals")—Hares, Rabbits, etc. . . . 39
   Ungulata ("Hoofed Mammals")—Deer, Wild Cattle, Sheep, and Goats 46

II. BIRDS 51
   Classification of Birds 55
   How to observe Birds 58
   Guide to British Birds 59
      I. Birds about the Size of a Sparrow 68

III. BIRDS (continued) 99
   II. Birds about the Size of a Blackbird 99
   III. Birds about the Size of a Wood Pigeon 112
   IV. Birds about the Size of a Rook 126
   How to attract the Birds 139
   How to identify Nests and Eggs 140

IV. REPTILES 143
   Lacertilia—Lizards 143
   Ophidia—Snakes 145

CONTENTS

V. AMPHIBIANS: FROGS, TOADS, AND NEWTS 147

VI. FISHES 150
    FRESH-WATER FISHES 151
    SALT-WATER FISHES 157

SECTION II.—INVERTEBRATES.

VII. ARTHROPODA 164
    I. CRUSTACEA—Fresh-water Crustacea 165
        Marine Crustaceans 166
    II. ARACHNIDA—Scorpions, Spiders, Mites, etc. 171
    III. MYRIAPODA—Centipedes 180
    IV. INSECTS 181
        I. APTERA—Bristle-tails, etc. 182
        II. DERMAPTERA—Earwigs 182
        III. ORTHOPTERA—Cockroaches, Grasshoppers, Crickets . . 183
        IV. PLECOPTERA—Stone-flies 184
        V. ISOPTERA—White Ant 185
        VI. CORRODENTIA—Book-lice, Bird-lice 185
        VII. EPHEMEROPTERA—Mayflies 185
        VIII. ODONATA—Dragon-flies 185
        IX. THYSANOPTERA—Thrips 186
        X. HEMIPTERA—Bugs, Aphides, etc. 186
        XI. ANOPLURA—True Lice 189
        XII. NEUROPTERA—Alder-flies, Lacewings 189

VIII. ARTHROPODA (CONTINUED) 191
    XIII. COLEOPTERA—Beetles 191
    XIV. MECOPTERA—Scorpion-flies 217
    XV. TRICHOPTERA—Caddis-flies 217

IX. ARTHROPODA (CONTINUED) 218
    XVI. LEPIDOPTERA—Butterflies and Moths 218
        British Butterflies: List of Species 224
        British Moths 237

X. ARTHROPODA (CONTINUED) 287
    XVII. DIPTERA ("Two-winged" Insects) 287
    XVIII. SIPHONAPTERA—Fleas 289
    XIX. HYMENOPTERA—Saw-flies, Wood-wasps, Ichneumons, Ants,
        Hornets, Wasps, Bees 289

CONTENTS

XI. MOLLUSCA ("SHELLFISH")	300
CUTTLE-FISH, ETC.	302
SNAILS AND SLUGS	303
FRESH-WATER MOLLUSCS	306
MARINE SHELLS	307
Univalves	307
Bivalves	310
XII. ECHINODERMATA	314
STARFISHES	314
SEA URCHINS	316
XIII. POLYZOA—ANNELIDA—PLATYHELMINTHES	318
POLYZOA—Sea Mats, etc.	318
ANNELIDA—Worms, Leeches, etc.	319
PLATYHELMINTHES—Flatworms	321
XIV. CŒLENTERATA	322
JELLY-FISH, ETC.	322
SEA ANEMONES	324
CORALS	325
XV. PORIFERA AND PROTOZOA	327
PORIFERA—Sponges	327
PROTOZOA—Animalcules	328

PART II.—THE VEGETABLE WORLD.

I. INTRODUCTORY	333
HOW TO DRY PLANTS	334
THE GENERAL STRUCTURE OF PLANTS	334
EXPLANATION OF THE LISTS	338
II. PHANEROGAMIA—FLOWERING AND SEED-BEARING PLANTS	341
ALPHABETICAL LIST OF FLOWERS—ENGLISH	437
,, ,, ,, LATIN	442
III. PTERIDOPHYTA	447
FERNS	447
CLUB-MOSSES AND HORSE-TAILS	451

CONTENTS

IV. BRYOPHYTA	453
Mosses	453
V. THALLOPHYTA	456
Fungi	456
Seaweeds	465

APPENDIX.

SOME WILD PETS I HAVE KNOWN.

No. 1. Paddy, the Otter	470
No. 2. Vicky, the Fox	472
No. 3. Joeee, the Starling	474
No. 4. Mr. Spines, the Hedgehog	477
No. 5. "Young Wisdom," the Little Owl	479
INDEX	481

LIST OF PLATES.
(FOR TEXT ILLUSTRATIONS SEE INDEX.)

	Facing page
I.—1. Hedgehog (basking); 2. Mole; 3. Water Vole; 4. Hedgehog	28
II.—1. The Otter at play; 2. Long-eared Bat; 3. Squirrels; 4. A Tame Otter	32
III.—1. Weasel; 2. Foxes; 3. Badger; 4. Rabbit	36
IV.—1. Short-eared Bats; 2. Bat, showing Structure of the Wings; 3. Common Mouse; 4. Old English Rat	40
V.—1. Common Rat; 2. House Mice; 3. Field Mouse in Nest; 4. Shrew	44
VI.—1. The Stoat; 2. Red Deer in Snow; 3. Skeleton of Mouse (found in an old piano); 4. Rabbit fostered by Cat	48
VII.—1. Common Curlew; 2. Snipe, with Eggs just hatching; 3. Wood Pigeon; 4. Song Thrushes	84
VIII.—1. Stone Curlew; 2. Green Plover; 3. Common Buzzard; 4. Tree Pipit	112
IX.—1. A Starling's Box; 2. "Starling Castle"; 3. Blackbird's Nest in Bucket; 4. Robin's Nest in a Tea-caddy	136
X.—Representative British Birds' Eggs	140
XI.—Representative British Birds' Eggs	140
XII.—1. Common Lizard; 2. Edible Snail; 3. Blind-worm; 4. Grass Snake	144
XIII.—1. Minnows and Sticklebacks; 2. Crayfish, with Eggs; 3. Adder; 4. Foraminifera	152
XIV.—1. Marine Zoophyte (*Coryne vaginata*); 2. Tube of Ship-worm; 3. Angular Crab; 4. Cuttle-fish, showing upper and under sides	164
XV.—1. Web of *Epeira callophylla*, covered with dew; 2. Spider guarding Eggs; 3. Commencing the Web; 4. Garden Spider in Web	168
XVI.—1. Garden Spider (upper side); 2. Garden Spider (under side); 3. House Spider; 4. Wolf Spider	172
XVII.—Some Representative British Spiders	176
XVIII.—1. "Money-spinner" or "Harvester"; 2. Hydra, budding (enlarged); 3. Water Flea (enlarged); 4. Millipede (enlarged)	180
XIX.—1. Head of Cockroach (from behind); 2. Front view; 3. "Cuckoo Spit"; 4. Aphides on a Rosebud	184

LIST OF PLATES

Facing page

XX.—1. A Spring-tail (*Papirius*); 2. Cockroaches; 3. Silver Lady (*Lepisma saccharina*); 4. Stag Beetle in defensive attitude . 188

XXI.—Representative British Beetles 192

XXII.—Representative British Beetles 197

XXIII.—Representative British Beetles 205

XXIV.—Representative British Beetles 209

XXV.—Representative British Butterflies 224

XXVI.—1. Black Hair-streak; 2. Camberwell Beauty; 3. Swallow-tail Butterfly, newly emerged; 4. Small Garden White Butterflies at sunrise 232

XXVII.—1. Vapourer Moths: Male, Female, and Eggs; 2. Lichenaria: Larvæ feeding; 3. Larvæ of Peacock Butterfly; 4. Pupa of Swallow-tail Butterfly 240

XXVIII.—1. Pupa of Purple Emperor; 2. Larva and Pupa of Black Hair-streak; 3. Five-plumed Moth; 4. Larva of Privet Hawk Moth 248

XXIX.—1. Pupa of Holly Blue Butterfly (*in situ*); 2. Death's-Head Moth; 3. Pupa of Orange-tip Butterfly; 4. Orange-tip, emerging . 256

XXX.—Representative British Moths 264

XXXI.—Representative British Moths 272

XXXII.—1. Protective Cases of Caddis-worms; 2. Great Ox Gad-fly; 3. Crane-fly (" Daddy-long-legs "); 4. Forest-fly; 5. Sheep-tick or " Ked "; 6. Rose leaves mutilated by Leaf-cutting Bee; 7. Female Leaf-cutting Bee, with eleven pieces of leaf . 288

XXXIII.—1. Hornet, Giant-tailed Wasp, and Common Wasp; 2. Humble Bees and their mimics; 3. Male Winged Ant; 4. Wood Ant (Worker); 5. Meadow Ant (Queen newly emerged, with wings still folded) 292

XXXIV.—Nest of Black Ant, showing Queen, Workers, etc. 294

XXXV.—1. Mason Bee's Nest in a Door Lock; 2. Hive Worker Bees with Queen; 3. First Stage of Wasp Nest; 4. Humble Bee's Nest . 296

XXXVI.—1. Dragon-fly; 2. Ichneumon Fly, emerged from Pupa of Swallow-tail Butterfly; 3. Pupa of Dragon-fly; 4. Glow-worms; 5. Ichneumon Flies, emerged from Magpie Moth Pupæ . . 298

XXXVII.—Marine Shells and Sea Anemones 308

XXXVIII.—Marine Shells 312

XXXIX.—1. Section of Spine of Sea Urchin; 2. Brittle Starfish; 3. Jaws of Brittle Starfish; 4. Part of Palate of Whelk, showing " Teeth " 316

XL.—Seaweeds and Annelida 320

AUTHOR'S NOTE

It must be obvious to every Nature student that in writing such a book as this the author must be very largely a compiler, and I desire, at the outset, to acknowledge the very great debt that I owe to the writings of many experts and specialists in the various branches of British Natural History referred to in the following pages.

Amongst many others, I would name with gratitude the following: Lydekker's *Mammals*, Sir Harry Johnston's *British Mammals*, Kirkman's *British Birds*, R. South's *British Butterflies and Moths*, Kirby's volumes on the same subject, Bastin's *Insects*, Bentham's *Flora*, Johns's *Flowers of the Field*, Hulme's *Familiar Wild Flowers*, etc., etc.

S. N. S.

BISHOPSTOKE,
April, 1921.

THE BRITISH NATURE BOOK

INTRODUCTORY.

"In the Beginning."

MANY years ago a famous book was written—*Madame How and Lady Why*: it was an attempt to answer many of the questions which arise in a child's mind concerning the things round about him.

Sooner or later, similar questions are bound to arise in the mind of every one who loves to observe Nature; but the biggest of all is the old, old question, concerning which wise men of all ages have written, and thought, and spent their labour—" Where did the life which we see round about us come from ? " or, as the query frames itself in the mind of a little child, " Who made the flower, the butterfly, the fox ? "

There has never been any answer except that contained in the first verse of the first chapter of the first book in that sacred library which we call the Bible—

" IN THE BEGINNING GOD CREATED THE HEAVEN AND THE EARTH."

Now most of the grown-up folks who have reached middle life were taught when they were children that what follows after that grand statement in the first few chapters of Genesis was literally true, and that God made the world and all that is in it, one thing after another, in six days, as a man might set himself to make toys. So we were taught that all this was as much a piece of actual history as the building of Eddystone Lighthouse, or the making of the first phonograph.

To-day we know better, and though we still believe that " in the beginning God created the heaven and the earth," we have learned that the story that follows is a wonderful parable or allegory—a story told originally, ages ago, and perhaps in words far less beautiful, by the bygone ancestors of the Jewish race—people who, compared with the present generation, were but children, knowing nothing of science or history, nothing of geology or biology. Age by age, this ancient story was repeated by story-tellers round camp-fires, or round sacred trees in villages and hamlets, until unknown men, inspired by

2   THE BRITISH NATURE BOOK

God, as we believe our great poets and thinkers to be inspired, turned it into the form of the immortal story which to-day we call the story of Adam and Eve. It seemed to them that they had found certain high thoughts about God: where they had come from, or how they came into their minds, they could not tell; but those thoughts they felt to be true, and so, in telling again the old story of the Creation and the first man and woman, they raised it to be a vehicle to convey these thoughts to others.

If ever you are able to read the Assyrian story of the Creation, you will see the difference between it and the story of Genesis in this respect; yet you will understand that both versions come from some still older story.

So we understand to-day that the books of the Old Testament were never intended to teach us science or history; but they help us to see what science cannot tell us. They show us that man is far more than an animal—that he has a spiritual character; that he is, in fact, a soul; and therefore there is something in him that reaches out after a knowledge of other things besides those that lie within the compass of his five senses—after a knowledge of God and the things of God—after that spiritual realm to which the best part of him belongs.

The Bible is the record, then, from the human side, of the reaching out of man's mind and soul after these things—it is, we also believe, far more than that: a record of how God has reached out after man's love—and not a science primer, or a history book.

From this point of view it is as valuable as it was before, and indeed more valuable: for instead of having to criticize and explain its imperfect science and history, we can leave them alone altogether, and see how it helps us to realize that higher life, and the relation of man to God, which those old story-tellers felt was true when they told the great tales of the first few chapters of Genesis.

Naturally, living as they did in times that we should call barbarous and uncivilized, compared with the present day, they could not put their thoughts into such words as a great thinker or poet would use in the twentieth century. They clothed their thoughts in very simple forms. They made them into tales, just as we often make up tales for little children, knowing that this is the best way to get them to understand things. That also helps to explain the stories of the beginning of the world, and the creation of man; and the proper way to read them to-day is to try to discover what are the lessons which are hidden under their surface. There are many such lessons, and the longer we live the more true we are finding them to be; but the first lesson, and the lesson from which all others start, is contained in the opening words: "In the beginning God created the heaven and the earth."

But though we believe this to be true, it is not long before we have to pass on to another question: "How did He do it?" Here Science steps in and tells us what she has found out after long and laborious investigation. Even now she does not pretend to be able to tell all the story; but she tells

" IN THE BEGINNING "

us as much as she can, and she is still tirelessly searching, and learning, and seeking to know more.

What Science tells us to-day about the answer to the question, " How did God make the world ? " is, and always will be, associated with the name of a famous man, Charles Robert Darwin, born at Shrewsbury in 1809, who died in 1882, and whose tomb is in Westminster Abbey.

In his young days, people who thought about the origin of life felt it was almost impossible to believe the old view that all the forms of life had been specially and separately made by God; they saw how closely related they were; and about some, indeed, they wondered whether they were animals or vegetables. But they could not find any explanation or theory that would agree with the facts. A few very great men went so far as to declare that all the different species had sprung from one another; but even then they could not explain their origin.

After many years of the greatest toil and study, Darwin wrote his book *The Origin of Species*, in which he gave what he believed to be the explanation. He found that men and animals and plants were not specially created as they are, but that these forms of life which we now see have grown out of other forms; and so on back into the past, until there was but one, or at the most a few very simple forms in which life came into this world. And this explanation of the different forms of life growing out of one another is called " Evolution."

His book created a tremendous stir; many people thought it was downright wicked, especially those who had been brought up to believe that the Creation story in Genesis was literally true.

But to-day every one acknowledges that it is the only explanation of life that fits the facts; and that, instead of denying God, it shows us more of His power, wisdom, and glory. So Darwin believed it would, for he ends his book with these words:

" There is grandeur in this view of life, with its several powers, having been originally breathed by the Creator into a few forms, or into one; and that, whilst this planet has gone cycling on according to the fixed law of gravity, from so simple a beginning, endless forms most beautiful and most wonderful have been and are being evolved."

What Darwin discovered was this—that there always has been a great competition between living things, a struggle for life. Watch, for example, the plants growing in a small bed, and see how, if they are left alone, the stronger ones will crowd the others out. That is an illustration of what has always been true of all life. There is not room for everything to live; and therefore those die out which are the least suited to live under the conditions in which they find themselves. But the young ones vary among themselves, and those that vary so as to adapt themselves best to their surroundings are able to survive, while the rest die.

This explanation Darwin called " Natural Selection," but to-day it is known as " the survival of the fittest "; and it helps us to understand why plants and animals of to-day are found so beautifully fitted for the lives they have to lead; and as you study this book, and go on to observe and study Nature, you will be constantly coming across remarkable illustrations of this law of life.

Of course much that Darwin suggested has since been discovered to be untenable. A very great deal more has been discovered in the last forty or fifty years; and if he were with us to-day, he would be the first to acknowledge that while "natural selection" is part of the truth, it is not the whole explanation of the facts.

But now, bearing this explanation in mind, we can go a step farther. How does a baby grow into a man? We know how a house is built, brick by brick being added *from outside;* but a baby grows by a force *from within,* in the same way as a seed becomes a plant. There is a power within the seed, a power of self-creation, so vital and strong that it grows at last into the perfect plant. Now what is true of a single seed or a single baby is equally true of life as a whole. Even the highest forms of life have grown or evolved, during millions of years, from the few simple forms (perhaps only one) into which God "in the beginning" breathed the breath of life. In other words, God put His power of creation into the first living things upon this earth, and ever since it is that power which has gone on working in the world—the power at work in the seed to-day, as in the new-born baby.

We should like to know all the history that lies behind the evolution of the living things on the earth to-day; but that is impossible. Part of it we know; Science is still at work puzzling out the difficulties and problems. By examining and comparing the bodies of living things much has been discovered. Much has been told us by the earth itself as to its past history. The fossils, the buried remains of strange animals and reptiles, the discovery of the traces of prehistoric man—all these things have been pages in the book of knowledge which wise men have learned to read; but much has still to be discovered: the wise man of to-day confesses that "all he knows is that he knows nothing"—there is so much more to learn.

But at least this much can be said to be known: that after a time, in the far-away history of life, the realm of living things divided into two parts— the *Animal* and *Vegetable Kingdoms*. There were, and there still are, living things that are neither animal nor vegetable; some of them are mentioned in this book. But the plants, as a whole, went on evolving in their own way, producing at last the highest possible kind—the tree; and the animals evolved, also, in their own way.

To-day we can divide all animals into two main groups—those that have backbones (*Vertebrates*) and those that have none (*Invertebrates*). No doubt exists to-day that those without backbones came first, and that the others were evolved from them. There are still a few animals left with only traces of a backbone, and they help us to understand how it came to be evolved.

"IN THE BEGINNING"

The simplest creatures with backbones are the fishes; and probably the first creatures with backbones sprang from some other marine animal, perhaps a kind of worm. Later on, some of these backboned animals came ashore, and learned how to breathe the open air instead of the oxygen in water. Instead of gills, these creatures used lungs; instead of fins, they evolved limbs. So from the fish we get the idea of the frog, a creature that is "amphibious"—double-lived, because when young it lives as a fish, when full grown it is an air-breathing animal.

From the amphibia came reptiles—and these are the undoubted ancestors of the birds; but from the amphibia also came the ancestors of man—a wonderful order of creatures which we call mammals—animals that feed their young with milk. The mammals nearest to man are the apes, especially the anthropoid apes, known as gorillas, chimpanzees, orang-utans, and gibbons. It is not true to say that man has descended from the apes; but it is true to say that man and the apes have come from the same far-away ancestors.

No one can say when the first human being was evolved, but we know that tens of thousands of years ago there were human beings of different kinds. Of these, all died out but the one kind best fitted to survive—and from that kind the human race of to-day was derived.

That first type of man was very different from his modern descendants. He was hairy, and had much larger teeth, and no chin, larger muscles and bones, and a head not so developed in front as to-day, and therefore with a lesser brain. None the less, that first type of man was cleverer than the other animals around him. We can still see the bones of the animals, larger and stronger than himself, which he killed for food; and we can see the stone weapons with which he overcame them.

That is the story of how man came to be what he is: it begins with some worm-like animal in the sea—where does it end? There is no end to the story. But if man can be evolved from that lowly form of life, what may not be evolved from man?

The power of God is still working from within; "Creative Evolution" (to give it the name by which it is called to-day) is still going on. Where it will end no one can tell; but one thing is quite clear: all life is divine—every living thing is an expression of the Spirit of God, in whom all things live and move and have their being. We look upon Nature with fresh light, and greater reverence, the more we realize this truth; all life becomes to us a holy and mysterious thing; and as we learn to understand and appreciate Nature round about us, in the gardens and the fields or at the seaside, we take off our shoes from our feet, because round about us, in truth, is holy ground.

[NOTE.—Much of the material in the above is derived from the charming articles by Dr. Saleeby written for *The Children's Encyclopædia* and elsewhere, to which, not for the first time, I am greatly indebted.]

THE BRITISH NATURE BOOK

Some Necessary Apparatus for the Naturalist.

I HAVE written somewhat extensively in *The Young People's Nature Study Book* on sundry simple apparatus for the would-be naturalist; to this I venture to refer any reader who would wish to know how to make a simple "observing glass" or a "naturalist's walking-stick."

In this chapter I deal with an entirely new set of suggestions for those who like making their own instruments, or, like the majority of us to-day, cannot afford to buy expensive articles such as binoculars, microscopes, cameras, and lenses—all of which are great aids to the study of Nature.

One piece of apparatus alone I suggest that a student should buy, and by means of that one instrument he can construct, with very little skill or trouble, both microscope and camera, as well as discover how to increase the utility of the instrument itself. I refer to a cheap pocket telescope.

Before the Great War this instrument could be bought for 6s. 6d. at a house such as Gamage's. It has the advantage of taking up very little room, measuring 6½ inches when closed; it is invaluable for observing birds or animals at a distance, and gives a much higher magnification than any pair of binoculars; while practice will enable its possessor to focus it quickly on any small object. But in addition it can be used, with a very slight alteration, for observing insects and flowers at a distance of two or three feet; it contains an excellent microscope, which can be used either in the fields or on a stand at home; out of it also can be obtained a whole battery of magnifiers for use when necessary, together with a lens which serves as the important part of a simple Nature camera.

Few people realize what a *multum in parvo* a small telescope is; but several of the illustrations in this book (for example, the Camberwell Beauty) were taken with its aid.

For use in the fields, to observe birds or animals, the only disadvantage I know of is the difficulty of steadying it in prolonged observations. If a convenient fence or tree is not at hand on which to support it, a walking-stick is useful if applied in the following manner: A piece of string or a strap is fastened round the right knee, into which the end of the stick is lodged; then the end of the telescope is supported on the top of the stick, at eye-level. This is so simple a dodge that I am surprised that it does not appear to have been known before; at any rate, I have never seen it in print.

It requires a little knack to be able to centre a distant object quickly within the field of the instrument; but practice makes perfect. I find that the quickest way is to hold the telescope to the eye and take a sight along the top of it at the object; then, by slowly tilting up the end in a vertical direction, the object is sure to enter the field of vision.

In order to be quite accurate, and to enable readers to have no difficulty in purchasing a similar instrument to that to which I refer in this chapter, I

A POCKET TELESCOPE

add that my instrument measures when extended just over 17 inches, and the object lens is 1 inch in diameter, or, with the mount, 1¼ inch. It will focus objects fifteen feet away, but no nearer—which is exasperating sometimes, until you discover the dodge by which you can focus objects as near as three feet away.

It is, then, with the expenditure of 6s. 6d. that we are going to provide ourselves with telescope, microscope, camera, etc. Whatever other disbursements are necessary in the making of the accessories will be chiefly a matter of pence only.

Let us begin by taking the telescope to pieces (Fig. 1). It consists of four tubes, three of which slide into the fourth, AB, at the end of which is the object lens. This can be unscrewed, and consists of an achromatic doublet (that is, two lenses, a positive and a negative, in contact with each other). This lens is about 10 inches focus, and can be used, as I shall show, as a photographic lens in a simple Nature camera. If dust gets between the two glasses, they can be taken out of the mount for cleaning purposes by unscrewing the inner ring to be found at the back of the mount. In replacing them, remember that the negative, or diminishing, lens must go behind.

The second tube of the telescope, on being unscrewed, is found to contain

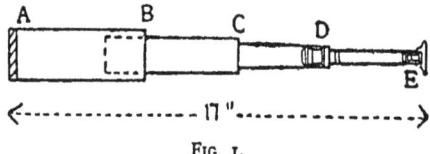

Fig. 1.

a fixed diaphragm, with an opening of ⅝ of an inch. But the third tube, CD, has no such diaphragm. It is, however, an advantage to have one here, when one is using a much higher eyepiece than the normal, and I have added one, made of cardboard, with an aperture of ⅜ of an inch in diameter, which increases the brilliancy and definition of the object.

There was no difficulty in making it. A little cardboard tube an inch long was rolled up and glued together to fit into the end of the tube at C, and a disc of cardboard, with a hole in the middle of the required size, was glued on to the top of it. This diaphragm, then, is removable, being placed in position only when required.

We now come to the last tube, containing the eyepiece of the telescope, and this is the most elaborate part of the instrument. There are four lenses of high magnifying power, contained in two small tubes, of which one is screwed into the bottom end, and the other fits loosely into the other end of the tube DE, the latter being held in position by the cap at E. It will be noticed that between each pair of lenses there is a small fixed diaphragm. Three out of four of these lenses can be used as pocket magnifiers when required. They can easily be used in the hand, held between finger and thumb; but it is not a difficult matter to make a little wooden holder for them, if considered necessary.

This fourth tube, called the "eyepiece," is really a small microscope, the two lower lenses in their mount being the "objective," the two upper ones the true "eyepiece"; and this is the portion we shall use, later on, when we fit up our microscope as a table instrument. Meanwhile, it is a delightful thing to take the tube as it stands into the garden and examine leaves, flowers, and insects with it. Holding it about an inch from the object, you will find that very slight movement to or from the object will bring it into sharp focus. Fig. 3 shows how to hold an object in one hand and the microscope in the other, and get a perfectly steady view—three fingers of the left hand touching the lower edge of the right hand.

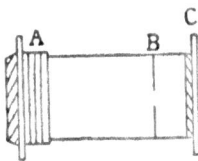

FIG. 2. The objective at D in Fig. 1.

Having thus dissected the telescope, fit it together again, taking care not to force the screwing, or the threads will be destroyed. If you give a light and easy turn to each section, you will find the screws bite almost at once; when the process is complete, do not screw tight home, but use just sufficient pressure to make each screw-joint hold, and that is all.

Now, as pointed out above, these telescopes are excellent for observation of distant objects, but they will not focus anything within fifteen feet of the observer. It must happen often that the Nature student would like to be able to watch insects and other small creatures at a much shorter distance—a spider, for example, at work upon its web, aphides on the rose bushes, bees gathering honey, and so forth. With a very slight addition the telescope can be used upon objects as near as three feet. All that is required is a spectacle lens, placed in front of the object lens A.

The more powerful this additional lens is, the nearer you can get to the object; but there is nothing to be gained by having this lens of a higher power than is actually necessary. I find that a spectacle lens of the power $\times 1$ or $\times 0.5$ is ample. Opticians and spectacle makers have a large number of chipped lenses, which are useless to them, and these can be bought extremely cheaply—I have bought many at the rate of six for a penny—and there will almost certainly be found among them one or more of the strength required. The fact that they are chipped will not matter at all, as, in any case, you will have to take off the edges to make the lens fit. If you have no glazier's diamond, use a pair of pliers, and pinch off the

FIG. 3.

A POCKET TELESCOPE

edges until the lens is a rough circle instead of being oval. Make a little cardboard cap to fit over the object lens. This can be done by taking a strip of brown paper and rolling it round the end of the telescope, gluing it down upon itself, until a ring of sufficient stiffness has been made. (Do not, of course, stick it to the brass.) When dry, stick a circle of cardboard on the top, cutting out of it a hole about $\frac{3}{4}$ of an inch in diameter. On the inside of this cap fasten your spectacle lens. The rough edges of the glass will not show, being hidden behind the overlapping portion of the cap. There, then, is your auxiliary lens, costing a fraction of a penny.

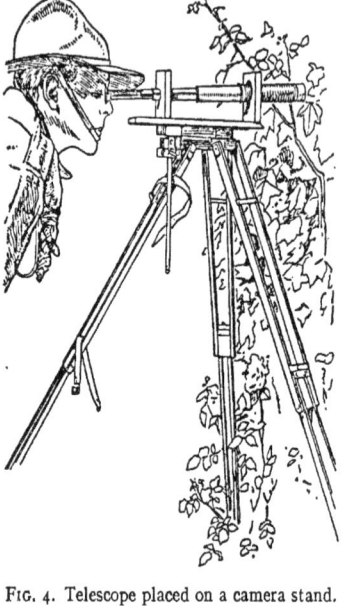

With one of these lenses added to your telescope you can make out the veining upon a leaf, and the stinging hairs of the nettle, at a distance of three feet or so; and you can watch, as I have done, ants milking aphides, as big (apparently) as rats!

When the telescope is thus used it will be found necessary to place it on a stand of some sort, as it cannot be held steadily enough in the hands. If you want to use it in comfort—in the garden, for instance—use a table, or, better still,

FIG. 4. Telescope placed on a camera stand.

a camera stand, placing on the top of it some form of holder. The simplest arrangement in the world will serve; Fig. 4 shows a rough-and-ready method. This has the advantage that the telescope is set independently of the person who is looking through it, and so you may show your friends the particular object at which you have been looking. In the open country, a walking-stick and an elastic band will make a stand sufficiently stable (Fig. 5).

When once the fascination of examining small things in this way has taken hold of you, it will not be long before you crave for still greater magnification. And here, again, another simple and cheap addition will give you what you want: you must add an extra magnifier to the eyepiece at D.

FIG. 5. Telescope fixed to walking-stick.

Purchase, for this purpose, a sixpenny "finder" (Messrs. Houghton and Co. and Butcher and Sons stock them), and take out the lens. This, you will find, will just fit inside the inner tube which is at D; it must be put at the end nearest your eye, close to the diaphragm at E. This will almost double the size of the object at which you are looking.

A Simple Microscope.

We next deal with the use of a portion of the telescope mounted on a stand as a "table" microscope. The illustration (Fig. 6) shows a simple form of stand. As arranged, it possesses several powers of magnification, and its maximum will be found equal to that of an objective of about $\frac{4}{10}$ of an inch.

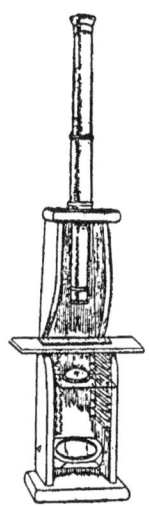

Fig. 6. A home-made microscope stand.

The stand is made of wood, and any one who is handy with a fretsaw can easily make it. The dimensions of the one illustrated are: height, 9 inches; the top board which supports the telescope tubes being 2½ by 3 inches. These dimensions can be varied, of course. The middle stage has a hole in the centre 1 inch in diameter, and is intended to carry the object. In the base is a little mirror—which can be bought for a penny at a Penny Bazaar—mounted on wood, and pivoted so that it can reflect the light upwards through the hole in the object stage.

It will be noticed that under the stage are two sets of cardboard grooves. These are not really necessary, but are intended for a luxury known as a "spot lens" (described below), and also for diaphragms and "tinters."

Diaphragms of various apertures, from ½ to ⅛ inch, are cut in the centre of rectangular black cards, which slide in these grooves when required. Or they may be placed on the object stage, and the object placed above them. I need scarcely add that only one is used at a time; and that its object is to concentrate the light reflected upwards by the mirror upon the object under observation. Actual experiment will show in which pair of grooves the card should be placed for any particular object.

The spot lens consists of a bull's-eye lens on the flat side of which a little disc of black paper is stuck centrally. As various sizes of discs may be required, it is well to "stick with a lick," and not with any more adhesive liquid.

The bull's-eye is placed on a slip of glass which fits these grooves, and the proper distance from the object is found by experiment. The use of this simple spot lens is to obtain what is called "dark-ground" illumination, the effect of which on many objects is to make them appear brilliantly lit on all sides against a background of rich dark velvet. The bull's-eye can be obtained for 2d. from any shop where electric torches are sold; or a cycle shop will

A SIMPLE MICROSCOPE

supply a larger lens, used on many modern cycle lamps, for sums from 1½d. upwards. These cheap lenses answer the purpose perfectly well.

As for the "tinters," these are made of strips of cardboard which fit the grooves; each piece has a hole in the centre about an inch in diameter, and over this is gummed a piece of tinted gelatine, such as may be found on Christmas crackers—red, blue, green, and so forth.

Now let us examine the portion of the telescope used. Notice, first, that the two top tubes are used, and not simply the top tube alone. Unscrew the telescope at C, and make the hole in the top of the wooden stand just large enough to take the screw-piece. There should be no difficulty in identifying this, as it is marked clearly C in the diagram.

The lowest power is obtained by shutting up the top tube DE into the lower one CD. This is just making use of the "eyepiece" of the telescope as it stands.

The second magnification is obtained in the following way: You will remember that when we took the telescope to pieces we found at D a little tube with a powerful lens at each end, and a small diaphragm between.

Here (Fig. 2) is a diagram of that objective. To increase your magnification you must take out this compound lens, unscrew the top lens, marked C in the diagram, and put the rest back in its place. You will now find on focusing your object afresh that it appears at least twice as big as before.

The third magnification is actually shown in the drawing of the microscope. This time you put back your little lens C, and having thus reconstructed your compound lens, you place it, not in its usual position at the end of the first tube, but at the end of the *second* tube, and you open out the two tubes to their farthest length (which is about 9 inches). Notice in the drawing the end of the "objective" just protruding from the bottom tube. It is held there in position by a small tube of cardboard, the edge of which can also be seen. Now examine your object again, and you will have it appearing at least as large again. (I have no means of accurately determining these magnifications, but these are approximate.)

The fourth magnification is obtained by taking off lens C again, and replacing the rest of the objective in the same place at the bottom of the second tube.

This is the greatest magnification obtainable by manipulating the telescope lenses themselves, and will probably suffice most of my readers. But if the extra lens (extracted from the sixpenny finder mentioned above) is dropped into place (as suggested on page 10), you can now get two further magnifications: the first with the whole objective plus your extra lens inside it, the second with the lens at C removed.

You have now no less than six different "powers" or magnifications, and to show the difference between first and last I have experimented with a micro-slide of *Volvox globator*. With the first magnification I could see practically the whole cell full of these minute organisms. With the highest power I could just get three of them into view in the field of vision.

12 THE BRITISH NATURE BOOK

It is hardly necessary to point out how to focus the object. The telescope tubes must be slid downwards towards the object, which is observed all the time through the eyepiece, until it is perfectly sharp and clear. In focusing with both tubes extended, take care to focus with the lower tube, and not the upper.

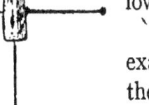

FIG. 7.

A great many objects—perhaps the first to be examined by the young microscopist—are opaque, and therefore cannot be lighted by transmitted light— that is, by light thrown from the mirror below them. Instead, light must be concentrated upon them from above. For this purpose a condenser is necessary, and this, like the rest, is easily and cheaply made.

Figs. 7 and 8 show two roughly made condensers, the lens of which is a bull's-eye, obtained at a cycle shop for a few pence. In Fig. 7 it is shown mounted in a block of wood. The rest of the apparatus consists of a hat-pin, a knitting needle, a cork, and a block of wood. With this the condenser can be moved and rotated vertically or horizontally, and set at any angle, and so will cast the rays of light from a lamp in a concentrated spot upon the object under the microscope. It will be found that the condenser must be two or three inches away from the object. The second form (Fig. 8) shows the lens mounted in a penny candle-shade holder, supported on a rod of wood stuck into a lump of plasticine. It needs no further description.

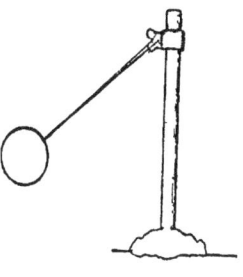

FIG. 8.

A few slips of glass are required upon which to place the objects under observation. These should be 3 inches by 1 inch—the standard size. They can be cut from disused quarter-plates, the glass used in photographic plate manufacture being very thin and free from flaws.

I venture to add that details as to simple mounting and preparing of objects, and all other necessary information as to the use of a simple microscope, can be found in *The Young People's Microscope Book.*

A Simple Nature Camera.

" Buy an 'am and see life," says Kipling's Mr. Pyecraft; and it will appear to some of my grown-up readers as if I were parodying the advice and saying, " Buy a cheap telescope and—see Nature " : for once again I propose to show how to use the " object lens " of the telescope as a photographic lens in a simple home-made camera.

I am not going to pretend that this lens will be of any use for instantaneous photography—though it could be so used, provided it was fitted into an instantaneous shutter ; but as this would involve more expense, I propose that

A NATURE CAMERA

at first, at any rate, the camera shall be used for "time exposures" only. At any future time the camera can be fitted with a more expensive lens and shutter—and that without any alteration; but at first we will be content to use a cap in the old-fashioned way.

I suggest to my younger readers that the camera, fitted as I am about to describe it, will enable them to take photographs of their friends, and that it can be thus made to earn a more efficient lens and shutter. Such a lens and shutter (for example, a Rectilinear or Symmetrical lens of 6-inch focus, in a Unicum shutter) can be bought second-hand, for sums from 10s. upwards, from any of the well-known firms.

In the meantime the camera, with the telescope lens, can be used for a very great many branches of Nature study, especially of "still life" subjects. Nests and eggs, flowers and trees, museum specimens, butterflies, moths, beetles, shells, can all be taken with it; so that it will be a really useful instrument for many purposes of Nature study. What is more, the camera has a fine focusing power, and can be used later on for taking photomicrographs.

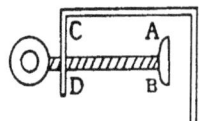

FIG. 9. The cramp as bought.

First of all, a dark slide will be required to hold the plate. A quarter-plate metal dark slide is the best to buy, and will cost, new, 1s. or 1s. 6d. In addition, for focusing purposes you will require a "cramp," which can be bought for a penny at a Penny Bazaar. Fig. 9 shows such a cramp. When bought, prepare it for transformation into a "focusing screw" by cutting off the arms at C and D, and drilling two holes for screws at C, and also at A and B, which mark the cup at the end of the screw. If you have no tools for cutting or drilling the metal, you will find a good-natured blacksmith or a working ironmonger able to do it for you. Fig. 9a shows the result.

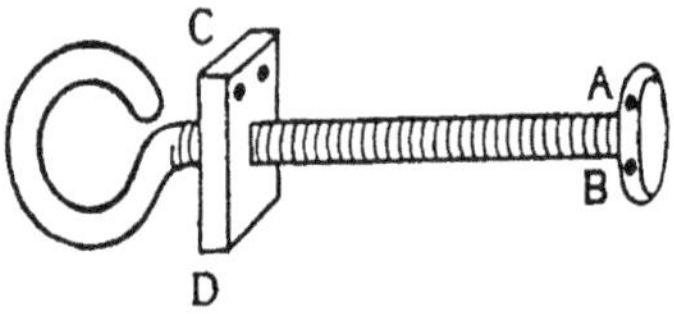

FIG. 9a. The cramp cut for use in camera.

Next, build a box to form the body of the camera—Fig. 10. To the back of this box (AB) the dark slide is to be attached. The latter must run in grooves, which are best made by bending over two strips of zinc and attaching them by screws to two opposite sides. Fig. 11 shows one of these bent strips in position. Glue strips of velvet on to the edge of the wood, to form a light-tight bed on which the dark slide will rest. The length of this camera body is about 4½ inches; the width and depth must depend on the size of your dark slide, and will correspond to its length and width. On the other end of the box is a square opening of about 2½ inches.

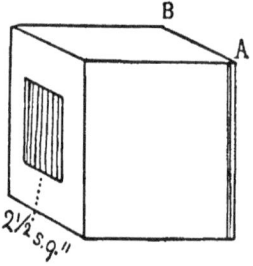

FIG. 10. The camera body.

14 THE BRITISH NATURE BOOK

The next step is to make a base-board and front—Fig. 12. The front (ABCD) is a plain piece of wood, of the same dimensions as the back of the body, allowing for an extra edge by which to join it to the base-board. In the centre is a hole 1 inch in diameter. This is attached, at right angles, to another piece of wood, ½ an inch longer than the camera body, and the same width. On the outer sides (DE and CF) are fixed two slips of wood, to act as runners. If you are clever enough to be able to groove these, so much the better, as then you

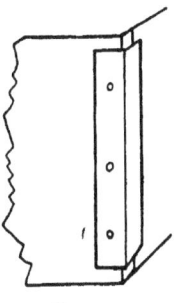
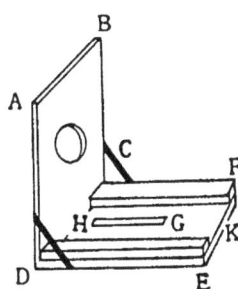

FIG. 11.   FIG. 12. Base-board and front.

will be able to affix corresponding runners to the under side of your camera body, so that it slides to and fro along the base-board. But if you cannot manage the neat grooving, leave the slips of wood plain, and instead cut a narrow slot, 3½ inches long, in the centre of the base-board at GH. Attach the front and base-board together, and strengthen them by two strips of wood or brass, as shown in the diagram at C and D.

Now turn again to the camera body. You have to attach to the under side of it a piece of wood, of the shape shown in Fig. 13. This must be of a width

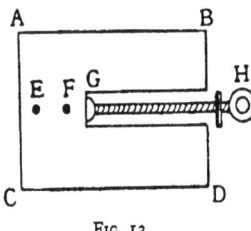
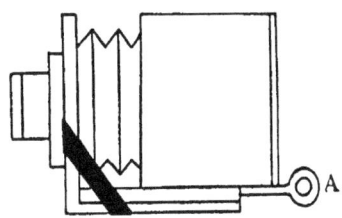

FIG. 13.   FIG. 14. The camera complete.

to fit neatly between the slips of wood on the base-board; its length must be the same as that of the camera body. A rectangular strip is cut out of the centre (GH), and the portion of the cramp which contains the screw is to be fixed there. Note that the cup of the cramp is screwed to the wood at G; the rest is left loose for the moment.

This odd-shaped piece of wood is screwed to the bottom of the camera body, so that the unattached end of the screw juts out below the dark slide (see A in Fig. 14). And you now attach the loose plate (CD in Fig. 9a) to the

A NATURE CAMERA 15

base-board at K (Fig. 12). Now fix two screws, with small washers on them, through the slot in the base-board, into the bottom of the camera body, and you will find that, by turning the finger screw or cramp, your camera body will move in or out along the base-board for some two inches. This will enable you to focus any object you desire when the camera is complete.

The next business is to make a short bellows, to be attached to the camera body and the front.

The simplest way of making this is as follows: Make a box to act as a "mould," about 3½ inches wide by 3 inches deep—the length being immaterial, say 6 inches. The material for the bellows (the covering of an old umbrella will do excellently), 7 inches long by 14 inches wide, is wrapped round the box; there will be an inch to spare, which is glued down upon the cloth it overlaps. The whole then forms a sort of sleeve over the box. Now you require twelve slips of cardboard—stout postcard —cut into the shape of one of the sections in Fig. 15, each ½ an inch wide and 3½ inches long. In addition twelve other similar pieces, 3 inches long, are needed. These are to be glued down upon the material, six on each side, with an interval of ⅛ inch between each piece. Fig. 15 shows the pattern of one side. Then another piece of material the same size as the first is glued down over the whole, and the box is put aside for the glue to get nearly dry. When that is the case, you draw off this "sleeve" and fold in the corners between the cardboard slips; this is a simple process and is quickly accomplished, and has the effect of turning the "sleeve" into a neat, strong bellows, to be attached to the camera body and front.

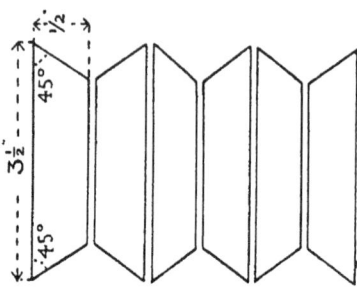

Fig. 15. The bellows.

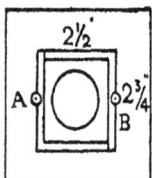

Fig. 16. The lens board.

Fig. 17. Lens panel.

The last business is the making of the lens board. On the outer side of the camera front fix four small slips of wood to enclose a square, in the centre of which is the lens hole, about 2½ inches each way (Fig. 16). Make a panel (Fig. 17) to fit inside this square, to be held in place by two small turn-pins (which can be seen at A and B, in Fig. 16). In the centre of this small panel is another hole, of the same size or a trifle smaller than that in the camera front.

Now you require a wooden pill-box, with a hole (of the same size) in the bottom, which is to be glued or screwed down upon the panel. The lid of the pill-box will act as the cap by means of which you make your exposures.

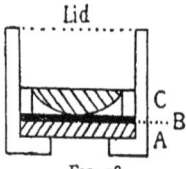

Fig. 18.

Now for the lens. The telescope object lens is of too long a focus to be used as it stands, and you must use with it a spectacle lens to shorten the focus.

Find, among your chipped lenses, one of about × 2.50; this goes at the bottom of your pill-box (A, in Fig. 18). Next comes a circle of black cardboard (B), with a small hole in the centre not more than $\frac{1}{4}$ inch in diameter; put that upon the spectacle lens; and then add your telescope object lens, with the curved side down (the flat surface being nearest the box lid). You will find out how to fix these in position so that you can remove them readily.

All is now complete. But note that the inside of the camera body should be blacked all over; and if any light should show through the corners or joints, this must be stopped out. The outside of the camera can be covered with American cloth, painted or varnished according to taste.

A focusing screen is required at the back; and if you have a metal dark slide of the ordinary pattern, the following is a simple way of making a ground-glass screen: First get a piece of cardboard—stout postcard, about $\frac{1}{18}$ inch— and cut it to the same size as your dark slide, so that it will slide in and out of the grooves at the back of the camera. Obtain a piece of ground glass of the same size. Out of the middle of your cardboard cut a rectangle 4 by 3 inches, and glue the frame that is left upon the ground side of your glass. If you like to make a neat job of it when dry, bind the edges with strips of black lining.

Your camera, if made according to these instructions, will now have a "compound" lens of about 6 inches focal length, and the focusing arrangement will enable you to take photographs of objects as near as two and a half or three feet—a very convenient distance for such subjects as birds' nests or flowers.

If you would wish to photograph smaller objects, to appear a good size on the plate, you must take out your spectacle lens and put in its place a stronger one (× 4.75); this, combined with your telescope object lens, will enable you to photograph objects such as beetles and moths from a few inches away.

It is necessary to have a cardboard disc for such purposes, with a smaller hole than $\frac{1}{4}$ inch. And I should advise your making one with an aperture of $\frac{1}{8}$, and one with $\frac{1}{12}$ of an inch.

As already stated, some of the photographs in this book were taken with this camera.

When you are able to afford a more expensive lens and shutter, all that will be needed is to make a new panel upon which to mount your purchase.

The camera, thus made, focuses at the back. Practically the majority of modern cameras focus by drawing out the front; but, after many years of Nature photography, I have no hesitation in saying that for taking photographs of small objects (and these form the greater part of the living things around us) it is far better to have a camera focusing from the rear. In photographing butterflies, beetles, small flowers, etc., it is necessary to have the camera within a very few inches of the object, and in this case it is very difficult to focus from the front of the camera; but the difficulty vanishes entirely if there is a means of focusing from the back.

A NATURE CAMERA

I need scarcely add that if a camera of longer extension is required, it can be made on the same lines · but instead of a "cramp" costing a penny, a proper "rack and pinion" set of fittings would be required, or what is known as a "focus screw," costing about 5s.

One other advantage of the camera, made as I have described it, is that it is fairly substantial and solid, and will stand a good deal of hard wear.

I do not deal with the question of stands, or the other adjuncts of a photographer's outfit, which belong more properly to a book on photography pure and simple. Nor do I think it necessary here to treat of the subject of bird photography, with its devices for concealing or disguising the camera.

The special object of the camera designed above is rather the photography of "still life": a hobby to which there is no end, and one which, if adopted, will prove of the greatest value to the Nature student—I may add, of great interest to others besides himself, if he is able to turn his pictures into lantern slides.

Those of my readers who are interested in the microscope and desire to take photographs of mounted objects can use this same camera, using, instead of the telescope objective, the other end of the instrument. Either the whole of that portion DE (in the diagram of the telescope) can be used whole, or the little objective which is at D, or half of that objective. No cap is required for making the exposures, but a piece of black cardboard is interposed between the lens and the object, which is removed when the plate is ready for exposure.

For further details on this most fascinating branch of Nature study I must refer readers to *The Young People's Microscope Book*.

PART I.
THE ANIMAL WORLD.

SECTION I.
VERTEBRATES.

CHAPTER I.
British Mammals.

WHAT is an animal? A good many people, grown up as well as young, make the mistake of answering this question by saying that an animal is a four-footed creature. They would not, therefore, call a butterfly or a fish an animal. But the fact is—as any one would know who thought of the Latin from which it is derived—that the word animal applies to every living thing except those of the Vegetable Kingdom, and we have to find some further means of classifying them.

The word Mammal is applied to all air-breathing animals that have warm blood and suckle their young; and of these there are still some fifty to sixty species to be found in Great Britain and its seas.

(i.) Mammals are subdivided into six chief orders: (1) Bats (*Cheiroptera*, "hand-winged"); (2) Hedgehog, mole, shrews (*Insectivora*); (3) Wild cat, fox, pine marten, polecat, stoat, weasel, badger, otter, seals (*Carnivora*); (4) Squirrel, dormouse, rats, mice, voles, hares, rabbits (*Rodentia*); (5) Deer (*Ungulata*); (6) Whales and porpoises (*Cetacea*). These form the highest class in the list of Vertebrates, and are followed by—(ii.) Birds (*Aves*); (iii.) Reptiles (*Reptilia*)—lizards and snakes; (iv.) Frogs, toads, and newts (*Amphibians* and *Batrachians*); (v.) Fishes (*Pisces*). The lowest of all in the scale are lampreys and hag-fishes, the latter to be found off the North Coast of Scotland and in the North Atlantic.

All the above are *Vertebrates*—that is, possess backbones. Whales and porpoises are true mammals, because they bring forth their young alive, and suckle them like any other animal possessing *mammæ*, or teats. Young people, realizing this fact, will not be surprised that these creatures are not included among the fishes, although they live in the sea.

Where did they come from? That is a question which arises sooner or later. Where did the mammals of the British Isles come from?

It is impossible to answer with any certainty; but the following is one of the most probable of scientific theories. In the Secondary Epoch,* Great Britain, instead of being an island, was probably a peninsula attached to the North American continent, and from that direction there came the first primitive types of some of the mammals. In the ages that succeeded, the British Isles became disconnected from the Western Hemisphere as the great oceans were formed, though they were connected for a time with Northern Europe, till finally separated by the shallow sea we now call the Channel. So, in the Tertiary Epoch, Britain received its mammals from Europe; and as the North of Europe, together with Scotland, Ireland, and much of Wales, was at the close of the Tertiary Epoch under ice, the chief mammals were found in the South of England, and, as has been discovered, in East Anglia, at that time joined to Holland and Belgium.

It is known, from remains that have been discovered, that at least 113 different species inhabited the British Isles from the end of the Pliocene Period onwards; but of their descendants only seventy are now to be found, and of these at least fifteen are so rare that they need not be counted. The total number of species within British confines is fifty-seven.

Order: CETACEA—Whales and Porpoises.

The Whales are easily the largest of British mammals.† They were originally land animals, which have become completely adapted to living in water.

* The following are the great epochs into which geologists have divided the past history of the world:—
SECONDARY.—The *Triassic* Period, in which the first Reptiles (*Anomodontia*) and a few Mammals of low type began to appear.
The *Jurassic* Period, when Birds began to originate from Reptiles.
The *Cretaceous*, or Chalk, Period, which was the great age of Reptiles, and when, possibly, some of the later types of Mammals had their first forms.
TERTIARY.—The *Eocene* Period (*Oligocene*), when many of the present-known *orders* of Mammals were first evolved.
The *Miocene* Period, in which the *families* of Mammals developed.
The *Pliocene* Period, in which MAN originated.
The *Pleistocene* Period, when many modern *species* were first distinguished, and Man became established in Great Britain.
QUATERNARY.—The *Prehistoric* Period, in which Neolithic Man lived, and most of our domestic beasts originated.
The *Recent* Period, from somewhere about 7000 B.C. to the present time.
† The following is a list of all the orders of mammals to be found in Great Britain:—
Ungulata: Single-hoofed mammals—example, the Horse.
Ruminantia: Cud chewers—Deer, Cow, Sheep.
Cetacea: Whale-like, including Porpoises and Dolphins.
Pinnipedia: Fin-footed—the Seal.
Carnivora: Flesh-eating—Weasel, Stoat, Cat, Dog, etc.
Rodentia: Gnawing mammals—Rat, Rabbit, Squirrel.
Insectivora: Insect-eating mammals—Shrew, Hedgehog, Mole.
Cheiroptera: Hand-winged—the Bats.
Primates: "Highest" mammals—Man.
This classification is based chiefly on the character and arrangement of the teeth, but also upon the form of the limbs. If you examine your own teeth, you will find that you possess three kinds:

WHALES AND PORPOISES

They depend upon the air for breathing, like any other animal, and would drown if kept below water too long. Some can only stay an hour, others as long as twelve hours, beneath the sea. Once, in the ages long past, they had legs; but of these no vestige remains to-day except some very small fragments of bones to be found in the lower muscles. These are said to be the remains of the thigh and one of the leg bones. Their fore-limbs, or flippers, are really hands—in those species that possess teeth, being five-fingered, whilst in those that have plates of baleen, or whalebone, in place of teeth, they are four-fingered.

Whales are encased in a thick padding of blubber, which serves to keep them warm in Arctic seas, and also acts as a cushion, protecting the body from the pressure of the water when they dive deep. They have no ears, but small holes in the head which answer the same purpose. Some species have one nostril, and others two, through which they breathe. When they exhale the vast bulk of air from their lungs after having been submerged, the moisture from the lungs condenses into vapour, and produces an appearance called "spouting." A whale does not throw up water in a regular fountain, as so many old pictures represent; but just as human breath becomes visible on a frosty morning, their exhalation looks almost like a fountain of spray.

Their food consists of many of the crustaceans—the young of crabs, shrimps,

---

those in front, called incisors, which have a sharp edge; those at the back, which are molars or grinders, because with them we masticate our food; and between them come the sharp-pointed "dog" teeth, or canines. These three kinds are represented in much-modified forms in the other mammals. In the Carnivores—such as the Cat, for instance—the incisors are small, but the canines are very long and pointed, since with these the animal seizes its food. The molars are ill-adapted for grinding, being sharp and pointed. Such mammals cannot "chew" their food, but bolt it in pieces, to be digested after swallowing.

A Ruminant, such as a Cow or Sheep, has good incisors, but only in the lower jaw; they meet upon a pad of gristle in the upper jaw, by means of which the vegetable food is torn; the other teeth are specially formed, as we should expect, for grinding.

Another noticeable difference between Carnivores and Herbivores will be found in the fact that the former can only move their jaw up and down; the latter can move it sideways: the reason is obvious.

The Rodents have an entirely different arrangement of teeth. The incisors are very long and sharp; there are no canines, and but a few smallish molars. The front teeth are specially formed for their work of gnawing, and are kept sharp by actual exercise. If anything happens so that a Rat or Rabbit loses one of its incisors, the consequences are very serious, as the opposite tooth grows, unchecked, and may at last become so big as to prevent the animal from eating at all!

This very general description will serve to suggest to young students the lines upon which they may study the mammals. But in addition, of course, attention must be paid to the formation of the limbs, hoofs, claws, fingers, toes, and so forth. Interesting questions will at once arise, which a little thought will answer, as, for instance: Why does a cat turn its head on one side when eating? Why are a dog's claws blunt, and a cat's not? Why are a rabbit's eyes at the side of its head, and so large and staring?

A collection of the skulls of the smaller mammals and birds is of no small value for purposes of comparison. To prepare a skull—or, for that matter, a skeleton—the specimen should be first skinned. Make an incision from the vent upwards, and press the skin back, so that, if properly done, it comes off like a glove. Open the abdomen and take away as much flesh as possible; and place the body that is left in a vessel of water—in the open air. Here it must remain until the rest of the flesh has decomposed and loosened. Examine it from time to time, and when possible take away, with a small brush, what softer portions you can.

etc.—cuttles, squids, and fish, except in the case of the Grampus, or Killer Whale, which preys upon its own brothers! Whilst some species possess teeth, others have instead plates of whalebone, or baleen; these are plates of thin horny matter, attached to the gum or palate—sometimes more than 300 in number. Their lower edges consist of a fringe of threads acting as a sieve or strainer, through which the water which the whale takes into the mouth passes out, leaving the living organisms which are its food behind.

The whale's method of obtaining its meals is to open its mouth when in the middle of a shoal of tiny crustaceans; then, closing its mouth, it blows out the water through these plates of baleen, while its living food, unable to escape, remains behind to be swallowed through the very narrow gullet. The "Right" Whale's principal food is the small, inch-long mollusc, *Clione limacina*, of a very vivid purple colour.

1. **The Common Porpoise** (*Phocæna communis*) is seldom more than 5 feet in length. This creature, with its blackish back and flippers and its long white waistcoat, is a familiar sight all round the coast, and frequently ascends our British rivers. It breeds in the spring, producing one young one at a birth. Its food consists of fish, usually mackerel or salmon, or other species of that size. Its hide is used for leather, and its blubber makes a valuable oil.

2. **The Grampus**, or COMMON "KILLER" WHALE (*Orca gladiator*), is frequently met with round the British Isles, especially off the East and West of Scotland, and the Shetlands and Orkneys. It may reach a length of 20–30 feet, though the average is smaller. It is very curiously marked, its dark back being enriched with several white patches, and the white of the under parts extends in a curious bay into the black of the sides towards the tail. Its back fin is long and terminates in a sharp, hard point. This mammal is extraordinarily ferocious, attacking and eating porpoises, dolphins, seals, and even the biggest whales.

3. **The Lesser Killer** (*Pseudorca crassidens*) is seldom more than 12 feet in length, and is almost completely black; it is to be met with all over the world. Fossil remains have been found in Lincolnshire, and it is not infrequently met with in the North Sea.

4. **The Black Fish** (*Globicephalus melas*), often called the PILOT WHALE, is well described by its Latin name, being entirely black but for a strip of white beneath the throat, and having a very round-shaped head. It attains a length of some 20 feet. Its food consists of cuttle-fish, mackerel, and other fish. It is frequently seen round the coast, especially near the Orkneys and Shetlands, and is noticeable for its gregarious habits, herds of two or three hundred being seen together, under the leadership of one of their number, whom they follow blindly.

5. **The Common Dolphin** (*Delphinus delphis*) is often mistaken for the Porpoise; but all dolphins are easily distinguished by their pronounced "beak," and this is accentuated by the bulging appearance of the forehead above it.

Indeed, there is an undoubted similarity in shape between the dolphin's head and beak and a duck's. This mammal is unique in possessing more *teeth* than any other—sometimes as many as sixty-five on each side of the jaws. It has also a much bolder eye than the Porpoise, and is far more handsome in colour, having a black back, yellowish stripes on the sides, and white under parts. It often appears to have an iridescent sheen whilst alive. Its average length is from 6 to 8 feet, and it may often be seen in the English Channel, with sportive gambols accompanying the ships in herds. Its food is herrings, mackerel, and other small fish. It is notable for its remarkable care for the single young one produced at birth. Like the Porpoise, it is said to possess a voice, with which it produces a gentle lowing sound. Occasional specimens of a larger species, the BOTTLE-NOSED DOLPHIN (*Tursiops tursio*)—so called from its shorter beak—are found round the coasts.

6. **The Sperm Whale**, or CACHALOT (*Physeter macrocephalus*), attains a length, in the male of some 60 feet at greatest, in the female of some 30 feet, and has an enormous head about one-third of the whole length. It is from this whale that spermaceti and ambergris are chiefly obtained, and in consequence of this, together with the oil made from the blubber, it has been hunted down almost to extinction, so that its appearance off Great Britain is to-day rare compared with former centuries. It feeds on cuttle-fish and squids, as well as on other fish.

7. **The Common Beaked, or Bottle-nosed, Whale** (*Hyperoodon rostratus*) is common round the Shetlands, and is frequently seen off Norfolk and in the Bristol Channel. Its length is from 20 to 30 feet, and, as its name implies, it has a short beak and a large, "lumpy" head. It does not go about in herds, but singly or in pairs.

8. **Sowerby's Whale** (*Mesoplodon bidens*) has two of its teeth, in the middle of the lower jaw, prolonged into tusks. It is some 15 feet long, and is occasionally stranded or captured off these shores; its home is the Atlantic.

We now pass on to the *Whalebone* Whales, divided at the present day into two families—the " Right " Whales and the Rorquals.

9. **The Right Whale**—so called by the whalers, in contradistinction to all others, as being most valuable for oil and whalebone—is in its prototype, the GREENLAND WHALE, almost extinct, and even the SOUTHERN RIGHT WHALE (*Balæna australis*), which was once an inhabitant of the Channel and the North Sea, is now practically so; but the Rorquals are still represented by various species.

10. **The Hump-backed Whale** (*Megaptera boops*) is often seen off the East Coast of Scotland and the North of Ireland. This species eats larger molluscs and crustaceans than the Right Whales.

11. **The Common Rorqual** (*Balænoptera musculus*) may grow to a length of 70 feet, the female being the larger of the two sexes. It is blackish grey above, and white or yellowish white below. It feeds on small fish as well as on the crustaceans and molluscs, and is frequently seen in the English and

Irish Channels and elsewhere. Its whalebone and blubber are so inferior in quality as to be scarcely worth obtaining. Possibly this accounts for its existence still in such numbers.

12. **Sibbald's Rorqual,** or the "BLUE" WHALE (*Balænoptera sibbaldii*), is the largest of all the whales, sometimes measuring 90 or 100 feet in length. The colour is dark grey above and lighter grey below, and frequently appears of a blue shade : hence its name. It is still fairly abundant in the North Sea, and has been washed ashore on the North-east Coast of England.

13. **Rudolphi's Rorqual** (*Balænoptera borealis*) is found in the Atlantic, North Sea, and English Channel. Its length is under 50 feet. A specimen was captured in the Thames in 1887 ; and another, stranded near Rochester in 1888, was said to cry like a child in distress.

14. **The Lesser Rorqual,** or PIKE WHALE (*Balænoptera acuto-rostrata*), is quite common round the British Isles. It is some 30 feet long, and comes near land, apparently, when about to produce its young.

Order : INSECTIVORA ("Insect-eaters").

1. **The Common Hedgehog** (*Erinaceus europæus*).—This is one of the oldest genera of mammals which still exist, its remains having been found, unaltered, dating from the Miocene Period. Every one is familiar with this curious if common creature, with its covering of spines, and, on its under parts, coarse hair. It is to be found practically all over England and Scotland, and, not quite so commonly, in Ireland. It feeds on all kinds of insects, and slugs, snails, spiders, and worms. It is known to kill and eat snakes and frogs, and even small birds, mice, voles, etc. It is very partial to eggs. Those which I have kept as pets have eaten practically all sorts of food—scraps from the table, bread and milk, vegetables, etc. One lived under my study table for a year, and used to come out from his box and lick my boots, apparently finding the blacking to his taste ; and another, which was brought to me quite wild, within an hour made himself at home on the hearth-rug in front of the fire, having successfully ousted a dog and a cat. A hedgehog is a useful pet if the house is infested with " cockroaches " ; but it is worth adding that the creature will require other food. I have known at least one family who believed it was sufficient to lock the hedgehog up in the kitchen for the night, to get all the meals he required from " black beetles " and a saucer of water !

The young are born, in a litter of four to six, in July or August ; sometimes a second litter is born in October. They are quite blind, and, like young rabbits, almost naked, their spines being soft and white. This species hibernates during the winter, often under a heap of dead leaves, where it lies torpid until March.

The hedgehog takes its walks abroad chiefly at night, but I have several times seen it by day. It can utter a squeal or mew, though it is seldom

HEDGEHOG AND MOLE

heard. Shakespeare, however, is accurate in his famous line: "Thrice and once the hedgepig *whined*." A remarkable description has been given of the hedgehog's fight with the viper, which is not unlike the famous duel between Rikki-tikki-tavi and the cobra. The hedgehog dashes in, dodging from side to side until the adder has exhausted itself or has injured itself by striking at the hedgehog's prickly back. Then the spine is bitten through, and the little creature passes the whole body through its teeth, cracking every joint of the backbone, before making a meal—from the tail end upwards! I have never had the opportunity of witnessing such a duel, though I have seen a hedgehog play with a dead grass snake, almost as a puppy will play with a slipper. The hedgehog pranced and gambolled round the snake, then pounced upon it and worried it, and, occasionally pretending it was alive, would leap away and roll himself into a ball. It was not difficult to imagine what the scene would be between my tame hedgehog and a live snake.

Hedgehogs are very thirsty creatures, and, I believe, will soon die without water. Every summer a number of them come from the fields around to drink at night at a little fountain in my garden, and occasionally tumble in and get drowned. They can swim, however, quite easily, and lie very flat on the water, with little but the head exposed, much after the same manner as the "Water Rat," or Vole.

Their thirsty habits may account for the legend, so often repeated in country parts, of the hedgehog's sucking the cow's udder. There is probably more truth in it than is generally supposed. A cow lying down at night, if in full milk, would have a few drops exuding from the teats, and a hedgehog which discovered the fact might very readily proceed to suck. Be that as it may, any one who has kept these creatures in captivity knows with what avidity they drink from a saucer; indeed, I have drawn mine out of their sleeping boxes by rattling the saucer, and have had them sit up and drink out of a spoon.

The hedgehog's flesh is not very palatable, but according to the gipsy method it may be cooked by being rolled up in a lump of clay and put in the embers. When the ball is hard it may be broken, and the spines come away with the clay.

2. **The Moles** (*Talpidæ*).—Every one is familiar with the general characteristics of the "little gentleman in black," and only too often a lawn is ruined in a single night by the tunnelling of one of these creatures.

The Mole is a distant cousin of the Shrews. Though it is common in Great Britain, it is not found in Ireland. Its fossil remains have been found, showing that it existed in this country before man. Popularly it is supposed to be blind, and to have no ears; but the fact is that it possesses very small eyes, and a pair of very acute ears, though they are completely concealed in the fur. The extraordinary development of its fore-limbs, or hands, is an instance of adaptation. To all intents and purposes, only the wrist and hand extend from the body, the "arm" being concealed within it, and these "hands" are splayed outwards from the body in what appears to be a most ungainly position, but is peculiarly convenient for the mole's underground work.

The fur is also a remarkable feature, the hair being set vertically in the skin, so that there is no right or wrong way of stroking it. This enables the animal to pass backwards or forwards through its passages without getting its coat caked with mud. The colour is not a real black, but a very dark brown; occasionally I have seen specimens with a light patch on the chest. The nose is long and extremely sensitive, a very slight blow upon it being fatal. The young are born in June, and number generally four or five. They are born devoid of fur and quite helpless, but rapidly attain maturity, being three parts grown in a few weeks.

Most of the tunnels which a mole excavates are made in the search for worms and grubs; but in addition, the creature excavates a regular fortress, very often at the root of a tree, complete with bolt holes, and chamber lined with dead leaves and grass. The female constructs her own fortress for her young, and permits no male to approach it. In making the heaps of earth which so often

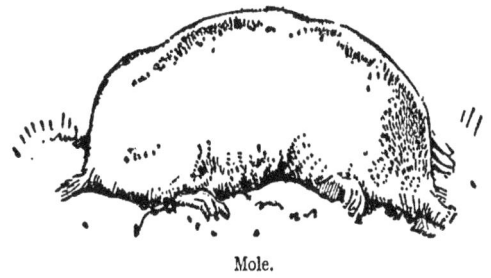

Mole.

mark the windings of the tunnels, the mole pushes the earth forward with forehead and nose; and it is remarkable to notice the rapidity with which it works. If a mole is observed during the day—and I have on several occasions seen them above ground in daylight—it immediately attempts to burrow. If the ground is too hard, it can only move over the surface very slowly and clumsily; but should the ground be favourable, the mole will sink out of sight with astonishing speed, and without, apparently, much disturbance of the soil. Generally, however, the animal only comes to the surface during the night.

During the winter moles are just as active as in the summer, except that they have to sink their shafts and borings rather deeper, as the worms retire from the frozen surface of the ground. They are very voracious, and will eat their weight of worms in a very short time; on the other hand, they quickly die of starvation. One such mole which I had in my possession, and which lived in a tub of earth, would actually sit up to eat worms, holding them very awkwardly in its "hands" whilst it chewed its victims with a very audible crunching sound. In addition to worms, its chief article of diet, the mole does not

PLATE I.

1. Hedgehog (basking).   2. Vole.   3. Water Vole.   4. Hedgehog.

THE SHREWS

despise slugs, snails, frogs, small birds, and even its own offspring or its neighbour's! It is a very thirsty creature, and can swim well, as may be guessed from its broad "hands." The mole is undoubtedly useful, not only in ridding the land of many of the larval pests of the farmer, but also in bringing up to the surface the virgin soil of its tunnels: it does not always deserve the fate which it meets at the hand of the farmer and gamekeeper. Its sense of smell is very acute—the female will almost always desert her young if they have been handled—and the mole-catcher has to take special precautions not to leave the scent of human hands upon his traps. The Latin name for the Common Mole is *Talpa europæa*.

3. **The Shrews**, which are distant cousins of the Mole, are represented in Britain by two species—the Common (*Sorex vulgaris*) and the Pygmy or Lesser Shrew (*S. minutus*).

The Common Shrew is reddish grey in colour, with a longish snout, sharp pointed, and a tail that looks as if it had been cut short. It is noteworthy as possessing a pair of glands which secrete a very offensive fluid, the consequence being that no cat or other carnivore will eat it. Its dead body is often found lying on paths or roads, and country people have a belief that a shrew cannot cross a road but dies in the attempt. The truer explanation is either that the little creature has been killed by a cat or other animal, and left uneaten on account of its odour, or else that it has died of starvation through lack of its proper food. The latter is all the more probable since large numbers of dead shrews are often observed in the autumn, the season when there is least insect life to be found. For the food of the shrew consists of insects of all kinds (though it does not despise worms and snails). It is, therefore, one of the most valuable helpers of the farmer, consuming as it does great quantities of noxious grubs and slugs, whilst it does no harm whatever to the crops. It does not burrow, but makes a nest in the springtime of soft grass, rudely roofed over, in a bank or hole in the ground. Here it gives birth to five or six young. For their size, shrews are extremely pugnacious, and may sometimes be seen fighting and uttering the shrillest of faint squeaks. I have watched them so engaged two or three yards away, totally engrossed in their warfare. It is on account of these spiteful proclivities that the name of "shrew" (which means "to bite" or "reprove") has been applied to certain human beings, as, for instance, to that "Katharina Minola, renowned in Padua for her scolding tongue."

The Lesser Shrew (*Sorex minutus*) is only $1\frac{3}{4}$ inch long in body, and so is easily the smallest of British mammals, and is browner in colour than the common species. It is not so frequently met with in England and Scotland, though it is abundant in Ireland; this is all the more remarkable as the Common Shrew is quite unknown in the Green Isle.

The Water Shrew (*Crossopus fodiens*) is of a different genus from the preceding, and is much larger and more handsome, being a rich blackish grey on the back, and white beneath. This species makes a burrow with a chamber at the end in which the young are born—generally in number from five to ten—towards the end of May. As its name implies, it can swim and dive remarkably well, and, in addition to land insects, it hunts for the larvæ of water insects, shrimps, frog spawn, and even tiny fish. It is commonest in Wales, but is to be found in England and Scotland, though not in Ireland.

Order: CHEIROPTERA ("Hand-winged")—Bats.

Bats present some unique features which should be noted first of all. First, they are the only mammals in the world which can really fly. If the wing is examined, it will be seen to be in reality a modified hand, with very long fingers and a very short thumb. Between the fingers comes the thin, tough membrane which transforms the hand into a wing (Titania's description of the "*rere-mice*" with their *leathern* wings, in *A Midsummer Night's Dream*, is singularly apt). The ears are remarkable, as in certain species the tragus, or flap of skin which human beings possess guarding the entrance to the ear-hole, is developed into a strange shape and size, and presents the appearance of an inner ear. Many species have a curious development of cartilage round the nose, known as a "leaf"; but in British species this is not to be found to any marked degree, though the Barbastelle Bat has a most eccentric-shaped and grooved nose and lips, which at first sight suggest a crumpled leaf.\

Bats are not "blind," in spite of the proverb, but possess very small eyes. They are chiefly nocturnal in their habits, and depend, therefore, upon hearing and smell; though they may be seen by day occasionally. I once observed a large bat daily which left its hiding-place in my roof almost always between twelve and one o'clock, and after a short flight duly returned. It is said that they possess some remarkable power, beyond ordinary hearing and smell, which guides them in avoiding obstacles in the dark. No doubt the curious glands and bulges upon their faces—which will be at once observed if they are examined closely—serve some such purpose.

These remarkable mammals hibernate in the winter, but not to that thoroughgoing extent usually associated with hibernation. Occasionally on a mild winter's day they may be observed flying—no doubt tempted forth by hunger. They breed in the spring, the young, in England, consisting of one, though in Europe two are produced at a birth. They are born blind and naked, and cling to the mother's breasts until old enough to leave her. The latter literally folds them in her arms: for she bends one wing over her body while she hangs suspended by the other.

Bats can walk, or rather crawl, and climb—and swim, if need be. I need scarcely mention that they sleep upside-down; but I have known a printer, before now, insist upon setting the photograph (Plate II.) the other way about, because he thought that was the "right way up." Some species are gregarious in their habit: I once had to get rid of nearly a hundred which had taken

BATS

possession of the roof of my house—and their smell was most offensive! Others are solitary in habit, and find some secure hiding-place by themselves.

It must be remembered that bats are some of the most useful of our country's creatures, as they live entirely upon insects. In captivity, however, they show a distinct liking for scraps of raw meat. They eat considerably more than their own weight in food each day—if they can obtain it; they are, therefore, public benefactors in helping to keep down the noxious insect life for the farmer and the gardener.

Only some twelve or thirteen species may be considered truly British, though a few others have occasionally been found. The most common is the Pipistrelle, which is also the smallest; the Noctule, which is the largest British bat, comes next in numbers.

1. **The Serotine Bat** (*Vespertilio serotinus*)—so called because it appears *late* in the evening—has ears comparatively small, with a short tragus; a blunt, wide muzzle, almost naked except for a slight fringe of hair on the upper lip. Length of body, excluding tail, $2\frac{3}{4}$ inches. Dark brown above, greyish yellow beneath. Found in the South of England. Hibernates singly, generally in trees.

2. **The Noctule, or GREAT BAT** (*Pterygistis noctula*).—Body 3 inches long; spread of wings up to 14 inches. Has widely spread nostrils; short, broad ears; tragus is bean-shaped. Colour, yellow-brown; very silky hair. A rapid flyer, often uttering shrill squeaks. Gregarious; feeds chiefly on beetles. Possesses scent glands in the mouth, which emit a very offensive odour. Commonest in the Midlands, but widely distributed, though not in Wales or Scotland.

3. **The Hairy-armed Bat** (*Pterygistis leisleri*)—so called from the fore-arm being furred. Length, $2\frac{1}{4}$ inches. Not common; chiefly found in Western Midlands, Lake District, and East Ireland.

4. **The Pipistrelle, or COMMON BAT.**—Length, $1\frac{3}{4}$ inch. Head rounded; ears large and triangular; glandular swellings on face well marked. Colour, reddish brown, shading into grey. Breeds in June and July. Hibernates during depth of winter, but often comes out on a sunny day; sleeps in crevices of buildings, etc. Flight resembles that of a moth. Feeds on small insects, gnats, and moths. Common everywhere.

5. **Daubenton's Bat** (*Myotis daubentoni*).—Under 2 inches. Oval-shaped ears, large in proportion to head; inner ear nearly half the size of outer. Colour, reddish brown, shading off to grey. Often seen over water. Possesses large feet. Chiefly found in West Midlands and Lake District.

6. **The Reddish Grey Bat** (*Myotis nattereri*).—Body under 2 inches in length. Ears $\frac{3}{4}$ inch, with a narrow, pointed tragus. Colour, light red-brown, shading to almost white beneath—an unmistakable characteristic. Gregarious in habit; found in eaves and roofs, sometimes in trees. Fairly common in South and Midlands; occasional in Scotland and Ireland.

7. **Bechstein's Bat** (*Myotis bechsteini*).—Length, 2 inches. Ears nearly

1 inch; tragus small, thin, and pointed. Longish snout. Rare: chiefly found in woods; hides only in hollow trees.

8. **The Whiskered Bat** (*Myotis mystacinus*).—Body just over 1½ inch. Identified by its distinct "moustache." Fur black with chestnut tips. Hides in crevices in walls and roofs; frequently observed over water. Fairly generally distributed, but not found in Scotland.

9. **Barbastelle Bat** (*Barbastella barbastellus*).—The ears in this species are so closely set that the inner edges are united at the base; the face appears to be enclosed in a band of ear-cartilage. Triangular-shaped tragus. Short, bare muzzle. A curious notch along the nose; two other grooves below the nostrils. Length of body, about 2 inches. Colour, deep black; grey tips to the hair. Hibernates at the first approach of winter—not in trees, but in caverns and earth-crevices. Not gregarious. Not common; chiefly met with in the South-east and Midlands. Unknown in Ireland and Scotland.

10. **The Long-eared Bat** (*Plecotus auritus*).—Distinguished by its very long ears. Tragus leaf-shaped, and small in proportion to the ear. This species can droop its ears, so as to bring them over the chest. Length of body, under 2 inches. Colour, pale reddish brown, shading to grey. Frequents caverns, trees, and buildings.

The ears of this bat are extraordinarily sensitive, and from actual experiments have been found almost to take the place of *sight* when meeting with any solid obstacle in flight.

This bat frequently remains out all night—far longer than other species; it also possesses a very thin, piercing voice. Is easily tamed in captivity. Its distribution is general.

11. **The Greater Horseshoe Bat** (*Rhinolophus ferrum-equinum*).—Length, 2¼ inches. Possesses a "nose leaf," the portion above the lip being shaped like a horseshoe. This curious formation, being very sensitive, serves to enable the bat to fly without colliding against obstacles, and yet without using its very insignificant eyes. The ears are large and broad, without a tragus. This bat lives largely on cockchafers; it flies high, frequently round trees. It hides in old buildings and caves. Chiefly found in the South and West of England. Unknown in Ireland and Scotland.

12. **The Lesser Horseshoe Bat** (*Rhinolophus hipposideros*) is a smaller species than the above, but its general characteristics are the same. Its distribution is chiefly in the South of England, but it has also been found in the West of Ireland.

Order: CARNIVORA ("Flesh-eaters").

Modern carnivorous animals are divided into two classes: *Fissipedia* ("Separate-toed"), among which come Dogs, Cats, Weasels, etc.; and *Pinnipedia* ("Web-footed"), such as the Seals and Walruses.

PLATE II.

1. The Otter at play.
2. Long-eared Bat.
3. Squirrels.
4. A Tame Otter.

CARNIVORA—THE FOX 33

Fissipedia.

1. **The Common Fox** (*Canis vulpes*).—Every one is familiar with some facts about this mammal, even though not every one has seen it. Its average length is 3 feet, though I have seen specimens larger; and it is so great an enemy to farmers, in its propensity for killing chickens, lambs, geese, pheasants, and other creatures, that it would long ago have become extinct but for its preservation for the sake of the " noble sport " of fox hunting. The fox is perhaps the most cunning of our country's wild animals, and whilst, on the one hand, he often kills for the pure sake of killing—I have known the whole of a poor

Fox Cubs at play.

man's fowl shed to be destroyed in a night and left by the fox—on the other hand, he will leave a wild duck undisturbed on her nest until the eggs are almost hatched, in order that he may make a meal of the mother and the young ducklings at once. Foxes are really very beautifully marked creatures, with their white cheeks and throat, the generally light-coloured waistcoat, and orange-red back and sides, ornamented black on the feet, ears, and muzzle. The tail also is reddish, with black fringe and a white tip. Being a nocturnal animal (though it sometimes hunts by day), its eyes are very large, and there is a curious characteristic of the pupil, which, instead of narrowing under strong light to a round *spot*—as all " dogs' " eyes should—becomes a *slit*, as does the cat's.

The fox, in common with other kinds of dogs, has a strong odour, due to the possession of a scent gland, which is found close to the tail and emits a fœtid smell. It is this "scent" which becomes the means by which he is hunted down by the hounds.

Foxes breed in February, and one of the eerie sounds of the real country-side is the bark of the vixen at night, calling the males to her. After marriage the lady separates from her husband and makes a burrow for herself, where the young are born, generally in April. The litter consists of from three to seven cubs, which are born blind and remain in that condition for ten days. After being nursed for a month, they are able to tackle the young rabbits and other food which the mother brings to them. They are very delightful creatures in their infancy, and easily tamed. I have seen them playing at the mouth of their home in early morning, worrying a dead rabbit which their mother had brought—*obviously not for food, but as a toy*—and racing backwards and forwards between their "earth" and the tree which made their "long-distance mark." Young foxes in their frolics make a well-beaten track for games, which is quite plainly seen by those whose eyes are alert. It may be round the base of a tree, where the grass will be found quite bare ; or, more probably, in addition, it will consist of a path running more or less straight for fifty yards or so to some point such as a tree, hillock, or rock, doubling back by a lower track "home." Those who practise "woodcraft" should look out for these "playing sites."

The fox can make his burrow for himself, but frequently he enlarges one made by the rabbit ; I have found his "earth" in the midst of a rabbit warren on more than one occasion.

As for food, the fox will eat pretty well anything. Besides the farmer's poultry, he feeds on wild rabbits, hares, game, hedgehogs, rats, mice, moles, frogs, beetles, and worms. On the coast he does not despise fish, crabs, or shellfish ; and everywhere he will eat carrion if he can find it.

Foxes are easily tamed, and I place in an appendix a short account of one I have known.

As for the fox's cunning, that is proverbial. Every one, I hope, knows "Brer Fox" : that name, with "Reynard" in English, *Reinaert de Vos* in German, comes into a group of stories older than any books in the world, told by primitive man round his camp-fires. They show that Master Fox's character was well known in those dateless days.

Fox hunting is not the ancient sport that we should at first sight imagine. It became a vogue in England about the beginning of the seventeenth century, though previously the fox was *occasionally* hunted—on foot—as a beast of venery, though an inferior one.

2. **The Common Otter** (*Lutra vulgaris*).—This handsome mammal is the "weasel" of the river, and is, I fear, becoming rarer. When full grown it measures, from nose to tip of tail, over a yard in length. Its general shape is clear from the photographs (Plate II.). Its head, or face, is really pretty,

from a front view not unlike that of a cat, with its short, thick whiskers and short ears. The fur consists of two kinds—a close, soft coat of greyish yellow, tipped with brown, close to the skin, and, set with it, the longer " external " fur, of a rich dark brown.

The otter feeds chiefly on fish, but will attack poultry and young lambs; it also eats the wild water-fowl, such as dabchicks and wild duck, and is fond of frogs. It is said to destroy far more fish than it eats, for the sheer love of killing. But even so, fish are plentiful, and otters rare; all possible effort should be made to preserve it from extinction.

Otters breed once a year, the young being born in March or April. They are three or four in number, and are quite blind for a few days, like kittens. The nest, or "holt," is generally in a hole in the river bank, under the roots of a tree. The tame otter's story in the Appendix illustrates the other points—cry, method of swimming, etc.—of the otter's character.

The otter does not attack human beings, but can, none the less, inflict a really severe bite when roused, and becomes most pertinacious in returning furiously to the charge, even when kicked off.

3. **The Common Badger** (*Meles taxus*) is the heaviest of all our British carnivores, as well as of the weasels, to which group it belongs. A full-grown badger weighs between 30 and 40 lb., measures about 2½ feet from nose to root of tail, and stands about 1 foot high. Notice from the photograph (Plate III.) that it stands on the *toes* of the fore-feet, but on the whole foot (up to the *heel*) of the hind-legs. Its coloration is well seen from the same photograph, the remarkable motley of face and head being strikingly like that of the Racoon. The whole back is grey, deepening to black beneath. There is little doubt that the colour is protective to a very remarkable degree; and one would be glad to think that on this account badgers are supposed to be much rarer than they really are. A badger standing motionless in a hedgerow or amongst bracken is practically invisible, the white patches on the face breaking up the shape so that it appears to mingle with the play of light and shade on the leaves and branches. Unfortunately, however, the badger possesses those scent glands which have made his "stink" proverbial, and though those I have seen in captivity seldom smelt offensive, yet in a wild state the scent is sufficient to betray him to any dog, and often to human smell. Many years ago I saw eight badgers dug out from one set of "earths," and the fœtor then was more than proverbial! That occasion also impressed on me the tremendous power of the badger's *jaw*, and the fact that, like the otter, the skin is so loose and baggy that the animal can turn in it, when seized, with extraordinary facility. To see, as I did on that day, a labourer at full speed across the fields, yelling for help, with a badger holding on to the loose part of his corduroys—but I must refer readers to the story, which belongs to *The Young People's Nature Study Book*. Suffice it to say that the badger's jaw is so articulated that it cannot be dislocated, and it is capable of crushing bones, roots, and other hard articles of diet. The animal's food consists of everything eatable

that comes its way, besides roots and nuts, eggs, fruit, larvæ, honey, frogs, and snails.

Badgers breed in late summer or early autumn, the young being born in May or June; they are blind, like those of the otter, for ten days or more.

The female inhabits a solitary burrow during the rearing of the young, but otherwise several badgers live in close proximity to one another in a sort of "city" of separate burrows. The badger's cry is generally a short yelp or low grunt; but it is seldom heard, since its habits are nocturnal, and all night-using mammals are impressively silent.

Reference must be made to the burrows, which the badger digs generally on some slope in a wood or quarry. There is often a sharp turn in the tunnel a little below the surface, where the badger waits in case of attack, and so pins its enemy as it turns the corner. The sleeping chamber is kept clean and bedded with dried grass, ferns, and leaves. The inmate is said to gather these materials into heaps in the autumn and leave them to dry, clearing out its hole and replacing the old litter with the new before settling down for the winter's hibernation. Badgers do not, however, sleep the whole winter, but wake from time to time and sally forth in search of food.

The word "badger" is an interesting one, and has been given various derivations—(a) a "badge" or stripe, referring to its face coloration; (b) a stealer of corn; (c) a creature caught in a *bag* (in old days sacks were thrust into the holes at night, and the creatures caught when returning home). Badger baiting has given a metaphor to the language—to "badger." The Old English name was "brock," and is found in names such as "Brockenhurst" and "Brockham."

4. **The Pine Marten** (*Mustela martes*), once common, but now, alas! rare, is found in Ireland, the Highlands, and occasionally in England. Upper parts chocolate-brown, throat and chest yellow; length about 20 inches, with a tail some 9 or 10 inches more. It gets its name from being found frequently in woods where the Scotch pine grows. Like its near relatives the stoat and weasel, it catches birds, young rabbits, rats, mice, poultry, and game. It does not despise fruit and berries. When in flight it makes astonishing leaps of five or six feet, and it climbs trees with the greatest of ease.

5. **The Common Polecat** (*Putorius foetidus*) is rare as a wild creature, though known familiarly enough as the "Ferret," which, indeed, is simply a domesticated variety which came to us from Rome—perhaps a sporting centurion of Cæsar's was responsible for its introduction to these shores. Certainly it was used for hunting rabbits in those days.

The wild species is found occasionally in the New Forest, Devon, the Lake District, and Scotland, but not in Ireland.

In early English it was called "Foul Marten," from its filthy smell, as it possesses a pair of very active glands at the base of the tail. The male measures some 17 inches; the female is shorter. It is handsomely coloured, with white tips and white edge to the ear; a band of grey over the forehead;

PLATE III.

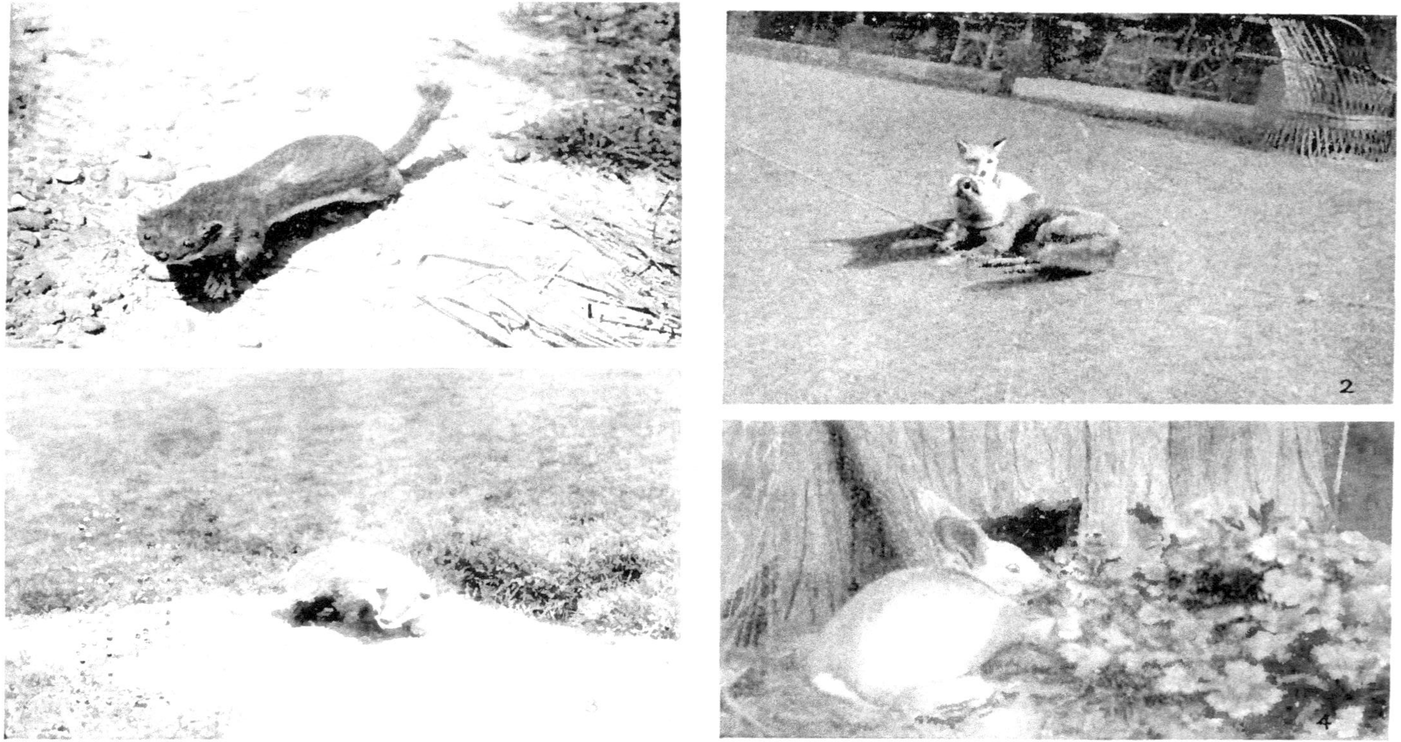

1. Weasel. 2. Foxes. 3. Badger. 4. Rabbit.

the rest a general dark brown tending to black on the legs. The dense under fur is a lighter brown. The polecat feeds on birds, rabbits, hares, frogs, eggs, and fish, and often kills for the sake of killing, sucking the blood of its victim and then leaving the carcass.

6. **The Stoat, or** ERMINE (*Putorius ermineus*).—This mammal is often confused with the weasel, owing to their similarity; but there can be no difficulty in distinguishing them if seen side by side. The weasel is only half the size of the stoat, and though the general colour is the same, there is *no black tip* to the weasel's tail.

The stoat is about 12 inches long from nose to root of tail, the latter being another 6 inches or so. The photograph (Plate VI.) shows the great length of this animal compared with the shortness of its legs. As it moves after its prey with relentless certainty and great speed, it appears to resemble a thick, yellow-brown arrow, or a snake, *hovering a few inches above the ground*, but going forward as if impelled by some unseen magic force. This is due, first, to its method of progression, a series of bounds or gallops, and, secondly, to its coloration, reddish brown above and white below (with a broad black tip to the tail). In winter the colour changes to pure white, the tail alone remaining black, and in this state the stoat is much sought after for "ermine fur," associated for centuries with the dress of royalty or nobility. (Apparently this change is not complete, but only partial, with stoats inhabiting the Midlands and South of England, probably because of the comparatively mild winter.)

The stoat makes a nest of leaves and grass in a hole in bank or tree, and the young are born about April or May. The animal hunts more by smell than sight, though its eyes are large and full; having once scented the trail of a victim, it holds tenaciously to its course, and becomes a veritable Doom in the inevitable end of its prey, which it kills generally by a bite at the back of the head (in larger victims, the throat).

It hunts in absolute silence; but it has a voice, described as a low chuckle or clucking sound, which is rarely heard except when it is defending its young.

It is said to fascinate the rabbit by performing all kinds of gambols before it, edging nearer and nearer to its victim until within leaping distance.

Though it devours hares, rabbits, and eggs, the stoat kills an enormous number of rats, mice, and voles, and so is, to a large extent, a valuable servant of man; the young, in fact, are fed mainly on these smaller animals.

The true stoat is not found in Ireland, but is fairly common in England and Scotland; there is a *smaller* and quite distinct species some 9 inches long (*Putorius hibernicus*) found in the sister island.

7. **The Weasel** (*Putorius vulgaris*), 7 or 8 inches long, a graceful and pretty beast, is the smallest of all the flesh-eaters, its thinness of body making it resemble a snake more closely than the stoat, to which in general coloration it is similar, except that there is *no black tip* to the tail, nor does the fur change colour in the winter *in Britain*.

It breeds twice a year, the young being born in April and July, generally four in number, blind but not naked. They are, in their infancy, some of the most playful of all Nature's children, ten times more sportive than kittens.

The weasel's habits of hunting and killing resemble the stoat's, but it chooses *smaller* victims, especially mice. Lucky the farmer who finds one near his ricks, for the weasel can enter all the mouse tunnels, and will practically wipe all the mice out. Occasionally weasels may be seen hunting in companies of four or five.

8. **The Wild Cat** (*Felis catus*).—Though once common in Britain, this carnivore is almost extinct to-day, being found only in the North of Scotland. It is about 2 feet in length, and has a handsome, bushy tail with dark bands and tip. The whiskers are white, the eyes yellow; the general colour like a domestic tabby, but lighter and yellower. It lives in forests, often making its nest in a hollow in a tree, or even in the old nest of hawk or crow. It breeds twice a year, and there is little doubt that the common domestic species has descended from the Wild Cat in past generations. It is very savage, and attacks not only rabbits, hares, and birds, but even lambs.

Pinnipedia—The Marine Carnivores.

As previously mentioned, this order includes Sea-lions, Walruses, and Seals—the "fin-footed" mammals. Of these, only the seals can now be found round Great Britain, and these are, I fear, in danger of extinction, through the brainless folly of the so-called "sportsmen," who, when one is seen, attempt to shoot or capture it.

1. **The Common Seal** (*Phoca vitulina*) is found round the coasts of Ireland, North and West Wales, North, East, and West Scotland, and the northern islands. At one time it was common all round the coasts, in the sense that it was abundant, but to-day it is practically never seen in our eastern or southern waters.

The general character of the seal is fairly well known. The Common Seal measures, in the male, 5 feet long, the female being smaller. The young seals, born generally in June, are pretty creatures, covered at first with a coat of thick, soft fur almost white; but this is shed shortly after birth. The ordinary colour of the hair is a dirty nondescript white, with a touch of lemon in it, but with all sorts of odd-shaped spots and patches of a dark stony colour worked over it. There is no doubt that this coloration is protective, resembling the broken lights and shadows on a pebbly or rock-strewn beach. Young seals can swim a few hours after birth; but on land all, young and old alike, can make but slow progress, though they manage to travel considerable distances at night. The short, webbed fore-feet, armed with stout claws, have to serve ashore as hands and feet, since the two back limbs are useless as legs, being *always turned back* and incapable of forward movement for walking purposes. Seals can haul themselves forward out of water by

SEALS, HARES, AND RABBITS

their fore-limbs, but the rest of their progress has to be a clumsy wriggle. They live in colonies, and are "sociable" animals. When at ease ashore they grunt like so many contented pigs—a sound exchanged for a snort or bark or cough of defiance when courting or playing. The babies bleat like lambs.

Seals are attracted by sound, and will follow a boat where music is being played—

> "Rude Heiskar's seal through surges dark
> Will long pursue the minstrel's bark." (*Scott*.)

A quaint old writer speaks of the seals swimming straight to shore when the church bells of Hoy (Orkney) were rung,* and they are easily tamed, and become as attached to their human masters as dogs.

The skin, with its glossy, silken hair, is of some value—for motorists and other creatures!

The food of the seal consists of fish of every sort, including shellfish and starfish, varied sometimes with sea-gull or other bird.

2. **The Grey Seal** (*Halichœrus grypus*).—This species is twice as large as the Common Seal, a male measuring often 9 or 10 feet. In colour, as its name implies, it becomes a beautiful silver-grey when full grown.

The young are born later than those of the Common Seal, in the autumn, the mother generally finding some cave or grotto for her home. The young cubs do not take to the water like the Common Seals, but when some six weeks old have to be taught to swim by their mother—not without some reluctance on the youngsters' part.

The mother will protect her young with ferocity, and will attack an enemy or an intruder. When she leaves her babe ashore, the latter is always *silent;* and its sallow-white fur and large black eyes form a splendid protection, rendering it almost indistinguishable from the boulders and whitened rocks scattered on the shore.

The Grey Seal is found on the coasts of Ireland, and the Hebrides and western islands of Scotland, but is practically never seen in English waters. There are some famous seal caves on Achill Island.

Order: RODENTIA ("Gnawing Mammals")—Hares, Rabbits, etc.

In this order, notice that the *canine teeth* are completely absent (see page 23, *note*), the incisors are specially developed, and the mouth is really divided into two, there being between the entrance and the back a narrow passage where the *palate is covered with hair*. This prevents the animal from swallowing any material it is gnawing which is unsuitable for food.

1. **The Common Rabbit** (*Oryctolagus cuniculus*).—Though hares and rabbits are so much alike in general appearance, they belong to different genera,

---

* Quoted by Sir H. Johnston in *British Mammals*.

and differ very much in detail. Young rabbits are born naked, helpless, and blind; young hares furred, with eyes open, and able to run. Rabbits burrow; hares do not, being content with the concealment afforded by the long grass in which they make their " forms." The habits and general characterization of rabbits are so well known that I draw attention only to one or two details. The under side of the tail is white, to serve as a signal to its neighbours. In a warren, when the first rabbit spies an intruder and moves off to its hole, the flickering of the white tail immediately informs the others that flight is necessary.

The female makes a separate burrow when about to have young, with only *one* entrance (instead of the usual two). On leaving her nest for food, she closes the hole with earth to prevent foes from scenting her babies.

2. **The Common Hare** (*Lepus europæus*).—This mammal is always larger than the rabbit, with much longer ears in proportion, and tail; the hind-legs are also much longer. Hares breed twice a year, and have two to five young at a birth, known as leverets; these are the most appealingly pretty and timid babes in Nature's nursery.

The " form " or nest of the hare consists of a smooth space in a tuft of grass or other vegetation, stamped flat by the hare's feet, and " cooked " into dry hay by the heat and pressure of the creature's body lying upon it.

Note that neither hares nor rabbits can *walk*. Their method of progress is by galloping and jumping. The hare is not only remarkably swift, but extremely clever and agile in eluding pursuers. It can " double " instantaneously, and would always escape the dogs, except when the course is over carefully arranged ground.

It is said that the origin of the famous " Brer Rabbit " is not the rabbit, but the hare. Early American colonists (says Sir H. Johnston) called all hares rabbits, and the slaves brought from West Africa, with their folk-lore of beast tales, adopted the word " rabbit " for their four-legged hero. Certainly it is the hare that figures in the Greek stories.

This hare is not found in Ireland, but is common in England.

3. **The Mountain Hare** (*Lepus timidus*) is slightly smaller than the above, and is coloured a yellowish grey in summer, whilst in winter it becomes *white*, like the stoat. This variety is found in Ireland and the Highlands, but not in England; the Irish hare does not, however, become white in the winter.

4. **The Common Squirrel** (*Sciurus vulgaris*).—The squirrel belongs to a group of rodents known as *Simplicidentata*—possessors of but *one* pair of incisor teeth in both jaws. This group includes by far the greatest number of rodents, and in England is represented by (besides squirrels) dormice and rats. It used to include BEAVERS, but the latter species has been extinct for centuries (though of late years experiments have been tried in various parts of the country to acclimatize it again), and there is nothing of it left but its name, which still clings to some localities—Beverley, in Yorkshire, is a corruption of *Beaver-lac* (the " Beaver's Lake "); probably Beverston = " Beavers'

PLATE IV.

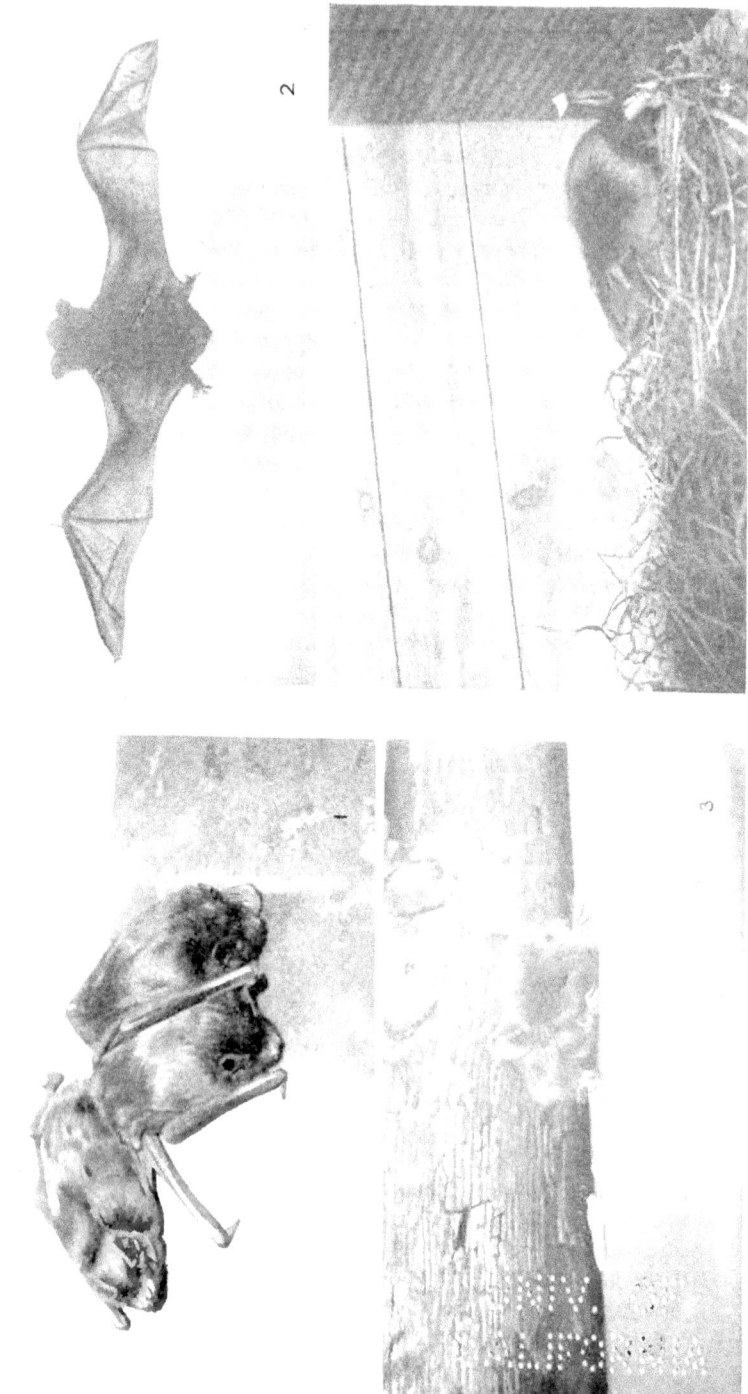

1. Short-eared Bat.   2. Bat, showing Structure of the Wings.   3. Common Mouse.   4. Old English Rat.

THE SQUIRREL

Town "; and there are other places. Beavers disappeared before Chaucer could write of a " Flaundrish bever hat " (see *Chambers's Encyclopædia*).

This beautiful and fascinating creature is common throughout England and Scotland, but is scarce in Ireland. I am sorry to say, however, that in parts of England it has been exterminated, owing, I fear, to its wanton pursuit and capture or death at the hands of boys.

I know no more delightful creature to keep as a pet, and no more delightful denizen of our woods and forests. Its impudence and inquisitiveness ought to be proverbial; for no one can have sat still in a wood where squirrels are plentiful without finding them about him in the trees, swearing and scolding, pretending at one moment to be terrified, at another staring boldly round a branch, or chasing one another with bravado from tree to tree.

They are much like monkeys, not only in their climbing antics and in intelligence, but in the untidy and wasteful way they eat, to say nothing of their chattering. I have known tame squirrels to live indoors by night, but to scamper out along a rope stretched from the bedroom window to a tree on the lawn by day; one got accustomed to being wakened early in the morning by the clacking and squeaking of the most saucy of the family, sitting on one's pillow and demanding " nuts " !

The Common Squirrel's colour is a chestnut-red, with grey sides and white chest and under parts; in the winter the colour dulls and the grey predominates, but in spring the grey tends to disappear, and the rich red and white combine to make a pretty contrast. The tail itself is more bushy in winter than in summer; it is carried over the back when the owner sits up, but streams out behind when the squirrel runs. The hair on the ears also varies enormously, entirely altering their apparent shape. In summer the ear appears round and wide; but the winter hair growing into a thick tuft makes the ear look long and pointed. It is scarcely necessary to point out that in this way the squirrel's ears are protected from frost-bite during its hibernation.

The squirrel's nest or " drey " is a well-made structure of moss, leaves, and stalks, covered over and set either in a fork of a tree, or it may be in an old bird's nest. The young, generally four in number, are born in June, and are able to look after themselves in a month or so, though they keep together as a family until the next spring. The parents (unlike most mammals) remain attached to one another for several seasons.

For food, the staple diet is fruit, nuts, pine cones, acorns, and seeds; but the squirrel steals eggs, and even nestlings. In addition, it sometimes does a limited amount of harm by eating the tender bark and tender shoots of young trees.

In autumn the squirrel lays up stores in different hiding-places for use in winter. This is especially true of those which inhabit the colder, bleaker districts, where food is scarce. Here the squirrel lies in a torpid condition in some hole or nook, only waking up on a bright, warm day to find its hoard and get a meal. But in the south it may be said that the squirrel does not hibernate at all, nor does it store up food if there is plenty to be obtained, either from human habitations or from the pine woods close at hand.

5. **The Common Dormouse** (*Muscardinus avellanarius*).—This small rodent is not unlike a "toy" squirrel, with somewhat similar habits. Its body is about 3 inches long; it has a bushy tail, though not so thick as the squirrel's; very large, bead-like eyes, and in colour is light fawn, fading into white or yellow-white on throat and under parts.

The feet—and this is a noteworthy characteristic—are *padded*, to stand the shock of a big jump (a dormouse will leap six feet *upwards* as well as downwards), or to move absolutely silently from place to place.

The young are born in the spring, about May (blind and helpless), the nest being in a hole in a bank or tree, or sometimes in a disused birds' nest. Occasionally a second litter is born in the year. In the autumn the dormouse

Dormouse.

constructs a winter nest. If it is set in a bush or hedge (and not a hole or hollow), it is a beautiful, ball-like structure, 6 or 8 inches across, of interwoven blades of grass, with no visible entrance. Here, at the end of October, the dormouse, grown enormously fat, and having stored up in the nest a supply of hazel nuts, goes to sleep for the winter, coiled into a complete circle, with tail over face. On a specially warm day in December it may wake up and eat a little, but generally it requires a good deal of warmth to waken it into activity.

Its food consists of corn or any grain, hazel nuts, acorns, the buds and tender shoots of young plants, some fruit, and also a considerable number of various grubs and larvæ. It will also take birds' eggs. It makes a delightful pet, is easily tamed and fed, and is a most cleanly animal; but let it escape to the garden, and it is off into the bushes or the hedge with extraordinary rapidity.[1]

RATS AND MICE

This rodent is still common in a good many parts of England, but is practically unknown in Scotland, and altogether in Ireland.

6. **The Brown Rat** (*Mus decumanus*).—If any of our mammals deserve extinction, it is the Brown Rat, which is a loathsome and repulsive as well as a savage creature. Yet it is cleanly in its habits, though it is found in the foulest places. What is more, it is an alien, coming originally from Central Asia. It is said to have migrated into Russia in the early part of the eighteenth century, and to have been brought to England by ships from the Baltic. Now British vessels have carried it to all parts of the world. Apart from its ferocity (it has been known to attack man), it is a disease carrier. In India it spreads the plague; in England, owing to the garbage on which it feeds, its bite is dangerous—I have known cases of severe blood-poisoning as a result.

Its colour is a grey-brown, lighter underneath; but in Ireland a variety is met with which is much darker, almost black, and has a white patch on the chest and white feet.

It multiplies fast, being capable of breeding when three or four months old, and having several litters in the year. As for food, it eats anything; and does not stop at killing small birds and mammals. It can eat its way anywhere —can burrow easily, can swim, can climb—so that its presence is ubiquitous.

7. **The Black Rat** (*Mus rattus*) is smaller than the former, but it has, in proportion, longer ears and tail, and much bolder eyes. This species is also alien in origin, and is said to have come to this country with William the Conqueror, and was once known as the " French Mouse." It has been almost exterminated by the Brown Rat; but is still found in various parts of the British Isles, and of late years has apparently increased in numbers. Rats have become a " fancy " of recent years, and it is by no means uncommon to see tame specimens in cages at shows.

The Black Rat is undoubtedly a more graceful and pretty creature than its brown cousin, and makes an interesting pet; but it is very shy. It is the ancestor of the common " White " Rat, which has been kept as a pet for at least 200 years. The Black Rat's fur is very fine, and used to be of some value; the White Rat's fur is still largely used by furriers.

Its food is very much of the same varied nature as the Brown Rat's; but it is not so ferocious in disposition, and therefore is less carnivorous.

8. **The Common Mouse** (*Mus musculus*).—This little rodent needs no description; it is a pity that so pretty and captivating a creature should be such a nuisance. It varies in size and colour, but is generally about 3 inches long, and of uniform grey-brown, lighter underneath, its fur being beautifully kept and very glossy. It breeds all the year round, and the young are capable of breeding when two months old. Occasionally one hears strange accounts of " singing " mice; but any one who has kept " white " mice knows that the curious twittering or chirping which some mice emit is only the result of some form of asthma or bronchial trouble.

44   THE BRITISH NATURE BOOK

The Common Mouse is easily tamed, and the story of the prisoner whose only friend was the mouse may be imitated in any house where food is regularly put down for the mice, if any one likes to try the experiment!

9. **The Long-tailed Field Mouse** or WOOD MOUSE (*Mus sylvaticus*).—There

Wood Mouse.

are (says Mr. G. C. H. Barrett Hamilton) five varieties of this species found in the British Isles; but the average length is 4 inches, and the colour a handsome fawn above and pure white below, except on the chest, where there is a fawn spot; the ears are hairy on the outside. These points alone should serve to distinguish it from the Common House Mouse. Like the latter, the Field Mouse is a most prolific creature, capable of breeding when two months old, and having ten or twelve litters in a year. As the average number of babies in the litter is seven or eight, it is not difficult to calculate how many children, grandchildren, and great-grandchildren one original pair will have in twelve months.

If it were not for the work of owls, hawks, weasels, stoats, snakes, and other rodent-eating creatures, these mice would devastate the country. Foxes also eat them, and rooks and crows dig up their nests and swallow the helpless, naked litter.

This mouse is, perhaps, the handsomest of all our British mice, and I confess I have always had compunction in killing it. Some years ago one of them discovered the advantages as a food supply of my outdoor aviary, and took up his abode in the ivy close by. When my birds were fed, the mouse would appear *the moment I retired* and feed with them. In this case I found the mouse tenanting an old robin's nest; but the Wood Mice can burrow if they wish (they often use the moles' runs), or can build a round, woven nest of their own in hedges or low herbage or wheat. They store up large quantities of food, wheat, bar-

Wood Mouse jumping.

ley, oats, acorns, haws, hazel nuts, etc., upon which they feed during the winter.

There is little doubt that this is the "wee timorous beastie" of Burns's famous poem, and not, as Sir Harry Johnston points out, the Harvest Mouse, which is rare in Scotland.

PLATE V.

1. Common Rat.   2. House Mice.   3. Field Mouse in Nest.   4. Shrew.

THE VOLES 45

10. **The Harvest Mouse** (*Mus minutus*).—Next to the Lesser Shrew, this is the smallest mammal in England—2½ inches long, a bright red-fawn above and white below, and possessing a really *prehensile* tail, unlike the other mice, who use their tails chiefly as *balancers* when climbing.

The wonderful round nest of the Harvest Mouse, built off the ground on stalks, needs no description; but it is so cleverly constructed that, when there is no visible aperture, the mouse can pass in and out by pressing open any point of the woven surface. This nest is only occupied in the summer, the mouse retiring to a hole in the ground or a tree in the winter.

Its food is grain and seeds in general; but it also devours flies, worms, and *bees*; it is said to be particularly fond of the humble-bee. It is not found in Ireland, but *I have seen it in Wales* (in spite of statements to the contrary). It is met with in parts of the East and South of Scotland, and here and there in England, especially in the south and south-west.

11. **The Water Vole** (*Microtus amphibius*) is often called a Water Rat, though it is not a rat, being easily distinguished by its stouter build, its shorter tail with hairs thickly growing on it, and its smaller ears. In addition, the three pairs of molar teeth in each jaw are of an extraordinary and unique shape and pattern, utterly different from those of the rat (see general remarks on teeth of mammals, page 23, *note*); whilst the incisors are a deep orange or yellow in colour.

The fur is of a beautifully fine silky texture, and probably every reader has noticed the way in which air bubbles cling to it when swimming under water. Though mixed with a good deal of grey, it will be found on observation that the vole's hair is really fawn, or chestnut.

It breeds once or twice a year only, in a burrow on the bank of a stream, the entrance being below the level of the water. Here five or six young are produced in a cosy nest lined with dry grass, above the water level; and here the vole also stores up food for the winter.

Its food is entirely vegetable, consisting of the pith of rushes and reeds, duckweed, water plants, etc.; but owing to the fact that many true rats have taken to living on the banks of streams, their depredations among chickens, ducklings, and fish have been charged to the voles—quite without foundation —a sad instance of the consequence of bad company.

12. **The Short-tailed Field Vole** (*Microtus agrestis*)—often called FIELD MOUSE—resembles the preceding in general characterization, but is less than half its size, some 4 inches long in body, and the tail 1½ inch. The short, blunt head, and stumpy tail covered with hair (and not with scales), distinguish it from the true mouse. It is brown in colour above and a dirty grey below.

It is found in meadow and pasture land, and after a series of mild winters often becomes a veritable plague; for, like the mice, it is remarkably prolific, having four or five litters during spring and summer. The remark is obvious that man deserves some punishment for his folly in persistently killing off the Field Vole's natural enemies—owls, hawks, crows, and weasels.

In the spring field voles will do untold mischief by gnawing the bark of young trees. I have seen a small copse devastated in this manner, the trees having been killed by the removal of the bark in a perfect ring at their bases. They will destroy turf—thereby starving the sheep; they will strip the heather of its young shoots. In one place in Germany 1,500,000 of these pests were caught in fourteen days.

It is of interest to note the one occasion when they served a nation's turn. According to Herodotus, the destruction of Sennacherib's host (2 Kings xix.) was the result of the invasion of a plague of field mice into the camp, which gnawed the *bowstrings* of the Assyrians, rendering them useless. Another reference, in 1 Sam. vi., points to the " golden mice "—models of " your mice that mar the land "—as offerings to Israel's God from the Philistines, in consequence of the havoc wrought by field mice and the famine and pestilence which ensued. In ancient Egypt the mouse was the symbol of pestilence.

The Irish may well be thankful for this, among other small mercies—that the Field Mouse is unknown in Erin !

13. **The Bank Vole** (*Arvicolus glareolus*)—sometimes called the WOOD VOLE)—is chestnut-red in colour in the upper parts, its chief point of distinction from the Field Vole; in habits it is similar to the others, except that it is found in woods and forests much more than in open fields. It is even more destructive to young trees, devouring bark, buds, and tender shoots, and wreaks havoc in the garden.

Order : UNGULATA ("Hoofed Mammals")—Deer, Wild Cattle, Sheep, and Goats.

1. **The Roe Deer** (*Capreolus caprœa*).—This animal is some 26 inches in height at the withers—*that is*, where the shoulder bones meet at the top of the back—and in summer is foxy-red in colour. In winter, when the fur is much thicker and coarser, it appears a dark brownish grey. It possesses a very distinctive mark in its black-and-white muzzle and mouth, the colouring of which adds materially to the pretty appearance of this deer.

It was once common in England, and there are still a few said to be living in Cumberland, the descendants of the old English stock ; but those that are found in parks to-day have been reintroduced, since the beginning of the nineteenth century, from abroad. In Scotland, however, they are still native in the Highlands.

The horns of the male are shed in December, and the new antlers are nearly perfect by the end of February. Fawns are born in June.

The Roe Deer are *monogamous*—an unusual feature among deer, where generally one stag has several hinds.

The male utters a cry like a dog's bark or yelp ; the female has a softer cry, seldom uttered except in the breeding season. At this season the males are very savage and dangerous.

DEER 47

2. **The Red Deer** (*Cervus elaphus*).—This deer is a native of our islands, and is found on Exmoor, in the Highlands of Scotland, the wilder parts of Ireland, and the Hebrides. A full-grown stag (the male) is at least 4 feet at the antlers, the hind only slightly smaller. Its winter colour is brown, tinged with grey, with a certain amount of black, a stripe down the back, and on the tips and edges of the ears. On the rump is a well-defined patch of dingy yellow, roughly shaped like a heart, and turning gradually to white near the tail. The summer coat is, as the name implies, a rich red, with touches of bronze-gold in specimens in first-class health and condition. The hair on the under side of the neck is so thick as to become a real mane. In common with most deer, there is a gland marked by a tuft on the outer side of the hind-leg below the hock, and a face gland or " tear pit."

The story of the deer's horns is one of the most remarkable in Nature.

Roe Deer.

They are shed every year, until the stag is fourteen years old, and grow again in increased weight and size. A full-grown horn weighs about 24 lb., and this is made in ten or twelve weeks. When the animal has cast its antlers it frequently eats them, or at any rate gnaws them. The new antlers are at first covered with a soft, downy skin, very tender and sensitive, filled with blood-vessels; but as soon as the antlers have reached their full size the blood-vessels dry up, and the " velvet," as the skin is called, is rubbed off against trees, rocks, or other hard obstacles.

The horns have three (roughly horizontal) prongs or tines—the one next to the head called the brow or frontal tine, and the others the *bez* and *trez* tines—old Norman-French terms (meaning " twice " and " thrice "), dating from the Conquest. Above the third tine, the " trunk " of the antler broadens

48 THE BRITISH NATURE BOOK

and divides into a number of prongs, this time pointing more or less vertically; in the centre is a " cup " or hollow.

For a good many years in the stag's life his age may be told by the development of his antlers—

A one-year-old stag carries a simple prong, 8 or 10 inches long (perhaps ending in a knob).

At two years old, a small brow tine and *trez* appear.

At three years old, the *bez* tine first appears.

At six years old, the cup begins to form.

Fallow Deer.

At seven years old, the cup has three points, from which the prongs are to grow.

After this come years of development of this series of prongs: a stag with three prongs is called a " Royal."

After fourteen years the horns develop no further, but even degenerate.

The Red Deer speaks to its kind in several " voices "—a gentle bleat of friendship; a kind of bark of alarm; and, when angry or excited (as in the rutting season), a strange and awesome roar. I have heard this roar of challenge or jealousy in the semi-darkness of a late autumn morning, and it has wanted but a little imagination to believe it came from a lion.

The breeding season is in the autumn, beginning in September, when the

PLATE VI.

1. The Stoat. 2. Red Deer in Snow. 3. Skeleton of Mouse (found in an old piano). 4. Rabbit tostered by Cat.

DEER AND WILD CATTLE 49

stag, which has a harem of as many hinds as he can get, is very savage. The photograph (Plate VI.) was obtained only with difficulty, for this reason: that the photographer could not approach the wire fencing with his camera without the stag charging (fortunately, the *other* side), and getting out of focus. It was necessary to use strategy, and get an assistant to distract the stag's attention until the proper moment.

Fawns are born in May and June, and are guarded with the most devoted care. They may live to thirty years (in the male) and twenty (in the female), but have passed their meridian at fourteen.

3. **The Fallow Deer** (*Cervus dama*).—It is a question whether this species is not a native of this country; there may have been an indigenous species, though it has been reintroduced since (probably) Roman times, and it may be seen in many parks to-day. It is not as large as the Red Deer—the males standing about 3 feet high at the withers. In summer it is a rich yellow-brown in colour, dappled or spotted with white. In winter it becomes a uniform dark brown above, shading off into grey. The antlers are "palmated"—that is, hand-shaped towards their ends. They are cast in May, and the new horns are full grown by the middle of August—a shorter rate of growth than in the case of the Red Deer.

There were once **Wild Sheep** in this country, the remains of which have been found in East Anglia; but to-day the only Wild Sheep to be found alive are confined to Soa and St. Kilda, the islands forty miles north-west of the Outer Hebrides—and these were introduced there by the Vikings.

The Wild Cattle—or, rather, the preserved remnants of the ancient Wild Cattle—are to be found only on a few private estates. There is a famous "herd" in the forest of Cadzow, in Lanarkshire, in the possession of the Duke of Hamilton; and others at Chillingham (Northumberland), Lyme Park (Cheshire), Chartley, and Vaynol.

They are generally white, shaggy creatures, with black ears and muzzles, and other black flecks about them (or, as at Chillingham, *red* ears). They show the habits of their ancestors in feeding—at any rate, in summer—chiefly at night. The cows hide their calves in the thick brushwood for the first week or two, and may then be dangerous to passers-by in their desire to protect their young.

[I desire to acknowledge my indebtedness to Sir Harry Johnston's *British Mammals* and other works throughout this chapter.]

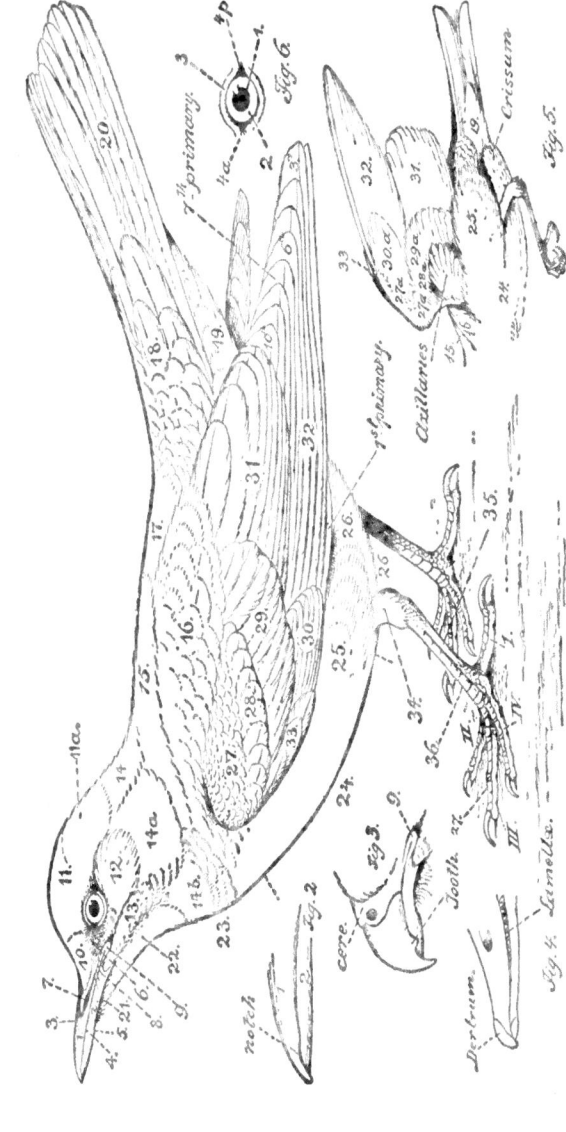

TERMS ILLUSTRATED BY THE FIGURES.

FIG. 1.—1. Upper mandible of beak (see Fig. 2); 2. Lower mandible of beak (see Fig. 2); 3. Ridge; 4. Cutting edge (or commissure); 5. Angle or gonys; 6. Lores (space between base of bill and eye); 7. Nostrils; 8. Gape bristles; 9. Flanges (see Fig. 3); 10. Forehead; 11. Crown; 11a. Nape; 12. Ear coverts (auricular); 13. Cheek; 14–14b. Neck; 15. Back; 16. Scapulars (shoulder feathers); 17. Rump; 18. Upper tail coverts; 19. Under tail coverts; 20. Tail feathers; 21. Chin; 22. Throat; 23. Gorget (pectoral band); 24. Breast; 25. Flanks; 26. Belly (abdomen); 27. Minor, lesser, or upper wing coverts; 28. Median or middle coverts; 29, 30. Major or greater coverts of primaries (30) and secondaries (29); 31. Secondaries; 32. Primaries; 33. Bastard wing; 34. Tibial feathers; 35, 36. Metatarsus, or tarsus (popularly leg or shank); 37. Toe. FIG. 2.—See 1 and 2 above. FIG. 5.—Terms for the under surface of the wing correspond to those for the upper—for example : 27a. Lesser coverts, etc. FIG. 6 (EYE).—1. Pupil; 2. Iris (plural, irides); 3. Eyelid.

CHAPTER II.
Birds.

THE one chief characteristic by which birds are distinguished from all other animals is that they alone have their bodies covered with *feathers*. These are of two kinds—the "down" feathers and the "contour" feathers—the latter arranged on certain definite parts of the body so methodically that they can be identified, practically in all cases, in the same place on every species. A glance at the diagram (page 50) will show the arrangement of the chief feathers and groups of feathers better than any description.

Birds are warmer blooded than mammals, their temperature being 106° to 108° F. This is due, in part, to the more extended development of their breathing apparatus, as well as to the superior protection of their feathers. In addition to their lungs, birds have certain air spaces in different parts of their bodies communicating with them, so that they can make use of more *oxygen* than mammals, and thus produce greater heat. In addition, some of their *bones* are hollow, and contain air. These characteristics make the bird very light in weight, and so specially adapted for flying.

Note also that, instead of teeth, birds possess a gizzard, which serves as the masticating organ. This is in reality a *mill* in which the food is ground up, and consists of two strong and muscular portions covered with a tough skin. Within are always some small stones or pieces of grit, which are in a constant state of movement as the two parts of the gizzard rub together.

It is worth while to observe the skeleton of a bird, with its special points of difference from our own—the many bones in the neck, which enable the bird to revolve the head with far greater freedom; the extraordinary breast-bone with its keel, to which the powerful wing muscles are attached; and the fewness of the ribs.

I am not in favour of "collecting" eggs, unless it is done with a purely scientific aim. The student will do far better to observe birds and their nests than to take their clutches. Many of our British birds are in danger of extinction at the hands of would-be collectors. What is to be said, for instance, of one who told me with triumph that in one season he had taken eight nests of kingfishers! If eggs are taken, for purposes of study and comparison, it is sufficient to take *one* from a nest; the rest—number, and general colouring and size—can be made a matter of notebook and pencil, and if need be, of camera and lens. *There is no necessity whatever for the taking of the whole clutch.* I therefore give no directions for the making of such a collection; if it must be done, it should be left to those who are making a really scientific study of the subject.

I feel sure that if my readers are able to take up the charming hobby of photographing eggs and nests, they will have in their finished prints an infinitely more delightful record of their observation than in any number of cabinets filled with empty egg-shells.

The eggs of some species are very much alike, and to distinguish them readily it may be necessary to see them side by side. Here comes in the value of a good museum. Those who live in a big city, where there exists such a place, can go and study the collection there. It is well worth while to do so methodically, with notebook and pencil, marking down the essential differences in colour, shape, size, and markings of eggs that at first sight appear similar. Notes made in this way, directly in your *own* pocket-book, are worth more than any printed matter. It is only where there is no local museum or collection that it may be necessary, if you really and truly are desiring to *learn* to distinguish the eggs and nests of British birds, for you to take occasional eggs, so that you can compare them at home; but I strongly advise you to make this practice as rare as possible, for the passion of collecting grows, and it may become a veritable " kleptomania." An enormous amount of harm is done every year by those whose passion for collecting sends them out to take birds' eggs or to shoot rare birds.

The chapter on Apparatus gives directions on how to photograph nests, eggs, and birds, amongst other things; the only thing to be said here is with regard to the few eggs that come into your possession. To blow an egg properly, only one hole should be drilled in it, not at either end, but in the middle. A blowpipe can be made out of a piece of glass tubing, drawn out to a point in a gas flame, and preferably bent at an angle. The glass tubes used for filling fountain pens serve the purpose very well.

The egg should be drilled with as small a hole as possible, and held with the hole *downwards* whilst the blowpipe is used. The end of the latter should *not* be inserted into the hole, but placed close by. Then when air is blown into the hole, the contents of the egg are discharged easily. When empty, the egg should be washed out by blowing water into it, and drawing it out again. If the egg should be " set," get rid of as much of the contents as possible, using a needle to loosen them. If the contents are fairly solid—that is, if incubation is advanced—I know no plan so effective for emptying the egg as that suggested, I believe, first by Mr. C. Kearton, of putting it into an ants' nest, and letting them do the work. This is best done by putting the egg into a little tin box, with holes in it through which the ants can pass and repass. Bury the tin an inch or so below the surface, and leave it. It must not be left *too* long, or the ants will devour *shell* and all.*

Every now and then you may come across a *dead* bird which you may

* Do not *wash* any of the eggs you collect, or varnish them!

BEAKS AND BILLS. "As birds feed, so are their beaks shaped."

wish to preserve. Once again, I emphasize the point that the *young* Nature student *will only be doing harm*, in the long run, by making a collection of *dead birds or their skins*. Occasionally, for purposes of study, such as that of the differences in the sexes, or changes in plumage at different ages or seasons, it is an advantage to be able to inspect a preserved specimen; but the place for this is the museum or the local art gallery.

But it often happens in the course of one's rambles that one finds a dead bird, recently killed—my own youthful memories remind me of many such discoveries—and the wish presents itself immediately to preserve the skin, or even make an attempt to stuff it! The latter task is too involved for this book, but the following simple directions will be useful for preserving it.

First, to *skin* the bird. Put it on its back, with head towards you, and blow aside the feathers from breast to vent. Then, on the bare flesh thus exposed, cut with a sharp pair of scissors a slit (take care to cut the *skin* only, and *not* the flesh) from the *end of the breastbone* to the vent. Raise the skin, forcing the flesh away from it with some suitable instrument—the thin blade of a small paper-knife will do, or the *handle* of a tea-spoon. When you come to the legs, you must push them *in* from the outside until the shank or knee is exposed, and then the leg must be cut through, leaving the bony lower part in the skin. Similar cuts have to be made (1) at the vent itself, (2) the tail-bone, and (3) the shoulder joints of the wings. The head is the most difficult of all, and is left till last. The skin comes away over neck and head as far as the ears fairly easily; but when the ears are reached, a sharp blade of pocket-knife or scalpel must be used to cut round the membrane. Then the skin is pushed back until the eyes are just cleared. The knife is again used to slit their membranes, and they are scraped out. The skin is now hanging loose, fixed only to the fore-part of the head. Cut the head off the body, then open the *lower part* of the skull, and remove the inside. Then go back over the skin, which is now inside out, and clear away any adhering flesh or fat. Put the preservative mentioned below freely over the skin and in the skull, and hem the skin right way in—beginning at the head, *pressing this inwards*, for this is the first move in the game. The feathers will be much disturbed, but can be stroked smooth with a pad of cotton wool. A little wad or roll of wool is prepared for the neck, and pushed into position. A second wad, egg-shaped, forms the body of the bird. Shape the latter into a firm contour, with thread wound round it tightly. Powder these wads with the preservative before putting them in place. Finally, stroke and arrange the feathers in position with a pad, or even a fine brush.

There is one hint of great value in handling a bird in this manner. Have some plaster of Paris at hand, and if the feathers get stuck, or your fingers in any way messy, *dust* them with the powder freely. It will all brush off afterwards. Treat the body of the bird and the inside of the skin in the same manner.

The preservative can be bought ready made, but the following is as good as anything: six parts of whiting; three of burnt alum; one of camphor, naphthalene, or "carbon." Make this into a fine powder, and mix it well up. This is applied *dry*, but sometimes it must be used in the form of a soap, and rubbed into the skin. For this purpose, add one part of soft soap, mix all together with water to a thick paste, and stir it all up over a fire till thoroughly mixed. Then bottle it. Dry "carbolic" soap may be used instead of the "soft soap."

These instructions are necessarily very brief; but I would suggest that the young student should, if possible, get round some good-natured taxidermist, and watch him at work. He will learn more from one such ocular demonstration than from many printed words.

Classification of Birds.

There are more than 470 species of birds known to these islands, but of these only some 190 nest in this country. The rest are visitors, or birds of passage. The coming and going of our bird visitors is a matter upon which there is still much to learn. It is important to record the first observation of the coming of the summer visitors and of their departure in the autumn; and here there is undoubted opening for many readers of this book who wish to add to the general knowledge of birds. Keep a notebook for this purpose, and put down the first and last date on which you saw any particular bird *in your district*.

The British Isles undoubtedly possess some special attractiveness to the migratory birds, probably because they form a most convenient resting-place on the long journeys which these birds make.

Some 50 summer visitors come in April and May from Southern Europe and Africa; whilst 100 more arrive as winter visitors from September to November, driven by approaching winter from their nesting sites farther north—in Iceland, Greenland, and Northern Europe. There is thus a remarkable series of movements going on amongst our birds, and to it we must add the *local* movements of the birds which reside with us all the year round. There is far more migration amongst the most familiar of our common birds than is generally imagined. For instance, while some song thrushes are known to have remained in the same neighbourhood, others have been found to have travelled northwards or southwards, as the case may be. I am myself convinced that even the ubiquitous sparrow changes his quarters very frequently, and the scoundrel who nips your buds in the early spring is often *not* the same as the one who nests in your tits' boxes.

In addition, a large number of birds simply use these shores as a resting-place on their journey, and do not spend a season here. These are called birds of passage.

We can thus classify our birds under the heads of Residents, Summer Visitors, Winter Visitors, Birds of Passage, and Irregular Visitors, as follows:—

I. RESIDENTS.*

Raven.
Common Crow.
Hooded Crow.
Rook.
Jackdaw.
Magpie.
Jay.
Chough.
Greenfinch.
Hawfinch.
Chaffinch.
Goldfinch.
Siskin.
Lesser Redpoll.
Twite.
Linnet.
House Sparrow.
Tree Sparrow.
Crossbill.
Bullfinch.
Corn Bunting.
Yellow Bunting.
Cirl Bunting.
Reed Bunting.
Snow Bunting.
Skylark.
Woodlark.
Red Wagtail.
Grey Wagtail.
Meadow Pipit.
Rock Pipit.
Eider.
Scoter.
Goosander.
Red-breasted Merganser.
Creeper.
Wren.
Dipper.
Mistle Thrush.
Song Thrush.
Stonechat.
Redbreast.
Dartford Warbler.
Goldcrest.
Hedge Sparrow.

Starling.
Long-tailed Tit.
Great Tit.
Coal Tit.
Marsh Tit.
Willow Tit.
Blue Tit.
Crested Tit.
Nuthatch Tit.
Bearded Tit.
Green Woodpecker.
Great Spotted Woodpecker.
Lesser Spotted Woodpecker.
Barn Owl.
Tawny Owl.
Long-eared Owl.
Short-eared Owl.
Little Owl.
Heron.
Bittern.
Cormorant.
Shag.
Gannet.
Kingfisher.
Wood Pigeon.
Stock Dove.
Rock Dove.
Razorbill.
Guillemot.
Black Guillemot.
Black-headed Gull.
Common Gull.
Herring Gull.
Lesser Black-backed Gull.
Pintail.
Great Skua.
Richardson's Skua.
Woodcock.
Common Snipe.
Ringed Plover.
Golden Plover.
Lapwing.
Oyster-catcher.
Dunlin.
Ruff.

Redshank.
Greenshank.
Curlew.
Water-rail.
Great Crested Grebe.
Slavonian Grebe.
Black-necked Grebe.
Moorhen.
Coot.
Capercaillie.
Black Grouse.
Red Grouse.
Ptarmigan.
Pheasant.
Partridge.
Red-legged Partridge.
Golden Eagle.
White-tailed Eagle.
Marsh Harrier.
Hen Harrier.
Sparrow Hawk.
Buzzard.
Kite.
Osprey.
Peregrine.
Merlin.
Kestrel.
Greylag Goose.
Mute Swan.
Tufted Duck.
Shelduck.
Mallard.
Gadwall.
Shoveller.
Blackbird.
Teal.
Widgeon.
Pochard.
Great Black-backed Gull.
Kittiwake.
Little Grebe.
Black-throated Diver.
Red-throated Diver.

---

* These birds are with us all the year round; but while some do not move away, others shift their quarters locally, or even come or go as migrants. The starling, for example, is found with us always; yet while some will leave these shores, or even perhaps the neighbourhood where they nest, others come from Europe in the spring in great flocks, and yet others migrate in the autumn. The starling therefore, though resident, is also a summer visitor, a winter visitor, and a bird of passage.

BIRDS

II. SUMMER VISITORS.*

These begin to arrive at end of March from their winter quarters in Southern Europe or Africa. Many, it is known, travel from as far away as South Africa along the Nile Valley, and crossing the Mediterranean, bear westwards. Others follow the shore line of Spain and France, and so cross the Channel. The migration takes place in waves—that is, a small vanguard comes early, and then two or more vast flights of birds follow.

Yellow Wagtail—Africa.
Blue-headed Wagtail—Africa.
White Wagtail—Africa.
Garden Warbler—Africa.
Chiffchaff—shores of Mediterranean.
Yellow Wren—Africa and Persia.
Wood Warbler—Africa.
Reed Warbler—Africa.
Marsh Warbler—Africa.
Sedge Warbler—North Africa and Asia Minor.
Grasshopper Warbler—North Africa and South Europe.
Golden Oriole—Africa, Sind.
Red-backed Shrike—Africa.
Spotted Flycatcher—Africa.
Pied Catcher—Africa.
Tree Pipit—North Africa, Persia, India.
Ring Ouzel—Central Africa, Asia Minor.
Wheatear—West and North Africa, Persia, North India.
Swallow—Ethiopia, North India, India.
House Martin—South Abyssinia.
Sand Martin—India, Africa.
Wryneck—China, North Africa.
Swift—Africa.
Nightjar—Algeria, Egypt, Asia Minor.
Hoopoe—North and Central Africa to Abyssinia.
Cuckoo—Central Africa, South India.
Turtle Dove—North Africa, Egypt, Nubia.
Puffin—New England states of North America, Azores, Canaries, West Mediterranean.
Common Tern—Africa, Asia, India.
Arctic Tern—Africa.

Whinchat—North Africa.
Redstart—North Africa.
Nightingale—Africa.
Roseate Tern—South Africa.
Sandwich Tern—South Africa, Red Sea, Persian Gulf, etc.
Little Tern—East Africa, Asia.
Red-necked Phalarope—Mediterranean, India, China, Japan.
Dotterel—South Europe, North Africa, Palestine, Persia.
Kentish Plover—Africa, India, South China.
Common Sandpiper—Africa.
Whimbrel—South-West Asia to India, Madagascar, South Africa.
Corncrake—Algeria, Egypt, Asia Minor.
Whitethroat—South Africa.
Lesser Whitethroat—Africa.
Blackcap—North Africa, South Europe.
Spotted Crake—Canaries, Africa, Mesopotamia, North India.
Quail—Egypt, North Africa.
Montagu's Harrier—Canaries, Africa, India, Ceylon, Burma.
Hobby—Africa, India.
Garganey—Sudan, British East Africa.
Storm Petrel—On migration, Norway, Iceland, Greenland.
Leach's Fork-tailed Petrel—East of North America, Azores, Canaries, Madeira, etc.
Manx Shearwater—Very widely distributed.
Fulmar—As far as 43° south in Europe, Massachusetts, Maine, North America.

III. WINTER VISITORS.

These birds begin to arrive as our summer visitors depart; really, all alike taking part in the enormous tide that sets from the east or north-east southward. So not only do we get birds which will spend the winter with us,

* The places following the names indicate the winter quarters. The references to India, China, and the far East apply to those species which, during the migration-waves westwards and northwards, move into Europe. In case of sea birds, their winter quarters can only be very broadly defined.

but in their company hosts of passers-by, on their way beyond us to the south. Generally speaking, our familiar winter visitors have come from Iceland, Greenland, Scandinavia, Russia, Siberia, where they have bred.

Brambling.	Buffon's Skua.	Barnacle Goose.
Mealy Redpoll.	Jack Snipe.	Brent Goose.
Shorelark.	Grey Plover.	Great Northern Diver.
Redwing.	Turnstone.	Whooper Swan.
Fieldfare.	Purple Sandpiper.	Bewick's Swan.
Black Redstart.	Knot.	Scaup.
Waxwing.	Sanderling.	Golden-eye.
Snowy Owl.	Green Sandpiper.	Long-tailed Duck.
Little Auk.	Bar-tailed Godwit.	Velvet Scoter.
Little Gull.	Greenland Falcon.	Smew.
Glaucous Gull.	White-fronted Goose.	Red-necked Grebe.
Iceland Gull.	Bean Goose.	Great Shearwater.
Pomathorine Skua.	Pink-fronted Goose.	

IV. BIRDS OF PASSAGE.

Obviously, this is a difficult class to separate from the "visitors," because these birds, in some cases, linger or travel slowly through our domains; in others, even remain all the summer. The list, therefore (which is the work of Mr. Kirkman), represents those birds which may really be regarded as "passers-by."

Scarlet Grosbeak.	Barred Warbler.	Little Stint.
Ortolan Bunting.	Great Grey Shrike.	Temminck's Stint.
Little Bunting.	Woodchat.	Curlew Sandpiper.
Lapland Bunting.	Red-breasted Flycatcher.	Wood Sandpiper.
Richard's Pipit.	Roller.	Spotted Redshank.
Tawny Pipit.	Black Tern.	Black-tailed Godwit.
Water Pipit.	White-winged Black Tern.	Rough-legged Buzzard.
Firecrest.	Sabine's Gull.	Honey Buzzard.
Norwegian Bluethroat.	Grey Phalarope.	Spoonbill.
Yellow-browned Warbler.	Great Snipe.	Glossy Ibis.
Icterine Warbler.	Avocet.	

V. IRREGULAR VISITORS.

These form a long list, which is scarcely necessary in this book. Readers are referred to *The British Bird Book*, Vol. IV., page 592, to which superb work I owe a great debt for much in this section.

How to Observe Birds.

There is an immense amount of work to be done in this direction, and young readers *who are careful* may be able to add to the sum of our knowledge about our birds. As Cap'en Cuttle says, "*When found, make a note of*": put down *accurately* whatever notes you make; keep your notebook at hand; be careful

BIRDS

about the date. Cultivate *two* important qualities—patience, and the ability to sit still. Do not theorize—simply record the facts that you are sure of.

As for equipment : I refer to the use of the pocket telescope in another chapter. It is *cheaper* and less bulky than binoculars. If you photograph, the camera described will be most useful; but perhaps most important of all is *the pencil and notebook*. If you are to sit still for some time, take a piece of brown paper, or a more permanent material, such as waterproof, for a seat. To those who use the telescope, I add, take your walking-stick stand, referred to in the chapter on Apparatus.

Guide to British Birds.

In the following pages an attempt has been made to provide a means of identifying a large number of our British birds. Such details of size, plumage, note, etc., are set down as, I trust, may enable the reader to distinguish the different species. The further table is to provide a simple key to the identification of nests and eggs which are met with, when the young naturalist has no opportunity of seeing the birds themselves.

Obviously the first feature which will be observed in a bird is the *size*, and if it be remembered that the Common House Sparrow is 6 inches long, the Blackbird and Mistle Thrush 10½ inches, the Wood Pigeon 16 inches, and the Rook 19 inches, we have here four standards of comparison. Placing birds as near to these sizes as possible, we have the following lists.

The next step is to find the picture which the bird most closely resembles. For this purpose the illustrations are grouped according to the four standards of sizes.

Then pass to the detailed description given ; specially noting whether the bird is stated to be in the district where you think you have seen it, and, if possible, corroborate by the description of the nest and eggs.

For those who wish for a classified list of birds, the following* is added.

I. Order : PASSERIFORMES.

1. Family : *Corvidæ*—CROWS.

1. Raven—*Corvus corax corax.*
2. Carrion Crow—*Corvus corone corone.*
3. Hooded Crow—*Corvus cornix cornix.*
4. Rook—*Corvus frugilegus frugilegus.*
5. Jackdaw—*Corvus monedula spermologus.*
6. Magpie—*Pica pica pica.*
7. Jay—*Garrulus glandarius rufitergum.*
8. Chough—*Pyrrhocorax pyrrhocorax.*

---

* Adapted from *Kirkman*. The first name gives the *genus*, the second the *species*, the third the *sub-species*, when clearly recognized. The *number* in the alphabetical description following corresponds with this list.

THE BRITISH NATURE BOOK

2. Family: *Fringillidæ*. (a) Sub-family: *Fringillinæ*—FINCHES.

9. Greenfinch (Green Linnet)—*Chloris chloris chloris*, or *Ligurinus chloris*.
10. Hawfinch—*Coccothraustes coccothraustes coccothraustes*, or *C. vulgaris*.
11. Chaffinch—*Fringilla cœlebs cœlebs*.
12. Brambling—*Fringilla montifringilla*.
13. Goldfinch—*Carduelis carduelis britannica*.
14. Siskin—*Carduelis spinus*.
15. Lesser Redpoll—*Linota linaria cabaret*, or *L. rufescens*.
16. Mealy Redpoll—*Linota linaria linaria*.
17. Twite—*Linota flavirostris flavirostris*.
18. Linnet (Brown Linnet)—*Linota cannabina cannabina*.
19. House Sparrow—*Passer domesticus domesticus*.
20. Tree Sparrow (Mountain Sparrow)—*Passer montanus montanus*.
21. Crossbill—*Loxia curvirostra*.
22. Bullfinch—*Pyrrhula pyrrhula pileata*, or *P. europæa*.

2. Family: *Fringillidæ*. (b) Sub-family: *Emberizinæ*—BUNTINGS.

23. Corn Bunting—*Emberiza calandra*, or *E. miliaria*.
24. Yellow Bunting or Yellowhammer—*Emberiza citrinella*.
25. Cirl Bunting—*Emberiza cirlus*.
26. Reed Bunting—*Emberiza schœniclus schœniclus*.
27. Snow Bunting—*Plectrophenax nivalis*, or *Passerina nivalis*.

3. Family: *Alaudidæ*—LARKS.

28. Skylark—*Alauda arvensis arvensis*.
29. Woodlark—*Alauda arborea arborea*.

4. Family: *Motacillidæ*—WAGTAILS AND PIPITS.

30. Pied Wagtail—*Motacilla alba lugubris*.
31. White Wagtail—*Motacilla alba alba*.
32. Grey Wagtail—*Motacilla boarula boarula*.
33. Yellow Wagtail—*Motacilla flava rayi*.
34. Tree Pipit—*Anthus trivialis*.
35. Meadow Pipit (Titlark)—*Anthus pratensis*.
36. Rock Pipit—*Anthus spinoletta obscurus*.

5. Family: *Certhiidæ*—TREE-CREEPERS.

37. Tree-creeper—*Certhia familiaris britannica*, or *C. familiaris*.

6. Family: *Troglodytidæ*—WRENS.

38. Wren—*Troglodytes troglodytes troglodytes*.

7. Family: *Cinclidæ*—DIPPERS.

39. Dipper (Water Ouzel)—*Cinclus cinclus britannicus*, or *C. aquaticus*.

8. Family: *Turdidæ*. (a) Sub-family: *Turdinæ*—THRUSHES.

40. Mistle Thrush (Missel Thrush)—*Turdus viscivorus viscivorus*.
41. Song Thrush—*Turdus philomelus clarkei*, or *T. musicus*.
42. Redwing—*Turdus musicus*, or *T. iliacus*.
43. Fieldfare—*Turdus pilaris*.

BIRDS

44. Blackbird—*Turdus merula merula*.
45. Ring Ouzel—*Turdus torquatus torquatus*.
46. Wheatear—*Œnanthe œnanthe œnanthe*.
47. Whinchat—*Saxicola rubetra rubetra*, or *Pratincola rubetra rubetra*.
48. Stonechat—*Saxicola torquata hibernans*, or *Pratincola rubicola*.
49. Redstart—*Phœnicurus phœnicurus phœnicurus*, or *Ruticilla phœnicurus*.
50. Redbreast (Robin)—*Erithacus rubecula melophilus*.
51. Nightingale—*Luscinia megarhyncha megarhyncha*, or *Daulias luscinia*.

8. Family : *Turdidæ*. (b) Sub-family : *Sylviinæ*—WARBLERS.

52. Whitethroat—*Sylvia communis communis*, or *S. cinerea*.
53. Lesser Whitethroat—*Sylvia curruca curruca*.
54. Blackcap—*Sylvia atricapilla*.
55. Garden Warbler—*Sylvia borin*, or *S. hortensis*.
56. Dartford Warbler—*Sylvia undata dartfordiensis*.
57. Goldcrest—*Regulus regulus anglorum*, or *R. cristatus*.
   (In winter, a continental variety, *Regulus regulus regulus*, visits us.)
58. Chiffchaff—*Phylloscopus collybita collybita*, or *P. rufus*.
59. Willow Warbler (Willow Wren)—*Phylloscopus trochilus trochilus*.
60. Wood Warbler—*Phylloscopus sibilatrix sibilatrix*.
61. Reed Warbler—*Acrocephalus streperus streperus*.
62. Marsh Warbler—*Acrocephalus palustris*.
63. Sedge Warbler—*Acrocephalus schœnobœnus*.
64. Grasshopper Warbler—*Locustella nævia nævia*.

9. Family : *Accentoridæ*—ACCENTORS.

65. Dunnock (Hedge Sparrow)—*Accentor modularis occidentalis*.

10. Family : *Sturnidæ*—STARLINGS.

66. Starling—*Sturnus vulgaris*.

11. Family : *Paridæ*—TITS.

67. Long-tailed Tit—*Ægithalos caudatus roseus*, or *Acredula rosea*.
68. Great Tit (Ox-eye)—*Parus major*.
69. British Coal Tit—*Parus ater britannicus*.
70. Irish Coal Tit—*Parus ater hibernicus*.
71. Marsh Tit—*Parus palustris dresseri*.
72. Willow Tit—*Parus atricapillus kleinschmidti*.
73. Blue Tit (Tom Tit)—*Parus cœruleus obscurus*.
74. Crested Tit—*Parus cristatus scoticus*.

12. Family : *Sittidæ*—NUTHATCHES.

75. Nuthatch—*Sitta europæa britannica*, or *S. cæsia*.

13. Family : *Panuridæ*.

76. Bearded Tit—*Panurus biarmicus biarmicus*.

14. Family : *Laniidæ*—SHRIKES.

77. Red-backed Shrike (Butcher Bird)—*Lanius collurio collurio*.

15. Family · *Muscicapidæ*—FLYCATCHERS.

78. Spotted Flycatcher—*Muscicapa striata striata*, or *M. grisola*.
79. Pied Flycatcher—*Muscicapa atricapilla*.

THE BRITISH NATURE BOOK

16. Family: *Hirundinidæ*—SWALLOWS AND MARTINS.

80. Swallow—*Chelidon rustica rustica*, or *Hirundo rustica*.
81. House Martin—*Hirundo urbica urbica*, or *Chelidon urbica*.
82. Sand Martin—*Riparia riparia riparia*, or *Cotile riparia*.

II. Order: CORACIIFORMES.

1. Family: *Picidæ*—WOODPECKERS.

83. Green Woodpecker—*Picus viridus pluvius*, or *Gecinus viridis*.
84. Great Spotted Woodpecker—*Dryobates major anglicus*, or *Dendrocopus major*.
85. Lesser Spotted Woodpecker—*Dryobates minor comminutus*, or *Dendrocopus minor*.

2. Family: *Iynginæ*—WRYNECKS.

86. Wryneck—*Iynx torquilla torquilla*.

3. Family: *Cypselidæ*—SWIFTS.

87. Swift—*Apus apus apus*, or *Cypselus apus*.

4. Family: *Caprimulgidæ*—NIGHTJARS.

88. Nightjar (Goatsucker)—*Caprimulgus europæus europæus*.

5. Family: *Strigidæ*—OWLS.

89. Barn Owl (White Owl, Screech Owl)—*Tyto alba alba*, or *Strix flammea*.
90. Long-eared Owl—*Asio otus otus*.
91. Short-eared Owl—*Asio flammeus flammeus*, or *A. accipitrinus*.
92. Tawny Owl (Brown Owl, Wood Owl)—*Strix aluco aluco*, or *Syrnium aluco*.
93. Little Owl—*Athene noctua noctua*.

6. Family: *Alcedinidæ*—KINGFISHERS.

94. Kingfisher—*Alcedo ispida ispida*.

III. Order: CUCULIFORMES.

Family: *Cuculidæ*—CUCKOOS.

95. Cuckoo—*Cuculus canorus canorus*.

IV. Order: CHARADRIIFORMES.

1. Family: *Columbidæ*—PIGEONS.

96. Wood Pigeon (Ring Dove, Cushat)—*Columba palumbus palumbus*.
97. Stock Dove—*Columba œnas*.
98. Rock Dove—*Columba livia livia*.
99. Turtle Dove—*Turtur turtur turtur*, or *T. communis*.

2. Family: *Alcidæ*—AUKS.

100. Razorbill—*Alca torda*.
101. Guillemot—*Uria troille troille*.
102. Black Guillemot—*Cepphus grylle grylle*.
103. Little Auk—*Alle alle*, or *Mergulus alle*.
104. Puffin—*Fratercula arctica arctica*.

BIRDS 63

3. Family : *Laridæ.* (a) Sub-family : *Sterninæ*—TERNS.

105. Sandwich Tern—*Sterna sandvicensis sandvicensis*, or *S. cantiaca.*
106. Common Tern—*Sterna hirundo*, or *S. fluviatilis.*
107. Arctic Tern—*Sterna paradisæa*, or *S. macrura.*
108. Little Tern (Lesser Tern)—*Sterna minuta minuta.*

3. Family : *Laridæ.* (b) Sub-family : *Larinæ*—GULLS.

109. Black-headed Gull—*Larus ridibundus.*
110. Common Gull—*Larus canus canus.*
111. Herring Gull—*Larus argentatus argentatus.*
112. Lesser Black-backed Gull—*Larus fuscus fuscus.*
113. Great Black-backed Gull—*Larus marinus.*
114. Glaucous Gull—*Larus glaucus.*
115. Kittiwake—*Rissa tridactyla tridactyla.*

3. Family : *Laridæ.* (c) Sub-family : *Stercorariinæ*—SKUAS.

116. Great Skua (Bonxie, Skooi)—*Megalestris skua*, or *M. catarrhactes.*
117. Arctic Skua (Richardson's Skua)—*Stercorarius parasiticus*, or *S. crepidatus.*

4. Family : *Œdicnemidæ*—STONE CURLEWS.

118. Stone Curlew (Thick-knee, Norfolk Plover, Great Plover)—*Œdicnemus œdicnemus*, or *Œ. scolopax.*

5. Family : *Charadriidæ.* (a) Sub-family : *Scolopacinæ*—WOODCOCK AND SNIPES.

119. Woodcock—*Scolopax rusticola.*
120. Common Snipe—*Gallinago gallinago gallinago*, or *G. cœlestis.*
121. Jack Snipe—*Gallinago gallinula.*

5. Family : *Charadriidæ.* (b) Sub-family : *Charadriinæ*—PLOVERS.

122. Dotterel—*Eudromius morinellus.*
123. Ringed Plover (Ringed Dotterel)—*Ægialitis hiaticula hiaticula.*
124. Golden Plover—*Charadrius apricarius*, or *C. pluvialis.*
125. Grey Plover—*Squatarola squatarola*, or *S. helvetica.*
126. Lapwing (Green Plover, Peewit)—*Vanellus vanellus*, or *V. vulgaris.*

5. Family : *Charadriidæ.* (c) Sub-family : *Hæmatopodinæ.*

127. Oyster-catcher (Sea-pie)—*Hæmatopus ostralegus ostralegus.*
128. Turnstone—*Arenaria interpres*, or *Strepsilas interpres.*

5. Family : *Charadriidæ.* (d) Sub-family : *Tringinæ.*

129. Dunlin—*Erolia alpina alpina*, or *Tringa alpina.*
130. Purple Sandpiper—*Erolia maritima maritima*, or *Tringa maritima.*
131. Knot—*Erolia canutus*, or *Tringa canutus.*
132. Sanderling—*Calidris leucophœa*, or *C. arenaria.*
133. Common Sandpiper—*Tringa hypoleuca*, or *Totanus hypoleucus.*
134. Green Sandpiper—*Tringa ocrophus*, or *Totanus ocrophus.*
135. Redshank—*Tringa totanus*, or *Totanus calidris.*
136. Bar-tailed Godwit—*Limosa lapponica lapponica.*
137. Curlew—*Numenius arquata arquata.*
138. Whimbrel—*Numenius phæopus phæopus.*

V. Order: GRUIFORMES.

Family: *Rallidæ* — RAILS.

139. Corncrake (Landrail)—*Crex crex*, or *C. pratensis*.
140. Water-rail—*Rallus aquaticus aquaticus*.
141. Waterhen (Moorhen)—*Gallinula chloropus chloropus*.
142. Coot—*Fulica atra atra*.

VI. Order: GALLIFORMES.

Family: *Phasianidæ*. (*a*) Sub-family: *Tetraoninæ*—GROUSE.

143. Capercaillie (Capercailzie)—*Tetrao urogallus urogallus*.
144. Black Grouse (Black Game, Blackcock, Greyhen)—*Tetrao tetrix*.
145. Red Grouse—*Lagopus lagopus scoticus*.
146. Ptarmigan—*Lagopus mutus mutus*.

Family: *Phasianidæ*. (*b*) Sub-family: *Phasianinæ*—PHEASANTS.

147. Pheasant—*Phasianus colchicus*.
148. Partridge (Grey Partridge)—*Perdix perdix perdix*, or *P. cinerea*.
149. Red-legged Partridge (French Partridge)—*Caccabis rufa rufa*.
150. Quail—*Coturnix coturnix coturnix*.

VII. Order: ACCIPITRES. Sub-order: FALCONES.

1. Family: *Buteonidæ*. (*a*) Sub-family: *Aquilinæ*—EAGLES.

151. Golden Eagle—*Aquila chrysaëtus chrysaëtus*.

1. Family: *Buteonidæ*. (*b*) Sub-family: *Buteoninæ*—BUZZARDS.

152. Buzzard—*Buteo buteo buteo*, or *B. vulgaris*.

1. Family: *Buteonidæ*. (*c*) Sub-family: *Accipitrinæ*—SPARROW HAWKS.

153. Sparrow Hawk—*Accipiter nisus nisus*.

2. Family: *Falconidæ*.

154. Peregrine Falcon—*Falco peregrinus peregrinus*.
155. Merlin—*Falco regulus regulus*, or *F. æsalon*.
156. Kestrel (Wind-hover)—*Falco tinnunculus tinnunculus*.

VIII. Order: ANSERIFORMES. Sub-order: ANSERES.

Family: *Anatidæ*. (*a*) Sub-family: *Anserinæ*—GEESE.

157. Greylag Goose—*Anser anser*, or *A. cinereus*.
158. Barnacle Goose—*Branta leucopsis*, or *Bernicla leucopsis*.
159. Brent Goose—*Branta bernicla bernicla*, or *Bernicla brenta*.

Family: *Anatidæ*. (*b*) Sub-family: *Cygninæ*—SWANS.

160. Mute Swan—*Cygnus olor*.

BIRDS

Family: *Anatidæ.* (c) Sub-family: *Anatinæ*—SHELDUCK AND SURFACE-WATER DUCKS.

161. Common Shelduck—*Tadorna tadorna,* or *T. cornuta.*
162. Mallard (Wild Duck)—*Anas platyrhyncha platyrhyncha,* or *A. boscas.*
163. Shoveller—*Spatula clypeata.*
164. Pintail—*Dafila acuta.*
165. Teal—*Nettion crecca crecca.*
166. Widgeon—*Mareca penelope.*

Family: *Anatidæ.* (d) Sub-family: *Fuligulinæ*—DIVING DUCKS.

167. Pochard (Red-headed Pochard)—*Nyroca ferina ferina,* or *Fuligula ferina.*
168. Tufted Duck—*Nyroca fuligula,* or *Fuligula cristata.*
169. Scaup Duck (Scaup)—*Nyroca marila marila,* or *Fuligula marila.*
170. Golden-eye—*Clangula clangula,* or *C. glaucion.*
171. Long-tailed Duck—*Harelda hyemalis,* or *H. glacialis.*
172. Common Eider—*Somateria mollissima mollissima.*
173. Scoter (Black Duck)—*Oidemia nigra nigra.*

Family: *Anatidæ.* (e) Sub-family: *Merginæ*—SAWBILL DUCKS.

174. Goosander—*Mergus merganser merganser.*
175. Red-breasted Merganser—*Mergus serrator.*

IX. Order: CICONIIFORMES. 1. Sub-order: ARDEÆ.

Family: *Ardeidæ*—HERONS AND BITTERNS.

176. Common Heron—*Ardea cinerea.*

IX. Order: CICONIIFORMES. 2. Sub-order: STEGANOPODES.

1. Family: *Phalacrocoracidæ*—CORMORANTS.

177. Cormorant (Great or Black Cormorant)—*Phalacrocorax carbo carbo.*
178. Shag (Green Cormorant)—*Phalacrocorax graculus graculus.*

2. Family: *Sulidæ*—GANNETS.

179. Gannet (Solan Goose)—*Sula bassana.*

X. Order: PROCELLARIIFORMES. Sub-order: TUBINARES.

Family: *Procellariidæ*—PETRELS.

180. Manx Shearwater—*Puffinus puffinus puffinus,* or *P. anglorum.*
181. Fulmar—*Fulmarus glacialis glacialis.*
182. Storm Petrel—*Hydrobates pelagica,* or *Procellaria pelagica.*

XI. Order: COLYMBIFORMES. 1. Sub-order: PODICEPEDES.

Family: *Podicepididæ*—GREBES.

183. Great Crested Grebe—*Colymbus cristatus,* or *Podicipes cristatus.*
184. Little Grebe (Dabchick)—*Colymbus ruficollis,* or *Podicipes fluviatilis.*

THE BRITISH NATURE BOOK

XI. Order: COLYMBIFORMES. 2. Sub-order: COLYMBI.

Family: *Colymbidæ*—DIVERS.

185. Great Northern Diver—*Gavia immer*, or *Colymbus glacialis*.
186. Red-throated Diver—*Gavia stellata*, or *Colymbus septentrionalis*.
187. Black-throated Diver—*Gavia arctica*, or *Colymbus arcticus*.

These numbers correspond with those in Kirkman's *British Birds* (Jack), the most excellent pocket-book on the subject published. The intention is that the young reader should carry one of these about with him on his rambles. Indeed, I most strongly advise him to get a copy, and *interleave it with blank pages* on which he can make notes. I can scarcely over-emphasize the value of the pocket-book thus made, if the young student will add his own original notes to the admirable descriptions given by the author. It is the sort of book which should accompany him on every bird-observing expedition. Another most valuable exercise is to *colour* the plates of birds from direct observation.

I. BIRDS ABOUT THE SIZE OF A SPARROW—6 INCHES FROM TIP OF TAIL TO BEAK.

103. Auk, Little, 7½ in.
54. Blackcap, 5¾ in.
12. Brambling, 6 in.
22. Bullfinch, 6 in.
25. Bunting, Cirl, 6½ in.
23. ,, Corn, 7 in.
26. ,, Reed, 6½ in.
27. ,, Snow, 7 in.
24. ,, Yellow, 6–7 in.

11. Chaffinch, 6 in.
58. Chiffchaff, 4½ in.
37. Creeper, Tree-, 5½ in.
21. Crossbill, 6½ in.

39. Dipper, 7 in.
129. Dunlin, 7½ in.

79. Flycatcher, Pied, 5 in.
78. ,, Spotted, 5 in.

57. Goldcrest, 3½ in.
13. Goldfinch, 5 in.
9. Greenfinch, 5½ in.

10. Hawfinch, 7 in.

94. Kingfisher, 7½ in.

18. Linnet, 5½ in.

81. Martin, House, 5⅛ in.
82. ,, Sand, 4⅞ in.

51. Nightingale, 6½ in.
75. Nuthatch, 5¾ in.

182. Petrel, Storm, 6¼ in.
35. Pipit, Meadow, 5¾ in.
36. ,, Rock, 6¼ in.
34. ,, Tree, 6 in.

150. Quail, 7 in.

50. Redbreast (Robin), 5¾ in.
15. Redpoll, Lesser, 4½ in.
16. ,, Mealy, 5 in.
49. Redstart, 5½ in.

77. Shrike, Red-backed, 7 in.
14. Siskin, 4½ in.
28. Skylark, 7 in.
121. Snipe, Jack, 7½ in.
65. Sparrow, Hedge, 5½ in.
19. ,, House, 6 in.
20. ,, Tree, 5½ in.
48. Stonechat, 5½ in.
80. Swallow, 7½ in.
87. Swift, 7 in.

76. Tit, Bearded, 6¼ in.
73. ,, Blue, 4½ in.

69. Tit, British Coal, 4¼ in.
74. ,, Crested, 4½ in.
68. ,, Great, 5¾ in.
70. ,, Irish Coal, 4¼ in.
67. ,, Long-tailed, 5½ in.
71. ,, Marsh, 4½ in.
72. ,, Willow, 4½ in.
17. Twite, 5 in.

32. Wagtail, Grey, 7 in.
30. ,, Pied, 7 in.
31. ,, White, 7 in.
33. ,, Yellow, 6 in.
56. Warbler, Dartford, 5 in.
55. ,, Garden, 5¾ in.
64. ,, Grasshopper, 5½ in.
62. ,, Marsh, 5¼ in.
61. ,, Reed, 5¼ in.
63. ,, Sedge, 5 in.
59. ,, Willow, 4¾ in.
60. ,, Wood, 5¼ in.
46. Wheatear, 6 in.
47. Whinchat, 5½ in.
52. Whitethroat, 5½ in.
53. ,, Lesser, 5¼ in.
29. Woodlark, 5½ in.
85. Woodpecker, Lesser Spotted, 6 in.
38. Wren, 3½ in.
86. Wryneck, 7 in.

BIRDS

II. BIRDS ABOUT THE SIZE OF A BLACKBIRD—10½ INCHES LONG.

44. Blackbird, 10½ in.
139. Corncrake, 10½ in.
122. Dotterel, 9 in.
99. Dove, Turtle, 11¼ in.
43. Fieldfare, 10 in.
184. Grebe, Little (Dabchick), 9¼ in.
102. Guillemot, Black, 11 in.
131. Knot, 10 in.
155. Merlin, 11–12 in.

88. Nightjar, 10¼ in.
45. Ouzel, Ring, 10¼ in.
93. Owl, Little, 9–9¼ in.
148. Partridge, 12½ in.
124. Plover, Golden, 11 in.
126.   „ Green (Lapwing), 12¼ in.
125.   „ Grey, 11½ in.
123.   „ Ringed, 8 in.
135. Redshank, 11 in.
42. Redwing, 8½ in.
132. Sanderling, 8 in.

133. Sandpiper, Common, 8 in.
134.   „ Green, 9¼ in.
130.   „ Purple, 8¼ in.
120. Snipe, Common, 10 in.
66. Starling, 8½ in.
108. Tern, Little, 9½ in.
40. Thrush, Mistle, 10½ in.
41.   „ Song, 9 in.
128. Turnstone, 8 in.
140. Water-rail, 11½ in.
84. Woodpecker, Great Spotted, 10 in.
83. Woodpecker, Green, 12½ in.

III. BIRDS ABOUT THE SIZE OF A WOOD PIGEON—16 INCHES LONG.

8. Chough, 16 in.
142. Coot, 15 in.
95. Cuckoo, 14 in.
118. Curlew, Stone, 16 in.
98. Dove, Rock, 13¼ in.
97.   „ Stock, 13¼ in.
168. Duck, Tufted, 17 in.
154. Falcon, Peregrine, 15–18 in.
136. Godwit, Bar-tailed, 15½ in.
170. Golden-eye, 18½ in.
145. Grouse, Red, 15¼ in.
101. Guillemot, 18 in.
109. Gull, Black-headed, 16 in.
110.   „ Common, 18 in.

153. Hawk, Sparrow, 13–15½ in.
5. Jackdaw, 14 in.
7. Jay, 14 in.
156. Kestrel, 13–14 in.
115. Kittiwake, 16 in.
6. Magpie, 18 in.
89. Owl, Barn, 13½ in.
90.   „ Long-eared, 14 in.
91.   „ Short-eared, 14½ in.
92.   „ Tawny, 15–18 in.
127. Oyster-catcher, 16½ in.
149. Partridge, Red-legged, 13½ in.

96. Pigeon, Wood, 16 in.
146. Ptarmigan, 14½ in.
104. Puffin, 13 in.
100. Razorbill, 17 in.
180. Shearwater, Manx, 15 in.
165. Teal, 14½ in.
107. Tern, Arctic, 14½ in.
106.   „ Common, 14½ in.
105.   „ Sandwich, 16½ in.
141. Waterhen, 13 in.
138. Whimbrel, 16–18 in.
166. Widgeon, 18¼ in.
119. Woodcock, 14¼ in.

IV. BIRDS ABOUT THE SIZE OF A ROOK—19 INCHES AND LARGER.

152. Buzzard, 21–23 in.
143. Capercaillie, 35 in.
177. Cormorant, 36 in.
2. Crow, Carrion, 19 in.
3.   „ Hooded, 19 in.
137. Curlew, 21–26 in.
187. Diver, Black-throated, 27¼ in.
185.   „ Gt. Northern, 31 in.
186.   „ Red-throated, 24 in.
171. Duck, Long-tailed, 22–26 in.
169.   „ Scaup, 19 in.
162.   „ Wild (Mallard), 23 in.
151. Eagle, Golden, 32–36 in.
172. Eider, Common, 23 in.

181. Fulmar, 19 in.
179. Gannet, 33 in.
174. Goosander, 26 in.
158. Goose, Barnacle, 27 in.
159.   „ Brent, 22 in.
157.   „ Greylag, 34 in.
183. Grebe, Great Crested, 21 in.
144. Grouse, Black, 23 in.
114. Gull, Glaucous, 29 in.
113.   „ Great Black-backed, 30 in.
111.   „ Herring, 24 in.
112.   „ Lesser Black-backed, 22 in.
(188. Harrier, Montagu's.)

176. Heron, Common, 36 in.
175. Merganser, Red-breasted, 24 in.
147. Pheasant, 35 in.
164. Pintail, 26–29 in.
167. Pochard, 19 in.
1. Raven, 25 in.
4. Rook, 19 in.
173. Scoter, 20 in.
178. Shag, 26 in.
161. Shelduck, Common, 25 in.
163. Shoveller, 20 in.
117. Skua, Arctic, 20 in.
116.   „ Great, 21 in.
160. Swan, Mute, 60 in.

THE BRITISH NATURE BOOK

I. BIRDS ABOUT THE SIZE OF A SPARROW—6 INCHES LONG.

Auk, Little.—This bird does not breed in Great Britain, but visits our north and east coasts irregularly in the winter, coming from its home in the Arctic Ocean. It is recognizable *by its small size*. In its winter plumage, the upper parts are chiefly black, with a touch of white on the shoulder feathers and " secondaries," and a white spot over the eye; white belly and breast, and a collar of black round the throat. Its food consists of small crustaceans (*Entomostraca*). It is a restless, noisy bird, its call being said to resemble " Perre-rett-tett-tett." The eggs are laid on the bare rock in deep crevices and under boulders.

Blackcap.—One of our summer migrants, generally (though locally) to be found in wooded districts, where its very pleasing song, containing very mellow full notes, generally preceded by a short, quiet, subdued phrase, may be heard flooding out from some leafy clump—" second only to the Nightingale," though bearing a general resemblance to that of the Whitethroats. The alarm note or call is a sharp " Tock-tock." The bird is rare in Ireland and the North of Scotland; though sometimes it winters in the South-west of England. It is distinguished from our other warblers by the glossy black cap in the male and reddish brown in female and young. Upper parts light olive-brown, almost ash-grey. Wings and tail sepia-brown. Throat and under parts ashy white, tinged with brown on flanks.

Blackcap.

The nest, a fragile structure of grass and bents, lined with finer material and hair, is found in bushes, brambles, hedges, undergrowth. The eggs (four to five), dull white blotched with olive-brown and grey, may be found in May.

Brambling.—A winter visitor and bird of passage, which breeds in Scandinavia; does not sing with us, though its harsh chirping call-note can be heard. It is frequently seen with chaffinches in autumn and winter, and is at once distinguished from them by the white rump seen when it flies. It is also identified by the chestnut throat and breast. In winter the head, cheeks, and upper part of the back are black, the feathers edged with ruddy brown; the belly is dirty white. The female is not so bright. Its haunt is beech woods.

Bullfinch.—Resident and widely distributed. The male has head, wings, and tail black, back grey, rump white. Throat and breast red, under parts greyish white. The female has a brown back and breast. Note the strong short beak. The nest is of twigs and moss, lined with roots, sometimes hair. The eggs—four to six—bluish-green, streaked or spotted with red-brown, chiefly at the larger end, generally laid in May. Its favourite nesting-place is in evergreens, but also found in hedges and bushes. Its note is a low, soft

22. Bullfinch. 11. Chaffinch. 79. Pied Flycatcher.

23. Corn Bunting. 21. Crossbill. 13. Goldfinch.

24. Yellow Bunting, or Yellowhammer. 39. Dipper, or Water Ouzel. 57. Goldcrest.

26. Reed Bunting. 129. Dunlin. 10. Hawfinch.

54. Blackcap. 56. Dartford Warbler. 20. Tree Sparrow.

Birds about the size of a Sparrow.
(The numbers correspond with those in the alphabetical list, page 66.)

whistle, often repeated—"Dee-ew, dee-ew." Its food consists chiefly of seeds, hawthorn berries, and—alas!—fruit buds.

Bunting, Cirl.—A local bird in England and Wales—rarely seen in Scotland and Ireland, and not in the North of England. In appearance it resembles the Yellowhammer, but has a black throat and an olive-green rump. Below the black throat comes a yellow band, then a green one, and stripes of red-brown on the flanks. Underneath yellow. Female has a yellow throat with streaks of black. The eggs (three to five) are bluish white with markings like the Yellowhammer's, but usually darker and bolder. The nest, found in May, is like the Yellowhammer's.

The song is said to resemble "Zee-ree-ree-ree-ree" repeated monotonously, the call-notes being "Zip-zip" and "Basta."

Bunting, Corn (Resident).—This is a bird of heavy build, much like a lark in appearance, and is at once distinguished from the other buntings by the absence of any white in the tail. Its general colour is brown above, the under parts greyish white with streaks and spots of dark brown. In autumn and winter it becomes a lighter brown, tinged with yellow. The young are like the parents in their winter garb, but have a reddish tinge on the throat and bright yellow edges to the tail and other feathers. The song is a short strain, constantly repeated, like that of the other buntings. The nest is found on the ground in tufts of grass, furze, or small bushes, on downs and cornlands, and is of grass and roots, *lined usually with grass.* The eggs, which vary in colour, are generally grey-white with dark spots and scribbles: number, four to six; generally found in June and July.

Bunting, Reed, often called "REED SPARROW."—Common in marshy districts and reed-beds; is at once distinguished by the black head *and* the white collar. Upper parts reddish brown streaked with black, rump greyish; under parts white with brown streaks on sides. The female has a reddish brown head. The song is a slight one, short and repeated, which has been vocalized thus: "Tsza, teet, taee, tziziz, taee, tseer," etc. The nest is usually in tussocks of grass or rushes, close to the ground, in marshy places, and is made of dried grass, lined with finer material and hair. Four or five eggs are laid, greenish or creamy white, spotted and streaked with rich dark brown (generally smaller than those of the preceding), and may be found as early as April.

Bunting, Snow.—This bird breeds rarely in the Highlands, but is generally a winter visitor to coast districts. It is distinguishable from all other buntings by the large amount of white on the wings. In fact the male, in breeding plumage, is all white except on the back, centre tail quills, and wings. The nest, composed of grass with a lining of feathers, fine grass or hair, is found in crevices among rocks on a mountain side. The eggs are white or greenish white with red-brown markings, and are laid in May or June.

Bunting, Yellow, or YELLOWHAMMER.—A quite common resident, the song of which—"A little bit of bread and no chee-eese"—is familiar to everybody,

Birds about the size of a Sparrow.

as is also its beautiful plumage. It is easily identified by the yellow head, neck, and under parts, the chestnut rump, and the white feathers in the tail visible when flying. No other British bird except the Yellow Wagtail shows so much yellow, and there is no likelihood of mistaking one for the other. The females and young are much duller, as is so generally the case.

The eggs, slightly smaller than those of the Corn Bunting, are of a purplish white, with deep brown marking and "scribbles"—hence the country name "SCRIBBLING or WRITING LARK." The nest is generally in a hedge bank or tuft, and is made of grasses, roots, etc., *lined with horsehair.*

Chaffinch.—Resident and widely distributed. Can be recognized by its smart, upright bearing, its jerky, quick motion on the ground, the large amount of white on the wings, and its sharp call-note "Pink-pink." The cock has slate-blue crown and nape, chocolate back, red throat and breast. Hen is duller, with breast grey-brown. The nest, built in hedges, bushes, and trees, is one of the most beautiful and symmetrical of British birds' nests; built of moss, ornamented with lichens, lined with hair and feathers. Once seen, its beautiful character renders it unmistakable. The eggs (four to six), greenish or bluish white, spotted and streaked with dark brown.

Chiffchaff.—A summer migrant, scarce in Scotland, a harbinger of spring, though a few spend the winter with us. It is identified by its note, "Chaff-chaff" repeated eight or ten times, and generally from a tall tree. The only bird which has a note at all resembling it is the Great Tit with its spring call; the latter, however, is heard much earlier, in January or February, and is quicker and shriller.

The bird is very small (4½ inches), and much like the Willow Wren, from which it is distinguished by the dark legs and feet, and generally duller plumage—dull olive-green above, wings and tail brown, under parts dingy yellowish white, eyebrow dull greyish white. The nest, often on the ground, or in some mixed tangle of brambles and herbage, is a domed structure, made usually of dead leaves, grass and moss, lined with feathers. The eggs are white, spotted with light red—generally six in number.

Creeper, Tree-.—This little bird is distinguished by its habit of creeping up and round the trunks of trees like a mouse, seeking insects in the crevices of the bark. It appears usually to ascend spirally; and if it notices its observer, will immediately run round the opposite side of the tree. It possesses a foot large in proportion to its size, with very mobile claws, a long slender curved beak, twelve specially stiffened and curved feathers in the tail—all obvious adaptations for its special habit of tree climbing. Its usual note is "Zib"; but it possesses a little song, which few naturalists hear, not unlike the Hedge Sparrow's—"Ticka-tee-tee-tee-tee-tee-ticka-ticka." The upper parts are chiefly brown; a silvery white throat, breast, and under parts.

Its nest, of twigs, moss, roots, etc., lined with wool or down, is usually behind the loose bark of a tree, or in some crevice in a wall or wooden building. The eggs, five or six in number, are white, with red spots, and may be found in May.

Birds about the size of a Sparrow.

74 THE BRITISH NATURE BOOK

Crossbill.—A special form or variety of this species is found only in the North of Scotland, where it breeds. The more familiar and bright-coloured form is chiefly a winter visitor, though some stay to breed. The bird is recognized by its " crossbill "—the tips of the beak actually crossing. The cock has a gaudy crimson plumage, with brown wings and tail. The hen is a yellowish green. The nest is high up in larches, firs, and other conifers ; a foundation of larch or fir twigs, with a superstructure of dry grass, wool, moss, etc., lined with grasses or hair, contains three or four eggs, like a large Greenfinch's, but with darker and fewer markings, greenish white, with a few dark purple spots or streaks. The birds begin laying *very early*—January to March. The call is " Yip-yip," or " Gip-gip."

Dipper, or WATER OUZEL.—This bird, like a large Wren with a white bib, gets its first name not from its habit of diving into water for food, but from its constant " curtseying," with downward jerks of the tail, on land. It is found by swift, rocky streams in the North and West of England, in Scotland and Wales, and is resident all the year round except in winter, when it makes local movements to open water. After having once been seen, there is no difficulty in identifying other specimens. Its erect attitude, with the short, stumpy tail almost at right angles to the back, its dark colour above, with the white breast plainly showing, distinguish it at once. The bird feeds on water insects, snails, and crustaceans, which it enters the stream to get, possessing the power of walking underneath the water. But it can also swim, and looks not unlike a miniature Dabchick, bobbing about at ease on the quickest running stream. The nest is usually near the water, in the bank or under a bridge, or on a stump or thick branch, and is a large domed structure of felted moss, with a hole at the side, containing an inner nest of dried grasses lined with leaves. The eggs (four to six) are pure white, and may be found as early as February, though generally in March to April. The Dipper has a charming song, mild and sweet, and may be heard specially in the winter, sometimes at night.

Dunlin.—This is a small member of the Sandpiper family, a common winter visitor on our coasts, but breeding only in Scotland (very occasionally elsewhere). It inhabits moors and marshes and low-lying land on the sea edge. The nest is a mere hollow of the ground, concealed by grass, heather, or similar herbage. It is lined sparsely with roots or grasses. The four eggs, pear-shaped, are greenish white blotched and spotted with reddish or dark brown, and are found in May. The summer plumage is as follows : Crown and nape chestnut streaked with black, mantle black with chestnut edges, remainder of upper parts grey, upper portion of breast grey-white, lower breast black, belly white, legs black. The winter plumage is chiefly grey above, white below, banded with grey on the lower breast. The spring call is a loud trill, " Whiz-whiz-whiz-whiz-whiz," not unpleasing compared with its usual purring winter note. The call-note is a clear whistle, " Trui," or " Pe-pe-pe."

Though classed according to *size* in this first list, it should be remembered that this bird (7½ inches long) is utterly unlike the sparrow in every other particular. Being a water bird, it has the long legs and long beak of the waders. The figure (No. 129) gives a good general idea of the family.

Flycatcher, Pied.—A summer visitor, but very local, almost entirely confined to mountainous valleys in northern counties and Wales. In the time of arrival, the construction of its nest, and its song, it resembles the Redstart, but the male is clearly distinguished by its black upper parts, the white bar on its forehead and white patch on the wing. The female is olive-brown, with no patch on forehead, but a whitish patch on the wing. It has a cheery little song—" Tickee-tickee-chuck-chuck-chee " is one constant phrase of it, and " Cheety-cheety-cheety-chee." The cock's alarm note is " Tit-a-tit " ; the hen's, like a Chaffinch's, " Wit-wit." The nest is almost always in a hole, and is of grass, moss, and leaves, lined with finer grasses, hair, wool, or feathers. The eggs (six to eight) are pale blue ; occasionally with a few red speckles.

The bird frequently returns to the same nesting site year by year : generally in well-wooded country, not far from running water.

Flycatcher, Spotted—often called " GREY FLYCATCHER."—One of the last of our summer immigrants, yet a very common bird, though scarce in Scotland. If a small brown bird is seen perching on the top of a fence or post or tennis net, and making repeated short flights from it after insects, it is almost certain to be the Spotted Flycatcher. A characteristic feature is its horizontal pose on the post, in order to " take off " instantaneously after the insect it sees. In Kent it is nicknamed the " POST BIRD," while, from its habit of often building its nest on a beam, it is known elsewhere as the " BEAM BIRD." Whilst mostly brown above, its under parts are ashy white, streaked with brown. Its food is entirely insectivorous, and the " gape " is provided with a set of stiff short " bristles," which are said to be useful in preventing the escape of its prey, forming a sort of " *cheval de frise* " round its mouth. The nest, which is generally near human habitation, is placed in many various situations, not only on beams, as mentioned above, but in holes, thatch, ledges, ivy, and so forth, and often in the deserted nest of some other bird, such as a chaffinch. It is built of grass, roots, etc., lined with hair or wool. The few notes of the so-called song, " Utik-utik-utik-tik," may be heard in May and June. The eggs are four or five in number, a bluish white, fading to creamy white, freckled and spotted with red-brown.

Goldcrest (GOLD-CRESTED WREN), the smallest British bird, generally resident throughout Great Britain and Ireland. There is also a continental variety, which appears on our eastern shores in the autumn on its migration to Northwest Africa; but this is larger and lighter in colour.

The Goldcrest is distinguished by its small size and " gold crest "—really a bright lemon crest—passing, in the cock, to an orange-red behind, edged with a line of black. Upper parts olive-green. Wings dusky brown with two bars of yellowish white. Under parts dull white ; in the female, dull buff.

It seems almost incredible that this tiny bird, with wings scarcely 2 inches across, can cross the Mediterranean or find its way to Africa ; yet in the autumn great flocks of these birds are to be seen on the East Coast, uttering their call-note—"Hüt-hüt-hüt"—as they make their way southwards, ever southwards. In addition to the call-note, the Goldcrest has a very bright, merry little song, though it consists of but two notes uttered five or six times, ending in a rapid trill. The bird haunts practically every wood of conifers—firs, pines, or yews—and builds a beautiful cup of a nest, which is generally *suspended* from three or four of the slender twigs. In addition, note that the nest is of green moss and *spiders' webs*, lined with feathers. The little eggs are whitish or ochreous, with tiny red-brown spots. The bird feeds on spiders, beetles, aphides, and other insects, and (during autumn and winter) on American blight. The deserted nest I have often found tenanted by humble-bees.

Goldfinch.—Resident and migrant. This charming bird is recognized by the flash of yellow on the wing, the crimson face, white cheeks, and black head. The back is a beautiful fawn-brown, which shades off into white beneath. The hen is duller, the crimson patch not extending behind the eye. The young, known as "Greypates," have a *brown* head.

The nest is a neat structure of moss, lichens, and roots, lined with hair, wool, etc., in trees, shrubs, and hedges; an apple tree is a favourite site. The eggs—four to six—pale bluish white, spotted purple and brown. In the autumn flocks of goldfinches may be seen on the common lands plucking the thistle seeds. The song is a delightful, varied composition, with a number of rich skylark notes, rattled off with tremendous "vim." The call-note is a defiant whistle—"Tu-whittu." The antics of the cock when courting are very noticeable. He turns rapidly from side to side, with tail spread out, so as to display himself to his mate "from both points of view," at the same time uttering his persuasive call-notes.

Greenfinch—often called GREEN LINNET—a resident and migrant. This bird is recognized by his general green colour, the yellow patches on the wings and base of the tail, and his heavily built, bulldog head, shoulders, and beak. The hen is duller in colour. This is one of the few birds which sing (if you can call it so) on the wing. The song is not melodious, consisting of a few low notes. The noticeable note is a long-drawn "wheeze"—"Twee-ee-ee"— which the bird will repeat for hours from its covert in the bushes or plantations. At the same time I should like to state that I had a pair of greenfinches, the male of which, very early in the morning, and only then, sang a very full and melodious song, not unlike but richer than the Goldfinch's. Greenfinches appear to like to build near houses—a shrubbery is a favourite haunt—and here, or in the adjoining hedgerow, you may find their nest, larger than but like the Chaffinch's, though untidier—of twigs, moss, and grass, lined with hair and feathers.

The eggs—four to six—are whitish, with a tinge of green-blue, and with purplish spots and markings.

Hawfinch—so called from its habit of eating the seeds of haws. This is the largest of the finches, and though at one time scarce, is now on the increase, and is resident in woodlands throughout the country, but rare in Ireland. It is a heavily built bird, with a huge beak (from which its old name of "GROSBEAK" came), and can be distinguished by its general build, the white (a good deal) showing in tail during flight, and chestnut-brown of the upper parts. The throat is black.

The call-note is a sharp "click"—a "clinking" note—like "Krupps," heard during flight, and unmistakable. The song is a soft and simple one of low, plaintive notes, not unlike those of the Bullfinch.

The nest is a characteristic, built first of a layer of twigs, on which is a shallow cup of bents, fibres, etc., lined with rootlets, hair, grass, etc., and is found in bushes, trees, and hedges. The eggs are large and handsome, bluish green, with bold marks and streaks of olive-brown.

The food consists of the kernels of hawthorn berries (hence "*Haw*finch"), cherries, plums, yews, peas, etc., the Hawfinch having a pair of remarkable horny plates, or crushing pads, inside the bill, with which he can break most kernels. It is a common sight to see him adroitly bisect a cherry stone "at one bite," the two halves falling neatly from each side of that heavy bill.

Kingfisher.—Recognized by the brilliant blue of the upper and chestnut-red of the under parts, the long beak, stumpy tail, and red feet. This bird is resident in the British Isles, but scarcer in Scotland. The nest is generally in the steep bank of a stream, though I have seen its tunnel some distance away in a bank and a sand-pit. The tunnel is some 3 feet long, with a rounded chamber at the end, and slopes slightly upward. The nest is often used in consecutive years. The eggs are laid on the bare earth, but, as incubation proceeds, the fish-bones which the birds eject accumulate until they form a considerable amount of debris round the eggs: hence the popular fallacy that the bird builds its nest of fish-bones. The eggs (six or seven in number) are almost round, a pure glossy white, and are laid in early April; I have known them laid in mid-March. The bird feeds on fish, and also on aquatic insects, slugs, and snails. The note is a shrill "H'wee—h'wee" or "Peep-peep," uttered in flight.

The feet of the Kingfisher are very small, the front toes being united in a common sheath (*syndactylous*). The sexes are indistinguishable in colour. Though popularly supposed to use the burrow of a water vole, the birds always dig their own tunnel, except when utilizing a sand martin's "dug-out."

Linnet—often called "BROWN LINNET"—a common bird, resident with us; a favourite cage bird, easily tamed, and with a very fascinating song. It is distinguished, in the male, by its crimson forehead and breast in the summer; chestnut back; forked tail with white edging; the quills black, edged with white, which shows as a white streak when the wings are closed. The female is browner and duller, without the crimson colour.

It has a sweet, varied song—much prized in captivity—a call-note which consists of "a rapid chuckle followed by a twitter," and a quaint alarm note like a timid whistle of interrogation. The nest—in bushes, especially gorse, and hedges—is a neat structure of roots, moss, and grass, lined with hair, wool, and feathers. The eggs (four to six) are a bluish white, marked with red, often at the larger end. The Linnet has two broods in the year. Its food consists almost entirely of seeds, though it brings larvæ, etc., when feeding young.

Martin, House.—This bird, with the Swallow and Sand Martin, form one family—the *Hirundinidæ*, with which the Swift, though similar in habits, is not connected. The notes on the Swallow and the Sand Martin should be compared; they both come in this section.

The House Martin is a summer visitor, very generally distributed, and is distinguished from the Swallow by the *white* patch on the *rump*. Otherwise the upper parts are a dark, glossy blue; wings and tail brown; under parts white right down to the feet—in fact, when seen on the ground its white "gaiters" are very noticeable. The nest is found under eaves or under a ledge on a cliff, and, being usually placed with the top touching the eave or ledge, is really a closed nest with a hole at the side. Compare this characteristic with that of the Swallow's nest. The nest, like the Swallow's, is made of mud, and takes some ten days to build. Both birds—male and female—share in the work, bringing wet mud in and on their beaks, and, beginning at the *bottom*, pressing it on to its place with their *chins* (the under part of the beak and throat). As this species has a sticky secretion in the mouth (which serves to hold fast the insects on which they feed), it is probable that the mud they use is mixed with it, and is rendered more adhesive thereby. I have noticed that, when beginning to build, they place a good many "dabs" of mud on the site, which begins to look as if some mischievous boy had been flinging or spattering it there. There is no apparent reason for this, and the untidy smudges remain after the finished nest is completed close by. Many of the mud patches drop off; in fact, in one season I calculated that at least as much mud fell off from a site over my door as was used for the actual nest. Generally the first layer is allowed to dry before the next is added. In order to help the birds one very dry year, I kept a small patch of path wetted, and it was of the greatest interest to note how eagerly the birds availed themselves of it.

In order, doubtless, to add to the cohesiveness of the nest, hay and straw are mixed with the mud; the interior is lined with feathers.

House Martins breed in colonies. Sometimes many nests may be found under the same roof; if not, on neighbouring buildings.

The sparrow is a great enemy to the nest builders, and it is more than probable that when the work is done he will take possession, keeping the owners out by his stout bill. I remember as a boy reading of the revenge of a pair of martins who, finding it impossible to turn the intruder out, calmly closed up the entrance with fresh mud, and thus immured her in a living tomb. I believe the story to be true; but I have more than once found that the best way to defeat the designs of the sparrow was to knock a hole in the bottom of the nest: the martins speedily put a new floor in when once the sparrow had been ejected.

The song is a very charming and musical twitter, which may be heard *in* the nest as well as when the birds are flying. It has been written down as "Chur-r-ruee—chur-r-ruee—ruee—ruee." The young ones have a pretty call-note—"Chirrup." The eggs are a pure white, laid at the end of May, and often again for a second brood.

Martin, Sand.—This is the smallest of the Swallow family, less than 5 inches in length, and is distinguished from the others by its mouse-brown back and upper parts, the under parts being white, with pale brown on the flanks. The tail is shorter and less forked than the Swallow's. The Sand Martin makes its nest in a rounded hole at the end of a burrow, 2 or 3 feet long, excavated by the birds in the side of a sand-pit or bank, generally in the neighbourhood of water if possible; occasionally in holes in walls and trees. The bird begins by scrambling along the face of the sand-pit till it finds a spot to its purpose, when it commences digging with its beak. It is said that one pair of birds bored a tunnel 20 inches long in forty-eight hours; another pair bored one 4 feet long in sixteen days. More observation on this point, together with the state of the weather, and the hardness or softness of the soil, would be of value—and here is an opportunity for the young student to do some original observation work. In the rounded chamber at the end of the tunnel the bird builds the nest proper of feathers, and lays four or five *white* eggs, breeding twice in the season.

The note is a slight chattering, often uttered as the birds chase one another in their flights. There is also a low chirp, which develops into a scream when alarmed or disturbed. The Sand Martin builds in colonies. The tunnels are often infested with fleas—*nota bene!*

Nightingale.—The king of the Thrush family, famous for its song, which has been shown to possess at least twenty different phrases and fifty notes. It is a summer visitor, appearing in April and leaving us in August and September; found in the South of England, omitting Cornwall and most of Devon; in the Midlands, as far north as Yorkshire; and the eastern borders of Wales, chiefly Glamorganshire. It is unknown in Ireland and Scotland. It returns to the same nesting site each year, as I know to my joy, having a visitor every year in a little copse with tangled brushwood close to the church. Its song is its distinguishing feature, but it must be remembered that it is not the only bird that sings at night (for example, the Sedge Warbler does). It is recognized by its uniform russet-brown upper parts; its handsome chestnut tail; the under parts white, shading into grey and brown on flanks and breast. The nest is almost always on or near the ground, among herbage in undergrowth, and is made of dead leaves and grass (so deep as to appear domed), lined with finer material. Oak leaves are a favourite choice. The bird is very tame on first arrival, and will sing on a low branch overhanging the road without fear of passers-by; but when once mated it appears to become much

80   THE BRITISH NATURE BOOK

shyer, and disappears among the trees and brushwood. The eggs are a pure olive-brown—occasionally blue—four to six in number, and are laid in May.

Nuthatch.—One of our residents, rare in the west but fairly common in wooded districts elsewhere, this bird is readily identified by its shape: stiffly built, thick, stumpy tail, powerful beak, and thick-set head. It feeds on insects (all injurious species, weevils, and beetles), which it seeks for by creeping up and *down*—I sometimes think chiefly *down*—trees, in the crevices of the bark; but, as its name suggests, it is fond of nuts, which it wedges into some crevice and then hammers and cracks. I have seen it take a dozen, one after the other, in a few moments from my bird table. It also takes acorns, beech nuts, and berries; whilst in winter it comes for the cocoanut and fat which I put out for the tits. It appears to pair for life, as I find both birds together in the autumn and right through the winter. Its blue-grey back and head (with a dark streak through the eye to the ear), reddish white throat and chest, deepening into chestnut-red on the flanks, make it a handsome bird.

It has a musical note—"Wheet-wheet"—always the signal of its approach in my garden, and a call-note—"Be quick—be quick"—as it arrives on a post outside my study window and makes a headlong, very business-like descent to the nearest food. The nest is usually in a hole in a tree (or a nesting box); if too large, the orifice is plastered up with clay. The interior is furnished with dry leaves or grass, and five to eight eggs are laid, white spotted with red.

Petrel, Storm, the smallest web-footed bird known—"Mother Carey's Chicken"—one of the four species of petrels that breed on our coasts. The name "Petrel" is derived from "Peter," and is due to the habit of paddling or treading on the water, characteristic of them all. The Storm Petrel is seen off all our coasts, especially in spring and autumn, but it breeds only in certain places—namely, the islands off the west coasts, from Scilly to the Shetlands; off the Irish coasts, and chiefly on the West Coast of Scotland. Here its nest may be found on some rocky islet, under stones or boulders, in crevices, or it may be in a rabbit burrow. It is generally a mere scrape, though sometimes a few grasses are used as a lining, or as a pad under the one chalky white egg which is laid. Occasional eggs with a circle of reddish spots round the bigger end are found. To its nesting site, even to the same burrow, the bird will often return year by year. It is recognized by its small size ($6\frac{1}{4}$ inches), black plumage, with a patch of conspicuous white at the root of the tail, long, black legs (their length no one has yet explained, as the bird does not appear to *walk* on land, going straight from its nest to sea and back again), webbed feet, black beak, and short tail. It appears to eat small molluscs and other fish; like the other petrels, it is fond of "sorrel." The young, which are downy, are fed with regurgitated oil.

The rare LEACH'S FORK-TAILED PETREL is much like this species, but is distinguished by its larger size and distinctly forked tail, as well as by the grey on the wing coverts. It nests in very rare places in the St. Kilda group of

BIRDS

islands, in County Kerry, and on the coast of Mayo. It is, however, generally distributed during the winter on most of our coasts. Its food consists of fish-fry, small crustaceans, cuttle-fish, and sorrel.

Pipit, Meadow (often called the TITLARK).—Is a resident with us all the year round; slightly smaller than the Tree Pipit (which see), and not so tawny, an olive shade pervading its "colour scheme." In the autumn its plumage is still further tinged with buff. The *hind-claw is longer than the toe.* Its song is not so rich as the Tree Pipit's, but is uttered in much the same way, except that, instead of starting from a tree-top, the bird starts from the ground or a low bush, and sings as it descends from a height of fifty feet or so. It is not found so much on cultivated land, but prefers marsh pasture and moor-land, where it builds a nest on the ground or in a bank, in the shade of a tussock or under a bush, using the same materials as the Tree Pipit. The eggs—smaller than the Tree Pipit's—are so covered with dark mottles that it is hard to discover the ground colour—in reality, "grey-white, mottled with brown"—but they are equally described as "red-brown, mottled with darker brown." The nest is frequently used by the Cuckoo as the depository for its egg. Both these pipits feed upon insects and larvæ, as well as on seeds. The song has been syllabled thus: "Vitge, vitge, vitge, vitge, vitgevitge-vitgevitgevitge, zickzickzickzickzickzick, yeckyeckyeckyeckyeck, terrrrr" (Naumann).

Pipit, Rock.—Is to be found on our rocky coasts, where it is a resident. It has the same charming song-flight as its relatives, but the song is a weaker, more tinkling strain. The call-note is "Weet-weet." The bird is distinguished by the complete absence of white on the tail feathers, its place being taken by grey. The upper parts are olive-brown—in autumn with a distinct *greenish* tinge; the under parts whitish with brown striations, becoming yellowish after the summer. The nest is cunningly hidden in a crevice or under stones, sometimes on a cliff ledge, occasionally in a rabbit's burrow; I have found it in the middle of a bed of sea campions. It is made of dry grass, some-times seaweed, lined with finer grass and hair. The eggs are greyish brown, speckled with darker shades; four to five in number; larger than the Meadow Pipit's.

Pipit, Tree.—This bird is a summer visitor, rare in the North of Scotland and entirely absent from Ireland; noted chiefly for its song and manner of singing, which is extremely characteristic. It sings on the topmost bough of a tree, or often may be seen on a telegraph wire, from which it frequently mounts into the air, and, rising high, descends with outspread wings and tail to its starting point, singing in a crescendo of rich notes as it descends; the last notes consisting of "Twee-twee-twee"—a sort of "coda" as it drops to its perch. It is often confused with the Meadow Pipit, but this characteristic song, its larger size, richer tawny colour, and its wagtail carriage on the ground suffice to distinguish it at a distance. In detail, note that the hind-claw is not so long as the toe itself. In colour the bird is tawny-brown above, with dark

82 THE BRITISH NATURE BOOK

Tree Pipit.

centres to the feathers; under parts buff-white, with some dark streaks; white on outer tail feathers.

The nest is in woodland, on the ground or in a bank or tuft of grass, constructed of grass, stems, and moss, lined with finer material. The eggs (four to six) vary in colour—bluish, greenish, pinkish, or brownish white, mottled with purplish brown or grey. It begins to lay in May.

Quail.—A young reader will be fortunate to see the nest of this bird, which, once so common, is diminishing in numbers every year. It is a summer visitor (though some remain through the winter), chiefly to the South of England and East of Ireland. Although it can fly but feebly, it is the only member of our native game birds that migrates, appearing among us about the second week of May, and departing about October. There is no likelihood of its increase, unfortunately, owing to the tastes of gourmets, for whose sake these beautiful little birds are netted in thousands as they migrate over Egypt and Italy, and, packed alive in cages by hundreds of thousands, are consigned to all parts of Europe—for the appetites of the luxurious!

Recognized by its small size, general sandy colour striped with pale buff (there is a long buff stripe over the middle of the crown, *like a parting*), it is found on rough pastures and cultivated land, where the cock's challenge, "Click-a-lick, click-a-lick"—or, as country folk have named it, "Wet-my-lip, wet-my-lip"—may be heard by the fortunate, and the hen's gentle reply, "Phew-phew." The nest, a scrape among crops or rough grass, lined with grass or leaves, contains seven to twelve eggs, *about the size of a Blackbird's*, yellowish, with dark brown patches and blotches.

BIRDS 83

Redbreast (ROBIN).—So familiar that little need be said about it. Note, however, that while a common resident, a paler-coloured sub-species visits us as a bird of passage to and from North Europe. The bird's habit of making a " claim " on a particular strip of land, be it garden or hedgerow, and attacking pugnaciously any intruder of its own species, should also be noted. As for its colour, its olive-brown, crimson, and greyish white mark it at once, as well as its impudent carriage. The young are quite unlike the parents, being yellowish brown, speckled and spotted, more like a miniature Thrush, until the autumn, when the regular mature colours appear.

The song is a delightful tinkle; the call-note a "Tick-tick"; and there is also a plaintive, weeping note when disturbed or alarmed. The nest is placed in the most various receptacles—a hole in a bank, an old kettle, or any other position that affords cover. The eggs are dull white spotted with red.

Redpoll, Lesser—in the Midlands known as a " PUEY," from its plaintive little call-note—recognized by its small size, its rosy cap (the Linnet has the red on the *forehead*), and, in the male, the summer garb of rosy waistcoat. The bird is resident in most parts, though it does not breed in the South-west of England. The nest may be in a high tree or in a bush or hedge, and is made of twigs, moss, and grass, *usually lined with down*. The eggs are distinguished by their dull surface and greenish colour with red and purplish brown spots. The song is a low twittering, the alarm note a scolding chatter like the Linnet's. The bird is a very graceful, active creature, remarkably bold and agile, and, when caged, is very quickly tamed.

Redpoll, Mealy, or GREATER REDPOLL.—Does not breed here, but is a regular winter visitor, especially on the eastern side. It is larger than the former, and is less chestnut-coloured on the back. Its call-note is " Chizzzz," and its song has been written as " Zig, wig, chutta chutta, che-we-we."

Redstart.—This handsome bird, locally known as the " FIRE-TAIL," is a summer visitor, arriving in April. Distinguished by the *white* forehead on a jet-black head, throat, and neck. A rich chestnut on the lower rump and tail coverts, the breast, and flanks; the tail the same, but duller, the two middle feathers of which are a light brown. The rest of the upper parts are grey. The female is brown-grey above, dull white below, but having the chestnut tail and rump, and a rufous tinge on the breast.

Redstart.

The constant flicking of the tail is characteristic, and its resemblance, when suddenly seen among the leaves, to a flickering tongue of fire no doubt suggested its name to our Anglo-Saxon forefathers—" FIRE-START" or "FIRE-TAIL." It haunts the edges of woods and gardens near buildings, and generally places its nest in a hole in a tree or a wall, though sometimes in odd places—on the ground, or in a pot. Materials: dry grasses, fibre, strips of bark, and mosses, lined with horsehair and feathers. The eggs—five to seven—are a pale blue, lighter than the Hedge Sparrow's but practically the same size, occasionally spotted with red. The bird is an insect-eater. It has a low, soft, but disappointing song, opening with a robin-like warble, and then breaking down suddenly into a mere succession of gurgles. The song reminds one closely of the Pied Flycatcher's, and is often uttered on the wing. The alarm note is a "Ptui" like the Chiffchaff's, and a sharp "Tick" like the Robin's.

Redstart, Black—marked by its black and grey hue, lacking the white patch on the forehead and chestnut on the breast, but retaining the "fire"-tail—is an autumn and winter visitor, fairly common. It *may* occasionally breed here, but so far no positive instance is known. The nest is generally in a shed or wall or a rock crevice, and is rather bulky; the eggs are white.

Shrike, Red-backed—the "BUTCHER BIRD"—classed by old naturalists amongst the birds of prey because of its well-known habit of killing young birds, lizards, mice, bees, beetles, and other insects, and impaling them on thorns, as a sort of "larder." The bird, however, possesses no sort of relationship to the *raptores* except this rapacious characteristic. It is a summer migrant, one of the last to arrive and first to depart, chiefly found in South and Central England and Wales, very scarce in the extreme west. Its name, *shrike*, doubtless refers to its shrieking note—" Chack-chack," though it has also a low warbling song, very seldom heard, but used intimately when *en famille*. Its distinguishing features are the reddish back, grey head, the black streak over the ear coverts, and hooked beak; but only the cock bird has the back red, the female's being a dull chestnut, and the young are " barred with black on red or reddish grey."

The nest is placed in bushes, straggling hedges, and tangled undergrowth, and is a bulky structure, in which plenty of moss is used, with stalks and roots, lined with finer material, and hair or down.

The eggs (five or six) vary in ground colour—white, cream, brown, or greenish, spotted and blotched at the larger end with brown or red. In fact, to my mind, in their variation they bear a close resemblance to a miniature Sparrow Hawk's eggs. They are laid in May.

The Red-backed Shrike returns regularly to its old nesting place year by year; so that when once seen, it is probable that in every succeeding season a pair of birds may be found in or near the old haunts.

The GREAT GREY SHRIKE, $9\frac{1}{2}$ inches in length, is an irregular winter visitor, chiefly on the East Coast; but other continental species occasionally visit

PLATE VII.

1. Common Curlew. 2. Snipe, with Eggs just hatching. 3. Wood Pigeon. 4. Song Thrushes.
(*Photos by W. P. Green*)

these shores. One, the WOODCHAT SHRIKE, recognized by its red crown and nape, has been known to breed in the Isle of Wight and Hants.

Siskin, chiefly known as a winter visitor. This active and fearless little bird is resident in pine forests in Ireland and Scotland (above Perth), but nests only sparingly in the South of Scotland and the North of England. It is distinguished by its small size, its black head and chin, and yellow and green plumage. The female is greyer, and lacks the black on head and chin.

The nest is generally high up in coniferous trees; made of twigs, roots, grass, and moss, lined with wool, down, etc. The eggs are bluish white with reddish brown spots. The call is a simple piping note; but the bird has a noisy little song of its own, not very musical.

Skylark.—Although this bird is a common resident, it is also a migrant with the most bewildering movements, thousands of the birds moving in spring and autumn to and from the North and South. Its sober colours are too well known to need describing; but note that it has an erectile crest and a curiously long spur on the hind-toe, the purpose of which is not known. The old countryside explanation was that the lark used it to blind sheep when they came too near the nest, and the expression "lark-spurred" is still, I believe, used for one kind of ophthalmia in sheep. The bird's song is heard regularly from January to July, and again from September to November. But it is almost truer to say that it sings all the year round, for I have heard larks singing in August plentifully on Portland Bill, and every Christmas Day for some years past I have seldom been disappointed on listening for the welcome sound.

The wonderful song, generally heard in the air, sometimes lasts without a break for half an hour; but the bird also sings on the ground or from a bush. In spite of popular statements, the bird can and does perch in trees, but rarely; on the ground it is more at home; and it displays a marked characteristic in running, not hopping. During the autumn it gathers into large flocks. Thousands of birds fall victims, unfortunately, to the tastes of men, and I know no sadder sight than that of the bodies of scores of these glorious songsters hanging up for sale in the shops. However, in spite of this fact, the lark does not appear to diminish in numbers.

The nest is always on the ground, usually in grass or amongst corn, and is made of grass bents, lined with finer material and hair. The eggs (three or four) are greyish or greenish white, closely mottled with olive-brown and grey.

Snipe, Jack, the smallest of the family of *Scolopacinæ*, embracing the Woodcock and Snipes, is a winter visitor, and does not breed in the British Isles. Its general habits and characteristics are like those of the Common Snipe (which see), from which it is distinguished by its smaller size. It has twelve instead of fourteen tail feathers. The centre of the crown is *black*, with a vague band of chestnut down the middle (the Common Snipe has a clearly marked buff stripe). There is a remarkable metallic sheen on the purple of the rump and the green of the scapulars; four buff stripes on back. Under parts dull white, streaked with brown.

The bird breeds in Lapland, Finland, and Russia, and arrives in England from October till April. It feeds on beetles, snails, seeds when necessary, as well as on the worms and grubs it obtains from beneath the surface of the ground in the marshy or coastal districts which it haunts. It is a solitary bird, and when disturbed flies up *without uttering* the "Scape-scape," so marked a feature of the Common Snipe.

Sparrow, Hedge (DUNNOCK is a common local name).—This bird is one of the commonest visitors to any garden, and one of the most charming,

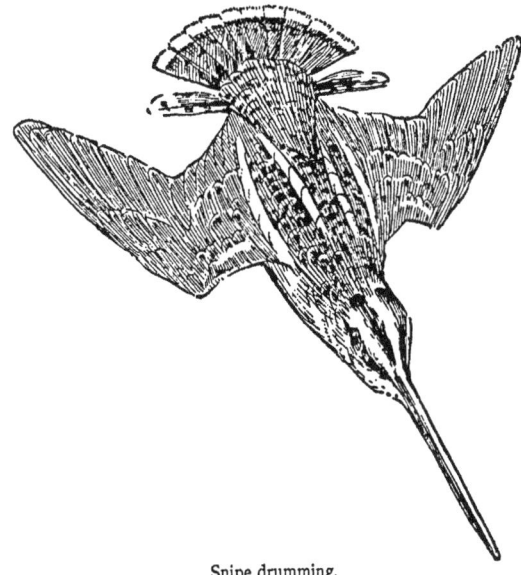

Snipe drumming.

having quiet, unobtrusive ways of appearing at the bird table, or amongst the poultry, and slipping in and out among the flowers and bushes like a mouse. His "piping-plaintive" call-note may be heard, like his sweet, joyous little song, all the year round. This is a bird of true British race; for though there is a continental variety, lighter in colour and with a finer bill, that visits the East Coast in the winter, our own bird is nowhere found but in the British Isles.

It is a "pretty" bird, daintily made, a great contrast to the House Sparrow, with whom it has no connection save in name. It is distinguished by its head of soft grey, its thin, delicate beak, and "mouse-like" carriage when on the ground searching for food. It feeds on insects, spiders, etc.; though in winter time, like the Wren, it appears to find specks of food invisible to the other birds. I have had it in captivity with my "domesticated" birds in an aviary in winter, and it has fed then entirely on seeds, which it swallowed whole. I found it very gentle, and, though shy at first, easily tamed.

Its nest may be found in every hedge or bush : a neatly constructed home of moss, wool, and grass, lined with hair, etc., and containing four or five eggs of pure unspotted blue. It is an early nester—generally in March—and its nest is frequently chosen by the Cuckoo for its own egg.

In the pairing season the cock has a habit of showing off to the hen by drooping its wings and "shuffling" them: hence one of its rustic names is "SHUFFLE-WING."

Sparrow, House.—Common as this bird is, I doubt whether one person out of a hundred could describe his plumage, beyond saying it was "brown." The coloration in spring when examined in detail is beautiful. He has a white cheek patch and a black bib, which alone make him handsome ; the crown and rump are ash-grey, and the mantle is chestnut, the beak black. The hen has browns instead of greys, a buff eye stripe, under parts dirty white, beak brown. In winter the cock is much duller in colour.

There is no real *song*, but the chirp is known to every one. There are various alarm notes and courting notes, which must be familiar to dwellers in town and country alike.

From the Hedge Sparrow this bird is distinguished by the thicker and more stumpy bill and the bold, impudent carriage, as well as by differences of plumage.

As for its nesting site, the sparrow will place its untidy bundle of straw, hay, and feathers anywhere—in any hole or crevice in trees, houses, rocks, under eaves, in pipes, and in every convenient or inconvenient situation. I made a nest box one year of a box with an entrance consisting of an empty carbide tin. The sparrows occupied it, though it took "superhuman" exertions to get into and along the tin tunnel. Another box, with a small hole and no perch (intended for tits), just outside my window, was commandeered by sparrows, although in this case also it was extremely difficult for the birds to enter. When the nest is built in a tree it is always domed ; there is never any mistaking it, owing to its large size and untidy structure. The eggs vary very much—pale bluish white, with spots of grey and brown; sometimes reddish, sometimes almost white.

Sparrow, Tree (MOUNTAIN SPARROW).—Resident, but a local species, found in all counties but Cornwall and Devon ; scarce in the Lake District, increasing in Ireland. Like the House Sparrow, but distinguished by its chestnut crown and nape, a detached spot of black on the white cheek, and two white bars on the wing. It nests in holes in trees, buildings, walls—an untidy nest of straw, grass, etc., lined with feathers. The eggs are smaller than the House Sparrow's, whitish with brown spots ; often one or two eggs in the clutch are lighter than the rest. Its food is the same as the House Sparrow's, and its note is much the same, but rather more musical.

Stonechat.—This bird, in general coloration often confused with the

Whinchat, is a resident, whilst the other is a visitor. It may be distinguished by its stout, almost corpulent build (as compared with the Whinchat's slenderness), its habit of jerking its tail, and the black throat and large white neckspot in the male; the female having a black spot on the throat and a complete absence of white on the tail. The cock is a handsome bird, with his jet-black head, throat, and eyes; white on rump and neck sides; bright chestnut-red breast, inclining to buff on the belly; black wings and back, and tail edged with reddish brown. The hen is dusky coloured above, with feathers edged with light chestnut. She has a black throat, spotted with white and reddish, and a dull red breast.

The bird is found on commons, heaths, and moorlands, especially near the coast, where the nest, carefully hidden, is placed in heather or grass, or most usually at the foot of a bush. It is composed of moss, grass, etc., lined with finer materials and hair. The eggs are pale bluish green, with light brown spots.

The call-note resembles the sound of two pebbles being clinked together, hence the name "Stonechat"—"Utack-tack-tack." There is a famous Highland curse associated with it, of which the last two lines are—

"De'il break their long back
Who my eggs would tak'."

But the Stonechat has a delightful song of its own, consisting of a "rapid series of double notes." Its food is chiefly insects and their larvæ, and spiders; but it also eats small lizards. In autumn the birds assemble nearer the coasts.

Swallow (see notes on MARTIN).—The Germans call this bird the "inside swallow," to distinguish it from the House Martin—the "outside swallow"—in regard to its choice of a situation for the nest. For the Swallow's nest is usually *under cover*—in a porch, shed, or cave—and is placed *on*, not *under*, a ledge or beam. It is made of mud with hay or straw like the House Martin's, but is either cup-shaped or like a bisected basin, according to its place.

The bird is the earliest of the *Hirundinidæ* to arrive—some time in March—and it departs last. Woe betide it if a sharp frost should come after its arrival, and the insects on which it depends wholly for food be killed, for then it starves to death.

Certainly three-parts of its time are spent on the wing, catching its food—not only small flies and gnats, but moths and butterflies as well. In fact, it *drinks* and *bathes* on the wing, as any one will note who watches a pool or stream over which it flies.

The bird, in common with the others of its family, returns to the same place each year, often uses the same nest, and pairs for life.

It is distinguished from the House Martin by its uniform blue-black upper plumage, its longer wings, and more deeply forked tail. In addition, it has a patch of beautiful chestnut-red on its forehead and throat; the tail is a dull greenish colour, with some white spots towards the tips of the feathers, showing plainly when it is expanded. The under parts are chiefly dull yellow-brown, with a blue band below the throat.

The song is a cheerful musical twitter, and there is a shrill alarm note, "Tisit-tisit." The eggs, five in number, are larger than the House Martin's, and longer in shape, white, with reddish brown markings. It breeds twice in the season.

Swift.—Note that this bird comes under the order *Coraciiformes* (that includes the Woodpeckers), although most people would place it in the Swallow family. It differs from the Swallow in having all four toes pointing forward, and is distinguished by its larger size, its soot-black plumage (except the throat, a dirty white), and the long, scimitar-shaped wings. Every one is familiar with its shrill scream in the air, and its marvellous flight—"JACK SQUEALER" is a common country name in consequence. There is no other bird like it for its command of the air, and its mysterious disappearance in the sky at night. There seems no doubt that the male Swifts rise upwards and *sleep* on "widespread, tranquil wings" in the upper air, though no one has ever seen them descend in the early morning. Otherwise the cocks roost in the nest holes, or cling to a branch or some other hold on a building or wall. The food is entirely insectivorous, especially beetles and flies, which are held by a sticky saliva in the mouth. It has been calculated that a Swift catches at least 2,000 insects a day. It is also, alas! the prey of insects, being terribly infested with parasites. In spite of the old popular belief, the bird can rise from the ground, or any level surface, though it is rarely seen there.

Its nest is placed under eaves, or in holes and crevices, and consists of a scanty lining—often a mere ring of straw, feathers, etc., picked up on the wing, and cemented together with its saliva. Fierce fights for its nesting place have been observed between the Swift and the *Starling*. The eggs are two or three in number, a chalky white. The bird arrives in Great Britain during the first half of May, and lays its eggs at the end of the month or in June, leaving our shores very early in mid-August.

Tit, Bearded, BEARDED REEDLING, or REED PHEASANT.—Found practically only on the Norfolk Broads; distinguished in the male by the "beard," or more properly "sideboards" of black feathers hanging from between the eye and the beak. It is recognized otherwise by its deep tawny upper colouring, and the russet-grey of its under parts. The nest is generally among the reeds and sedges in a reed bed or marsh, and is often lined with reed flower heads, with occasional feathers. The eggs (five to seven, sometimes more) are white, with a few scattered chocolate-brown streaks and scrawls. There is no "song," for the birds are peculiarly silent in coming to and from their nest; but there is a thin call-note, "Ping-ping," not unlike the Reed Warbler's, and a short scolding note, "Phwut." The young have four rows of remarkable white tooth-like projections on their palates, their presence or purpose an unexplained mystery.

Tit, Blue.—Is distinguished by its blue cap and general blue and yellow plumage; greenish back, cheeks white, with a blue-black line through the eye. Every one must know this familiar bird-acrobat, which invariably utters its note, when alighting, like the clown's "Here we are again!"—"Chee-chee-chee," and "Chee-chee-chee, chit, te-de-dee-dee," the last five syllables uttered quickly and on a lower note. The bird nests in any convenient hole, and its presence within may be known by its *hisses* when disturbed. It lays seven to twelve eggs, white, with red spots. This is one of the birds which it is a sheer delight to watch at the cocoanuts and suet, which should be hung up during the winter for its food. I once took a photograph of an incident much later in the year, when in *June* a Blue Tit brought its family to be fed from the remains of a cocoanut in my garden.

Tit, British Coal.—This little bird ($4\frac{1}{4}$ inches) has a black head and throat, white patch on each cheek, and *a noticeable white patch on the nape*, which distinguishes it from the Marsh Tit. The back is olive-brown; wings dusky brown, with two white bars; the under parts greyish white. The song is a weaker edition of the Great Tit's, but without the final "Wheat." Its nest is generally in a hole in a tree or wall, and the eggs are white, with many pale red spots.

Tit, Crested.—Is a rare bird, confined almost entirely to the valley of the Spey, and is distinguished by the crest.

Tit, Great.—This is the largest of the British tits, and is distinguished by the white cheeks surrounded by black, and the black band that runs from the throat down the centre of the yellow breast. The spring note, often said to sound like a saw cutting wood—"Wheet-tu, wheet-tu, wheet-tu-wheat"—is one of the first bird notes that announce the coming of spring. The bird also utters a sharp "Pink-pink," like the Chaffinch. The Great Tit is "resident and generally distributed." Head and throat black; cheeks white, white patch on nape; breast yellow, with black streak down the middle; back yellowish green; wings and tail grey-blue.

The nest is a biggish structure, usually in some hole—from a letter-box to a tree-stump—made of moss, wool, fur, hair, etc. The eggs are white, with red spots.

The Great Tit, like the others of its family, has popularly a bad character for destroying fruit-buds, etc.; but it has been proved that the tits, even the Great and Blue, feed chiefly on injurious insects—the Great Tit's young are fed generally on moth larvæ, and it is calculated that one pair in rearing their nestlings destroy between 7,000 and 8,000 larvæ; the Blue Tit even more.

Unfortunately, as I have seen to my cost, the Great Tit has a partiality for *hive bees* as well, and I fear I must state that when once it is discovered that the hives are being molested, there is nothing to be done but to destroy the robbers!

Tit, Irish Coal.—This bird was only recognized in 1910; is found only in Ireland, and is distinguished by the sulphur-yellow which replaces the white patches in the British variety.

Tit, Long-tailed (BOTTLE TIT).—This little bird, generally distributed and resident in the British Isles, is unique in its shape and the character of its nest. The bird has a long tail quite out of proportion to its size, and appears like a tiny ball of fluff with a long feather stuck in it. It is distinguished by the long tail, its white, black, and rose-coloured plumage. The head is mostly white, with some streaks of black; the back is black in the centre, but sides and scapulars are rose-red; the under parts white, with a rosy tinge. There is a curious ring of orange-yellow round the eye, which when first seen gives the appearance of an inflamed eyelid. The *note* is a tiny rattling sound, and the " Zee-zee-zee " common to all the tits. The nest is quite unique, built like an oval ball or bag, with entrance at the side near the top. It takes ten or twelve days to make, is placed in thick bushes or hedges and trees, and is made of moss, wool, and *cobwebs*, decorated with lichens and lined thickly with feathers—in one case 2,379 were counted in one nest. Ten to twelve eggs are laid, white, with a few pale red specks; sometimes unspotted. When sitting, this tit brings its long tail backward over its head, and it may be often seen sticking out of the entrance, a sign that the bird is " at home."

Tit, Marsh.—Only found in England and Wales. Head and throat black, *no* white on nape (the feature distinguishing it from the Coal Tit); upper parts greyish brown; wings and tail bluish grey; cheeks white, inclining to buff; under parts greyish white. A silent bird on the whole, except for its family call-note. Its true " song " begins with a loud, clear note, repeated seven times. Its nest, generally placed in a *natural* hole in a decayed tree, is a bulky structure of moss lined with fur, hair, or down; the eggs are white, with a few dark red spots. The bird is not confined, as its name would suggest, to marshy districts, but may be found in woods and gardens. Its food is chiefly insects, but in autumn and winter it also eats berries, beech mast, nuts, seeds of the larch, etc.

Tit, Willow.—Has only recently been recognized as a distinct species. Breeds in Scotland as well as England. The absence of gloss on its black head and neck—as well as its *rounded* tail when partly closed—are said to distinguish it from the Marsh Tit. The nesting hole is stated to be *excavated* by the bird, and the material used is scanty.

Twite (locally known as " MOUNTAIN LINNET," etc.), a little brown bird, grey beneath, like a Redpoll, but differing in having the *red* colour on the rump only; white edges, showing plainly to the inner primaries; a yellow beak, and no black on the chin. The hen and young lack the red altogether. Does not breed in the South and East of England, where it is only seen in the winter; but is resident on moorland in Central and Northern England, and in Scotland and Ireland. It nests in very variable places—bushes, heather, creepers, on the ground under stones, in walls, crevices, rabbit-burrows—constructing its nest of roots, grass, moss, twigs, lined with wool, hair, and feathers. It is stated to adorn its nest conspicuously in many cases with one or at the most two feathers from a cock's hackle. The eggs (four to six) are blue streaked with dark red-brown, like a Linnet's, but more strongly coloured.

It is a seed-eater. Its call-note is syllabled as "Jegegegeck," and an alarm note, "Sheh-she-shy"; and it has a curious little song which it rattles off, containing, among other chattering phrases, "Lazy Jenny!"

Wagtail, Grey.—The wagtails are a very familiar family, with the distinctive characteristic that gives them their name—the balancing tail, moved up and down as if it were on a spring slightly touched by a finger. The Grey Wagtail is increasing in numbers in the South (in Hants, for example, where it breeds regularly), though it is said to be distributed generally in the hilly districts and to be rare in or absent from the South. I have, however, every year for the past ten years, seen its nest under the bridges and on the walls or woodwork of the locks and hatches of the river. There is no mistaking its uniform slate-blue upper parts, and longish tail; the cock's black throat, white stripe above and below the eye, the yellow under parts.

The hen has little black on the throat. The note is a simple "Tweet." The nest is almost always near water, in a bank, wall, or part of a bridge or lock: moss, etc., lined with hair. The eggs (four to six) are yellowish white, with brownish spots.

Wagtail, Pied.—This species is easily recognized by its constantly repeated note, "Tisit-tisit-tisit," as well as by its black-grey and white plumage, and black tail with white edges. The female is greyer. The birds are often found near water catching insects, but they haunt gardens as well. They may also be seen following cattle as they graze, catching the insects stirred up by the animals' feet.

There is a "gentle, warbling song," somewhat resembling a weak robin's and lark's, but it is seldom heard.

The nesting site is usually in a recess in a wall or bank: dried grass, moss, etc., lined with hair and finer grasses, etc. The eggs are five or six in number, white, with numerous grey spots and dots.

Wagtail, White.—This is a *summer* visitor (the foregoing being a resident), which breeds to some extent in the South and East of England. The male in summer plumage differs from the former species in having back and rump grey instead of black. In winter the male has more white on the wing, a lighter grey on the back, and grey instead of black on the tail. This bird is said to sing "continuously," the hen as well as the cock.

Wagtail, Yellow (or RAY'S).—One of our summer migrants; a bird of slender shape, marked by its *olive-green* upper parts, the bright *yellow* eye stripe, and yellow under parts. The nest is generally on the ground in a field or a meadow, often under a clod of earth or tuft of grass, and the eggs are whitish, with small spots and dots of greyish brown. There is a shrill call-note; the species nests later than the preceding, beginning to lay in May.

Warbler, Dartford.—A rare bird, very local, to be found on heaths and commons where there is plenty of gorse, chiefly in the South of England, especially Hampshire, where it remains all the year round. It is like a very dark Wren with a very long, fan-shaped tail. Upper parts dark brown, under parts dark chestnut-red. The iris is dark red. It has a subdued liquid song or warble, the call-note being syllabled as "Pit-it-chou," or "Pit-cha-cha." The nest, usually 18 inches above the ground, is placed amongst gorse bushes or heather, and is composed of grass stems (often goose-grass) interspersed with moss, wool, or a few feathers. The eggs, four in number, are like the Whitethroat's but smaller, light greeny white with distinct markings of dark brown and grey. It breeds twice in the year, beginning to lay in March to April. A noticeable characteristic is the posture of the male on the topmost twig of a bush of gorse singing defiance at the human intruder. In winter the birds are very shy, though sometimes they may be seen in the garden looking for food.

Warbler, Garden.—A summer migrant, of a uniform olive-brown above; under parts dull greyish white. The olive-brown distinguishes it from the Blackcap or other bird of its size or shape; both sexes are alike. The nest is generally placed where there are plenty of low-growing bushes or undergrowth—on the edges of woods, in hedges, in bushes in gardens, or any tangled herbage. It is a frail structure, rather larger than the Blackcap's but somewhat similar, of grass stalks, lined with finer material and hair; the eggs, like the Blackcap's, but glossier and more distinctly marked—rarely almost pure white. The Garden Warbler is a delightful singer, having a liquid, rapid song like the Blackcap's; its alarm note, when the nest is approached, is "Tit-tit-tit," changing into an angry "Teck" and the scolding "Cha-ah."

Warbler, Grasshopper ("REELER").—Is so called from its peculiar song, which resembles the noise of the reel used by hand-spinners of wool. It is a curious rhythmical sound, growing louder and diminishing, often mistaken for the continuous chirping of the grasshopper; heard especially in the evening or early morning. The bird in singing moves its head from side to side, thus effectually "throwing" its voice, and making it difficult to locate the sound. In moving through the herbage it is extraordinarily noiseless, gliding like a mouse—as a matter of fact, running, not hopping. It has an alarm note, "T'wit-t'wit," and a long-drawn cry like a weasel. The upper parts are a rufous brown, marked with blackish lines; the under parts brown, with a few darker streaks on the breast. There is a fine eye stripe. The nest is carefully concealed, and difficult to find; placed in low bushes, undergrowth, or heather, near the ground; made of coarse grass, leaves, etc., lined with finer materials. The eggs, six in number, are thickly spread with small reddish brown spots.

Warbler, Marsh.—A very local bird, but a regular summer visitor to South and Midlands; much like the Reed Warbler, but lacking the reddish tinge in the under parts. Its song is said to be far superior to the Reed Warbler's, which otherwise it resembles. It also imitates and mimics the notes of other birds. The nest, also, is like the Reed Warbler's, but is placed, not over water among reeds, but in the midst of herbage—meadow-sweet being a favourite, and osiers,

94 THE BRITISH NATURE BOOK

etc. It is not so deep or compact, and it will be noticed that the material used in the rim to fasten the nest to the supporting stems is only woven into the nest at the ends, assuming the appearance which Mr. Warde Fowler describes as "basket handles." The eggs are very much the same as the Reed Warbler's, greenish white, with prominent dark spots and many fine speckles.

Warbler, Reed.—This bird's uniform olive-brown colour distinguishes it from the Sedge Warbler, but the only means of distinguishing it from the Marsh Warbler (which see) is by its nest, eggs, and song. This latter is decidedly inferior, and is a hurried chattering, with many "Tack-tacks" in it (like the Sedge Warbler's). The under parts are white tinged with buff, inclining to a rufous tinge, which the Marsh Warbler entirely lacks. The nest is a wonderful structure, attached to reeds over water, generally suspended between three or four reed stems, and constructed chiefly of the dead flower heads of old reeds, interwoven to make a clean round rim. (*Note.*—Sometimes found amidst vegetation some distance from water.)

It is a deep nest, to prevent the eggs from falling out when the reeds sway in the wind, and generally contains four or five eggs, of a pale green colour, thickly blotched with greenish brown spots.

Warbler, Sedge.—This bird is identified by the plumage markings, the upper parts being a russet-brown, with black centres to the feathers, a pale eyebrow, and a dark line above it, the under parts white, with tawny-buff sides. It is a very voluble singer, and like all the Marsh Warblers often sings at night. There are many chattering, scolding notes in its song, and it is an excellent mimic. It is often found in many places where the Reed Warbler would not occur, such as near small streams and ponds. And it does not keep to marshy ground, but places its substantial nest usually in mixed herbage, in hedges and bushes ; occasionally, it suspends it like the Reed Warbler.

The nest is composed of grasses and moss, lined with hair, sometimes with feathers and other materials. The eggs, like the Yellow Wagtail's, are greenish white, clouded all over with brownish, and a thin line or two of black.

Warbler, Willow (WILLOW WREN).—A very common summer visitor, with a simple, pleasing song, slower than the Wood Warbler's, and with notes that fall in a descending scale. It has the plaintive, piping call-note "Wheet," which is a characteristic of all the family. It is smaller than the Wood Warbler and duller in colour, while its pale brown legs distinguish it from the Chiffchaff. Olive-greenish above, wings and tail brown, a yellow eyebrow, and a dark streak through the eye ; under parts yellow-white. The nest is *domed*, with entrance at side, made of grass, leaves, etc., and *lined with feathers* (a distinguishing feature) ; generally placed on or near the ground in grass or other herbage, or on the side of a bank, in woods or open ground. The eggs are white, with light red spots.

Warbler, Wood (often called WOOD WREN).—This bird is larger and more brightly coloured than the Willow Warbler and Chiffchaff. Upper parts yellowish green, a broad eyebrow of yellow, yellow throat ; under parts whitish.

BIRDS

Tail and wings brown, edged with yellow-green and tipped with white. The hen is, as usual, duller. Its song, generally heard in woods or from the top of tall trees, is very characteristic. It begins with a "Tick-tick-tick," and ends with a remarkable shivering trill, in which the bird sings with head thrown back and the whole body quivering. Once heard, it can always be recognized. It has been syllabled as follows: "Wheeou-wheeou-wheeou-ip-sip-sipp-sipsip-sipsipp-srreeeeee"; but generally the latter part only is sung. The call-note is "Wheet." The nest is on or near the ground, in dead bracken or tangled herbage. It is a domed structure of bracken, leaves, grass, etc., lined with grass and hair—but without feathers (this is a distinguishing feature). The eggs are white, with red spots.

Wheatear.—This bird gets its name from the Anglo-Saxon "whete-aer," white rump, the conspicuous mark which serves to distinguish it readily. This patch shows most plainly when the bird is flying. On alighting and closing its wings, it disappears in such a way that the bird in its full plumage seems to vanish into the tones of its surroundings. Probably this same protective coloration explains its consistent habit of always flying low, so as to harmonize with the ground. Its upper parts are a blue-grey, a black streak passing through the eye to the ear coverts; the tail is black, except the base of the outer feathers, which is white; wings blackish brown; cheeks, throat, and breast tawny buff; the rest of the under parts creamy white. The hen is duller brown, except for the white markings. The bird haunts moorlands and wild pastures; in the North it is considered "unlucky"—probably from its habit of frequenting old disused churchyards. Its note is "Tack-tack," but it has a short, joyous song not unlike the opening of the Skylark's; it also mimics other birds. The nest is placed on the ground, on downs or open country under rocks or among stones; sometimes in curious places—an old kettle or a drain pipe. It is of dry grass lined with hair, wool, etc., and generally where one nest is found, others may be discovered. The eggs are pale blue, sometimes with speckles of red. The food consists of spiders, insects, and their larvæ. The bird is a summer migrant.

Whinchat.

Whinchat.—This small sandy-brown bird—short, thick-set, with black streaks; blackish wings with white spot (sometimes two), a prominent white streak over the eye, a white patch at base of tail, rosy breast—is to be seen on commons and moorlands, singing a low, persistent, warbling song, sometimes for half an hour at a time.

This is the cock Whinchat—the hen is duller, with a yellow or buff eye streak. The note is like the Stonechat's, "Tza-tza"; but if you get too near the nest there is an unmistakable call, "Utick-tick-tick—utick-tick-tick," accompanied by fluttering wing and jerking tail.

The bird is a summer visitor, arriving later than the Wheatear. It places its nest of grasses and moss, lined with finer materials and hair, on or near the ground, in a bank or the bottom of a bush. The eggs are a greenish blue with pale spots of "faded" russet-brown—not so bright or large as the Wheatear's.

Whitethroat—often called "NETTLE-CREEPER" and "PEGGY WHITE-THROAT"—a summer migrant, widely distributed. Head ashy grey, back brownish grey, wing coverts edged with chestnut, wings dark brown, tail the same, edged with white. Throat pure white, breast tinged with pink, legs pale brown. Female browner above, and breast whiter. The bird is distinguished by the pure white throat, the blue-grey head, and chestnut on wings. When seen close, the pale brown or flesh-coloured legs distinguish it from the Lesser Whitethroat, which has bluish grey legs.

Whitethroat.

It has a very lively song, uttered in a characteristic way, the bird fluttering up a little way into the air and singing as it descends. There is also an unmistakable scolding note, "Cha-ah," repeated in a torrent of expostulation when the nest is approached too closely. This is placed usually quite close to the ground in herbage and undergrowth, often in a clump of nettles (hence the local name); it is a fragile structure, but rather deep, of bents lined with fine roots and hair. The eggs—four or five (sometimes more)—are greenish white, spotted and speckled with grey and greenish brown.

Its food is insects; in the autumn, fruits such as blackberries, elderberries, etc.

Whitethroat, Lesser.—This is only half an inch smaller than the preceding, from which it is distinguished by its general lighter appearance, the prevailing colours being grey and white. It is more shy and retiring; there is no bright chestnut on the wings, and the legs are lead coloured, not flesh coloured. It is rare in Devon, absent from Cornwall, rare in Western Wales and the northern counties, but fairly common elsewhere. It has a quieter song, but a loud rattling call like the first part of a Chaffinch's song broken off short. It also utters a rapid clicking note when the nest is approached. The nest is the most fragile and the smallest made by any British bird, *flat* compared with the Whitethroat's; placed in bushes, hedges, and undergrowth, usually near the ground. Made of the same materials as the former bird's. The eggs (five or six) are white, spotted chiefly at the larger end with brown and grey.

Woodlark.—Resembles the Skylark in general colour, but is distinguished by its smaller size, shorter tail, and absence of white in the tail. Many may be said to be *lighter* in appearance, having a buff and even white colour in the under parts. This species is getting less common, and more local; but it breeds generally in both England and Wales. Its nest is on or close to the ground, almost always sheltered by bracken, heath, or grass, generally near trees. The eggs are four in number, ashy white, spotted with brown or grey. The song is superior in compass to the Skylark's, and lasts even longer. It is uttered on the wing, but the bird flies in wide circles, not perpendicularly, and descends also in graceful spirals; it also sings on the ground, and in trees more frequently.

The SHORE LARK is a winter visitor only, on the East Coast, and is marked by two narrow black feathers like two horns on the sides of the head.

Woodpecker, Lesser Spotted.—There are three members of this family— the *Picidæ*—all of which find their food in the crevices of the bark of trees. Hence they are specially adapted for the work of climbing and searching, having feet with strong, sharp claws, two of the toes placed forward and two backward; a longish, sharp bill—a veritable pickaxe; a very long tongue, barbed at the end and sticky; and a short, strong tail, which with its pointed feathers serves as a prop and a lever. All nest in holes, generally bored by the bird, and all have eggs of a beautiful glossy white. None breed in Ireland. Only one of the family comes within this first group as to size—the Lesser Spotted Woodpecker, 6 inches in length. Its colour is principally black and white in bars and patches, but the male has a crimson crown, the female a whitish one. The nest is hollowed out of a decayed tree, the nesting material being chips of the wood. The bird has a preference for tall trees, especially elms, for its insect-hunting expeditions; but for nesting purposes it often chooses orchard trees, such as pear or apple. It utters a curious call-note, "Kink-kink-kink-kink," like that of "a noisy Blackbird going to roost," and it also signals by drumming on the tree with its beak, like the others of its family (which see). The eggs are small, and of a pure white.

Wren (JENNY WREN).—This "jolly" little bird is with us all the year round, and besides his curious note, like the winding of a clock, has a loud and passionate song, extraordinarily powerful from so small a creature. It is at once recognized by its small size, its nut-brown plumage, and short stumpy tail, carried at right angles to the body. It builds its nest in any convenient shelter—wall, bank, ivy, and in such odd places as a hat or a sack. The nest is beautifully made—domed, with a hole at the side, well matching its site—of leaves, bracken, moss, etc., lined with feathers. Many more nests are built than are used. These are unlined, and are supposed to be built by the cock bird for roosting places; but I have known them to be furnished completely (with feathers) some weeks after they were finished, and apparently abandoned. The eggs, from five to ten, are white with red-brown speckles. The food consists of wood-lice, spiders, insects, and their larvæ; in the winter of seeds and other minute particles which the Wren may be seen searching for methodically in shrubberies and hedgerows, as well as farmyards. The strange fallacy still remains popular that the Wren is the hen Robin! As a matter of fact, it is far more akin in structure to the Dipper, and occasionally has been seen to enter shallow water and hunt beneath its surface like that bird.

Wryneck—"Cuckoo's Mate."—The last of this first group of birds—approximating to a Sparrow—is distinguished by the beautiful mottled greys and browns of its plumage, which reminds one of the Nightjar. The upper parts (male) are of silver-grey freckled with darker colour; the crown adorned with bars of chestnut and white spots; brown wings with checks of chestnut. The under parts are a rich buff with dark bars and lines; a large broad tail. The female is rather duller and smaller than its mate.

The bird has the "zygodactylous" feet of the Woodpecker—that is, two toes in front and two behind; a long, protrusible tongue, and an erectile crest. It is a rare summer visitor, except in South-east England, Essex to Hants; in the latter county, at any rate, it is fairly common, generally arriving in May.

The nest is a *natural* hole in a tree, but I have often seen it in a nesting box. No material is used unless the bird has adapted another bird's old nest, such as the Starling's. Seven to fourteen eggs of a glossy whiteness are laid, but not so glossy as the Lesser Woodpecker's. The bird feeds on ants and other insects; in autumn on berries.

The Wryneck gains its name from its habit of twisting its long, lithe neck from side to side, almost with a snake-like motion. The pretty name, "Cuckoo's Mate," comes from the observed habit of the bird's arrival about the same time as the Cuckoo. Its call-note, "Pee-pee-pee-pee-pee" (like the Lesser Woodpecker's), is a welcome sound in spring. When disturbed sitting, the hen hisses like a serpent, almost too realistically. If held in the hand, the bird writhes its head, erects its crest, darts out its tongue, as if imitating a snake, or it will even feign death with closed eyes.

CHAPTER III.

Birds (*continued*).

II. BIRDS ABOUT THE SIZE OF A BLACKBIRD—10½ INCHES LONG.

(Smallest, 8 inches; largest, 12½ inches.)

Blackbird.—One of our most familiar residents. The male is jet-black, with yellow bill and eye-rim. Female is brownish black above, with a rufous tinge in the brown of the under parts. Her bill is brown. The nest is composed of dried grass, made into a solid structure with mud; it is lined with mud, within which is a layer of fine grass. The nest is in bushes, trees, or banks, on the ground, often on a beam in an outhouse, or some other odd site.

The eggs are bluish green, with spots of reddish brown.

The song consists of a series of rich mellow notes, so musical that they may be actually written down on a stave. This should make it easy to distinguish it from that of the Song Thrush, which is always noticed to contain notes and phrases repeated several times, a familiar one being "Duty, duty, duty," or "Pretty boy, pretty boy, pretty boy." The alarm cry, so often heard when the bird flies suddenly out of hedge or copse, is a loud chattering, scolding series of notes, quite unmistakable.

Corncrake (LANDRAIL).—A bird which I remember as much more common in the Midlands when I was a boy than to-day. I have still a memory that belongs to the romance of a boy's summer holiday attached to this bird—hearing the harsh, monotonous "crake" for the first time—"Kray, kray," or "Crex-crex"; catching a glimpse of the little bird, not unlike a Partridge, but smaller and slimmer (wedge-shaped like all the Rails); and at last—it must have been in June—finding the nest in some high grass. After that my memory seems to be that it was the one and only nest worth finding that holiday, and was regarded as a treasure most rare.

As a matter of fact, the bird has decreased in numbers in the South and Midlands, but is fairly common in the North or grass-lands. It is a summer visitor, coming from Central Africa to us towards the end of April. It is distinguished by its chestnut wings and general yellow-buff plumage, as well as by its cry. This can be imitated by rubbing two stones together, or drawing a finger nail over a comb.

If the bird is suddenly disturbed, it will sometimes feign death, like the

THE BRITISH NATURE BOOK

Wryneck; but in spite of its being a migrant from Africa, it seldom takes to flight, but prefers to run.

The nest is almost always in tall grass, and consists of a few leaves and grasses, placed in a depression in the ground.

The eggs, seven to twelve, are reddish white, spotted with reddish brown and ash-grey, and are generally laid in May.

[Note the family (*Rallidæ*) to which the bird belongs, which contains both *Coot* and *Moorhen*. All the members possess the same characteristic shape.]

Dotterel.—This is one of the rarest of our British Plovers, a very handsome, upright-standing bird, identified by a white band across the upper portion of the breast, and by the beautiful chestnut colour below. The head has a distinct white line over each eye, joining in a sharp point at the back of the neck, making a V shape behind. Upper parts, a bluish grey, with pale margins to the feathers. Belly, white.

The bird is a summer visitor, appearing at the end of April or early May, and making its way northwards to its breeding places in Scotland, and (very sparsely) in the Lake District. Its nest, a mere scrape in the ground, with a scanty lining of dried grass, is only found *high up* on a mountain slope, generally 2,500–3,000 feet above the sea.

The eggs are usually three—" clay-yellow, blotched with black markings " —and are found in June.

The food consists of insects, chiefly beetles and their larvæ, land shells, and a little vegetation.

The call-note is a sweet " Wit-a-wee "; but there is also an ugly and common cry, " Peek-peek," said to resemble the regular creak of an unoiled wheelbarrow.

Dove, Turtle.—There are four species of the " Pigeon " family (*Columbidæ*) which breed in these islands, of which the Turtle Dove is the smallest (11.25 inches). Its colour is a chestnut-brown above, with a tinge of slate-blue, and black centres to the feathers; a bluish grey head; on each side of the neck a patch of black and white feathers, in alternate bars. The wings are of rich red-brown on the wing coverts and scapulars (with black centres to the feathers). The tail is noticeably broad and tipped with white. The sides of the face and throat are a buff colour, with a tinge of pink, deeper on the chest, and passing to white on the belly.

The bird is easily distinguished in flight by the chestnut colour and the white margin to the tail, and otherwise by its soft purring " Coo-coo-coo."

This species is a summer visitor only, disappearing, unlike the British pigeons, during the winter. It is somewhat rare in the North and in Ireland, and is chiefly found in the South. It winters in North Africa. The nest is a very flimsy structure of twigs, placed in a tree, bush, or hedge, generally low down. The eggs are two in number, white, and rather long in shape. Its food consists of grain, seeds, and berries, and also small mollusca. It appears fond of salt water, and is often abundant near the coast.

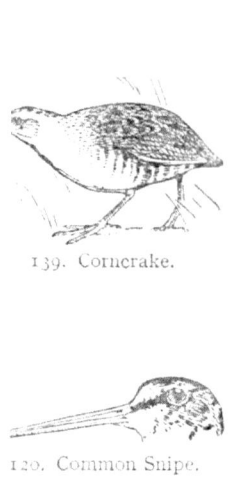
139. Corncrake.

126. Green Plover, or Lapwing.

184. Little Grebe, or Dabchick.

120. Common Snipe.

133. Common Sandpiper.

88. Nightjar.

108. Little Tern.

99. Turtle Dove.

83. Green Woodpecker.

123. Ringed Plover.

43. Fieldfare.

66. Starling.   41. Song Thrush.    124. Golden Plover.    45. Ring Ouzel.

Birds about the size of a Blackbird.

THE BRITISH NATURE BOOK

Fieldfare.—This bird does not breed in England, but is a common winter visitor, usually seen about grass-lands in flocks, arriving about October and leaving in April. It is not so large as the Mistle Thrush, but larger than the Song Thrush, and is recognized by its chestnut and grey back, contrasting with its black tail. The head is grey, throat and breast yellowish white.

The only notes heard during the bird's sojourn with us are a chattering cry overhead when the flock is moving, and a sharp alarm note, "Tsak," uttered often from a tree.

Grebe, Little—DABCHICK—the smallest of the British grebes. The Grebe family are noted for two well-marked characteristics: first, the almost total absence of a *tail;* and second, the curious lobed toes. The Dabchick is a very familiar sight on any pool, lake, or stream, where it looks like a large stumpy blackbird, smoky-black, except for the sides of neck and breast, which (with the lower flanks and a patch on each side of the rump) are a deep chestnut colour. There is some whitish colouring on the under parts. The legs are a dull green.

In the winter, however, the chin and throat are white, and the chestnut on the neck fades to a yellowish brown. At this time of the year it is often seen near the coast. It is a most expert diver; in fact, the young can dive as soon as they are hatched.

The nest is a mass of decaying rushes and water plants, usually placed among reeds, sometimes built in the open in shallow water, and the eggs are usually covered over by the bird on leaving the nest. These are originally a bluish white, but they rapidly become stained in browns or reds through being covered with the wet vegetation. The note is a mere shrill chatter. The bird is said never to be seen on land, but this is an exaggeration, though, owing to the legs being placed very far back, walking is a difficult process. It does, of course, walk on land, and when surprised shows remarkable speed in getting to the water.

Greenshank.—Is a much rarer bird than the Redshank (which see), breeding only in Scotland, though sometimes seen as a bird of passage on our coasts. It is a larger bird (14 inches), and has olive-green legs, a beak slightly upturned, and dark-grey upper parts. Its call is like the Redshank's, but sharper—"Tijü-tijü." Its nesting habits are much the same, but it is not so sociable. See also SANDPIPERS.

Guillemot, Black.—This bird does not breed in England, but in Scotland, Ireland, and the Isle of Man, where it is practically stationary all the year round. It is, as its name implies, chiefly black in colour, but is at once recognized by its *scarlet legs* and a *large white patch* on the wings. It feeds on crustaceans and small fish. It does not breed in large colonies, though it is not a "solitary" bird, one or more pairs being found together. The eggs, two in number, are laid on the rock in a cliff-crevice or under boulders, and are whitish in colour, with dark-brown and grey markings; to be found in May or June. The call is a clear "Ist-ist-ist," and there is a low, plaintive whine or whistle.

BIRDS

Hobby (*Falco subbuteo*).—"A peregrine in miniature," the male being 12 inches long, slate-grey above, white throat and cheeks, buffish white under parts with black stripes, rust-red shank feathers and tail coverts. Is found in the South of England from Devon to Norfolk, but scarce elsewhere. It is a summer visitor, arriving in May, nesting in an old nest of crow or magpie. The eggs, three or four, are lighter and yellower than the other falcons', mottled with light yellow or pale brown-red. Food consists of dragon-flies, butterflies, and beetles, with an occasional swift, swallow, or martin; in winter (when it is occasionally seen), of larks and other birds. The Hobby is a "forest bird," hunting on the outskirts of woods; very swift of wing.

Knot.—This bird does not breed in the British Isles, but is a winter visitor, feeding on molluscs, especially small mussels. It derives its name from its hoarse, grunting call, "Knot" or "Knut"; but it has also other notes—"a curious warbling" when in flocks, and a "Tullawee-tullawee-whee-whee" when courting. It is one of the family of Sandpipers, long-legged and long-billed. In its breeding plumage it is recognized by its *red-brown under parts*, head, and neck. The back is black, with light buff margins to the feathers. In winter garb it becomes an ash-grey, with darker shades above and lighter below.

Lapwing. See PLOVER, GREEN.

Merlin.—This bird is the smallest of the British falcons; but it is only the cock bird that comes within measurable distance of this classification by size, being 10–11 inches; the female is larger. Its small size, therefore, distinguishes it from any other British falcon. The upper parts are slate-blue; the under parts white, tinged with a rufous shade, and barred with black. The legs are yellow, the beak hooked. The female has brown upper parts, and underneath whitish, with dark-brown stripes.

The Merlin is resident in Great Britain, and is also an autumn immigrant. It breeds in Wales, North of England, Scotland, and Ireland (possibly Exmoor), on the hills and moors. In winter it is found on the coast.

Its nest is a hollow scratched out among heather on a hillside, with a few scanty dried stalks for lining. It also breeds in old nests of raven and carrion crow, and on cliff edges. The eggs, four to six, are mottled with red-brown or chocolate so thickly as to hide the ground colour. They are usually to be found in May. The cry is a "Kek-kek-kek." The food consists of larks, linnets, and other small birds, also large moths, especially the "eggars."

Nightjar (GOATSUCKER, NIGHT-HAWK, FERN-OWL, etc.).—No one who has once heard the peculiar jarring cry of this bird at night can fail afterwards to identify it. It is a long drawn-out "Churr"; but in flight there is a call-note syllabled as "Co-ik," and an alarm note, "Quik-quik." Its characteristic "Churr" has been compared to the tearing of calico, or the rattling of a mowing machine.

The bird has several striking peculiarities, and is easily identified by its huge mouth, guarded with bristles (a portcullis from which no insect can escape), its flat, toad-like head, its small feet and legs, and its remarkable plumage, lichen-grey in colour, barred and streaked with buff and chestnut. It is so like the branches and boughs and bracken where it nests that it is extremely difficult to discover. It has a habit of crouching *along*, and not across, a branch, thus enhancing its similarity to its environment; when in daylight, it keeps its eyes nearly closed to lessen the possibility of being discovered by them. It haunts commons, uncultivated lands, and open woods, where it nests on the ground, the eggs being laid among dead sticks and leaves, usually among bracken. These are two in number, a creamy white, with spots and mottlings of brown and grey, very long and elliptical.

It flies at night, catching insects, chiefly beetles and moths. It has a curious middle claw, serrated along its inner edge like a saw. The purpose of this peculiarity is unknown. Gilbert White thought it caught insects with its foot, this saw-toothed claw helping it to retain its prey; but this is not proved. Other explanations are: the claw is used to clean the mouth bristles; or to help it to clutch firmly the bough on which it rests longitudinally. None of these theories are proved.

The chicks are hatched covered with down, and are able to move about at a day old; and thus quickly leave the " nest " to hide in the neighbouring undergrowth. The parent birds will try to distract the attention of an intruder by feigning to be injured, their movements being those of a wounded or dazed bird.

Ouzel, Ring.—This bird is found on moors and hillsides, where it is a summer visitor, arriving about the middle of March. It is the same size and build as a Blackbird, but the plumage is a rusty black, and the bird is at once identified by the crescent-shaped patch of white on the breast. The hen is browner, with a narrower and indistinct crescent. The note is like the Blackbird's, but not so sweet and mellow. The nest is also like the Blackbird's, but is placed far more frequently on the ground, among rocks or heather, and only rarely in a bush; and the eggs also resemble the Blackbird's, but with bolder markings.

Owl, Little.—The smallest British owl, no larger than a Thrush; distinguished by its size, its greyish brown colour, spotted and barred with white. It is increasing as one of our residents in Southern England and Wales, owing to its importation by Lord Lilford and others. Like other owls, it makes no nest, but lays four or five white eggs in a hole of some sort, whether in tree, wall, or bank.

Though so small, it is a bold and even savage species, and is said to attack small birds and game more than other owls, and to feed by daylight as well as night. In addition, it devours voles, mice, and beetles.

The introduction of this bird has not proved an unmixed blessing, for gamekeepers charge it with working no small havoc amongst young pheasants and partridges. There is no doubt, however, of its usefulness in destroying beetles, such as cockchafers. Its cry, unmistakable, is " Cu " or " Cu-cu."

Partridge (GREY PARTRIDGE).—A familiar resident, widely distributed, but local in Scotland, distinguished by having eighteen feathers in the tail. In colour, brownish buff above, with fine black markings; under parts chestnut and grey; a large horseshoe patch of chestnut on the male bird's breast. Its plump appearance and the swift whirr with which it gets up serve additionally to identify it.

It has a creaking call-note, heard chiefly in spring—" harsh, guttural, and complaining." It nests on the ground, in long herbage, a hedge bottom, or under a bush, laying from ten to twenty eggs of an olive-brown-grey colour. The nest is a scrape lined with leaves and grass, which sometimes are pulled over the eggs when the bird leaves them. It feeds on young shoots and leaves of grass and clover chiefly, and also on insects and their larvæ. (For Red-legged Partridge, see next section.)

Plover, Golden.—All the Plovers come under the same category as to size (though they vary in size from the 9 inches of the Dotterel to the $12\frac{1}{2}$ inches of the Lapwing); and as they have many characteristics in common, it is well that they should be grouped together here. (See also DOTTEREL.)

The Golden Plover is far more general in the hilly districts of the West of England, Wales, Scotland, and Ireland than in the South, for it breeds but sparingly in Devon and Cornwall; and though a British resident, is practically only a winter visitor in the South. It is recognized by the dark upper parts with their rich golden spots; its black face and under parts, which have a wide margin of white on each side, from the forehead, behind the eyes, and down to the white tail coverts; the beak and legs are black, and the foot lacks a hind-toe. A striking seasonal change of plumage takes place in the autumn, the under parts becoming all white, with a tinge of dusky yellow mottlings on the neck.

The bird utters a shrill, musical note; its breeding cry is syllabled " Taludl-taludl-taludl " ; its call-note is " Tlüi " or " Tlüei." It feeds on snails, slugs, worms, insects, and some herbage; inland, especially on beetles.

The nest is a scrape on rough lands, among heather or tussocky grass, sometimes sparsely lined. Four eggs are laid, of a warm stone colour, with blackish spots and blotches.

Plover, Green (LAPWING, PEEWIT).—A familiar and widely distributed species, recognized by its note " Pee-wit," as also by its beautiful recurved crest of black, glossed with green; its metallic green back and wings, with their coppery lustre; the black on the throat and breast; the chestnut on the tail coverts. Otherwise the under body is white, a feature showing distinctly when the bird is in flight, when its broad rounded wings will also be noticed.

The nest is a scrape in the ground on pasture or marsh lands, generally, I believe, on very slightly rising ground. It is scantily lined with dried grass or roots.

The neighbouring ground is sure to contain two or three " cock's nests "

THE BRITISH NATURE BOOK

—scrapes made by the cock bird in the course of his curious courting; and in many of them (as in the nest proper) a stone is frequently found. I believe the cock bird lies on this, and uses it to round the nest—if not, to derive some ecstatic pleasure from riding it. I have seen a domestic pigeon do the same thing. The eggs, four in number, are yellow or olive-brown, spotted and blotched with darker colour. Unfortunately, they are too often taken for the market, to satisfy the gourmet's appetite; yet the bird is one of the most useful existing, feeding entirely upon insects, slugs, and other creatures injurious to the crops.

Plover, Grey.—Does not breed in Great Britain, being only a winter visitor, the young birds arriving in flocks from Russia in September, followed by the older ones in October and November. A few remain with us for the winter, but most pass on to their destination in Africa, returning in spring till May. The call-note is a double whistle, first short and then drawn out.

The bird is distinguished from the Golden Plover, which it otherwise resembles, by the black-and-white bars and checks on the back and head in its summer plumage; it possesses also a short hind-toe. In winter the under parts are chiefly white, but the upper parts become "an almost uniform ash-brown," with whitish edges to the feathers.

Plover, Kentish.—Is a very rare bird, only found breeding on the coast of Kent and Sussex, where it is a summer visitor only. It has a black beak and legs, and the black on the breast is broken into a patch on each side of the neck. It lays its eggs in a scrape on the beach. They vary in colour from a light stone to deep tawny brown, and have some well-defined streaks and scrolls besides the spots.

The bird is "a noisy little bird," flying in a bat-like manner, with quick wavering movements, and utters an alarm note, "Fluit," its call-note being "Pui," uttered at fairly long intervals. Its food is the same as the Ringed Plover's—marine animals, crustaceans, and insects.

Plover, Ringed.—Is a fairly common resident, especially on the coast, though it is found sometimes inland, on waste grounds and open spaces. Generally its nest will be found on a shingle beach, or on sands near the sea, and it varies from a mere scrape to an actual attempt to line a nest with pebbles, broken shells, and dried grass or other material. The eggs (usually four) are, like those of the other plovers, pear-shaped, of a yellowish stone colour, blotched and spotted with dark brown or black. It will be observed that these always lie with the pointed ends towards each other, in which position they occupy less space, and are more easily covered by the bird than in any other.

The bird itself is distinguished by its grey-brown crown and back, the broad black band which passes across the white breast, right round the neck, the characteristic black-and-white face markings, and the yellow legs. It has also an orange beak with a black tip. Its plaintive alarm note is a kind of whistle, "Tuli-tuli," uttered often when on its graceful flight, skimming

BIRDS

low for a moment, then circling high, and sweeping down almost to the ground. It looks a much larger bird in the air, owing to its spread of wings, long and pointed, and showing much white; but once on the ground it appears almost transformed (the white disappearing) into another bird—small, plump, and grey, moving with short, quick steps.

Redshank.—There are very few counties in which this bird does not breed locally, especially in low-lying meadows by rivers, and marshes. In fact, on beach, or marsh, or moorland, salting or rough pasture, it may be heard, acting as a sentinel, giving all too speedy an alarm cry at the approach of strangers—"Too-oo-ee, too-oo-ee!" The Redshank frequently breeds in companies, and nests are generally found close to one another. They are a deep scrape, generally well hidden in herbage, and lined with grass.

The eggs, two to four, are a deep cream colour, speckled and spotted with dark brown, larger than the Dunlin's or Sandpiper's. The bird is like the Common Sandpiper in shape (see Fig. 133). In summer it is coloured on the upper parts pale brown, streaked and barred with umber; white rump, flecked with dusky; white tail feathers, barred with blackish; white under parts; streaked with umber on neck and breast. It may be identified by its long orange-red legs and feet, and the white on the wing and rump. In winter the upper parts are ash-coloured; rump and under parts white, slightly spotted, and streaked with grey on neck and breast.

Redwing.—One of the Thrush family, often seen flying about in flocks during the winter, like the Fieldfare. It is only a winter visitor, and does not nest with us, preferring Norway, Scandinavia, and other countries. Its distinguishing feature is the rich red (not on the wing, in spite of its name, but) on the flanks, under the wing coverts. Otherwise it resembles the Song Thrush. It feeds on worms, insects, snails, and berries.

Sanderling.—One of the Sandpiper family—has no hind-toe. In summer plumage has the upper parts, including the upper breast, a mahogany-brown, streaked with black, and touches of white on the margins of some of the feathers; the under parts are white : in the winter the upper parts are grey, under parts all white. It does not breed in the British Isles, but is often seen in the winter on the coasts, where it feeds on worms, small crustaceans, and molluscs. A quiet bird compared to other waders. Its alarm note, something like a Chaffinch's, " Wick-wick," or " Swink-swink."

Sandpiper, Common.—Notice that the Sandpipers belong to a family represented by quite a number of species, including Dunlin, Knot, and Redshank. The Common Sandpiper is a summer visitor, fairly common in Cornwall and Devon. More numerous west of Severn and north of Trent; rare in the south-eastern counties. Recognized by its brown back, with arrow-shaped markings of black on the feathers. Below white, with a few dark spots on chest. Tail short, barred with blackish, tipped with white; outer feathers nearly all white. Bill rather long, but not so long as the Snipe's.

Its note is " Peep-peep," or " Teet-teet."

It is distinguished by its brown back and white under parts. A graceful bird on slender legs, often seen running along the edge of a lake or stream. When disturbed, it flies away, just skimming the surface, uttering "Peep-peep," showing white margin to the inside of wings and round tip of tail.

The nest, a depression among the pebbles or shingle near a stream or lake, lined with grass, etc. The eggs (four) are buff-white, with dark brown and grey spots and blotches, pear-shaped; about the size of a Blackbird's, but of course very different in shape.

Sandpiper, Green.—Easily distinguished from the others by its larger size (9.5 inches), the bronze-green upper surface, and the dull black underwing and axillaries, the latter having white bars. [The rare WOOD SANDPIPER is smaller (3½ inches), and is distinguished by the *white* underwings.] Does not breed, so far as is known, in Great Britain, but is a winter visitor and bird of passage. The bird has a strong smell, like the woodpeckers.

Sandpiper, Purple.—This bird is much like the Dunlin (which see), but has yellow legs. In *breeding* plumage, the male has a purple gloss on the black upper parts. It appears as a winter visitor, young birds arriving during September, the adults in October. It does not breed in the British Isles; prefers wild, rocky coasts more than sandy shores. Its note is "Weet-wit," or "Tee-wit."

Snipe, Common (see notes on JACK SNIPE in the preceding group).—Is smaller than the Woodcock (which see), possesses a long bill, flat head, and neat, "compact" body, beautifully coloured so as to resemble the foliage and soil of its haunts.

The long beak is used (a characteristic common to all the family) for thrusting into the earth in search of worms, and possesses this remarkable feature —the end of the upper jaw is movable, capable of being raised up and brought down on the lower jaw without moving the rest of the bill. It is, in fact, a sort of "upper lip," and is an instrument of great grasping power. Its purpose is obvious. When the bill is thrust into the ground after a worm, to open the whole beak and close it would fill the mouth with dirt; but the bird is thus able to keep its bill shut and open just the extremity to secure its prey. The feeding haunts of these birds may be found by noticing the neat holes which they have made in the ground. In colour the Snipe is distinguished by the three stripes of yellow on the crown from front to back, and four stripes along the back. The upper parts are of a black and buff variegated pattern, with grey on the wings, the under parts being whitish with shades of grey.

The bird may be recognized by its peculiar twisting flight, as well as by its alarm cry of "Scope-scope."

Its food consists of worms, insects and their larvæ; in winter, when the ground is frost-bound, it seeks the coast, where it finds food in the sand or mud of the sea-edge.

The nest is a cup-shaped hollow in the ground in a marshy spot, often under a tussock of grass, in rough pasture land near water; it is lined with dead grass.

The eggs are pear-shaped, pale olive-brown (varying to greenish), spotted and blotched with reddish brown, black, and purple-grey. Just as the Woodcock (which see) has its own peculiar flight—"roding"—so the Snipe is noted for its "musical ride," when it mounts high in the air, then flies in wide circles, dropping sideways every now and then some fifty feet, and uttering as it falls a series of high notes called "drumming," "bleating," or "neighing." It begins at daybreak for an hour or so; again at midday and sunset; and on a moonlight night on and off through the night, several birds taking part. It has now been proved that this curious "humming" sound is produced by the wind passing through the wide spread feathers of the tail, the two outside feathers being of peculiarly stout construction.

The hen bird when disturbed will frequently feign injury, and—at a safe distance—scold unmistakably, "Chack-ach-chack-wach-chack-a-a-h-chacka-a-ah!"

The Snipe does *not carry* its young, as the Woodcock does, to the feeding grounds.

Snipe, Great ($10\frac{1}{2}$ inches).—Does not breed here, but is a bird of passage, coming in small numbers to the South and East Coasts. It may be distinguished by the *white* outer tail feathers; and, if the bird be handled, by the sixteen tail feathers, instead of the Common Snipe's fourteen.

Starling.—There is no need to describe this common but beautiful bird, with the metallic blues and greens of his black spangled plumage, his long yellow bill, flat head, and short tail. Whatever harm he does to the fruit (for example, the cherries), he more than equalizes by his persistent hunt for injurious insects and larvæ, wire-worms, weevils, and grubs. There are two varieties in this country, a purple-headed and green-headed, and though resident with us all the year round, enormous flocks migrate to and from these shores. The song with its bubbles and castanets and imitations is unique, and to watch the cock bird giving his vocal performance is, or may be, the delight of every one who lives under a roof. Any sort of a hole serves for a nest, and some "nesting boxes" occupied every year by starlings are shown in this book. Among noticeable features of this bird, it may be remarked that it *walks*, instead of hopping on the ground; that it has a curious way of parting the grass blades by thrusting in its bill and then opening it—an operation which I have endured upon my hair from a tame starling; and it devours, and brings to its young, the obnoxious *cabbage butterflies* (an inestimable service to the gardener and farmer). Its eggs are a beautiful pale blue, and it sometimes has *two* broods in a season.

Thrush, Mistle.—This bird is so familiar that brief notes will suffice. It is larger than the Blackbird; is distinguished from the Song Thrush by its large size, its *greyer* appearance (the upper parts being greyish brown), its *spotted* flanks—no other thrush being so marked—and the white edging to the tail, showing up especially in flight; also by its harsh, grating alarm note.

It is one of the earliest birds to sing; in fact, it may be heard from September

THE BRITISH NATURE BOOK

to June, but at its best from the end of December to April. Its name of STORM COCK comes from its habit of singing in rough weather. The song consists of a short phrase or two repeated.

The nest is a rough structure of grass, wool, etc., with an inner cup of mud lined with dry grasses, usually placed in the fork of a tree. Four eggs are the usual number, but I have found five more than once, and even six are recorded. They are greenish or buff-white, with red-brown and pale purple spots. Generally two broods in the season.

Thrush, Song.—*Smaller* than the Blackbird, *olive-brown above*, under parts white tinged with yellowish brown, with black spots except on the flanks, which are *streaked*. Its song consists of a number of notes, each being repeated several times. The nest is of dried grass and mud, lined with small fragments of rotten wood, etc., laid on a coating of wet mud, making a hard, smooth surface.

The eggs (four or five) are greenish blue with black spots.

The bird has two or three broods every season. The song has been syllabled thus: " Tea, tea, quickly—Below, below, below—Teete, teete, teete—Pretty boy, pretty boy, pretty boy—Cup-o'-tea, cup-o'-tea, cup-o'-tea—Worry Lill, worry Lill, worry Lill—Kiss her now, kiss her now, kiss her now—Peep-bo, peep-bo—Chee-he-he, chee-he-he."

Tern, Little (compare notes on COMMON TERN in next group).—This is the smallest of the Terns—or Sea Swallows, as they are frequently called on account of their resemblance to the swallows (disregarding size and colour). This bird has the black, grey, and white plumage of the others, but is distinguished by its smaller size (only slightly larger than a thrush). It has also a broad white forehead, with a broad black stripe from the beak to the eye, a yellow beak tipped with black, and yellow legs. It is a noisy bird, and from its rapid wing-beats appears to be always in a hurry. Its usual cry is " Kweek," and often " Kweek-tik-tik—kweek-tik-tik-a-tik," and as it flies off to sea, in company with its mates, it utters a " Tiri-wiri-tiri-wiri-tiri-wiri."

The nest is only to be found on sandy or shingly beaches; it is a shallow depression, either in the sand or amongst stones, and is very occasionally lined with a little vegetation—seaweed or grass; usually there is nothing to distinguish it from the ground round about.

The eggs (two or three) are light brown, yellow, or grey stone colour, with spots and blotches of deeper colour; about the size of a Mistle Thrush's.

There are other species of terns which are occasional visitors, and in some rare instances breed here. The BLACK TERN (9½ inches) appears in small numbers as a bird of passage, on the South Coast. The ROSEATE TERN, distinguished by its black beak and rosy tinted breast, is extremely local, one colony being carefully preserved in Wales.

Turnstone.—The delightful Norfolk name for this bird is the TANGLE PICKER, and the two names indicate the well-known habit of this species of turning over stones, seaweed, driftwood, etc., to search underneath for food such as small crustaceans, tiny crabs, shrimps, sand-hoppers, and insects. Frequently it works in *parties*, two or more birds combining to turn over some object too heavy for one to move. The bird is not unlike a miniature Oyster-catcher, especially in flight, when the large patches of white on wings and body make it conspicuous and give it a distinctly pied appearance. As a matter of fact, together with the Oyster-catcher (which see), it belongs to the sub-family of *Hæmatopodinæ*—" Red-legged " Plovers.

It is chiefly known to us as a spring and autumn bird of passage, but some are almost always to be seen in summer. It may possibly breed in Ireland or on islands off the West and North of Scotland, but there is only the scantiest evidence of this.

Its cry on the wing is a " long, chuckling twitter "—" Cheeka-cheeka-cheeka-chee." In searching for it through a glass, remember it is *smaller than a Blackbird*, with (in summer) white crown and nape, streaked with black; a black and chestnut back and wings. Under parts white, except upper breast which is black; black beak, red legs. In winter it becomes browner above, and the throat white.

Water-rail.—A resident—of the same family as the Corncrake, Waterhen, and Coot. It is identified by a red beak, brown back with black streaks, blue-grey neck and breast, and a conspicuous patch of black-and-white bars on the flanks. A shy bird like the Corncrake, it breeds locally—for example, on the Norfolk Broads—the nest being generally well hidden in swamps and marshes, sometimes on a tussock, or in osier beds; it is a largish nest, built of dead leaves of flags, reeds, etc., well rounded, and lined with leaves. The eggs (seven to twelve) are like those of the Land-rail, creamy white with a few small reddish spots, chiefly at the big end (very rarely, bold blotches of red-brown). The Water-rail feeds on worms, slugs, snails, and some vegetation. It has a " loud, explosive call," which the country folk call " sharming"; but except for this, it is a silent and furtive bird.

The SPOTTED CRAKE, or SPOTTED RAIL, is a rarer bird, olive-brown, with white spots on neck and fore-breast; a summer visitor; has occasionally bred, and may still do so, in several southern counties, choosing marshy ground, where plenty of rank growth is to be found. A large nest; eight to twelve eggs, stone-buff, with dark red spots.

Woodpecker, Great Spotted.—Less common than the Green Woodpecker; prefers oak woods, hedgerows with large ash trees, or riversides where rows of pollarded willows may be found. It is a shy and solitary bird—uttering an occasional " Guet-guet " and other notes, and when alarmed a loud " Chink-chink." It does not, like the Green Woodpecker, eat ants, but other insects; also fruit such as cherries in their season, and, in the autumn, berries. It may be recognized by its black-and-white plumage, the patch of red on back of the head, and the red under the tail coverts.

The *drumming*, of which it is a great exponent, peculiar to all the Wood-peckers, is produced by the bird striking the tree with its beak. This is done so

THE BRITISH NATURE BOOK

rapidly that the head appears blurred, and the sound can be heard half a mile away. The nest and eggs as Green Woodpecker's.

Woodpecker, Green—often called the YAFFLE, from its familiar laughing cry, which has been syllabled "Plen-plen-plen." There is no mistaking this brilliant coloured bird, with its bright green upper parts, its crimson crown and nape, white spots on wing, and yellowish under parts. It has a curious undulating flight, which is very characteristic, as if "riding on invisible waves." It prefers light sandy soils, where ants and their nests may be found abundantly, for on this insect it is fond of feeding, as well as on other insects and their larvæ. Here a curious point may be noted. Both this bird and the Great Spotted Woodpecker have a strong, pungent *smell*, which is said to be due to their eating the offensive-smelling larvæ of the Goat Moth. It appears to prefer old and decaying oak trees for nesting purposes. The nest is bored by the bird, chips of wood being the material on which the five or more glossy white eggs are deposited. The bird possesses a wonderful tongue, capable of being protruded a long distance from the mouth. This weapon is barbed at the tip and is covered with sticky saliva. Its value in "sticking" insects is apparent.

III. BIRDS ABOUT THE SIZE OF A WOOD PIGEON—16 INCHES LONG.

(Those under this head vary from 13 inches—for example, Waterhen—
to 18 inches—for example, Common Gull.)

Chough—the RED-LEGGED DAW, or CORNISH DAW—one of the Crow family, distinguished by its black coat gleaming with blue and purple metallic gloss, its *red legs*, and long *red, curved bill*. A scarce bird, practically confined to Devon, Cornwall, Isle of Man, and West Coast of Ireland.

It nests in holes and crevices, in cliffs, caves, and occasionally old buildings —using sticks, stems, roots, etc.; the eggs (three to five) sometimes white, creamy, brown, or even pinkish white, darker spots and blotches.

The Chough eats "everything"—its usual food being worms, insects, crustaceans, berries. Its ordinary note is a loud, clear "K'chare."

Coot.—A rather thick, heavy-looking bird, of a uniform dark colour, with a *white* forehead and beak, and green legs (the feet having curious lobed toes). Dives much after its food; often seen with the Moorhen; makes a large nest of dead vegetation in reeds or sedges, with seven or eight eggs, pale buff-white with small brown spots; haunts large ponds and lakes.

Utters long single call-notes, one of which is like "Coot."

It is found with us all the year round. It feeds chiefly on water plants, but also on insects and molluscs, grain and berries.

Cuckoo.—Every one knows *something* at least about this bird, but not all can describe its appearance. In flight, it has somewhat the appearance of a hawk, with its rather long, fan-shaped tail and general colouring. Above

PLATE VIII.

1. Stone Curlew. 2. Green Plover. 3. Common Buzzard. 4. Tree Pipit.
(Photos by W. P. Green.)

BIRDS

slate-grey; tail dark bluish, spotted with white; the breast with black bars. The toes are very characteristic, two being pointed forward and two back. The hen is smaller, and has a ruddy tinge on neck and upper breast.

The hen places her eggs in the nests of other birds—Hedge Sparrow, Wagtail, Pipit, etc. The eggs vary a great deal; usually larger than the foster-bird's own eggs; whitish with markings of various shades. They sometimes *resemble* the other eggs in the nest, especially on the Continent.

A summer visitor—" in April come he will." The food consists of insects, especially *hairy caterpillars*—" woolly bears," which few other birds will touch. The remaining brief notes must suffice on this unique bird. Frequenting open woodland, each Cuckoo has its own " beat " or district. The hen is polyandrous. It is *not* true that " in June he changes his tune "—the " Cuck-cuck-oo " referred to being heard in May. There are other notes as well, particularly a hoarse cry, like half a cough and half a laugh—" Kwow-wow-wow."

The hen sometimes lays her egg directly in the nest, but frequently lays it on the ground and *carries* it to the nest in her beak. In so doing, she often removes one or more of the original owner's; but these ejected eggs are *seldom*, if ever, eaten by the bird. The young Cuckoo, when hatched, proceeds to eject the other eggs or young from the nest. This it does by getting its victim on to its back (where there is a strange hollow), then, climbing up the side backwards, it jerks its burden off. But after three or four days the desire to eject its neighbours ceases—in fact, the hollow in the young bird's back itself disappears.*

Curlew, Stone—often called "NORFOLK PLOVER," "THICK-KNEE," etc.—Is the sole member of the family *Œdicnemidæ*, which is included in the sub-order of *Limicolæ*, and so is related to that of the Snipes, Sandpipers, Plovers, etc. The bird is distinguished by its very large yellow eye and long yellow legs. Otherwise it is sandy-buff above, with dark brown streaks; under parts whitish, with pale brown tinges on the upper breast and flanks. Some white on the face, two white bars on wing; a touch of white on tips of the outside wing quills, which just shows when bird is on ground. Yellow beak with black tip. Chiefly a summer visitor in the South and East of England, and breeds locally and sparingly in Dorset, Hants, and other counties; but chiefly in Norfolk and Suffolk. Nests in a hollow in ground on commons and waste land covered with stones—hence "Stone" Curlew. Very often rabbit droppings are found in the nest, but little or no other lining. The eggs (two) are buff or stone colour, blotched and spotted with darker brown and grey; often carelessly deposited, a little distance apart—good examples of " protective coloration."

The food consists chiefly of insects (especially beetles); also small mammals —for example, field mice.

* Since the above was written, I have had a young cuckoo under observation, and have seen what has never been remarked before—namely, that the female Cuckoo visited the young bird regularly every morning and evening. The egg was placed in a Wagtail's nest, built in a cold frame, and continually passed by gardeners at work, so that there can be no mistake about the facts. The mother bird, usually but not invariably accompanied by the Wagtail, came down to the nest in the early morning and late evening, disappearing during the rest of the day.

The cry is "Cour-li-vee—cour-li-vee." This is uttered in flight. On the ground often a shrill note, "Dew-leep."

Dove, Rock.—Is identified by the large white patch on the rump. It also shows white plainly on the coverts of the under wing when in flight. It has a darker blue on the head, neck, and tail. It is scarcely ever found away from the sea cliffs which it frequents, placing its nest on a ledge or in a crevice; the nest is generally a rough structure of grasses, seaweed, etc., containing two white eggs. It feeds on grain, seeds, and the roots of noxious weeds. It never alights on a tree. From this bird all our domestic pigeons have descended, and it still interbreeds with them; in fact, species shot are often almost identical with the "Blue-rock."

Dove, Stock.—Another of the four species of "pigeon" found in Great Britain. This bird is often confused with the Rock Dove, but it can be distinguished by the fact that it has *no* white in the plumage. Otherwise it is a slaty blue bird, with two broken black bars on the wing. It is a resident, not uncommon, but somewhat local; much smaller than the Wood Pigeon. Its food consists of grain, with seeds of weeds, acorns, beech mast, etc. Its nest is almost always in a hole—whether in tree, building, or ground; often in a rabbit burrow. Very little material is used; the eggs (two) are cream-white.

Duck, Tufted.—This bird is at once identified by the pendent crest, as also by the uniform black (male) or brown (female) upper colours. The male has belly and flanks white, but from July to October his plumage is like that of the female. Until 1849 the bird was not known to breed in Britain, but since it has spread to every part. It is a social bird, breeding when it can in colonies. Its harsh note, "Karr, karrkarr," is often heard on our canals and inland waters, especially in winter, when, besides those which are *resident*, others visit us on migration, and like the Pochard, prefer fresh water to salt.

The nest is generally close to the water, in a hollow under a bush, and is lined with a few dead leaves or grasses, becoming mixed with down (of a dully dusty brown). The eggs (eight to twelve) are olive-brown, much *longer* than the normal duck's egg, and are laid quite late in the season—from mid-May to June.

Falcon, Peregrine.—The largest of the falcons which breed with us; haunts moors and cliffs, where its cry of "Kek-kek-kek" may be heard. A resident (specially in the Devonian peninsula). Feeds on puffins and other sea birds, pigeons, rabbits, etc. It is of a slate-blue colour above, buff-white below. It makes its nest almost always on the face of a cliff, a mere scrape or hollow, with no attempt at lining. The eggs (three or four) are whitish, almost entirely hidden by mottles and shades of chestnut and red-brown.

Godwit, Bar-tailed.—Remembering that this is one of the "Dunlins" (which see), a general idea of its figure and shape comes to mind. It does not breed here, but is a winter visitor to our coasts, especially Northumbria. Note its large size ($15\frac{1}{2}$ inches), the bright brown of the head, neck, and upper parts (only in breeding plumage), the long, upturned beak, the tail white

Birds about the size of a Wood Pigeon.

barred with black. [The rarer BLACK-TAILED GODWIT is known by the broad black end to the tail.] In winter it is a grey bird, darker above. It feeds on worms and burrowing crustaceans. The call is " Kew-it."

Golden-eye.—One of the Duck family, to be recognized (when in full plumage) by the round white patch at the base of the beak—almost like a large white " dimple "—the green-black head, and a large amount of white on the wing. It has a black back and white under parts; the female has a chestnut-brown head, the rest being grey (above) and white.

It is a winter visitor only, to be found on our coasts and inland lakes, feeding on molluscs, crustaceans, tadpoles, and frogs. It has a harsh, rasping double note, " Zee-at," heard chiefly at the breeding season. Otherwise it is a silent bird.

Grouse, Red.—This is the one and only species of bird inhabiting our country that is not known in any other part of the world (except where it has been deliberately introduced, as, for example, into Germany and Sweden). It is not known in the South; but on the Lancashire and Yorkshire moors, and in North Wales, Scotland, and Ireland it may be found breeding. The changes in plumage are of great interest, the male moulting in autumn and winter, the female in summer and autumn. The general plumage is reddish brown on neck and head; upper parts chestnut-brown, barred and speckled with black; black breast tipped with white. In summer the colouring is lighter, in winter there is a certain amount of white mottling on the under parts. The male has a small red " comb " above each eye.

The alarm note is " Cock-cock-cock "; the call-note, a harsh " Go-back, go back-back-back." The nest is a scrape among heather or herbage, lined with heath, grass, fern, etc. Eight or nine eggs are laid, varying in colour—yellowish, creamy, and reddish, blotched and mottled with darker brown.

The Red Grouse feeds on young shoots of heather or ling, and in autumn on seeds of sedges, grains, and wild fruits. In winter it often burrows beneath the snow, making a remarkable and intricate series of tunnels.

Guillemot.—One of the Auks. May be confused with the Razorbill at first sight; but it is easily distinguished by its *long* and *slender* bill, more graceful neck, and grey-brown upper parts (slate-grey in summer, browner in autumn); the under parts are mostly white. The bird is found in colonies with the Razorbill (which see) on our sea cliffs all the year round. On the Yorkshire coast quite a large trade is done by cliff climbers in collecting the eggs. Only one egg is laid, on the bare rock of the cliff ledges or the top of stacks. It is pear-shaped, and varies extraordinarily in colour, having green, white, or yellow ground colour, blotched and spotted with darker colours. The bird sits bolt upright, reminding one of the Penguin. It feeds on fish. The notes are various—some like gulls, others like the commencement of a dog's howl, others a succession of laughing cries, its most familiar call being syllabled as " Murr."

[Many of these birds have a white circle round the eye, and are known as " bridled " or " ringed."]

6. Magpie.

101. Guillemot.

170. Golden-eye.

107. Arctic Tern.

142. Coot.

100. Razorbill.

168. Tufted Duck.

141. Waterhen.

127. Oyster-catcher.

118. Stone Curlew.

109. Black-headed Gull.

104. Puffin.

Birds about the size of a Wood Pigeon.

THE BRITISH NATURE BOOK

Gull, Black-headed.—The family of *Larinæ*—Gulls—is a large one, and consists of several species. This one, however, is not likely to be confused with any but the Common Gull and the Kittiwake (the notes of each should therefore be compared). The Black-headed Gull is a common resident, yet the whole species is *migratory ;* the gulls which appear in London in the winter are of this species, though the so-called *black* colour of the head is absent till the next spring.

The general colour is: on the back, pearl-grey; wings same, but black ends to the outer primaries, and a broad edge of white (a distinguishing mark). The rest white. In the breeding season the *dark coffee-brown* plumage of the head appears. The bird may be always identified by its blood-red legs and beak. It nests in colonies on the ground, in marsh land or near lakes, sometimes on sandhills near the sea, using for material such grass or reeds as abound in the neighbourhood. Scoulton Mere, on the Norfolk Broads, is a famous nesting site. The eggs (three) have shades of stone colour, varying from buff to green, with dark brown blotches and spots.

The birds are often seen on ploughed land close to the sea, and they are of the utmost value to the farmer, as their staple food consists of worms and insects—especially crane-flies and wire-worms.

The note is a kind of laughing call.

Gull, Common.—Though labelled "common," this species does not breed in England, but in Scotland and Ireland. It is a familiar winter visitor to England and Wales. It is identified by its size (18 inches), its pearl-grey back, and yellowish green beak and legs. It chooses low grassy islands, grass-grown cliffs, and loch sides for its nests—often found in colonies—substantially built of heather, seaweed, reeds, etc. Three eggs form the usual clutch. These are a broader oval than the Black-headed Gull's, the ground colour varying from buff to olive, blotched and spotted darker. The species eats " everything "— worms, insects, fish, garbage, etc. Its call-note is a sound like " Yak," and it possesses a laughing cry like " Luka-luka-luka."

Hawk, Sparrow.—In spite of its enemies the gamekeepers, this is one of the commonest of our " hawks," and may be seen about any of our wooded districts. It may be recognized by its relatively short wings, long tail, and long legs. The female is larger (15 inches) than the male (13 inches). The general colour is slate-grey; there are three or four bars of darker colour across the tail; the under parts whitish, with delicate ripples of grey; and there is a noticeable touch of rufous or chestnut colour about the head and face.

The bird flies close to the ground when hunting; but whilst the female sits, the male often soars to a great height above the nest, uttering a silvery cry, " Kick, kick, kick." The nest is a neat and substantial one of twigs, bark, etc., placed on the old nest of some other bird—Crow or Wood Pigeon. The eggs (four to six) are white, with bold blotches of reddish or dark brown. The bird feeds on young rabbits, rats, mice, small birds, and frogs; and though it sometimes does harm to young game (in which case there is nothing for it but to kill the marauder), it is otherwise a useful member of society as a destroyer of vermin.

Jackdaw.—Though much might be written about this interesting and well-known bird, space forbids more than a brief description. It is a common resident, though it accompanies the Rook (which see) on its strange migrations. It may be easily distinguished by remembering that it is a much smaller bird, black with a patch of grey on the back of the head and sides of the neck; the eye also is light grey. When flying in the company of rooks, the jackdaws may be picked out by the quicker beating of the wings.

Both birds are fond of the proximity of human habitations: the Jackdaw building in any convenient hole, building, tree, or cliff. Occasionally, also, it builds a *domed*, as also an open, nest in a tree; the species nests in colonies. The eggs (four to six) are bluish white, with spots of dark brown. The well-known call is "Jack," but the bird has also a spring song described as a "prattle." Jackdaws are very fond of "leather-jackets" and other larvæ, but they will also rob nests of eggs and young birds. They make interesting pets and are easily tamed. I know one soldier who refused to be parted from his bird, which, when last I saw him, was busy sharing his master's rations.

Jay.—This bird is identified by its pinkish brown back, prominent white on the rump, black tail, and patch of white, black, and blue on the wing. [An Irish variety is darker.] The bird is fairly common in woods and forests. It places its nest usually high up in the fork of a tree, using twigs and stems, lined with grass, etc. The eggs (four to six) are greenish, thickly freckled with fine green-brown; sometimes almost uniform. The note is a harsh scream or chatter, "Shushushusha"; but there is also a real song, "a variety of low warblings"; and the bird is also a notable mimic. It is, like the others of its family, omnivorous, but is especially fond of acorns, chestnuts, etc. It also robs nests and kills "vermin." During the winter, like the Magpie, it will make a hoard of food.

Kestrel.—A common resident—in fact, the most familiar of the falcons—on moor, marsh, cliff, or in forest. It is the *only* falcon which hangs stationary in the air, and may be at once distinguished by the chestnut colour of the upper parts, and the tawny under parts. It takes but few birds, preferring mice, moles, frogs, and beetles, and has therefore no right to be labelled "vermin." It is a silent bird, placing its nest in various sites—on cliff edges, in ruins, in old nests in trees, and even on the ground. The eggs (four to six) are whitish, blotched and mottled with red-black shades. Its cry is like the plaintive call of a cat.

Kite (22 inches, female larger).—Is very rare, some twenty birds being closely preserved in mid-Wales. It may be identified by its chestnut-coloured, deeply forked tail.

Kittiwake.—This bird acquires its name from its well-known cry—"Kittiway-ek." Though widely distributed, it is *local* as a breeding species in England and Ireland. It places its nest on ledges of sea cliffs, constructing it of sea plants, lined with dry grass. It is to be found in colonies with guillemots, razorbills, and other sea birds. It breeds late in the season, and young may be found in the nest in July. The three eggs are stone-coloured, olive-tinged, or bluish in ground colour, with dark brown and grey spots and blotches.

The bird may be identified by the black or dark-coloured legs, the absence of the white "mirror" on the tips of the outermost primaries, and the plain triangular black tip to the wings, seen when flying. Only the mantle and wings are grey, the rest is white.

The food is chiefly small fish and their ova.

Magpie.—This handsome black and white bird, with its long, wedge-shaped tail, can hardly be mistaken. It is a resident, common throughout the British Isles, but is often massacred wholesale by the gamekeepers. It has a harsh, grating cry.

It builds a massive nest of sticks, domed or roofed above, with only a small opening, usually high up in a tree or bush. (A curious habit of the Magpie is to commence building more than one nest at a time.) It lays five or more eggs, greenish white, thickly spotted and speckled with brown. It will eat almost anything, but, like the Jay, performs some useful work in killing mice and other "vermin." One of the interesting features of this bird is its habit of assembling in companies in spring, apparently for the purpose of selecting mates. In the winter also it is seen in flocks.

Owl, Barn (WHITE or SCREECH OWL).—When flying in the evening appears white, and has a very quiet, noiseless flight. This owl may be distinguished by its orange-buff upper parts and white under parts. Its note is not a "hoot," but a screech. The young emit a sound like a *snore* when disturbed. It nests in holes in trees, ruins, or rocks, laying four to six white eggs on the bare floor. It is a fairly common resident, but scarce in Wales, Scotland, and Ireland. Its staple diet consists of field mice, shrews, and rats; sparrows and other small birds are also taken.

Owl, Long-eared.—Noted for its long "ear" tufts, which are $1\frac{1}{2}$ inch; its *yellow* eyes, and its general buff colour; is a resident and winter visitor, not rare in our wooded districts. It prefers the flattened nest of some other bird, such as crow or hawk, but occasionally uses the ground. The eggs are white, rounder and more glossy than the Barn Owl's. The food is much the same—field mice, voles, rats, sparrows, etc.

The note when disturbed is like the spitting and swearing of a cat, whilst the female "quacks"—"Kyack-kyack." The call-note is a long-drawn "Oo."

Owl, Short-eared.—As its name implies, has *short* ear tufts, and has a less decorated buff plumage than the preceding. Whilst the Long-eared Owl prefers woods, this species chooses open country, moorland, etc., where it makes a scrape in the ground, among heather, rushes, or grass, for its four or more white eggs. It is found chiefly in the north as a breeding species, but is fairly widely distributed as a winter visitor, often found at the lanterns of lighthouses, preying on the other birds attracted by the glare. It feeds very largely on field voles.

Its note when alarmed is a bark, like " Whowk," but it also utters the cry, " Kyak, kyak."

Owl, Tawny, or Brown.—Distinguished by its densely feathered legs and toes, its familiar "Hoo-hoo, hoo-hoo-hoo," and its dark coloration—upper parts reddish brown, under parts lighter; some varieties being grey. It has another cry at night "Ewick, ewick." It nests usually in a hollow tree, ruin, or cliff, but also chooses deserted nests, and sometimes a burrow. The eggs (two to four) are white. It is resident in Great Britain, chiefly in wooded districts. It is the *largest* of the British owls (15-18 inches), and whilst preying on the smaller mammals, such as field mice and voles, can also manage a *rabbit* or *hare*, starling or pigeon.

[All the owls, be it noted, have very soft plumage, which serves to "muffle" their flight. It is a great pity that these birds, so useful to the farmer, should be so often shot by gamekeepers as "vermin," for they keep down rats and mice to an enormous extent; in fact, it is stated that "the recent outbreak of plague spread by rats would never have occurred" if only the owl had been unmolested.]

Oyster-catcher (SEA-PIE).—A bird with a bright red and very long bill, flesh-coloured legs, black upper parts, and white below, found on all our coasts in the winter, breeding on the West, and in Scotland and Ireland, but very rarely on South and East Coasts. The nest is a scrape, on rock, sand, or rough ground, sometimes lined with grass, shells, or pebbles; the three eggs being yellow stone-colour, boldly marked with dark brown.

The food consists of mussels, limpets, and other shellfish, worms, crustaceans, and seaweed.

The call-note is a loud, shrill monosyllable — " Kwick-kwick-kwick." When flying in flocks, as during the autumn, the bird has a noticeable habit of keeping *time* with its wings to the alarm note—" Heep-a, heepa, heepa."

It may sometimes be seen on ploughed lands some distance from the sea, in company with rooks and gulls.

Partridge, Red-legged (FRENCH PARTRIDGE).—Only slightly larger (13½ inches) than the Common Partridge (12½ inches), which is placed in Group Two. This species was introduced into England in 1770, where it is now resident. It is distinguished by the pale grey flanks, plainly barred with black, white, and chestnut. The legs are a bright coral-red (the Common Partridge's being grey-black). The skin round beak and eye is also plainly red. The bird at a glance appears to be dressed in lavender and slate-grey, with delicate browns on the upper parts, in contradistinction to the other partridge, which has much more chestnut and dark grey about it. On the whole the Red-legged Partridge prefers wilder, more uncultivated country than the Grey Partridge. The nest is like the Grey Partridge's; the eggs (ten to twenty) are buff-coloured, with fine specks of red-brown.

THE BRITISH NATURE BOOK

Pigeon, Wood (RING DOVE).—Distinguished by its large size, and large patch of white on the neck, and white on wing when flying. The bird is resident, but its numbers increase in winter by immigration from North Europe. Generally builds in high trees a slight structure of twigs, but sometimes uses old nests or squirrels' dreys, laying two glossy white eggs. Its food is grain, peas, beech mast, acorns, clover and turnip leaves. Its note is the familiar cooing—"Take two coo-oos, Paddy." At times the bird is a veritable plague to the farmer, in destroying his crops.

Ptarmigan.—One of the Grouse family, but you must journey to the mountains of Scotland to see it. It breeds entirely on the Scottish hills, where it is stationary except for its descents to the valleys and moors for the winter.

The nest is to be sought high up—seldom below 2,000 feet—a mere hollow, more or less scantily lined. The eggs are like those of the Red Grouse (which see), "whitish with a reddish tinge, blotched and spotted darker."

The bird is to be distinguished from its relatives by the *white* on the wings. The Red Grouse is the only one which comes near it in size, being only slightly larger; but the colouring is quite distinct.

The Ptarmigan undergoes three changes of plumage in the year, as follows:—

	MALE.	FEMALE.
April–July.	Blackish upper parts, decorated with grey; whitish under parts, with brownish upper breast.	Brownish upper parts, decorated with buff, grey, and white.
Aug.–Oct.	Grey upper parts, decorated with black and white; under parts almost entirely white.	Darker than the male.
Nov.–March.	All white except tail feathers and round the eye.	Like male, but no black on the head at all.

The bird feeds on the shoots and fruits of "blaeberry," blackberry, and small red cranberry; also on young plant leaves and lichens, especially reindeer moss.

The note is a mournful croak, and an alarm of "Ack-ack-ack."

Puffin.—One of the most singular of the Auk family—indeed, of all British birds. It is a summer visitor which breeds on all our coasts, but chiefly where cliffs are found—not in great numbers in the south. Nothing is known of its journeys, but it appears with the utmost regularity each year at its breeding places. It is recognized by its curiously coloured beak and orange-red legs; and its strange, dignified pose has given it the nickname of "POPE," whilst that red beak has won for it the opprobrious name of "BOTTLE-NOSE." As a matter of fact, the beak is larger in summer than in winter, for the hinder part, which is slate-blue, scales off after the breeding season, together with the other facial adornments. The upper parts of the plumage are black; there is a black band round the throat; grey cheeks; white under parts. It is a rather silent bird, but can give vent to a loud alarm note—"Owk" or "Ow"—and a long-drawn "Oo." It has a light and graceful flight, and is an expert diver. It makes a nest of grass and feathers in a burrow, either a rabbit's or else excavated by the bird, which always breeds in colonies. One whitish egg is laid, slightly marked with brown. The Puffin feeds on fish and crustaceans. Its chief enemies are gulls and hawks, which will often attack the young at the entrance of the burrow, or kill the adult birds.

Razorbill.—This bird, so often found with the Guillemot, is present with us all the year round, and breeds in colonies on the sea cliffs. It prefers to lay its one egg in a crevice or *under* a ledge (compare GUILLEMOT); the egg being more oval than the Guillemot's, but of much the same varying colour. The black, axe-like beak, with a prominent white crescent-shaped mark across it, is sufficient to distinguish it; but it is altogether a more thick-set bird than the Guillemot, with greenish black upper parts, dark brown on the throat, white underneath. The note is a long-drawn-out cry; also a low, guttural call.

Shearwater, Manx.—One of the "Petrels." This bird is seen on all our coasts throughout the year, but breeds only on the west and in Ireland, the Orkneys and Shetlands. It used to breed on the Calf of Man. It is called by a variety of names—"MANX PUFFIN," "MACKEREL COCK," "LYRE BIRD," etc. It is readily identified by its slender, hooked beak, long body, black upper and white under parts, and short tail. It feeds on surface fish, small cuttle-fish, free-swimming mollusca and crustaceans, and offal. It breeds in burrows (often made by the bird itself) on the slopes of cliffs and islands, making a slight nest of grasses. One egg is laid—smooth, dead white.

Three species of Shearwater may be seen in our waters, but this is the only one that breeds here. The name is apparently given from their oblique manner of flight when feeding, rising and descending with the waves, the downward flight being sideways—"shearing." It should also be remembered that, whilst taking most of their food from the surface of the water, they are also dexterous divers.

Teal.—These "Ducks," which are residents, to be found on fresh water, may be recognized by their small size ($14\frac{1}{2}$ inches) and by the glossy green patch on the wing. The male has a very handsome head, bright chestnut, with a beautiful violet-green band from the eye to the neck, margined with pale buff; the female being brown-headed. From July to October the male loses his bright colours, becoming more like the female. The beak is black; the general colours buff and brown. The nest is frequently found in heather on moors and marshes, a hollow scantily lined with leaves and grasses, and becoming filled with down. From eight to sixteen eggs are laid—cream-white slightly tinged with green.

The Teal is the smallest British duck, and, after the Mallard, the most numerous. Large numbers arrive in the autumn from North Europe. It is a silent bird, but on the wing emits a low double whistle. Both sexes " quack," but in a lower key than other "ducks."

Tern, Arctic.—Does not breed on our southern shores, and generally is a more *northerly* summer visitor; it is also less of a fresh-water-haunting species. It is distinguished from the Common Tern by its uniform blood-red beak, its dark grey under colouring, and the narrower band of grey on the outer primaries (see COMMON TERN). The nest is the same; but there are more often two than three eggs, and they are usually deeper in ground colour and bolder in markings, slightly smaller in size.

The note is " Kerr," occasionally " Kerr-err."

Tern, Common.—This species is widely distributed in the British Isles wherever the coast makes a suitable breeding ground, which may be bare, water-worn rock, shingle beds, sandy flats with or without vegetation. The nest is a scrape, with or without a scanty lining of bents or other material. The eggs, generally three, vary in ground colour, dull grey to brown, boldly blotched and spotted. I have found them of a beautiful sea-blue on a famous shingle beach in Dorset. In any case, they are so like the ground upon which they are laid that they are difficult to see. I have taken a friend amongst the colony, and had to check him again and again to prevent his treading on nests which he did not see. The bird is so like the Arctic Tern that the two species are often confused. Both possess the beautiful coloration of black, grey, and white. The Common Tern has, however, an orange-red beak for two-thirds of its length; the remaining third is black; and the band of dark grey on the inner side of the white shaft of the outer primaries is *much broader* than that of the Arctic Tern. In addition, the under parts are a *pale* vinaceous grey, the Arctic Tern's being darker. It is also distinguished by its cry, a long-drawn and plainly two-syllabled " Keee-yerrr."

Tern, Sandwich (see notes on LITTLE TERN in preceding group).—This bird (16½ inches) is the largest of the British terns, and may be identified by its stouter build, its *black beak* (with yellow tip) and legs, and the long, pointed feathers on the nape—a sort of black mane. When flying, note its shorter tail, and longer beak, and also its distinctive cry—" Kirr-whit." There is also an alarm note, something like " Quk " or " Keek."

In the British Isles the colonies of this species are not numerous, but it has bred in Kent and Norfolk. There are large colonies in Cumberland, and in certain parts of Ireland and Scotland. It is a summer visitor, arriving first towards the end of March. It breeds in close colonies on sandy flats, often with a scanty growth of plants, such as marram grass. The nest is generally a slight hollow, sometimes lined with scanty dried grass, etc. The eggs (two, rarely three) are grey or brown stone-colour, with blotches and spots of deeper brown. Note their size: $2 \times 1\frac{1}{2}$ inches.

These birds feed on small fish, aquatic insects, and small crustaceans.

Waterhen (commonly MOORHEN).—A bird to be found on almost every pond and river, recognized by the white markings on the under tail—which it constantly flicks up as it swims—as also by the red forehead and beak, the latter tipped with yellow. Otherwise it is a slate-black bird. Its nest is generally among rushes, but it also builds in hedges and trees—a strong structure of water plants, lined with grasses, etc. The eggs (six to ten) are light brown, with spots and blotches of brown-red. It feeds on aquatic plants (duckweed, etc.), and insects. Its note is a rather loud " cluck "—" Krek, krek-krek "— and a metallic " Ts-ack."

The bird often builds extra nests, used as roosting and resting places. It may often be heard at night, uttering a curious " Kick-kick-kick."

Whimbrel.—A bird very like the Curlew, but much smaller, possessing a long, curved bill. Its plumage is brown and grey, with a light-coloured band down the " forehead " and over the crown. It breeds only in the Orkneys and Shetlands, but is seen as a bird of passage, chiefly in the spring, on our coasts. The four eggs are laid in a scrape; they are pear-shaped, greenish brown, blotched darker. Its call has been syllabled, " Tetty, yetty, yetty betty, yetty betty, tet " (seven times). Its whistle in the winter sounds like " Whee-whee-whee-whee-whee-whee-wit."

Widgeon.—A " duck " often to be found on estuaries in the winter months, where it feeds on the zostera grass. Its note is a loud " Whee-ou." The species breeds only in Scotland (very exceptionally in the North of England and in Wales). It is recognized by its small slate-blue bill tipped with black, and the wing patch, green surrounded by *velvet-black* (the Teal's wing patch is green surrounded by *buff*). The drake has a bright chestnut head, with green " freckles."

The nest is on the ground, generally near water—of grasses and sedges, later mixed with down. The eggs are creamy white.

Woodcock.—It is impossible to write as one would wish of all the remarkable characteristics and habits of this bird, one of the most interesting of our British birds. It is, as its name implies, a wood dweller, as compared with the *Snipe*, which prefers to frequent marshes. It is resident with us all the year round, and though local in breeding, and to be sought in well-wooded districts, there are few counties where it has not bred. Like all its family, its plumage is so coloured as to afford the most wonderful protection for the bird, by rendering it indistinguishable from the soil and vegetation around it, being a variegated pattern of chestnut, buff, and black. The Woodcock is the largest of the family, and may be distinguished by the *broad black bands crossing the back of the head and nape*, separated by narrow bands of buff; as also by the closely barred under parts (it has the long beak and flattened head of all the Snipe family). During the winter large numbers of woodcocks arrive on migration, beginning from October. These fly in flocks, and chiefly by night. The species is, in fact, a " night," or rather a " twilight," bird in its habits, as may be guessed from the size of its eye. By day it remains quietly in its haunt in the wood, but when sunset comes, at practically the same hour each evening, the woodcocks leave the woods—*and almost always by the same exit*—one after another, for the hunting grounds, near stream or pond. So fixed is this habit that from old times the fowlers used to spread nets across these openings in the woods and catch the birds at what Shakespeare, for example, calls " cockshut " time. Another interesting habit is called " roding " or " roading "—a flight during the breeding season, which also takes place at the same observed hour at dusk and dawn: the courting birds in play fly swiftly side by side for a few hundred yards out of their exit from the wood, and, often making a triangular course, return. This also is so regular a habit that man has made use of it in setting his nets.

The bird feeds, like the Snipe, on worms, slugs, insects, small crustaceans and molluscs. Its nest is a depression in the ground, often amongst bracken, in a wood, and lined with dead leaves. The eggs (four) are not so pear-shaped as the Snipe's—rather a broad oval—yellowish brown (varying from light cream to warm brown) in body colour, with spots and blotches of darker and greyer colour; laid in March to April. The Woodcock's most familiar note is a curious croak, often said to resemble " More rain to-morrow "—" Croho-croho " ; but there is also a screeching cry—" Chizzie."

The mother birds, as the young grow, *carry them to and from* the feeding grounds in their claws; and often, if the nest (or young) is approached too closely, will flutter off feigning to be injured.

IV. BIRDS ABOUT THE SIZE OF A ROOK—19 INCHES AND LARGER.

Buzzard.—This bird used to be far more numerous than at present, but it is still to be found in wild and hilly districts such as the moors of Devon, Wales, the Lakes, and elsewhere. It has a hooked beak and yellow legs, the latter differentiating it from the ROUGH-LEGGED BUZZARD, whose legs are feathered, and which is only a winter visitor. The bird is of a general brown colour, and may often be seen above its haunts, soaring high in the air in small parties. It nests in cliffs and high trees—most of the birds I have been familiar with in Devon have nested in the latter. The nest is a huge structure of sticks, lined with leaves and grasses. The eggs (two or three) are a dirty white, with blotches of red-brown or blackish brown.

The food consists of mice, rats, moles, frogs, snakes, beetles, etc.

Capercaillie.—A splendid bird, the cock nearly a yard in length; to be found only in Scotland, where it nests in a hollow at the foot of a tree in a pine forest, laying six to eight yellowish eggs with reddish tint, spotted and speckled with brown. It feeds on the buds of trees, on insects and their larvæ, berries, grain, and shoots of larch and fir.

The cock is a grey bird, enriched with touches of glossy green and purplish black beneath; the hen, much smaller, is altogether a browner bird.

Cormorant.—This bird, known as the BLACK or GREAT CORMORANT, is likely to be confused only with the Shag, but is distinguished by its larger size and the blue-black metallic lustre of its plumage. It is a silent bird, though it can utter a hoarse, croaking note, and feeds on fish, especially eels, for which it dives. It is a large species, 3 feet in length, to be found on most of our precipitous coasts, where it breeds in colonies on ledges or islets. It is to be found also on some of our larger inland waters; and though not breeding in such situations in England, it is known elsewhere to nest on islands in lakes, and even to build in trees. The nests are made of sticks and other material, and seaweed, and are generally very offensive.

The bird, like the others of its family, has webbed toes, a straight, hooked bill, and short legs. In the breeding season it has a crest of white plumes and white collar; also a white mark on the thigh. The eggs are blue, with a chalky incrustation.

Crow, Carrion (CORBIE, GORCROW).—The only difference between this bird and the Hooded Crow is that this is black and the other *black and grey*. They are so akin as to interbreed, especially on the Continent. The Carrion Crow is general throughout England, not uncommon in Scotland, but absent from Ireland. It nests in trees and on cliffs, building a large nest of sticks, roots, etc., lined with fur, wool, grass, etc. It lays four or five eggs, greenish white, thickly spotted and blotched with greenish and reddish brown. The bird is usually seen singly or in pairs, and builds solitary nests, unlike the Rook. The note is a hoarse croak or caw. Food, as Hooded Crow.

Crow, Hooded.—Distinguished by its grey back and under parts. Is found in Ireland and the North of Scotland, but is rare in England, although in winter large numbers from the Continent visit the Eastern and Northern Counties. The nest and eggs are like those of the former. The food is practically "everything and anything"—carrion; young, weakly animals, such as lambs; small rodents, birds, eggs, fruit, and grain.

Curlew.—This bird is known by its whistling cry, resembling its name, "Curlew"—"Too-ee, too-ee, too-ee"; its winter cry being expressed "Quoi-ee, quoi-ee." Like the Whimbrel (a much smaller bird), it is distinguished by its down-curved, long bill. Its colour is brown, with narrow dark centres to the feathers; white rump with black streaks; tail nearly white, with black bars; under parts white with black streaks. It is common on the coast in winter, but breeds inland on uplands and moorlands where there are soft, boggy patches. The nest is a shallow depression, scantily lined, the four eggs being olive-brown, well marked with darker brown. The food consists of insects, their larvæ, worms, snails, etc.; on the shore, sandworms and small shellfish.

Diver, Black-throated.—This is a much rarer bird than the two following, not unlike the Great Northern Diver, but smaller in size and having a smaller bill. It may be distinguished by its grey head and purple-black throat. The back is—like that of the Great Northern Diver—black, with rows of white spots; there are two patches of white with dark stripes on neck; under parts white. In "winter" plumage, the colours become browner. It nests only in Scotland, but is found round our coasts in winter, though not commonly. It nests on islands on mountain lochs, close to the water's edge, laying two eggs, deep brown to olive-green, with a few darker spots, in a mere depression, scantily lined. It feeds chiefly on fish.

Diver, Great Northern.—A very handsome bird, like a large duck when seen swimming, but with a pointed beak. The head and neck are a glossy greenish black; there are two curious white bands on the throat, striped with dark lines reaching down to the sides of the lower breast; the black back is covered with white spots in rows; the under parts are white. In the winter the black changes to brown. The bird is only a winter visitor, its nearest breeding place being Iceland, and is chiefly found in Scotland, Yorkshire, North Wales, and the North and West of Ireland, from October to May. It is a voracious feeder on fish.

Diver, Red-throated.—Distinguished by its grey head and chestnut-coloured throat, brown back and wings; under parts white. It is much smaller than the Great Northern Diver, and in breeding plumage without the rows of white spots on the back, although in winter these appear. The bird is resident in parts of the North of Scotland, where it breeds, but is only a winter visitor to our other coasts—from August to April.

It nests generally on the edge of a small lake, making a shallow depression, lined scantily with rushes or heather. Two eggs are laid, chocolate to olive-brown in colour, spotted slightly with black. The bird is mainly a fish eater.

[*Note.*—All the Divers utter a loud wail, often when on the wing—" a blood-curdling scream, often at night." Besides this there is a loud, trumpet-like " Hoo-hoo-hoo-hoo," a curious " yapping " like that of a little dog, and other notes.]

Duck, Long-tailed.—This is a large bird (22–24 inches), and is distinguished (in the drake) by the long, thin, pointed tail. It is never a common bird in British waters, and is only a winter visitor, almost entirely confined to the seashore, where it feeds chiefly on molluscs. The drake in winter plumage has a whitish head, shading into brown on the cheeks, and a short black bill, the centre of which is pink. The general appearance is *pied* (grey, white, brown, and black); the duck is a much browner bird.

The male bird has a loud, musical call—" Coal and can'le licht "—as the Scots syllable it, or " Calloo "—as the bird is nicknamed in the Orkneys. This may be heard often at night as well as by day, and penetrates to a great distance.

Duck, Scaup (19 inches).—The drake has a great deal of black about it, with greenish lustre, the rest being grey and white, with a distinct white patch on the wing. The duck has a conspicuous blaze of white round the beak. This bird breeds very rarely in Scotland; elsewhere it is a winter visitor and bird of passage, almost entirely in coastal waters. The bird has a harsh call-note, from which its name " Scaup " is derived; as also a loud cry like " Karr-karr-karr." Large flocks are sometimes found far out at sea by day, only coming to the shore at night.

Duck, Wild, or MALLARD.—This bird is distinguished by its wing spot of steel-blue, with the two sides edged with white and black margins. The

Birds about the size of a Rook and larger.

drake in full plumage has a velvet-green head, and a white collar round the throat. It is a common species, the nest being generally on the ground not far from water, and hidden in long grass or other vegetation. Sometimes, however, it may be placed in a tree, such as a pollarded willow. It is lined with grass, etc., and the bird's down; the eggs are greenish or grey. This is one of the surface-feeding ducks, eating minute organisms, insects and larvæ, worms, slugs, small fish, etc. It is the species from which our "domesticated ducks" have been derived.

Eagle, Golden.—This splendid bird (male 32 inches, female 35 inches) is resident in Scotland, and possibly Ireland, nesting in trees or precipitous crags, where the same site is used every year, so that the structure in time becomes an enormous mass, composed of sticks and branches lined with grass and heather and clumps of woodrush. Usually two eggs are laid, varying in colour—*white* or *grey*, with or without spots and marblings of red-brown. The bird feeds on grouse, rabbits, and other small animals. The Eagle is recognized by its legs feathered to the toes. [The rare " WHITE-TAILED " EAGLE has no feathers on the legs, and the tail is white.]

Upper parts chocolate brown; head lighter brown, shading into gold on the neck; under parts generally chocolate colour; the skin round eye and toes is yellow; the young are covered with white down.

Whilst the Eagle is resident only in Scotland, it appears as an occasional visitor even in the South of England. The bird utters a strange hoarse cry, and also a note between a whistle and a whine.

Eider, Common.—A handsome bird; the drake has much white about it, a tinge of green on the nape of the neck, and a distinct pinkish colour on the breast, the other coloration being a dark brown. The duck is uniformly brown. Both sexes may be distinguished at all times by the way in which the feathers of the face extend along the sides of the beak (see Fig. 172). The bird is a resident on our coasts from Northumberland and Argyllshire upwards, but is a very scarce winter visitor elsewhere. The nest is to be found close to the water on islands, on the ground, where it is soon lined with the down for which this species is famous. The eggs vary much in number, from four to eleven. They are a large oval in shape, grey-green and olive-brown in colour. The bird feeds chiefly on sea molluscs and small crustaceans. It utters a curious wailing or mourning note, " Wow-wow-wow."

Fulmar.—This "petrel" is much like a Gull, but may be distinguished by its curious tubular nostrils; the back, wings, and tail are grey, the rest white. It is generally distributed, but is seldom seen near land except in the breeding season, when it visits the north isles and mainland of Scotland for that purpose. It deposits its egg in a depression in the soil or turf, often on the ledges of inaccessible cliffs, or on tops of stacks. One egg only is laid, white, coarse-shelled, sometimes with faint red spots.

The St. Kilda folk depend largely on this bird, for its oil and its flesh and feathers.

179. Gannet.

164. Pintail.

181. Fulmar.

117. Arctic Skua.

137. Curlew.

178. Shag.

172. Common Eider.

159. Brent Goose.

158. Barnacle Goose.

2. Carrion Crow.

Birds about the size of a Rook and larger.

THE BRITISH NATURE BOOK

Gannet (SOLAN GOOSE).—This bird's pointed beak distinguishes it from the Cormorant, which has a hooked beak. Otherwise it is recognized at once by its colour: all white except the wing quills, which are dark brown; but the head and neck are yellow-buff during the breeding season, against which the eye rim and beak make a striking contrast, being a clear slate-blue in colour. The bird is found all the year round in our waters, and breeds in large colonies on precipitous islands, chiefly off Scotland, Wales, and Ireland. The nests are built on cliff ledges, of seaweed, grass, and odds and ends of material. Only one egg is laid (larger than a Cormorant's), blue, covered with a chalky incrustation, which soon becomes stained.

The bird feeds on fish. The courting cry, heard on the cliff ledges, is "Urrah-urrah"; but there is also a long-drawn wail—"Yee-orrr"—when taking to flight. A very unique point observed in the incubation period is that the Gannet covers the egg *with her foot*, placing first the web of one foot and then the other over the egg, and then lowering the body into the sitting position.

The bird is a most expert diver, dropping from a height into water after a fish, which it never fails to secure; and it loves also to sail through the air with outspread wings (nearly 6 feet from tip to tip), almost without a movement.

Goosander.—This bird, together with the Merganser and Smew, form a sub-family—"Saw-billed Ducks," from the serrated edges of their mandibles. (The SMEW is a winter visitor, in rare numbers, commonest on our Eastern seaboard.) They all possess straight, slender, hooked bills. The Goosander drake is a handsome bird in breeding plumage: black-green head; blackish mandible; rest chiefly white; red beak and legs. The duck has chestnut-red head; upper parts chiefly grey; lower parts whitish.

The nest is in a hollow tree, or a hole in a bank, or among rocks, generally on an islet or close to a river, and contains seven to twelve creamy eggs. See also notes on MERGANSER.

Goose, Barnacle.—Only a winter visitor; has a white face and throat; glossy black head, back, and breast; grey to white under parts. Chiefly found on the West Coast, especially on the Solway.

Goose, Brent, not unlike the preceding, except that it is smaller, and has no white on the face, and only a very small patch on the neck. It is a winter visitor, chiefly to our eastern coasts (exactly the reverse of the Barnacle Goose), often in large numbers.

Goose, Greylag.—This bird only breeds in the North of Scotland, but is rather more abundant as a winter visitor; uncommon on most parts of our coasts. Upper parts light greyish brown; under parts lighter; belly white; differing from the other rarer geese (BEAN GOOSE, PINK-FOOTED GOOSE) by the white tip on the bill, and from the WHITE-FRONTED GOOSE by the absence of the prominent white patch on the face which the latter possesses.

The nest is often amidst deep heather, or on an island: a slight depression, scantily lined—though sometimes a more bulky structure is made. The eggs (four or more) are yellow-white, soon becoming stained. This species feeds on corn, grass, and roots.

[*Note.*—The geese are famous for their formation in flight, travelling in "skeins" ∧ or "gaggles" M. A century or more ago the Greylag bred in large numbers in our fens, where the young were caught, and kept with flocks of tame geese. The cry is a loud clanging "Honk-honk."]

Grebe, Great Crested.—The largest and handsomest of the Grebes, distributed over the greater part of Great Britain, wherever there is open water and reeds, during the spring and summer, but migrating to the sea invariably in winter from November to February. The bird is an expert swimmer and diver, and can sink its body till only its head and neck can be seen. It feeds chiefly on small fish and aquatic larvæ and vegetation. Both birds join in building the nest, a mass of floating water plants, anchored amid reeds, or built up from the bottom. Here four chalky white or slightly blue-tinted eggs are laid (always covered by the bird with some of the debris of the nest when leaving it, and hence soon becoming stained a dirty brown). A charming trait of the parent birds is their habit of carrying their young on their backs, one at a time, when first hatched, for a sun bath. This generally falls to the "father's" share.

The species is undoubtedly coloured "protectively," for whilst the birds are visible enough on open water, they become difficult to see against a background of weeds. The bird is distinguished by its large size and long beak. The upper parts are a dark brown; the under parts a most beautiful satiny white. In breeding plumage, there are two tufts of feathers, like little horns or ears, on the head, and a rich chestnut frill round the head, which can be erected like an old-fashioned "ruff." Like its "family," the Great Crested Grebe has practically *no* tail, and the toes are lobed.

[The RED-NECKED GREBE is only a rare winter visitor on the eastern seaboard; the SLAVONIAN GREBE is known to breed on one loch in Scotland, otherwise only a cold-weather visitor; the BLACK-NECKED, or EARED, GREBE is equally rare.]

Grouse, Black (BLACKCOCK ♂, GREYHEN ♀, BLACKGAME).—Known at once by its lyre-shaped tail, its black plumage with blue metallic lustre (male), and large patch of white under the tail. The female is brown and buff-marked, with bars and freckles of lighter colour. The male has a prominent wattle of red above the eye. In July to September the male's black becomes mixed with brown feathers.

The bird is diminishing in the British Isles; very scarce in the South, breeding chiefly in the North of England and in Scotland. The nest is a scrape made by the hen in woods or open country, scantily lined, containing six to ten eggs, yellow-white, slightly spotted and blotched with red or orange-brown.

The bird utters a hoarse cry when challenging, and a curious call, like "a cat on the housetops."

Gull, Glaucous.—This species has no black upon it at all. Upper parts grey, the rest white; legs pink, bill yellow. It is a regular winter visitor, though rare on the South and West. It does not breed here. [The rarer ICELAND GULL is of the same colour, but smaller in size.]

The cries and calls are much like those of the other Gulls—" Kau-kau-kawkawkaw," and " Keeaw-keeaw."

Gull, Great Black-backed.—As its name implies, much larger than the Lesser Black-backed Gull (30 inches). It has a dark slaty black back and wings, and flesh-coloured legs. Does not breed on the East Coast, rarely on the South, chiefly in Scotland and the West of Ireland; but in winter is more widely distributed. It nests often singly on a small islet in a loch or top of some isolated rock; sometimes in colonies, but these are small. The eggs are like those of the Lesser Black-backed Gull, but larger, and with more prominent markings. The species is omnivorous, and it preys upon small mammals and birds, such as wounded ducks and game birds.

This bird, like its family, utters a hoarse cry, like a laugh, and also a high-pitched cry like " Kiow."

Gull, Herring.—This bird is larger than the Common Gull (24 inches), and has flesh-coloured legs, and a grey back and wing coverts; a certain amount of black on the primaries; rest white; bill yellow. The young are brown. Found everywhere except where coast is flat. Often breeds in colonies on cliffs, shingle, and grassy islands; a bulky but neat nest of grass, etc. Two or three eggs, varying in colour and markings—stone-coloured, buff, brown, green, with darker streaks and blotches. The alarm notes are hoarse cackles or barks—" Kak."

Gull, Lesser Black-backed.—Distinguished from the Herring Gull by the darker grey on back and its yellow legs, but not so widely distributed—for example, only sparsely breeding on the South Coast, east of Devon, preferring Western England and Scotland.

It only occasionally nests on cliffs, preferring grass-covered tops of islands, moors, or bogs, where it is found in colonies. The eggs are much like the Herring Gull's. Like the latter, it is an omnivorous feeder. Alarm note, " Ha-ha-ha-ha."

Harrier, Montagu's.—The Harriers are very rare: the MARSH HARRIER (21-24 inches) is almost extinct; the HEN HARRIER (19-21 inches) nearly as rare; Montagu's Harrier (18-19 inches) generally breeds in Norfolk, and from Cornwall to Surrey on arriving as a summer visitor. But it is a rare bird, and owes its survival to the protection afforded it by the landowners on whose property it nests. The nest is usually on moorland or among reeds. Generally three eggs are laid, white, exactly like a bantam's.

Heron, Common.—There is no mistaking this grey bird, so often seen standing in water, or with slow flapping wings, and head curved right back, making for the distant heronry. It has a long yellow beak, long legs, grey and white plumage, a V-shaped cap of dark blue-black on its white head, the plumes being so long as to form a drooping crest. The female is slightly smaller.

BIRDS

The bird is widely distributed, nesting in colonies, and is very general in England, and in parts of Scotland and Ireland. There are some two hundred colonies in England, about the same number in Scotland, and forty in Wales; more than fifty in Ireland. In winter other herons migrate to our shores from abroad, but probably our native herons remain sedentary.

In most parts the colonies nest in trees; but the ground is also used, or even a low bush or a reed-bed. The nest is flat, but substantially built of sticks and branches, lined with finer twigs. Four or five eggs are laid, of a dull light green.

The species feeds on fish, but small reptiles and amphibia and even water voles are also caught. The usual note is a harsh shriek, not unlike a Goose's cry heard in the distance, and also a low "Ka" when near the nest.

[It is sad that the BITTERN can scarcely rank as a British bird, being nearly extinct. In old days, its strange booming was a familiar sound in the fens. It is now a cold-weather visitor in small numbers. Its near relative, the LITTLE BITTERN, is a still rarer occasional visitor.]

Montagu's Harrier.

Merganser, Red-breasted.—Is distinguished from the Goosander (which see) by its smaller size, its reddish throat, and the curious double crest of long feathers (p. 129). The drake has a black-green head, white throat, mottled brown-red breast, the rest of the coloration being black and white. The duck has a dull chestnut head, neck, and throat.

The nest is usually near water on the ground, in herbage, under bushes, or some other natural protection. The eggs are grey, of lighter or darker shades, to olive.

[All the Saw-billed Ducks are expert at swimming and diving, as well as flying. Unfortunately, they cause great havoc among the trout and salmon fry, and are therefore kept down as much as possible by fish preservers. The Goosander utters a harsh guttural quack; but the Merganser is a much more silent bird, for while the duck quacks when disturbed, the drake seldom utters any note except a loud rough purring note when courting.]

Pheasant.—There is no need to describe this familiar bird, whose short abrupt crow, "Cock-up, cock-up, cock-up," is so often heard in the woods on spring and summer evenings. Its distinguishing feature is the brilliant

THE BRITISH NATURE BOOK

colouring of the cock, and its long tail. The nest is almost always on the ground, under a hedge or bush. The eggs are a uniform olive-brown colour.

It is said that the species was introduced by the Romans, but many other species and varieties have been added from time to time. The bird is "polygamous," and often several hens lay in the same nest. It is an omnivorous feeder, eating grain, seeds, berries, fruits, acorns, caterpillars and other insects, slugs, worms, and even mice and vipers; the young eat insects, "ants' eggs," etc.

Pintail.—Another of the Surface-feeding Ducks (26–29 inches). It may be identified by the "speculum" of rich dark green, with a front margin of cinnamon. The bird gets its name from the sharp, slightly forked tail, the drake, in full plumage, being distinguished by the white stripe which passes down from the crown of the head and descends into the white of the breast. The head is brown, the back a beautifully patterned grey. The duck is a brown bird, with delicate crescent-shaped patterns of lighter brown or buff.

The bird is not common, breeding in Scotland only, but found more numerously on our coasts in the winter. The nest is placed on the ground, in the shelter of some vegetation, dry grasses and other material being used, lined with sooty-brown down. Eggs, seven to ten, are buff or yellow-green.

Large estuaries are the favourite haunt, though the bird may also be found on inland lakes. It is shy, and feeds at night rather than by day. The male, usually silent, utters a low whistle sometimes when in flight.

Pochard.—The drake is recognized by its chestnut head and neck, dark breast, and light grey back and under parts. The duck is brown. The bird is now well established as a breeding species in the British Isles, chiefly in Scotland and the Eastern Counties of England. The nest is generally in a wet and inaccessible place—in rushes or flags—made of dead reeds, etc., much like the Coot's. The eggs are large and broad, of a smooth surface, leaden grey or drab in colour. The drake utters a hoarse "Charr-charr-charr" when courting.

The species appears to prefer fresh to salt water for its winter resort.

Raven.—This bird is rare except in hilly and coast districts of Devon, the Lakes, Wales, and Scotland. It is the largest of all the Crow family (25 inches), a funereal black, polished with blue and violet gloss. Its nest is usually on some crag, though it also chooses high trees, and has been known to build in a ruin; it is a very large, untidy structure of twigs, etc., lined with wool and other materials. The eggs are greenish white, blotched with darker colours—brown, black, and grey. The bird is known in captivity as a great mimic, with a "strong love of drawing corks." In a state of freedom, it has a loud and commanding caw, and a love-song of hoarse eccentric chuckles. It is, like the other members of its family, omnivorous.

Rook.—Much might be written of this familiar but interesting bird, whose ecclesiastical gravity contrasts with the pert, dapper roguery of the Jackdaw,

PLATE IX.

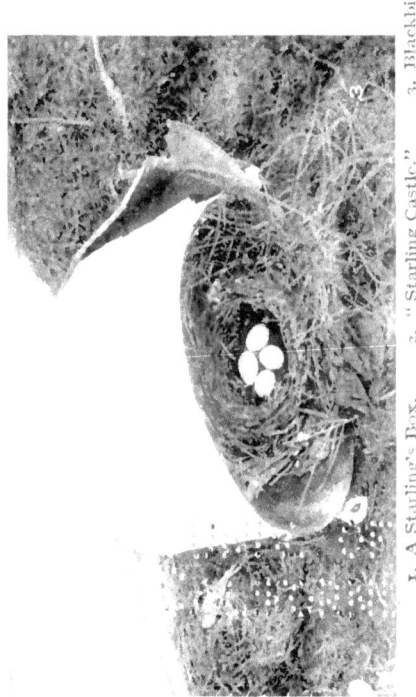

1. A Starling's Box.   2. "Starling Castle."   3. Blackbird's Nest in Bucket.   4. Robin's Nest in a Tea-caddy.

almost always to be found in its company. It is considerably larger than the Jackdaw, and is distinguished from the Crow by the white skin round the base of the bill. (The young Rook, however, has the base *feathered* up to the second moult.) The species has a remarkable interest in point of view of its curious migrations, flocks of birds coming and going from Europe and the North in September to November, and again in February to April, returning in due course to their breeding lands. Our own native Rooks also migrate —to Ireland and back.

The Rook nests in colonies, as is well known, beginning its courtship in February, and repairing its nest in the middle of March. It appears to pair for life. Though one is accustomed to its familiar "Caw," it has many other notes and tones. The eggs, three to five, are greenish, with brown markings. The Rook is credited with great sagacity and cunning; but, amongst other popular statements, the one that it *posts a sentinel* when at its meals in the farmer's fields lacks proof.

It is, however, a valuable friend to the farmer, its food consisting of worms, insects, slugs, etc.

Scoter (BLACK DUCK).—This member of the "Diving Ducks" is at once distinguished by the complete black plumage of the drake (the duck being a sooty brown, with greyish cheeks and whitish throat), and the peculiar bill, black and yellow, with a curious excrescence at the base. [The Velvet Scoter, sometimes found in its company, has a *white patch on the wing* of both sexes. It is a rarer winter visitor.]

The Scoter is very restricted in its breeding area—a few places in the North of Scotland, especially Caithness and Sutherland—but appears sometimes in large flocks, in the winter, round our coasts.

The nest is usually in water-logged moorland, under a bush or among heather, in a depression scantily lined with bents, dead leaves, etc., and plenty of down. The eggs are light buff or cream in colour, large, and pointed oval.

In winter the Scoter is entirely a marine bird, feeding on mussels and other molluscs. The usual call is the drake's "Kr-kr-kr," answered by the duck's "Re-re-re."

Shag (GREEN CORMORANT—see notes on CORMORANT).—Is distinguished from the Cormorant by its smaller size, twelve tail feathers, and the greenish tinge in its black plumage. In the spring both sexes have a recurved crest on the head, but this is soon lost. It breeds locally, on rocky coasts, but is absent from the South-east and East Coasts from the Isle of Wight to Northumberland; more generally distributed in winter.

It is entirely a marine bird. Its call is "Gau-gau" and "Crew-a-oop." It prefers sea caves to nest in, or some rocky cover (differing from the Cormorant in this respect). Seaweed and coarse vegetation form the material of the nest. Three to five eggs are laid, blue, with a chalky incrustation, like but smaller than the Cormorant's. It feeds on fish.

Shelduck, recognizable by its size and patched plumage: head and neck greenish black; body white, chestnut band round upper part; black on shoulders; tail black; beak red. The strange fact about the coloration is that at a distance it appears simply black and white, magpie-hued in fact. It is a resident, found in large estuaries chiefly, scarce in the South-east. Large flocks of migrants also arrive for the winter. It generally makes a nest in a tunnel or burrow, near the sea, laying seven to twelve eggs, creamy white. It feeds on sand-hoppers and other small crustaceans, etc., obtaining worms by rapidly beating the sand with its feet.

While feeding it is a noisy bird, the drake uttering a curious hissing whistle, the duck a real "Quack." In the North Frisian Islands artificial burrows are made for the bird, and the eggs are regularly taken by the people until June.

Shoveller.—The drake has a beautiful plumage: glossy green head, and handsome chestnut under parts, conspicuous against the white of the neck and rump; but the species is identified by the remarkable beak, which is specially broad and dark-coloured. It is chiefly a fresh-water bird, feeding at night. Its powerful and noisy flight has earned for it the local name of "Rattle-wings"; the drake utters a croaking "Honk-honk." The nest may be anywhere on the ground in a meadow or marsh; the eggs are greenish or grey-buff.

Skua, Arctic.—The Skuas are the "pirates of the bird world," robbing other birds of the fish they have caught, and taking the eggs and young of other species. In addition, they feed on carrion, molluscs, and crustaceans, etc. The Arctic Skua is smaller than the Great Skua, and has a long-pointed tail. There are two distinct varieties, the first being all brown, the second having white on the neck and under parts. This bird only breeds in a few places in Scotland, being elsewhere a winter visitor only. It breeds in colonies on hummocky moorland, the nests being some distance apart; they are depressions lined scantily with bits of grass and heather. Two eggs are laid, varying in shape and colour from pale olive-green to deep brown, with spots and blotches. [The POMATHORINE SKUA and BUFFON'S, or the LONG-TAILED SKUA, are only rare cold-weather visitors.] The Arctic Skua utters a wild mewing call; the Great Skua a croaking "Ag-ag," or a loud "Ay-er, ay-er."

Both species defend their nests with ferocious courage, attacking even a human intruder with violent blows, not of wing or beak, but of *feet*.

Skua, Great (BONXIE).—This species, a large brown bird, with hooked upper mandible and white patch on the wings, breeds only in the Shetlands, but is an uncommon winter visitor to other parts. It breeds in colonies, on slopes high above the sea, laying two eggs of olive-brown or green, with darker blotches and spots.

Swan, Mute.—This bird is familiar to everybody. Its red beak and black "berry" above the beak identify it from the WHOOPER (60 inches) and the BEWICK (50 inches), which have yellow bills, and are only winter visitors. The Mute Swan is said to have been introduced into this country by Richard Cœur de Lion. The earliest reference in writing is found in a MS. of 1272.

BIRDS 139

A large number of these birds are bred at certain swanneries, such as that of Abbotsbury, where in some years the stock consists of more than a thousand. The eggs are a greeny white.

How to attract the Birds.

I trust that every reader of these chapters upon Birds will not forget that the nearest place in which to study many of them is his own garden. Here a great deal may be done to attract and tame—(1) by putting up suitable nesting places for them ; and (2) by feeding them during the winter months. The never-ending interest and pleasure derived from watching them will more than repay the cost and the trouble. I venture to refer readers to the detailed description of " nest boxes " and " foods " in *The Holiday Nature Book*.

As a matter of fact, any sort of a box placed in a bush or against a tree, or even on the wall of a house will serve for many of the common birds of the garden. An old tin kettle, a sack, a worn-out boot—these and many other curious shelters have been chosen again and again by robins, tits, wrens, and other birds. The starlings will fight for the possession of any box which is dark within and has for entrance a small hole.

Very delightful natural wood boxes are made by the Selborne Society, and may be purchased from them ; but there is no need to use natural wood —any sort of box will answer the purpose, provided it is toned down in colour, to harmonize more or less with its surroundings. Boxes for the tits should have a small hole, and no perch outside, otherwise the sparrows will take possession of them. As it is, they wrangle daily with the starlings for the ownership of their boxes.

I think that, as a general rule, it may be said that birds prefer a box hung on the outer edge of a wood or copse, and the southern side should be avoided, unless the nest is sheltered from the direct rays of the sun.

For thrushes a light tray of twigs nailed to a tree provides an excellent foundation. In other cases, the branches of a bush may be tied together to form a natural cup or cylinder.

I need scarcely add that all such artificial arrangements should be placed high enough to escape the cats, and such boys as would be tempted to disturb the birds perpetually by too many inquisitive visits.

With regard to the feeding of the birds, some people use a bird table— a small platform four or five feet above the ground, placed on legs, or even attached to the house close to a window. On this there should always be kept fresh water, and in the winter, when the frost is keen, this will be greatly appreciated by all sorts of birds, both for drinking and bathing purposes.

Whatever food is placed there should be put out regularly every day at the same hour ; and the birds will speedily grow accustomed to the hour, and will be found often waiting round in the trees for their breakfast.

The sparrows are the greatest nuisance to the bird lover, as they are ex-

SITES OF BRITISH BIRDS' NESTS.

(Note that the eggs of birds, the names of which are shown in *italics*,

A. Shrubs, Hedges, Trees.	B. Bushes, Hedges, Thickets.	C. Long Grass, and on or near Ground near Hedges, etc.	D. Bare Ground. (See also under Seabirds.)
...ackbird (B, C).	*Blackbird* (A, C).	*Blackbird* (A, B).	Black Grouse.
...affinch.	Blackcap.	Capercaillie (pine forest,	Common Sandpiper
...ossbill (conifers) (F).	Bullfinch.	foot of tree).	(K).
...ldcrest (conifers).	Chiffchaff (C, N).	Chiffchaff (B, N).	Common Snipe (H).
...ldfinch.	*Corn Bunting* (C, O).	Cirl Bunting.	Corncrake (C).
...eenfinch.	Dartford Warbler (gorse	*Corn Bunting* (B, O).	Curlew (H, O).
...awfinch.	or heather).	Corncrake (D).	Dotterel (P).
...ouse Sparrow (G).	Garden Warbler (C).	Garden Warbler (B).	Golden Plover (C, O).
...ty (F).	Grasshopper Warbler (C).	Golden Plover (D, O).	*Lapwing* (O, H).
...sser Redpoll (B).	*Hedge Sparrow*.	Grasshopper Warbler (B).	*Long-eared Owl* (F).
...ng-tailed Tit (B).	Lesser Redpoll (A).	Lesser Whitethroat (B).	Meadow Pipit (C, H,
...agpie (F, N).	Lesser Whitethroat (C).	Meadow Pipit (D, H, O).	O).
...stle Thrush.	Linnet.	*Nightingale*.	Merlin (E).
...skin (coniferous trees)	*Long-tailed Tit* (A).	Partridge.	*Nightjar*.
(F).	Red-backed Shrike.	*Pheasant*.	Ptarmigan (P).
...ng Thrush (B, C).	*Song Thrush* (A, C).	Pintail (K).	Quail (C).
...urtle Dove.	Twite (C, G).	Quail (D).	Red Grouse.
...'ood Pigeon (F).	Willow Warbler (C, N).	*Redbreast* (G, I, L).	Ringed Plover (K, M)
	Wood Warbler (C, N).	*Red-legged Partridge*.	Ring Ouzel.
	Wren (G, N).	Redshank (O, P).	*Short-eared Owl*.
		Redstart (G.	*Skylark* (C).
		Reed Bunting (H).	Stone Curlew (O).
		Sedge Warbler (H, K).	Tree Pipit (in wood-
		Skylark (D).	land) (C).
		Song Thrush (A, B) (un-	Wheatear (O).
		Stonechat (O). [usual].	Whimbrel (H, O).
		Tree Pipit (in wood-	Whinchat (C, O).
		land) (D).	Woodcock (C).
		Twite (B, G).	Woodlark (C).
		Whinchat (D, O).	Yellow Wagtail (C).
		Whitethroat.	
		Willow Warbler (B, N).	
		Woodcock (D).	
		Woodlark (D).	
		Wood Warbler (B, N).	
		Yellow Bunting.	
		Yellow Wagtail (D).	

E. Cliffs and tall Trees.	F. Tree-tops.	G. Holes, Buildings, Crevices.	H. Marshy Ground.
...uzzard (F).	Buzzard (E).	*Barn Owl*.	Bearded Tit (K).
...arrion Crow (not Ireland	Common Heron.	Blue Tit (I).	Black-headed Gull
or Isle of Man).	Crossbill (A).	British Coal Tit (J).	(K, M).
...hough (G).	Jay (A).	Chough (E).	Common Snipe (D).
...ormorant (M).	Long-eared Owl	Crested Tit (I).	Curlew (D, O).
...ulmar (M) (not in trees).	(deserted nests)	Great Tit (I).	Dunlin (M, O).
...annet (M) (not in trees).	(D).	*House Sparrow* (A).	*Lapwing* (D, O).
...olden Eagle.	Magpie (N, A).	Irish Coal Tit.	Meadow Pipit (C, D, O).
...erring Gull (M) (not in	Rook.	Jackdaw (N).	Pochard (K).
trees).	Siskin (A).	*Kingfisher* (K).	Reed Bunting (C).
...ooded Crow.	Sparrow Hawk.	*Little Owl* (N).	Scoter (K, O).
...ouse Martin.	Wood Pigeon (A).	Nuthatch (I).	Sedge Warbler (C, K).
...estrel.		Pied Flycatcher.	Shoveller (K, O).
...ittiwake (M) (not in trees).		Pied Wagtail (L).	Teal (K, O).
...erlin (D).		*Redbreast* (C, I, L).	Whimbrel (D, O).
...eregrine Falcon (not in		Redstart (C).	Widgeon (K, O).
trees).		*Sand Martin* (bank).	
...aven (occasionally ruins),		Snow Bunting (High.) (P).	
hilly and coast districts.		Spotted Flycatcher.	
...ock Dove (not in trees).		Starling (I, L).	
...ock Pipit.		Stock Dove (I).	
...hag (M) (not in trees).		Swift (E).	
...wallow.		*Tawny Owl* (E).	
...wift (G).		Tree-creeper.	
...awny Owl (G).		Tree Sparrow (E, I).	
...ree Sparrow (G, I).		Twite (B, C)	
		White Wagtail (L).	
		Wren (B, N).	

PLATE X.

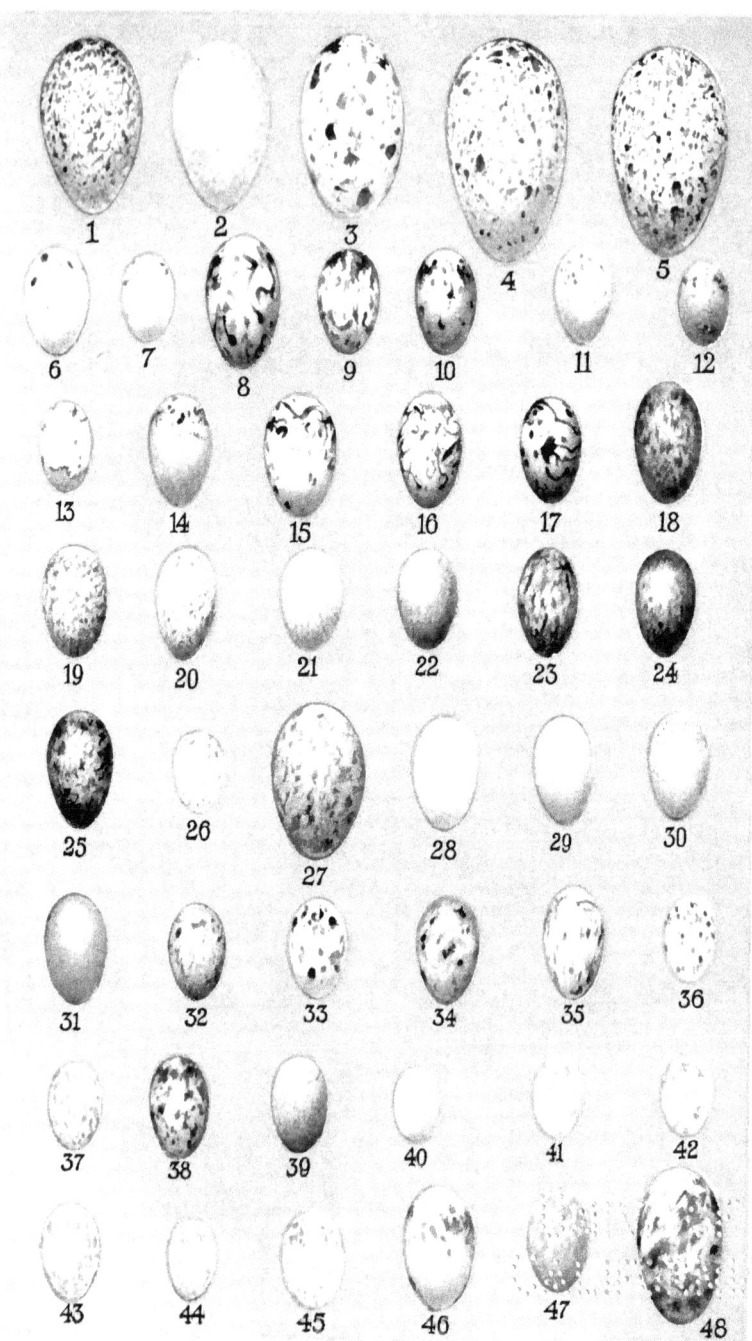

PLATE XI.

49. Puffin. 50. Razorbill. 51. Guillemot. 52. Common Tern. 53. Common Gull. 54. Woodcock.
55. Snipe. 56. Ringed Plover. 57. Common Sandpiper. 58. Lapwing. 59. Waterhen.
60. Coot. 61. Corncrake. 62. Partridge. 63. Pheasant. 64. Sparrow Hawk. 65. Kestrel.
66. Merlin. 67. Great Crested Grebe. 68. Little Grebe.

SITES OF BRITISH BIRDS' NESTS.

(can be identified from some characteristic feature of nest or egg.)

I. Holes in Trees.	K. Near Water.	L. Under Cover.	M. Sea and Fresh-water Birds.
Blue Tit (G). British Coal Tit (G). Crested Tit (G). Great Spotted Woodpecker. Great Tit (G). Green Woodpecker. Lesser Spotted Woodpecker. *Little Owl* (G). Marsh Tit. Nuthatch (G). Pied Flycatcher. *Redbreast* (C, G, L). *Starling* (G, L). *Stock Dove* (G). Tree Sparrow (E, G). Willow Tit. *Vryneck*.	Bearded Tit (H). Black-headed Gull (H, M). Black-throated Diver. Common Sandpiper (D.) Coot. *Dipper*. Goosander. Great Crested Grebe. Greylag Goose. *Kingfisher* (G). Little Grebe. Mallard. Marsh Warbler. *Mute Swan*. Pintail (C). Pochard (H). Red-breasted Merganser. Red-throated Diver. *Reed Warbler*. Ringed Plover (D, M). Scoter (H, O). Sedge Warbler (C, H). Shoveller (H, O). Teal (H, O). Tufted Duck. *Waterhen*. Water-rail. Widgeon (H, O).	*House Martin*. Pied Wagtail (G). *Redbreast* (C, G, I). *Starling* (G, I). *Swallow*. *Swift*. White Wagtail (G).	Arctic Skua (slopes near sea—colonies) (P). Arctic Tern (sand, shingle —colonies). Black Guillemot (bare rock —singly). Black-headed Gull (H,K) (on ground and sandhills). Common Gull (islands, cliff tops, sandhills). Common Eider (islands). Common Shelduck (holes). Common Tern (sand, shingle —colonies). Cormorant (E) (colonies). Dunlin (H, O) (high-lying marshes). Fulmar (E). Gannet (E) (ledges). Great Black-backed Gull (islet or stack—singly). Great Skua (slopes near sea) (P). Guillemot (bare rock—cols.). Herring Gull (islands, cliff-tops, sandhills, ledges) (E). Kittiwake (cliffs, caves— colonies) (E). Lesser Black-backed Gull (O) (tops of islands, moors —colonies). Little Tern (beach—cols.). Manx Shearwater (burrows —colonies). Oyster-catcher (rough ground, rocks, or sand). Puffin (burrows—colonies). Razorbill (bare rock—cols.). Ringed Plover (D, K) (sand or shingle). Sandwich Tern (sand, shingle —colonies). Shag (E) (ledges in caves— colonies). Storm Petrel (islands).

N. Domed Nests.	O. Commons, Downs, or Moors.	P. Mountain side.	Q. White Eggs.
Chiffchaff (B, C). *Dipper*. Jackdaw (when in trees) (G) Magpie (when in trees). *Nightingale* (?) Willow Warbler (B, C). Wood Warbler (B, C). *Wren* (B, G).	*Corn Bunting* (B, C). Curlew (D, H). Dunlin (H, M). Golden Plover (C, D). *Lapwing* (D, H). Lesser Black-backed Gull (M). Meadow Pipit (C, D, H). Redshank (C, P). Scoter (H, K). *Short-eared Owl*. Shoveller (H, K). Stonechat (C). Stone Curlew (D). Teal (K, H). Wheatear (D). Whimbrel (D, H). Whinchat (C, D). Widgeon (H, K).	Arctic Skua (M). Dotterel (D). Great Skua (M). Ptarmigan (D). Redshank (C, O). Snow Bunting (G).	*Dove*. *Kingfisher*. *Martin*. *Owl*. *Pigeon*. *Swallow*. *Swan*. *Woodpecker*. *Wryneck*.

THE BRITISH NATURE BOOK

traordinarily bold and impertinent; but by spreading black thread across the table, an inch or two above it, and altering its position from time to time, something may be done to keep them off.

For the seed-eaters, seed can be provided in a bottle, turned upside-down upon a small tray, so that there is only the space of $\frac{1}{8}$ inch or so between the mouth of the bottle and the bottom of the tray.

As for the tits, their food—consisting of fat, suet, cocoanut, etc.—can be suspended on strings, and this plan will keep most other birds away from it. But not all, for, as the winter advances, it is astonishing to note how a few of the other birds learn to flutter up to the food and snatch odd mouthfuls. I have seen robins, sparrows, and chaffinches thus making use of a cocoanut.

I find it an advantage to mix some of the birds' food into a solid mass with melted fat, so that it is not easily scattered, and lasts longer. Chicken-meal, powdered dog-biscuit, desiccated cocoanut, etc., mixed with any kind of fat can be served thus.

The illustrations (Plate IX.) show some of the rather uncommon nest boxes which a little ingenuity helps to make.

How to identify Nests and Eggs.

With many of our British nests and eggs the student will have no difficulty, because of some well-marked characteristics. No one, for example, would mistake the Long-tailed Tit's nest or the Chaffinch's; but in other cases the *site* will serve as a rough guide, and then the detailed description given in the text must be consulted.

The following table (pages 141, 142) gives the approximate *sites* of most British birds' nests, and the *plates* will help to distinguish some of the commoner eggs, which may be at first mistaken.

NOTE: THE CUCKOO.

OUR knowledge of the habits of the Cuckoo has been added to, since the section on pages 112–13 was written, by the remarkable investigations and observations of Mr. E. P. Chance. His "Cuckoo Film" picture will become famous. He shows beyond question that in many cases the female cuckoo marks down all the nests of the foster-parents in her particular district; and in most cases flies to the nest, takes out one of the eggs, holding it in her beak while she lays her own in its place, and then flies off to devour her booty.

In one case, Mr. Chance actually saw both mother and daughter lay an egg in the same nest.

Another point which he elucidates is that the mother bird pays periodic visits to the nests where her young ones are being brought up. I am able to confirm this from my own observations of a cuckoo in 1921, which came regularly every morning to see her nestling in a meadow-pipit's nest within a hundred yards of my house.

S. N. S.

CHAPTER IV.
Reptiles.

REPTILES (from Latin *repo*, " I creep ") are represented in Great Britain by very few species. They are *cold-blooded* animals—that is, the temperature of the blood is much lower than that of mammals or birds. They do not pass through any such changes as in the life-history of the frog, but the young are like their parents, differing only in size, and they breathe by means of lungs. Two classes or sub-orders of reptiles are known to us in Great Britain —the *Ophidia*, serpents ; and *Lacertilia*, lizards. The latter have jaws so connected that they cannot be distended ; but the serpents have jaws joined together by an elastic ligament which allows them to be opened to such an extent that they can swallow far larger victims (such as frogs and mice) than at first would seem possible.

The skin of reptiles is a characteristic feature : the upper, or epidermis, is in reality of a very thin and transparent, horny nature, and looks like *scales*, like those of fishes. It is shed, or cast off, by the reptiles, from time to time, and very often you may find the skin of a snake, very fragile and light, lying where it has been discarded by its owner.

Most lizards have four legs ; but one—the Blind Worm—be it noted, has no external limbs, and so is often mistaken for a snake. They are coloured in such a way as to harmonize with their surroundings (many other instances of " protective coloration " are given in this book), the result being that it needs an experienced eye to distinguish them when motionless. A dry heath or a sunny bank is the place to find them, but the slightest unwary movement will cause them to vanish from sight. It is well known that when caught a lizard will frequently snap off the end of its tail in the hope of escaping. After a time the injured portion grows again to more or less of its original state.

Some reptiles are *oviparous*—that is, they lay eggs from which the young are hatched ; others are *viviparous*, bringing forth their young alive ; and still others are *ovo-viviparous*, laying eggs in which the young are already well developed and about to hatch out.

Sub-order : LACERTILIA—Lizards.

Only three species are found in the British Isles.

1. **The Common Lizard** (*Zootoca vivipara*), to be found on banks, heaths,

moors, especially where there is plenty of sand. The male is about 6 inches long, the female about 7 inches. They are reddish brown above, spotted, and marked with a lighter and darker colour. The male has a brighter red or orange-blue below, spotted with black; the female, a paler orange or yellow under side. The young are almost black at first. This species produces its young alive, six or more at a time, about 1 inch long. For a few days they require no food, existing on the "egg-yolk" still within them; then they begin to feed as the adults, on flies and other insects. When seen basking in the sun, the movement of the sides of the neck, expanding and contracting, will be noticed —the method of inflating the lungs.

2. **The Sand Lizard** (*Lacerta agilis*) is much rarer, though fairly common in Hants and Surrey and Dorset. This species has teeth, but though it may attempt to bite, they are too small to do harm. It varies very much in colour —greyish and greenish or brownish in general colour, decorated with blackish brown and white spots. It is entirely *oviparous*, the six to twelve eggs being laid in July in a depression in the sand, where they are hatched out by the sun.

The best way of distinguishing these two species is to remember that the snout of the Sand Lizard is *blunt*, and the tail nearly twice as long as the body and head together. Like the Chameleon, the Lizards *change colour* rapidly when in active life.

3. **The Slow-worm**, or BLIND-WORM (*Anguis fragilis*), is unfortunately often killed because of its snake-like appearance; yet it is really a legless lizard, and is, as a matter of fact, neither blind nor slow. It has movable eyelids (which snakes do not possess), rows of scales on the belly, and its tongue is not forked like a snake's, but *notched* like the other lizards. Its length is from 12 to 15 inches, and the prevailing colour is grey or brown, with coppery tinge. It is a species that is both *viviparous* and *ovo-viviparous*, and breeds in August or September. During the winter it hibernates, but may sometimes be seen on a sunny day in early spring. It feeds on slugs, worms, and small caterpillars.

These lizards may easily be kept in captivity—a Tate's sugar box with a glass top, containing plenty of sand, moss, and "rocks" and some virgin cork, is as good as anything: a saucer should be kept filled with clean water; but the soil is better kept *dry*, though if a plant is kept in the box it should be sprinkled with water, that the lizards may drink, as they will, the little drops of water which gather on the leaves. They quickly get accustomed to being handled, and I have seen some kept as pets emerge from their hiding-places to be fed *when called*. They should be supplied with flies, small smooth caterpillars, worms, etc., and when this supply fails, it is always easy to get *meal worms*, which will form a staple article of their diet. In the autumn they should be put into a cold room and allowed to hibernate.

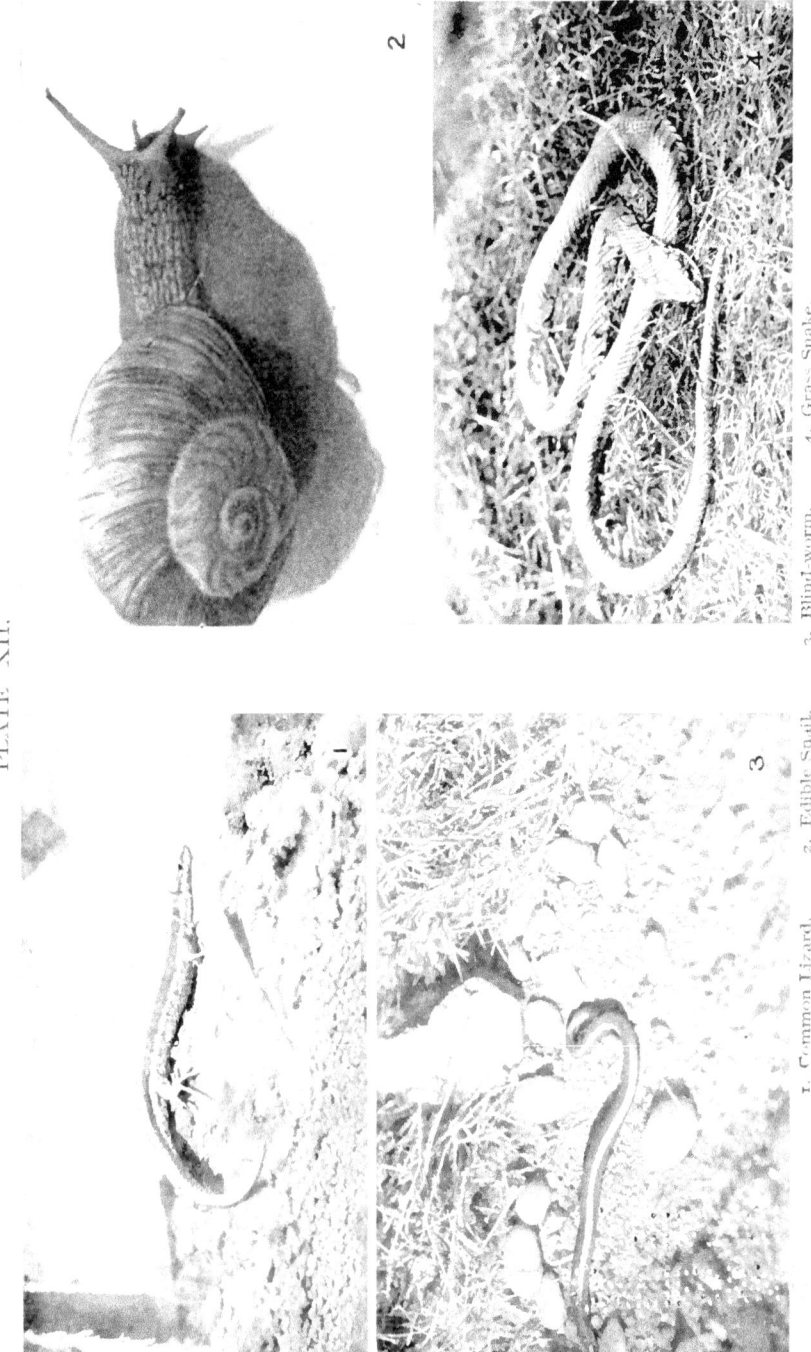

PLATE XII.

1. Common Lizard.   2. Edible Snail.   3. Blind-worm.   4. Grass Snake.

REPTILES

Sub-order: OPHIDIA—Snakes.

There are only three species of snakes to be found in Great Britain; of these one alone is venomous, and one is very rare and local. None of them is found in Ireland.

1. **The Grass Snake** (*Tropidonotus natrix*)—also called the COMMON or RINGED SNAKE—is the commonest. This is perfectly harmless, yet I fear that in most cases where it is found it is at once killed as if it were dangerous. The only offensive power it possesses is that of exuding an abominable smell when first approached or handled; but this is fortunately soon exhausted, and the reptile soon gets accustomed to being handled. Perhaps a personal illustration may be permitted here. Some years ago one of my neighbours rushed into my house with the alarming story that a large snake was hiding in one of his trees, and that he was afraid it would attack his children. I went up to his garden to find that it was a splendid specimen of the Grass Snake, a female, which had climbed into a tree, apparently after birds' eggs. I had no difficulty in picking it up, but it emitted the most offensive odour, which clung to my hands for a long time in spite of washing. I placed it in my vivarium, and within an hour or two it would allow any one to handle it without making itself a nuisance.

There can be no mistake about this species, for it has a yellow patch on the side of the head, and dark markings on the side of the body, and is generally of a greyish olive-green colour. It varies in length, up to about 3 feet. It feeds on frogs, newts, mice, small birds, and birds' eggs, all of which are swallowed whole. As already pointed out, the jaw can be "disjointed" so as to open extraordinarily wide, and the neck is like a rubber tube capable of a remarkable enlargement.

Occasionally this snake may be seen *swimming*. This is a strange sight, as the creature swims with its head and neck well out of the water, the rest of the body being submerged. It lays a number of eggs—fifteen to twenty—white, oval bodies about the size of a blackbird's egg. They have a soft parchment-like skin, and are often laid in a dunghill or a heap of rotting vegetation, where the warmth helps to hatch the young.

2. **The Adder**, or VIPER (*Pelias berus*), is our one poisonous snake, generally *smaller* than the former, and altogether differently marked. It has a dark zigzag pattern down the back, and a V-shaped mark on the head. In spite of common opinion, the forked tongue often seen flickering from the mouth is not its "*sting.*" But if a dead specimen is examined, two long curved teeth will be seen in the upper jaw, which are movable. These are its *fangs*. Each is in reality a hollow needle connected with a gland behind, which contains the venom. The Viper when about to attack raises its head and strikes its victim, making two small punctures, and thus injecting the poison.

Obviously, you must be extremely careful in capturing a viper alive; and if bitten, suck the wound immediately, and rub some liquid ammonia well into it. The viper is ovo-viviparous, its young either being born alive, or hatching out of the egg as soon as it is laid. The stories of adders swallowing their young, though very common, are not really to be depended on; and much closer observation is necessary before the truth can be established. Like the other British reptiles, these all hibernate in the winter.

3. **The Smooth Snake** (*Coronella levis*) is reddish brown or brownish black, and has a double row of black spots upon its back. The New Forest is the locality where it is most often caught, but it is very rare even there. Its natural food consists of lizards and blind-worms; it seldom exceeds 15 inches in length, is an expert tree climber, but often *burrows* underground during the heat of the day.

[*Note.*—The Grass Snake subsists chiefly on frogs and newts, and is therefore most usually met with in the neighbourhood of water. The Viper appears to prefer field-mice, voles, and young birds, and chooses dry plantations or exposed heather moors.

If a harmless snake be *kept in captivity*, it needs a box with a glass front, which can be set in the *sunlight* when required, the bottom covered with turf or pebbles, and a bath sunk flush with the surface of this material. For food it needs small frogs or fish; the latter must be placed in the bath. Very small specimens may be fed on tadpoles and meal worms or other insects. To *preserve a specimen*, the best way is to place it in a bottle of spirit or equal quantities of spirit and water, or a ten per cent. solution of formalin, tightly corking the bottle to avoid evaporation.]

CHAPTER V.
Amphibians: Frogs, Toads, and Newts.

THE Amphibians, as their name implies, lead a *double life*, on land and in water, and differ from mammals, such as the seal or the otter, in possessing *gills* like a fish during the early stages of their existence. They are all produced from *eggs*, and undergo a remarkable series of metamorphoses in reaching their adult state. The life-history of the frog is so well known that I take for granted that it is familiar to all my readers. Suffice it to say that the stories of the other Amphibians are much the same. If, however, an attempt is made to rear tadpoles in an aquarium, the following hints may be of use :—

1. Have plenty of mud to begin with in the water, as at first they are vegetarians.

2. Remember that the tadpoles must have food as they develop (I have known too many *teachers* who thought that somehow or other tadpoles live on water !). Give them water-fleas and other minute water creatures. If you have the proper means of catching these (see Chapter VII.) it takes but a few minutes to get a supply.

3. Tiny pieces of raw meat may be placed in the water for a meal, or squeezed so that the "juice" runs out ; but after half an hour the whole of the water *must be changed*, or it will become foul.

4. As the tadpoles grow, they will eat small worms or larvæ and "ants' eggs."

There are only seven species of Amphibians found in this country—two species of Frogs, two of Toads, and three of Newts. The eggs of the frog are laid in masses ; those of the toad, in long double chains ; and those of the newt, one at a time, and deposited in the leaf of some water plant.

1. **The Common Frog** (*Rana temporaria*) needs but little description; but it is worth while to draw attention to the well developed web on the hindfeet, the ear-drums, and the tongue, which is attached to the *front* of the mouth, its tip extending backwards. With this organ, tipped with a sticky secretion, the frog often catches the insects on which it feeds. Popular fancy still credits the frog and toad with the power of "spitting," as if they were venomous creatures, but there is no truth whatever in the legend ; and though the toad can exude a sticky secretion when attacked, it is its only means of defence.

The frog, be it noted, changes its colour so much that often people may imagine that they have found a new species; but the fact is that the frog possesses the power of matching its colour to its surroundings. In water, amidst the rank growth of water plants, it appears greenish yellow; in a coppice or shrubbery it may be almost red; whereas in a vivarium, against dark earth, it will become a dark brown.

2. **The Edible Frog**, which is generally slightly larger than the foregoing, is an introduction from France, where, as is well known, its legs form a favourite dish. It is increasing in this country. Its colour is greenish, with black markings on the back, and white lines.

3. **The Common Toad** (*Bufo vulgaris*) differs from the frog in having no teeth; it possesses a dark, warty skin, and conspicuous swellings over the eyes. It is comparatively clumsy and bulky in appearance, and instead of leaping like the frog, generally prefers to crawl. It *can* jump, however, when necessary, but not so well as the frog, since its hind-legs are shorter. In addition, the hind-feet are only slightly webbed; and it is not, in consequence, so aquatic in its habits as the frog. Like the Reptiles, all the Amphibians cast their skins periodically; the toad has the economic habit of rolling its discarded suit into a ball sometimes and swallowing it!

4. **The Natterjack Toad** (*Bufo calamita*)—sometimes locally known as the RUNNING TOAD, because it travels faster than the common species— is easily distinguished by the thin yellow line straight down the middle of the back. Its hind-legs are also shorter, and when on the move it attracts notice by its method of raising its body from the ground, as if it were walking on tiptoe.

Newts—often called EFTS or EVVATS—are regarded with repulsion by many people, though they are perfectly harmless. The female places each egg in the folded leaf of a water plant; it hatches in about a fortnight, and the tadpole emerges, to grow to maturity in about a month. It then leaves the water, and does not return for three or four years (though it must be noted that the Great Water Newt is much more aquatic in its habits). Two interesting features should be noted: (1) Newts can breathe through their *skins*, as well as by means of lungs; (2) in the breeding season they become much more brilliant in colouring, and the males assume a handsome ornamental crest on back and tail.

5. **Common or Smooth Newt** (*Lophinus punctatus*).—About 4 inches long; in colour brownish grey, spotted with black; under parts yellow, spotted with black. The tail of the male is red underneath, with blue markings; the female lacks the bluish colour. In the breeding season both sexes grow a "frill," the male's being much the larger. Often the cast skin, exceedingly delicate, like gossamer, may be found in an aquarium where newts are kept.

6. **The Great Water Newt** (*Triton cristatus*) is sometimes 6 inches long; black above, and yellow spotted, with black below. The skin is covered with little wart-like projections. The female is larger than the male, but lacks the

FROGS, TOADS, AND NEWTS

handsome frilled crest possessed by the latter in the spring. These creatures feed on worms and tadpoles.

7. **The Palmated Newt** is the smallest and rarest of our British species—about 3 inches long. The species may be identified by the curious filament on the tail, and the fact that the crest has black edges and is not *frilled*.

It should be noted that all the Amphibians are useful. Whilst in their tadpole stage, they keep the water sweet by eating the vegetable growths. When adult they feed on all kinds of aquatic creatures, and ashore devour large numbers of insects. They can be kept in captivity in a simple vivarium, such as a fern case, or glass-fronted box, provided a bath or dish of water is placed within. It should not be of *metal*, however, as, for some unknown reason, these creatures do not like it. The bottom of the case should be strewn with loam, leaf-mould, sand, and pieces of stone, in which a few coarse ferns may be planted.

If newts are kept in an aquarium, it is essential that they should have some means of leaving the water when they wish. I have often found that they have been *drowned* in aquariums for lack of this means. It must be remembered that they all spend more time in nature out of water than in it. Flies, earwigs, small worms, meal worms may be given for food. In the autumn a plentiful supply of moss should be put into a corner, in which your pets can hibernate during the winter.

Toads and frogs are easily tamed, and if fed at regular times will come out from their hiding-places to get their meals. Many times I have seen toads kept in a greenhouse or conservatory actually come to take worms from their owner's fingers.

CHAPTER VI.
Fishes.

FISHES belong to the last or lowest class of the Vertebrates which we have been considering. They are, as is well known, entirely aquatic animals, and are naturally specially adapted for their life in the water.

Notice, first of all, their characteristic *shape*, which enables them to move with ease and swiftness beneath the surface. The fins, arranged in pairs, correspond to the four limbs of all back-boned animals. They are used, not for swimming, but for steering and directing purposes, as well as keeping the body upright. The fish swims by means of powerful strokes of its tail, and can swim as easily against as with the current, whilst, owing to its peculiar structure and shape, it is not affected by the swiftness of a stream. Fishes are cold-blooded animals, of approximately the same temperature as the water. Their method of obtaining air is unique amongst animals. The water, which they continually swallow, instead of passing into the stomach, is discharged through the gill-covers, the wide slits at the back of the head familiar to all who have handled fish. In these slits are the *gills* proper—organs of fringed or feathered membranes (generally *four* on each side of the head) of a deep red colour, being abundantly supplied with blood-vessels.

Here the water is only separated from the blood by a very thin membrane, through which the air in the water is easily absorbed into the blood. But the gills cannot perform their functions unless kept damp, for which reason a fish speedily dies of suffocation when out of the water.

Most fishes have an air bladder, by which they can rise or sink. To rise to the surface, the fish fills its air bladder with the quantity of air required; to go lower or to sink, it presses out the air by muscular contraction.

Some species which live at the bottom do not possess this organ, but all surface-swimming species have it.

Fishes lay enormous numbers of eggs, known as spawn, deposited in various places, sometimes at the bottom of a stream, on sand or gravel, sometimes on seaweed or water plants. Some species—for example, salmon—ascend the rivers to spawn; others, like the eel, go down to the sea for that purpose. The roe of a single fish may contain over a million eggs. The cod, for example, lays several million a year, and if it were not the case that the majority of these eggs are devoured by enemies, our rivers and seas would literally be blocked by solid masses of fish.

# FISHES

Note the large eyes of most species, which enable them to see in water with great sharpness, but which would be useless to them out of water. There are ears as well, but these are difficult to find in most fishes.

The fish, being cold blooded, requires no special warm covering, but its skin is meant to protect it from harm. Generally it has a covering of overlapping scales, of a horny or bony substance. These differ considerably in form : some are square, others rounded on two sides (cod and haddock), others almost circular (herring). They fit over one another, like a bird's feathers, or the slates of a roof ; and to prevent water getting between them, a coating of slime oozes out from beneath many of them, through pores in the skin.

There are some two hundred British salt and fresh water fish, but only a few of the commoner ones can be dealt with in this chapter.

Fresh-water Fishes.

Many of our fresh-water fishes belong to the Carp family (*Cyprinidæ*). These are known as " Coarse Fish."

THE CARP (*Cyprinus carpio*)

was introduced from the Continent before the fifteenth century. It is hardy and prolific, having often more than 500,000 eggs in a single roe.

It is a very hardy species, and will live to a great age. There are still some very large specimens, for instance, in the fishponds at Emmanuel College, Cambridge, said to have been placed there more than one hundred years ago. The average weight up to six years is from 4 to 10 lb. ; the record for the largest fish is 24 lb. It is a greenish bronze in colour, with scales which have black margins ; there is a large barbel at the corner of the mouth, and a small one on the upper jaw.

It is a slow moving fish, feeding chiefly on vegetable matter, as well as on larvæ and worms.

1. **The Crucian Carp** (*Carassius vulgaris*) is much smaller, and has no barbels on the jaws. It rarely exceeds 1½ lb. in weight, and is a rather more thickset fish than the former, with which it freely interbreeds.

2. **The Golden Carp** (Goldfish) (*Carassius auratus*) is a universal favourite with aquarium keepers. It is really a Chinese or Japanese fish, in its native waters a dark brown in colour, but in a domesticated state losing the black and brown pigment and becoming golden-yellow, and in some cases silver. It was introduced into England in 1691.

3. **The Barbel** (*Barbus vulgaris*) is very common in the Thames, and is fond of muddy ponds. It grows to a great length, as much as 3 feet, and up to 15 lb. in weight. It obtains its food by rooting in the mud with its snout like a pig, as well as by feeding on aquatic vegetation. The mouth is furnished

with four soft barbels. The general colour is greenish brown, becoming yellower on the sides, white belly, red fins, and tail of deep purple. The eggs are deposited in strings among stones. The upper jaw extends considerably beyond the lower.

4. **The Gudgeon** (*Gobio fluviatilis*).—A small fish, rarely more than 8 inches in length, abounding in many English rivers. The upper colour is olive-brown, spotted with black, the under parts being white. It possesses two small barbels. This species swims in shoals, and feeds on worms, molluscs, and other small creatures. It is one of the easiest fishes to catch.

5. **The Roach** (*Leuciscus rutilus*).—This species is abundant in England and, like the former, is gregarious in habit. It measures from 10 to 15 inches, but whilst attaining to a weight of 3 lb., a specimen weighing a pound or more may be regarded as a good catch. The body has a silvery appearance; the back is dull green, the lower fins are red, and there are no barbels.

6. **The Rudd** (Red eye) (*Leuciscus erythrophthalmus*).—This fish resembles the roach, but is much shorter and deeper. It is found in rivers, lakes, and fens. It is richly coloured, and as its name implies, has red fins and a red eye. It attains a weight of between 2 and 3 lb.

7. **The Chub** (*Leuciscus cephalus*).—This, though in reality a common inhabitant of many of our rivers, is a difficult fish to catch, being extremely wary. It prefers rapid water and a clear bottom. I have seen numbers of Chub slowly parading up and down the Mole in the summer between the " swallows," ignoring every kind of bait set out for them. They are a bluish black above, with white beneath. The cheeks and gill covers are a rich golden brown. A fish of 2 or 3 lb. is a good catch; but specimens have been taken from 5 to 7 lb. in weight. The scales of this fish, as indeed of several others, are used in the manufacture of artificial pearls.

8. **The Dace** (*Leuciscus vulgaris*).—This is a local species, though common enough where found. It prefers the deep clear water of quiet streams. It is not unlike the Roach in shape, but rather longer, and the scales are smaller. It seldom exceeds a pound in weight. It is a dusky blue above, paler on the sides and white below, and has a beautiful silvery appearance throughout. It swims in shoals, feeding on insects and vegetable matter, and spawning in May or June. It is, perhaps, the liveliest and most " sporting " of all its family.

9. **The Minnow** (*Leuciscus phoscinus*).—This species seldom exceeds 4 inches in length. It is a very active and common fish, generally found in swarms in rivers and swift-running streams. In the breeding season it is exceedingly handsome—olive-brown on the back, and a metallic lustre on the sides. The fins are a beautiful silver-grey, tinted with rose or pink at the base, and marked during the height of the season with small pure white spots or knobs. After spawning the colours become duller. It is a voracious feeder, eating aquatic plants, worms, insects, etc., but it is, in its turn, preyed upon by many other fish. It spawns in June, and the eggs hatch in a few days. The Minnow

PLATE XIII.

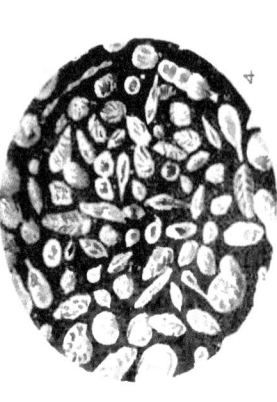
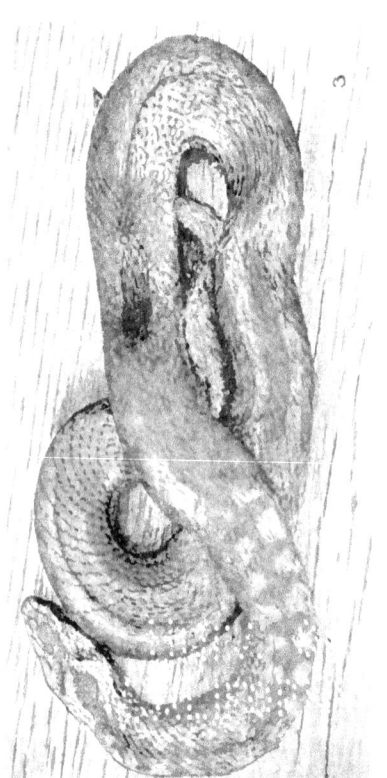

1. Minnows and Sticklebacks.   2. Crayfish, with Eggs.   3. Adder.   4. Foraminifera ($\times$ 20).

FISHES

has a curious power of changing its colour rapidly ; the presence of food appears to excite this power, and it is noticeably brighter by day than by night.

10. **The Tench** (*Tinca vulgaris*).—This fish has a thick body, covered with small scales, and very slimy. It is fond of mud, and indeed spends the winter lying dormant in the mud and ooze at the bottom of a pond or river. Though it occasionally grows to a great size (up to 3 feet), a specimen of 2 or 3 lb. weight is a good catch. It is of a deep yellowish brown colour, approaching sometimes a golden or greenish hue. It spawns in May or June, laying its eggs amongst water plants. Like the Carp, it will live for some time out of water.

11. **The Bream*** (*Abramis brama*), a common little fish, closely related to the Bleak, possessing a long body, a short blunt snout, and long anal fins. Its colour varies from silver-grey to dark brown. It lives in shoals, showing a preference for quiet waters, and feeding chiefly on water plants. It may reach a weight of 8 or 10 lb., but generally a 4-lb. fish would be considered a good specimen. During the breeding season the males are adorned with curious whitish excrescences, which become a golden colour.

12. **The White Bream** (*A. blicca*) is another common species, which has more red upon the body and fins, and the scales are larger. Its flesh is seldom eaten, or, at any rate, is not esteemed highly.

13. **The Bleak** (*Alburnus lucidus*), a small species 6 or 7 inches long, possessing an elongated and compressed body ; its mouth points upwards, and the lower jaw projects noticeably beyond the upper. The upper parts are bluish green, the sides and under parts silvery, the fins white and transparent. Its activity on the surface makes it familiar to most anglers. The scales are used, like those of the Chub and other fish, in the manufacture of artificial pearls.

14. **The Loach** (*Nemachilus barbatulus*) is about 4 inches long, of a yellowish white colour, with brown spots. It is distinguished by the six or more barbels on its mouth. It has very small scales and is very slimy. It hides beneath stones, and is a difficult creature to catch. It makes an interesting occupant of an aquarium, and soon gets remarkably tame.

THE PERCH FAMILY.

This is a genus of spiny-finned fish, of which a familiar marine species is the **Bass**, whilst the **Fresh-water Perch** (*Perca fluviatilis*) is the best known British representative in fresh water. It is a handsome fish, distinguished by its conspicuous front dorsal fin, which is very prickly. It is a bronze-green colour on back and sides, whiter underneath, with red fins, and has six or seven dark bands on the sides. It may reach as much as 9 lb. in weight. The eggs are laid in spring, in long sticky strings attached to weeds. It is an omnivorous feeder, and will even pull down young moorhens and water-voles as well as devouring other fish.

* The Sea Breams, or *Sparidæ*, are quite distinct from this species.

THE BRITISH NATURE BOOK

The Pope, or RUFFE (*Acerina cernua*), is common in lakes and slow rivers. It is not more than 6 inches in length, and has the spiny fins of its family. Instead of the dark bands of the perch it is mottled and spotted with brown, whilst it possesses only one dorsal fin.

The Bullhead, or MILLER'S THUMB (*Cottus Gobio*), belongs to a family represented in salt water by the familiar FATHER LASHER (*C. Scorpio*). To most people this is rather a repulsive little fish, owing to its ugly large head, its slippery skin, and the spines on its crown. But it has a beauty of its own when examined in detail, and makes a quaint inhabitant of an aquarium. In addition, though it is so small, its flesh is delicate, and when boiled is reddish like a Salmon's. It buries its spawn in a hole which the female makes with her tail, and over this nest the male keeps a courageous guard.

STICKLEBACKS.

With this genus we deal with a family of fishes in which the dorsal fin has been replaced by strong spines, which vary in number according to the different species. They are small fish, and the male is brightly coloured, especially during the breeding season. One of our British species (the FIFTEEN-SPINED STICKLEBACK) is marine; the other two are found in fresh or brackish water.

1. **Three-spined Stickleback** (*Gasterosteus aculeatus*), which by-the-bye is sometimes four-spined, is the commonest, and is known to most boys by its nickname of "Soldier," from its bright red colouring during the breeding season. The remarkably interesting story of the Stickleback has been told so often that it may be mentioned with brevity here. The male makes a nest of grass and stems—or, in salt water, of seaweeds—cemented firmly together into a barrel shape, with openings at front and back. When completed, the male sallies forth to find a wife, and endeavours to coax her inside to deposit her eggs. When she has finished her task, and the eggs are fertilized, the male induces other females to enter, until the nest is filled, when he sets himself to guard it with jealous vigilance, allowing no other fish to come within reach of it. Even when the ova are hatched his labours do not cease, but are increased by the difficulty of keeping the "babies" in the shelter of the nest until they are big enough to look after themselves.

The Three-spined Stickleback is covered with plates instead of scales, and is greenish, silver, and brown, except in the male during the breeding season.

2. The **Ten-spined Stickleback** (*G. pungitius*) possesses no plates on the sides of the body; and the male, during the breeding season, becomes a deep black.

3. The **Fifteen-spined Stickleback** (*G. spinachia*) is olive-brown and white in colour, and may be identified not only by the number of spines but by the long body and snout and large size. On the Continent it is both a marine

FISHES

and fresh-water species, but occurs round England only in the sea. It makes its nest of seaweeds.

THE EELS (*Anguilla*).

The **Common Eel** (*Anguilla vulgaris*) needs no description, but note that the species possesses only rudimentary scales, and, instead of separate fins, has them united in a long fringe, except one pair behind the head. The life-history of the eel has only in late years been discovered. It breeds only in the sea and in very deep water. There the young, 2 or 3 inches long, known as "elvers" at first shaped like very thin, transparent leaves, gradually assume the eel shape, and make their way to the shores, where they ascend the rivers and streams in thousands. They thus find their way inland, and when necessary will even leave the water and travel over the land, in this way reaching pools and lakes far from the sea. Here they grow to maturity —the males at five years, the females at seven years of age. Then they make their way downstream again to the sea, where they breed. It is in autumn that the migration to the sea takes place, and large numbers are caught in eel pots and traps at this time of the year. (I may perhaps be allowed to refer to the Eel's Story in *Nature's Nursery Tales* for further particulars.)

THE SALMON FAMILY (*Salmo*).

This is a large and important family, about a hundred species in all, among which are the Salmon itself, Trout, Grayling, Smelt, and others. Their scales are generally round shaped, and they have no barbels. By far the most important in our waters is the **Salmon** (*Salmo salar*), one of the largest of the family, which has been known to attain a weight of 80 or even 100 lb. It is almost a perfect fish in symmetry and shape, a rich bluish or greenish grey above, and silvery white underneath, sprinkled above the lateral line with somewhat large black spots. After being in fresh water some time reddish spots and lines appear, and the bluish tinge becomes duller. The Salmon are then considered "foul fish," unfit for food. During the breeding season the male assumes a curious hooked growth on the under jaw, which is used as a weapon in its frequent combats with rivals. This fish preys on almost any creature it can capture, but feeds chiefly in the sea. Indeed it is asserted that it never feeds in fresh water. Whilst the Eel descends to the sea to breed, the Salmon, on the contrary, ascends some fresh-water river, where the spawn is deposited, from the autumn to the spring, in a bed of fine gravel. It appears to return year by year to the *same* river: marked Salmon having been observed several seasons running. To enable it to ascend over weirs and waterfalls, fish-steps or ladders have in some cases been provided. A whole vocabulary has sprung up round the Salmon. The fish after spawning are called "foul" or "spent fish," or "Kelts." The males are "Kippers," (kip being the name of the horny hook on the lower jaw); the females "Shedders"

THE BRITISH NATURE BOOK

or "Baggits." The young fish, when an inch or so long, are known as "Parrs" or "Samlets" (also "Pinks," "Brandlings," and "Fingerlings"). As they grow older they become "Smolts," when they assume their silver coats and for the first time go down to the sea. Those that come back early to spawn are "Grilse," and not until descending to the sea for the second time do they become mature "Salmon."

The **Salmon Trout** (*S. trutta*, or *Fario argentius*), also called SEA TROUT, is a rather thicker fish, marked with many X-shaped darkish spots. It does not grow so large as the Salmon, though sometimes it reaches from 20 to 25 lb. Its habits are much the same as the Salmon.

The **Grey Trout**, or BULL TROUT (*S. eriox*), called the SEWEN in Welsh rivers, is not so frequent or so large.

The **Trout**.—This is the name given to many species and varieties of the genus *Salmo*.

The **Common Trout** (*Salmo fario*, or *Salar ausonii*) is the favourite fish of many anglers, and is found in almost all our rivers. Occasionally a very large fish is caught—for example, a monster in the New River at Harringay Park, 1907, weighed 18 lb.; one caught at Salisbury weighed 25 lb. None the less a fish of 1 lb. is considered a fine specimen in most of our rivers. In colour the trout varies a good deal; it is more or less yellow, but sometimes almost black or violet. On the back and sides are many spots of black and red; the under parts are silvery white or yellow. The colour varies according to the character of the water in which it lives and the food it can obtain.

It is a voracious species, taking worms, slugs, and insects, small crustaceans and shell-fish, as well as other small fish. It spawns in October and November, when the male acquires a peculiar elongation of the lower jaw, like that of the Salmon, but not so accentuated. The ova is deposited in gravel beds, like the Salmon's. The young fish is called an "Alevin."

The **Lochleven Trout** (*S. levenensis*, or *cœcifer*) and the **Great Lake Trout** (*S. ferox*) are two other British species.

The **Charr** (*S. salvelinus*) is found only in the English Lake District, and in the breeding season is known by its bright red and orange-coloured abdomen; but at all seasons it is a handsome fish of bright and pleasing colour.

The **Grayling** (*Thymallus valgaris*) is distinguished by the many rays on the dorsal fin and the smaller mouth. In colour the back and sides are silver-grey, spotted with black on the head and body and light on the fins, the latter in the spawning season being banded with red. It gets its Latin name from the fact that when freshly caught it has a smell like wild thyme.

THE PIKE (*Esox lucius*).

This well-known fish—the pirate of fresh water—has a long body, with its dorsal fin set close to the tail; a great mouth armed with strong teeth, the under jaw projecting. It is olive-grey above, silvery-white beneath, banded

FISHES

and spotted with yellow. Its length is from 2 to 4 feet, and its weight up to 20 lb., though much larger specimens have been taken. The Common Pike or Jack (Scots, Gedd) spawns, when three years old, in March. It lives to a great age, feeding on any living creature it can catch, not only fish, but ducks, geese, water-voles, etc. "To watch it lurking with cruel eye, in some coign of vantage among reeds or lilies, and suddenly rushing like a torpedo upon its prey, to swallow it at a gulp, is to give an impression of something almost sinister, cruel, and malignant, hidden beneath the beauty of the lily-pads, or amidst the waving forests of the lake's green weeds."

Salt-water Fish.

It is impossible to deal here with any but a few of the commonest of the sea fish, and after a brief reference to some of those which are used for food, we will pass on to discuss some of the common *shore* fishes which many of my readers will find on their visits to the seaside.

Reference has already been made to the family of the PERCHES and SEA BREAMS. Here we begin with a salt-water "Perch" known as the BASS (*Labrax lupus*).

1. **The Bass** (BASSE) (*Labrax lupus*).—This fish affords good sport to sea anglers, and migrates in shoals to our South Coasts from June onwards. It ascends our rivers, and can live in fresh water. It was known as "Labrax" to the Greeks, and the great Aristotle made notes of the tough teeth on its tongue, and other features which distinguish it from the other perches. It is a voracious fish, sometimes reaching 15 lb. in weight. Shaped like a Salmon, it has two dorsal fins, and is dark green on the back, shading off to silvery white beneath. It is often taken with Sand Eel as bait, and it will also rise to the fly. It spawns in July.

2. **The Sea Bream** (*Pagellus cent. rodontus*) has one long dorsal fin, very spiny. It runs up to 5 or 6 lb. in weight, is found all round our shores, but especially where rocks and reefs abound, and is bright red in colour, with a noticeable black spot on the shoulder. The young are called "Chad," and in a maturer stage "Ballard."

3. **The Mackerel** (*Scomber scomber*), a member of a family which includes the Tunny, Bonito, and Sucking Fishes, is known to every one by sight and taste. The temperature of its body is higher than that of other fishes. It feeds on the fry of herrings, sprats, and pilchards, etc., and moves about in shoals, coming coastwards either to spawn or to prey upon the shoals of other fishes. It spawns in May or June, depositing its eggs some distance from the shore on the surface of the water. The Mackerel migrate in a remarkable manner, moving from the deep water of the Atlantic in early spring towards our coasts; in May or June they appear with regularity off the Scillies; then, whilst some go up St. George's Channel, the majority proceed up the English Channel. An interesting feature of their migrations is that they are accompanied by other

fish—for example, by one long-beaked species known as the "Mackerel Guide," or to the fishermen as "Long-nose."

4. **The Grey Mullet** (*Mugil capito*).—The family of *Mugilidæ* contains some seventy species. They possess few and only rudimentary teeth, living on mud, which they sift by means of a specially adapted pharynx, the stomach being not unlike a bird's gizzard. The Grey Mullet is a silvery fish, with darker markings, and attains a considerable weight, some specimens reaching a length of 3 feet.

5. **The Red Mullet** (*Mullus*) belongs really to the Perch family, and is esteemed a great delicacy. Its colour is pale pink, with three or four yellow stripes. It seldom exceeds 2 lb. in weight.

6. **The Cod** (*Gadus morrhus*) belongs to a large family, including Haddock, Whiting, Pout, Hake, and others.

The Cod is the largest of the family, and sometimes attains a length of 4 feet and a weight of 100 lb. It has a sensitive barbel or "beard," by which, no doubt, it is enabled to locate the various crustaceans on which it feeds. It spawns from January to May, being extremely prolific—in fact, the roe of a large female may contain nine million eggs.

7. **The Haddock** (*Gadus æglefinus*) much resembles the Cod, but possesses a black spot behind each of the pectoral fins, sometimes extending to meet on the back. The fisherman's story is that these are the marks of St. Peter's finger and thumb, the Haddock being reputed to be the fish from which he took the tribute money. It appears in great shoals on our coasts, those taken on the East Coast and in Dublin Bay being of specially fine quality. When cured, it is, of course, so flattened out as to be difficult to recognize as the same fish seen in the water.

8. **The Pout** (BIB, BRASSY, WHITING POUT) (*Gadus luscus*) is seldom more than a foot long, and is a much deeper-bodied fish than the other members of the family. It is brown in colour, deeply banded, and white beneath. It has a curious loose membrane on the head which it can dilate at will.

9. **The Whiting** (*Gadus merlangus*), of great service as a food fish, possesses no barbel on the chin, and is of a pure silver colour, with a dark spot on the pectoral fin. It gains its English name, however, from the pearly whiteness of its flesh. It is a voracious species, feeding not only on the bottom on small crustacea, but also on small fish such as sprats. It attains a maximum length of 16 inches, and a weight of 3 to 4 lb. It is abundant, especially on our South and West Coasts. It breeds in spring, the eggs floating on the surface of the water.

10. **The Pollack** (*Gadus pollachius*) is known in Scotland and Ireland as the LYTHE. It is an active fish, green in colour, possessing no barbel, and the lower jaw projects beyond the upper. Its maximum weight is some 20 or 25 lb. It is a common fish; but as its flesh deteriorates quickly, it is not often on view at the fishmonger's, generally being disposed of to customers as soon as it is brought ashore.

FISHES

11. **The Hake** (*Merluccius vulgaris*), a very voracious species, attacking herrings and pilchards, and hence known as the "HERRING HAKE." Length, 3 or 4 feet; colour, whitish, greyer on back. A valuable fish, known in its dried state as "stock-fish."

12. **The Ling** (*Molya vulgaris*).—This is a much longer-shaped species than the Cod, and reaches a weight of 70 lb. The colour is grey, with an olive tinge, silvery underneath, the fins edged with white. It is found chiefly where the sea bottom is rocky.

FLAT-FISH.

Under this head come more than two hundred species, among which are many of our British fish, such as the Turbot, Halibut, Flounder, Plaice, and the Soles. They all keep (in the adult stage) to the sea bottom, are all carnivorous, and all have a remarkable life-history. They are not really "flat," but "thin" fish. When first hatched, the young resemble ordinary "round" fish, except that they are almost transparent; they swim vertically, and have an eye, as usual, on either side of the head. But very early in life they take to lying down on their sides, and then the upper side becomes a darker colour, curiously marked and patterned so as to resemble very closely the nature of the ground on which they are lying. Indeed many of them possess the power of altering their coloration to suit their surroundings. The under side does not change colour, but remains white. In addition, the skull becomes twisted, so that the eye, which is at first beneath, comes round to lie beside its fellow on the upper side. If it be remembered that the edges of a flat-fish are really its back and belly, this strange history will become clearer.

1. **The Turbot** (*Rhombus maximus*) has its eyes on the left side, is about 2 feet long, and reaches 30 lb. and more in weight. It feeds on crustaceans and other fish, and is found on sandy bottoms round our coasts. It is extremely prolific, the number of eggs in one female having been estimated at fourteen millions.

2. **The Halibut** (*Hippoglossus vulgaris*) is the largest of all our flat-fish, having its eyes on the right side. Specimens have been taken 500 lb. in weight, and as much as 20 feet in length.

3. **The Plaice** (*Pleuronectes platessa*), one of our commonest flat-fishes, is distinguished by the orange spots on its olive-brown side. It inhabits sandy and muddy banks, where it lies partially covered, but with its eyes exposed, and watchful for its prey. It feeds on molluscs, crustaceans, and worms. Its average weight is between 2 and 3 lb. It spawns in early spring.

4. **The Dab** (*Pleuronectes limanda*) is distinguished by its light brown colour, small, irregular dark spots, and the roughness of its small scales.

5. **The Flounder** (*Pleuronectes flexus*) has an olive-green or brown upper side, sometimes with yellow spots. The species prefers river mouths, where the eggs are deposited; in fact, the Flounder often leaves the sea and goes upstream, and can thrive in fresh-water ponds.

THE BRITISH NATURE BOOK

6. The Soles.—The **Common Sole** (*Solea vulgaris*) is the largest of the British species, sometimes reaching 2 feet in length. The colour is a yellowish brown covered with black blotches. It has well-developed pectoral fins, and sensitive filaments on the snout. It appears to find its food (crustaceans and worms) by means of smell, moving over the sea bottom, tapping with its head. It is a night fish, hiding in the sand by day. It haunts river estuaries.

The **Lemon Sole**, or SAND SOLE (*S. lascaris*) has specks instead of blotches on its coloured side, and the nostril on the under side larger than that on the upper. It is very scarce.

THE EELS.

We have already dealt with the COMMON EEL, which lives in rivers and fresh-water lakes, and only returns to the sea to spawn.

1. **The Conger Eel** (*Conger vulgaris*) is entirely a salt-water fish, common off our coasts, especially Cornwall. It is a very powerful and voracious species, feeding on large prey, such as lobsters and cuttle-fish, and has been known to attain to 10 feet in length. Much smaller specimens are ugly creatures to deal with on board a small boat at night, as I discovered when fishing for them. Apart from their biting powers, which are not small, they are so muscular that they can move with extraordinary rapidity, and they have a habit of grasping with their tails, and using the leverage thus obtained for aiming a blow at their prey. Little is known of the life-history of this species, but the eggs, of which enormous numbers are laid (one female has been known to contain eight million eggs), hatch out into larvæ much resembling those of the fresh-water eel, but with a longer snout.

2. **The Sand Eel**, known as the LAUNCE (*Ammodytes tobianus*), belongs to an entirely different family, and is only so called from its long thin shape. It is really allied to the Cod. This fish, often caught in enormous shoals in bays and harbours, where it is preyed upon by mackerel and other fishes, as well as by gulls, can bury itself almost instantaneously in the sand. It has a protruding lower jaw, which is a useful instrument for piercing the soft sand when seeking refuge from its pursuers.

THE HERRING.

The **Herring** (*Clupea harengus*) belongs to a family which includes the Sprat, Pilchard, Shad, and others. The so-called "whitebait" is chiefly composed of the fry of the Herring. The species is a surface-feeder, living on small crustaceans and other organisms, and approaches the shore in summer in enormous shoals for the purpose of spawning. The eggs are heavy and adhesive, and stick to the stones, rock, etc., at the sea bottom, in this respect differing from those of the Sprat and Pilchard, which float on the surface. The Herring has large thin scales and a keeled body, with no lateral line; and is thus distinguished from the Shad and Pilchard, which have much larger scales and radiating ridges on the gill covers.

FISHES

The larva, when hatched, is a minute transparent creature, very slender, and elongated, which lives on the surface of the sea, and grows at the rate of $\frac{1}{2}$ an inch per month; at twelve months it is $6\frac{1}{2}$ inches long. The full-grown fish is therefore three or four years old.

The **Sprat** (*Clupea sprattus*) is a very abundant species, much smaller than the Herring, being only 5 inches long when full grown. It has a *serrated* belly, a distinguishing mark from the Herring, which is smooth underneath. It is caught in immense shoals, and is used, not only for food, but by farmers as manure. "Sardines," "Norwegian Anchovies," as well as "whitebait," are largely composed of this species.

The **Pilchard** (*Clupea pilchardus*) is nearly as large as the Herring, but thicker, and is found in more southerly seas, being abundant off Devon and Cornwall, where the Pilchard fishery is an important industry. Most "sardines" are young Pilchards, the French "sardine" fishery being valued at £400,000 a year. Most of the Devon and Cornish Pilchards are salted for the Mediterranean market, especially Italy.

The **Anchovy** (*Engraulis enchrasicholus*) is usually about 3 inches long, but while abundant in the Mediterranean and elsewhere, is not common round our coasts, although its eggs have been obtained off Lancashire. At one time, however, it was far more common in the British seas.

The **Smelt** (*Osmerus eperlanus*), known as the SPARLING in Scotland and EPERLAN in France, is related to the Salmon, and grows to a length of 8 or 10 inches. It is shaped like a Trout, but more slender, and has a whitish back, tinged with green, bright silver underneath and on the sides. It has a distinct smell like a cucumber; is often found in estuaries and rivers.

THE SKATE.

The popular name of several species of RAY. The **Common Skate** (*Raia batis*) is plentiful on the British coasts. Pale grey in colour, the body is spotted with black, the under side being white, with black speckles. It is an ugly species, with two large spineless pectoral fins and a long tail. Like the Sharks, to which it is allied, the Skate deposits "purses," which are often found dry and empty on the beach. These egg-cases differ from those of the Shark in having no tendrils. The largest Ray in British waters is the **Sharp-nosed Ray**, which is sometimes 6 feet in length and 400 to 500 lb. in weight.

The **Painted Ray** is common in the English Channel; the **Sting Ray** ("FIREFLARE") is also common off our coasts, and attains a length of 3 feet or more, and 80 lb. in weight. It has a sharp-toothed spine on its long tail, which it uses as a weapon of defence, being able to inflict a serious wound.

THE DOG-FISH

is the popular name given to a number of fishes allied to the Shark. The **Picked Dog-fish** (*Acanthias vulgaris*) is more abundant off our coasts than any other, and measures some 3 feet in length. It is not oviparous, but is said to produce young almost daily for several months a year. It does great damage to nets and lines, and is equally hated by fishermen for the damage it inflicts on the shoals of herring and other food fishes. Other Dog-fish (such as the Rough Hound or LESSER SPOTTED DOG-FISH, *Scyllium canicula*) are found off our shores; the so-called " Mermaids' purses," yellow horny envelopes with long tendrils, are their eggs, the tendrils being used to attach the cases to weeds, thus ensuring their safety till the young have been hatched out. A good deal of the flesh of the Dog-fish is prepared and sold for food under other names.

Of the smaller fishes found in the rock pools and close to the shore edge, a few must be mentioned, because no reader can spend a holiday at the sea without coming across them.

THE BLENNIES, OR SHANNIES,

are among the commonest, though they will escape observation by hiding under sand or stones, and their curious mottled colour, green and yellow, brown and black, serves to render them indistinguishable from their surroundings when at rest. They are distinguished from other species by their crimson-ringed eyes. The **Smooth Blenny** (*Blennius pholis*) has the peculiar characteristic of being able to move its eyes independently of each other, so that it may turn one upward as if to look out for enemies from above, whilst the other surveys the bottom for food. It is generally found in some small crevice, into which it retreats backwards at any alarm. It has sharp teeth, and a large blenny (4 to 5 inches long) will hold on to your finger almost like a marine bulldog. It is in this way that the fish will seize a limpet which has slightly raised its shell from the surface of the rock, and with a wrench will twist it off its resting-place and devour it. This species has a short snout, and its head is not unlike a bulldog's, and there is a clearly defined dent in the middle of the upper fin.

THE GOBIES

are generally common also, and can be identified by the formation of the lower fins, which, being placed close together, form a kind of sucker, enabling the fish to cling firmly to a rock or stone. The **Black, or Rock, Goby** (*Gobius niger*), 5 or 6 inches when full grown, is coloured to match the ground on which it rests. The male builds its nest under an empty shell or seaweed, and, like the Stickleback, guards the eggs jealously until they are hatched. The **Little Goby** (*Gobius minutus*) is only 2 or 3 inches long, yellowish in colour, and marked with brown specks.

The **Spotted Gunnel**, or BUTTER FISH (*Centronotus gunnellus*), is a deep olive colour, with a row of black spots bordered with white under its one narrow fin. From these curious spots it is known as "Nine-eyes." Its skin is thickly coated with a slippery mucous secretion, hence its nickname of "Butter Fish." It belongs to the Blenny family.

Father Lasher (HORNY COBBLER, STING FISH) (*Cottus scorpio*) is an ugly fish, like the Miller's Thumb or Bullhead of our fresh-water streams. It has a broad head covered with spines, is protectively coloured in brown, green, and grey, to suit its surroundings, and has a habit of dashing out at anything that moves within its view. Most of us have found it a nuisance when fishing from a pier or breakwater.

The **Cornish Sucker** (*Lepadogaster gouani*)—so called because it was first found on the Cornish coast—is 4 inches long, with a distinct red or crimson tint. It is provided with discs or suckers, by means of which it can attach itself to rocks or weeds. It is one of a family of SUCKERS (*Liparis*), which may be found under stones at low water. The **Two-spotted Sucker** (*Lepadogaster bimaculatus*), 2 inches in length, is identified by the eye-like spot on each side behind the pectoral fin.

The **Worm Pipe Fish** (*Syngnathus lumbriciformis*), a relation of the SEA-HORSE, is a long snake-like fish with a remarkable mouth, the two jaws of which are united into a long thin tube or beak.

The **Greater Pipe Fish** (*S. acus*) is much larger, 12 to 15 inches, and the males have a pouch (like that of the kangaroo), inside which the female transfers her eggs, and the young use it as a shelter for the first few days of their life.

THE ROCKLINGS

are not unlike the Gunnels, but rounder in shape and deeper in colour. They may be distinguished by the barbs on their jaws. The **Five-bearded Rockling** (*Motella mustela*) has four barbs on the upper and one on the lower jaw, the **Three-bearded Rockling** has two on the upper and one on the lower jaw. These fish build a sort of nest by packing fragments of coralline into a crevice, where they deposit their eggs.

The FIFTEEN-SPINED STICKLEBACK has already been referred to above.

The **Lesser Weever** (*Trachinus vipera*) may also be found occasionally half buried in the sand. It possesses a sharp spine on each side of the gill covers, which will inflict a bad wound if any attempt is made to catch the fish in the hand.

SECTION II.
INVERTEBRATES.

CHAPTER VII.
Arthropoda.

WE have so far completed our survey of most of the British Vertebrates, from Mammals to Fishes, and we next proceed to the *Invertebrates*—that is, to the animals that do not possess backbones. These are divided into thirteen groups, of which the following are important for students of British Nature.

1. *Arthropoda* ("Jointed-limbed")—a group which includes Crabs, Lobsters, Shrimps, Wood-lice, Spiders, Insects, etc.

2. *Mollusca*—Shellfish, including Cuttle-fish, Snails, Whelks, Oysters, etc.

3. *Echinodermata* ("Spiny-skinned"), in which are placed Sea-urchins, Starfish, etc.

4. *Polyzoa*, or Moss Animals, such as Corallines, Sea-mats, etc.

5. *Annelida*, or Worms, such as Earthworms, Sea-mice, etc.

6. *Platyhelminthes*, or Flatworms.

7. *Cœlenterata* (Zoophytes), to which belong Sea-anemones, Corals, and Jelly-fishes.

8. *Porifera*—Sponges.

9. *Protozoa*, or Animalcula.

The first group—ARTHROPODA—contains as its first class the **Crustacea** (Crabs, Lobsters, Crayfish, Shrimps, etc.). Most of the Crustacea are aquatic, living either in salt or fresh water, or in damp places. Their bodies are composed of a number of ring-like segments jointed together, each segment having a pair of limbs. They have no inner skeleton, the flesh being supported and protected by a "crust" (hence the name *Crustacea*, from the Latin, *crusta*, which in common parlance is a *shell*)—as, for instance, that of the Crab. They breathe by means of gills. They shed their shells periodically; and if they lose a limb, they can grow a new one to take its place.

Most of the Crustaceans lay eggs, and the young when hatched pass through various stages until they reach their mature or adult form. Many of them feed on dead creatures or decaying organic matter, a few being herbivorous.

PLATE XIV.

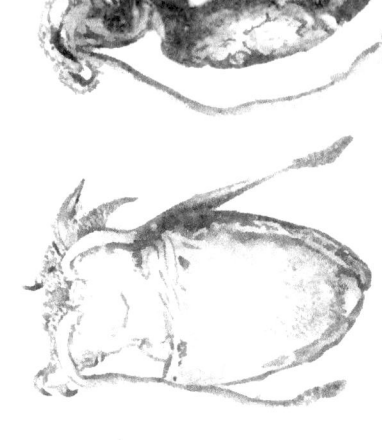

1. Marine Zoophyte (Gorgon azonia). 2. Tube of Ship-worm. 3. Angular Crab. 4. Cuttle-fish, showing upper and under sides.

Class I. CRUSTACEA—Fresh-water Crustacea.

The smallest are to be found in the water from any stagnant pond or pool. If a bottle of such water be examined closely, you are sure to see a number of minute creatures darting and jerking about in all directions. These are Water-fleas and Cyclops, in size less than ⅛ of an inch, which, to examine thoroughly, should, be watched through your microscope (the home-made apparatus described elsewhere in this book will serve excellently for this purpose).

1. **The Water-flea** (*Daphnia pulex*) is not to be confused with the House-flea, the latter being a real insect. It is recognized by its oval shape and its

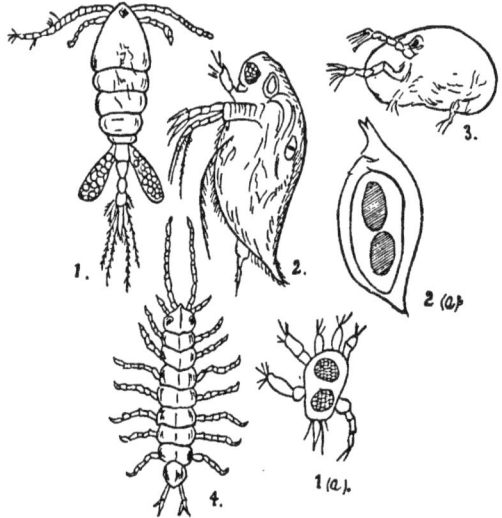

Crustaceans. 1. Cyclops, the one-eyed crustacean. 1 (a). Young cyclops. 2. Water-flea.
2 (a). Egg-bag of water-flea. 3. Cypris. 4. Asellus aquaticus.

prominent beak. Under the microscope its shell (or carapace) is so transparent that you may watch its inner organs working, its heart beating, and its eggs *in situ*. The male is very rare. The female produces two kinds of eggs— winter and summer. The former remain inside the carapace, which is shed by the female in due time and drops to the mud, where the eggs are thus protected till the spring. They may freeze, or the pond may dry up, but yet they survive. Indeed, the carapace may be blown by the wind far from its original resting-place and find a home in a new pond. This accounts for the presence of these creatures in practically every piece of water in the country. The *summer* eggs are laid when food is plentiful, and they hatch almost immediately. Notice (under the microscope) the remarkable single eye.

2. **The Cyclops** is, as its classical name implies, a one-eyed crustacean. It is a tiny, pear-shaped creature, with long antennæ and four pairs of legs. The male is smaller and much rarer than the female, which may always be identified by the two egg-bags which she carries attached to her abdomen, containing fifty or sixty eggs apiece! The larva when hatched is almost invisible, and is not in the least like its parents until it assumes the adult form.

3. **The Fresh-water Shrimp** (*Gammarus pulex*) is also found in every pond and stream. It feeds on decaying animal matter, and is a good scavenger for an aquarium. The eggs are carried by the female in her front legs; and the young, on hatching out, remain with their mother until scattered.

Fig. 3 in the illustration is another Water-flea, *Cypris*, an insect with a bivalve shell, about the size of a grain of millet, and not unlike a miniature mussel shell. It possesses a single eye and two pairs of antennæ. A *male* Cypris has never been found.

Fig. 4 is the Water-louse, *Asellus aquaticus*, a scavenger to be found in the mud and on weeds. Its breathing apparatus, a series of flat appendages beneath the abdomen, is worth observing.

4. **The Crayfish** (*Astacus fluviatilis*) is to be found in many of our streams, especially in limestone districts. These creatures make a burrow in the bank or find a natural crevice, in which they reside for the winter; but in warmer weather they emerge much more frequently. They eat all kinds of food, not only vegetable, but animal—snails, meat, fish; they will even devour one another, and I have photographed crayfish engaged in a tremendous battle for supremacy.

The female lays eggs in November and December, and carries them fixed to her abdominal legs till they hatch in the following June. The Crayfish moults—that is, casts off its outer shell—eight times in the first year, five times in the second, twice in the third, and once a year for the rest of its existence. This is accounted for by the fact that, as the creature grows, the shell does not grow with it, and therefore has to be discarded when too small, and a new one formed.

Marine Crustaceans.

1. **The Barnacle.**—The most familiar species is the **Acorn Barnacle**, or ACORN SHELL (*Balanus*), found on almost every rock on our coasts, and sharp enough to cut hands and feet as we clamber about. Inside the cone-shaped shell is a small creature belonging to the *Cirripedia*, or Curl-footed Crustaceans. When first hatched it swam about freely, a minute creature with three pairs of legs, one eye, and a delicate shell on its back; but after moulting several times it settled down on a rock, a shell, or a piece of wood, glued itself firmly to its support by means of suckers, and gradually assumed the acorn shape. These *Balani* feed by protruding their six pairs of legs through the slit in the lid

MARINE CRUSTACEANS 167

or operculum of the shell, sweeping them to and fro like a net, and thus bringing the minute animals on which they feed to their mouths.

Another well-known barnacle is the **Goose Barnacle** (*Lepas anatifera*), frequently found attached to the wooden bottoms of ships which are brought into dock to be " scraped "—that is, to be cleaned from the thousands of barnacles which have fixed themselves there. They attach themselves head downwards upon a kind of stalk (peduncle), really consisting of the pillar of cement with which the little animal covered its feelers before it changed into its final form. There are many other kinds, some found attached deeply to whales—most uncomfortable parasites !

2. **The Brine Shrimp** (*Artemia salina*) is a reddish animal about half an inch long, with eleven pairs of legs and a long, jointed tail. It is to be found in every salt lake, as well as on the shore.

3. **The Sand-hopper** (*Talistra locusta*) may be found in hundreds by turning over any bunch of seaweed on the shore, or burrowing in moist sand. Its three pairs of hind-legs have joints that bend forward, while those of the front legs bend backward. It breathes by means of gills, and feeds upon decaying seaweed and other matter, being the most useful scavenger of the sea-edge. It is the prey of all the shore birds and of crabs, and at least one beetle tunnels after it in the sand, and devours it in its burrow!

4. **The Sand-screw** is closely allied to the Sand-hopper; but whilst the above sinks its burrows almost vertically in the sand, the Sand-screw drives them horizontally just below the surface, and, instead of jumping like the Sand-hopper, it screws itself along on its side.

5. **The Shrimp** (*Crangon vulgaris*) is so familiar as to need no description. It is so transparent as to be almost invisible in the water, and when resting at the bottom its speckled body looks almost exactly like the sand. As if this were not sufficient protection, it can bury itself in the sand, rapidly scooping a furrow with its hind-limbs, sinking into it, and then covering itself with sand by means of its feelers. The female carries her eggs on her swimming feet, and as she is found thus laden at all seasons, there appears to be no special breeding time.

6. **The Great Prawn** (*Leander serratus*) is a bold and fearless animal in its native element, and a handsome creature when examined in detail. Note the pear-shaped eyes, the antennæ, two pairs of " hands " (*chelæ*), and three pairs of walking feet. Behind these are five pairs of swimming organs, or legs, and a four-plated, fan-shaped tail, by means of which the prawn can leap backwards with astonishing speed. Both prawns and shrimps feed on carrion. There are several species of both these animals (the **Æsop Prawn**, for example, to be found in summer in the rock pools, distinguished by the hump on its back). Many small prawns are sold as shrimps, but there is one striking difference easy to observe—the long beak or spike projecting from the edge of the shield, or carapace, which covers the back is set with sharp teeth, like a saw, in the prawn, whilst in the shrimp it is perfectly smooth.

THE BRITISH NATURE BOOK

7. THE LOBSTER (*Homarus vulgaris*).

Shrimps, prawns, crabs, and lobsters all have five pairs of walking feet, including the large claws, and are therefore grouped as *Decapoda* (" Ten-footed "), and the student should take the trouble to dissect specimens in order to see their general similarity. All of them, be it remembered, " moult " or cast their skins, retiring to some secluded retreat until the new " shell " has hardened. Whilst, however, the likeness between the lobster and the shrimp is fairly obvious, the crab's similarity is not so plain, the fact being that the crab's tail, instead of stretching out behind him and being a most powerful weapon, is permanently bent underneath, and fixed close to the under surface.

The lobster, as is well known, is black until it is boiled. Its claws are invariably of odd sizes, the larger one being used as a weapon for fighting, the smaller as a hand with which to hold on firmly to the weeds or rocks at the sea bottom. The tail is used as a powerful oar, the animal " doubling it up," so to speak, beneath him with such a powerful stroke—and with the plates of the tail outspread—that he can shoot a distance of thirty or forty feet with extraordinary swiftness. When moving forward the lobster makes use of the five pairs of swimming legs underneath the tail, and it is to these " swimmerets " that the female glues her eggs. They may vary in number from 2,000 to 12,000, and are thus carried for several months, hatching in June and July. There is one other species frequently taken on our coasts, known as the **Norway Lobster** (*Nephrops norvegicus*). This has kidney-shaped eyes, whereas those of the Common Lobster are round, and it is of a pale flesh colour. The **Spiny Lobster** (*Palinurus vulgaris*), with its purplish brown back and red-tinted white legs, is not a true lobster; nor are the so-called " SPANISH LOBSTER," really the **Scaly Squat Lobster** (*Galathea squamifera*), and the **Spinous Squat Lobster** (*Galathea strigosa*), both of which may be found under stones below low-water mark, and are identified by the spines and " bayonets " on the back and claws.

8. CRABS.

There are many species of crabs round our coasts, of which only a few can be mentioned here; but so common is this animal that it is worth while to know something of its strange life-history (that of the lobster being very similar). From the egg a strange minute creature emerges called a " Zoëa," about the size of the top of a small pin, not unlike a spiked helmet, with two large eyes in front of it, and a long, jointed tail behind. This swims by turning somersaults as a means of progress, and feeds upon almost invisible decaying matter. To a great extent it is upon myriads of these " crab caterpillars," if they may be so called, that the whale feeds. Later on the Zoëa throws off its skin and changes into a " Megalopa " (in reality the " chrysalis " or " pupa " of the crab caterpillar), so called because of its enormous eyes. It is now not unlike a lobster in shape—of course very minute still—with tiny claws and a long tail.

PLATE XV.

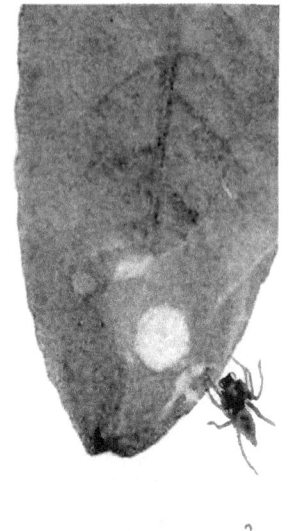

1. Web of *Epeira callophylla*, covered with dew.   2. Spider guarding Eggs.
3. Commencing the Web.   4. Garden Spider in Web.

CRABS 169

And after a few weeks the form is changed once more, the skin thrown off, and a perfect crab appears, about $\frac{1}{8}$ of an inch long. A shell-less crab—that is, one which has "moulted"—may often be found hiding in some crevice in a rock pool. It is then quite soft to the touch, though the "shell" soon hardens. A crab has to shed its skin frequently while growing, but as soon as it is mature, once a year is sufficient. In so doing it loses even the coverings of its gills, its stomach, eyes, antennæ, jaws, and all its other parts. The eyes are on stalks, and are like those of insects, compound, consisting of 3,000 or 4,000 square facets, and thus enabling their owner to see in all directions without moving them. On the head are two pairs of feelers. The lesser feelers have on each a small gland containing salt and water—these are the "ears" of the crab; while on the first joint of the greater feelers are similar glands by means of which it "smells."

The **Edible Crab** (*Cancer pagurus*) is by far the most important of those in the British seas. Small specimens may be found in rock pools, but the larger ones can only be caught in deep water, by means of the well-known crab or lobster pots baited with pieces of fish. This crab is brown in colour on the back, possesses enormous claws, and is a tremendous fighter. An old specimen is very often covered with barnacles and the tubes of some of the sea worms.

The **Common Shore Crab** (GREEN CRAB, or HARBOUR CRAB) (*Carcinus mænas*) is known to every seaside visitor. Its back is coloured protectively with tints of yellowish green and brown, sometimes with black markings. It spends a great part of its life out of water, possessing gills so made that they will keep moist for a long time.

The **Velvet Fiddler** (*Portunus puber*).—This is one of the swimming crabs, having its hindmost pair of legs flattened out into broad oval plates fringed with hairs. Its name is given to it for the short, soft down like velvet covering its blackish shell. The legs are striped with blue, with some scarlet on the claws.

The **Slender Spider Crab** (*Stenorhynchus tenuirostris*) has a very small, triangular body, bright pink in colour, and long spider legs. Its carapace is drawn out into a kind of beak. It is often found covered with seaweeds or sponges.

The **Large Thorny Spider Crab** (*Maia squinado*), or "THORNBACK," has its carapace covered with spikes, and frequently tufts of seaweed, which are planted there by the crab itself as a sort of disguise. It is sometimes of considerable size—carapace 8 inches long, and legs 14 or 15 inches.

The **Common Swimming Crab** (*Portunus variegatus*), common on Scottish coasts, has the last pair of legs flattened into paddles. The swimming species attack live fish, and are thus adapted for pursuing their prey.

The **Masked Crab** (*Corystes cassivelaunus*) has, in the male, very long claws, and is distinguished by the curious markings on the back, which resemble a human face. The carapace is long and narrow, differing thus from that of all other crabs.

The **Four-horned Spider Crab** (*Pisa tetraodon*), the commonest of the spider crabs, has four horns on its very long beak, and many short spikes and hairs on its back. It is frequently covered with seaweeds or corallines.

The Pea Crab (*Pinnotheus pisum*) when full grown is about half an inch across, and very round; yellow in colour. It lives inside the shells of living mussels and other bivalves—a very remarkable instance of "partnership" in animals.

The Hairy Crab (*Pilumnus hirtellus*) is a small species covered with hairs and spines, with large claws; common on the South and West Coasts.

The Angular Crab (*Gonoplax rhombides*) is identified by the many sharp angles of its back, which is reddish brown in colour, and its long pincer claws. It has specially long eye-stalks, and lives in mud.

"Zebedee" (*Xantho hydrophilus*) is one of a genus of yellowish-coloured crabs known as Devil-crabs, or Zebedees, having the shell much wrinkled and with the fingers of the pincer-claws brown (in *X. incisus*, black).

The Broad-claw (*Porcellana platycheles*) is a very flat and dirty species inhabiting mud, found in tidal estuaries. It is quite small, hairy on the back, but a smooth, creamy white below: hence the name "HAIRY PORCELAIN CRAB."

Hermit Crabs.—There are many species known by this name from the fact that, having soft tails, they protect them by living in the abandoned shells of molluscs, which they thus carry about with them, like snails! They are very pugnacious, and often fight one another for a coveted shell. The commonest is *Eupagurus bernhardus*—when full grown 5 inches long, inhabiting large whelk shells. One of the most interesting is *Eupagurus prideaux*, which plants an anemone (the Cloaklet, *Adamsia palliata*) on its shell. This " friendship" serves both parties well, for as no fish will devour an anemone, the crab is thus protected from enemies, whilst the anemone profits by being carried to any meal which the crab obtains.

These crabs make interesting inhabitants of the aquarium.

The Wood-louse belongs to a family included in the order known as *Isopoda* (" Equal-footed "), and it is well to be reminded that the curious little creature found in our gardens, under stones and decaying wood, is *not* an insect, but a crustacean. Its strong armour of grey plates, its long antennæ, and its seven pairs of walking legs, are its most familiar characteristics; but it is worth a closer inspection. Then it will be seen that the abdomen has six pairs, the first five overlapping like tiles, the sixth modified to hold air. The process of reproduction is most remarkable, but it must suffice here to refer to the fact that the eggs are carried in certain brood chambers on the legs until they are hatched. Wood-lice feed on vegetable matter, both fresh and decayed. At least one species (*Armadillidium vulgare*) is able to roll itself into a ball when alarmed. In old days this habit was considered to show its value as a medicine, and it was actually used as a pill!

A large marine species is often found under stones on a rocky shore—the Sea-slater (*Ligia oceanica*).

Class II. ARACHNIDA—Scorpions, Spiders, Mites, etc.

This is a group of animals which are distinguished from insects by having only *two* divisions of the body—the cephalo-thorax (head and thorax united) and the abdomen. There are usually *four* pairs of walking legs on the thorax. Insects, on the other hand, have three divisions of the body—head, thorax, and abdomen—and only three pairs of walking legs. There are no true Scorpions in this country, and therefore we pass on to the

SPIDERS,

of which there are about 500 British species, divided into two tribes: (1) *Octonoculina* (eight eyes), and (2) *Senoculina* (six eyes). Their general appearance needs no description, but certain points are worth noting. In the first place, the young when once hatched pass through no larval or pupal stages like insects, but are perfect specimens of the adult spider, though very small. They "moult" or change their skins several times before reaching maturity, and frequently reproduce at this time any part which has been broken off or injured. They have been known to live three or four years, and the female to produce several broods, but in most cases they do not long survive the laying of eggs. The eyes of spiders are simple, and not compound, as is the case with those of insects, and are either six or eight (in British species). They vary in size and in grouping, thus forming an important detail in distinguishing the different genera. It is worth while to examine them under a microscope or magnifying glass to realize their brilliancy and colour, some being of a beautiful ruby colour. Some are set in parallel rows on the "forehead" thus: $\begin{smallmatrix}\circ&\circ&\bullet&\bullet\\\circ&\circ&\circ&\circ\end{smallmatrix}$, in oval or circular form $\begin{smallmatrix}\circ&\circ\\\circ&\circ\end{smallmatrix}$, or in pairs $\begin{smallmatrix}\bullet&&\circ\\&\circ&\\\circ&&\end{smallmatrix}$, and, in fact, in many other combinations. Below the eyes and above the mouth you will notice the falces, or poison fangs, formidable weapons, of which the fang closes down upon the base into a groove like a pocket knife. With these the spider catches, holds, and kills its prey, the poison being contained in a gland at the base, and emitted through a small opening at the point of the fang. The legs have seven joints, and on the foot are two or more curved claws, sometimes plain, sometimes toothed like a comb. At the end of the abdomen are the spinnerets or organs of spinning, in two, three, or four pairs. These contain many minute openings through which the silk issues as a sticky fluid, which hardens immediately on contact with the air. The breathing apparatus consists of two or four yellowish or brownish scales or gills slit at their hinder edge.

The web of the Garden Spider is a most wonderful construction, and there is no more interesting work to be observed than the actual building of this beautiful snare. First a number of irregular threads are fixed as a roughly four-sided framework to certain firm points, and these are furnished with other threads as guys or stays. Then from the centre point the spider spins its radiating lines, all of which are double. Finally, beginning again at the centre, the spider weaves its spiral lines from one radial to another, until, in something like an hour's time, the task is complete. If the web is examined through a lens, it will be found that the spiral lines (except those near the centre) are covered with sticky globules, and it is these lines which hold fast the insects which touch them. As is natural, these spiral lines have to be renewed, as the globules dry up in the air.

The House Spider's snare is a gauzy sheet of fine lines, none of them sticky, in which the insect is literally entangled.

The eggs of spiders are usually laid from June to October, and are covered with a cocoon of yellow silk until September or the next spring.

Spiders can be kept in captivity with very little trouble. A glass jar makes a good prison, and it is interesting to discover how intelligent your captive becomes, recognizing the time when you are about to " feed " it. I have frequently kept specimens for the whole season in this way. Care should be taken to provide *water* as well as insects for these " pets." Spiders, if collected as specimens, should be killed by dropping either into boiling water or spirit, and should be kept in a small glass tube filled with turpentine, formalin, or other preservative.

In studying these animals, take notice of the *kind* of web, the position (whether in bushes or grass, on a tree trunk or wall, etc., whether in a dry or damp situation). The spider itself may be found either by just touching the web gently, when the chances are that the animal will dart forward, expecting a victim, or by tracing the clue line which leads from the centre of the web to the hiding-place. The courtship of spiders is very interesting. The males fight one another for the possession of a female, and then pose before her in the most grotesque attitudes. The lady, however, is not easy to please, and may kill and eat her would-be suitors before yielding to a favoured one. Opposed to this unmaiden-like ferocity, the mother spider often evinces real care for her eggs and young, the Wolf Spider, for example, carrying her eggs in a round cocoon attached to her body until hatched, and then carrying the young till they are old enough to shift for themselves.

Gossamer.—Many young spiders travel by means of a sort of gossamer parachute. Standing on tiptoe, with abdomen elevated, the young spider spins out into the air a silken thread which floats upward. When this is sufficiently long the spider gives a slight jump into the air, and is thus launched on its aerial voyage, to descend at last some distance—perhaps miles—from its starting point. It is these floating threads which, whether in the air or at last entangled in vegetation, are known as gossamer.

One other point I mention in the form of a question which has often been put to me, and *the answer to it is not to be found in any popular book on the subject of spiders* which I have read: When a spider ascends its thread, what does it do with the thread? It does not climb it like

PLATE XVI.

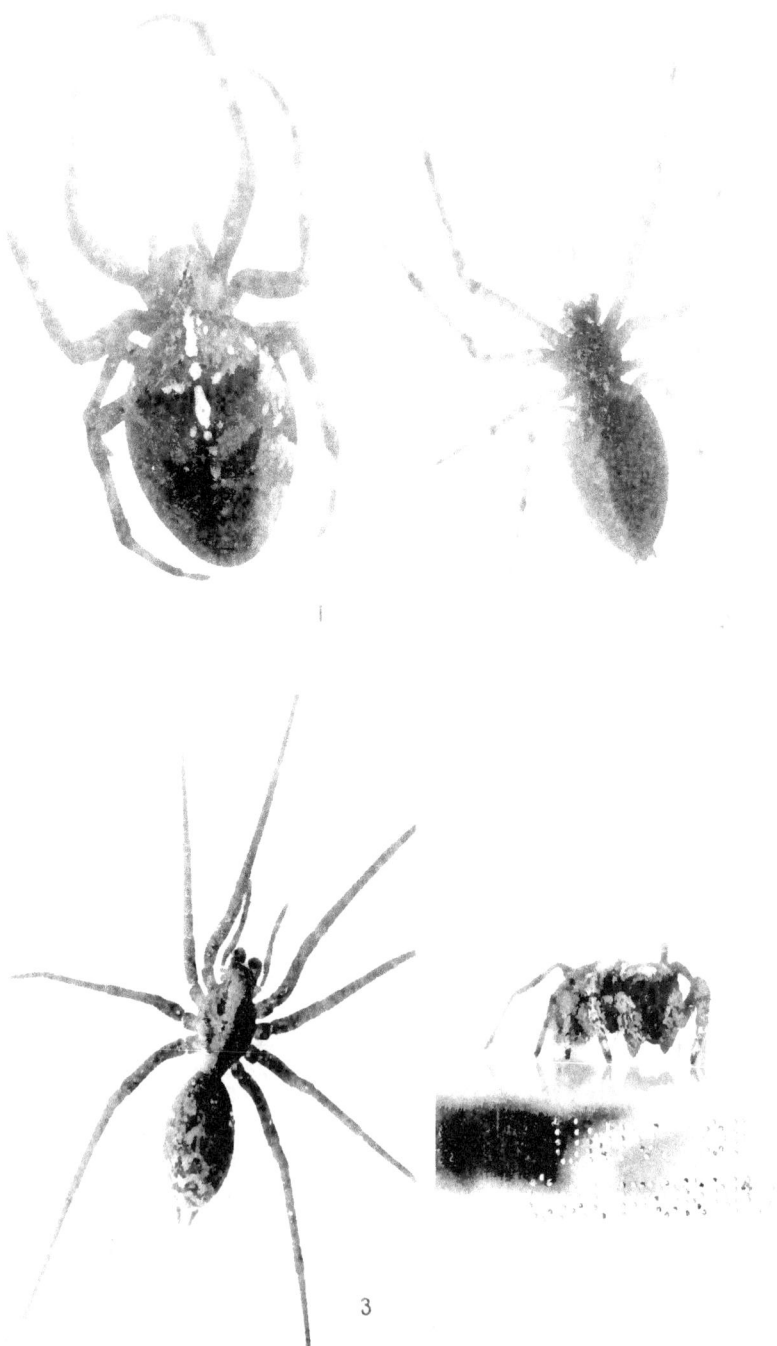

1. Garden Spider (upper side).   2. Garden Spider (under side).
3. House Spider.   4. Wolf Spider.

SPIDERS 173

a rope, leaving it dangling below. It cannot *eat* it, for it climbs too fast for such an operation—though on other occasions it does so. Then what is the answer? It is that the spider rapidly winds up the thread upon its legs in a sort of skein as it ascends. This it can rapidly pay out for the purposes of descent, as may be noticed when a spider ascending its rope suddenly drops four or five inches instantaneously.

The following are the chief families of British spiders:

Tribe I. OCTONOCULINA ("Eight-eyed").
Family i. *Mygalidæ* (only one British representative).
    ,, ii. *Lycosidæ* (Wolf Spiders).
    ,, iii. *Salticidæ* ("Leaping" Spiders).
    ,, iv. *Thomisidæ* (very crab-like in appearance).
    ,, v. *Drassidæ* (including the Water Spiders).
} All catch their prey by hunting; all have three pairs of spinnerets.

    ,, vi. *Ciniflonidæ* (four pairs of spinnerets).
    ,, vii. *Agelenidæ* (weave webs of great extent).
    ,, viii. *Theridiidæ* (snares of irregular masses).
    ,, ix. *Linyphiidæ* (fine horizontal sheets of web).
    ,, x. *Epeiridæ* (the well-known geometric webs).
} All weave snares, and have three pairs of spinnerets (except Family vi.).

Tribe II. SENOCULINA ("Six-eyed").
Family i. *Dysderidæ* (making lairs beneath stones, etc., and hunting their prey).
    ,, ii. *Scytodidæ* (making a slight web; female carrying her cocoon with her, but not attached, as in the case of the *Lycosidæ*).

As so little information is given on this subject in most books, the following notes on some of the species may be of value.

Tribe I. OCTONOCULINA.

Family i. *Mygalidæ*. Genus i. *Atypus*.—Eyes arranged thus: $\overset{\circ\;\circ}{\underset{\circ\;\circ}{}}\quad\overset{\circ\;\circ}{\underset{\circ\;\circ}{}}$; recognized by the great size of the cephalo-thorax and falces; reddish brown. Makes a tunnel in the ground, lined with white silk.

Family ii. *Lycosidæ*. Genus i. *Lycosa*.—Position of eyes: $\begin{smallmatrix}\circ&\circ\\\circ&\circ\\\circ\circ\circ\circ\end{smallmatrix}$ These "Wolf Spiders" make no snares, but carry cocoon and young upon their bodies. The female fights to protect her cocoon, and if deprived of it will remain in the same spot hunting for it—sometimes until she dies. Very rapid in movement when darting on their prey. *Lycosa piratica* pursues its prey on the surface of water, and will dive, if necessary, for refuge. See also ARGYRONETA.

Genus ii. *Dolomedes*.—Position of eyes: $\begin{smallmatrix}\circ&\circ\\\circ&\circ\\\circ&\circ\end{smallmatrix}$; found in wooded districts. One of these carries her cocoon until the time of hatching, when she weaves a large dome on grasses or bushes, under which she remains with the young until they are old enough to manage for themselves.

Genus iii. *Hecaërge.*—Position of eyes: ⁘ ; found in woods. Cocoon flattened, attached to the under side of a stone.

Genus iv. *Sphasus.* Position of eyes: ⁘ . Has a habit of leaping upon its prey, resembling in this way the *Salticidæ*.

Family iii. *Salticidæ.* Genus i. *Eresus.*—Very rare. Crimson and black in colour; not more than ⅓ of an inch. Position of eyes: ⁘ .

Genus ii. *Salticus.*—Eyes thus: ⁘ ; the two middle eyes of the front row being larger than the rest. *S. scenicus* is very common, about ¼ of an inch long; recognized by its zebra-like markings, and its habit of stalking and leaping upon its prey. In so doing it always secures itself by fixing a silk thread to its starting-point, and drawing it out as it jumps. It is thus saved from falling headlong. *S. cupreus*, which is about ¼ of an inch long and has a metallic sheen on the back, places her eggs in some crevice in a nest of silk, and appears to try to disguise it by sticking small particles of earth, etc., on the outside.

Family iv. *Thomisidæ.* Genus i. *Thomisus.*—Position of the eyes: ⁘ ; the larger ones being on slight elevations. They are a very short and broad species, with the first two pairs of legs very long. *T. cristatus* is the commonest, and is one of the species which float on gossamers. It is found hunting on bushes, where it spins long lines to serve as tracks for pursuing its prey; in the autumn this consists of other spiders. *T. citreus* is a species that hides in flowers to await its prey.

Genus ii. *Philodromus.*—Position of the eyes: ⁘ . *P. cæspiticolis* is found on heaths, where its nest, with one or two cocoons, flat and white, may be found on a branch, amidst a cluster of leaves which have been drawn together. The female will savagely defend her eggs if attacked.

Genus iii. *Sparassus.*—Eyes thus: ⁘ ; a very active species in chasing its prey on the ground or grass. *S. smaragdulus* makes a large round cocoon, green in colour, which she places in a cell made of leaves rolled together.

Family v. *Drassidæ.* Genus i. *Drassus.*—Position of eyes: ⁘ . *D. ater* is a nearly black species, which is nocturnal in habit. The nest is a cell of white silk in a hole in the earth or under a stone, and the female keeps close guard on the eggs, which she places in a cocoon within.

Genus ii. *Clubiona.*—Position of the eyes: ⁘ . *C. holosericea*, about

SPIDERS

½ an inch long, is common in wooded districts, on leaves and flowers, under stones, etc. The cell containing the cocoon is under a leaf or in a crevice. Here the female stays, only emerging to seize an insect. The interesting point about this cell is that it contains two chambers, in one of which the male, and in the other the female, resides. They prey largely on the eggs of other spiders, and are themselves liable to attack from predatory insects and other spiders. One insect is known to lay an egg in the cocoon, the larva from which quietly devours the whole of the eggs. *C. corticalis* adorns her cell with particles of earth, sand, fragments of insects, etc., either to disguise it or to make it stronger.

Genus iii. *Argyroneta.*—Position of eyes: °° °°. *A. aquatica* is one of the most remarkable of the British species. The male is larger than the female, which in itself is exceptional among spiders. The abdomen is thickly coated with hairs. These spiders live almost entirely under water, the fine hair of the abdomen being used to entangle a large bubble of air, so that when beneath the water the animal appears to be surrounded by a silver globe. These species are easy to keep in an aquarium, and make most interesting "pets." The female constructs the cell under the water, attached to some plant, in shape like a miniature thimble, and this she fills with air, round it extending threads which serve to entrap various water insects, although occasionally she will leave the water to hunt her prey on land, carrying it when captured to her nest. Here the eggs are laid in the dome, the young on hatching having the air bubble like the adults. During the winter they hibernate in their cells under the water.

Family vi. *Ciniflonidæ.* Genus i. *Ciniflo.*—Position of eyes: °° °°. This species has a fourth pair of spinnerets, and a curious double row of curved spines on the upper joint of the foot, known as the *calamistra*, and used for constructing the remarkable web. This appears at first sight dirty and ragged, but is in reality composed of compound threads curled and twisted in every direction, and covered with almost invisible "flocking," which appears to give a bluish tinge to the whole structure. *C. atrox*, about ⅜ of an inch, has a very poisonous bite, and can attack wasps with impunity. In winter it swathes itself in a warm covering of this flocculent silk.

Genus ii. *Ergatis.*—Position of eyes as in the preceding, but all more nearly of equal size. *E. benigna* makes quite a small web on grass or small plants. Her Latin name indicates that she lives peaceably with her mate; and, indeed, the pair take shares in making the nest. The female is about ⅙ of an inch long.

Genus iii. *Veleda.*—Position of the eyes is uncommon, being in two crescents curved away from the face °° °°.

Family vii. *Agelenidæ.* Genus i. *Agelena.*—Eyes °° °°. *A. labyrinthica* is one of the commonest of this family, found on commons and heaths, where its large, compact white net, spread horizontally, is a familiar sight. From some portion of this web a long tube leads downwards into one or more chambers, open at the farther end. In the mouth the spider may often be seen on the watch for its victims. Another species (*A. elegans*) spreads its snare over holes in the earth, such as hoof-marks of cattle.

Genus ii. *Tegenaria*.—Eyes thus ∴∴, the four middle eyes making almost a perfect square. To this genus belong the Common House Spiders. *T. domestica* places her dusty web in corners of old buildings, covering the cocoon with fragments of whitewash and plaster. The web may last for several seasons, and if vacated by its owner is taken possession of by a newcomer. *T. atica* is found in houses, conservatories, etc. *T. civilis* has been known to live for *four* years in her corner of the ceiling, and to produce several broods.

Genus iii. *Cælotes*.—Eyes ∷ ∷.

Genus iv. *Textrix*.—Eyes ∴ ∴, the middle pair of the back row being largest.

Family viii. *Theridiidæ*. Genus i. *Theridion*.—Position of eyes ∴ ∴. Snares spun on bushes and plants horizontally. *T. lineatum* is very common, and is greenish or yellowish white, sometimes with crimson markings. The cocoon is bluish or greenish in colour. *T. nervosum* ($\frac{1}{6}$ of an inch long) may be found in a bush or shrub in June or July. The web is slight, but forms a kind of pent-house, the nest being quite tent-like in shape, and frequently covered with small dead leaves, or parts of flowers and insects. Within is a round green cocoon, almost always embraced by the female upside down.

Genus ii. *Pholcus*.—Position of eyes ℘∙ ∙℘. *P. phalangoides* has very long legs, and a long narrow abdomen, thus making it easy to identify. Its snares may often be found in the corners of ceilings. The female carries her cocoon in her falces, or jaws, and continues to do this even when the eggs are hatched. The species has a curious habit (shared by a very few species) of agitating the body when alarmed, or when an insect is snared, thus vibrating the web and causing the insect to entangle itself still more firmly by its struggles.

Family ix. *Linyphiidæ*. Genus i. *Linyphia*.—Position of the eyes ∴ ∴. *L. montana* weaves a horizontal snare in hedges, and generally remains in an inverted position on the web, even when moving swiftly. *L. crypticoleus* is found in cellars and dark places, and carries her cocoon fastened to her spinneret.

Genus ii. *Neriene*.—Position of eyes ∴ ∴.

Genus iii. *Walckenaera*.—Some of these have eyes placed on curious projections. The male of *W. acuminata* (about $\frac{1}{7}$ of an inch long) has a high slender horn, on the top of which are two pairs of eyes, and about the middle

PLATE XVII.

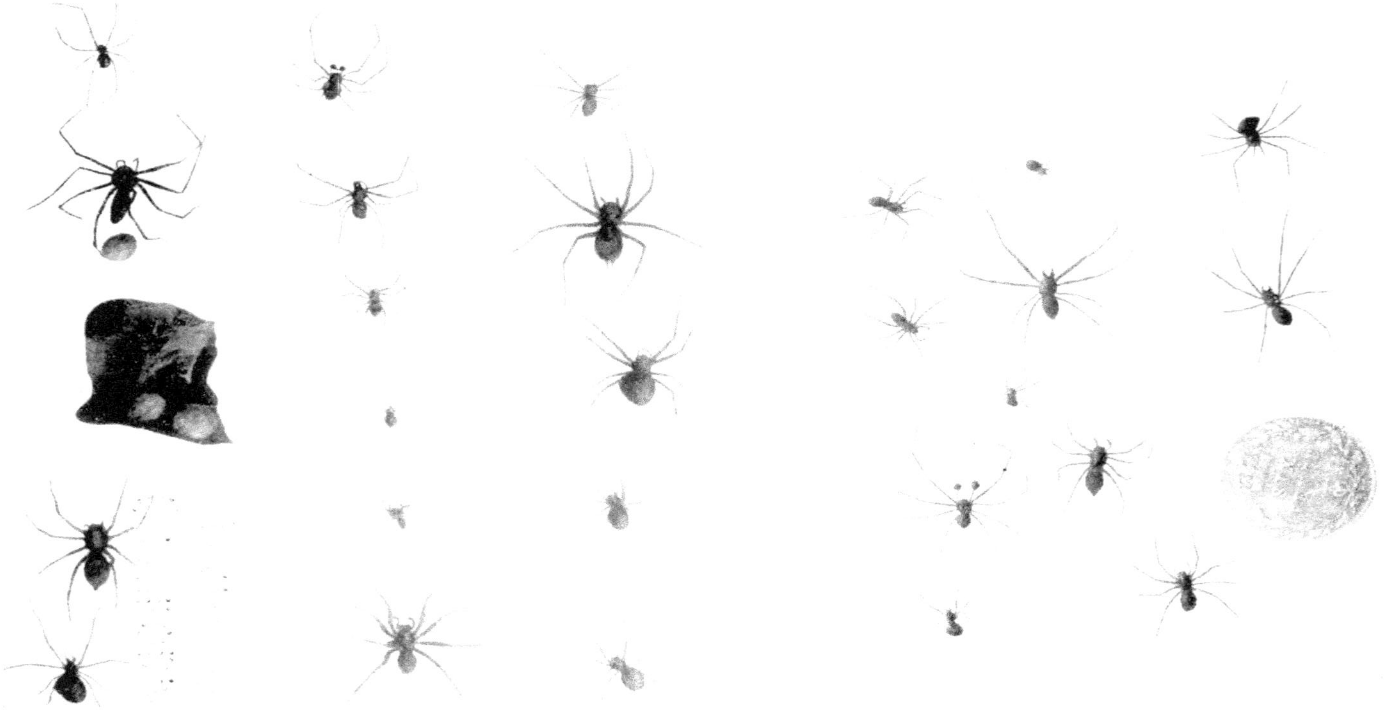

Some Representative British Spiders.

SPIDERS

the other two pairs. All the species have some peculiarity about the cephalothorax, and all are exceedingly small.

Genus iv. *Pachygnatha.*—Eyes ∘∘∘∘ ∘∘∘∘, the outside pairs nearly touching.

Family x. *Epeiridæ.* Genus i. *Epeira.*—Position of eyes, ⁀∘∘⁀, forming three groups, the centre four forming almost a square. These are the most familiar of all the spiders, forming the beautiful geometric webs, already described under the Garden Spider. *E. quadrata* has four principal marks, consisting of four large oval white spots on the abdomen, as well as other white marks. It makes a dome-shaped cell close to its web. *E. umbratica* is an ugly creature of dingy blackish brown, and makes a peculiar web of very large size, with no spiral lines, but curious forked meshes of very irregular dimensions. *E. diadema* is recognized by the cream-coloured cross on its back, made of two chains of spots. This is the species known best as "the Garden Spider." The cocoon is made in October, and the young spiders on emerging the next spring are often seen clustered together in a tiny ball, dispersing in all directions when disturbed, only to collect together again when peace returns. *E. angulata* is recognized by the two humps or projections on each side of the abdomen. *E. callophylla* has a web which is at once recognized by the frequent peculiarity that one section is altogether missing, and the space is intersected by one thread, generally connecting the web with the hiding-place.

Genus ii. *Tetragnatha.*—Eyes ∘∘ ∘∘ ∘∘ ∘∘ on black spots. This species has very large, distending jaws. *T. extensa* has very long front-legs and a long, narrow abdomen, quite unmistakable.

Tribe II. SENOCULINA.

Family i. *Dysderidæ.* Genus i. *Dysdera.*—Eyes six, ∘∘∘∘∘ or ∘∘∘∘∘∘, in a full or partly open circle. These hunt their prey, lurking in crevices and crannies in walls; they are nocturnal in habit. *D. erythrina* is often found in an anthill, where it preys upon the ants.

Genus ii. *Segestria.*—Position of eyes ∘∘∘∘∘∘.

Genus iii. *Schœnobates.*—Position of eyes ∘∘ ∘∘.

Genus iv. *Oonops.*—Position of eyes ∘∘∘∘.

Family ii. *Scytodidæ.* Genus i. *Scytodes.*—Position of eyes ∘ ∘ ∘∘.

It is hoped that this very brief description of a few of the British spiders will at least help the young Nature student to place those he finds in their right family and genus. For further details, he should refer either to Blackwall's great work, or to the most useful book, *British Spiders*, by E. F. Staveley, to which I desire to acknowledge my own indebtedness.

The study of British spiders forms a hobby which comparatively few people have made their own; yet it has some advantages, apart from its intrinsic interest, shared by few other branches of Nature Study. For example, it can be indulged in all the year round, for spiders are found in their natural haunts right through the year—in the winter as well as the summer.

Not very much is needed in the way of paraphernalia. A few chip boxes, or one or two small wide-mouthed bottles, such as pomade bottles; a good net, or an umbrella; a small tin or two in which to carry nests and cocoons; and a few tubes, such as those in which homœopathic remedies are sold, about 3 inches long. The net should be about the size of the ordinary butterfly net, and made of jean, about 16 inches deep. The tubes should be filled with either methylated spirits and water (three parts of spirit to one of water), or a ten per cent. solution of formalin. Personally, I prefer the latter.

The net is used to sweep bushes or grass, when large numbers of spiders may thus be taken and transferred to the tubes. I prefer to kill them at once by placing them for a few minutes in a bottle containing crushed laurel leaves, or a little chloroform, and then to transfer them to the tubes. The spiders from each district should be kept separately, and their place of capture should be written on the label.

Many of the orb-weaving spiders—the *Epeiridæ*—may best be found in the early evening, when they appear upon their webs, constructing or repairing them. It is not a difficult matter to get them to fall direct into the poison bottle if it is held beneath them. During the day many species of ground spiders, and the jumping and wolf spiders, hide under bark or stones, or behind woodwork; whilst decayed trees, old willows, wall-copings, corners of sheds and outbuildings, cellars and lofts should be searched carefully.

Live specimens, brought home in the chip boxes, may be kept alive, a suitable observation cage being made of any small box fitted with a glass front, movable, so that the inmate may be fed with flies or other insects.

Another method of obtaining specimens is to sift over the dead leaves and debris of woods and hedgerows. A simple sieve can be made of 1-inch wire netting; a sheet of newspaper spread below will catch any spiders that fall from the sieve.

Generally the small tubes containing the specimens are placed in larger bottles (wide mouthed and preferably stoppered) containing the same solution as that in the tubes.

A writer in *The Countryside* some years ago advocated an excellent method of preserving spiders which I think is new. He mounted his spiders on strips of porcelain—glass would serve the purpose as well—covered with paraffin wax, the body and legs being placed in position, and fixed by melting the wax in contact with the spider with a hot needle. These slips of porcelain were then kept in bottles, with either methylated spirit or formalin solution.

Unfortunately spiders cannot be mounted or " set " like insects and exposed to the open air. But if it is desired to make the attempt, the spider should be mounted on cardboard, in much the same way as a beetle, and saturated with gumtragacanth, when it will keep fairly well. If it should get covered with mould, a brushing with methylated spirits will remove it instantly.

Harvest Men (*Phalangida*).—These long-legged animals might easily be mistaken for spiders, but are distinguished by their segmented abdomens, and the absence of a definite " waist " (the spider's abdomen has no segmentation). They have two eyes, large pincers, in addition to their long thin legs, and feed upon plant-lice and other small insects.

MITES AND TICKS

are related to spiders, but form a distinct order (*Acarina*). Most of them are exceedingly small, and must be studied with a pocket lens or the microscope. They have oval bodies, and there is no distinction between the cephalothorax and the abdomen. In the adult forms there are eight legs, but some in their earlier stages have only six. The mouth may be an organ for biting, but usually it is adapted for sucking. Some are found in water, others on land. Many are parasites living on the blood of their hosts, others infest insects, still more feed on decaying matter.

Almost any pond will yield specimens of a minute scarlet mite (*Hydrachna*) very active in swimming, with eight legs thickly fringed with hairs. The female makes a puncture in the leaves of pond-weed, and deposits its eggs therein in May or June; from these a red larva with six legs emerges. The mite is a parasite on water beetles in the next stage, driving its sharp beak into the body of its host. Here it often appears to lose or absorb its legs, and grows in size until it becomes the adult eight-legged free swimming **Water Mite**.

Another mite (*Gamasus coleoptratorum*) is exceedingly common on beetles and bees. Examine a Watchman Beetle, or a Humble Bee, and frequently you will find it covered underneath with these creatures. The so-called " RED SPIDER " is in reality another mite most destructive to plants.

The **Cheese Mite** (*Tyroglyphus siro*) is another familiar species, the larvæ having three pairs of legs, and passing through a " nymph " or pupal stage with eight legs before assuming the adult form.

The **Harvest Bug**, which so torments people with delicate skins, is really the *larva* of the mite *Trombidium holosericeum*. It is a bright scarlet, but so small as to be hardly visible to the naked eye. The eggs are laid in June and July, and produce a six-legged larva, almost round, which finds a host to live on, and thrusts its sharp mandibles into the skin. Then it swells to nearly five times its original size with the fluid it imbibes, drops off and hibernates, turning next spring into an eight-legged nymph, which feeds upon vegetation only.

Class III. MYRIAPODA—Centipedes.

Centipedes and Millipedes are to be found in the earth, under stones and logs, amongst grass, and in many other places. There are more than fifty species to be found in England; but little is known of them, as they have not been studied to any great extent. They are worm-shaped creatures, and breathe by means of air tubes. The Centipedes have flattened bodies, divided into many segments, with a pair of legs on each segment, the first pair being modified into piercing poison organs, with which they seize their prey. They are swift and ferocious, feeding on worms, flies, and larvæ. One species (*Geophilus electricus*) emits light in the dark like a glow-worm; but, unlike that insect, leaves a slight trail upon the ground behind it.

The commonest is the **Red Centipede** (*Lithobius forficatus*), often found under stones. It has fifteen pairs of legs, and possesses eyes. It attacks worms, pursuing them, like a weasel, down their burrows. I have kept this species for a long time in a case containing damp earth, feeding them on insects and worms. When the female lays an egg, she grasps it in two small hooks on her under surface, and rolls it round and round on the earth till it is covered with soil. This is done to disguise it from the male, which would otherwise devour it. In fact, on occasion the female has to run away from the male with her egg to reach some secure spot, where she can deposit it and cover it with earth.

Millipedes have rounded bodies and very numerous legs—for example, the Common Snake Millipede has ninety-nine pairs! They are slow-moving creatures, feeding entirely on vegetable diet; they possess along the body certain "stink-glands," through which they can emit an unpleasant smell, presumably to ward off animals or birds eager to devour them.

One of the most common, *Julus terrustris*, is miscalled the WIRE-WORM, a name that belongs really to the larva of the CLICK BEETLE (which see). It can be kept under observation, using for food slices of apple, grass, etc. When alarmed, it rolls itself into a ring and feigns death. In early summer the female makes a "nest," consisting of a hollow ball of particles of earth, glued together by a sticky secretion, about as large as a small acorn, and placed if possible under ground. Through a small hole in the top she passes from sixty to one hundred eggs, which are covered with some sticky fluid, and thus adhere together. Then she closes the hole and leaves the eggs to hatch, which they do in about twelve days. At first they possess but three pairs of legs, but each time they moult they increase the number of segments and limbs. The Wire-worms may be distinguished from Centipedes by the absence of any poison claws as well as by the rounded body.

PLATE XVIII.

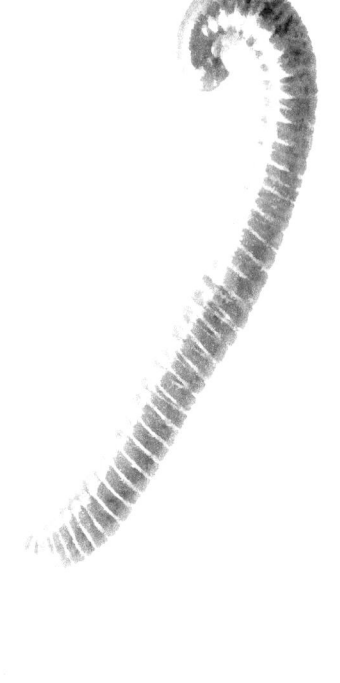

1. "Money-pinner" or "Harvester."   2. Hydra, budding (enlarged).   3. Water flea (enlarged).   4. Millipede (enlarged).

INSECTS 181

Class IV. Insects.

The word *insect* is popularly but mistakenly used of all sorts of small creatures—not only of Flies, Moths, and Butterflies, but also of Spiders, Centipedes, and others. It is necessary therefore to define as briefly as possible the kind of creature to which the term is properly applied. First, its derivation teaches us something. It comes from the Latin "to cut into," and therefore refers to the three distinct divisions of a true insect's body—head, thorax, and abdomen—which are often separated from each other by an exceedingly small neck and waist. No such threefold division characterizes the Spider or the Centipede. Second, all insects reach their full adult stage through certain changes or *metamorphoses*—from the egg to the grub, larva, or caterpillar. This, when full grown, changes to a *pupa* or chrysalis, and from this the perfect insect, or *imago*, finally emerges. The larvæ are usually very voracious feeders, and as they grow, change or moult their skins several times; but the pupæ, as a rule, are inactive, eating nothing, and generally encased in cocoon or hidden underground, or in some other place of concealment. During this period a remarkable change gradually takes place, the organs of the larval form disappearing, and those of the perfect insect being formed.

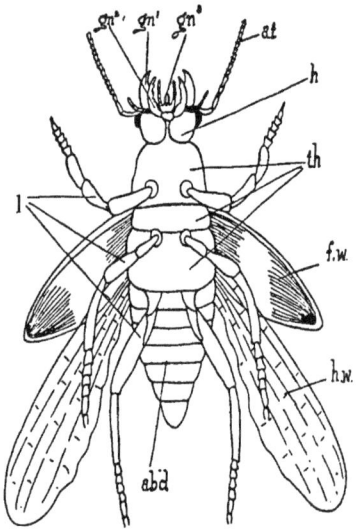

A Beetle viewed from below as an example of Insecta: *at*, single pair of antennæ; *abd*, abdomen; *f.w.*, fore-wing; gn^1, gn^2, gn^3, the three pairs of gnathites; *h.w.*, hind-wing; *h*, head; *l*, walking legs; *th*, thorax.

The perfect insect has always three pairs of legs, and generally two pairs of wings, though many, such as flies and gnats, have but one pair; and some, like fleas, have none developed for flying. All insects breathe by means of air-tubes, called tracheæ, opening along the sides of the abdomen into stigmata, or spiracles—very minute "little mouths" through which the air enters. They also possess two sensitive organs of touch—the antennæ, or feelers, which are of very varied form, and by which it is probable they hear, smell, and touch. They live by gnawing or sucking—in the former case having mouths specially formed for the purpose; in the latter having a *proboscis* or trunk (often called the tongue) running out from the lower lip. Again, most insects have two large eyes, consisting of a vast number of small lenses grouped together, thus

THE BRITISH NATURE BOOK

enabling the insect to see in many different directions without turning its head. In addition, there are often three or four single eyes set between them.

An insect, then, is an animal whose body is in three divisions, and has six legs in the perfect state; it breathes through tracheæ, and attains its full development through changes or metamorphoses.

The insect world is so vast that it has been necessarily classified into the following groups or orders:—

I. ORTHOPTERA (Straight-winged Insects—Earwigs, Cockroaches, etc).
II. NEUROPTERA (Nerve-winged Insects—the Dragon-flies, etc.).
III. COLEOPTERA (Sheath-winged Insects or Beetles).
IV. HYMENOPTERA (Membrane-winged Insects—such as Ants, Bees, and Wasps).
V. LEPIDOPTERA (Scale-winged Insects—Butterflies and Moths).
VI. and VII. DIPTERA and HEMIPTERA (Two-winged and Half-winged Insects—such as Bugs, Frog-hoppers, Gnats, etc.).

In the first three orders the mouth parts are adapted for biting. In the fourth (*Hymenoptera*), usually for licking and sucking. In Orders V., VI., and VII., for sucking, or for piercing and sucking. This arrangement, however, is inadequate, and the most modern classification recognizes nineteen orders; and though it is impossible to deal with them in any detail, it will be best to adopt this latest scheme, in order that students may have at least the right basis for their future studies.

Order I. APTERA.

As the name signifies, this order consists of "wingless" insects, and contains the lowest of all the insect species, the "**Bristle-tails**" and "**Fish-insects**," many of which are covered with shining scales. They are all very small. One, *Campodea staphylinus*, is nearly white, and may often be found in gardens under dead leaves. Another, *Lepisma saccharina*, known as the "**Silver-fish**," is found in pantries and cupboards. It feeds upon all sorts of materials, and often damages prints and books. Another species is found in bakehouses.

"**Spring-tails**" are included in this order. They possess a curious fork beneath the abdomen, by means of which they can jerk themselves into the air. They may be found in decaying vegetation, in stagnant pools, under bark, etc.

Order II. DERMAPTERA.

In this order the **Earwigs** are found. These insects have no fore-wings proper, but in their place a pair of oblong plates, under which the hind-wings are sheltered. These are beautiful fan-like structures, not often used, shaped like an *ear*—hence, according to some, the name "earwings," corrupted to "earwigs"; but the popular derivation of the word is connected with the supposed habit of this insect to crawl into people's ears! This is, however,

EARWIG, COCKROACH, GRASSHOPPER 183

a very exceptional occurrence, and quite obviously can only take place when an insect has fallen on one's head, and is seeking a hiding-place. The formidable forceps or pincers at the end of the abdomen are sometimes used for folding and packing up the wings after flight. Although the insect can cling to your finger with these pincers, it cannot pierce the skin. It is nocturnal in habit, hiding by day under stones or in crevices. It feeds generally on vegetation, though it also attacks and devours other insects. The young pass through an imperfect metamorphosis, and resemble their parents, except that the wings are absent. The common British species, *Forficula auricularia*, is too well known to need further description, but there are several species characterized by their varying size and by the shape of the forceps.

The female earwig shows remarkable maternal care; she lays her eggs in a depression in the ground, sits on them, and when hatched, attends upon them like a hen with her chickens!

Order III. ORTHOPTERA.

To this order belong the British Cockroaches, Grasshoppers, and Crickets, and the foreign (but well-known) Locusts, Stick-insects, and Praying Mantids.

THE COCKROACH.

There are three true British species, found in moss, dead leaves, and low vegetation; but others which have come to us from abroad are all too well known—for example, the **German Cockroach** (*Phyllodromia germanica*), the **American Cockroach** (*Periplaneta americana*), and the common "**Black Beetle**" (so-called) of our kitchens (*Blatta orientalis*)—the latter said to have been introduced to this country two hundred years ago. The female, whose wings are undeveloped in some species, lays sixteen eggs in a curious purse-like capsule, which is placed in some secluded crevice. The young when first hatched are colourless, except for their black eyes. It is not until it is three years old that the adult form is assumed. Most species are nocturnal in habit, feeding on most varied menus.

GRASSHOPPERS (*Locustidæ*).

Several species of these insects are found in Great Britain; all are distinguished by the great length and power of the hind-legs in leaping, and they have remarkable organs of hearing, or "ears," as well as an apparatus for producing chirping sounds. The "ear" is found at the base of the last pair of legs, upon the abdomen, and the chirping sound is produced by the male's wings in the following manner. On the right wing-cover (and sometimes the left as well) is a transparent round membrane stretched on a ring—a kind of drum, in fact—and on the under side of the opposite wing-cover is a serrated ridge, a small file; this is the bow, while the membrane aforesaid is the fiddle of the insect's music, the grasshopper producing it by rubbing the left wing over a ridge on the right. The females have long "tails"—in reality ovipositors—that is, instruments by which the eggs are laid. Whilst many feed on vegetation, most species catch (with their fore-legs) and devour flies and caterpillars. The eggs are laid in the earth, or in some dry stem in the autumn, from which larvæ very like the adults are produced in the following spring; these moult five or six times before assuming the adult form.

The **Great Green Grasshopper** (*Locusta viridissima*) belongs to the LONG-HORNED or TREE GRASSHOPPERS (*Phasgonuridæ*), which feed on leaves. It is about 2 inches long, and green in colour. The **Common Grasshopper** is smaller, and belongs to the SHORT-HORNED GRASSHOPPERS, or true LOCUSTS. Another British species is *Decticus verrucivorus*, which gets its name from the habit of Swedish peasants who make it bite their warts, which the fluid secretion from the insect's mouth is said to cure.

CRICKETS (*Gryllidæ*).

These resemble the grasshoppers in many respects, having "ears" and chirping organs. Four species are found in Britain. The **Wood Cricket** (*Nemobius sylvestris*) is very local—only found in the New Forest. The **Mole Cricket** (*Gryllotalpa vulgaris*) is a very curious species, about 2 inches long, having enormous, broad fore-legs, like the fore-limbs of a mole, specially adapted for burrowing underground. It is by no means common, but may sometimes be seen flying in the evenings. It is of a greyish brown colour, with a silken sheen. The eggs, encased in a cocoon, are laid underground, the larvæ taking some years to mature. Whilst the Mole Cricket does some damage by destroying the roots of crops, it is far more largely carnivorous. I have kept this curious insect for some time in a glass-covered box in damp soil, and have seen it attack small worms, grubs, and larvæ.

The **House Cricket** (*Gryllus domesticus*), the most familiar of all insects of the house, and regarded as "lucky," as witness Dickens's *Cricket on the Hearth*. It has a whitish yellow body about half an inch long, hiding in chinks and crevices, close to the fire. Indeed, away from the heat it becomes dormant in the winter. The larva is wingless, the pupa also having only rudimentary wings. It hunts actively at night for crumbs and other scraps of food.

The **Field Cricket** (*Gryllus campestris*) is a very local species, black in colour, burrowing underground, and doing damage to vegetables. It is common on the Continent.

Order IV. PLECOPTERA.

Stone-flies.—Of these some twenty-four species occur in Britain. The eggs are laid in water, and the larvæ and nymphal forms are aquatic, resembling

PLATE XIX.

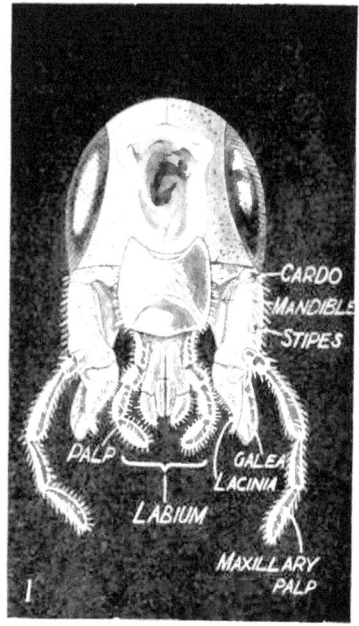
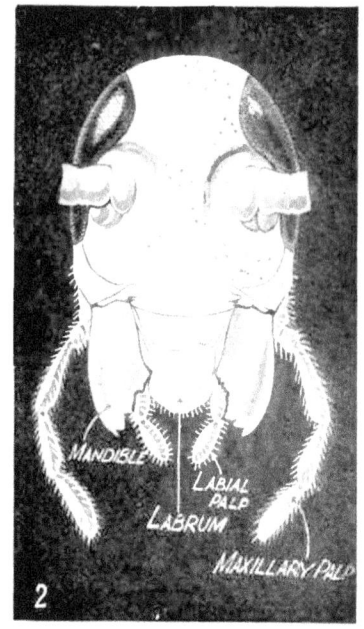

1. Head of Cockroach (from behind).
2. Front view.
3. "Cuckoo Spit."
4. Aphides on a Rosebud.

INSECTS—MAYFLIES AND DRAGON-FLIES

the perfect insect, but without wings. The adult insect is "stone-coloured"; one of them, *Perla bicaudata*, is well known as a good bait for trout and other fishes.

Order V. ISOPTERA.

None of these occur in Britain; the **White Ant**, or TERMITE, is the representative.

Order VI. CORRODENTIA.

Under this order come the **Book-lice** and **Bird-lice**. The former are minute, soft-bodied insects, which never develop wings. *Atropos divinatoria* is common in damp housés. Some damage books and papers, and others destroy entomological collections. The Bird-lice are also wingless, and spend their lives on the plumage of birds or the fur of animals, feeding on the delicate feathers and hairs.

Order VII. EPHEMEROPTERA.

Mayflies.—These insects, familiar to all dwellers by streams and rivers, are a very large family—more than 300 species in all parts of the world. Their adult form is very peculiar, owing to the fragile wings (very delicate and beautiful), their two or three long tails or *cerci*, and their short bristle-like antennæ. The mouth parts are very undeveloped, and in some cases absent altogether, which means that the adults do not feed. Indeed, they require no food, since they live for a few hours only—" creatures of a day," as their name *Ephemera* signifies. Within a single twilight, it may be, they dance jerkily up and down over the water, in a characteristic flight, deposit their eggs, and fall dead; but some two years are spent in the earlier stages. Their eggs, united into a little mass, are allowed to fall into the water, where the larvæ burrow into the mud, feeding on decaying vegetation; the pupa, or nymph, also is aquatic, and leaves the water to change into the adult form. This is called a "false imago," kn‚wn to anglers as the **"Green Drake."** Within a short time the skin splits, and the true imago emerges, being called by fishermen the **"Grey Drake."** The commonest are *Ephemera vulgata* and *E. danica*.

Order VIII. ODONATA.

Here we meet the

DRAGON-FLIES,

more than forty species of which are found in Britain. Their shape and form are well known, the characteristics being a very large head, which can be moved freely; enormous compound eyes, consisting of thousands of lenses, and three simple eyes on the forehead or brow; remarkable mouth parts, formed for biting, the jaws or maxillæ forming a kind of trap for holding the insects on which the Dragon-fly feeds; a thorax, which slopes forward so that

THE BRITISH NATURE BOOK

the legs, grouping beneath the mouth, form an additional basket for holding the prey; while the abdomen is very long and slender and ends in a pair of forceps, which look formidable enough, but are quite harmless. In spite of popular belief, no Dragon-fly can sting. The wings are of glassy, lace-like texture, all four being approximately the same size.

The eggs are laid in or near the water, the larvæ being aquatic. They are ferocious creatures, living upon other larvæ, worms, tadpoles, and any living thing they can master. They can swim rapidly, possessing a special organ by which they discharge a jet of water, thus propelling themselves forward. The pupa is very similar, but possesses rudimentary wings. The larvæ are provided with a curious underjaw, or "mask," which is folded beneath the head, but can be shot forward to seize the prey, which are held by means of terminal hooks and drawn back to the mouth. When the time for emergence comes (after eleven months) the pupa leaves the water, and climbing up a rush or other water plant, its skin splits down the back and the winged insect appears.

The following are some of the commoner species:—

The Great Dragon-fly (*Æschna grandis*), about 4 inches long, with proportionate wings of light brown colour with paler markings.

The Horse Stinger—an entire misnomer—(*Libellula depressa*), which has a much shorter body, very much flattened, yellow in the female and blue in the male.

The Demoiselle, a most beautiful species about 2 inches long, very graceful and slender—the male coloured a deep metallic blue, with prominent black patches on the wings; the female green.

This species is often found in large numbers, the pupæ (nymphs) having emerged practically all at the same time. I have seen fifty or sixty at once hawking over a few yards of river.

Calopteryx Virgo—a deep metallic blue on the wings as well as the body of the male, the female being of a coppery lustre.

Order IX. THYSANOPTERA.

THRIPS.

These are very minute insects, frequently found in flowers. Many possess no wings, but others have exceedingly narrow wings, fringed with hairs; the larvæ are very much like the parents, but lack wings. Many do considerable damage to crops. The **Corn Thrip** (*Thrips cerealium*) sucks the sap from wheat and other cereals, whilst *Thrips pisivora* attacks peas and beans.

Order X. HEMIPTERA.

Sub-order i. *Heteroptera*.

Bugs, Aphides, etc., are included in this large Order.

These are true bugs, having fore-wings of a leathery texture, with a

INSECTS—BUGS

small portion near the tip transparent; the hind-wings are membranous, and are folded beneath the others except when in flight. There are more than 10,000 species; but fortunately few, comparatively speaking, are British. They possess a long sucking proboscis, curved down beneath their bodies. Most suck the juices of plants, but some prey on smaller insects and a few on animals. **Shield-bugs**, of which we possess but few species, are identified by the shield or plate which covers the whole of the wings. **Pentagonal Shield-bugs** have five-sided shields. These may be found among bushes; they are brown or green in colour and about half an inch long. The most notorious of all is the **Bed-bug** (*Cimex* or *Acanthia lectularia*), a wingless insect, with a very flat body and almost circular abdomen. During the day it lurks in crevices and cracks, to emerge at night in search of its victim, from which (and all too frequently from *whom*) it sucks the blood until it is enormously distended. The female lays fifty eggs four times a year, between March and September, the larvæ being like the parents. The first three broods reach maturity in about eleven weeks, the last brood appears to perish, while the adults survive through the winter. This insect appears to have come from the East, and was known both to Greeks and Romans. It emits an offensive smell (like the Pentagonal Shield-bugs). Other species infest pigeons and swallows.

There are many other species known as **Field-bugs** and **Water-bugs**, the latter being entirely *aquatic*. One of the former, *Acanthosoma griseum*, a British species, found in birch trees, shows remarkable maternal care, the female conducting her thirty or forty young as a hen with her chickens, showing great uneasiness when they seem threatened with danger, and waiting by them instead of trying to make her own escape.

There are three familiar "Water-bugs," to which a brief allusion must suffice.

The Water-boatman (*Notonecta glauca*).—The third pair of legs are remarkably long and fringed with hairs, and are used as oars; the insect rows itself along on its back, and when resting with these rowing legs thrown out " looks like a waterman resting on his sculls." The insect is about half an inch long, and usually a brownish green in colour. It can fly well, but prefers to keep in the water. It can remain under water for some time, taking down a supply of air entangled in the hairs that fringe certain ridges on the abdomen, which thus serve as air chambers. The food consists of animal substances, and it attacks and devours small larvæ, fish spawn, etc.

Corixa is a similar Water-bug, but swims the right way up. It has a curious habit of rubbing its fore-legs across its forehead, probably producing a *call-note*; for it is an ascertained fact that these insects can do so, and, conversely, can hear.

The Water Scorpion (*Nepa cinerea*) is to be found in many shallow ponds and pools, where it will be almost buried in the mud, with its remarkable seizing legs extended. These are the first pair, which have been modified

THE BRITISH NATURE BOOK

into limbs like the pedipalps of a scorpion—hence the name. I have kept these insects under observation in a small aquarium; they are extremely interesting but very rapacious, and no other small aquatic creatures must be kept with them. They measure about an inch long, and are identified by their scorpion-like "jaws" and the long tube (often miscalled tail) at the end of the abdomen, by which the insect breathes. This it does by coming to the surface, turning upside down, and pushing its tube through to the air. The "jaws"—that is, the front-legs—are not unlike a pocket-knife in action, the first joint being the blade, which fits into a groove in the second joint, and thus holds its victim in a veritable vice. It feeds on all sorts of small water-creatures, larvæ, shrimps, tadpoles, and small fish. The insect can fly well, and indeed leaves the water frequently at dusk; therefore, if kept in confinement the top of the aquarium must remain covered.

It is a peculiarly fierce creature in the water, and will destroy far more victims than it requires for food.

Sub-order ii. *Homoptera*.

Under this heading come the *Cicadas* (of which one small species is occasionally found in Britain), Lantern-flies, Froghoppers, Aphides, scale insects, and others.

Lantern-flies, several small species of which are found in Britain, are so called from the curious processes projecting from the head of some species. Many have brilliantly coloured wings.

Froghoppers.—The commonest British species is well known as the **Cuckoo-spit Insect** (*Philænus spumarius*), so called because the white froth found on grasses and bushes in spring time, in which the larva (and nymph) resides, was supposed to be the saliva of the cuckoo. The fact, however, is that the little yellowish green creature sucks the juices of its plant-host, and therewith surrounds itself with the "froth" which issues from its body. What purpose this serves is not known, but probably it helps to protect the insect from its foes. The nymphs may be distinguished by their rudimentary wings. The perfect insects have remarkable leaping powers, as the name suggests.

Plant-lice (*Aphides*), known as GREEN-FLY, or BLIGHT, found too numerously on our rose trees, consist of many species, which live by plunging their piercing proboscis into the juicy tissues of the young shoots to suck the sap. Many species have a pair of teats or tubes on the abdomen which secrete a waxy substance appearing at first as oil-like globules. Ants frequently find their way up rose trees for the purpose of "milking" these insects. The sweet liquid called "honey-dew," noticeable under lime trees, was supposed to be this substance; but it is now known to be derived, not from the tubes, but from the alimentary canal of these plant-lice. Typical aphides have two pairs of wings, but most (in the majority of species) are quite wingless.

PLATE XX.

1. A Springtail (*Papirius*). 2. Cockroaches. 3. Silver Fish (*Lepisma saccharina*). 4. Stag Beetle in defensive attitude.
(*Orchesella*)

INSECTS—APHIS, SCALES 189

The life-history of the aphis is very remarkable. Their extraordinary abundance is due to their peculiar method of reproduction. In the autumn numerous eggs are laid in the crevices of bark, which hatch the next spring, producing wingless females. These females actually produce *young* like themselves, no male being necessary; and this remarkable reproduction goes on for several generations, the young aphis herself becoming a mother in ten or fifteen days. Hence in a few weeks the offspring of a single individual become very numerous. Some of the young aphides of these broods have two pairs of wings: these are usually females. In the autumn, both males and females are born, and these pair, the fertilized eggs which ensue being those which will hatch out the next spring.

Many insects feed on the aphides, and are therefore friends of the gardener; especially Wasps, Lady-birds (larvæ and imagoes), the larvæ of the Lacewing-fly and of Hover-flies.

THE SCALE INSECTS AND "MEALY BUGS" (*Coccida*)

are very small, but many are most injurious to plants. The males have long antennæ and a pair of wings; the females are slow-moving, grub-like creatures. The best known is the **Mussel Scale**, or BARK-LOUSE, found on apple trees. Another is the **Brown Scale** of the gooseberry and currant trees, the male of which has not yet been discovered. The female is unable to move long before she lays eggs, owing to her bulk; and as she lays, her under surface shrinks until she assumes a sort of dish-cover appearance, under which are hundreds of whitish eggs. She dies in this position, her dead body, the so-called scale, acting as a protection to the eggs, and for a short period to the larvæ.

Order XI. ANOPLURA.

The True Lice.—These are wingless, possibly having lost their wings and become simplified through their parasitic habits. They possess flat bodies, legs furnished with grasping claws, and a sucking beak provided with a circle of hooks near the end. The eggs known as "nits" are pear shaped, and are attached to hairs, feathers, and the like.

Order XII. NEUROPTERA.

ALDER-FLIES, ANT-LIONS (not found in England),
LACEWINGS, AND OTHERS.

Alder-flies (*Sialida*), well known to the angler, are slow and heavy-flying insects, distinguished from Caddis-flies by the fact that the wings are not folded longitudinally when at rest. They lay their eggs in clusters on the leaves or stems of aquatic plants, and the larvæ when hatched enter the water, where they prey on other creatures. When full fed they leave the water and burrow in the earth, where they pupate, eventually changing to the perfect insect about midsummer. The **Common Alder-fly** is *Sialis lutaria*. **Snake-flies** (*Raphididæ*) are recognized by their large heads and long necks, these and the thorax having a distinct snake-like appearance. There are four British species; the larvæ live in rotten wood or under bark and prey upon small insects, throwing themselves when alarmed into very grotesque positions.

Lacewing-flies.—These are pale green, with beautiful eyes of a metallic lustre, and are to be encouraged, for the larvæ feed on aphides, from which they suck the juices. The eggs are most remarkable objects, each on a long stalk, and laid in clusters. The female lays on the leaf or twig a drop of sticky substance, and draws it upwards into a thread, at the top of which the egg is attached. Some of the larvæ cover themselves with the dried bodies of the aphides on which they have fed, thus obtaining a protective device which effectively conceals them from their enemies.

CHAPTER VIII.

Arthropoda (*continued*).

Order XIII. COLEOPTERA.

THIS, the largest order of insects, comprises the beetles, of which we have nearly 4,000 species in Great Britain alone. Obviously, therefore, it is impossible to deal with more than a selection in this book. The collecting of these insects makes a fascinating hobby for the young nature student, and therefore some brief directions may be given as to how to catch and mount them.

First of all, the would-be collector must know where to expect to find the specimens he is seeking—whether under stones or bark, in decaying wood, dung, or carrion, in low herbage and rough grass, and so forth; and as far as possible details are given in the following notes of the figured species. Some may be taken by beating the bushes, holding a cloth or an umbrella underneath into which they may fall, whilst others are taken by sweeping the bushes and rank grass with a strong net. They may be placed in small bottles or glass tubes alive, but carnivorous species should be confined separately, or they may attack the others. I think, however, that the best plan of all is to place them in a wide-mouthed bottle containing fresh crushed laurel leaves, for here they are quickly killed by the fumes given off by the leaves, and are also protected from damage amongst the fragments of laurel on which they lie. A pickle bottle with a metal-topped cork makes an ideal receptacle for this purpose. Otherwise all hard-bodied beetles may be killed by being put in boiling water, but the method advocated above is, in my opinion, preferable.

Most collectors set their specimens by gluing them to slips of cardboard, just touching their legs with the gum and then arranging them on the card. This is the simplest and easiest way, although they may also be set, like butterflies and moths, on a pin through the right elytron.

"Coleoptera" means "sheath-winged" (from the Greek *koleos*, "a sheath," and *pteron*, "a wing"). It is an obviously appropriate name for beetles, for their real wings are kept folded up under a pair of hard horny covers, or wing-cases (in reality, the specially modified fore-wings). These are called elytra, and are not used in flight, except as balancers or "planes." The true wings are membranous, of a peculiar parchment-like appearance. In many species the wing-cases do not completely cover the abdomen, and in others the true wings are only rudimentary or even non-existent. The male of the Glow-worm, for example, can fly, but the female has no wings or elytra.

The hard, shell-like material which protects the soft inner body is called "chitin," and is in reality the skeleton (technically, exoskeleton) of the insect. The eyes are compound, though some species have two simple eyes in addition. In some cases these compound eyes are divided nearly in two by a process on the side of the head, as, for example, in some of the Water Beetles.

It is, however, in the *antennæ* that the most striking feature of beetles is seen. These vary in shape in different species, and are thereby of great use in classifying the species. They may be simple, thread-like forms, known as filiform, serrate (or saw-like), pectinate (comb-like), capitate (with a head), clavate (clubbed), lamellate (plated), geniculate (elbowed), etc. The *foot* also is an important feature in classification. This (usually called the *tarsus*) has generally five joints, on the last of which are a pair of claws; but in many cases it will be found that this number varies. The five-toed species form a large section—the *Pentamera;* a second group, the *Heteromera*, have five "toes" on the first and second pair of legs, but only four on the third pair; the *Tetramera* have four "toes" to all their legs; whilst the *Trimera* have (apparently) only three "toes" to a leg.

The elytra—that is, the wing-cases—vary also in form. Some are grooved or furrowed, these marks being known as *striæ;* others are covered with tiny holes or punctures, which may be fine or coarse, deep or shallow. In many cases beetles are clad in soft down, usually called "pubescence."

The life-history is much the same as that of other insects. First the egg, generally laid by the female in a selected spot where the larva can find food without difficulty—in the ground at the roots of trees, in pellets of dung, rolled up in leaves, etc. The larvæ vary in the different species, some having three pairs of legs, but others being entirely legless. Some have bodies protected by flat horny plates, others are quite soft and easily damaged. Some reach their pupal stage in a few weeks, others remain as larvæ for two or three years. In the case of those which remain underground, feeding on roots, it may be imagined how destructive they are.

In the pupal stage some are encased in a cocoon, others suspended by the tail, others remain hidden in the old larval skin, on or beneath the ground. Whilst in this condition they take no food, but gradually darken in colour, and finally, shedding a transparent skin, appear as soft beetles, very soon hardening and assuming the perfect condition.

As soon as the collector makes a start, he will be surprised at the many varied colours of the species he captures, for beetles appear to be tinted in almost every metallic hue—green, blue, bronze, tinged with pink and yellow, as well as brown, black, and grey. The species vary also in size from the great Stag-beetle to the smallest, almost microscopic specimen that flies into one's eye.

Many, it is true, are injurious to plants and trees, feeding upon the roots

PLATE XXI.

Representative British Beetles.

BEETLES

or fruits; but against this must be set a multitude of species which are beneficial. The latter feed on carrion, dung, and other refuse, acting thus as Nature's dustmen, others devour aphides and other insects, whilst the Glowworm, for example, is the foe of snails and slugs.

Some Common British Beetles.

Sub-order i. ADEPHAGA (from the Greek *adephagos*, "ravenous").

This name is given because many of the beetles included are carnivorous and predaceous creatures, moving swiftly after the caterpillars, snails, and small insects on which they feed. Some live on the ground (*geodephaga*), others in water. They have filiform or thread-like antennæ; five joints to their feet, the legs being long and slender; mouth parts, as is obvious, adapted for their carnivorous habits.

Family: *Cicindelidæ*—"TIGER" BEETLES.

The eggs are laid in the ground. The larvæ have dark horny heads, and curious angular bodies, the eighth segment carrying two spines curving backwards. They make a burrow about a foot deep, using the spines as climbing hooks. When complete, the larva remains at the top with its head protruding, awaiting its prey, which is seized and conveyed into the burrow. The full-grown beetles have long thin legs, adapted for running.

C. campestris (Fig. 1), the **Green Tiger Beetle.**—About ½ inch long; bright green, tinged at the edges and on the legs with coppery red, five whitish yellow spots on the wing-cases. Common, found in sandy places; especially fond of sunshine.

C. germanica (Fig. 2), **Small Tiger.**—The smallest British "Tiger," dark green, with a few faint spots. Found in grassy places; seeks safety by running, unlike the other species, which usually take to the wing.

C. sylvaticæ, the **Wood Tiger Beetle.**—Larger than the Green Tiger Beetle; coppery black, with irregular whitish marks on the elytra, well-pitted. Found locally on sandy heaths in Surrey and Hants.

Blethisa multipunctata (Fig. 3).—Thorax flat and squarish. Found near pools and in damp meadows, often in decaying vegetation.

Family: *Carabidæ*—CARNIVOROUS GROUND BEETLES.

A large family (thirteen thousand known species in the world); generally black. Very useful, as they feed on worms, larvæ, and insects. Foot five-jointed; antennæ thread-like. Many species have only rudimentary wings, having lost the power of flight. Found under moss, stones, bark, dung, etc.

Cychrus rostratus (the only British representative of this genus).—Black;

¾ inch long; has a rounded pearl-shaped body, not so long as the typical beetle, head narrowing into a beak. Found in sand-pits and woods. Widely distributed.

Carabus catenulatus.—Black, with violet margins; about 1 inch long; wing-cases grooved with fine broken lines. Common. (The genus *Carabus* includes the true Ground Beetles, many of which are of bright metallic colouring. As a rule they seek their prey by night. They possess as a means of defence the power to eject a strong fluid, which has caustic properties.)

C. granulatus (Fig. 6).—A dark bronze-coloured beetle, with black antennæ. Common; found in swampy places.

C. niteus (Fig. 7).—The smallest of this genus in Britain; a brilliant green, with coppery red edges; three black ridges on the elytra. Found on moors and mosses.

C. violaceus (Fig. 8), the **Violet Ground Beetle.**—Length, about 1 inch; a black head, and black elytra and thorax, but tinged with purple metallic lustre, and edged by the same; long black legs. Common.

C. nemoralis (Fig. 9).—Length about 1 inch; head black, but rest of body coppery green; the elytra have three rows of punctures, easily visible. Common everywhere.

C. arvensis.—Not so large; colour a metallic lustre, varying from copper to greenish; legs black; three rows of small rounded points on each elytron. Found on sandy heaths. Local in England; common in the Highlands.

Notiophilus aquaticus (Fig. 5).—(*Notiophilus* is a genus of very small beetles about ¼ inch long; shining bronze in colour; eyes large; swift running. Found in damp places.) *N. aquaticus* is brassy in colour. Common under stones and moss in damp localities. *N. biguttatus* is bronze above; black, with greenish lustre, underneath; there is a dusky yellow on the thighs. Common.

Leistus spinibarbis (Fig. 10).—Blue-black elytra, with reddish brown legs; antennæ reddish; length about ⅓ inch. Found under stones and bark, especially in hilly districts. Generally distributed in England; rare in Scotland and Ireland.

Nebria brevicollis (Fig. 11).—Length about ½ inch; black, with reddish antennæ and legs. A rather flattish beetle, found under stones in damp places. Common.

Elaphrus riparius.—Length ¼-⅜ inch; very similar to a Tiger Beetle. Coppery green in colour; legs with yellow tibiæ; elytra have four rows of round punctures of lighter colour. Found in muddy places near streams. Fond of sunshine. Common.

Elaphrus cupreus (Fig. 4).—Much like the above, but a darker bronze. Similar eye-spots on the wing-cases; yellowish brown tibiæ. Common on the edges of ponds.

Clivinia fossor (Fig. 12).—(Only two of the genus *Clivinia* are found in Britain.) Length about ¼ inch; black, with reddish legs; distinct punctured grooves on the elytra. Common; often found in garden rubbish. Front-legs adapted for digging, as this species burrows in mud or sand.

Broscus cephalotes (Fig. 22).—Black, with reddish colouring on antennæ and palpi; thorax heart-shaped; elytra flat, with eight slight grooves; a distinct "waist"; two spines on front-legs. Burrows under stones. Feigns death when disturbed. Common on the coasts.

Panagæus quadripustulatus.—A small beetle, about $\frac{1}{4}$ inch long, with red elytra, the red divided into four parts by a black cross. *P. crux-major* is similar but larger.

Badister bipustulatus.—Head black; thorax red; elytra reddish yellow, with a blue-black patch; length $\frac{1}{4}$ inch. Common in damp places under moss or stones.

Harpalus ruficornis (Fig. 35).—Black thorax and head; elytra brownish black; legs red, covered with greyish yellow down; length, $\frac{1}{2}$–$\frac{3}{4}$ inch. Very common.

H. æneus (Fig. 33).—About $\frac{1}{3}$ inch; colour varies from blue-black to green; legs usually red; elytra finely grooved; parallel sides. Common.

H. proteus (Fig. 33b).—About $\frac{1}{3}$ inch; thorax and head black, with a distinct green lustre; elytra bronze, with green tinge; legs red-brown.

H. azureus (Fig. 34).—Elytra, with a bluish tinge; red legs. Found in chalk districts.

H. sabicula (Fig. 36).—Larger than above; legs reddish brown. Found in chalky and sandy districts.

H. caspius (Fig. 37).—Jet black, with a bluish metallic lustre.

Dichirotrichus obsoletus (Fig. 37b).—Dusky yellow, with a dark stripe on each elytra; length about $\frac{1}{4}$ inch. *D. pubescens* is slightly smaller and darker. Common in salt marshes and by tidal rivers.

Anisodactylus binotatus.—A dull-black beetle about $\frac{1}{2}$ inch long; some red on legs and tarsi; often head has two red dots between the eyes; elytra grooved. Common under stones.

Zabrus gibbus.—Length about $\frac{1}{2}$ inch; black, with reddish limbs. A humpbacked beetle. Found on field paths. Not only feeds on insects, but also devours the grain of wheat, the larvæ feeding on the shoots of young corn. Not very common.

Pterostichus vulgaris (Fig. 17).—A wingless genus, common in hilly country under stones. This species is completely black.

P. niger (Fig. 18).—Slightly larger; wing-cases without punctures.

P. cupreus (Fig. 19).—About $\frac{1}{2}$ inch; a rich metallic coppery green; elytra grooved and flattened. Common under stones.

P. madidus.—Shiny black, with reddish brown legs and antennæ; elytra grooved. Common under stones.

P. picimanus (Fig. 20).—Length about $\frac{1}{2}$ inch; brownish black, with reddish legs; a somewhat flat beetle.

P. striola (Fig. 21).—About $\frac{3}{4}$ inch; shining black; head large; deep grooves on thorax; elytra strongly grooved also. Common.

Amara communis (Fig. 25).—(The genus *Amara* consists of twenty-seven British species, not easy to distinguish. The terminal joints of the palpi are oval in shape, a distinctive feature.) This species is about ¼ inch long; has red antennæ; elytra simply grooved. Widely distributed.

A. fulva (Fig. 26).—Length about ⅓ inch; reddish yellow or "fulvous"; elytra with deep grooves; bear a bluish metallic tinge. Found in sandy places.

A. aulica.—About ½ inch, being the largest of the genus found in this country; black above, brownish below; red legs and antennæ; elytra deeply grooved. Common under stones and on plants.

A. spinipes (Fig. 27).—Slightly smaller; has reddish antennæ and femora. Common.

A. familiaris (Fig. 28).—Long shape; greenish bronze; reddish brown legs and antennæ. Common.

Calathus cisteloides (Fig. 28*b*).—About ½ inch; black, with touches of red on antennæ and palpi; legs may be red or black; four pits on the thorax; elytra grooved; wingless. Common under moss, stones, and decaying leaves.

Pristonychus terricola.—Nearly ¾ inch; bluish black, with a dull sheen; limbs all black; the grooves on the elytra join in pairs at the apex. Common under stones and in cellars.

Anchomenus prasinus (Fig. 29).—Belongs to a genus of twenty-one British species; all flattened and small, none more than $\frac{7}{16}$ inch in length. They inhabit decayed wood, leaf-heaps, etc. This species has brown wing-cases, with a greenish spot at the base.

A. albipes (Fig. 30).—Is larger; black, with yellow legs and antennæ. Common in damp places.

A. parumpunctatus (Fig. 31).—Thorax has a greenish tinge; the elytra a distinct coppery lustre.

A. fuliginosus (Fig. 32).—Much smaller; black thorax; elytra dark bronze tinge.

A. angusticollis.—Shining black; antennæ and legs blackish brown; elytra deeply grooved; length, $\frac{7}{16}$ inch.

Brachinus crepitans (Fig. 13).—The genus *Brachinus* has a remarkable method of self-defence. When disturbed, the beetle can discharge a caustic fluid from the abdomen, which volatilizes on contact with the air, making a slight report. The explosions may be produced several times in succession. The species live gregariously under stones. *B. crepitans* is known as the Bombardier Beetle from this curious characteristic. Length about ⅜ inch; elytra blue-black, the rest being red. Common on South Coast, on river banks, and on chalky ground. *B. explodens* is smaller, but very similar.

Demetrius atricapilla (Fig. 14).—Length, ¼ inch; black head, the rest tawny.

Loricera pilicornis (Fig. 15).—Length about ⅓ inch; black, with bronze

PLATE XXII.

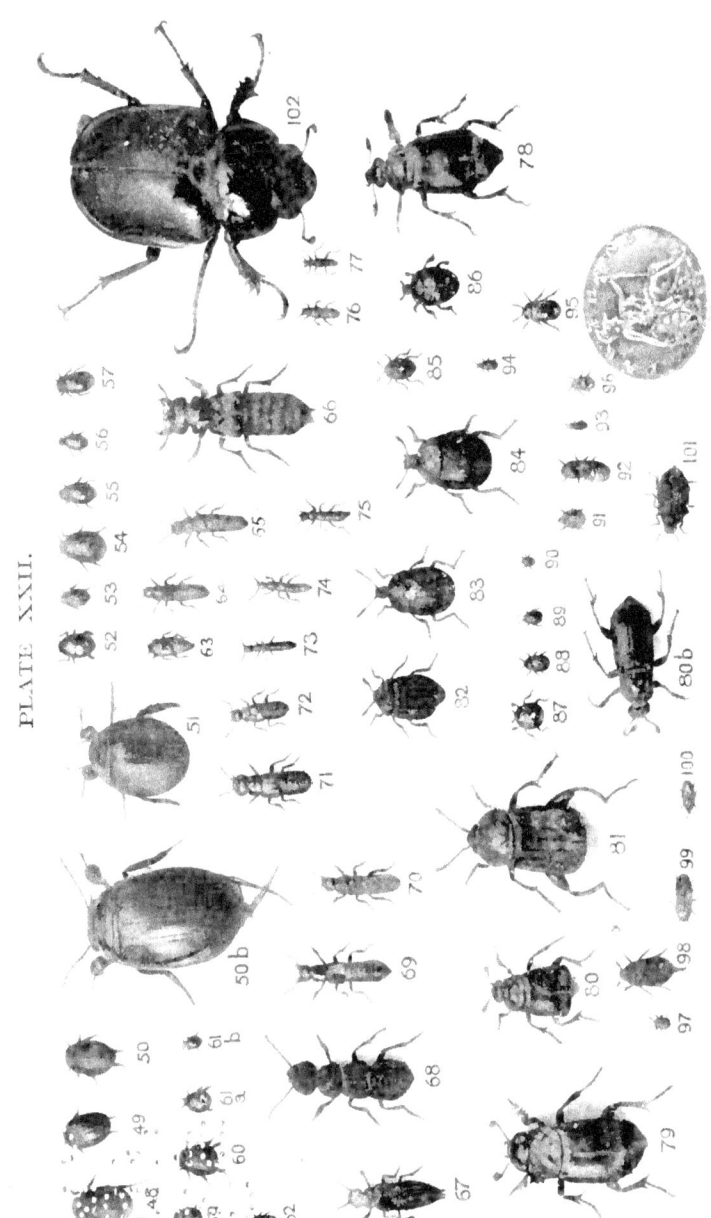

Representative British Beetles.

lustre ; legs reddish brown, except the femora, which are black. The only species of this genus in England. Found in dead leaf heaps.

Chlænius vestitus (Fig. 16).—Head, thorax, and elytra coppery green, the rest brown. Type of a genus found under moss and stones near water.

Licinus silphoides (Fig. 23).—A flattish, dull-black beetle, deeply pitted.

Steropus madidus (Fig. 24).—A dull black ; elytra with three deep punctures. Fairly common under stones.

Bembidium quadriguttatum (Fig. 38).—The beetles of this genus are very small, and have bright, vari-coloured elytra. They are common in damp meadows, sand, and under reeds. *B. quadriguttatum* is a shiny·black, with two pale yellow spots on the wing-cases, and also two similar coloured patches near the bases.

B. lampros (Fig. 39).—Elytra black-bronze ; legs red.

B. littorale (Fig. 40).—Greenish coppery colour, with two reddish coppery patches on each elytron ; legs reddish.

B. pallipenna (Fig. 41).—Head and thorax have a dark greenish lustre ; elytra yellowish, with a darker wavy patch crossing the apex.

Family : *Dytiscidæ*.

These are all **Carnivorous Water-beetles**, having taken to living in water, where they hunt their prey. Their hind-legs are adapted for swimming. They breathe by rising to the surface and getting a supply of air, which they store between the elytra and the abdomen. Both they and their larvæ are very fierce and voracious. The antennæ have eleven joints, and are entirely bare.

Agabus bipustulatus (Fig. 48).—The genus *Agabus* is represented by nineteen British species, very much alike and hard to distinguish ; but the photographs show that they are boat-shaped insects, without " waists," and with wedge-shaped wings under rounded elytra. They are found in running water, though they spend the winter in moss or at the roots of trees gregariously. This species (*A. bipustulatus*) is about $\frac{3}{8}$ inch long ; black, with a distinct coppery sheen ; legs brownish. Very common in ponds.

A. chalconotus (Fig. 49).—Slightly smaller ; black, with a slight metallic sheen ; legs and antennæ reddish.

A. maculatus (Fig. 50).—About the same size, but the back is black, with patches and streaks of coppery brown.

A. nebulosus.—A dusky yellow beetle, about $\frac{1}{3}$ inch. Common in stagnant water.

Ilybius fuliginosus (Fig. 47).—Length, about $\frac{2}{8}$ inch ; dark bronze, with a yellowish edge to the elytra ; under side yellowish red ; antennæ red. Common in running water.

I. ater.—Is a larger species, about $\frac{1}{2}$ inch ; black, with red antennæ and dark-brown legs. Common in ponds.

THE BRITISH NATURE BOOK

Colymbetes fuscus.—The only British species, ⅝ inch long; found in water; head black, tinged in front with red; thorax and elytra tawny brown, with yellowish edges; red antennæ; black and red parti-coloured legs.

Dytiscus.—This genus contains some of the largest British Water Beetles, and these may easily be kept in aquaria, provided that the top is covered; but remember that they are very voracious, and will attack all small fish and other living creatures in the aquarium. The perfect insect lives for several years, and in a state of nature frequently leaves the water for a flight, generally in the evening. The hind-legs are fringed with hairs, and are used as oars. The fore-legs of the male have a remarkable disc on the tarsus, which acts as a sucker, and is used to hold the female. It exudes some kind of sticky fluid, for it will be noticed that the male often gets entangled by its means in water-weed, and has to struggle to break away.

This beetle has an additional protection from its enemies in the form of an evil-smelling fluid, which it can eject from the thorax, and which is much disliked by birds. The female places her eggs in slits in the stems of rushes and other water plants. The larva hatches in three weeks, and soon grows, feeding on other small water creatures. It is most rapacious, and a vigorous swimmer, rising frequently to take in a supply of air from the surface of the water by means of a pair of spiracles at the tail. It has twelve eyes, and a cruel mouth and jaws. After moulting several times, it leaves the water, and buries itself in the damp earth by the water-side to pupate. In this condition it remains through the winter, emerging as a perfect beetle in the spring.

D. punctulatus (male) (Fig. 50b).—Note the discs on the fore-legs. Elytra black, shaded with yellow at the sides; antennæ red; legs dark brown. Fairly common.

D. marginalis.—Is larger, the thorax having a complete yellow edge all round. Very common.

Acilius sulcatus (male) (Fig. 51).—Note the discs on the fore-legs. Brown, with two black bands on the thorax. Common in ponds and ditches.

Haliplus flavicollis (Fig. 42).—Belonging to a genus of very small oval beetles; pale yellowish brown. Found in stagnant water.

Hyphydrus ovatus (Fig. 43).—Black, with a dull red tinge; almost round in shape. Common in pools.

Hydroporus planus (Fig. 44).—Black, with reddish brown head and legs.

H. palustris (Fig. 45).—This very small species looks black to the naked eye, but the magnifier shows it to be shaded with yellow, and to have two yellow or tawny patches on the elytra. Common in water.

Lacophilus minutus (Fig. 46).—Dark olive-brown, a very active species. Swims near the bottom of ponds.

BEETLES

Family: *Gyrinidæ*—WHIRLIGIG BEETLES.

These are the beetles so often seen on the surface of ponds, describing circles in company with others. When disturbed, they dive below for safety. They have an inner bladder at the end of the abdomen. They also possess curious divided eyes, making four in all—two on the upper, and two on the lower surface of the head. They are thus able to see below the surface and into the air as well.

G. natator (Fig. 52).—About ¼ inch; shining blue-black above, and black beneath; legs red.

Deronectus depressus (Fig. 53).—Tawny brown, with black pattern on the elytra, in which are four tawny spots. Found on water weeds.

Sub-order ii. CLAVICORNIA.

This sub-order, as the name (*clava*, " club"; *cornu*, " horn ") indicates, contains beetles with knobbed or clubbed antennæ, though in some cases the clubbing is not very marked. Their legs are clumsy and small, for they do not seek safety by flight, but when disturbed feign death, either by rolling up or remaining motionless. They feed on carrion or dung. Some thirty families are included under this heading.

Family: *Hydrophilidæ*.

Distinguished from other water beetles by their method of swimming, which is not by "rowing," but kicking their legs *alternately*. They live at the bottom of standing water, feeding on vegetable matter.

Hydrophilus piceus (the Great Water Beetle).—You will be fortunate if you find this species, for it is rare and local—chiefly in the fens and round London. There is no difficulty in identifying it, for it is the largest water beetle, and of a shiny black. The female lays her eggs in a shining silvery cocoon, which floats on the surface.

Hydrobius fuscipes (Fig. 54).—Black; elytra many-grooved. Common in stagnant water at the roots of plants.

Philhydrus maritima (Fig. 55).—Coppery brown. Found in stagnant water.

Berosus affinis (Fig. 56).—Head black; thorax a dark copper; elytra almost black, with some dark brown shading.

Helophorus aquaticus (Fig. 57).—A similar species, but slightly larger. Dark brownish yellow. Common on the edge of stagnant pools.

Ochthebius pygmæus.—Pale brown; very common, but very small; no bigger than a pin's head. Found in water, under stones, and on decaying vegetation.

Cyclonotum orbiculare (Fig. 59).—Shining black; hemispherical body. Not uncommon.

Sphæridium scarabeoides (Fig. 60).—A polished dark brown, with a blood-red spot at the base of the elytra, and a similar one at the apex. Found in fresh dung. Common.

S. bipustulatum (Fig. 61a).—Smaller, but very similar in markings, which, however, need a magnifying glass to distinguish.

Cercyon flavipes (Fig. 61b).—Shining black. Very common. Found in damp places, under stones, or in dung.

Family : *Staphylinidæ*.

These are "**Cocktail**" or "**Rove**" **Beetles**, distinguished by their short wing-cases, which leave the lower part of the long abdomen exposed. Many of them " cock " their tails when disturbed, emitting a disagreeable odour. They form a very extensive family, consisting largely of small, elongated, blackish species. To be found beneath moss, bark, stones, in decomposing vegetation and dung; also in fungi, ant-heaps, flowers, etc.

Myrmedonia canaliculata.—Brick red, with a black band crossing the abdomen. Common in ants' nests, under stones, etc.

Aleochara fuscipes.—About $\frac{3}{10}$ inch; shining black body; wing-cases brownish red, with dark edges. Very common in dung and refuse.

Tachyporus obtusus (Fig. 62).—Orange coloured, with upper half of wing-cases black, forming a kind of collar, and tip of the abdomen black. Fairly common in vegetable refuse.

Tachinus humeralis (Fig. 63).—About $\frac{1}{4}$ inch ; shiny black, with reddish borders on thorax; reddish elytra and legs. Found in dung, decaying fungi, and refuse.

Quedius picipes (Fig. 64).—One of twenty-nine British species comprising the genus. About $\frac{1}{2}$ inch ; shining black, with red elytra. Found amongst decaying leaves, fungi, and moss.

Q. fuliginosus (Fig. 65).—Entirely black, with rusty brown legs. Found in damp, dark places, cellars, etc.

Creophilus maxillosus (Fig. 66).—The only British species of this genus. Black, with grey hair on the wing-cases. Common in dead animals.

Leistotrophus murinus (Fig. 67).—About $\frac{1}{2}$ inch long. A shabby brownish species covered with downy hairs, living in dung and carcasses in summer and under moss in winter.

L. nebulosus.—The only other species of this genus, $\frac{1}{2}$–$\frac{3}{4}$ inch. Shabby black, covered with down; legs reddish. The abdomen has two rows of round black spots. Found in dung, decaying fungi, and dead creatures.

Staphylinus cæsareus.—Known as the Red Rove Beetle, the commonest of the British Rove Beetles. Found under stones, on warm sunlit paths, etc. ; $\frac{1}{2}$–$\frac{3}{4}$ inch in length. Dull black, with red elytra and legs ; patches of golden yellow down on thorax and abdomen.

Ocypus olens (the **Devil's Coach-horse**) (Fig. 68).—The genus *Ocypus* com-

BEETLES

prises ten British species, of which this is the most familiar. It is dull black in colour, and is provided with wings; has a pair of very strong jaws. When alarmed, " cocks " its abdomen, and opens its jaws for fight, and also emits a foul smell. Hides under stones and refuse. The larvæ make pits, in which they lie in wait for other insects.

O. ater (Fig. 69).—Smaller than above. Colour a more polished black.

O. cupreus (Fig. 70).—Bronze;' legs black, with some brownish red; winged. Common under stones.

Philonthus splendens (Fig. 71).—One of a large genus, comprising forty-six British species. Found in vegetable and animal refuse. Black, with metallic bluish tinge; elytra closely punctured; head and thorax very shiny.

P. æneus (Fig. 72).—Much smaller, but similarly coloured, with bronze lustre on the elytra. Common on dung and carrion, in which the beetles and larvæ prey on the larvæ of gnats and flies.

Xantholinus punctulatus (Fig. 73).—One of a genus of long, narrow beetles, which double up in repose. Black, with elytra dark green or rusty brown. Common in moss, cut grass, etc.

X. glabratus is the largest of the genus, being nearly ½ inch long; bright black, with red elytra. Common in dung and refuse, and under stones.

Lathrobium elongatum (Fig. 74).—The genus, comprising fifteen species, consist of elongated slender beetles. Found in damp woods. This species, about ⅓ inch, is bright black, with red elytra, black at the base; legs and antennæ reddish; head nearly round. Found in moss, marshy places, etc.

L. fulvipenna is about the same size, but the elytra are reddish brown.

L. boreale is also very similar, but narrower, the elytra being sometimes wholly red.

Pæderus litoralis (Fig. 75).—A small handsome species. Elytra metallic blue; head and tail black; thorax and other sections of abdomen orange-red. This genus lives gregariously near water, under stones and leaves, hibernating in decaying willows.

Stenus biguttatus.—The genus has sixty-three species, inhabiting damp localities, brook-sides and marshes. The species named is about ⅓ inch in length. Black, covered with silvery down; a round orange spot on each elytron. Common on margins of streams and ponds and sandy shores.

Oxyporus rufus (the only species of the genus), about ⅓ inch long. Shining black, with brilliant red thorax, red patches at base of elytra, and four red segments on abdomen. Found in decaying fungi.

Bledius tricornis (Fig. 76).—Black, with reddish brown antennæ. Red elytra, with a triangular black mark, V-pointed, formed by their contact. The end of the abdomen is red. Found in salt marshes. This wedge-shaped patch on the elytra seems to be a characteristic of the genus, *B. spectabilis* (¼ inch) and *B. arenarius* (⅓ inch) also possessing it.

Dianoüs cærulescens (Fig. 77) has a beautiful blue metallic lustre all over; two reddish spots on the wing-cases.

Family : *Silphidæ*.

Scavengers, living in the bark of trees or in carrion ; straight 11-jointed antennæ, more or less clubbed.

Genus *Necrophorus*.—These are the **Burying** or **Sexton Beetles**, and have antennæ with four joints expanded into a distinct club. These must be highly developed, sensitive organs, which enable the insects to detect the presence of any dead creature within range. A dead mouse or bird is sure to attract them, and they fly with little delay to it. They then proceed to bury it, having legs wonderfully adapted for digging. Several of them work at once, under or round the " corpse," throwing out the soil till the dead body sinks into the hole. The females then lay their eggs in it, so that the larvæ on hatching may find an abundance of food. Some species have a distinct musk-like smell (*N. vespillo*). Another remarkable feature of these beetles is their power of signalling to one another by making a curious clicking sound. This is produced by rubbing a bar which is found crossing the elytra against two files on the top of the abdomen.

N. humator (the **Black Burying Beetle**) (Fig. 78).—As its name implies, it is a uniform black, except the clubs of the antennæ and the claws of the forelegs, which are orange.

N. ruspator (Fig. 79).—About 1 inch long ; clubs of antennæ orange. Two orange bands cross the elytra, *the front band of which is not interrupted* at the suture ; there is a tuft of golden hair at the tail. Rather local, but quite common where it is found.

N. mortuorum (Fig. 80).—Similar to above, but much smaller—about $\frac{3}{5}$ inch. Antennæ entirely black ; two orange bands crossing the elytra, but *the upper one is interrupted* at the suture; *the lower one is really two irregular patches.*

N. vespillo (Fig. 80b).—Similar but slightly larger—about $\frac{4}{5}$ inch ; orange clubs. Distinguished by the golden or yellowish hair on the *thorax, abdomen*, and scantily on the elytra as well. Fairly common in the South.

Necrodes (Silpha) littoralis (Fig. 81).—The only British species of this genus (*Necrodes*) ; has longer clubs to the antennæ than the above ; pale orange colour. The elytra are flat and long, almost covering the abdomen ; blackish, with a chocolate tint, strongly ribbed. The thorax also has the same bronze tint ; eyes very prominent. Found in carrion.

Silpha rugosa (Fig. 82).—A thick-set, small, flattish species ; very common ; dull black. The elytra are ribbed both horizontally and vertically, giving a rough netted appearance. Head and thorax covered with grey down.

S. atrata (Fig. 83).—Slightly larger (about $\frac{1}{2}$ inch), of a bright black ; elytra pitted and crossed by three ribs. Common in carrion and decayed wood.

S. lævigata (Fig. 84).—About $\frac{3}{4}$ inch ; not so flat as the preceding ; black, of a medium brightness ; thorax has some grey down. Elytra pitted but not ribbed or grooved. Found in carrion, etc., especially on the coasts in chalky districts.

S. obscura is very much like *S. atrata*—shining black; the elytra *regularly* pitted.

S. quadripunctata (the **Four-spot Carrion Beetle**) is about ½ inch in length; has yellowish elytra with two black spots on each. The sides of the thorax are also yellow. It feeds on larvæ, and attacks gregarious caterpillars. Found in oak woods, chiefly in South.

S. thoracica.—About ⅜ inch, is distinguished by its black elytra and red thorax; covered, with the head, with golden down. Found in fungi and carrion.

Family : *Scaphidiidæ.*

Little shining, oval beetles; found in fungi and decaying wood, tree stumps, etc.

S. quadrimaculatum (Fig. 85).—Is shiny black, with two red spots on each wing-case. The feet are reddish (under a pocket lens). There is some scanty grey down on the back and wing-cases. This is a rounded insect, not to be confused with *M. quadripustulatus* (see below), which is longer shaped.

Family : *Histeridæ.*

Beetles which feign death when disturbed—hence the name (from *histrio*, an actor or mimic). The elytra are cut short, showing two sections of the abdomen. Found in carrion, dung, fungi, and refuse.

Hister unicolor (Fig. 86).—Shiny jet-black; nearly ¼ inch long; thick-set, powerful fore-legs; short antennæ, ending in a club. Elytra scored with seven lines. Common in cow-dung in the South.

H. cadaverinus is very similar but slightly smaller, with a dull metallic sheen.

H. bimaculatus is very small, about ⅛ inch long, distinguished by two red patches on the black elytra.

Saprinus nitidulus (Fig. 87).—Much like *H. unicolor*, but only one-quarter the size; shiny black. Common in dung and decaying fungi.

Family : *Nitidulidæ.*

Containing some ninety species; small flattish beetles with straight 11-jointed antennæ; feeding on dry animal matter and carrion. Many found on flowers.

N. bipustulata (Fig. 88).—About ⅛ inch long; black; two red spots on the elytra; reddish legs. Very common in carrion.

Epuræa obsoleta (Fig. 89).—A tiny tawny-coloured species; found under the bark of pine trees and exuded sap.

Meligethes æneus (the "**Turnip-blossom**" **Beetle**) (Fig. 90).—One of thirty-four British species in this genus, found in flowers. It eats into the bud, and the female deposits her eggs there, the larvæ feeding on the flower; very destructive to rape. Colour, a dark green or blue metallic lustre.

THE BRITISH NATURE BOOK

Cychramus luteus (Fig. 91).—A small tawny-yellow species, common on flowers, and flowering shrubs, such as hawthorn-blossom ; the elytra almost cover the abdomen, and have a slight covering of fine light hairs, scarcely visible to the naked eye. This beetle is very similar to *Byturus tomentosus* (Fig. 96), but a darker colour, and rounder in shape.

Ips quadriguttata—about ¼ inch—is a longish-shaped species, bright black, with four reddish spots ; found under oak and pine bark, and feeding on the sap of various trees.

Trogosita mauritanica (Fig. 92).—About ½ inch long, a flattish, elongated species, black or brownish, sometimes with a red tinge ; reddish legs, antennæ slightly clubbed, the club being three-jointed. Found among drugs and other merchandise all over the globe, in granaries, warehouses, etc.; also under the bark of decaying trees ; elytra grooved and faintly punctured.

Ditoma crenata (Fig. 93).—Black with reddish brown antennæ and legs. Elytra grooved and pitted, with two red spots or bands on each. Local, under the bark of dead trees.

Cryptophagus lycoperdi (Fig. 94).—Belonging to a genus (11-jointed antennæ) found in damp places, cellars, fungi, and decayed wood. Reddish brown; elytra slightly pitted.

Mycetophagus quadripustulatus (Fig. 95).—The name means mushroom eaters ; they are found not only on fungi but also under bark, in granaries, and rubbish. Eleven species in all. *M. quadrip.* is a long oval in shape ; elytra black with two brick-red spots on each; grooved and pitted; legs reddish. Local.

Family : *Coccinellidæ*—LADY-BIRDS.

This family of nearly hemispherical beetles is highly beneficial, since both the larval and adult forms devour the aphides. They may often be found on rose trees and other plants infested by the green-fly.

Hippodamia 19-*punctata* (Fig. 221), has nineteen black spots on its yellow wing-cases.

H. 13-*punctata*, with thirteen black spots on the yellow or orange elytra, is rare.

Subcoccinella 24-*punctata*.—The only species of its genus found in Britain ; is a vegetable feeder. About ⅛ inch long, with thick reddish down; spotted with variable dots and patches (sometimes absent). Common in certain localities among herbage, especially in South.

Anatis ocellata is the largest British lady-bird ; found on fir trees ; not very common. Head black ; thorax with white markings ; elytra red, spotted with yellow-ringed black dots, or " eyes."

Coccinella bipunctata (the **Two-spot Lady-bird**) (Fig. 222).—Elytra red. Common.

C. oblongo-guttata (Fig. 223).—A tawny brown, with lighter streaks and patches on the elytra.

PLATE XXIII.

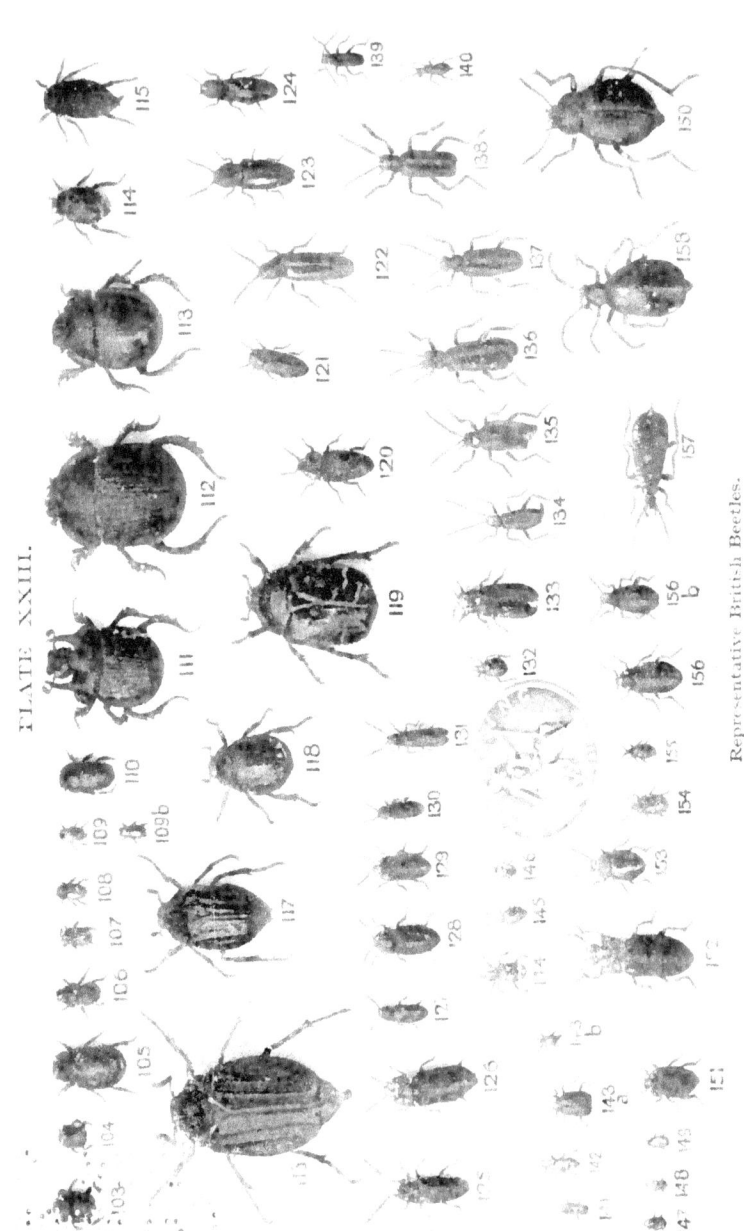

Representative British Beetles.

BEETLES

C. septem punctata (Fig. 224).—One of the commonest species; elytra red, with seven spots in all (the one at the base being common to both elytra).

C. 18-punctata (Fig. 225).—Reddish brown, with light ochreous spots.

C. 12 punctata (Fig. 226).—Red elytra; black spots.

C. variabilis (Fig. 226b).—In this species the black spots run into one another, forming a grill; yellow beneath.

Scymnus frontalis (Fig. 227).—Black, with grey down. Elytra with one or two red spots. Common at the roots of grass.

Coccidula rufa (Fig. 228).—Orange-red; found in marshy places, on plants.

Family: *Dermestidæ*—BACON BEETLES.

These are small oval or oblong-oval beetles found in furs, hides, cheese, bacon, etc.; some on flowers. Fourteen species in all, divided into six genera, in all of which, except the genus *Dermestes*, there is a simple eye on the front of the head, besides the usual compound eyes. The antennæ are short and clubbed.

Byturus tomentosus (Fig. 96). (See notes on Fig. 91.)—Yellowish brown (sometimes black), with some light down on elytra; orange legs and antennæ. Found on flowers.

Omosita discoides (Fig. 97).—Blackish brown, covered with grey down; two light brown patches on the elytra.

Dermestes murinus (Fig. 98).—A dull black species, covered sparsely with grey down. Feeds on animal substances and is found everywhere. The under surface is covered with dense white hair.

D. lardarius (the **Bacon Beetle**) (Fig. 99).—Rusty black, with a broad band of yellowish brown across the elytra. On this lighter patch are six blackish spots. Attacks any kind of animal substance, hides, bacon, and stuffed specimens; in reality a scavenger. The larvæ have thick, erect hair, and are frequently met with in the larder. When touched they feign death.

Attagenus pellio (Fig. 100).—Oblong-oval in shape; black, covered above with fine black down and beneath with yellowish hairs. There is a shade of red on the elytra, in the middle of each being a dot of white down. Often found in winter on furs and skins, or museum specimens.

Byrrhus pilula (Fig. 101).—One of twelve species belonging to the *Byrrhidæ* or **Pill Beetles**, which can draw their head and legs in close to the body so as to appear round, bead-like objects. This species is dark brown, with yellowish or brown down on the upper surface, found in pastures, at roots of grass, moss, etc., in spring. Feigns death when touched.

Sub-order iii. LAMELLICORNIA.

Leaf-horned Beetles.—So called because the ends of the antennæ are flattened into leaves, which are movable, or can be opened and closed like a fan.

THE BRITISH NATURE BOOK

Family: *Lucanidæ*—STAG BEETLES.

Lucanus Cervus (the **Stag Beetle**) (Fig. 102).—Antennæ with a comb-like club, the plates of which cannot be spread; 10-jointed. Mandibles like a stag's antlers. This species is so well known as to need little description. The larvæ live in decayed oak trees for five years before maturing. The adult beetle has a habit of standing in a war-like attitude when alarmed, but in spite of its formidable appearance it is quite harmless. The female does not possess the large " horns " of the male. A remarkable characteristic is the courtship period, when the male pursues his mate, and seizing her in his mandibles carries her off bodily, kicking and struggling, by main force.

There is a smaller species, *Dorcus parallelopipedus*, about an inch long, flattened and parallel-sided. The head of the male as broad as the thorax; mandibles not " antlered." Commonest round London and in the South. Found in decayed elm, beech, etc.

Sinodendron cylindricum.—Shiny black, with brownish elytra; is recognized in the male by the long, recurved horn—in the female this horn is reduced to a tubercle. About ½ inch long. Fairly common in the South of England and Wales.

Family: *Scarabæidæ*—CHAFERS.

This is a large family (many species being of great beauty and colouring), in which are to be found many useful beetles, such as feed on dung and refuse and act as scavengers. Legs adapted for digging; antennæ short, with movable terminal plates.

Onthophagus fructicornis (Fig. 103).—About ⅓ inch long; has thorax and head dull black, with a shade of bronze. The elytra are roughly punctured, of a fawn shade, with blackish patches; legs coppery. Found in dung, especially near the coast.

O. ovatus (Fig. 104).—A smaller species, dull bronze-black. Elytra streaked and pitted.

Aphodius fossor (Fig. 105).—Of the genus *Aphodius* there are thirty-eight British species, living principally in dung, in which they lay their eggs. *A. fossor* is about ½ inch long, black, with a copper-coloured tinge especially on the elytra, which are grooved and slightly pitted. The male has three tubercles on the head.

A. peteus (the **Small Dung Beetle**) (Fig. 106).—Black head and shoulders, shading into red at the edges. The elytra are red, deeply grooved. Common.

A. inquinatus (Fig. 107).—Shining black head and thorax; but the elytra are fawn coloured, ornamented with black patterns.

A. stricticus (Fig. 108), is similar but brighter in colour—the thorax black on the top, shading into bright fawn on the sides; the elytra shining fawn with darker markings.

BEETLES

A. prodromus (Fig. 109).—Very small, about ⅕ inch; black head and thorax; elytra a dull yellow with darker shaded patches.

A. pusillus (Fig. 109b).—A small, narrow, shining black species. Very common.

A. rufipes (Fig. 110).—This is as large as *A. fossor;* pitchy brown or black; elytra slightly grooved; under side brownish or reddish.

Genus *Geotrupes*.—Consists of beetles of large size, very powerful, living in dung, where the females burrow deep holes through to the earth—sometimes as much as 12 inches—where they lay their eggs. They carry dung down for food for the larvæ.

G. typhæus (Fig. 111) is a shiny black species. The male has three curious spikes, or horns, on the shoulders (or *pronotum*). The head is edged with stiff hairs or bristles.

G. putridarius (Fig. 112).—Black, with violet or purple sheen on the elytra, which are finely ribbed. This is not so common as the preceding.

G. sylvaticus (Fig. 113).—About ¾ inch; has a beautiful purple lustre under the blackish colouring of the whole body, which is thickly punctured, especially underneath. It is common in dung and fungi, especially in woods.

The **Common Dor Beetle** (which is not pictured), *G. stercorarius*, "DUMBLE-DOR" or "CLOCK" BEETLE, also known as the "WATCHMAN."—About 1 inch in length; is familiar from its clumsy, humming flights in the evening. It is generally infested with small mites. Its most curious peculiarity, however, is that it can utter a curious squeaking noise. In colour it is shiny black; steel-blue on the under sides and legs. It is common in dung.

G. spiniger is about the same size and colouring, but is identified by *a long, smooth space* along the centre of the under side of the abdomen, which is otherwise thickly clothed with hair.

Genus *Melolonthini* ("Cockchafers").—These beetles do a great deal of damage to trees and plants, as the larvæ feed on the roots, sometimes for three or four years.

Hoplia philanthus (Fig. 114).—About ½ inch long; head and thorax black; covered sparsely with yellow down. The elytra in the male are tawny; in the female, reddish brown or chestnut. Antennæ and legs of male black; of female red. This is not very common, though sometimes, especially in the South, it appears in large numbers. It is found on flowering shrubs, alders, etc.

Serica brunnea (Fig. 115).—A long, almost cylindrical species, reddish yellow in colour, except the head, which is dark brown. The elytra have nine deep grooves. Found in sandy places and woods. Rather local; flies by night.

Melolontha vulgaris (Fig. 116), the **Common Cockchafer** or **May-bug**.—A handsome species, too well known to need description; but its history is very interesting. The female burrows in soft soil, and the eggs hatch after a few weeks, the larvæ feeding on the tender roots of grasses and other plants. Sometimes these larvæ are in such numbers that they will destroy large patches of meadow grass. The mole does good work in devouring them. In the winter the larvæ burrow still deeper and hibernate. Not until the third year do they change into pupal state, from which in July and August the perfect beetles emerge. Even now they do not immediately come to the surface, but remain in the burrows till the spring of the fourth year, when they come to the surface and may be seen in flight. The perfect beetle only lives a few weeks, but during this time does fresh damage by devouring the leaves of trees.

This beetle is adapted for the life it leads, having a head covered with a strong shield, and a hard stout tail, which acts as a lever in the soil. Notice the spines on the legs, which also serve to give it support when pushing its way through the ground. The antennæ are beautiful objects, consisting of a fan of plates—seven in the male, six in the female; both have delicate organs of smell.

Rhizotrogus solstitialis (Fig. 117).—This is about half the size of the Common Cockchafer; a bright fawn in colour, covered with golden hair. It is quite as destructive as the former, but not so common.

Anomala frischii (ænea) (Fig. 118).—A most beautiful species. Head and thorax black, with a bright green metallic tinge. Elytra chestnut, with a similar metallic lustre. Found on sandy scrub on seacoast.

Cetonini.—Shining beetles living on flowers; larvæ in ground.

Cetonia aurata (the **Rose Beetle**) (Fig. 119).—Bright green above, with a golden sheen, coppery beneath; legs black; sometimes 1 inch in length. Found on flowers, and specially destructive to roses. Commonest in the South. Larvæ found in decayed wood and in ants' nests (especially the Wood Ant).

Sub-order iv. SERRICORNIA (Beetles with saw-like or serrate antennæ).

Family : *Elateridæ*—CLICK BEETLES.

Long species, which have the power of jumping from the ground, turning a somersault, with a clicking noise when placed on their backs.

Lacon murinus (the only British species) (Fig. 120).—A shabby brownish black species, covered with grey hair; short antennæ, which when the insect is at rest are received into grooves in the prosternum. Common in the Midlands and South on flowers or in moss.

Elater sanguinolentus (Fig. 121).—Black, with scarlet elytra, marked with black when they meet. Length about ½ inch. Local; found in pine stumps.

Melanotus rufipes (Fig. 122).—An elongated black species, covered with scanty down. Legs dull reddish; head and thorax pitted. Found in rotten wood, on flowers. Fairly common.

Athoüs niger (the **Black Skipjack**) (Fig. 123).—(Of the genus *Athoüs* we have eight species, two of which are figured.) Shining black, covered with greyish down. Head flattened and strongly punctured. Elytra striated; found on bushes, hedges, and in woods.

PLATE XXIV.

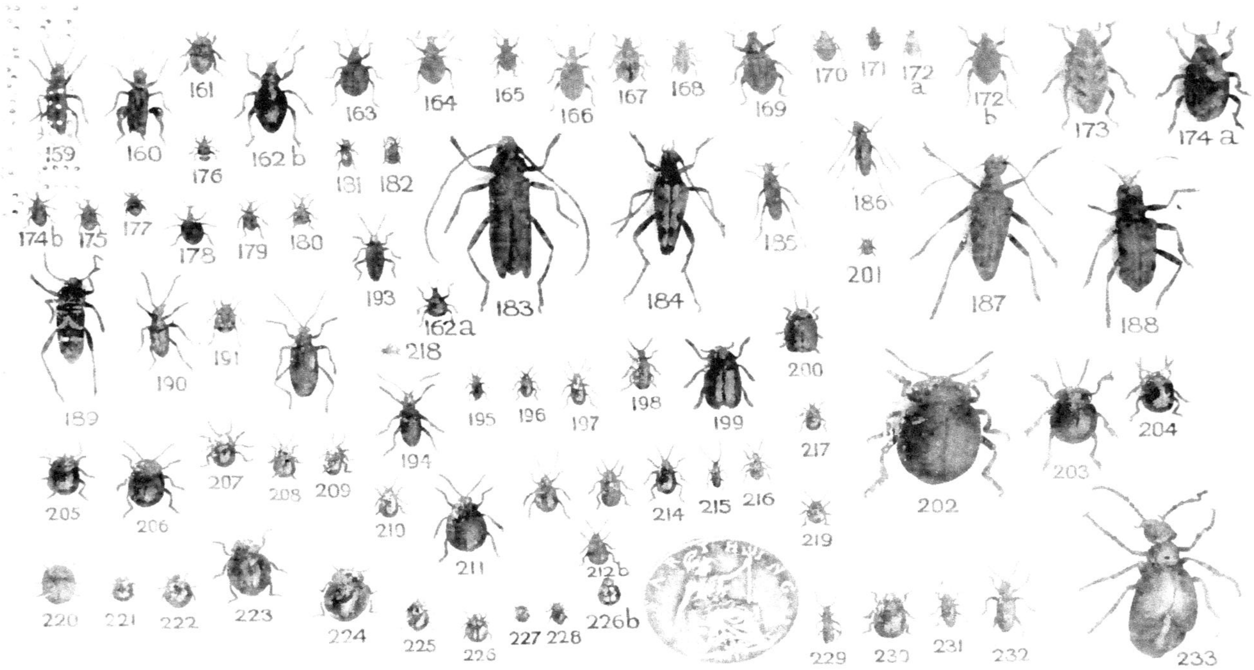

Representative British Beetles.

BEETLES

A. hæmorrhoidalis (the **Reddish Skipjack**) (Fig. 124).—Usually brownish black above, but the under side is plainly reddish, like the legs. Head and thorax strongly punctured; elytra striated and punctured. Very common on hazel, heath, bracken, etc.

Corymbites cupreus (Fig. 125).—Long and narrow, $\frac{1}{2}$–$\frac{3}{4}$ inch in length; has a violet-bronze tinge. The antennæ are quite plainly pectinate (comb-like). Found on grass, bushes, and stones.

C. tesselatus (Fig. 126).—About the same size; brown-bronze covered with greyish down, which in many specimens is in patches, giving a tessellated appearance. Found in moss and marshy districts.

C. quercus (Fig. 127).—Dull black; elytra striated, with faint pubescence. Length $\frac{1}{4}$ to $\frac{1}{3}$ inch. Found on oaks.

C. holosericeus (Fig. 128).—Length $\frac{1}{3}$–$\frac{1}{2}$ inch; dull black, with yellowish grey down on the back; legs rusty red. Found in grass.

Genus *Agriotes*.—A genus found on flowers. The larvæ are known as "wire-worms," and live in the ground on roots of plants. Very destructive.

A. obscurus (Fig. 129).—About $\frac{1}{3}$ inch in length; generally black, with brown elytra, finely grooved and punctured. Under side black or very dark brown. Common in moss and under stones. Larvæ feed on roots of grass and corn.

A. sabrinus (Fig. 130).—Yellowish brown elytra, with darker brown thorax. Length about $\frac{1}{4}$ inch. Equally injurious, but not so often seen.

Campylus linearis (Fig. 131).—The only species of this genus. Length, $\frac{3}{8}$–$\frac{1}{2}$ inch. A very narrow, elongated species, with light fawn elytra (male), black in female. The eyes are very prominent, standing out quite clear of the thorax. Legs frequently yellowish brown. Found on bushes and under bark.

Helodes minutus (Fig. 132).—About $\frac{1}{4}$ inch; oval shape; yellow-brown thorax; elytra a shade darker. Antennæ almost as long as the elytra. Found in marshes and water meadows.

Family: *Malacodermidæ*—" SOFT-SKINNED " BEETLES.

So called because the skin is softer and more flexible than in other families.

Lampyris noctiluca (the **Glow-worm**) (Fig. 133).—The only species of this genus. The male (which is figured) has wings, but the female none. The latter is larger than its mate. Colour, a dull brown. Both sexes can emit the light which gives rise to the name, but the female's power is greater than the male's. There is little doubt that the light is intended to act as a guide by which the male finds the female, and it can be controlled at will. Both sexes sham death when disturbed. The larvæ are much like the female in appearance, and feed on snails, rendering a beneficent aid to the gardener.

Genus *Telephorus*.—These are soft-bodied beetles with long antennæ and prominent eyes, frequently found in flowers; popularly known as " soldiers and sailors." The larvæ feed on earth-worms, etc. The species are very similar in colour.

Telephorus fulcus (Fig. 134).—About $\frac{1}{3}-\frac{7}{16}$ inch. Yellow elytra, with black tips; orange-brown head. Common on flowers.

T. rusticus (Fig. 135).—Length, $\frac{1}{2}$ inch. Orange body; on centre of thorax a black spot; elytra dull black, covered with grey down. Very common.

T. pellucidus (Fig. 136).—Slightly longer than preceding. No black spot on the elytra; black eyes, and elytra like preceding.

T. alpinus (Fig. 137).—Very similar, but with less black, and the legs are redder.

T. lividus (Fig. 138).—About $\frac{1}{2}$ inch.. Common on flowers in the South, but rarer in the North. Has dull *yellow* elytra, sometimes with a black spot on the forehead.

T. flavilabris (Fig. 139).—About $\frac{1}{4}$ inch. Orange body; blackish elytra, with scanty down; long antennæ.

T. testaceus (Fig. 140).—About $\frac{1}{4}$ inch. Light brown (sandy) elytra; orange body; black head and shoulders, shading into orange at sides.

Malthinus punctatus (Fig. 141).—About $\frac{1}{4}$ inch. A very thin and fragile species. Light brown elytra, with two pure yellow spots near tips; orange body; black head and eyes; yellow mouth. Found on bushes in woods, often in companies.

Dolichosoma nobile (Fig. 142).—About $\frac{1}{4}-\frac{1}{3}$ inch. A rich bronze-green; shoulders and elytra finely pitted. Found on flowers and bushes.

Malachius bipustulatus (Fig. 143a).—A species identified by its metallic green colour, and the scarlet tips to the elytra. Larvæ found in willows, etc. Beetle common on flowers.

Anthocomus fasciatus (Fig. 143b).—About $\frac{1}{8}$ inch. Head and shoulders dark metallic green; elytra black, crossed by two red bands.

Clerus formicarius (Fig. 144).—One of a genus which preys on other insects —some, for example, entering hives and killing the bees. Shoulders and tip of elytra red; rest of elytra black, crossed by two wavy symmetrical bands of grey. Found under bark, in rotten wood, and on fences. Larvæ devour destructive wood-boring beetles.

Corynetus cæruleus (Fig. 145).—Pear-shaped; about $\frac{1}{4}$ inch; has a blue metallic lustre; elytra pitted; antennæ clubbed. Found on decayed wood. Local.

Ochinus pederæ (Fig. 146).—Orange-brown, with two symmetrical patches of light down on wing-cases.

Cis boleti (Fig. 147).—Dull brown, with slight pubescence.

Lyctus canaliculatus (Fig. 148).—Brown, with clubbed antennæ.

Anobium domesticum (Fig. 149).—One of the **Death Watches**. A shabby brown. Common in old interiors and woodwork of houses. The male produces a clicking sound by knocking its head against wood, as a call to the female, which answers. The family *Ptinidæ*, to which these belong, are most destructive, the larvæ, white fleshy grubs, feeding, like their parents, upon waste substances, dry timber, woodwork, and stored goods.

Sub-order v. LONGICORNIA

(that is, "long-horned," the antennæ being usually very long, but not in all species).

Elongated, and generally flattened beetles, with short, sharply pointed mandibles.

Aromia moschata (Fig. 183).—The **Musk Beetle**, of a beautiful metallic blue or green colour, emits an odour like that of musk. Length, up to $1\frac{1}{4}$ inch. Found in decaying willows. Rare in North of England and Scotland.

Strangalia armata (Fig. 184).—Length $\frac{3}{4}$-1 inch. Elytra yellow, decorated with black spots and bands; head and abdomen black, clothed with yellowish down. Common on flowers in Midlands and South.

S. nigra (Fig. 185).—A glossy black, with a fine grey down, about $\frac{1}{2}$ inch in length. Found on flowers of Umbelliferæ and others.

S. melanura (Fig. 186).—Length $\frac{1}{2}$ inch; black, with reddish brown elytra, tipped with black. Found on yarrow and ox-eye.

Rhagium bifasciatum (Fig. 187).—Length about $\frac{3}{4}$-1 inch. Black, with a reddish tinge; two slanting yellow bands on elytra, set wide apart; antennæ rusty red; legs black. Found on firs and pines. Larvæ under bark.

R. inquisitor (Fig. 188).—A common species, with much shorter antennæ. There is no red tinge in the general colouring, which is black; but there are two yellow bands on each elytra, which are covered with grey down, like the rest of the body. Common in decaying fir, oak, and other trees.

Clytus arietis (Fig. 189).—About $\frac{3}{4}$ inch. Black, with symmetrical yellow curved and straight bands in the elytra, giving it rather a wasp-like appearance; legs chestnut. Found on oak, beech, and rose bushes.

Leptura livida (Fig. 190).—About $\frac{1}{4}$ inch. Black, with golden brown wing-cases; sparsely covered with scales. Found on flowers.

Bruchus pisi (Fig. 191).—The beetles of this genus are a great pest, inhabiting the seeds of leguminous plants. The female lays her egg on the flower or seed-vessel, and the newly hatched larva burrows through the pod and enters a developing seed. This species is found in pea-pods. A rich brown, with whitish down. On the wing-cases there are pairs of downless spots, patches and tips. The elytra are deeply striated.

Sub-order vi. PHYTOPHAGA—" PLANT-EATERS."

Closely allied to the foregoing sub-order, but with shorter antennæ. Feed upon leaves, and often are most destructive to gardens and crops.

Family: *Chrysomelidæ*.

Donacia menyanthidis (Fig. 192).—Length ½-¾ inch. Bronze-green in general colour; elytra pitted; legs red-brown. Found on reeds and water plants, as is general with the genus *Donacia*. The larvæ feed under water, and the perfect insects live in air, but can take to the water readily. Under side covered with silvery down, which resists water.

D. semicuprea (Fig. 193).—About ⅕ inch. Coppery green, but the centre parts of the elytra are purplish copper; under side silvery; thorax closely and plainly punctured. Found in similar situations.

D. sericea (Fig. 194).—A similar species, about ¼ inch, lacking the purplish hue on the elytra, which are metallic green.

Zeugophora subspinosa (Fig. 195).—Less than ⅛ inch. Orange body and legs; elytra black and pitted; tips of antennæ black. Lives on trees, the larvæ undermining the leaves.

Lema cyanella (Fig. 196).—Black, with a distinct blue lustre. Lives (like the others of its genus) on plants, and is said to be able to produce a sound of chirping by rubbing its elytra together.

L. melanopa (Fig. 197).—Slightly larger, with the same blue metallic tinge, but with red shoulders and legs; feet and antennæ black. These live on blades of grass and corn.

L. asparagi (*crioceris*) (Fig. 198).—The **Asparagus Beetle**. This has a pretty pattern on the yellowish wing-cases, consisting of a cross and six black spots connected together. Thorax chestnut red; legs black.

Clythra quadripunctata (Fig. 199).—Nearly ¼ inch. Head and thorax black; elytra yellow-orange, with two black spots on each. Lives on hazel, willow, birch, etc. The larvæ make hairy, leathery cases to live in, which they draw about with them when they move.

Cryptocephalus aureolus (Fig. 200).—About ⅛ inch. Oval shape; a rich metallic green in colour. Found on flowers.

C. pusillus (Fig. 201).—About 1/10 inch. A glossy yellow, the thorax being darker than the elytra. The antennæ are as long as the body. This genus lives on low plants, and the larvæ live in a case, like those of the preceding genus.

Timarcha tenebricosa (Fig. 202).—Known as the "**Bloody-nosed Beetle**," from its habit when disturbed of ejecting a red fluid from its mouth. This genus (*Timarcha*) consists of *wingless* beetles, very convex in shape. This species is nearly 1 inch in length; a dull black in colour. Found on grass and bushes in early spring.

T. coriaria (Fig. 203).—Length ⅓-½ inch. Shiny black; roughly pitted. Found on heaths and commons.

Chrysomela staphylea (Fig. 204).— About ⅛ inch; oval. Glistening reddish brown, with a bronze lustre; thorax a darker bronze than the elytra; legs lighter red-brown. Found under stones and on herbage.

BEETLES

C. polita (Fig. 205).—About ⅓ inch. Head, thorax, and legs black, with metallic green tinge; elytra reddish brown, finely pitted.

C. distinguenda (Fig. 206).—Slightly larger than preceding. Bluish black, but the edges of the elytra have a golden yellow margin. Frequent on flowers and in grassy places.

C. fastuosa (Fig. 207).—Length about ¼ inch. A most beautiful species. Coloured with a blue-green metallic lustre. On the elytra, when together, appear three longitudinal lines of violet hue, between which the green appears. Found on nettles and similar plants.

C. polygoni (*Gastrophysa*) (Fig. 208).—Length about ⅕ inch. Elytra bluish green; thorax and body clay-red. Common on knot grass.

C. raphæni (*Gastrophysa*) (Fig. 209).—About the same size as preceding. A bright metallic green. Common in grass.

C. vitellinæ (Fig. 210).—Black, with a dark green-blue tinge. Found on willows.

[*Note.*—The genus *Chrysomela* lives in large numbers on low plants, and is most destructive. The species are oval and very convex in shape, and of gorgeous metallic colours.]

Adimonia tanaceti (Fig. 211).—Under ½ inch. Dull black; under side having some scanty grey down; deeply pitted; pear-shaped. Found on wild tansy, chiefly on South Coast.

A. suturalis (Fig. 212).—Length ¼ inch. A dull fawn colour, with black head. Found on low plants.

A. sanguinea (Fig. 212b).—A similar species, but the elytra are blood-red, each with two black streaks; head black, with two reddish spots; thorax reddish, with a few black spots; legs black.

Galleruca sagittariæ (Fig. 213).—A brownish yellow. Found on water plants.

Agelastica halensis (Fig. 214).—About ¼ inch. Clay-yellow; but the elytra are a rich purplish black. Common on bed-straw.

Luperus flavipes (Fig. 215).—About ¼ inch. Very long antennæ; head and elytra shining black; thorax yellow. Found on pear and other fruit trees.

L. circumspexus (Fig. 216).—Black, with elytra yellow, edged with black.

Haltica erecta (Fig. 217).—The genus *Haltica* consists of small hopping beetles, living upon low plants and trees. Sometimes known as "Flea-beetles." This species is bluish green.

H. lepidii (*phyllotreta*) (Fig. 218).—Black, with a faint blue lustre.

H. testaceæ (*sphæroderma*) (Fig. 219).—Shining chestnut colour.

Cassida viridis (Fig. 220).—About ¼ inch. A flat oval shape. Elytra grass green; thorax yellowish; under side black. Lives on low plants. These beetles, as larvæ, have a curious fork on the back by which they carry the refuse of their food, like an umbrella. The genus *Cassida* (**Tortoise Beetles**) live on thistles, mint, and other plants, but look more like scale insects than beetles.

THE BRITISH NATURE BOOK

Sub-order vii. HETEROMERA (" Unequal-jointed "),

because the tarsi of the front and middle legs are five-jointed, the hind-tarsi four-jointed.

Family : *Tenebrionidæ*.

Usually black.

Blaps mucronata (the **Churchyard Beetle**) (Fig. 150).—About $\frac{7}{8}$–1 inch long. Dull black; pointed abdomen; wingless. Found in cellars, kitchens, and dark places at night. Common.

Opatrum sabulosum (Fig. 151).—Length about $\frac{1}{3}$ inch. A dull shabby brownish black. Scantily covered with grey down. Found under stones in sandy places.

Tenebrio molitor (the "**Mealworm**" Beetle) (Fig. 152).—Length about 1 inch. Black; finely pitted. Found in flour mills, rotten wood, and in stale flour. The larvæ, known as " Mealworms," are used by bird fanciers as food for young birds and soft-bills.

Helops striatus (Fig. 153).—About $\frac{1}{3}$ inch. Black, with fine lines on the elytra; legs have a slight reddish tinge. Found under bark of pine trees.

Cistela murina (Fig. 154).—Length $\frac{1}{4}$ inch. Black head and shoulders; elytra clay-yellow. Found on flowers in seacoast places.

Orchesia micans (Fig. 155).—Brown-black, with fine silky down. Lives on fungi. A type of a genus of hopping beetles.

Melandrya caraboides (Fig. 156).—Length about $\frac{1}{2}$ inch. Black, with bluish lustre; elytra thickly pitted; feet tipped with orange. Common on beech or oak.

Lagria hirta (Fig. 156b).—The only British species of this genus. Length under $\frac{1}{2}$ inch. Pear-shaped. Blackish body; yellow elytra. Soft, covered with light down. Found on flowering bushes.

Pyrochroa serraticornis (Fig. 157).—Length $\frac{1}{2}$–$\frac{2}{3}$ inch. Wedge-shaped. Dull red elytra; thorax and head covered with orange down; black legs and antennæ. Found in grassy shady places or under bark of trees.

Meloë violaceus (the **Violet Oil Beetle**) (Fig. 158).—Length very variable, $\frac{1}{2}$–1$\frac{1}{2}$ inches. Black, with a very pronounced bluish lustre. Wingless and soft-bodied. The elytra are short and cover only the upper part of the abdomen. The female is much stouter than the male. Common in grass.

These beetles have a very curious life-history. Their name " Oil Beetles " comes to them from the acrid, offensive oily fluid which is secreted at the joints of the femora and tibiæ of their legs. This contains cantharidin, an extremely caustic substance, which is an almost perfect protection against birds and other natural enemies, and accounts for the freedom with which they feed by day on open ground and for the lack of wings.

The female lays her eggs in a sticky mass in a hole which she excavates for them. When the larvæ hatch out (in about a month), they make their way

BEETLES

into flowers, where they remain until a bee arrives. Then the six-legged larva mounts the bee, and is carried to the nest, where it finds its way to a cell. There it devours the egg laid therein and lives on the food supplied ordinarily to the young bees. After passing through some strange changes of form, it pupates, and finally develops into the perfect insect.

The female lays some thousands of eggs, but few of which, fortunately, reach maturity.

Nacerdis melanura (Fig. 159).—Long, parallel-sided beetles about $\frac{1}{2}$ inch in length. Antennæ of male twelve joints; of female eleven. Head and thorax orange, shaded with black; elytra yellow, with black tips. Lives on flowers; larvæ in decaying wood. Found on seashore and estuaries.

Œdemera nobilis (Fig. 160).—A handsome brilliant green. Legs covered with hair. Thighs of hind-legs (of the male) much thickened. Found on flowers.

Phaleria cadaverina (Fig. 161).—An oval, convex species. Thorax dark brown; elytra fawn coloured, with a patch of black marbling in the centre of each. Plainly striated.

Sub-order viii. RHYNCHOPHORA—WEEVILS.

A very large group, containing more than twenty thousand species. Easily identified by the formation of the head, which is drawn out into a beak or trunk, with the mouth at the tip.

Family: *Curculionidæ*.

Vegetable feeders, most destructive, the larvæ being maggots without feet.

Attelabus curculionides (Fig. 162a).—Length about $\frac{1}{4}$ inch. Black head, antennæ, and legs; thorax and elytra chestnut red; antennæ clubbed. Found in oaks. Female lays her eggs in a mass of rolled-up leaves.

Otiorhynchus tenebricosus (Fig. 162b).—About $\frac{1}{2}$ inch long. Black; convex. Antennæ distinctly elbowed. Legs have a reddish tinge; feet heavy. Covered with fine long hairs. Found on fruit trees and at roots of grass.

O. scabrosus (Fig. 163).—Black head and thorax; elytra with a dull red tinge, much striated and roughly pitted; legs tipped with dull orange. Covered with scanty down.

O. picipes (Fig. 164).—Dull black, thickly covered with down; legs with a reddish tinge.

O. ligneus (Fig. 165).—Black wing-cases slightly ribbed, covered with fine light pubescence.

Phyllobius calcaratus (Fig. 166).—About $\frac{1}{4}$-$\frac{1}{3}$ inch long. A beautiful species under the magnifier. Black, but covered with golden green scales or down, so as to appear green; legs reddish. The femora are strongly toothed. Found on bushes in woods.

P. pyri (Fig. 167).—Slightly smaller, but very similar. Covered with bright shining green scales.

P. argentator (Fig. 168).—Long and slender, covered with red-golden scales.

[*Note.*—This genus, *Phyllobius*, has a short "beak" and long antennæ, and is found in numbers on bushes and trees, which they strip of their leaves.]

Barynotus obscurus (Fig. 169).—About ½ inch. Black. Elytra ribbed and pitted, covered with grey down. Wingless. Common under stones, at roots of grass, etc.

Strophosomus coryli (Fig. 170).—A rich fawn, covered with lighter satiny scales. Elytra pitted in rows. Found in hazel bushes.

Sitones lineatus (Fig. 171).—Black with brown scales. Makes havoc of clover fields.

Polydrosus pterygomalis (Fig. 172a).—A brilliant metallic green, with light brown legs and antennæ. Lives in shrubs.

Hypera punctata (Fig. 172b).—About ⅓ inch long. Blackish, with greenish down. Deep grooves on elytra. Found at roots of plants, especially in sandy districts.

Cleonus sulcirostris (Fig. 173).—About ¾ inch. A shabby black with thick grey down. Elytra very rough, marked by three slanting bands of black. Larvæ found on thistles, sometimes beet, especially on the coast.

Hylobius abietis (the **Pine Weevil**) (Fig. 174a).—Length ½–¾ inch. Black, with yellow scales, which form a rough pattern on the elytra. Coarsely punctured. Destructive to pines and firs.

Erirhinus tortrix (Fig. 174b).—A glossy dull chestnut; long trunk. Found on beeches and willows.

E. acridulus (Fig. 175).—A similar species, but black, with a faint dark blue tinge. Elytra striated and finely pitted; long and slender trunk.

Anthonomus ulmi (Fig. 176).—A beautiful dull red. A patch of golden scales at the base of each elytron, and a similar patch of light grey down about the middle, making a pattern. Found on elms and also on bushes.

Orchestes quercus (Fig. 177).—This genus has the power of hopping. Reddish brown, with grey down. The larvæ mine oak leaves, causing the familiar brown spots.

Cionus scrophulariæ (Fig. 178). — Blackish, covered with dense grey down, especially on thorax. Elytra ribbed and dentated. Feeds on figwort.

Apion miniatum (Fig. 179).—A beautiful red; black eyes; stout trunk; elytra elongated oval. Lives on galls on willows and aspens.

Rhynchites æquatus (Fig. 180).—Head and thorax a fine bronze colour; elytra chestnut red. Found on fruit trees and bushes, the larvæ living in fruits or rolled leaves.

Hylastes ater (Fig. 181).—Black; elongated and parallel-sided. Found under bark of pine trees.

SCORPION-FLIES

H. piniperda (Fig. 182).—Black, with reddish antennæ and legs. Larvæ live in pine shoots.

[*Note.*—As in other sections of this book I suggest here that the young student who is going to make a special hobby of " Beetles " should have one of the cheap pocket-books on the subject, which he should interleave, and use for handy reference on his walks. He will find *British Beetles* (price 1s. 9d.), published by Kelly, as useful as any, as it contains the greater part of the species referred to in this list, and illustrations very similar to those included here.]

Order XIV. MECOPTERA.

We now reach an order which contains one family only—

THE SCORPION-FLIES (*Panorpidæ*).

The **Common Scorpion-fly** is about ½ an inch long, shining black, with yellow legs, and long narrow transparent wings, spotted with brown. It possesses a curious three-jointed " tail," that of the male ending in a pair of forceps. This appendage is carried over the back like the tail of a scorpion—hence the popular name.

It is, in spite of its appearance, harmless, but feeds upon other insects. The eggs are laid in the ground or in rotten wood, where the larvæ, which are like caterpillars, but with eight pairs of prolegs, feed on refuse as well as other living insects.

Order XV. TRICHOPTERA.

In this order are placed the **Caddis-flies**, of which we have a number of species. The female lays her eggs in water, and the larvæ construct remarkable cases in which to pass the larval and pupal stages. Some use small bits of stick and leaves; others use leaves only, fastening them together by some sticky secretion; another species uses sand and small stones; while yet another uses the shells of small water-snails (often with the real owners still inside).

The head and front portion of the larvæ are well protected, but the rest of the body is soft, and needs the defence which these cases provide. Watching the bed of a clear stream numbers of these larvæ may be seen moving, dragging their cases behind them, as a Hermit Crab carries its shell. At the pupal stage, the creature retires into its case, and seals up the end, emerging after a few weeks, and leaving the water to pass into its mature form as the Caddis-fly. The larvæ feed on vegetation.

CHAPTER IX.

Arthropoda (*continued*).

Order XVI. LEPIDOPTERA.

Butterflies and Moths.

BUTTERFLIES and Moths belong to the Lepidopterous order of insects—that is, insects with scales (*lepis*) on their wings (*pteron*). The wing of a butterfly seen through a microscope is a most beautiful object, being covered, in regular lines, with minute scales or feathers of various shapes and characteristics. Butterflies are distinguished from moths, at any rate in the British species, by the fact that they have clubbed antennæ, whilst moths' antennæ come to a point, and are otherwise unmistakably differentiated. To put it in simpler language, the horns or feelers which protrude from a butterfly's head have small knobs at the end, whilst a moth's feelers have not. Another noticeable difference is to be found in observing the insects at rest. A butterfly's wings stand up at right angles to the body, a moth's wings are folded flat across the body. Butterflies are *Rhopalocera*, moths *Heterocera*. There are at the most some sixty-eight species of butterflies inhabiting, or known to have inhabited, Great Britain; of these some, like the Large Copper, are extinct, others are very rare. It may be said that there are some fifty to fifty-five species which may be met with generally, half that number being quite common, the other half needing looking for in the particular localities they are known to inhabit.

The eggs of butterflies are some of the most beautiful objects in Nature. Every one, I expect, who reads this book will have seen the clusters of eggs laid by the Common Large Garden Butterflies on cabbages or nasturtiums. (The number of eggs laid by the female varies in different species from 50 to 3,000.) View these small white specks under your pocket lens, and you find them beautiful miniature pyramids, ribbed and fluted with delicate lines. The eggs of the different species are all of varying shapes: some are round like balls, others oval, others flat; some are smooth and glossy, others ribbed and covered with delicate network. And they vary in colour—white, yellow, green, purple, red, black. Here, however, it must be noted that all the eggs change in colour as the young caterpillar inside develops. These changes are duly noted in the List of Species (pages 224–237).

When the larva emerges from the egg—after a period of from five to thirty-

BUTTERFLIES AND MOTHS 219

five days—its first meal in many cases is the discarded egg-shell. It is, of course, a most minute creature, but it speedily grows, and in the course of development changes its skin several times, as it becomes too small for it. The description of the larva in the List of Species is that of the caterpillar in *its last stage*, before it becomes a chrysalis. All larvæ have thirteen segments, excluding the head. The last two segments, however, are so closely united as to be difficult to distinguish in many cases, so that, popularly speaking, we may say that we shall easily count twelve segments, excluding the head. They have two kinds of legs, technically called true and false. The first three pairs are the true legs, and are horny jointed affairs, terminating in a useful claw. These are followed by four pairs of false legs, which are fleshy, and terminate in a number of most minute hooks, with which the creature clings to its support. There is also a last pair of legs on the "tail-part," called the "anal claspers."

Under the microscope or magnifying lens it will be noticed that all larvæ are covered with minute warts, from which spring the hair and spines, in some cases so fine as to escape observation by the naked eye, and along the sides are a row of circular marks called spiracles, through which the creature breathes.

The head of the larva is another object of interest. It contains some very minute eyes (*ocelli*), of little or no use to it; a complicated mouth with strong jaws; a pair of small antennæ; and a spinneret—the organ with which its silken line, and sometimes cocoon, is spun.

The pupa, or chrysalis, also is worth examining in detail. It is placed in characteristic positions by the different species. Some hang head downwards, others head upwards; others are supported by a girdle of silk round the body, the ends being fastened to the food plant or stalk. Others are held in position on the plant by a few cross lines of silk; a few are hidden in a cocoon, or sheath, made by bringing together the surfaces of blades of grass, or by rolling up a leaf. Again, they differ much in shape and colour: whilst some are green and quiet in tone, looking exactly like a portion of the plant they repose upon, others are of noticeable colours, even covered with gilt or silver metallic markings, which glitter in the sun. All these are points upon which the identification of different species is based. While some butterflies emerge in ten days or a fortnight, some of the moths remain for *years* in the pupal stage.

With regard to the imago, or butterfly itself, the young student must notice first of all the wings, divided by ribs or veins. Seen under the microscope, the wings are found to be covered with myriads of scales or "feathers," arranged in rows, not unlike the tiles upon a roof. These will be found to be of varying shapes in the different species; but, in addition, the males of many kinds have special scales or plumes, and I believe that the theory has been definitely proved to be a fact, whilst this very chapter was being written, that these plumes are scent organs, and emit a scent, much like that of different flowers, which is highly attractive to the females.

THE BRITISH NATURE BOOK

The brief description of the colour of the perfect insect in the List of Species cannot pretend to be more than an attempt to point out the salient features of each species, but I hope that, with the photographs as well, my readers will find it serviceable enough.

The student, however, has much more to note than the colour and shape of the wings. Let him look at a butterfly's head through his pocket lens. Here he finds striking and beautiful features. A pair of great compound eyes, and two simple eyes (*ocelli*) on the top of the head; the antennæ; the long tongue, coiled up when not needed like a watch spring, but in reality consisting of two tubes which, when brought side by side, form a central passage, through which the nectar and other sweets are drawn up into the throat.

The months of the year, placed in the List of Species, refer to the months when the butterfly itself may be seen. Common sense will suggest that eggs and larvæ are likely to be found in later months, and that, unless the butterfly hibernated all through the winter, there must have been either (1) larvæ, which had hibernated and then come out to feed and pupate in the spring; or (2) pupæ, which had been formed in the preceding autumn and had survived the winter; or (3) eggs, which, laid late in the autumn, did not hatch till the following spring. Such is, as a matter of fact, the case. Some butterflies— for example, the Small Tortoiseshell, the Peacock, the Brimstone—find a warm corner for the winter and sleep until the spring. Large numbers of pupæ must remain inert on their withered food plants till the spring sun warms them into activity. In addition, larvæ from eggs hatched in the summer and autumn feed for a few weeks and then hibernate for the winter.

To catch butterflies it is necessary to have a net, a killing bottle, and a store box, as well as a supply of pins. These latter should be the very thin black pins specially made for the purpose. The net should be ten to twelve inches in diameter, two or three feet long, preferably of green-coloured material (gauze or muslin), and fastened on a light but strong frame. A Y-shaped holder of tin can be obtained at any entomological shop, the base of which will slide on to a walking-stick, and a pliant cane on which the net is run will be held by the other two arms. This enables the apparatus to be "unshipped" and carried in the pocket till required.

The killing bottle has to be used at once, as it is impossible to carry live butterflies about without damaging them. Many of these insects can be killed instantaneously by pinching the thorax; but this is bound to damage them to some extent, and it is better to place them in a bottle containing poison. The simplest form of all is a wide-mouthed bottle containing crushed laurel leaves. These must be *freshly* used, and can be made effective by breaking them up and rubbing them between the palms of the hands. A "cyanide" bottle, containing cyanide of potassium in plaster of Paris, can be bought ready made. It is better for young people not to attempt to make one themselves, as it is a deadly poison; any chemist will supply one.

BUTTERFLIES AND MOTHS

Chloroform itself may be used, a few drops on a tuft of cotton wool being placed in the bottle in which the insect is confined.

I need hardly add that in all cases the bottle must be tightly closed, and the insect left long enough within to be actually killed, and not merely rendered "unconscious." When dead, it should be taken out and pinned into the collecting box.

A very useful "killing box" can be made out of an empty carbide tin—one of those long tube-like tins obtainable at any bicycle shop. A third of it may be filled with crushed laurel leaves, and a piece of perforated zinc placed above them; or, simpler still, the laurel leaves may be put in *a small muslin bag*, which is kept inside the tin.

As for the collecting box, it should be of a size convenient for the pocket. A cigar box, with a piece of sheet cork (or sections of ordinary bottle cork, about ¼ of an inch thick) glued to the inside of the lid and the bottom of the box, serves very well. To this the insects may be pinned. Keep a small piece of sponge, damped with water, in a corner of the box, to prevent the insects from getting too dry.

To "set" a butterfly for its place in the collection, care must be taken that it is not too dry, or its legs and antennæ will snap off when touched. If it has been kept unset for some time it must be *relaxed*. Place it on a piece of blotting-paper, resting on a layer of damp sand in an air-tight tin box, for a day or two, and it will then be softened and easily handled.

A setting board, of which a sectional sketch is given, must be used. This is made of cork, and has a groove in which the body of the insect lies. The wings are moved into position (*not* with the fingers, but with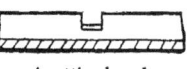

A setting board.

a blunt needle fixed in a handle), and fastened there by strips of thin paper, with pins at each end. The antennæ must be straightened out, and the easiest way of manipulating them is to use a small painting brush, moistening it with the lips, and, as it were, painting the antennæ forward into their proper position. The moisture thus used is sufficiently "sticky" to fasten the antennæ in place on the board till dry. This is a valuable hint which I do not remember to have seen given in print before.

I am not in favour of making large collections of butterflies or moths, unless it is purely for the sake of scientific work. At the most, the amateur will require only *four* of each species, male and female, showing upper and lower surfaces.

The specimens should be kept in air-tight drawers or boxes, preferably glass-covered, and a little lump of camphor naphthalene, or, cheapest of all, "carbon," should be pinned in a bit of muslin in one corner, to keep away mites or other destructive insects.

Nothing is more interesting than to rear butterflies, and this is a hobby which can be easily and successfully undertaken by anybody. Breeding cages can be bought at any naturalist's shop, but they can be made in very simple ways by anybody who is handy with tools. Any kind of case which will keep out a fly and keep in a caterpillar will serve, provided it gets plenty of light and air, and there is some arrangement for holding the food plant, and keeping it fresh. A small wooden box, set up on one end, with a sheet of glass in front in place of the lid, with some holes cut out in the top and sides, and pieces of fine perforated zinc or gauze tacked over them as ventilators, will house your larvæ perfectly well. Inside it you should place a smaller and quite shallow box, containing dried moss, or even mould or sand, in the middle of which set a small bottle full of water, in which some sprays of the food plant can be placed. Place this breeding cage somewhere in a good light, but not where the direct sunlight will reach it, or the insects will perish; and you can watch your insects hatch from the egg, and pass through all their stages up to the perfect butterfly.

An empty aquarium, or fish-globe, covered with fine muslin, is also a suitable home; and even a large pickle bottle will do, although the thick rough glass makes it difficult to view the insects within.

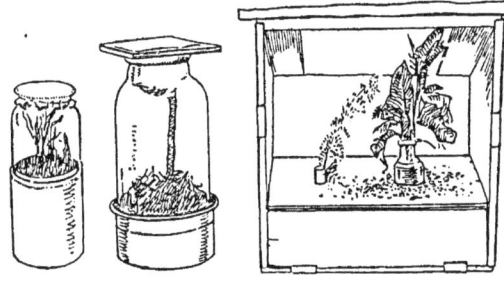

Home-made rearing cages.

It is most important to remember that the larvæ of butterflies feed on particular plants. There is still a very common notion that every caterpillar eats cabbage leaves, or that any kind of vegetation will serve it for a meal. This is, of course, a great mistake; and a glance at the List of Species will show the usual plants which the various species feed upon. In rearing butterflies, therefore, it is important to try to provide them with their natural food, or, if that should fail, with the nearest approach to it which can be found. For this reason an entomologist, you see, must be something of a botanist too.

Catching Moths is a rather different occupation from catching butterflies; for whilst the latter is done by day, much of the former is done by night. The majority of the moths fly only by night, though, of course, there are exceptions, such as the Foresters, the Clearwings, and others, which may be seen in broad daylight; and still many more may be captured during the day by beating bushes, herbage, and undergrowth, in which it will be found they are resting or sleeping.

For the rest, much can be done by collecting their larvæ, and rearing them

BUTTERFLIES AND MOTHS

at home, and by "sugaring" fences and trees after dark, thus providing bait to which many moths come eagerly. The larvæ can be obtained by shaking bushes and herbage. If a cloth or an umbrella is spread below, they will fall upon it, and may be easily captured.

Once again, the full-grown females may be taken home alive, and kept till they have laid their eggs. Care must be taken to observe the food plant upon which the larvæ are found, that fresh supplies of it may be provided.

Details of the way of making rearing cages may be found, if required, in *The Young People's Nature Study Book*.

Note also that in rearing larvæ the stale leaves should be removed from the cage when fresh food is put in, but on no account should the larvæ be forced to loose their hold on the old leaves. Take the stale food plant out first, and then if the new food is put in place and the old leaves put back, it will not be long before the larvæ find their way to it.

The cages should not be overcrowded with larvæ, otherwise they will not develop healthily, and may take to such depraved habits as eating each other. Some moss or fibre, or a little mould, or an inch or two of turf, should be put at the bottom of the cage for those larvæ which bury themselves when pupating.

Often, at the end of the summer and during the autumn, the larvæ of some of the larger moths may be found crawling across roads and paths, hunting for a suitable place to burrow for their pupal change. These should be taken home, and allowed to bury themselves in mould or moss in a suitable box.

Many pupæ of moths may be found if the proper places are well searched. "Such trees as poplar, willow, ash, elm, are certain to be the hiding-places of some. Trees which stand alone, or on the outskirts of woods or the banks of streams, yield richer finds than others. In the crevices of the bark, behind loose or decayed pieces, in clumps of moss, the debris of dead leaves, among the roots, three or four inches below the surface in dry, soft soil—all these are places where finds may be expected; and experienced entomologists tell us that, generally speaking, the majority of discoveries will be made on the north side of trees, because that is the side sheltered most from rain and sunshine, both of which are unhealthy for pupæ" (*Moths of the Months*). The net, poison bottle, and collecting box described above will serve again for moth-catching; but in addition some small boxes (pill boxes, or chip boxes), preferably those sold for the purpose with glass tops, must be taken. These are used for capturing moths found sleeping on trees or fences, placing the box close to the insect and sliding the lid over it. As moths are generally torpid during the day, they may often be taken home in the pill boxes without being killed first. Those that are wild and vigorous must be put into the poison bottle at once.

At night a great deal may be done by means of "sugaring." The moth hunter takes with him a bottle of sugaring mixture, and this is spread with a brush on trees or palings just after sunset. A dark, sultry night from June to September should be chosen. On going back later to the places thus "baited," if the night is a good one for the "sport," the moths will be found either greedily devouring the food, or already gorged with it.

Various recipes have been given for the sugar mixture, but any thick, *strong-smelling* (this is important) syrup will do. Treacle, in which a little beer or rum has been mixed, or sugar boiled till thick and mixed with the same "intoxicants," or flavoured with apple, pear, aniseed, etc., may be used. Many moths haunt the sweet-smelling and nectar-producing flowers by night, and a hunt in the garden in the dark with a lamp (an electric pocket torch, for instance) will often yield a succession of captures. Look especially at the following plants when in bloom—verbenas and pinks, honeysuckle, nettles, ivy, and sallow.

Many species also come to a light, and may be taken at a window or at a lamp fixed up outside. Some valuable prizes have been obtained round a street lamp before now, and indeed it is astonishing to notice how many moths are thus decoyed to their deaths by the street lamps in our suburbs.

What is said above as to the setting of butterflies applies equally to moths; but the latter need some special care if they happen to be large-bodied species. If left in a natural state, they either shrivel up when dry, or suffer from "grease"—that is, become saturated with an oily exudation from the abdomen. In the first case, the body can be stuffed. Cut the body off at the waist, extract the contents with a bent wire, and fill it with a tuft of cotton wool on which a few drops of some preservative may be put, afterwards seccotining it back in its place. In the case of the second calamity, dip the whole moth bodily into methylated spirits, and then leave it to dry. This is a complete cure.

BRITISH BUTTERFLIES: LIST OF SPECIES, WITH OCCASIONAL NOTES.

I suggest that my little book, *Butterflies, and how to identify Them*, should be used as a "handbook" to this section—as a pocket guide, which may be taken out, like the bird and flower books referred to in the sections dealing with these subjects.

Family: *Papilionidæ*. Genus: *Papilioninæ*.

1. **The Swallow-tail** (*Papilio machaon*).—Unmistakable.
Food plant—Milk parsley, angelica, fennel, wild carrot.
Larva—Green, with orange-spotted black bands.
Pupa—Sometimes green, sometimes a yellowish brown; fixed with girdle of silk, head upwards, on stems of reeds.
Eggs—Laid May or June.
Locality—Norfolk Broads and fenny districts.
Many larvæ I have found pierced by the ichneumon.

PLATE XXV.

1, Silver-washed Fritillary. 2, Pearl-bordered Fritillary. 3, Marbled White. 4, Wall. 5, Speckled Wood. 6, Large Heath. 7, Small Heath. 8, Painted Lady. 9, Purple Hairstreak. 10, Green Hairstreak. 11, Brown Argus. 12, Clifton Blue. 13, Swallowtail. 14, Little Blue. 15, Chalk Hill Blue. 16, Clouded Yellow. 17, Pale Clouded. 18, Large Skipper. 19, Small Skipper. 20, Dingy Skipper. 21, Grizzled Skipper. 22, Orange-tip, male. 23, Orange-tip, female.

BUTTERFLIES

Family: *Papilionidæ*. Genus: *Pierinæ*.

2. **Black-veined White** (*Aporia cratægi*).—Easily identified by black veins on wings.
Food plant—Sloe, hawthorn, plum.
Larva—Brown, with black stripes and paler hairs; congregate in silken home.
Pupa—Whitish, dotted with black; head upright, on food stem.
Eggs—Yellow, changing to grey; upright, with ornamented top like crown. Laid in July.
Locality—Kent (chiefly).

3. **Large White** (*Pieris brassicæ*).—Unmistakable; *male* is without the two black spots on upper wing, topside.
Food plant—Cabbage, tropæolum, mignonette.
Larva—Greenish grey, yellow lines, fine whitish hairs.
Pupa—Grey, spotted black and yellow; often fixed to palings, walls, etc.; upright, with silken brace.
Eggs—Yellow, ribbed, and cross-lined. Laid in batches (June to August).
There are two distinct broods—spring and summer—the latter being more richly coloured.

4. **Small White** (*Pieris rapæ*).—Unmistakable.
Food plant—Cabbage, mignonette, nasturtium.
Larva—Greenish, with blackish points; yellow line on back; yellow spots on sides.
Pupa—Grey-green, with faint black speckles.
Eggs—Greenish, changing to yellow; shaped like *Brassicæ*.

5. **Green-veined White** (*Pieris napi*).—Greenish veins. From May onwards.
Food plant—Hedge garlic, cruciferæ, nasturtium.
Larva—Green back; grey below; dark line on back; yellow line on sides.
Pupa—Green and brownish yellow; upright, with silken brace.
Eggs—Straw colour to green; fourteen ribs.

6. **Bath White** (*Pieris daplidice*).—Rare; like the *Napi*, but has green mottles on under side of hind-wing (like female Orange-tip), which is very transparent.
Food plant—Mignonette.
Larva—Grey-blue, black spots, yellow lines; short black hairs.
Pupa—Grey-blue, changing to white, black dots, yellow markings; braced to food plant.
Eggs—Said to be pinkish red; ribbed.
Locality—Occasionally visiting South Coast (August to September).

7. **Orange-tip** (*Euchloë cardamines*).—*Male* has "orange tips" to fore-wings; *female*, blackish grey tips. Hind-wings dappled with green.

THE BRITISH NATURE BOOK

Food plant—Hedge mustard, cuckoo flower, charlock, cresses.

Larva—Green-blue, white stripe on sides; like seed pods of food plant.

Pupa—Pale grey, sharp-pointed; braced to stalk, looking like withered fragment.

Eggs—White, changing to yellow, and purple. May, June (occasionally later).

Locality—Well distributed.

The illustrations show the emergence from the pupa found in the winter on the dead stem of hedge mustard by the river side.

8. **Woodwhite** (*Leucophasia sinapis*).—White, with black tip to fore-wings (*female* much fainter); thin, fragile body.

Food plant—Bird's-foot trefoil, yellow pea, vetch.

Larva—Green; yellow line on sides.

Pupa—Resembles *Cardamines*, but not so hollowed; green (sometimes with pink linings).

Eggs—Yellowish, ribbed, shiny. May and July.

Locality—South Ireland, New Forest, Worcester, Lancashire, Devon, and other counties; very local.

9. **Pale Clouded Yellow** (*Colias hyale*).—Scarce; *male*, light yellow; *female*, almost white. Blackish margins to fore-wings; orange spot on hind-wings.

Food plant—Clover, trefoil, etc.

Larva—Light green, but blackish, velvety back; orange lines on sides.

Pupa—Like *Edusa* (No. 10).

Eggs—Yellow-white, glassy, through orange to purplish; ribbed and reticulated. Larvæ feed in June and August.

Locality—Very local: Kent, South Coast, Essex, and other places.

10. **Clouded Yellow** (*Colias edusa*).—Orange, with black borders.

Food plant—Clover, lucerne, trefoils.

Larva—Dark green, tiny black dots; yellowish side lines.

Pupa—Yellowish green; row of red-black dots on body; upright; beak-like protrusion from head.

Eggs—Tapering, ribbed, yellow to pink; others in small batches. August and September.

Locality—Generally distributed, but very uncertain.

11. **Brimstone** (*Gonepteryx rhamni*).—Unmistakable; sulphur-coloured, with orange spot on each wing. Hibernates.

Food plant—Buckthorn, alder.

Larva—Green, black specks; pale low side-lines.

Pupa—Bluish green, of swollen, knobby shape, with pointed projection; braced with girdle.

Eggs—Pointed and ribbed; green to yellow and purplish. July and August.

Locality—Everywhere.

BUTTERFLIES

Family: *Nymphalidæ*. Genus: *Apaturinæ*.

12. **The Purple Emperor** (*Apatura iris*).—Unmistakable; fond of flying in tops of oaks.
Food plant—Sallow (occasionally willow and poplar).
Larva—Dull green, oblique yellowish stripes; two horns on head.
Pupa—Whitish; suspended head downwards from food plant; striped, and two horns.
Eggs—Green, ribbed, cylindrical. August to September.
Locality—Oak woods in South and Midlands, and Lincolnshire and Northamptonshire.
The males of this species can be attracted by means of a piece of decaying flesh. The pupa is very like the larva in its full-fed stage.

Family: *Nymphalidæ*. Genus: *Nymphalinæ*.

13. **The White Admiral** (*Limenitis sibylla*, or *camilla*).—Easily recognized by its white markings on dark wings.
Food plant—Honeysuckle.
Larva—Dark green, yellow dots; reddish bristles or spines.
Pupa—Remarkable shape; brownish, with metallic spots.
Eggs—Pale green. July.
Locality—South and East, especially New Forest.
Said to be getting rarer, but I have seen many specimens in the New Forest.

14. **The Comma** (*Polygonia C-album*).—Easily identified by irregular outline of wings and the white comma under hind-wings.
Food plant—Nettle, currant, hop.
Larva—Fore-part black, rear white; yellowish spines; two clubs on head.
Pupa—Brownish, silvery or golden spots.
Eggs—Green to yellow; ribbed. May and August. Hibernates.
Locality—Chiefly Hertfordshire, Worcestershire, and Monmouthshire.
I well remember the first pupa (from a Midland hop-field) which I obtained, with its wonderful silver spots.

15. **The Large Tortoise-shell** (*Vanessa polychoros*).—Unmistakable. Hibernates.
Food plant—Elm, willow, sallow, and other trees. Nettle.
Larva—Black with spines; lives in companies.
Pupa—Grey, often pink tinge, shaded with brown; metallic spots; suspended by tail.
Eggs—Dead-green; seven or eight ribs; June to August.
Locality—Fairly generally distributed, but not in Ireland.
This species also is associated with an incident of my schooldays, when I thought I had found a great rarity.

THE BRITISH NATURE BOOK

16. **The Small Tortoise-shell** (*Vanessa urticæ*).
Food plant—Nettle.
Larva—Yellowish, with black speckles; spines. Gregarious.
Pupa—Greyish, with metallic splashes.
Eggs—Green to yellow; ribbed; laid in clusters. May and July Hibernates.
Locality—Everywhere.
These breed regularly close to my church; the pupæ are almost always gilded all over. They hibernate in the church roof, waking up about Easter time.

17. **The Peacock** (*Vanessa io*).—Unmistakable from its "peacock-eye" markings.
Food plant—Nettle.
Larva—Black, with white dots; spiny. Gregarious.
Pupa—Varies from grey-green to brown; head downwards; metallic points, or gilded all over.
Eggs—Olive-green; ribbed. April to May onward.
Locality—Widely distributed, but not so common as in former years. Hibernates.

18. **The Camberwell Beauty** (*Vanessa antiopa*).—Unmistakable (see Plate XXVI.).
Food plant—Sallow, willow, elm, etc.
Larva—Black, with white spots; deep red markings on back. Gregarious.
Pupa—Black and orange, covered with a sort of bloom.
Eggs—Yellow, changing through brown to grey; ribbed; laid in batches. May onwards.
This butterfly is only an occasional visitor to England, but once used to breed here.

19. **The Painted Lady** (*Pyrameis cardui*).—Unmistakable.
Food plant—Thistle, generally.
Larva—Stoutish; varying from grey to black; yellow lines; makes a sort of lair on food plant.
Pupa—Grey-green, often with metallic points.
Eggs—Green; ribbed. Laid singly about June.
Locality—General, but very uncertain.
A large number of these butterflies immigrate from abroad.

20. **The Red Admiral** (*Pyrameis atalanta*).—Easily identified by its scarlet bands on upper side of wings.
Food plant—Nettle.
Larva—Sometimes blackish, or greyish, with white freckles; two yellow side stripes; spiny. Makes a lair.
Pupa—Greyish; head downwards under leaf; gold patches and points.
Eggs—Green; ten ribs; laid singly; darken very much. June to September.
Locality—Everywhere.

21. **Silver-washed Fritillary** (*Argynnis paphia*).—Largest of all the Fritil-

laries; recognized by the silver-washed marks on under side of hind-wing; almost like silver sand when tide is out.

Food plant—Dog-violet.

Larva—Black; spiny; two yellow lines on back; two spines, like horns, on head.

Pupa—Yellowish brown; gold lustre on back, and golden points; suspended by tail.

Eggs—Green-tinged; ribbed and notched; darken. Laid in June and July.

Locality—Southern woodlands.

A well-known variety of this species has a greenish coloration throughout instead of the beautiful rich brown hue. (*Valerina*.)

22. **High-brown Fritillary** (*Argynnis adippe*).—On under wing silvery spots, *as a rule*, but several varieties occur. Smaller than *Paphia*.

Food plant—Dog-violet.

Larva—Black; spiny; white line on back; grey patches on sides.

Pupa—Brown; greeny-gold points; head downwards.

Eggs—Yellowish green, changing through red to blue-green. Laid in July.

Locality—Southern woodlands chiefly, but also generally distributed in England.

23, 23 (a). **Dark-green Fritillary** (*Argynnis aglaia*).—Almost as large as *Paphia*, but easily distinguished by its regular silver spots on under side (no "washes").

Food plant—Dog-violet.

Larva—Grey and black; yellow back stripe; row of reddish spots at sides.

Pupa—Black, with pale brown markings; hung by tail.

Eggs—Yellow, changing to purplish, in rings; ribbed and reticulated. July and August.

Locality—Fairly common on moorland and sea cliffs.

23 (b). **Queen of Spain Fritillary** (*Argynnis lathonia*).—Resembling *Paphia*, but smaller in size, and many irregular pearly *patches* on under wings (not "washes").

Food plant—Dog-violet.

Larva—Black, plentifully dotted with white; spiny; two white streaks on each wing.

Pupa—Olive-brown, speckled with brown, black, and white; gilding on head and body; suspended by tail.

Eggs—Yellowish, changing to purplish grey; much ribbed and cross-ribbed. August to September.

Locality—South Coast, especially Dover, but *rare*.

24. **Pearl-bordered Fritillary** (*Argynnis euphrosyne*).—Like *Adippe*, but much smaller; and the pearl spots under hind-wing are placed like outline of anchor.

Food plant—Dog-violet.

Larva—Black; velvety; grey side-stripe; spiny.

Pupa—Brownish and grey; suspended by tail.

230   THE BRITISH NATURE BOOK

Eggs—Greenish white; ribbed and serrated. May or June.
Locality—Fairly common in wood clearings.

25. **Small Pearl-bordered Fritillary** (*Argynnis silene*).—Like above, but darker, and many more pearly or silvery spots.
Food plant—Dog-violet.
Larva—Dark velvet, with pink tinge; spiny, the first pair long, like horns; pink stripe close to feet.
Pupa—Brown marked with black; special black V mark on thorax; silver spots; head downwards.
Eggs—Green, changing yellow, grey, blackish; ribbed and reticulated. June to July.
Locality—As above, but more local.

26. **The Heath Fritillary** (*Melitæa athalia*)—sometimes called "PEARL-BORDERED LIKENESS."—Darker markings than above.
Food plant—Cow wheat (sometimes foxglove).
Larva—Black back; rich brown on sides; dotted white; orange spines.
Pupa—Pale brown, with black and orange markings; head downwards.
Eggs—Ribbed; green, becoming grey; in clusters. June and July.
Locality—Scarce: Essex, Kent, Surrey, Devonshire.

27. **Glanville Fritillary** (*Melitæa cinxia*).—Recognized by under side. Hind-wings pale yellow, crossed by two irregular orange bands. Pale yellow up to fore-wings (under side), dotted with black.
Food plant—Plantain, especially " narrow-leaved."
Larva—Black, white dots; red head and fore-legs; hairy tufts.
Pupa—Brown and orange.
Eggs—White, tinged yellow or green; clusters; ribbed, broad base. June.
Locality—Isle of Wight.

28. **Marsh Fritillary** (*Melitæa aurinia*).—Varies much in size and colouring, but identified by row of spots with black centres towards edge of hind-wing, under side.
Food plant—Devil's-bit scabious; also honeysuckle.
Larva—Black, spiny, tiny white dots; under side dull reddish colour.
Pupa—Pale brown, black and orange ornamentation: head downwards.
Eggs—Light brown, shiny; smooth base, ribbed upper half; clusters. May to June.
Locality—Water meadows; widely but locally distributed.

Family: *Nymphalidæ*. Genus: *Danainæ*.

29. **Milkweed Butterfly** (*Anosia plexippus*)—otherwise called "MONARCH." —Very rare; immigrant.

Family: *Nymphalidæ*. Genus: *Satyrinæ*.

30. **The Marbled White** (*Melanargia galatea*).—Easily identified.
Food plant—Grasses.

BUTTERFLIES 231

Larva—Whitish brown, with darker lines; a short forked tail—pinkish, like head; yellow back.

Pupa—Short, thick, same general colours as larva; unsuspended; often hidden.

Eggs—White; narrower apex; almost smooth; no ribs. July.

Locality—South and Midlands; especially south-west; rough fields.

31. **Small Mountain Ringlet** (*Erebia epiphron*).

Food plant—Grasses.

Larva—Green, with yellow lines.

Pupa—Little more than $\frac{1}{4}$ inch long; greenish.

Eggs—Yellow to darker colour; ribbed. July.

Locality—North.

32. **Scotch Argus** (*Erebia blandina*, or *æthiops*).—Dark brown; three black spots, with white centres on upper side of fore-wing.

Food plant—Grasses.

Larva—Light yellow-brown; dark stripe on back, etc.

Pupa—Head up; yellowish, with darker shadings.

Eggs—Creamy, round, ribbed, spotted. July to August.

Locality—Edges of woods, generally eastern side, North England and Scotland.

33. **Grayling** (*Satyrus semele*).—Lightish brown, with darker markings; two black spots on fore-wing, top side; one on hind-wing, top side.

Food plant—Grasses.

Larva—Yellow-brown, striped.

Pupa—Red, underground.

Eggs—Creamy, ribbed. August.

Locality—Common on open lands everywhere.

34. **Speckled Wood** (*Pararge egeria*).—Brown, with yellowish spots; one eye spot on fore-wing, three on hind-wing, top side.

Food plant—Grasses.

Larva—Green, with darker stripes.

Pupa—Green, suspended by tail.

Eggs—Greenish, not ribbed, but "roughened"; darken. May onwards.

Locality—Generally distributed.

35. **Wall Butterfly** (*Pararge megæra*).—Rich brown; darker markings. Eye spots, especially six or seven in row on hind-wing, under side.

Food plant—Grasses.

Larva—Whitish green, with white dots.

Pupa—Green, with yellowish markings; row of spots on body; tail upwards.

Eggs—Green, appearing smooth but finely ribbed. May to June, and July to August.

Locality—Fairly common.

36. **Meadow Brown** (*Epinephele janira*).—Shabby brown, with lighter markings; one eye spot on each fore-wing, upper side.

Food plant—Grasses.
Larva—Green ; line on back ; whitish side-stripes.
Pupa—Light green, brown spots and markings ; tail upwards.
Eggs—Greenish to yellow-brown, ribbed ; marked with brown blotches.
Locality—Everywhere.

37. **Gatekeeper** (*Epinephele tithonus*).—Like *Janira*, but smaller and richer colour.
Food plant—Grasses.
Larva—Light brown ; yellowish line near feet.
Pupa—Light brown, with darker streaks and spots ; head downwards.
Eggs—Yellowish, becoming blotched, to slate. July to August.
Locality—General.

38. **Ringlet** (*Aphantopus hyperanthus*).—Dark upper side ; under side, eight eye spots—three fore-wing, five hind-wing.
Food plant—Grasses.
Larva—Brownish grey, whitish below ; small forked tail.
Pupa—Brownish grey, with darker markings ; not suspended.
Eggs—Yellowish to brown ; pudding shaped ; not ribbed, but finely "pitted." July to August.
Locality—General.

39. **Large Heath** (*Cœnonympha typhon*).—Very variable ; tawny brown ; with eye spots.
Food plant—Grasses.
Larva—Green, white dots ; paler lines on sides.
Pupa—Green, brownish markings ; suspended by tail.
Eggs—Greenish yellow, becoming blotched, finely marked. June to July.
Locality—Northward and Midlands.

40. **Small Heath** (*Cœnonympha pamphilus*).—Light yellowish brown.
Food plant—Grasses.
Larva—Green ; striped ; divided tail.
Pupa—Pale green, with red-brown streaks ; suspended by tail.
Eggs—Green, ribbed, becoming blotched. May to June onwards.
Locality—Everywhere.

Family : *Lycænidæ*. Genus : *Lycæninæ* (Hair-streaks, Coppers, and Blues).

41. **Brown Hair-streak** (*Zephyrus betulæ*).— Hair-streaks usually have pale lines on under surface of wings, and projection from hind-wings called a tail.
Food plant—Blackthorn (will eat plum).
Larva—Green, with yellow lines ; Wood-louse shaped.
Pupa—Reddish brown ; on leaves.
Eggs—Flattened ; pitted, freckled. August to September.
Locality—General, but "local," and not common.

PLATE XXVI.

1. Black Hair-streak.   2. Camberwell Beauty (photographed with camera described in Introductory Chapter).
3. Swallow-tail Butterfly, newly emerged.   4. Small Garden White Butterflies at sunrise.

BUTTERFLIES

42. **Purple Hair-streak** (*Zephyrus quercus*).—So called from its purple hue; under side grey.
Food plant—Oak, sometimes sallow.
Larva—Red-brown, downy, whitish cross lines; Wood-louse shaped.
Pupa—Red-brown; on leaf generally.
Eggs—Light brown, with pinkish shade, covered with fine network; flattened. July to August.
Locality—Oak woods; generally distributed.

43. **Black Hair-streak** (*Thecla pruni*).—Brown-black; orange marks on border of hind-wing, upper side.
Food plant—Blackthorn.
Larva—Yellow-green, with darker markings; Wood-louse shaped.
Pupa—Black and white, on leaf; like bird's dropping.
Eggs—Red-brown; flattened. June to July.
Locality—Very rare.

44. **White Letter Hair-streak** (*Thecla W-album*).—Blackish; white "W" on under side lower wing.
Food plant—Elm.
Larva—Yellow-green; Wood-louse shaped.
Pupa—Brown; two purple lines on back; on or under leaf.
Eggs—Whitish, shape like other Hair-streaks. July.
Locality—A very local species; Essex and elsewhere.

45. **Green Hair-streak** (*Callophrys rubi*).—Unmistakable from its green colour, under side.
Food plant—Furze, rock-rose, broom.
Larva—Light green-yellow cross lines.
Pupa—Green, becoming purplish brown.
Eggs—Greenish. May to June.
Locality—Generally distributed.

46. **Large Copper** (*Chrysophanus dispar*).—Extinct.

47. **Small Copper** (*Chrysophanus phlœas*).—Coppery, with black marks; six spots on upper wing; very variable, however.
Food plant—Dock, sorrel.
Larva—Green, sometimes pinkish shade; Wood-louse shaped.
Pupa—Light brown, darker freckles and lines; hung by tail on leaf, supported by threads round body.
Eggs—Creamy; surface honeycomb pattern. May, July, October.
Locality—General.

48. **Long-tailed Blue** (*Lampides bœticus*).—Unmistakable from "tail" on lower wings.
Food plant—Seeds in pod, pea, and other Leguminosæ.
Larva—Green, double cross lines on sides; Wood-louse shaped.
Pupa—Red, with brown dots; suspended by waist girdle, head upward.

Eggs—Flat and disc-shaped.
Locality—Very rare.

49. **Short-tailed Blue** (*Cupido argiades*).—Very rare.

50. **Silver-studded Blue** (*Lycæna argus*, or *ægon*).—*Male*, purplish blue; *female*, sooty brown upper side, bluish metallic spots on hind-wings, under side.
Food plant—Gorse, vetch.
Larva—Brown.
Pupa—Brown (sometimes green); sometimes attached by tail, otherwise free.
Eggs—White; flat; roughened surface. July to August.
Locality—General, but not always common.

51. **Brown Argus** (*Lycæna astrarche*, known in Scotland as *Artaxerxes*).
Food plant—Rock-rose, stork's-bill.
Larva—Green; pinkish back line; black head.
Pupa—Yellowish green, pink shade; held by body threads to leaf.
Eggs—Greyish white; flat; roughened. May to June and August.
Locality—Widely distributed.

52. **Common Blue** (*Lycæna icarus*).—*Male*, blue; *female*, brown; hind-wings, under side, have row of black spots, with orange and white edges.
Food plant—Bird's-foot trefoil, rest-harrow, clover, etc.
Larva—Green; louse-shaped; ridged on back.
Pupa—Green; often in a slight lair or cocoon.
Eggs—Whity green; flat; with white netting, like a scraped sea-urchin. April to May and June to July.
Locality—Everywhere.

53. **Chalk Hill Blue** (*Lycæna corydon*).—*Male*, silvery blue, with blackish borders; *female*, sooty brown, top sides.
Food plant—Grasses and stunted herbage.
Larva—Bright green; Wood-louse shaped.
Pupa—Brownish.
Eggs—Light green; flat; netted design. July, August.
Locality—Chalk downs in many counties.

54. **Adonis Blue** (*Lycæna bellargus*).—*Male*, bright blue; *female*, brown, with edge of orange spots, upper side.
Food plant—Horseshoe vetch.
Larva—Deeper green than above; two well-marked yellow stripes; Wood-louse shaped.
Pupa—Greenish, becoming darker; frequently buried.
Eggs—Greenish white; flattened; reticulated like *Icarus*. May and August.
Locality—Kent, Surrey, and Sussex chiefly.

55. **Holly Blue** (*Cyaniris argiolus*).—*Male*, lilac-blue; *female*, lilac-blue, but with black border or tip to fore-wings. Under side unmistakable light blue, with black spots.
Food plant—Flower buds of holly; sometimes ivy buds.

BUTTERFLIES 235

Larva—Yellowish green ; back double-ridged ; pale side lines ; sometimes tinged with pink.
Pupa—Light brown, blotched with darker angular marks.
Eggs—Like above, but deeper indentation at top. May and August.
Locality—Common, but uncertain, in South; more local in Midlands and North.

56. **Small, or Little, Blue** (*Zizera minima*)—sometimes called "BEDFORD BLUE."—*Male* and *female* dusky brown upper side; grey-white under side, with black spots.
Food plant—Buds and flowers of kidney-vetch.
Larva—Brown, sometimes shaded with pink ; darker lines.
Pupa—Greyish, marked three rows of black dashes.
Eggs—Light green, like *Icarus*. May to June (sometimes also August).
Locality—Widely distributed, but not common everywhere.

57. **Mazarine Blue** (*Nomiades semiargus*).—*Male*, purplish blue ; *female*, dark brown, top side; under side light fawn, shading off to grey-blue ; clusters of eye spots.
Food plant—Thrift, kidney-vetch.
Larva—Yellowish green, with dark lines.
Pupa—Olive-green, darkening ; held by tail and girdle to food plant.
Eggs—Said to be white and round. July to August.
Locality—Rare, if not extinct, in Britain.

58. **Large Blue** (*Nomiades arion*).—Deep blue, with black border and black spots on upper wing ; under side grey-fawn, with eye spots and other markings.
Food plant—Buds of wild thyme.
Larva—Downy ; closely imitating the buds of the food plant ; pupates in the ground.
Pupa—Yellowish, gradually darkening.
Eggs—Whity blue, with all the characteristics of the " Blues."
Locality—Very rare ; the Cotswolds.
The larva is said to descend into an ants' nest, and to be fed by ants during its last stage.

Family : *Lemoniidæ*, or *Erycinidæ*. Genus : *Nemeobiinæ*.

59. **Duke of Burgundy Fritillary** (*Nemeobius lucina*).—*Male* has only four legs adapted for walking ; *female*, six. Chequered on upper surface with tawny and dark brown and black.
Food plant—Primrose, cowslip.
Larva—Wood-louse shaped ; reddish brown, with tufts.
Pupa—Greyish, hairy, with black dots and streaks; suspended head upwards on food plant.
Eggs—Glassy ; transparent. June to August.
Locality—Woodlands, chiefly in South.

Family: *Hesperiidæ*. Genus: *Hesperiinæ*.

60. **Grizzled Skipper** (*Hesperia malvæ*).—(The Skippers are easily identified by their thick-set bodies, broad heads, hooked tips to antennæ.) Blackish wings with white spots.
Food plant—Strawberry, bramble, raspberry, cinquefoil.
Larva—Greenish white, olive back and side lines.
Pupa—Enclosed in rolled-up leaf; brown, with darker markings; white spot, with black centre on each side of " neck."
Eggs—Green; ribbed and reticulated. May to June (occasionally August also).
Locality—Generally distributed.

61. **Dingy Skipper** (*Thanaos tages*).—Brownish, with darker bands and edges of small white spots.
Food plant—Bird's-foot trefoil.
Larva—Yellow-green, dark back line; red spiracles.
Pupa—Enclosed in leaf; " dark green, tinged red."
Eggs—Greenish white to orange; ribbed and reticulated. May to June, and sometimes August.
Locality—Generally distributed.

Family: *Hesperiidæ*. Genus: *Pamphilinæ*.

62. **Small Skipper** (*Adopæa thaumas*).—Orange-brown.
Food plant—Grasses.
Larva—Light green, darker lines; pinkish spiracles.
Pupa—In grass sheath; head upwards; coloration as larva.
Eggs—Said to be oval; smooth; white-yellow. July to August.
Locality—General.

63. **Essex Skipper** (*Adopæa lineola*).—Like *Thaumas*.
Food plant—Grasses.
Larva—Green; darker back stripe; yellow side lines.
Pupa—In sheath of grass blades; yellow-green.
Eggs—Greenish yellow; oval; smooth. July to August.
Locality—Essex chiefly, but occasionally elsewhere.

64. **Lulworth Skipper** (*Adopæa actæon*).—Dingy brown.
Food plant—Grasses; butterfly visits flowers of rest-harrow chiefly.
Larva—Grey-green; fine yellowish lines.
Pupa—Sheath of grass; pointed beak; and " eye spot," resembling bird's head.
Eggs—Whitish; roughened or finely pitted. July.
Locality—Lulworth Cove, and other coasts of Dorset, Devon, and Cornwall.

MOTHS 237

65. **Large Skipper** (*Angiades sylvanus*).—Light yellow-brown, with blackish shading and marking.
Food plant—Grasses.
Larva—Dark green ; brown head ; darker lines.
Pupa—Grass cocoon ; brown ; curious oval depression on " shoulders."
Eggs—Whitish ; finely reticulated ; often laid in a *line* on grass. June to July.
Locality—General.

66. **Silver-spotted Skipper** (*Angiades comma*).—Like above, but easily distinguished by greenish under colour and silvery spots.
Food plant—Grasses.
Larva—Olive-green ; lives in a *tube* of grass spun together.
Pupa—In grass sheath ; olive.
Eggs—White to yellow ; smooth ; slight cup depression on top. August.
Locality—Chalk hills ; generally distributed.

67. **Chequered Skipper** (*Carterocephalus palæmon*).—Distinguished by plain yellow spots on blackish ground colour.
Food plant—Grasses.
Larva—Light yellow ; living in tube of grasses.
Pupa—In grass cocoon ; light yellow ; beaked head and plainly marked " eyes."
Eggs—Whitish ; smooth ; glossy. May to June.
Locality—Rare ; chiefly woods in Lincoln, Northampton, and Buckinghamshire.

BRITISH MOTHS (*Heterocera*).

As there are more than 2,000 known species of Moths in Great Britain, it is obvious that they would require a large volume to themselves if they were to be dealt with thoroughly. They are divided into Macrolepidoptera and Microlepidoptera, the latter being by far the most numerous and consisting of the smallest-sized species. The plan adopted in the following pages is to describe each *family* and some typical *species* of each family, so that the student may, if he takes the trouble, be able to classify his finds, at least into their proper *genus*. Moreover, most of the *common* moths are described in some detail, in the hope that the beginner may be really helped in making his collection.

As in other sections of this book I have suggested a pocket book as a companion, I venture to refer here to my *Moths of the Months* (1s. 9d.), in which some 130 species are figured and described under the principal months in which they occur. If this book is taken on moth-collecting rambles, it will be rendered of greater usefulness if it is interleaved with blank pages, on which the notes of other species may be entered when found.

The chief distinctions between butterflies and moths have already been given on page 218, and need not be rehearsed again ; but whilst the butterflies have the tips of their antennæ clubbed, those of moths are not simply without clubs

238 THE BRITISH NATURE BOOK

or knobs, but are variously formed, and should be specially noted, as the shape and character of the antennæ form an important item in classification.

The following sketch gives the principal forms of the antennæ :—

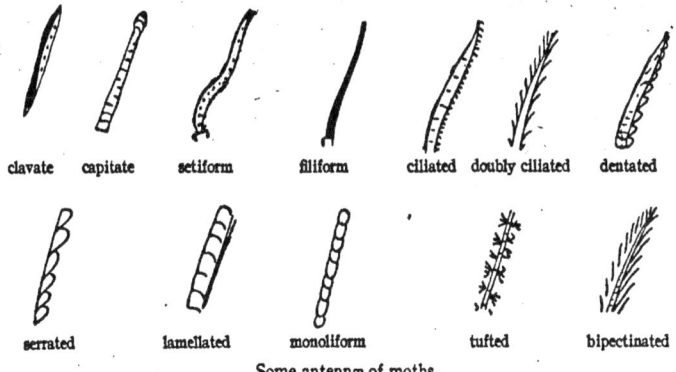

Some antennæ of moths.

It will be noted that some of the antennæ are bare and others hairy; and the hairs may be long, short, or in tufts.

The wings of both butterflies and moths are composed of a strong membrane spread over a frame of ribs, or nervures, as the material of an umbrella is spread

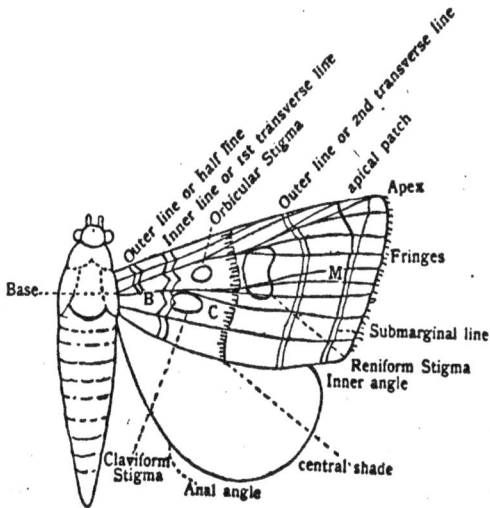

B, basal area; C, central area; M, marginal area.

over the wires; and the plan or map of these nervures is of great importance, as it enables the whole wing to be mapped out and any portion of it defined. In describing accurately the markings of a moth, a knowledge of this plan of the wing is essential.

MOTHS 239

The fore-wing with its markings is the more important. Note the inner and outer lines which divide it into three areas—basal, central or median, and outer or marginal. In the central area are three rings or dashes, called stigmata, which are found more particularly in the Noctuidæ.

I desire to acknowledge my great indebtedness to Mr. South's two volumes on *The Moths of the British Isles*, and to Mr. Kirby's *Butterflies and Moths of the United Kingdom*, the former of which I have followed in my classification.

It will be obvious to a reader who works through this long list that it is almost impossible to identify many species of moths from a short description of the moth itself. And if one would make a special study of the subject, the eggs or the larvæ must be bred at home, the food plant and locality being carefully noted, and then one of the sets of books referred to above (Mr. Kirby's *Butterflies and Moths of the United Kingdom*, and Mr. South's three volumes on the same subject) must be consulted; in these a detailed description of each species is minutely given. In addition, if an actual collection, such as that at South Kensington, can be examined, the young student will obtain great help by comparing his finds with the named specimens.

Where possible, in the following description some salient feature of each species is given, for the purposes of identification.

LIST OF BRITISH MOTHS, WITH BRIEF DESCRIPTIONS OF FAMILIES AND THE COMMONER SPECIES.

(*L.*=Larva ; *P.*=Pupa ; *E.*=Expanse of Wing; *Ly.*=Locality ; *F.p.*= Food plant ; *H.*=Hibernating.)

I. *Macrolepidoptera.*

Family : *Sphingidæ*—Hawk-moths.

The Latin name is given to this family from the supposed likeness of the larvæ to the Sphinx. They are all large and rather fearsome-looking. The majority burrow into the ground for their pupal change, though some make a cocoon of leaves on the surface. The name " Hawk-moths " is given to the full-grown insects on account of their rapid flight. They have stout bodies, tapering to a point. The antennæ gradually thicken and diminish. They are mostly night fliers. *Ten* species are found in the British Isles.

Lime Hawk-moth (*Dilina tiliæ*).—*E.* 2½-3 inches. Fore-wings pale pinkish grey, with irregular olive band across central area (often broken in middle). The outline of the wings is characteristic; fore-wings having two deep bays in hind-margin and hind-wings, one concavity close to anal angle. Appears May to June ; when resting, looks like a bunch of half-grown leaves ; common in South. *L.* green, roughened with yellow points ; seven yellow oblique stripes, edged with red or purple. A long curved horn, bluish green. A reddish shield on last ring of body. Feeds, July and August, on lime, elm, alder, and

240 THE BRITISH NATURE BOOK

other trees. Chrysalis is dark reddish, somewhat rough, underground, close to the tree.

Poplar Hawk (*Smerinthus populi*).—*E.* 2¾–3½ inches. Usually ashy grey, with darker brown central band, a white crescent-shaped spot on fore-wings, and a large red patch at base of the hind-wings. Common from May to July. *L.* is green, dotted with yellow points, with seven oblique yellow stripes, reddish spiracles, green horn; feeds on poplar, aspen, sallow, and willow, from July to September. *P.* dull black, found in the ground close to the surface.

Eyed Hawk-moth (*S. ocellatus*), recognized by the rosy red hind-wings, with a large eye-spot near the anal angle. *E.* 2¼–3¼ inches. *L.* is green with white points, and seven oblique whitish stripes; the horn is bluish. *F.p.*

Caterpillar of Death's-Head Moth.

Sallow, willow, apple, and other trees in July and August. Moth found May to July. Fairly common in South, but local in North.

Death's-Head Hawk-moth (*Acherontia atropos*).—*E.* 4–5 inches. The largest British moth; recognized by the mark on the thorax resembling a human skull. *L.* is sometimes 5 inches long, yellow or green, with violet dots and seven oblique stripes; purple-brown, edged with yellow. *F.p.* is the potato chiefly, but also woody nightshade, snowberry, and other plants, on which it may be found from June to September. When about to pupate it burrows some inches into the ground, and by revolving forms a cavity about the size of a hen's egg. The pupa is 2½–3 inches long, dark mahogany in colour.

The moth may be found from May to September, though it is not a common species. The larva, at least in the South of England, may be found from June to September, and is, I believe, much more frequently found than is

PLATE XXVII.

1. Vapourer Moths: Male, Female, and Eggs.
3. Larvæ of Peacock Butterfly.
2. Lichenaria: Larvæ feeding.
4. Pupa of Swallow-tail Butterfly.

supposed; but owing to its size and—to the inexpert eye—its repulsiveness, it is generally killed. So at least I have discovered in Hants.

The insect, both in the larval form and as a moth, has the singular power of emitting a shrill squeak or chirp when disturbed.

In many places it is known as the "BEE-ROBBER," owing to its fondness for honey, to obtain which it will enter a beehive. It is said that the squeak which it emits quiets the bees, being an imitation of the call of the queen bee herself.

Convolvulus Hawk-moth (*Sphinx convolvuli*)—" UNICORN or BINDWEED HAWK."—Almost the same size as the Death's-Head, but not so stout in body. Found occasionally in Great Britain, but only breeds exceptionally, most of the moths migrating from the Continent. It may be identified by the broad stripes on the abdomen, consisting of broad red and black, and narrow white bands, divided down the back by a broad grey stripe with a fine black line in the middle.

Privet Hawk (*Sphinx ligustri*).—E. 3-4 inches. This moth is not unlike the former, but is distinguished easily by the bands on the abdomen, which are red and brown (*no* white), divided by a brownish grey stripe down the back, with a blackish line in the middle. L. is 3 inches long, green, with seven oblique white stripes, each edged with purple in front; the horn is large and bristly, slightly forked at the tip. F.p. Privet, lilac, ash, elder, in July and August. P. underground, reddish brown in colour; often remaining there for two winters. Moth found in June or July, chiefly in South.

Pine Hawk (*Hyloicus pinastri*).—E. 3-3½ inches. An olive-brown moth, with bands of dark brown and white on the abdomen. Found in June and July occasionally, chiefly in Suffolk.

Small Elephant (*Metopsilus porcellus*).—E. 1½-2¼ inches. The wings are ochreous, with rose-pink margins; the head and body are pinkish, with yellowish variations. L. greyish brown, without a horn, but possessing in its place a double wart. F.p. Bed-straw, willow-herb, purple loosestrife, etc., on which it may be found in August and September. Flies from May to July, over honeysuckle and other flowers. Widely distributed.

The Elephant (*Chærocampa elpenor*).—E. 2¼-2¾ inches. Fore-wings olive-green and pink; hind-wings black and pink. Head and body olive-brown and pink. Appears in June, at dusk, hovering over honeysuckle, soapwort, petunias, and other flowers; also comes to sugar. L., full grown, measures nearly 3 inches; blackish grey; identified by the remarkable eye spots on fourth and fifth segments. The head and "eye" segments somewhat resemble an elephant's head and trunk: hence its name. It feeds in July and August on willow-herb, bed-straw, etc. P. encased in a cocoon of earth and leaves spun together on the ground. It is a fairly common species.

Humming-bird Hawk-moth (*Macroglossa stellatarum*).—E. 1¾-2 inches. Quite a common species; may be recognized by its brown fore-wings and orange hind-wings, with brownish edgings, and the black tuft on the end of the abdomen.

THE BRITISH NATURE BOOK

F.p. Yellow and hedge bed-straw, dyer's weed, and goose-grass. Flies by day, hovering from flower to flower; poising on vibrating wings, like a humming-bird, whilst thrusting its long proboscis into the flowers for their nectar. It is especially fond of jasmine. Larvæ found in July and August. Double brooded, June and October.

Broad-bordered Bee Hawk-moth (*Hemaris fuciformis*).—*E.* 1¾–2 inches. Recognized by its transparent wings, with broad reddish brown borders and short stumpy body covered with yellowish olive hair like a bee, crossed by a band of darker brown. Found in May and June. *L.* whitish green above, and reddish below; feeds in July and August on honeysuckle. The moth may often be found at rhododendron blossoms, and harebells, thistles, bugle, and other flowers. Common locally.

Narrow-bordered Bee Hawk-moth (*Hemaris tityas*).—*E.* 1½–1¾ inch. Like the former, but having narrower blackish borders to the wings. Flies in May and June. *Ly.* Rough meadows near woods. *F.p.* Scabious, honeysuckle. *L.* found in June or July. Like its predecessor, much resembles a humble-bee in flight.

Family: *Notodontidæ*—**Prominents.**

The members of this family fly by night, fairly rapidly; but some may be found by day on tree trunks and palings. The majority are distinguished by a curious projecting tuft of scales about the middle of the inner margin of the fore-wings. When the moth is at rest, these are brought together and raised, thus making a little " prominence " above the level of the closed wings. Antennæ are bipectinated in most of the males, and shortly pectinated, ciliated, or serrated in the females. They are attracted by light. Larvæ are mostly naked or have a thin coating of hair. The true Prominents have one hump on the back. Pupa is generally in a hard cocoon on tree trunks or in a soft cocoon underground.

Alder Kitten (*Cerura bicuspis*).—This species much resembles the Poplar Kitten and Sallow Kitten. *E.* 1¼–1¾ inch. May be distinguished by observing the central band of black or dark grey, which bends inwards *on both sides*— *L.* feeds on alder and birch in July and August. Cocoon placed on bark. Moth found in May and June. Local in woods.

Poplar Kitten (*Cerura bifida*).—*E.* 1½–1¾ inch. Grey fore-wings, distinguished by the shape of the dark grey central band, the inner margin of which is almost straight and outward curved— Found in June and July. *L.* feeds from July to September on poplars. Cocoon placed on the bark. Fairly common where poplars abound.

Sallow Kitten (*Cerura furcula*).—*E.* 1⅙–1½ inch. Distinguished by its smaller size and by the outer margin of the central band, which is sharply angled towards the edge of the wing— *L.* feeds from July to September on willow or sallow. Cocoon fixed to bark and covered like the preceding with fragments of wood. Moth appears in June and July, and is common.

Puss Moth (*Dicranura vinula*).—A common moth of great interest. The larva is green, with a purplish brown band or saddle on the back and a hump on the third segment. The head has a most curious "face" or "mask," and the tail is armed with two filaments or whips. When disturbed the creature assumes a terrifying attitude, with the head drawn back into the next segment, exposing the "mask" as if in a hood, while the two whips are raised and curved forward. In this position, it ejects an acid secretion, which is sufficiently powerful to sting and inflame the eyes, as I know from experience.

The pupa is enclosed in a very hard cocoon on the tree (willow or poplar), made of fragments of wood glued together by a very hard varnish. The moth ($E.$ $2\frac{1}{2}$–3 inches) appears in May and June. Head and body are fluffy, the whitish fore-wings have several ripple-like lines; the nervures are ochreous and blackish. Hind-wings whitish.

Lobster (*Stauropus fagi*).—$E.$ $2\frac{1}{3}$–$2\frac{3}{4}$ inches. The name is given to this moth from the extraordinary shape of the caterpillar, a reddish brown creature with six pairs of wedge-shaped humps on its back, two clubbed filaments on its "tail," which it twists about in a remarkable manner, intended to be alarming to its enemies. It possesses long, lobster-like legs. It feeds on beech, birch, oak, and other trees from July to September. Cocoon of dense white silk between dead leaves. The moth flies from May to July in most parts of England, but is not common. It is a large brown insect, central shade darker, a distinct sub-marginal row of dark-brown spots, with ochreous tips on the *inner* side.

The **Marbled Brown** (*Drymonia trimacula*) and **Lunar Marbled Brown** (*Drymonia chaonia*).—$E.$ $1\frac{1}{3}$–$1\frac{2}{3}$ inch. These are much alike. Fore-wings pale brown, marbled with dark brown and grey. Hind-wings pale grey or brown. $L.$ feeds on oak. Moth appears in May and June.

The **Swallow Prominent** (*Pheosia tremula*) ($E.$ 2–$2\frac{1}{4}$ inches), and the **Lesser Swallow Prominent** (*P. dictaeoides*).—These are much alike, the latter being smaller ($E.$ $1\frac{1}{2}$–2 inches). They have creamy white fore-wings, with a brown patch along the upper edge, and a variegated dark-brown band along the inner margin. They appear in May and June. $L.$ feeds on poplar, willow, and birch. Cocoon under the soil.

The **Pebble Prominent** (*Notodonta ziczac*).—$E.$ $1\frac{2}{3}$–2 inches. It has pale ochreous brown to darker brown fore-wings, tinged with reddish. Look for a pebble-like mark on the apical area, made by a blackish crescent and the curved outer line. This is characteristic. Hind-wings are pale ashy grey. $L.$ feeds on sallow, willow, and poplar, June to September. Moth flies in May to June, and August. *Ly.* Marshes and fens.

The **Iron Prominent** (*Notodonta dromedarius*) is much darker, and rather smaller. $L.$ feeds on birch, alder, and hazel from June to August.

The **Great Prominent** (*N. trepida*).—$E.$ 2–$2\frac{1}{2}$ inches. Grey or yellowish grey fore-wings, with dark cross-lines, and a sub-marginal line of dark, sometimes reddish, spots. Hind-wings whitish, or cream-coloured. Flies in May and June; is strongly attracted by light. *L.* feeds on oak, from June to August. These three moths have a distinct family likeness.

White Prominent (*Leucodonta bicoloria*).—*E.* 1⅓–1½ inch. A glossy white, identified by the rows of blackish dots running transversely across fore-wings, and the orange patch, resembling a Y on its side, or a roughly drawn T placed sideways. It is very rare. *L.* feeds on birch.

Coxcomb Prominent (*Lephopteryx camelina*).—One of the most familiar of the true Prominents; very variable in colour. Fore-wings are reddish brown and ochreous; there is a distinct dark-brown ragged line or shade running across the wing to the tuft or prominence on the edge. Hind-wings are a lighter ochreous shade, with a blackish patch at the anal angle. Flies from May to August. *L.* feeds on birch, oak, hazel, etc.

Plumed or Feathered Prominent (*Ptilophora plumigera*).—*E.* 1¼–1⅔ inch. So called from the plume-like antennæ of the male. Fore-wings are thinly-scaled, reddish ochreous; hind-wings paler. *L.* feeds in May and June on sycamore and maple. Moth flies late in October and November. Local in the South of England.

Pale Prominent (*Pterostoma palpina*).—*E.* 1½–2 inches. Common in most parts of England. Fore-wings pale ochre-yellow, with a darker grey central shade. Hind-wings the same, but without the shade. *L.* feeds on poplar, willow, and sallow in June and July, when moth is also on wing. Comes to light.

Caterpillar of the Buff Tip.

Buff Tip (*Phalera bucephala*).—*E.* 2¼–2¾ inches. Identified by its rich purplish grey fore-wings, flecked with silvery grey, and the more or less oval pale ochreous patch at the apex, the hind-wings being cream coloured. When closed the wings give the appearance of a twig broken short, with the breakage showing. It is common; flies in June and July. *L.* yellow and downy; feeds on lime, elm, hazel, willow, and many other trees in August and September.

The Chocolate Tip (*Pygæra curtula*) is smaller (1⅓–1½ inch) and darker, and has, as its name implies, a large reddish brown or chocolate patch towards the apex. *L.* feeds on poplar and aspen from May to June and August to September, the moth appearing in May and July. The SMALL CHOCOLATE TIP (*Pygæra pigra*) (*E.* 1–1¼ inch) has a less distinct chocolate patch. *L.* feeds on sallow and aspen from June to September. *Ly.* Fens and marshes.

Family: *Thyatiridæ*.

Medium-sized moths, with the apical angle nearly rectangular, and smooth, obliquely curved hind margins. Antennæ of males setiform, or pectinated. Flight is by day. Larvæ naked. Pupæ in slight cocoons between leaves.

The Buff Arches (*Habrosyne derasa*).—*E.* $1\frac{1}{4}$–$1\frac{1}{2}$ inch. Fore-wings pale olive-grey, with two whitish streaks across them : the first runs from the tip to the hinder angle, the second runs from close to the shoulder towards the middle of the lower margin, and has a small branch going off at right angles towards the base ; between the two streaks the wing is dull brown-orange in colour, with a whitish cloud on the upper edge. Hind-wings yellowish grey. *L.* feeds on bramble in August and September. Moth appears in June and July generally. Cocoon underground.

Peach Blossom (*Thyatira batis*).—Identified by its olive-brown fore-wings, with their five large round spots, pinkish white, with brown centres. *L.* feeds on bramble from July to September. Moths found in August and September.

Figure of Eighty (*Palimpsestis octogesima*).—*E.* $1\frac{1}{8}$–$1\frac{1}{2}$ inch. So called from the shape of the two stigmata, which resemble the figures 8 and 0. Sometimes, however, the lower part of the 8 is not very distinct. *L.* feeds on poplar in July and August. Moth emerges in May and June. Comes to sugar. *Ly.* Chiefly Eastern and South-eastern counties.

Poplar Lutestring (*Palimpsestis or*).—*E.* $1\frac{1}{8}$–$1\frac{1}{2}$ inch. It may be recognized by the four-lined bands—" lutestrings "—on the pale-brown wings, tinged with pinkish lilac. *L.* feeds on poplar, July to September. Cocoon spun between leaves. Moth found in June or July. Comes to sugar. Widely distributed.

Lesser Satin Moth (*Palimpsestis duplaris*). Light brownish grey fore-wings, whitish edged, with a broad dark central band ; has two *black dots on the outer edge of this band*—that is, in the position of the reniform stigma. These distinguish it from the SATIN CARPET (*Palimpsestis fluctuosa*), to which, otherwise, the remaining details apply. *L.* feeds on birch and poplar from August to October. *P.* in cocoon between leaves. Moth in June and July. Common.

The Lesser Lutestring (*Asphalia diluta*) has lighter wings of greyish brown, with two brown bands crossing them. *E.* $1\frac{1}{4}$–$1\frac{1}{2}$ inch. *L.* feeds on oak in May and June, at night. Moth generally found in September. Very partial to sugar. Widely distributed, most common in South.

Yellow Horned (*Polyploca flavicornis*).—*E.* $1\frac{1}{2}$ inch. Pale greenish grey fore-wings, with well-defined black cross lines. Generally a large greenish white orbicular stigma. *L.* feeds on birch in June and July. Moth appears in March or April. *Ly.* Birch woods. Visits sugar.

Frosted Green (*Polyploca ridens*).—Fore-wings greyish green, with plenty of brown markings. Two wavy whitish lines (sometimes broken) cross the wings, one near the base, the other near the outer-margin. *E.* $1\frac{1}{3}$–$1\frac{1}{2}$ inch. *L.* feeds on oak from May to July. Moth in June. *Ly.* Woodlands.

Family: Lymantriidæ—Tussock Moths.

Some of the larvæ of these moths have urticating hairs, which will cause a troublesome inflammation to a sensitive skin. They should therefore be handled with care, and on no account should the hands, after touching them, rub the face.

Vapourer (*Orgyia antiqua*).—*Male* has fore-wings dull orange-brown, with a conspicuous roundish white spot at the lower angle. *Female* is greyish, with small stumps representing rudimentary wings. Eggs are laid in a patch round small twig on many kinds of trees. Moth appears in August and October. *L.* very handsome, with four pairs of yellow tufts on back, and pencils of black hair on first and eleventh segments. (The SCARCE VAPOURER (*Orgyia gonostigma*)

Caterpillars of the Pale Tussock Moth.

has in the male an extra white mark near the tip of the fore-wing. It is a very local species.)

The Pale Tussock (*Dasychira pudibunda*).—*E.* 1¾–2½ inches. Has greyish white fore-wings (hind-wings almost white) sprinkled with darker grey. The central area is darker. *L.* is green or yellow, with four yellow tufts and a pencil of dull red hair. Feeds on hazel, oak, fruit trees, and hop (known to hop-pickers as the "HOP-DOG"), from July to September. Moth in May and June. Comes to light. Common. (The DARK TUSSOCK (*Dasychira fascelina*) is rarer, being chiefly a northern insect.)

Yellow-tail, or GOLD-TAIL (*Porthesia similis*), is white, with a golden yellow tuft at end of abdomen. *Male* has a black dot on the fore-wings. Larvæ hatch in August, hibernate, feed gregariously in spring on oak, poplar, hawthorn, and fruit trees. Moth appears in June and July. It has a habit of sitting still on leaves and branches, when it looks like a white feather. Attracted by light. *E.* 1¼–1¾ inch. (The BROWN-TAIL (*Euproctis chryorrhea*)

MOTHS

is very similar, having a brown tuft instead of gold, but it is a local species only, chiefly found on the coast.)

White Satin (*Stilpnotia salicis*), as its name implies, has glossy satiny wings, the body being black, with white hair; the legs black, with white rings. *L.* has clear white spots on the back; feeds on poplar, willow, and sallow from April to July. Moth in July and August. Widely distributed; most common in South.

Black Arches (*Lymantria monacha*).—*E.* $1\frac{1}{2}$–$2\frac{1}{4}$ inches. Identified by its fore-wings, which are creamy white, *with several zigzag black lines*, the middle ones generally blotched. Hind-wings greyish, with darker shading on margins. The abdomen is rose-pink, with blackish bands. *Female* has a longish, pointed "tail"—in reality the ovipositor. Flies in July and August, by night. *L.* feeds April to July, on oak, apple, and pine.

Family: *Lasiocampidæ*—Lackeys and Eggars.

These comprise rather small as well as larger species, with stout, hairy bodies; antennæ bipectinated. General colour brownish. Larvæ have soft hairs, and fleshy tubercles on the last segment.

The Lackey (*Malacosoma neustria*).—Colour pale ochreous, varying to reddish brown; generally has two cross lines on fore-wings, the space in between them being a darker shade. Moth found in July and August. Eggs are laid in a ring round a twig. Larvæ are gregarious, living in a silken tent, feeding on hawthorn, sloe, and fruit trees from April to June. Generally distributed. (The GROUND LACKEY (*M. castrensis*) has darker hind-wings; is found only in salt marshes of East Coast. *F.p.* Wild carrot, sea wormwood, etc.)

Pale Oak Eggar (*Trichiura crataegi*).—*E.* 1–$1\frac{1}{4}$ inch. Ashy grey, with a darker central area, generally well defined. Appears in August and September in wooded districts in South. *L.* feeds in April to June on hawthorn, sloe, and sallow.

December Moth (*Pœcilocampa populi*) has semi-transparent wings, sooty brown in colour; two pale buff cross lines on the fore-wings, the basal area of which is always a darker brown. Appears from October to December. Often seen round gas-lamps. Fairly common. *L.* April to June; feeds on most trees. Eggs are laid on the bark. *E.* $1\frac{1}{4}$–$1\frac{3}{4}$ inch.

Small Eggar (*Eriogaster lanestris*).—*E.* $1\frac{1}{4}$–$1\frac{3}{4}$ inch. Not unlike the preceding, but has a white spot at the base of the fore-wings, and another half-way across, nearer the upper margin; also a narrow wavy whitish line roughly parallel with the hind margins, continued on hind-wings. *Female* has a noticeable grey anal tuft, and uses the hairs to cover her eggs on the twigs where they are clustered. *F.p.* Hawthorn and sloe. The larvæ are gregarious, living in silken web, often found from May to July. Moth appears February and March.

Oak Eggar (*Lasiocampa quercus*).—A large and strikingly coloured species.

E. $2\frac{1}{2}$–$3\frac{1}{4}$ inches. Male deep reddish brown, with a wide yellowish band beyond middle of both wings; also a white central spot on fore-wings. Female larger, a brownish yellow colour, with paler bands and a larger central spot. Moth flies in July and August. L. found on various low plants—bramble, heather, hawthorn, etc. Female, if bred in captivity and placed in a jar in the open air, will attract the males from all directions. Almost my earliest peep, many years ago, into the life of a moth was the result of the taking of a female Oak Eggar in Wales, fresh from the chrysalis. I put her into a tumbler outside the window and went in to lunch. After lunch I went out to kill her, and found several males fluttering wildly round the glass.

The Grass Eggar (L. trifolii) is not so large (E. 2–$2\frac{3}{4}$ inches), but is very similar in colour, except that the male is not so dark, being the same reddish brown colour as the female. F.p. Trefoil, plantain, and other grasses. Local.

Fox Moth (Macrothylacia rubi).—E. $2\frac{1}{2}$–$2\frac{2}{3}$ inches. The male is fox-colour, the female greyish brown generally. Fore-wings of both have two pale yellowish lines across central area. L.—in June to October—is velvety-black (full-grown), with reddish hairs and blue incisions. Feeds on heath, bramble, etc. Moths emerge in May to June. Males fly by day very often, females only by night.

Drinker (Cosmotriche potatoria).—E. 2–$2\frac{1}{4}$ inches. Another reddish brown moth, with yellowish suffusions, the female being lighter than the male. Often there is a noticeable line (or band) from the apex of the fore-wing to middle of the inner margin; also a kidney-shaped spot surmounted by a smaller, rounder spot above middle of fore-wings. L. feeds on coarse grasses, August to October. It gets its name from a habit of the larva of drinking drops of dew. Moth found in July. Ly. Damp places, marshes, ditch-sides, etc.

Caterpillar of Drinker Moth.

Lappet (Gastropacha quercifolia).— The name arises from the curious fleshy lappets on the sides of the caterpillar, which is very large and dark grey or brown, having two white marks edged with black on the third ring. It feeds on sloe, hawthorn, apple, etc., from July to September. The moth (E. $2\frac{1}{4}$–$3\frac{1}{4}$ inches) emerges in June or July; flies by night. Colour, a warm reddish brown suffused with purple, with blackish lines. When resting the fore-wings are so folded over the others that it looks like a withered leaf. The egg is remarkably coloured—white with grey lines, like a boy's marble.

PLATE XXVIII.

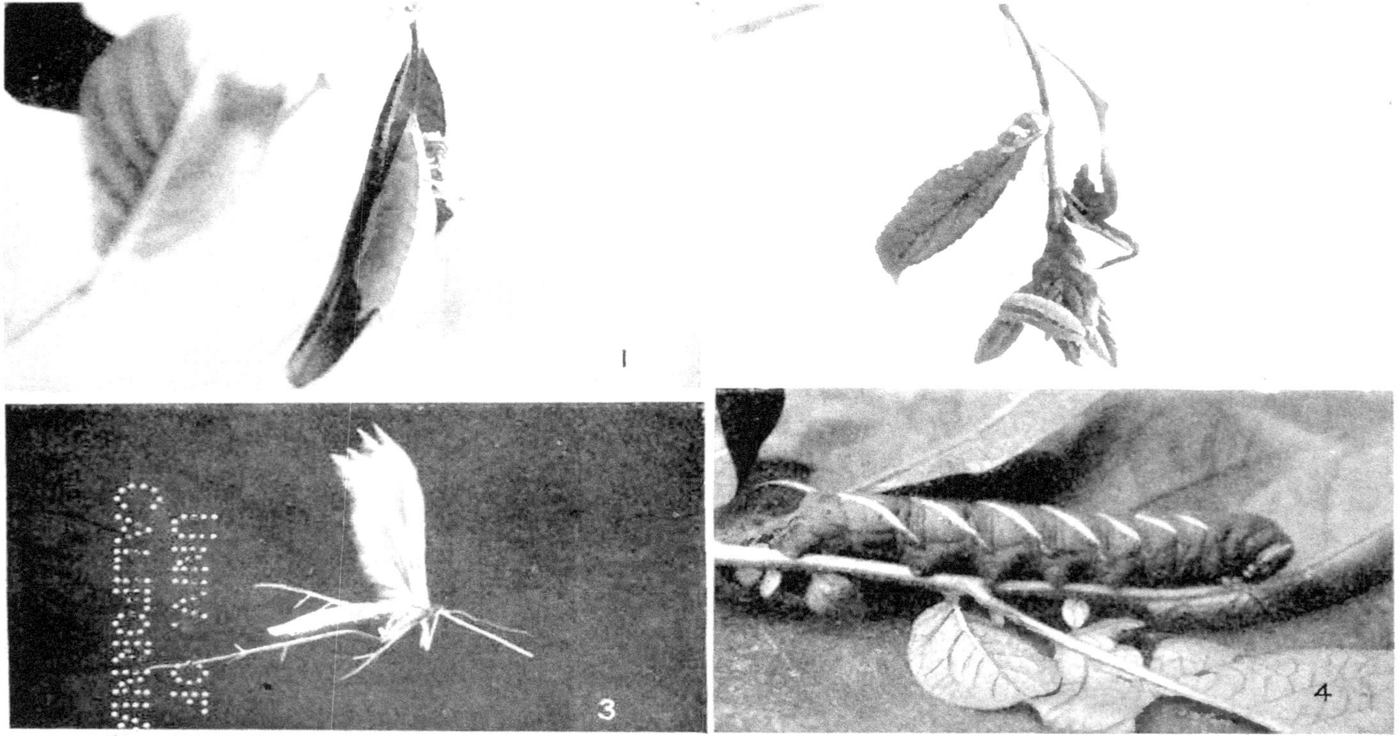

1. Pupa of Purple Emperor.   2. Larva and Pupa of Black Hair-streak.   3. Five-plumed Moth.   4. Larva of Privet Hawk Moth.

MOTHS 249

Family: *Endromididæ*.

The Kentish Glory (*Endromis versicolor*).—*E.* 2¼–3 inches. This is the only species of this family. *L.* feeds in June and July on birch, alder, sallow, and lime. Moth in April and May. *Ly.* Woods; but it is a local species, chiefly found in certain districts in Scotland.
Male has tawny-brown fore-wings with a white patch at base, some white marks and lines, three spots near the apex, two black cross-lines. Hind-wings are a more chestnut-brown, with a black central line and other markings. *Female* is larger and paler, appearing to be grey with brownish variegations. Eggs laid in rows on a twig.

Family: *Saturniidæ*.

Emperor Moth (*Saturnia pavonia*).—*E.* 2¼–3 inches. This species is unique in having a large eye-spot on each wing, by which alone it is easily identified. Eggs are laid round stems and twigs. *L.*, which is bright green with black markings, feeds from June to August on heather, bramble, sallow, and many other plants. It makes a curious flask-shaped cocoon with a kind of trap-door at the narrow end, which can only be opened from within, and closes again after the moth has emerged. In April and May the moths may be seen flying in sunlight. Generally distributed, but rare in places.

Family: *Drepanidæ*—Hook-tips.

The fore-wings have the tips pointed and curved so as to form a kind of hook. Larvæ have only fourteen legs.

Pebble Hook-tip (*Drepana falcataria*).—*E.* 1⅓–1½ inch. Brownish yellow moths, with three blackish zigzag lines on fore-wings, and a round spot in the middle through which the third zigzag passes. Hind-wings lighter, with four or five zigzag lines. *L.* feeds on birch and alder in June to July, and September to October. Widely distributed.

The Oak Hook-tip (*D. binaria*) feeds on oak. It is a smaller species (1–1¼ inch), ochreous brown. Look for two pale transverse lines on all wings, and two oblique almost central black dots. (The BARRED HOOK-TIP (*D. cultraria*) is the same size, and very similar, but markings less distinct. *F.p.* Beech.)

Scalloped Hook-tip (*D. lacertinaria*).—May be recognized by the " scalloped "—that is, dentated—edges of the hind margins of the fore-wings. Look for two nearly parallel oblique transverse lines, with a brown dot between them. *L.* feeds on birch in June to July, and August to September. Moth out in May to June, and August.

Chinese Character (*Cilix glaucata*).—*E.* ¾–1 inch. Whitish wings, with a brownish blotch on fore-wings starting upwards from the inner margin. Certain silvery scales on this patch give the suggestion of a "Chinese character" Appears in May and August. L. feeds in June and September on hawthorn, sloe, and apple.

Family: *Nolidæ*.

Rather small moths with broad fore-wings and short rounded hind-wings. Antennæ finely pectinated (in the *males*). Often found sitting head downwards on palings or trees. Fly by night.

Short-cloaked Moth (*Nola cucullatella*).—There is a dark patch, almost black, at the base of the whitish fore-wings, bounded by thick curved band; the second line is black and wavy; between these comes a clouded shade. Hind-wings grey. L. feeds on sloe, hawthorn, and fruit trees in May to June. Moth found in June and July, flying at dusk. Common in the South of England. E. ½–¾ inch.

Small Black Arches (*N. strigula*).—Pale grey, with fore-wings freckled with brown; two fine dentated black transverse lines, and other markings. Found in July. L. feeds in May and June on oak. A local species, common in woods in South.

The Least Black Arches (*N. confusalis*) is more widely distributed, about the same size (½–¾ inch); very similar in markings, but whiter. L. feeds in July and August on oak, beech, and apple. Moth in May to June. (The KENT BLACK ARCHES and SCARCE BLACK ARCHES are very rare.)

Family: *Chlöephoridæ*.

Cream-bordered Green Pea (*Earias chlorana*).—E. ¾–1 inch. Green fore-wings, with whitish on costa. White hind-wings. White head and shoulders. Found in May to June in the fens, and damp places in Southern and Eastern Counties. L. feeds on willow.

Green Silver-lines (*Hylophila prasinana*).—E. 1¼ to 1½ inch. Has its green fore-wings crossed by two silvery lines, and a silvery band from apex to inner margin. Hind-wings and abdomen yellowish white in *male*, silky white in *female*. L. feeds in August and September on oak, birch, and beech. Moth found in June to July in woods. (The SCARCE SILVER-LINES (*H. bicolorana*) is larger—1½–1¾ inch; the green colour paler, and the lines yellowish. Rather a local species.)

Family: *Sarrothripinæ*.

Large Marbled Tortrix (*Sarrothripa revayana*).—A most variable species, grey or brown in general colour. L. feeds in June and July on oak and sallow. Moth to be found from August to April; often in winter found hiding in holly, ivy, or yew.

MOTHS

Family: *Arctiidæ*

(divided into two sub-families—Tigers (*Arctiinæ*) and Footmen (*Lithosiinæ*)).

Arctiinæ—Tiger Moths.

White Ermine (*Spilosoma menthrastri*).—There are several Ermine Moths, so called from the markings on their fore-wings—black spots on a light-coloured background, not unlike ermine. They are therefore easily identified. In addition, the thorax is woolly. This species (*E.* 1½-1¾ inch) has creamy white fore-wings (sometimes pale buff) with many black spots, and white hind-wings with one or two black spots; abdomen yellow. *L.*—a brown "Woolly Bear" with red stripe down the back—feeds on dock, plantain, and other low plants in August and September. Moth flies in June and July. (The WATER ERMINE (*S. urticæ*) is white, with two black dots on fore-wings, none on the hind-wings; abdomen yellow. Is local in marshes. Slightly smaller than the White Ermine.)

The Buff Ermine (*S. lubricipeda*) is, as its name implies, buff-coloured, with a few scattered white dots (or dashes in some varieties). *L.* feeds on low-growing plants—for example, dock. Moth emerges in June. Quite common. Sometimes remarkable varieties are found. *E.* 1½-1¾ inch.

The Muslin (*Diaphora mendica*).—*Male*, reddish brown with a few indistinct spots; *female*, silky white, with more numerous and plainer black spots. Appears in May and June. *L.* in July and August on low plants.

Ruby Tiger (*Phragmatobia fuliginosa*).—*E.* 1-1½ inch. Fore-wings brownish, with two small black spots near middle. Hind-wings lilac (in South, rose-pink), with blackish hind margins and two or three spots in the centre. Common in the British Isles. Appears May to July, flying at night. *L.* feeds on low-growing plants.

Wood Tiger (*Parasemia plantaginis*).—A handsome and rather variable species appearing in May and June, the larva feeding in autumn and early spring on plantain, forget-me-not, and other plants. *Ly.* Heaths, moors, and thin woods. Fore-wings yellow with heavy black markings. The hind-wings vary from yellow to red, with black spots and patches. *E.* 1¼-1½ inch.

Clouded Buff (*Diacrisia sanio*).—*E.* 1⅓-1¾ inch. The *male* has yellowish fore-wings, with a reddish grey centre spot and margins; hind-wings cream-coloured, with a brownish centre spot and outer band, and pinkish fringes. *Female*, orange fore-wings with redder markings; hind-wings orange with a good deal of black. *Ly.* Heaths in June and July. *L.* in July and August, and in April and May, on low plants. Widely distributed.

Garden Tiger (*Arctia caia*).—This is the Common Tiger Moth, whose gaudy colouring is so familiar—fore-wings cream and chocolate, hind-wings orange with several round blackish spots. Found in May to July. *L.*, the "Woolly Bear," feeds on many low plants—nettles, dock, etc. *E.* 2½-3 inches. (The

THE BRITISH NATURE BOOK

CREAM-SPOT TIGER (*A. villica*), with black fore-wings with eight cream spots, and yellow hind-wings with five or six black spots, is not so common. *E.* 2-2½ inches.)

Jersey Tiger (*Callimorpha quadripunctaria*).—*E.* 2-2⅜ inches. Fore-wings chocolate, slashed with cream bands; hind-wings red, with three or four dark spots. Is found only in Devon. (The SCARLET TIGER (*C. dominula*) (*E.* 2-2⅜ inches)—fore-wings dark chocolate, with nine or ten cream and orange spots; hind-wings scarlet, with two or three dark patches—is local in Kent and Southern Counties.)

Cinnabar (*Hipocrita jacobeæ*).—*E.* 1¼-1¾ inch. Has greyish black fore-wings, with a scarlet stripe parallel to the upper edge, and two spots on the hind margin—one near the tip, the other near the anal angle. Hind-wings scarlet with black edges. Appears in May and June on wastes and heaths. *L.* feeds gregariously on ragwort.

Lithosiinæ—Footman Moths.

These moths get their name of " Footman " from their long, stiff appearance when at rest, their drab-coloured wings being folded close to the body. They fly at dusk.

Red-necked Footman (*Atolmis rubricollis*).—Sooty black wings, an orange-coloured " tail," and a red ring round its " neck." *L.* feeds from July to October on lichens. Moth flies in June and July. *Ly.* Woods. *E.* 1-1⅜ inch.

The Muslin (*Nudaria mundana*).—*E.* ¾-1 inch. Has semi-transparent greyish fore-wings crossed by two zigzag lines, the hind-wings being paler. *L.* in April and May on lichen. Moth in August and September. (The ROUND-WINGED MUSLIN (*Comacla senex*) has rounder wings, a larger central dot, and two rows of indistinct blackish dots instead of lines.)

The Rosy Footman (*Miltochrista miniata*) is recognized by the pink tinge on the yellowish fore-wings, and the rose-coloured margins. *E.* 1-1¼ inch. *L.* feeds on lichens. Moth out in July. *Ly.* Woods and heaths.

Dew Moth (*Endrosa irrorella*).—Yellowish buff, with three rows of black dots on fore-wings; hind-wings paler. It is said to get its name from its appearance when at rest, hanging from a leaf or grass-blade like a drop of dew. Moth flies in June and July. *L.* feeds on lichens. Widely distributed, but more common on South and East Coasts. *E.* ¾-1¼ inch.

The Four-dotted Footman (*Cybosia mesomella*) has two black dots on each creamy-coloured fore-wing—one near the upper and the other near the lower edge. *L.* feeds in April and May on lichens. Moth found in June. *E.* 1-1⅜ inch.

The Four-spotted or Large Footman (*Œonestis quadra*) is larger (1½-2 inches). The *female* has two spots on each yellowish fore-wing. The *male* has grey fore-wings tinged with yellowish, the basal area yellow, the outer edge blue-grey; hind-wings pale ochreous. *L.* in May and June on lichens.

Moth in July and August; flies at night. (The BUFF FOOTMAN (*Lithosia deplana*) (E. 1-1¼ inch)—ochreous grey—is scarce.)

The Dingy Footman (*L. griseola*).—*E.* 1¼-1½ inch. Has leaden grey fore-wings with a yellowish front edging, the hind-wings being yellowish grey. *L.* on lichens in fens and marshes. Moth in July and August. (Very similar in general appearance are the COMMON FOOTMAN (*L. lurideola*), found in woods in July; the SCARCE FOOTMAN (*L. complana*), a local species found in July and August in all the Eastern and Southern Counties; and the NORTHERN FOOTMAN (*L. serica*), only found in Lancashire and Cheshire.)

The Orange Footman (*L. sororcula*).—*E.* 1-1⅛ inch. Has orange-coloured fore-wings, the hind-wings being paler. It appears in May and June; the larva from July to September on oak lichens. *Ly.* Woods.

The Dotted Footman (*Pelosia muscerda*).—*E.* 1-1¼ inch. Has pale grey wings, and is identified by the six black dots on the fore-wings—two just above the inner margin, the other four in an oblique line from the top edge towards the anal angle. *L.* feeds on lichens and mosses. Moth out in July and August. Found principally in the fen district.

Family : *Noctuidæ*.

A very large section of medium and large moths, with well-defined markings, easy to recognize; divided into five groups. Antennæ usually finely ciliated. Mostly night fliers, coming readily to " sugar."

1. *Acronyctinæ*.

The Nut-tree Tussock (*Demas coryli*).—*E.* 1⅙-1½ inch. Fore-wings reddish brown on basal half, ashy grey on outer half; hind-wings greyish, with a broad dark marginal band. Moth in May to June, and August to September. *L.* in July and September on beech, birch, hazel, etc. Common.

The Miller (*Acronycta leporina*).—*E.* 1½-1¾ inch. Wings white dusted with grey, with a few black dots instead of lines. *L.* in July to September on birch and alder. Moth in May and June. *Ly.* Heaths and mosses.

The Sycamore (*A. aceris*).—*E.* 1½-1¾ inch. A dark grey mottled species with white hind-wings. *L.* feeds on sycamore and maple in August and September. Moth flies in June and July. (The POPLAR GREY (*A. megacephala*) is very similar, but has darker fore-wings. *F.p.* Poplar. Moth in May to August.)

The Grey Dagger (*A. psi*).—*E.* 1½ inch. Ashy grey fore-wings, with four short black forked streaks; the one near the hinder angle forms a mark like the Greek letter ψ. Hind-wings whitish, with slightly darker margins. Appears June to August. *L.* feeds on poplar, lime, birch, etc. (The DARK DAGGER (*A. tridens*) is very similar, but darker, and not so common.)

Knot-grass (*A. rumicis*).—*E.* 1⅓-1½ inch. Fore-wings brownish grey (sometimes appearing sooty brown), mottled with darker. Look for a white mark, something like a bracket [)] or a large comma [']. close to the inner margin, with a small spot sometimes below it. The hind-wings are a lighter brownish grey, shaded deeper towards the edge. Moth flies in June to July, sometimes August to September. *L.* feeds on knot-grass, dock, plantain, etc., in July to September. Common. (The LIGHT KNOT-GRASS (*A. menyanthidis*) is the same size and very similar, but lighter in colour. Orbicular stigma is usually a distinct small black ring with a lighter centre. Appears in June and July on moorlands in the North.)

The Coronet (*Cranisphora ligustri*).—*E.* 1⅛–1½ inch. Is similarly coloured. There is a pale greyish mark just beyond the reniform stigma like a coronet or crown. *L.* feeds on ash and privet in August and September. Moth in June and July.

Marbled Beauty (*Bryophila perla*).—*E.* about 1 inch. Fore-wings cream-coloured, marbled with darker. The orbicular and claviform stigmata are joined and make a figure 8 of dark grey. Hind-wings creamy white with dark lines. *L.* August to May on wall lichens. Moth in July and August. (The MARBLED GREEN (*B. glandifera*) is slightly larger and has a greenish tinge in fore-wings ; has no figure 8. A rather local species.)

2. *Trifinæ.*

Turnip Moth (*Agrotis segetum*).—Very variable. *E.* 1¼–1¾ inch. Fore-wings yellowish or brownish grey, sometimes orange-brown ; the markings darker and obscure. Hind-wings whitish, with brown margins and veins. Found in June. *L.* feeds from July to April on turnips and swedes, to which it is very destructive. (The DARK SWORD-GRASS (*A. ypsilon*) is similar in colour, but larger (*E.* 1⅞–2 inches). The markings are plainer. The submarginal line is yellowish and makes a W ; and bounded by it are two or three black arrow-headed streaks. Flies in August. *L.* feeds on cabbage, lettuce, swedes, etc. The PEARLY UNDERWING (*A. saucia*) is of the same size and colouring, but is a local species.)

Archer's Dart (*A. vestigialis*).—*E.* 1¼–1½ inch. A handsome species with pale brown fore-wings. Hind-wings whitish, margined with grey. Submarginal line is whitish and zigzag, and has some black arrow-headed marks in front of it. The three stigmata are generally clearly defined, enclosed in black, the orbicular being whitish with a dark pupil. *L.* in August to May on grasses, bedstraw, etc. Moth in July and August. *Ly.* Sandhills.

Heart and Club (*A. corticea*).—*E.* 1⅛–1½ inch. Fore-wings pale brown, with darker markings. Hind-wings lighter. Stigmata sharply defined in black, reniform being more or less heart-shaped ; and near the base there is a dark brown mark resembling a club. Appears in July. *L.* feeds on low-growing plants—dock, goosefoot, etc.—in March and April. (The HEART AND DART (*A. exclamationis*) is very similar, but has a distinct black mark on the front of the thorax. The CRESCENT DART (*A. lunifera*) is a coast species in July

and August; it gets its name from the crescent-shaped reniform stigma. The
SHUTTLE-SHAPED DART (*A. puta*) is smaller (*E.* 1⅛–1¼ inch), but similarly
coloured. *Ly.* Marshy meadows.)

The Light-feathered Rustic (*A. cinerea*).—*E.* 1¼–1½ inch. Has pale grey
fore-wings in the *male*, and dark brown in the *female*. Only the reniform stigma
is present; it is oval, with a dark edge. *Ly.* Chalky districts in May and June.

The Coast Dart (*A. cursoria*) is very variable, from lightish yellow to dark
reddish brown, and the markings also vary enormously. It is found on sandhills. *L.* feeds on grasses.

Garden Dart (*A. nigricans*).—Has sooty brown fore-wings. *E.* 1¼–1½ inch.
The reniform stigma is generally rather paler than the rest of the wing, and so
stands out with slight distinctness. Moth flies in July to August. *L.* from
September to June on clover, dock, and other low plants.

The White Line Dart (*A. tritici*) is very similar, and equally variable;
but a normal specimen has a whitish streak along two-thirds of the upper edge
(or costa). It is principally a coast insect.

The Heath Rustic (*A. agathina*).—*E.* 1–1¼ inch. Is a brownish species.
There is a blackish pyramid on the fore-wings, in which the grey orbicular
and reniform stigmata are situated. It is fairly common on heaths in August.

The Double Dart (*Noctua augur*).—*E.* 1½–1¾ inch. A dull brownish species
with a reddish tinge on fore-wings, the markings sometimes bold, at other times
indistinct. It is quite common from June to August. *L.* feeds on low-growing
plants from July to May.

The Grey, or Neglected, Rustic (*N. castanea*), is slightly smaller, but very
similar in its reddish-tinged brown colour; this in the South often varies to
grey. The markings are very obscure. Flies in August. Widely distributed.

The Dotted Clay (*N. buja*).—*E.* 1½–1⅝ inch. Fore-wings pale ochreous
brown (varying to darker); *but there is often a noticeable black spot near the apex
on the upper margin*. Moth in July and August. *L.* September to May on
hawthorn, bramble, etc. Common.

Setaceous Hebrew Character (*N. c-nigrum*).—*E.* 1⅜–1½ inch. This species
varies in colour from pale reddish grey to dark brown; but in the middle of
the costa there is always a light triangular spot, edged beneath by a black V-
shaped patch, supposed to represent a Hebrew letter. Moth in July and August,
sometimes earlier. *L.* on dock and other low plants in September onwards
to May.

Flame Shoulder (*N. plecta*).—*E.* 1–1¼ inch. This species is not unlike the
preceding, but smaller, and instead of a wedge-shaped light patch on the costa
there is a creamy stripe with black beneath it; hind-wings whitish. It is quite
common in May and June, and again in August to September. *L.* on low
plants, and lettuce and beet.

The Double Square Spot (*N. triangulum*).—*E.* 1½–1¾ inch. Has ochreous
brown fore-wings; has conspicuous marks in the discal cell, one of which
(farthest from the base) is a roughly outlined square. It is common in woods

THE BRITISH NATURE BOOK

in June and July. (The SQUARE-SPOTTED CLAY (*N. stigmatica*) is similar in size and markings but darker in colour. It is very local.)

Purple Clay (*N. brunnea*).—*E.* 1½–1⅔ inch. Has fore-wings varying from purplish brown to rusty ochreous. The markings also vary, but often the reniform stigma is outlined with an ochreous or whitish tint, and there is a whitish crescent within it. *L.* feeds on bilberry, wood-rush, and bramble—often attacking the buds of birch in the spring. Moth in June and July in woods.

The Ingrailed Clay (*N. primulæ*).—*E.* 1¼–1½ inch. Is so variable that it cannot be described in a few words. Fore-wings reddish or grey ochreous, with darker markings. It flies in June and July. *L.* feeds on primrose, bilberry, dock, etc., in August to May.

Barred Chestnut (*N. dahlii*).—*E.* 1⅜–1½ inch. Rusty brown fore-wings (*female* darker than *male*); hind-wings ochreous grey. Markings generally indistinct, but plainer in the *female*. Flies in July and August. *L.* on dock, plantain, etc., from September to May. *Ly.* Heaths and moorlands.

Small Square Spot (*N. rubi*).—Double-brooded in June and August. *E.* 1¼–1½ inch. Fore-wings pale or dark reddish brown. Hind-wings shining pale grey. Reniform stigma has a dark pupil. *L.* feeds on dandelion, dock, etc. Very common.

Six-striped Rustic (*N. umbrosa*).—Is somewhat similar, with dark or light coppery brown fore-wings; hind-wings shining pale ochreous. Common in July and August. *L.* feeds on dock, plantain, etc., August to May.

Square-spot Rustic (*N. xanthographa*).—*E.* 1¼–1½ inch. Very common and variable. Flies in August. *L.* on dock and low-growing plants. Fore-wings drab to dark brown, tinged with red. Reniform stigma more or less square—in some specimens conspicuous, in others almost absent.

The Flame (*Axylia putris*).—*E.* 1–1¼ inch. Fore-wings pale ochreous, with a broad reddish brown mark from base to apex, taking up nearly half the wing. This is slashed at the end by a lighter break. Generally common in June or July. *L.* on bedstraw, dock, nettle, etc., July to October.

Large Yellow or Common Yellow Underwing (*Triphæna pronuba*).—*E.* 2–2¼ inches. Fore-wings vary from buff to dark purplish brown. The hind-wings are bright yellow, with a narrow black submarginal band. It is common and abundant in June and July. *L.* feeds from August to May on grasses and low plants.

The Lesser Yellow Underwing (*T. comes*).—*E.* 1½–1¾ inch. Is common also, and very variable; its size distinguishes it from *T. pronuba*. Flies in July and August.

The Broad-bordered Yellow Underwing (*T. fimbria*).—*E.* 2–2¼ inches. Has variable brown fore-wings, the yellow-orange hind-wings having a very broad black band. The *abdomen* is yellow. Flies in June and July in woodlands. *L.* on primrose, violet, and dock, in autumn.

The Lesser Broad-bordered Yellow Underwing (*T. ianthina*).—*E.* 1½–1¾ inch. Has dark fore-wings, purplish or violet-tinged. Its name and size show

PLATE XXIX.

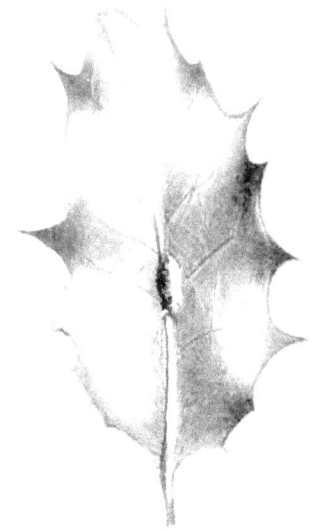

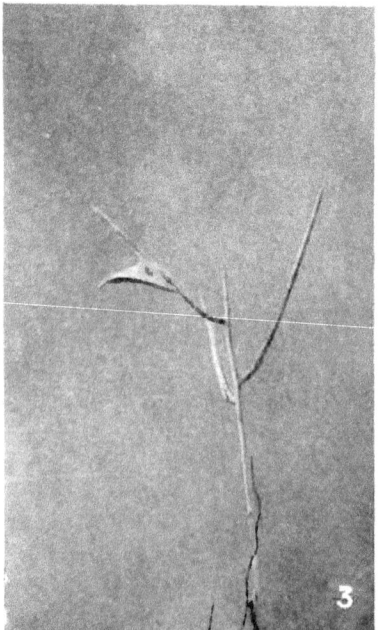

1. Pupa of Holly Blue Butterfly (*in situ*).
2. Death's Head Moth.
3. Pupa of Orange-tip Butterfly.
4. Orange-tip, emerging.

its distinguishing characteristics. Flies in July and August in lanes, hedgerows, and woods.

The Least Yellow Underwing (*T. interjecta*).—*E.* 1¼-1½ inch. Forewings rusty brown; hind-wings deep yellow ochre, *blackish at the base*, with a broad submarginal band. Flies in July and August. *L.* September to May on grasses, primrose, and dock. Not so common as preceding.

Green Arches (*Eurois prasina*).—*E.* 1¾-2 inches. The fore-wings, when fresh, have a green ground colour, but this often fades to an ochreous tint; black cross lines with whitish edges; and a distinct whitish patch on the outer edge of the reniform stigma. Hind-wings brownish grey, with straw-coloured edges. A wood-loving moth. Flies in June. *L.* on low plants from July to May; in spring on sallow and bilberry. Common in most parts. (The SILVERY ARCHES (*Aplecta tincta*) is the same size and very similar, but fore-wings are silvery grey, slightly tinged with purplish brown. Hind-wings smoky grey. It is a local species. The PALE SHINING BROWN (*A. advena*) has glossy pale reddish brown fore-wings, with faint but distinct markings. Local also.)

Grey Arches (*Aplecta nebulosa*).—*E.* 1½-2 inches. Fore-wings generally light grey, dusted with white, and varied with darker, but there is considerable variation. The three stigmata are large and whitish, with a darker centre, and a fine edging of black; hind-wings smoky grey. Flies in June and July in woods. *L.* from August to October on low plants. Common.

The Dot (*Mamestra persicariæ*).—*E.* 1½-1⅔ inch. Fore-wings violet-brown; hind-wings smoky brown, paler towards the base. The reniform stigma shows up very plainly, being white with a brownish centre. *L.* on many low plants from August to October. Moth flies in July and August. Common except in the North.

Cabbage Moth (*Barathra brassicæ*).—*E.* 1⅔-1¾ inch. A very common greyish moth, with obscure markings, but *generally the white edging of the reniform stigma is plain, and also the white submarginal line.* Feeds not only on cabbage but all sorts of low plants, July to October. Moth in June and July. Common and very destructive in kitchen gardens.

The White Colon (*Mamestra albicolon*) is much like the former, but lighter in colour; but *notice the two white dots like a* **:** *at the lower edge of the reniform stigma*, from which its name is derived. *L.* feeds on dandelion, plantain, etc. Moth double brooded in May to June and July to August. *Ly.* Sandhills.

Bright-line Brown-eye (*M. oleracea*).—Another very common species of similar general colour and size, distinguished, as its name suggests, by the yellowish reniform stigma—the " brown eye," and a fine white submarginal line—the " bright line." *L.* in July to September on low plants, especially goosefoot and tamarisk. Moth in June to July.

Light Brocade (*M. genistæ*). — *E.* 1½-1¾ inch. Fore-wings ochreous brown; the central area is tinged with reddish brown, and towards the bottom of this *there is a black bar*. Moth in May and June. *L.* in July and August on broom, persicaria, etc. Common in the South.

The Dog's Tooth (*M. dissimilis*) is another ochreous brown species, and gets its name from the shapes of the central markings. *L.* in June and July on dock, plantain, etc. Moth in June and July. Local in marshy places.

Pale-shouldered Brocade (*M. thalassina*).—*E.* $1\frac{1}{2}$-$1\frac{3}{4}$ inch. Rich chocolate-brown fore-wings, beautifully patterned. Its name is derived from a whitish patch at the shoulder—that is, at the base of the fore-wings. Moth in June. Common in woods. *L.* feeds on broom, honeysuckle, dock, etc., in August to September.

The Beautiful Brocade (*M. contigua*) has a *white or pale band* running across the fore-wings from the middle of the costa to the inner angle, crossing the large orbicular stigma. Moth in June in woodlands. *L.* in August to September on birch, oak, bilberry, dock, etc. Rather local.

The Broom (*M. pisi*).—*E.* $1\frac{1}{2}$ inch. Fore-wings reddish brown; markings more or less distinct, but the yellow submarginal line is usually clear, and ends in a pale blotch at the inner angle. Flies in June to July. *L.* in August to September on many plants—dog rose, brake fern, broom, etc. Common in most parts.

The Nutmeg (*M. trifolii*).—*E.* $1\frac{1}{2}$ inch. Fore-wings grey-brown, with darker patterning; cross lines pale, with black edging. Double brooded May to June and July to August. *L.* in July to September on goosefoot and orache. *Ly.* Market gardens and wastes, but especially in coastal districts.

The Shears (*M. dentina*).—*E.* $1\frac{1}{4}$-$1\frac{1}{2}$ inch. Brown varied with light grey; markings usually distinct; a dark central area, on which the nervures stand out as light grey lines. Hind-wings greyish brown. Moth in May to June. *L.* in July to August on dandelion, chickweed, etc. Common. (The GLAUCOUS SHEARS (*M. glauca*) is dark grey with purplish tinges, with plain whitish stigmata. Chiefly confined to northerly hilly districts.)

Marbled Coronet (*Dianthœcia conspersa*).—*E.* $1\frac{1}{4}$-$1\frac{1}{2}$ inch. Dark violet-grey fore-wings, with distinct creamy white markings and patches. Flies in June and July. Chiefly in seaboard counties. *L.* feeds on the seeds of catchfly, campion, etc.

The Lychnis (*D. capsincola*).—*E.* $1\frac{1}{3}$-$1\frac{1}{2}$ inch. Fore-wings greyish brown, with lighter marblings and lines. The orbicular and reniform stigmata almost join at the lower ends, making a Y-shaped pattern. Hind-wings grey shaded with brown. *L.* feeds on seeds of campion, ragged robin, etc., in July. Moth in May to June. (The CAMPION (*D. cucubali*) is very much the same in markings and general characteristics, but has a tinge of reddish violet.)

The Tawny Shears (*D. carpophaga*).—*E.* $1\frac{1}{4}$-$1\frac{1}{2}$ inch. Fore-wings ochreous brown, sometimes nearly white, with brown stigmata edged with black. Other particulars as in preceding.

Broad-barred White (*Hecatera serena*).—*E.* about $1\frac{1}{4}$ inch. Fore-wings almost white, sometimes with a greyish blue shade, but having a roughly triangular blackish grey band dividing each wing. Hind-wings shaded smoky grey. *L.* in July and August on hawk's-beard, lettuce, etc. Moth in June to August. Often seen in daytime at rest on fences and trees.

Bordered Gothic (*Neuria reticulata*).—*E.* $1\frac{1}{2}-1\frac{2}{3}$ inch. Brown fore-wings netted with pale brown cross lines and veins. Antennæ of *male* with minute hairs. *L.* in July and August on soapwort, knot-grass, etc. Moth in June and July. This moth may be confused with the GOTHIC (*Nænia typica*), but the latter is a darker brown, and has not so netted an appearance, besides having pectinated antennæ. The latter feeds on all kinds of herbage, and is gregarious when in early larval stage.

Feathered Gothic (*Epineuronia popularis*).—*E.* $1\frac{1}{2}-1\frac{2}{3}$ inch. Fore-wings brown with lighter nervures; orbicular and reniform stigmata showing fairly distinctly in the central area. Often seen in houses. *L.* feeds on grasses. Moth in August and September.

The Antler (*Charæas graminis*).—*E.* $1-1\frac{1}{2}$ inch. Another brown moth which gets its name from the supposed resemblance of the central markings, which are forked like a stag's horn. *L.* in March and June on grasses. Moth flies from July to September. *Ly.* Dry pastures.

Dark Brocade (*Eumichtis adusta*).—*E.* $1\frac{1}{2}-1\frac{2}{3}$ inch. Fore-wings usually dark reddish brown, the markings rather obscure. The hind-wings are lighter, shaded. *F.p.* Grasses, bladder campion, etc., in July to September. Moth flies in June and July. (The DUSKY BROCADE (*Apamea gemina*) is a smaller but somewhat similar species. *E.* $1\frac{1}{4}-1\frac{1}{2}$ inch. Fore-wings brownish grey, with purplish tinge. Other details as preceding. *Ly.* Moist places.)

Brindled Green (*Eumichtis protea*).—*E.* $1\frac{1}{4}-1\frac{1}{3}$ inch. Fore-wings brown, with *greenish* shades on the markings. *L.* March to June on oak; beginning by boring into the oak buds. Moth in September and October.

Minor Shoulder-knot (*Bombycia viminalis*).—*E.* $1\frac{1}{3}-1\frac{1}{2}$ inch. Fore-wings pale grey (in South—being darker in North), with a few dark brown lines; the reniform stigma pale greenish or yellowish within. *F.p.* Sallow and willow in April to June. Moth in June and July.

Dusky Sallow (*Eremobia ochroleuca*).—*E.* $1\frac{1}{3}-1\frac{1}{2}$ inch. Fore-wings ochreous, tinged with brown; two irregular white lines cross the wing, making a roughly shaped **X**. *L.* feeds on grasses and corn. Moth in July and August. *Ly.* Chalk districts.

Figure of Eight Moth (*Diloba cæruleocephala*).—*E.* $1\frac{1}{4}-1\frac{1}{2}$ inch. Identified by the figure **8** made by the orbicular and reniform stigmata touching. *L.* on hawthorn, sloe, wild crab, and fruit trees, in April to June. Moth in October and November.

Flounced Rustic (*Luperina testacea*).—*E.* $1\frac{1}{3}-1\frac{1}{2}$ inch. Pale brown (or darker) fore-wings, markings often indistinct. Hind-wings white, with a "flounced" black marginal line. *L.* on grass roots. Moth in August to September.

Straw Underwing (*Cerigo matura*).—So called from its straw-coloured or yellowish hind-wings, which have a marginal band of brown. Fore-wings reddish brown. Moth in July and August. L. on grasses in September to April. Common in most parts. E. 1½-1¾ inch.

Large Nutmeg (*Hama sordida*).—E. 1½-1⅞ inch. Fore-wings pale ochreous brown, mottled with darker; a black streak at the base; stigmata and submarginal line paler. Flies in June. F.p. Grasses. Common in most parts.

Rustic Shoulder-knot (*Apamea basilinea*).—E. 1⅓-1½ inch. Named after the *short black streak* from the middle of the base—" the shoulder-knot "— on the pale brown fore-wings. Tinged in some cases with rusty red. Flies in May and June. L. from August to March on grasses.

Small Clouded Brindle (*A. unanimis*).—E. 1¼-1⅜ inch. Fore-wings reddish brown; the *reniform stigma is outlined in white*, and is generally distinct. There are also two black streaks from the base. Flies in June and July. L. on grasses from July to April. Ly. Damp places.

Common Rustic (*A. secalis*).—E. 1-1¼ inch. A very variable species; ochreous or rusty brown fore-wings; generally the reniform stigma is conspicuous, with its white colour and edging. Flies in July and August. L. on grasses in autumn to May.

Marbled Minor (*Miana strigilis*).—E. about 1 inch. A very variable and common species. May be all brown, or slightly tinged with rose colour; but often fore-wings are brown, with the submarginal area grey. Moth in June and July. L. in March and April on grasses.

The **Middle-barred Minor** (*M. fasciuncula*) is slightly smaller, and has reddish ochreous fore-wings, with a darker central band; the transverse lines being distinctly white towards their lower part. Other particulars as preceding. (The ROSY MINOR (*M. literosa*) has pearly grey fore-wings, the base being clouded a claret colour, and a central reddish brown band. L. September to June on grasses. Moth in July and August. Chiefly on coasts. The CLOAKED MINOR (*M. bicoloria*) is another very variable species found on rough meadows by the sea. Fore-wings brownish on the basal area, whitish on the rest.)

Clouded Bordered Brindle (*Xylophasia rurea*).—E. 1½-1¾ inch. Fore-wings vary from grey-white to reddish ochreous. The outer transverse line consists of a row of dark brown dots. Stigmata usually lighter than ground colour. Moth in June and July. L. on grasses from August to May.

Clouded Brindle (*X. hepatica*).—E. 1½-1¾ inch. Fore-wings pale brown, with well-defined black markings. Orbicular stigma oval and oblique in a black margin. Moth in June and July. L. August to April on grasses.*

Light Arches (*X. lithoxylea*).—E. 1¾-2 inches. Pale ochre-yellow fore-wings, with indistinct markings; hind-wings whitish and semi-transparent. Moth in June and July. L. October to May on grasses.

Dark Arches (*X. monoglypha*).—A species of same size as preceding, but,

---

* In many cases the larva is noted as feeding from a midsummer month to the following spring. This means that it begins feeding up in the autumn, hibernates for the winter, and recommences in the spring.

as name implies, much darker in general colour. Moth from June to August. *L.* August to September on grasses.

Bird's Wing (*Dipterygia scabriuscula*).—*E.* 1¼–1½ inch. The dark brown, or blackish, fore-wings have on the inner margin a dull ochreous patch which resembles the wing of a bird. Moth in May and June. *L.* in July and August on dock, sorrel, etc. Chiefly confined to Eastern and Southern Counties.

Sprawler (*Brachionycha sphinx*).—*E.* 1½–1¾ inch. Fore-wings pale brownish grey, with numerous black streaks, one running from base well towards the centre. Moth in November and December. Rather local. *L.* on poplar, oak, lime, and other trees.

Green Brindled Crescent (*Miselia oxyacanthæ*).—*E.* 1½–1⅔ inch. Pale reddish brown fore-wings, with green metallic sprinklings on the hind margin and the nervures. Large pale brown stigmata. Moth in September and October. *L.* in April and May on hawthorn, sloe, etc.

Merveille du Jour (*Agriopis aprilina*).—*E.* 1½–2 inches. A pretty pale green moth with black and white markings; stigmata large and white with green centres; hind-wings dark grey. Moth in September and October. *L.* in April to June on oak.

Small Angle Shades (*Euplexia lucipara*).—*E.* 1¼ inch. Fore-wings dark brown, basal area lighter. Distinguished by the pale reniform stigma which is on the outer edge of the dark central area. Moth in June and July. *L.* in August and September on low plants.

Angle Shades (*Phlogophora meticulosa*).—*E.* 1½–2 inches. Fore-wings pinky brown, with triangular central area olive-brown, touched with green when newly caught. The pinkish hue and the contrasted colours serve to identify it. Moth and larva throughout the year; latter feeding on nettle, groundsel, dock, etc. When at rest, wrinkles the fore-wings, and looks like a withered leaf.

Old Lady (*Mormo maura*).—*E.* 2⅜–2½ inches. Often found indoors behind curtains, etc. Dark greyish brown wings, central area nearly black, crossed by paler nervures. Six dark spots or patches along the costa. Flies in July and August. *L.* in autumn on low plants, and in spring on young shoots of sallow, alder, etc.

Gothic (*Nænia typica*).—*E.* 1½–1⅔ inch. A very common species. Brown fore-wings, with whitish nervures, appearing like cracks in the brown. The three stigmata clearly defined, though the claviform is small. Flies in June and July. *L.* August to May on all kinds of herbage.

Crescent (*Helotropha leucostigma*).—*E.* 1⅓–1½ inch. This species, with its light or dark brown fore-wings, gets its name from the whitish crescent-shaped reniform stigma. *L.* feeds inside the stems of sedge and yellow flag, May to July. Moth in July and August. *Ly.* Fens and marshy lands.

Ear Moth (*Hydrœcia nictitans*).—*E.* 1⅛–1¼ inch. Fore-wings reddish brown; hind-wings grey. The name is given from the resemblance of the whitish reniform stigma to a human ear. Moth in August and September. *L.* May to August on grasses.

Rosy Rustic (*H. micacea*).—*E.* 1¼–1½ inch. Fore-wings light reddish brown, the darker central area separated from the outer by (generally) a well-defined paler line. Moth in August and September. *L.* in May to August on dock, plantain, potato; feeding on stems and down into the root.

Frosted Orange (*Ochria ochracea*).—*E.* 1¼–1½ inch. This species has bright yellow-ochre fore-wings, handsomely marked darker purple-brown. The stigmata are pale ochreous, the orbicular being very distinct and almost circular. Moth in August to October. *L.* April to July on stems of thistles, burdock, etc. *Ly.* Marshy lands.

The **Bulrush Wainscot** (*Nonagria typhæ*) gets its name from the food plant —the reed-mace—in the stems of which it feeds. *E.* 1½–2 inches. Usually pale whity brown colour, with a row of black wedge-shaped spots near the outer margin, and other scattered dots on the transverse lines. Moth in August and September. *L.* July and August.

Twin-spotted Wainscot (*N. geminipuncta*).—*E.* 1–1¼ inch. It has on its brownish ochreous fore-wings two small white spots for the reniform stigma. Moth in August. *L.* in May and June in reed stems. *Ly.* Fens.

Small Wainscot (*Tapinostola fulva*).—*E.* 1–1⅛ inch. A pale brown moth (some species reddish brown), with no distinct markings. Flies in fens and damp woods in August and September. *L.* in June and July on sedge stems.

Large Wainscot (*Calamia lutosa*).—*E.* 1⅜–2 inches. Fore-wings pale ochreous brown, with a faint row of black dots beyond the middle of the wing. *L.* in reed stems in April to June. Moth in August to October in marsh lands. (The FEN WAINSCOT (*C. phragmitidis*) is a smaller but similarly coloured species, with no markings, also found in the fens.)

Common Wainscot (*Leucania pallens*).—*E.* 1¼–1½ inch. Fore-wings pale ochre-yellow, with browner nervures, and with generally three black dots about the middle of the wing; hind-wings whitish. *L.* on grasses August to May. Moth in June and July. Everywhere common. (The SMOKY WAINSCOT (*L. impura*) is equally common, of similar size and colouring, but the hind-wings are darker grey.)

The **Striped Wainscot** (*L. impudens*) is larger than preceding. *E.* 1⅓–1½ inch. Often tinged with pink; the black streaks often very plain. It is found chiefly in fens and marshy districts.

Shoulder-striped Wainscot (*L. comma*).—*E.* 1¼–1½ inch. It has a white middle nervure, with a black streak below it, together with other black marks near the outer margin of its ochreous-brown fore-wings. *L.* on grasses in June to August. Moth in June and July. *Ly.* Meadows.

The Clay (*L. lithargyrea*).—*E.* 1½–1¾ inch. Fore-wings greyish ochreous, tinged with red. The reniform stigma represented by a small whitish crescent, and the transverse lines by a series of black dots; hind-wings paler. Common from June to August in woods. *L.* in April and May on grasses.

Brown-line Bright-eye (*L. conigera*).—Very similar to preceding, but the cross lines show up plainly in dark brown, the inner one being bent in a sharp angle. The reniform stigma is " bright," with a white spot. Other particulars as above.

Treble Lines (*Grammesia trigrammica*).—*E.* 1½-1½ inch. Pale greyish brown; the fore-wings crossed by three distinct brown lines, the centre one often being broad. Moth in June and July. *L.* from July to April on plantain, etc.

Mottled Rustic (*Caradrina morpheus*).—*E.* about 1¼ inch. Pale brown fore-wings, with stigmata and a band close to submarginal line dark brown and generally fairly distinct; hind-wings whitish (in *female*, with grey shading). Moth flies in June to August. *L.* on low plants from August onwards.

The Uncertain (*C. alsines*).—*E.* about 1¼ inch. Fore-wings rusty brown, tinged with ochreous, with dark brown distinct markings; hind-wings smoky grey. Flies in July to August. *L.* on dock, chickweed, etc., from September to March. (*Note.*—The fore-wings have a *rough* appearance.)

The Rustic (*C. taraxaci*) is very similar, and often confused with the preceding; but the fore-wings of *taraxaci* are browner and smoother, the markings being less distinct.

Pale Mottled Willow (*C. quadripunctata*).—*E.* 1-1¼ inch. Fore-wings ochreous grey, with brown markings. Note *the black spots along the upper margin;* these are a clue to identification. *L.* from September to May on grasses, peas, and grain—often in stacks of wheat. Moth in June to August.

Small Dotted Buff (*Petilampa arcuosa*).—*E.* 1-1¼ inch. Whity ochreous fore-wings, with (when present) two lines of brownish dots; hind-wings grey, with pale yellow fringes. Flies in July to August. *L.* on grasses (*Aira cæspitosa*) in May and June.

Brown Rustic (*Rusina tenebrosa* or *umbratica*).—*E.* 1½-1¾ inch. Fore-wings chestnut-brown, with blackish markings. Look for *three white dots* between the reniform stigma and the submarginal line. *L.* on grasses August to May. Moth in June and July.

Copper Underwing (*Amphipyra pyramidea*).—*E.* 1¾-2¼ inches. This handsome species is recognized by its coppery or sometimes reddish hind-wings; the fore-wings being rusty brown with blackish shading in the central area, bordered outwardly by dentated white line. Orbicular stigma is white, with a black dot. *L.* from March to June on oak, sallow, and other trees. Moth in July to September. *Ly.* Woods.

The Mouse (*A. tragopogonis*).—*E.* 1¼-1½ inch. Derives its name partly from its general colour, and partly from its mouse-like habit of running off when disturbed. Fore-wings greyish brown, with a black dot for the orbicular stigma, and two similar ones for the reniform. Moth common in July and August. *L.* April to June on sallow, hawthorn, willow-herb, etc.

Pine Beauty (*Panolis griseo-variegata*).—*E.* 1¼-1½ inch. Fore-wings reddish brown, varied with ochreous grey; dark transverse lines, edged with pink. The orbicular and reniform stigmata are white, often connected by a white line at the bottom; hind-wings dark grey-brown. *L.* feeds on needles of fir and pine in May to July. Moth in March and April. *Ly.* Pine or fir plantations.

Red Chestnut (*Pachnobia rubricosa*).—*E.* 1¼-1½ inch. Red-brown fore-wings, dusted with greyish, obscure markings; hind-wings ochreous grey. Moth in March and April. *L.* on dock, dandelion, etc., in April to June.

Hebrew Character (*Tæniocampa gothica*).—*E.* 1¼-1½ inch. So called from the shape of the black mark on the red-brown fore-wings, resembling the Hebrew ℶ, laid on its side. *L.* on dock and other low plants, also sallow and other trees in April to June. Moth April to July.

Blossom Underwing (*T. miniosa*).—*E.* 1¼-1½ inch. Fore-wings pinkish grey; central area salmon colour; the two stigmata darker. Hind-wings whitish, also shaded 'or tinged with pink. *L.* on oak; gregarious in early stages. Moth in oak woods in March to April.

Small Quaker (*T. pulverulenta*).—*E.* 1-1⅛ inch. Greyish ochreous fore-wings, with reddish tinge, the cross lines marked by blackish dots, sometimes indistinct. Reniform stigma dark grey and distinct. Moth in March to April. *L.* in April to June on oak, maple, sallow, etc.

Common Quaker (*T. stabilis*).—*E.* 1¼-1½ inch. Fore-wings variable, from light grey-brown to dark red-brown. Two stigmata large, often touching, and outlined in pale ochreous, filled with dusky brown. *L.* on oak, birch, sallow, etc., April to June. Moth March to April. (The POWDERED QUAKER (*T. gracilis*) is very similar, but has paler fore-wings, which are more pointed. It is out in April and May. *L.* feeds gregariously on meadow-sweet, bramble, sloe, etc.)

Clouded Drab (*T. incerta*).—*E.* 1⅜-1½ inch. Very variable. Fore-wings range from light grey-brown to reddish and deep purplish brown, and the markings are sometimes plain, at other times obscure. It is very common in April and May. *L.* feeds on oak, sallow, hawthorn, etc. The moth visits the sallow-bloom.

Twin-spotted Quaker (*T. munda*).—*E.* 1½-1⅔ inch. Another very variable species. Fore-wings from pale greyish to dusky brown; but the name is derived from *two distinct black dots* in the middle of the submarginal line (sometimes there are others above and below them). *L.* feeds on elm, poplar, and other trees in April to June. Moth in March and April. *Ly.* Woodland districts.

White-spotted Pinion (*Calymnia diffinis*).—*E.* about 1¼ inch. This pretty species has reddish brown fore-wings, and is distinguished by two large triangular white spots on the upper edge, from which the cross lines start. It flies in July and August. *L.* feeds on elm.

The Dun-bar (*C. trapezina*).—*E.* 1¼-1½ inch. Rather variable. Fore-wings greyish yellow or reddish yellow; a dark central shade, bordered

PLATE XXX.

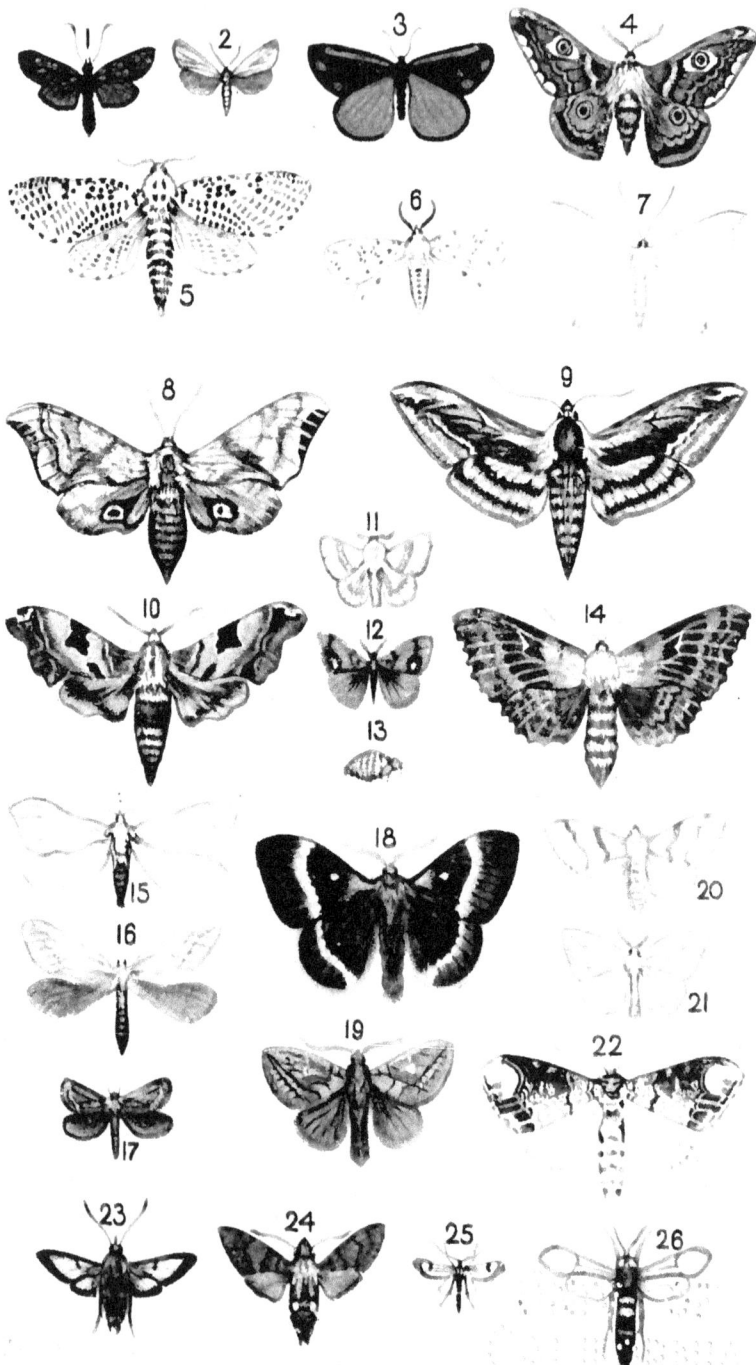

1. Six-spot Burnet. 2. Green Forester. 3. Goatmoth. 4. Emperor. 5. Wood Leopard. 6. White Ermine. 7. Swallow-tail Moth. 8. Eyed Hawk. 9. Privet Hawk. 10. Lime Hawk. 11. Lackey. 12. Vapourer, male. 13. Vapourer, female. 14. Poplar Hawk. 15. Ghost Swift, male. 16. Ghost Swift, female. 17. Common Swift. 18. Oak Eggar. 19. Drinker. 20. Pale Tussock. 21. Gold Tail. 22. Buff-tip. 23. Bee Hawk. 24. Humming-bird Hawk. 25. Currant Clearwing. 26. Hornet Clearwing.

usually by dark brown lines, forming more or less of a triangle. Hind-wings greyish brown. Moth in July and August in woods. *L.* in April to June on oak, elm, birch, and other trees. Common.

Dingy Shears (or DISMAL MOTH) (*Dyschoriata fissipuncta*).—*E.* 1¼-1½ inch. Fore-wings pale grey ground colour; but the markings are a dark brown, so that at first sight the moth would be described as dark brown. Orbicular and reniform stigmata are bordered with light brown. The submarginal line is whitish and dentated. Appears in July. *L.* on willows in April to May; comes to sugar. More common in South.

Olive (*Plastenis subtusa*).—*E.* 1-1¼ inch. Olive-grey fore-wings; the lines and stigmata generally clearly picked out by pale yellowish edges. Moth in July to August. *L.* in April and May on poplar and aspen. Widely distributed.

Lunar Underwing (*Omphaloscelis lunosa*).—*E.* 1¼-1½ inch. Fore-wings vary from pale ochreous red to dark brown. The stigmata are distinct, of dark brown; the submarginal line has a row of black dots alongside. The under-wings are greyish white, with some broken patches or spots of dark grey. Moth in September and October. *L.* on grasses October to May. Commonest in South and West.

Red-line Quaker (*Amathes lota*).—*E.* 1¼-1½ inch. Dark brownish grey, sometimes with a reddish tinge. The submarginal line is brick-red; border, pale ochreous. There is a noticeable black spot on each wing (the reniform). Moth in September to October. *L.* in April and June on willow and sallow. (The YELLOW-LINE QUAKER (*A. macilenta*) is smaller, has pale ochreous brown fore-wings, marked like the preceding, the hind-wings being a dark grey. Moth in September to October. *L.* in April and June on beech, oak, heather, and low plants. Common except in Midlands.)

The Brick (*A. circellaris*).—*E.* 1¼-1½ inch. Fore-wings ochreous, tinged with red; brown transverse lines; markings not very distinct. Moth in August to October. Very common. *L.* on wych-elm and ash flowers and seeds in May and June.

Flounced Rustic (*A. helvola*).—*E.* 1¼-1½ inch. Usually the fore-wings are a chestnut colour, but in some species olive-green; central and marginal areas brown; cross lines paler. *L.* feeds on oak and elm in April to May. Moth flies in September to October. *Ly.* Woodlands. (The BEADED CHESTNUT (*A. lychnidis*) is very similar in some varieties, but when well marked is beautifully patterned with dark brown, almost black, dots. There are generally three or four black dots in all the varieties along the costa. Moth in September to November. *L.* on grasses and low plants March to June.)

The Brown-spot Pinion (*A. litura*) is similar in general colour; but in some varieties the ground colour is lighter, and the stigmata show up plainly in darker brown, together with some three or four spots on the costa. Moth in September to October. *L.* in April to May on bramble, rose, oak, and low plants.

Orange Sallow (*Cirrhia* (*Xanthia*) *citrago*).—One of a group of moths which have fore-wings of an orange-yellow colour, and are much alike; all about the same size—*E.* 1¼–1½ inch. This species has *two rust-brown cross lines almost parallel;* hind-wings cream-coloured. Moth in September to October. *L.* in March to June: first on sallow catkins; later on low plants. Widely distributed.

The **Sallow** (*Xanthia fulvago*) is distinguished by the irregular dark brown bands or patches on the fore-wings, also the row of dots for the submarginal line. Other details as preceding.

The **Dusky-lemon Sallow** (*Mellinia gilvago*) is heavily mottled and clouded with purplish brown on the fore-wings. It is rather local, though widely distributed.

Orange Upperwing (*Xantholeuca croceago*).—*E.* 1¼–1⅜ inch. It is similar in colour to the Orange Sallow, but has *five small white spots along the costa.* *L.* feeds on oak in May and June. Moth flies in September to October, and again in spring. Local in the South and Midlands.

The **Chestnut** (*Orrhodia vaccinii*).—*E.* 1¼ inch. It has usually dark chestnut fore-wings, with indistinct markings, except for a more or less defined black central spot; but the species varies considerably from pale ochreous to dark grey. Moth in autumn and early winter. *L.* in May to June on oak, elm, etc. *Ly.* Woods.

The **Dark Chestnut** (*O. ligula*) is similar, but has darker chestnut brown fore-wings, and in the typical form has a series of white dashes forming a band on the outer area. *L.* on oak, sallow, etc., and low plants. Moth in October to November.

The **Satellite** (*Eupsilia satellitia*).—*E.* 1½–1¾ inch. Reddish brown fore-wings, with dark purple-brown cross lines, and a crescent-shaped white spot (or yellow) for the reniform stigma; hind-wings brown-grey. Moth in September to November. *L.* in May to June on oak, maple, beech, and low plants.

Pale Pinion (*Lithophane socia*).—*E.* 1½–1⅔ inch. Fore-wings pale grey-brown, tinged ochreous, with darker markings, not very distinct; the hind-wings are almost the same colour. *L.* feeds on blackthorn, lime, oak, etc. Moth flies in September to October. Absent from east counties. (The TAWNY PINION (*L. semibrunnea*) is more local, and has darker fore-wings, the lower half being a darker brown than the upper.)

Grey Shoulder-knot (*Graptolina ornithopus*).—*E.* 1½ inch. Fore-wings pale grey, with dark marks. *There is a distinct blackish streak at the base, which forks at the end.* Hind-wings fawn-grey. *L.* on oak in May to June. Moth in autumn and spring.

Early Grey (*Xylocampa areola*).—*E.* about 1½ inch. Usually grey wings, but sometimes tinged with pink, with darker markings. There is a short dark streak from the middle of the base, and just beyond it a ∪ shaped patch, in reality supporting the orbicular and reniform stigmata, which are conjoined. Moth in March to April. *L.* on honeysuckle in May to June.

The **Sword Grass** (*Calocampa exoleta*).—This is a larger moth, about 2¼ inches extended; common all over England and Wales, but more so in the North. Fore-wings are pale grey-brown, a broken patch of dark brown partially enclosing the reniform and orbicular stigmata, and *usually two small blackish arrow-heads pointing inwards* from the submarginal line; hind-wings brownish grey, with yellowish fringes. Moth in autumn and spring. *L.* in April to May on low-growing plants. (The RED SWORD GRASS (*C. vetusta*) is very similar, but has a reddish tinge; and the orbicular stigma is, though indistinct, rounder; the lower half of the fore-wings is shaded with dark brown; and there is *one* long black wedge pointing from the submarginal line. Other details as preceding. Less common.)

The **Mullein** (*Cucullia verbasci*).—One of a group having dentated edges to the wing, and a curious hood-shaped collar. Fore-wings brownish ochreous, with darker margins, the lower margin being broken by a lighter streak, intercepted by two small crescents. Moth in April to May. *L.* on mullein in June to July.

The **Star-wort** (*C. asteris*) is very similar, but with narrower dark margins, the lower containing a whitish curved mark. *F.p.* Golden rod and sea starwort. It is local in South and East Seaboard Counties.

The **Shark** (*C. umbratica*).—*E.* 1¾-2 inches. Fore-wings brownish grey, with faint (or pronounced) streaks, and two black dots in place of stigmata. Hind-wings in *male* whitish, in *female* grey-brown. *L.* in August to September on sow-thistle. Moth in June and July. Widely distributed, but commoner in South.

The **Chamomile Shark** (*C. chamomillæ*) is very similar, but darker. *L.* on chamomile, mayweed, etc. Moth in April to May. Widely distributed, but chiefly in Seaboard Counties.

Beautiful Yellow Underwing (*Anarta myrtilli*).—*E.* about 1 inch. Fore-wings blackish or purple-brown (in some varieties reddish tinged), with a central white spot, and other light markings. The hind-wings are light yellow, with a broad black margin. Moth May to July on heaths. *L.* feeds on ling and heath. (The SMALL YELLOW UNDERWING (*Heliaca tenebrata*) is smaller, and has no prominent white spot. Moth in May and June. *L.* on chickweed in June to July. Most frequent in Southern Counties.)

The **Straw Dot** (*Rivula sericealis*).—*E.* about 1 inch. Fore-wings straw-coloured, with a distinct dark-brown reniform stigma; hind-wings also straw coloured. *L.* feeds on grass. Moth out in June to August. *Ly.* Marshes, damp heaths. Widely distributed, but less frequent in Midlands.

Small Purple-barred (*Prothymia viridaria*).—*E.* about ¾ inch. Olive-brown fore-wings, with two reddish or purplish bands. *L.* on milkwort in August to September. Moth in May to June. Often very common.

3. *Gonopterinæ.*

The Herald (*Scoliopteryx libatrix*).—*E.* 1½–1¾ inch. A very handsome species, with a hooked apex and curiously excavated and dentated hind margins. Fore-wings sandy-brown tinged with red, and the central areas are usually brighter red; cross lines light grey; a white dot in middle of base. Moth in August to October, and in spring. *L.* on sallow, osier, etc., in June to August. Common.

4. *Quadrifinæ.*

Golden Plusia (*Plusia moneta*).—A migrant to England in recent times, but now established, and in some gardens a pest. The usual food plants are monkshood and larkspur, in May to June, and July to August. Moth in June to July; sometimes again in July and August. *E.* 1½–1¾ inch. Fore-wings pale golden, with dark brown lines. The orbicular and claviform stigmata form an 8-shaped figure. Hind-wings ochreous-grey.

Burnished Brass (*Plusia chrysitis*).—*E.* 1¼–1½ inch. Metallic-looking brownish fore-wings, with two broad golden-green areas or bands; the apex is slightly hooked. Hind-wings greyish brown. *L.* feeds on nettles. Full grown in May. Moth in June to August. *Ly.* Hedges and ditches. (The SCARCE BURNISHED BRASS (*P. chryson*) has one golden patch on the fore-wing. Is very local.)

The Gold Spot (*P. festucæ*).—*E.* 1¼–1½ inch. Fore-wings purplish brown, burnished with gold near margin and base. In middle two silvery pear-shaped spots, one larger than the other, with a third near the apex. *L.* feeds on sedge, coarse grasses, etc., April to June. Moth in June to July, sometimes August to September. Widely distributed, but rather local.

Plain Golden Y (*Plusia iota*).—*E.* 1⅛–1¼ inch. Fore-wings reddish violet, with olive-brown markings; identified by the V-shaped light gold spot, with a small dot close to it, forming a broken script "*Y*" (sometimes conjoined). *L.* in spring on dead nettles, mint, etc. Moth in June and July. Common. (The BEAUTIFUL GOLDEN Y (*P. pulchrina*) is very similar, the V and the dot being generally broader, and the wings being rather more mottled.)

The Silver Y (*P. gamma*).—*E.* 1¼–1½ inch. Has grey-brown fore-wings, suffused more or less with violet, and containing a silvery Y-shaped mark, rather like the Greek γ, below the orbicular stigma. *L.* feeds on low-growing vegetation in spring and summer, when moth also is to be found. Very common. (The SCARCE SILVER Y (*P. interrogationis*) is local on heaths and moors in the North. It has a very broad U-shaped mark, with a dot below it or conjoined.)

The Spectacle (*Abrostola tripartita*).—*E.* 1¼–1½ inch; has a spectacle mark of whitish grey, ringed with black before the thorax. The fore-wings are greyish brown, with darker mottles in the central area, the rest being a whitish grey. *L.* in July on nettles. Moth in June and August. Common.

The Dark Spectacle (*A. triplasia*) is similar, but the fore-wings are much darker, and there are two curved chocolate-brown cross lines, touched with dull reddish, bounding the central area. Two red-brown marks on the collar give it the name of "spectacle." Common, but local in North.

Mother Shipton (*Euclidia mi*).—*E.* 1⅛-1¼ inch. Fore-wings ochreous brown, with paler cross lines, edged internally with dark brown. The markings are supposed to resemble a ludicrous mask, and to be like the letter M. Moth in May and June. *Ly.* Meadows and banks. *L.* feeds on clover and grasses in July to September.

The **Burnet Companion** (*E. glyphica*) is often found in company with it. Fore-wings purplish brown, with blackish cross lines. Hind-wings dark brown, with a dull orange-yellow patch, crossed by a dark line.

Red Underwing (*Catocala nupta*) is a large species, nearly 3 inches across, with red hind-wings, having a broad marginal band of black and a black median band. Moth in August and September. *L.* on poplars and willows. *Ly.* South and East. (The DARK CRIMSON UNDERWING (*C. sponsa*) (*E.* 2¼-2½ inches) is found chiefly in the New Forest, July and August. The LIGHT CRIMSON UNDERWING (*C. promissa*) is smaller; also chiefly found in Hants.)

5. *Hypeninæ.*

Beautiful Hook-tip (*Laspeyria flexula*).—*E.* 1-1¼ inch. Fore-wings notched near the apex, giving a hooked appearance to the tip. They are pale grey-brown, with a tinge of red; crossed by two light lines edged with reddish brown. The reniform stigma consists of two black dots, set in paler rings. *L.* on lichens, September to May. Moth in June to August. Widely distributed in Southern Counties.

Fan-foot (*Zanclognatha tarsipennalis*).—The "Fan-foots" get their name from the fan-like tufts of hair on the front femora and tibiæ. This species has pale clay-brown wings, with two transverse lines. Moth in June and July. Common, except in North. *L.* on withered leaves, such as blackberry, etc. *E.* 1-1¼ inch.

The **Small Fan-foot** (*Z. grisealis*) is similar, but smaller. *E.* ¾-1 inch. The submarginal line is plainer, and runs to the apex of the wing. *L.* on oak.

The **Dotted Fan-foot** (*Herminia cribrumalis*).—*E.* ¾-1 inch. Has creamy-brown fore-wings, crossed by two series of black dots (sometimes indistinct). It is found in marshes and fens. *L.* on grasses.

The **Common Fan-foot** (*Pechipogon barbalis*).—*E.* 1-1¼ inch. Is common in woods, especially in south-eastern counties. It has greyish brown fore-wings, with three darker cross lines, the outer one edged with whitish. *L.* on withered oak and birch leaves. Moth in May to July.

The **Snout** (*Hypena proboscidalis*).—*E.* 1-1¼ inch. Common wherever there are nettles. The "Snouts" are so-called from the length of the palpi, which look like a long beak. This species has yellowish brown fore-wings, with two reddish brown cross lines, and a submarginal line of black-and-white dots (often indistinct). It flies in June and July.

The **Beautiful Snout** (*Bomolocha fontis*) is smaller (1-1¼ inch), and has far more prominent markings. *Male* has fore-wings of ashy grey, with two dark brown patches, the smaller at the apex; the *female* has *whitish* fore-wings, with the same two dark patches, the smaller one being shaded. *L.* feeds on bilberry in August to September. Moth in June to July. Local in Southern Counties chiefly.

The **Buttoned Snout** (*Hypena rostralis*).—*E.* 1-1¼ inch. Fore-wings grey-brown, the basal half a much darker shade, and a triangular brown patch close to the apex. The stigmata are two raised black patches (the "buttons"). *L.* feeds on hop. Moth in August and September, and again in May. Moderately common in Southern Hop Districts.

The **White-line Snout** (*Hypenodes tænialis*).—*E.* ¾ inch. Is light ochreous-brown. Two plain black lines cross the fore-wings, the outer one edged with whitish; the central mark is X shaped. *L.* said to feed on heather and thyme. Moth in July to August. *Ly.* Hillsides, wood edges. (The PINION-STREAKED SNOUT (*H. costæstrigalis*) is distinguished from preceding by the whitish streak from the apex of the fore-wings.)

Family: *Brephidæ*.

Orange Underwing (*Brephos parthenias*).—*E.* 1¼-1½ inch. Known by its orange hind-wings, with black margins, a black patch from the base, and a central crescent-shaped spot of black. *L.* on birch April to June. Moth in March to April. Common. (The LIGHT ORANGE UNDERWING (*B. nopha*) is similar, but smaller (*E.* 1-1¼ inch). *F.p.* aspen. It is a local species.)

Family: *Geometridæ*.

This family gains its name "geometers," or "measurers," or "loopers," from the mode of movement of the larvæ. These have only two pairs of claspers or fore-legs; and so, in moving, the larva first stretches out its full length, moving from side to side as if measuring the distance, and then, arching or looping its body, brings up its hinder part to the point held by the true legs. They feed chiefly on the leaves of trees and low plants. Many of the moths may be obtained in the daylight by "beating." There are five sub-families, four of which are represented in Britain.

1. *Geometrinæ.*

Grass Emerald (*Pseudoterpna pruinata*).—*E.* 1¼-1⅓ inch. At first the colour is a bluish green, which fades later to a grey-green. The cross lines, when visible, are darker. *L.* feeds on petty-whin, broom, etc. Moth in June to July. *Ly.* Moors and commons.

The Large Emerald (*Geometra papilionaria*).—*E.* 1¾–2¼ inches. Is also of a lovely green colour, with whitish scalloped cross lines. *L.* on birch, beech, hazel, in June to August. Moth in June to July. *Ly.* Woods and heaths.

The Small Emerald (*G. vernaria*).—*E.* 1⅓–1½ inch. Has a softer green colour, and the white cross lines are not scalloped. *L.* in May to June on wild clematis (traveller's joy). Moth in July to August. Chiefly in chalk districts.

The Blotched Emerald (*Euchloris pustulata*).—*E.* 1¼ inch. Has a creamy white blotch, with brown centre on fore-wings and others on the margin of the hind-wings. *Ly.* Oak woods. Local in Southern and Eastern Counties.

The Little Emerald (*Iodis lactearia*).—*E.* ¾–1 inch. Has delicate pale green wings, fading to white after death. Common in May to June. *L.* on birch, hawthorn, sallow, etc.

The Common Emerald (*Hemithea strigata*).—*E.* 1–1¼ inch. Dingy green, fading to grey; distinguished by its waved hind-margins and cream chequered fringes. Common in south and east in June and July. *L.* on hawthorn, rose, oak, etc.

2. *Acidaliinæ.*

Purple-bordered Gold (*Hyria muricata*).—A pretty moth, ¾ inch expanded, with reddish ochreous wings, margined with golden yellow, and patched with the same colour. *L.* feeds on knot grass and plantain. Moth in June and July in fen land. A local species.

Small Dusty Wave (*Acidalia virgularia*).—*E.* about ¾ inch. Straw coloured, with dusky brown dots. *L.* feeds on withered leaves of low plants. Moth in June to August. Common in South.

The Dwarf Cream Wave (*A. interjectaria*) is slightly smaller; has lighter straw-coloured wings, with a central black dot. It is also plentiful in the South.

The Satin Wave (*A. subsericeata*).—*E.* ¾–1 inch. Has glossy white wings, with a slight grey or yellowish tinge, and grey cross lines. Widely distributed. *L.* on knot grass, dandelion, etc. Moth in June and July.

The Plain Wave (*A. inornata*) is slightly larger; fore-wings shining ochreous-grey, with a central black dot, and dusky cross lines. *L.* on low weeds from August to June. Moth in July. Widely distributed.

The Riband Wave (*A. aversata*).—*E.* 1¼ inch. Is of same colour, but duller; and the space between the two cross lines is darker, giving the appearance of a ribbon across the wings. *L.* on low-growing plants. Moth in June and July.

The Small Fan-footed Wave (*A. bisetata*) is less than an inch expanded; has whitish wings, with a deep grey border. Common.

The Single-dotted Wave (*A. dimidiata*).—*E.* ¾ inch. Wings whitey-brown, cross lines of dots; a brown patch near the hinder angle of the fore-wings. *L.* on bed-straw, saxifrage, etc. Moth in June to August. Often common.

The Lace Border (*A. ornata*).—*E.* ¾-1 inch. White wings, with central black dots; two brown spots near the apex and anal angle, and a grey margin. *L.* on thyme and marjoram in October to May, and July to August. Moth in May to June, and August to September. *Ly.* Chalk district.

The Cream Wave (*A. remutaria*).—*E.* 1¼ inch. Common in May to June in woods; creamy white, with two dark cross lines forming a ribbon across wings (sometimes indistinct). *L.* on bed-straw, dock, etc.

The Lesser Cream Wave (*A. immutata*).—*E.* about 1 inch. Is similar, but with central black dots, specially noticeable on hind-wings. Common in fens and damp woods in Southern and Eastern Counties.

The Mullein Wave (*A. marginepunctata*) is greyish white, with three zigzag grey cross lines. A coast species, found in June to July, and August to September.

The Small Blood-vein (*A. imitaria*).—*E.* about 1 inch. Has pale red-brown wings, with a conspicuous reddish stripe crossing them both—hence the name. *L.* on dandelion, dock, etc., and privet. Moth in July to August. Common, especially by the sea.

The Blood Vein (*Timandra amata*) is similar, but larger. Most common in South.

The Smoky Wave (*A. fumata*).—*E.* about 1 inch. Pale grey, dusted with brown, and faint cross lines. Widely distributed, but most common in Scotland and Ireland. Moth in June and July. *L.* on bilberry, sallow, heather, etc.

Small Scallop (*Ania emarginata*).—*E.* ¾-1 inch. Scalloped wings, pale ochreous brown, with central dot, and fine cross lines. *L.* on bed-straw, bindweed, etc. Moth in July. *Ly.* Fens and marshes; rare in North.

The Mocha (*Ephyra annulata*) gets its name from the resemblance of the wings to the mocha stone, a kind of agate. *E.* about 1 inch. Straw-coloured wings, *the second cross line being plainly blackish and toothed*, a dark central shade, and deep brown rings. *L.* on maple in June. Moth in May to August. Common in most parts.

The False Mocha (*E. porata*) is slightly larger, with pale ochreous brown wings, tinged with reddish; with cross lines of indistinct blackish dots, dark central rings enclosing white dots. *L.* on oak and birch, June and September. Moth in May and August. Chiefly in South and West.

The Maiden's Blush (*E. punctaria*), rather like the former (*E. porata*), but has a more conspicuous central line, and no ringed dots. *L.* on oak. Moth in May to June. *Ly.* Woodlands.

Clay Triple Lines (*E. linearia*).—*E.* 1-1¼ inch. Is also like preceding, but, besides the distinct dark central line, there are often two others, more or less distinct; sometimes absent; and the ringed dots also are often obscure. *L.* on beech in June to July and September. Moth in May to June, and August to September. *Ly.* Beechwoods.

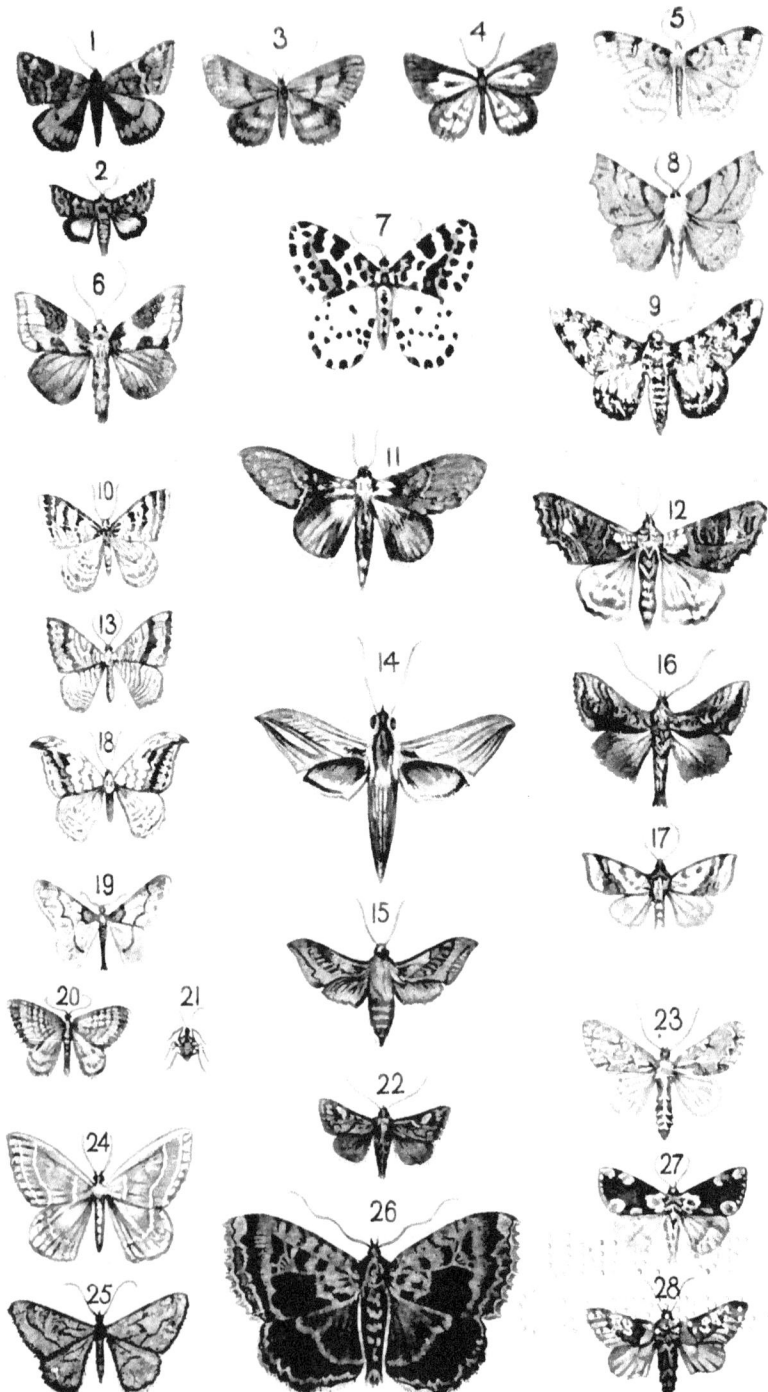

PLATE XXXI.

1. Orange Underwing. 2. Beautiful Yellow Underwing. 3. Bordered White, female. 4. Bordered White, male. 5. Brimstone. 6. Burnished Brass. 7. Magpie. 8. Canary-shouldered Thorn. 9. Pepper and Salt. 10. Garden Carpet. 11. Lobster. 12. Angle-shades. 13. Yellow Shell. 14. Elephant Hawk. 15. Small Elephant Hawk. 16. Silver Y. 17. Pink-barred Sallow. 18. Pebble Hook-tip. 19. Spring Usher. 20. Winter Moth, male. 21. Winter Moth, female. 22. Pine Beauty. 23. Grey Dagger. 24. Large Emerald. 25. Willow Beauty. 26. Old Lady. 27. Peach Blossom. 28. Figure of Eight.

3. *Hydriomeninæ*.

The Belle Moth, or LEAD BELLE (*Ortholitha plumbaria*).—*E.* 1¼–1⅓ inch. Fore-wings greyish, varying in depth; three cross lines, two being distinct and straight; also a short oblique streak from tip, and a small black central dot. *L.* on furze and broom, August to April. Moth in May to June. Common.

The Mallow (*O. cervinata*).—*E.* 1½–1¾ inch. Fore-wings chocolate or ochreous brown, with a central darker wavy band, with still darker edges, and an undulating whitish sub-marginal line. *L.* in May to June on mallow. Moth in September to October. Widely distributed, chiefly in South.

The Shaded Broad-bar, or SMALL MALLOW (*O. limitata*) is somewhat similar to above, but smaller (*E.* up to 1½ inch). Fore-wings ochreous brown, with a darker central band, a short streak at the apex; whitish clouded hind-wings. *L.* on clover, vetch, etc., September to June. Moth in July and August. *Ly.* Grassy places.

Chalk Carpet (*O. bipunctaria*).—*E.* 1¼–1⅓ inch. Is local, but plentiful in chalky districts. Fore-wings greyish white, speckled with brown; there is a pretty central band of darker brown, containing two black dots (sometimes conjoined) like a : in the lighter central space. *L.* on clover, etc., September to June. Moth in July to August.

The Oblique Striped (*Mesotype virgata*).—*E.* about ¾ inch. Is a greyish white moth (sometimes brownish), with two oblique dark stripes, edged with white, and a black dot in centre. *L.* on yellow bed-straw in May to June, and August to September. Moth the same. *Ly.* Chiefly coastal.

The Drab Looper (*Minoa murinata*).—*E.* about ¾ inch. Has wings of uniform grey or ochreous brown, with silky lustre. *L.* on spurge, July to September. Moth in May to June, chiefly in South and East Counties. (The CHIMNEY SWEEPER (*Odezia atrata*) is larger (*E.* about 1 inch), but is like above in having wings of uniform colour—black, with a touch of white on the tip. *L.* on blossoms of the earth-nut in spring. Moth in June to July. Widely distributed.)

The Treble Bar (*Anaitis plagiata*).—*E.* 1½–1⅔ inch. Has greyish white fore-wings, with three cross bars of black and brown; the one nearest the base is little more than a slender line sharply angled close to the costa; also a smeared streak at the apex; hind-wings sandy grey. *L.* on St. John's wort in June to July. Moth in May to June, and August to September. Common in most parts, but specially on cliffs and sandhills.

The Streak (*Chesias spartiata*).—*E.* about 1½ inch. Identified by the two oval spots (like slanting eyes) and the long whitish streak running to the tips of the fore-wings, which are shining brownish in colour. *L.* on broom in spring. Moth in September and October. Common.

Early Tooth-striped (*Lobophora carpinata*).—*E.* about 1¼ inch. Fore-wings greyish white, with an ochreous touch; two indistinct brown cross

THE BRITISH NATURE BOOK

bands, a dark line near hind margin, broken into a series of dashes. Hind-wings paler. *L.* on honeysuckle, sallow, willow, in June to July. Moth in April to May. Common. *Ly.* Woodlands.

Seraphim (*L. halterata*).—*E.* 1–1⅛ inch. Fore-wings whitish, speckled with dark grey. Two greyish bands on basal area, a black central dot. *L.* on aspen and poplar in June to July. Moth in May to June. Widely distributed, but local.

The Small Seraphim (*L. sexalisata*) is much smaller. *L.* on sallow in August to September. Moth in May to June. Local.

Winter Moth (*Chæimatobia brumata*).—*E.* 1–1⅛ inch. The *female* is almost wingless, and crawls on fruit trees, the larvæ being very destructive. The *male* has greyish brown fore-wings, with darker indistinct cross lines. It appears in the winter months from October to February. Generally distributed.

The Northern Winter Moth (*C. boreata*) is larger, the *male* having paler and more glossy fore-wings. *L.* on birch in May to June. Moth in October to November. Widely distributed, in spite of its name.

The Tissue (*Triphosa dubitata*).—*E.* 1½–1¾ inch. Fore-wings shining pale brown, tinged with rose colour, with numerous pale and dark cross lines. The edges of the wings are scalloped, especially the hind-wings. *L.* on buckthorn. Moth in August and September, and again in April to May. Common, except in North. (The SCARCE TISSUE (*Eucosmia certata*) is very similar, but not so glossy. *L.* feeds on barberry in June to July. Moth in May to June. Widely distributed, but only common in Eastern Counties.)

The Scallop Shell (*Eucosmia undulata*).—*E.* 1¼–1⅜ inch. Derives its name from the similarity of its colour and markings to those of the shell of that name. Ochreous grey wings, crossed by many brown wavy lines and a zigzag white submarginal line. *Male* has tufts of blackish hair about the middle of the inner margin, most noticeable on the under side. *L.* in August onwards on sallow, aspen, and bilberry. Moth in June and July. *Ly.* Woods. (The BROWN SCALLOP (*Scotosia vetulata*) is much smaller, and the markings are less distinct. *L.* on buckthorn in May to June. Moth in June to July. Found only in England.)

The Dark Umber (*Scotosia rhamnata*).—*E.* up to 1½ inch. Reddish brown wings, with numerous lighter cross lines. Fore-wings have an oblique darker central area, and a whitish submarginal line. *L.* in May to June on buckthorn. Moth in July. Common in South; rare in North.

Small Phœnix (*Eustroma silaceata*).—*E.* about 1⅛ inch. Fore-wings dark brown with a paler band near base, and another, much broken, near the margin, forked at the tip. Hind-wings pale grey, shaded. *L.* on nightshade, willow-herb, in July. Moth in woods in May to June. Local.

The Phœnix (*Lygris prunata*) is larger (*E.* up to 1⅜ inch), and chocolate brown, the markings being very similar. *L.* on currant and gooseberry in April to May. Moth in July to August. Local, but widely distributed. *Ly.* Gardens.

The Chevron (*L. testata*).—*E.* about 1¼ inch. Fore-wings reddish or yellowish grey, with darker central band and basal area. A triangular patch below the tip is edged with white, as also the outer edge of the central band. *L.* on sallow and birch in May to June. Moth in July to August. *Ly.* Heaths and woods.

The Spinach (*L. associata*).—*E.* about 1½ inch. Fore-wings pale ochre-yellow, clouded with darker, with two prominent bent cross lines, and a third nearer the base, less distinct. Hind-wings paler ; fringes of all wings chequered with brown. *L.* on currant in May to June. Moth in July to August. *Ly.* Gardens. (The BARRED STRAW (*Cidaria pyraliata*) resembles the Spinach, but there is less shading on the wings. *L.* on goose-grass and bed-straw in April to May. Moth in June to July. Chiefly in South.)

Barred Yellow (*Cidaria fulvata*).—*E.* about 1 inch. Deep yellow fore-wings, with a distinct central area, bounded by black angular cross lines, meeting in a blackish patch in middle. *L.* on wild rose in May to June. Moth in June to July. Common.

Broken-barred Carpet (*C. corylata*).—*E.* about 1⅛ inch. Fore-wings creamy, with an olive-brown patch at the base, and a central band often broken towards the bottom ; both edged with white ; marginal area marbled with brownish. Rather variable. *L.* in July to September on sloe, birch, oak, etc. Moth in May and June. *Ly.* Woods and hedgerows.

Common Marbled Carpet (*C. truncata*).—*E.* 1⅛–1½ inch. Very variable. The typical form has greyish brown fore-wings, with numerous dark waved cross lines, and a greyish white central patch. *L.* in autumn and spring on sallow, birch, hawthorn, etc. Moth in May to June and autumn. Common. *Ly.* Woods and hedgerows. (The DARK MARBLED CARPET (*C. immanata*) is somewhat similar, and equally variable. *L.* in April to June on sallow, birch, etc. Moth in July to August. Common. *Ly.* Woods and moors.)

Red-green Carpet (*C. siterata*).—*E.* about 1¼ inch. Has grey-green fore-wings, suffused with red, the basal and central areas being darker green. Hind-wings dark greyish brown. *L.* on oak, birch, apple, etc., in July to August. Moth in September to October. *Ly.* Woodlands. (The AUTUMN GREEN CARPET (*C. miata*) is similar, but the fore-wings are paler, and without the rosy tint ; other details as preceding.)

Grey Pine Carpet (*Thera variata*).—*E.* 1¼–1½ inch. Another common and variable species. Fore-wings greyish, with a dark, ill-defined patch at the base, and a central angulated brownish band across the wings. *L.* on fir and pine needles in May and July. Moth in June and September. *Ly.* Pine woods.

The Chestnut-coloured Carpet (*T. cognata*) is smaller, but very similar ; with a reddish tinge on the wings. It feeds on juniper ; is common where its food plant grows. (The PINE CARPET (*T. firmata*) has similar markings ; reddish grey fore-wings ; the patches being pale ochreous ; hind-wings whitish. *Ly.* Pine woods.)

The Water Carpet (*Lampropteryx suffumata*) is the same size, with whitish fore-wings, with basal, central, and marginal areas dark brown; in some varieties more or less clearly defined. F.p. goose-grass. Ly. Lanes and hedges.

Dark-barred Twin-spot Carpet (*Coremia unidentaria*).—E. about 1 inch. Fore-wings ochreous grey, with central band smoky black; just above middle of wing, close to the hind margin, are two black dots, like a ":". L. on various low plants, June to July, and September to October. Moth in May to June, and August to September. (The RED TWIN-SPOT CARPET (*C. ferrugata*) (E. ¾–1 inch) is very variable; fore-wings ochreous grey, with the patches reddish brown; hind-wings greyish white. Other details as above.)

Flame Carpet (*C. designata*).—E. about 1 inch. Fore-wings pale grey, with purplish chocolate base and central patch. L. on cabbage and cresses, June and July, and August to September. Moth in June and August. Ly. Damp woods. (The BEECH GREEN CARPET (*Amoebe olivata*) is somewhat similar, but when fresh has greenish fore-wings. L. on bed-straw. Moth in July to August. Local.)

The Green Carpet (*Amoebe viridaria*) has greenish fore-wings; the central patch is a deeper green, with two dark triangular top corners, and another at the wing-tips. L. on bed-straw. Moth in June. Ly. Commons, heaths, and hedges.

The Mottled Grey (*Malenydris multistrigaria*).—E. about 1¼ inch. An ochreous grey moth, with many brown dots on fore-wings; the central area defined by two lines of dots. L. on bed-straw in May to June. Moth March to April. Ly. Damp woodlands and heaths.

The Twin-spot Carpet (*M. didymata*).—E. about 1 inch. Fore-wings greyish brown, with a dark central band. Close to the outer margin above the middle are two black spots (with a third nearer the tip). The *female* is smaller and paler. L. on bilberry, campion, primrose, and grasses in April to May. Moth in July to August. Very common.

November Moth (*Oporabia dilutata*).—E. 1⅓–1½ inch. Fore-wings ochreous grey, with darker lines and shades. Hind-wings lighter, with line round margin. L. on elm, oak, birch, and fruit trees. April to June. Moth in October to November. Ly. Woodlands. Common.

Silver-ground Carpet (*Xanthorhoë montanata*).—E. 1–1¼ inch. Wings in some species silvery white, varying in others to brownish grey; a slight patch at base; an irregular darker central band, roughly Y-shaped. L. on low plants, such as bed-straw, August to April. Moth in June to July. Common.

Garden Carpet (*X. fluctuata*).—E. 1–1¼ inch. Variable; greyish wings. The fore-wings with basal and central bands; the central often ending halfway across the wing. Also often a dark patch near the tip, with another smudge below. L. on cabbage, and other garden plants, June to October. Moth practically from May to October. Common. When at rest looks like an irregular grey patch.

Common Carpet (*X. sociata*).—E. 1–1¼ inch. Very similar to the Wood-

Carpet. Fore-wings greyish white, with darker shadings on basal area; an angular dark central band, margins of dark grey, the narrow white area between this and the central band having a grey line down the middle. Hind-wings have broad darker margins, intersected by a zigzag white line. *L.* on bedstraw. Moth in May to June, and August to September. Very common.

Beautiful Carpet (*Mesoleuca albicillata*).—*E.* $1\frac{1}{4}$-$1\frac{1}{2}$ inch. Wings white or creamy, fore-wings having a purplish brown patch at the base, another at the tip; broad shaded hind margins, a slender line separating this portion from the white central area, continued on hind-wings, which have also dark margins. *L.* on bramble and raspberry in August to September. Moth in June. *Ly.* Woodlands.

The Pretty Chalk Carpet (*Melanthia procellata*) is somewhat similar, but the basal patch is smaller; there is a second patch extending from the middle of the costa, and the broad hind marginal band has a large round white patch in the middle, and a row of white dots from the tip. *L.* on clematis. Moth in July to August. Local in South and Midlands.

The Purple Bar (*Mesoleuca ocellata*).—*E.* about $1\frac{1}{8}$ inch. Whitish fore-wings tinged in the lower marginal area with ochreous; a prominent bluish black central band, and small basal patch. *L.* on bed-straw in June to July. Moth in June to July. Widely distributed.

The Blue-bordered Carpet (*M. bicolorata*) is like the PRETTY CHALK (see above) in markings, but much smaller. *E.* about 1 inch; the hind margins of all wings are bluish grey. *L.* on alder, birch, sloe, etc., April to June. Moth in July to August.

The Rivulet (*Perizoma affinitata*).—*E.* 1-$1\frac{1}{4}$ inch. Has smoky brown wings, and on the fore-wings a wavy white cross band just beyond the centre—the "rivulet." *L.* in the seed capsules of campion, July to September. Moth in June to July. Widely distributed. (The SMALL RIVULET (*P. alchemillata*) (*E.* $\frac{3}{4}$-1 inch) is almost similar, but of a greyer brown colour. *L.* in capsules of hemp nettle.)

Sandy Carpet (*P. flavofasciata*).—*E.* 1-$1\frac{1}{8}$ inch. White wings; fore-wings with light sandy patches, filling the greater portion. *L.* on flower-beds of campion. Moth in July to August. Common in most counties.

Grass Rivulet (*P. albulata*).—*E.* $\frac{3}{4}$ inch. Fore-wings ochreous grey, with a white wavy band beyond the centre, and a zigzag sub-marginal line. *L.* on capsules of yellow rattle. Moth in May to June. (The BARRED RIVULET (*P. bifasciata*) is a darker brown, with two distinct "rivulets." *L.* on capsules of eyebright. Moth in July to August. Commonest in South.)

The Yellow Shell (*Camptogramma bilineata*).—*E.* about $1\frac{1}{4}$ inch. Yellowish wings, with numerous brownish cross lines, and two whitish cross lines, bounding the central area, which is sometimes shaded at the edges with darker brown. *L.* on grass and low plants, August to May. Moth through summer. Very common.

July High Flyer (*Hydriomena furcata*).—*E.* $1\frac{1}{4}$-$1\frac{1}{3}$ inch. Very variable.

Fore-wings olive-grey (varied reddish or brownish) ; the darker markings vary also ; generally three or four broken, irregular cross lines on narrow bands. Hind-wings uniform brownish grey. *L.* in May to June on sallow, poplar, hazel, etc. Moth in July to August. Very common.

May High Flyer (*H. impluviata*) is slightly smaller, with greenish grey fore-wings, tinged with brown ; hind-wings ochreous grey ; the central portion of the fore-wing is frequently lighter. *L.* on alder in summer and autumn. Moth in May onwards. Very common.

The Ruddy High Flyer (*H. ruberata*) is very similar, but has a short black apical mark on the fore-wings. *L.* on sallow and willow during summer. Moth in May and June in hedges and woods. Widely distributed.

The Shoulder Stripe (*Anticlea badiata*).—*E.* $1\frac{1}{4}$-$1\frac{1}{3}$ inch. Fore-wings reddish brown with a pale central band ; three dark cross lines. Hind-wings ochreous grey. *L.* on wild rose. Moth in March and April in hedges. Common.

The Streamer (*A. nigrofasciaria*).—*E.* 1-$1\frac{1}{4}$ inch. Fore-wings have grey-brown central areas, with darker basal and marginal patches. There is a broad dark line bounding the base, and a dark wedge beyond the middle of the upper edge. *L.* on wild rose in May and June. Moth in April and May. Widely distributed.

Dingy Shell (*Euchœca obliterata*).—*E.* $\frac{3}{4}$-1 inch. A pale ochreous brown species, with faint markings. *L.* in July and August on alder. Moth in June and July. Common wherever the alder is found.

Small White Wave (*Asthena candidata*).—*E.* about $\frac{3}{4}$ inch. A delicate white species, common in woods, especially in the South. *L.* on birch, wild rose, etc., in July and August. Moth in May to June, and sometimes a second generation in August to September.

The Small Yellow Wave (*A. luteata*) is about the same size, and appears to be dappled with white. *L.* in August to September on alder and maple. Moth in June to July. Widely distributed.

Lime-speck Pug (*Eupithecia oblongata*).—*E.* $\frac{3}{4}$-1 inch. Cream-coloured wings ; on the front margin a prominent grey-blue blotch. *L.* in summer on ragwort, scabious, yarrow, etc. Moth in May to August and September to October. Common.

Foxglove Pug (*E. pulchellata*).—*E.* $\frac{3}{4}$-1 inch. Fore-wings pale brownish ochreous, with beautiful markings ; look for a reddish or chestnut stripe across the, wing on each side of the centre patch. Hind-wings greyish white. *L.* lives in July in the flowers of the foxglove, entering by piercing a hole in the side. Moth in May to June. Common.

The Toadflax Pug (*E. linariata*) is very similar, but usually smaller, and the central area is darker. *L.* feeds on flowers of toadflax. Moth in May to June.

The Netted Pug (*E. venosata*).—*E.* $\frac{3}{4}$-1 inch. Has ochreous grey fore-wings netted with black lines. *L.* from June to August on the seeds of catchfly. Moth in May to June. Widely distributed and common.

Currant Pug (*E. assimilata*).—*E.* $\frac{3}{4}$ inch. Has broad, rounded fore-wings, dark brownish grey, with a tinge of red; a black central spot, sub-marginal line ending in a white dot. *L.* on currant and hop in June and July. Moth in May and June. Widely distributed.

The **Wormwood Pug** (*E. absinthiata*) is very similar, but slightly larger. *L.* feeds on yarrow, ragwort, hemp agrimony, etc. Moth in June to July. Common.

The **Ling Pug** (*E. minutata*).—*E.* ¾ inch. Has also reddish brown fore-wings. *L.* is found on the flowers of heath and ling in August and September. Moth in June to July.

Common Pug (*E. vulgata*).—*E.* ¾ inch. Has rusty brown fore-wings, varying to pale grey-brown; with markings generally indistinct, though the central black dot and a white spot at the hinder angle are usually fairly defined. *L.* on sallow, hawthorn, etc., in June to July, and autumn. Moth in May to June and August.

The **Golden-rod Pug** (*E. virgaureata*) is very similar; with ochreous grey wings, a black discal spot, and a white spot at end of the sub-marginal line. *L.* feeds on flowers of golden-rod in autumn. Moth in May to June. Widely distributed.

The **Grey Pug** (*E. castigata*).—*E.* ¾–1 inch. Ochreous grey. *L.* on most low plants August to October. Moth in May to June. Common.

The **Satyr Pug** (*E. satyrata*).—*E.* ¾ inch. Has reddish grey wings, though specimens vary in darker colour. Often the markings are distinct and beautiful, consisting of light and dark zigzag transverse lines. *L.* on knapweed, bedstraw, etc., August to September. Moth in May to June on woodlands and heaths.

The **Slender Pug** (*E. tenuiata*).—*E.* ⅝–¾ inch. Short grey fore-wings, with darker cross lines and black centre-spot. *L.* feeds in spring on catkins of the sallows. Moth in June and July, in fens and marshy places.

Ash Pug (*E. fraxinata*).—*E.* ¾ inch. Has greyish brown fore-wings, crossed by indistinct markings. *L.* feeds on ash in August and September. Moth in June to July.

Narrow-winged Pug (*E. nanata*).—*E.* ¾ inch. Is recognized by its narrow pointed fore-wings, whitish grey, with brown cross lines, black central dot, with a white spot on the inner side. *L.* on heather and ling in autumn. Moth in May and June. Common on heaths.

Juniper Pug (*E. sobrinata*).—*E.* ¾–1 inch. Widely distributed. The larvæ may be beaten from juniper bushes in April to June. Moth from July to October.

Green Pug (*Chloroclystis rectangulata*).—*E.* ¾–1 inch. Fore-wings green, with many wavy dark markings, and a black centre spot. *L.* on flowers of wild apple and orchard apples and pears in April and May. Moth in June and July.

The **V Pug** (*C. coronata*).—*E.* about ¾ inch. Also has green fore-wings, with zigzag markings, most prominent of which is a black V-shaped

THE BRITISH NATURE BOOK

form set sideways just beyond the middle of the costa. *L.* in June to July and autumn on flowers of hemp agrimony, golden-rod, clematis, etc. Moth from May to August.

Dark Spinach (*Pelurga comitata*).—*E.* $1\frac{1}{2}$ inch. Fore-wings pale ochreous with darker bands and shadings. Hind-wings ochreous grey. *L.* on goosefoot and orache in autumn. Moth in July and August on waste places.

4. *Boarmiinæ*.

The Common Magpie (*Abraxas grossulariata*).—*E.* $1\frac{1}{2}$-$1\frac{2}{3}$ inch. This very familiar moth needs no description, with its creamy-white wings and black spots, and on the fore-wings yellow bands. It is a highly variable species, and specimens of unique colouring have a considerable value. *L.* feeds on currants and gooseberries, also on sloe and hawthorn, August to May, hibernating in the winter. Moth in July and August.

Clouded Magpie (*A. sylvata*). About same size as preceding. Creamy white, with pale violet-grey central spot, a double row of spots on submarginal line, ending in a brown patch. Fore-wings have a brown and ochreous patch at the base, and a triangular spot on the upper edge. *L.* on wych elm (also beech and hazel), August to October. Moth in May to June.

Clouded Border (*Lomaspilis marginata*).—*E.* $\frac{3}{4}$-1 inch. A pretty species; creamy wings, with dark brown hind margins, a wavy internal line, and basal patches. *L.* on sallow, aspen, and willow from June onwards. Moth in May and June. Common in moist places.

Scorched Carpet (*Ligdia adustata*).—*E.* about 1 inch. Cream coloured. Fore-wings have a dark brown patch at base and a broad submarginal band of similar colour. *L.* on spindle in June to July and August to September. Moth May to June and August.

Clouded Silver (*Bapta temerata*).—*E.* 1-$1\frac{1}{4}$ inch. Shining white wings, with greyish clouding round the outer cross line; a small central dot on fore-wings. *L.* on sloe, plum, and bird-cherry, July to August. Moth in May to June.

Common White Wave (*Cabera pusaria*).—*E.* $1\frac{1}{6}$-$1\frac{1}{3}$ inch. White, with three dark grey cross lines on fore-wings and two on hind-wings. *L.* in July and September on birch, alder, etc. Moth in May to June and August. Common.

The Common Wave (*C. exanthemata*) is very similar, but sprinkled with pale ochreous tints. Food plants and months the same. Common.

Barred Umber (*Numeria pulveraria*).—*E.* $1\frac{1}{4}$-$1\frac{1}{2}$ inch. Reddish brown, with darker freckles. On the fore-wings a broad dark red-brown band. *L.* on birch, sallow, etc., June to August. Moth in May to June. Widely distributed.

Barred Red (*Ellopia prosapiaria*).—*E.* $1\frac{1}{3}$-$1\frac{1}{2}$ inch. Reddish flesh-coloured wings, with whitish cross lines enclosing a darker band. The outer line continued on hind-wing. *L.* on pine, fir, larch, September to May. Moth in June to July. *Ly.* Fir-woods.

Light Emerald (*Metrocampa margaritaria*).—*E.* 1½–2 inches. Wings a delicate whitish green; two transverse lines on fore-wings, the outer continued on hind-wing. *L.* on oak, beech, elm, etc., September to May. Moth June to July. *Ly.* Woodlands.

August Thorn (*Ennomos quercinaria*).—*E.* 1⅓–1½ inch. Pale ochreous yellow wings with two dark cross lines on fore-wings, which are shaded and sprinkled finely with brown. *L.* on oak, lime, beech, etc., June to July. Moth August and September. Widely distributed.

The Canary-shouldered Thorn (*E. alniaria*) is somewhat similar, but recognized by the canary-yellow hair on the thorax. *L.* on birch, alder, etc.

The Dusky Thorn (*E. fuscantaria*) is like the above, but has some pale brownish shading from margin of fore-wings towards the base. *L.* on ash. Moth August and September.

September Thorn (*E. erosaria*) is a deeper ochre-yellow in colour, with two distinct cross lines on fore-wings. *L.* on oak, also lime and birch, May to July. Moth August to September.

Early Thorn (*Selenia bilunaria*).—*E.* 1½–1⅔ inch. Wings pale ochreous, sprinkled with brown; fore-wings with three dark transverse lines, the middle one being fainter. *L.* (very twig-like in appearance) on birch, alder, sallow, etc., May to June and August to September. Moth in April and May.

Lilac Beauty (*Hygrochroa syringaria*).—*E.* 1⅓–1½ inch. The wings of the *male* are brighter than those of the *female*, being ochreous, with a prominent reddish line crossing to the hind-wing, and a roughly parallel pale rose line, ending on the hind-wing in a row of dots. On the upper edge of the fore-wing are some delicate mauve patches and streaks. *L.* on honeysuckle, lilac, and privet in May and June Moth in June and July.

Scalloped Hazel (*Gonodontis bidentata*).—*E.* 1½–1¾ inch. Wings greyish or whitish brown, much scalloped at the edge; a dark brown eye-spot on each wing; two wavy lines on fore-wings, one on the hind-wings. Ground colour very variable. *L.* on oak, birch, hawthorn, etc., July to October. Moth in May and June.

Feathered Thorn (*Himera pennaria*).—*E.* 1½–1¾ inch. Tawny fore-wings, with two darker lines and a central dot. Hind-wings paler, with one indistinct line and a central dot. *Female* paler than the *male*. *L.* on oak, poplar, birch, etc., April to June. Moth in October and November (attracted to light frequently).

Scalloped Oak (*Crocallis elinguaria*).—*E.* 1½–1¾ inch. Colour, a light ochre-yellow; fore-wings with a central light brown area, marked by a black central spot; hind-wings have one faint cross line, and a centre spot. *L.* on many trees and bushes in spring. Moth in July and August.

Orange Moth (*Angerona prunaria*).—*E.* 1¾–2 inches. *Males* orange; *females* ochre-yellow, sprinkled with rusty brown; a crescent-shaped mark on each fore-wing. *L.* on sloe, hawthorn, honeysuckle, and many other plants from June to October. Moth in June.

Swallow-tailed Moth (*Ourapteryx sambucaria*).—*E.* 1¾–2¼ inches. Pale sulphur-yellow tinged with green, and delicately shaded. Two olive cross lines on fore-wings, one on hind-wings, which have a short tail, on each side of which is a black spot. *L.* on ivy specially, also hawthorn, sloe, etc., August to June. Moth in July.

Scorched Wing (*Eurymene dolabraria*).—*E.* 1⅛–1¼ inch. The dark brown blotches and marks and the general shrivelled appearance of the wings account for the apt name. General colour brownish ochreous. *L.* on oak, beech, birch, etc., July to September. Moth in May and June.

Brimstone (*Opisthograptis luteolata*).—*E.* 1⅓–1½ inch. Sulphur-yellow, the fore-wings having several reddish marks on the upper edge, the middle one having a white centre; faint wavy cross lines. *L.* on hawthorn and other trees in spring. Moth in May and June. Common.

Bordered Beauty (*Epione apiciaria*).—*E.* 1–1¼ inch. Deep yellow, sprinkled with orange, with a broad purplish grey margin, bounded inwardly with a black line. Also a black centre dot, and a fainter inner cross line on the fore-wings. *L.* on willow, poplar, alder, etc., in May and June. Moth in July and August.

Speckled Yellow (*Venilia maculata*).—*E.* ¾–1 inch. Yellow, with many purplish brown spots and blotches. *L.* on dead-nettle, wood-sage, etc., July and August. Moth in woods in June. Common in South, rather local in North.

Tawny-barred Angle (*Semiothisa liturata*).—*E.* 1⅛–1¼ inch. Ochreous grey, with a distinct dull orange band close to the margin of both wings. Three dark cross lines on fore-wings (sometimes faint), beginning from dark spots on the edge. *L.* on needles of Scotch pine July and August. Moth in June and July in fir woods.

Early Moth (*Hybernia rupicapraria*).—*E.* 1⅛–1¼ inch. Fore-wings of *male* ochreous grey, two cross lines and a central spot. Hind-wings paler, with one line and a central dot. *Female* almost wingless. *L.* on hawthorn, sloe, etc., in April and May. Moth in January and February. Common, but only found at night.

The Spring Usher (*H. leucophæaria*).—*E.* 1⅛–1¼ inch. A grey-coloured *male* (*female* being wingless), with dark basal patch and dark submarginal area on fore-wings, hind-wings being paler. *L.* on oak in April to May. Moth in February. Rather local, but widely distributed.

Scarce Umber (*H. aurantiaria*).—*E.* 1½–1⅔ inch. Orange-yellow *male* (*female* apterous), with two cross lines of brown and central dot. Hind-wings paler. *L.* in spring on oak, hawthorn, etc. Moth from October onwards. Widely distributed. Common in some woods.

Dotted Border (*H. marginaria*).—*E.* 1⅓–1½ inch. Rather variable. *Male* has pale ochreous brown fore-wings, with a *row of dots* on margin; central area paler than the rest. Hind-wings cream-coloured, with characteristic line of marginal dots. *Female* almost wingless. *L.* in April and May on hawthorn, sloe, oak, etc. Moth in March and April. Common.

Mottled Umber (*H. defoliaria*).—*E.* $1\frac{3}{8}$–$1\frac{3}{4}$ inch (*female* wingless). *Male* has pale ochreous brown wings, varying to darker; fore-wings with two cross lines, bordered with a rusty brown band, and a brown centre dot. Hind-wings paler. Some specimens have uniform darker fore-wings, with cross lines only faintly marked. *L.* in spring on forest trees and fruit trees. Moth from October to December; sometimes January to March. Common.

March Moth (*Anisopteryx æscularia*).—*E.* $1\frac{1}{4}$–$1\frac{1}{2}$ inch. *Female* apterous. *Male* pale or dark grey; two cross lines on fore-wings, a central dot; central area often smoky tinged. *L.* on hawthorn, sloe, currant, etc., April to June. Moth in spring.

Pale Brindled Beauty (*Phigalia pedaria*).—*E.* $1\frac{1}{2}$–2 inches. Pale grey with green tinge. Fore-wings four blackish cross lines, rather broken; thorax thick and hairy. *L.* in spring on birch, oak, and many trees. Moth in January and February; also found in November and December.

The Brindled Beauty (*Lycia hirtaria*).—*E.* $1\frac{3}{4}$–2 inches. Fore-wings greyish ochreous, tinged with brown, six thick black cross lines; thick, hairy body. *L.* on lime, elm, etc., and fruit trees May to July. Moth in March and April. Widely distributed, but most plentiful in *London*.

Oak Beauty (*Pachys strataria*).—*E.* $1\frac{3}{4}$–$2\frac{1}{4}$ inches. A large, handsome moth. Fore-wings white, dusted and speckled with black, crossed by two zigzag bands of brown edged with black. Hind-wings are duller, and have one of these bands more faintly marked. Body thick and downy. *L.* on oak, birch, elm, etc., May to July. Moth in March to April. Widely distributed.

Peppered Moth (*P. betularia*).—*E.* $1\frac{1}{2}$–2 inches. Dull white "peppered" or sprinkled with black (there is also a variety almost uniformly black). *L.* on oak, birch, elm, etc., July to September. Moth in May to June. Generally distributed.

Waved Umber (*Hemerophila abruptaria*).—*E.* $1\frac{1}{4}$–$1\frac{1}{2}$ inch. Brownish ochreous, with broad band of darker colour and shading on both wings. *L.* on privet and lilac May to August. Moth in April and May. Widely distributed, frequent in London.

Willow Beauty (*Boarmia gemmaria*).—*E.* $1\frac{1}{2}$–$1\frac{3}{4}$ inch. Brownish grey, dusted with darker; two blackish cross lines, and a zigzag pale submarginal line. *L.* on ivy, hawthorn, etc., in August and spring. Moth in July and August. Common.

Mottled Beauty (*B. repandata*).—*E.* $1\frac{3}{8}$–$1\frac{3}{4}$ inch. Wings grey, mottled and dusted with brown, two black cross lines, whitish submarginal line, edged with black scalloped line. *L.* on hawthorn, birch, etc., in July to May. Moth in June to July. Common.

The Engrailed (*Tephrosia bistortata*).—*E.* $1\frac{1}{4}$–$1\frac{1}{2}$ inch. Pale grey tinged with ochreous, dusted with dark brown; fore-wings have two cross lines of dark brown, edged with a band of lighter brown; a zigzag broken submarginal line of whitish grey. *L.* on foliage of many trees May to June and August to September. Moth March to April and May to June. Common.

284   THE BRITISH NATURE BOOK

Common Heath (*Ematurga atomaria*).—*E.* 1–1⅛ inch. A very variable species. *Male* ochreous; *female* creamy, sprinkled with brown. Fore-wings have four dark brown cross lines, the two centre ones uniting. Hind-wings have three lines; often the lines are broadened and partially united. *L.* on ling and heath July to August. Moth in May and June. Common on all heaths.

Bordered White (*Bupalus piniaria*).—*E.* 1¼–1⅜ inch. *Male* has pale ochreous or cream wings, with apex and margins broadly dark brown, the nervures also. *Female* orange, more or less tinged brownish. *L.* on pine and firs in August to October. Moth in May to June.

The "**V**" Moth (*Thamnonoma wauari*).—*E.* 1⅛–1¼ inch. Pale grey, tinged with violet. Four dark red-brown spots on fore-wings, the second of which is large and shaped like a **V** on its side. *L.* on gooseberry and currant April to June. Moth in July to August in gardens. Common.

Brown Silver-line (*Lozogramma petraria*).—*E.* 1⅛–1¼ inch. Fore-wings pale brown, with two cross lines edged with white; hind-wings shining creamy colour. *L.* on bracken in June. Moth in May to June wherever the bracken is common.

Latticed Heath (*Chiasmia clathrata*).—*E.* ¾–1 inch. Wings yellowish white, chequered or "latticed" with blackish cross lines and veins. *L.* on clovers and trefoils June to September. Moth April to May and July to August. Common in clover fields.

Family: *Zygænidæ*.

To this family belong the Burnets and Foresters species, which live gregariously; daylight fliers, with long, narrow wings, densely scaled. The following are the commoner species.

Five-spot Burnet (*Zygæna trifolii*).—*E.* 1¼–1½ inch. Greenish black, with five (sometimes six) carmine spots on fore-wings, the basal spots being united; and the hind-wings almost all carmine, edged with black. *L.* on clovers and trefoils July to May. Moth in May to August in damp meadows and marshes.

Narrow-bordered Five-spot Burnet (*Z. loniceræ*) resembles the preceding, but has longer fore-wings and more pointed hind-wings, the dark borders of which are narrower. It is *bluer* in colour than the above. *L.* on clovers and trefoils. Moth in June and July.

Six-spot Burnet (*Z. filipendulæ*).—*E.* 1–1½ inch. Six spots *in pairs*, the basal pair often united. *L.* in autumn and spring. Moth in July and August. The commonest of all.

The Forester (the GREEN FORESTER) (*Ino statices*).—*E.* 1–1¼ inch. Fore-wings bronze-green; hind-wings dark grey. *L.* on sorrel March to April. Moth in June. Frequent in meadows on flowers of ragged robin. Widely distributed.

The Cistus Forester (*I. geryon*) is smaller, and local.

Family: *Cochlidida*.

The Festoon (*Cochlidion limacodes*).—*E.* ¾-1⅛ inch. Fore-wings orange-brown in the *male*, with two straight diverging cross lines. Hind-wings dark brown; *female* paler. *L.* on oak in autumn. Moth in June and July. Local in Southern Counties.

Family: *Cossida*.

The Goat Moth (*Cossus cossus* or *ligniperda*).—So called from the odour of the caterpillar, which is a pinkish ochreous, ugly creature, with a black shiny head, and a black mark on the first ring. It feeds on the wood of trees such as elm, ash, and willow for three or four years, only leaving its tunnel to pupate. The moth (*E.* 2¾-3¾ inches) has pale grey fore-wings, clouded with brown, and a network of dark brown lines. The hind-wings are brownish grey, less netted; a stout thorax and body. It may be found in June and July.

The Leopard Moth (*Zeuzera pyrina*).—*E.* 2-3 inches. White, spotted like a leopard. *L.* feeds on wood in branches and stems of trees and shrubs for two or three years. Moth in summer. Local in South and East.

Family: *Sesiida*.

All the members of this family have "clear" wings and resemble hornets. They possess stout abdomens. The larvæ live in the stems and branches of trees, taking two years to arrive at maturity.

The Hornet Moth (*Trochilium apiformis*).—*E.* 1¼-1½ inch. Has transparent wings, and a body of yellow and black bands like the hornet. *L.* on poplars. Moth in May and June, chiefly in Eastern Counties.

The Lunar Hornet (*T. crabroniformis*) is very similar, but has a yellow collar behind the black head. *L.* on sallow, willow, and poplar. Moth in June to July. Generally distributed.

Currant Clearwing (*Sesia tipuliformis*).—*E.* about ¾ inch. Transparent wings with bronzy-tinged borders; body belted with yellow bands. *L.* in stems of currant bushes; full grown in May. Moth in June to July. Generally distributed.

The Red-belted Clearwing (*S. myopæformis*) has a single belt of *red* round the body. *L.* on apple. Moth local, often in gardens and orchards round London. (There is a LARGE RED-BELTED CLEARWING (*S. culiciformis*), very similar, found in most English counties.)

Family: *Hepialida*—"Swifts."

Ghost Moth (*Hepialus humuli*).—*E.* 1¾-2¾ inches. *Female* larger than male. Wings of *male* shining white with reddish brown edges. *Female* has pale yellowish fore-wings, smoky hind-wings. *L.* on roots of burdock, deadnettle, etc.; full grown in May. Moth in June and July. *Male* often seen swaying to and fro in flight like a pendulum. Generally distributed.

Orange Swift (*H. sylvina*).—*E.* 1-1½ inch. *Male* orange-brown with greywhite markings on fore-wings; *female* grey-brown. *L.* on roots of dock, bracken, etc.; full grown about July. Moth in July to August. Common.

Common Swift (*H. lupulina*).—*E.* 1-1½ inch. Fore-wings yellowish brown in *male*, with white markings in stripes and dashes. *Female* pale brownish grey, with less distinct markings. *L.* on roots of grass; full grown in April. Moth in June. Common; often seen flying at dusk.

II. *Microlepidoptera.*

These are much smaller moths, far more numerous than the larger ones, and requiring far more treatment than can be given here, but attention may be drawn to the *Tortrices*, or **Bell Moths**, which have broad fore-wings; the *Tineæ*, to which the **Clothes Moths** belong; the *Pterophori*, or **Plume Moths**, which have their fore-wings divided into two, and the hind-wings into three separate feathers; and the *Alucitæ*, of which only one British species is known —the beautiful though common **Twenty-plume Moth**, each wing having six feathers.

CHAPTER X.

Arthropoda (*continued*).

Order XVII. DIPTERA ("Two-winged" Insects).

HERE we have the true flies, which may be distinguished from all other winged insects by one simple fact: the hind-wings have vanished, and in their place are a pair of stalked *knobs*, known as balancers or halteres.
The mouth parts are adapted for piercing or sucking. There are two sub-orders. To the first—*Orthorrhapha*—belong, amongst others, the gall-midges, fungus midges, the true midges (*Chironomidæ*), and the gnats (*Culicidæ*).

Sub-order i. ORTHORRHAPHA.

The adult midges are frequently seen dancing in swarms in the air. Their larvæ are generally aquatic.

The gnats, of which there are at least nine British species, are specially numerous in marshy districts. The **Common Gnat** (*Culex pipiens*) is a beautiful object under the magnifier, the glossy wings bearing numerous hairs, and the antennæ having an exquisite feathery appearance. The female has mandibles. The male is harmless, living on nectar, but the female sucks blood (working by day and night) both from men and beasts, being armed with a remarkable proboscis used for piercing and sucking. The humming sound is produced by the female in flight, and is doubtless intended to attract the male. As many as 300 eggs are laid at a time in water, anchored to a floating leaf or twig. The larvæ and pupæ may be found in any water-butt.

Crane-flies or DADDY-LONGLEGS (*Tipulidæ*) are destructive, as their larvæ feed on roots of grass and plants, being known as leather-jackets. The general appearance of the adult is too well known to need description, but the female has a hard horny "tail"—the ovipositor, and may frequently be seen hovering up and down over grass, in the act of laying her eggs, which are glittering black in colour, and laid in damp places.

Gadflies (*Tabanidæ*) are notorious for the way in which the females suck the blood of horses and cattle; but the larvæ live in damp earth, where they feed on snails, slugs, and beetle larvæ.

Robber-flies (*Asilidæ*) prey upon other insects, their larvæ living in damp earth.

The Bee-flies (*Bombyliidæ*) are interesting as illustrations of protective mimicry, for they resemble humble bees in appearance and suck nectar from flowers. The larvæ of some species live upon the larvæ of the bee.

Sub-order ii. CYCLORRHAPHA.

To this belong the **Hover-flies** (*Syrphidæ*), which resemble to a remarkable degree both wasps and bees. They may be frequently seen in our gardens, where the perfect insects feed upon pollen chiefly, and the larvæ (in many species) prey upon *aphides*. The name is derived from the familiar and characteristic hovering of the insect, poised over flowers. The eggs are deposited on leaves, and the larva, armed with a three-pronged beak, sucks the juices from aphides, until it changes into the pupal state, in which, attached to some leaf, its skin becomes horny and golden-brown in colour.

BOT-FLIES (*Œstridæ*)

are hairy, bee-like insects, the larvæ of which actually live in the bodies of large animals. The **Horse-bot** lays her eggs on the hair of horses, where they (or the larvæ) remain till licked off. Then they live in the stomach all the winter, the mouth of the larva being furnished with two hooks, by means of which it clings to the inner coat of the horse's stomach. In the next summer it loses hold, and passing out of the horse burrows in the ground, where it assumes the pupal form. The **Ox-bot** or WARBLE-FLY is the most troublesome of all, much resembling a small humble bee, with whitish face and abdomen, the latter crossed by a band of black. The female pierces a hole by means of its remarkable horny " telescopic " ovipositor in the hide of an ox's back, in which an egg is placed. Cattle rush wildly about to escape her attentions; for the larva under the skin does great injury, causing a warble or sac of matter to form.

The **Sheep-bot** is the most serious of all these pests, laying its eggs in the nostrils of the sheep, the larvæ sometimes getting into the brain.

Muscidæ form an enormous family, which includes the **Common House-fly** (*Musca domestica*).

The briefest reference must be made to the **Tachnid Flies**, bristly-headed insects, whose larvæ, like those of the Ichneumon, live upon living caterpillars; and the **Grey Flesh-flies,** which actually produce their larvæ *alive* (not in eggs), and place them on animal refuse.

The **House-fly** is a pest so well known as to require no detailed description, but by all means examine it under the microscope, and note the marvel and beauty of its parts. Beyond any question this insect is, as Mr. F. W. Fitzsimmons, F.Z.S., calls it, a " slayer of men," in that it disseminates disease. From one single house-fly 100,000 fæcal bacteria have been discovered, and it must be obvious that a foul creature that settles on our food, bread, milk, meat, etc., is most dangerous to health. Every larder ought to be fly-proof on this account, and all refuse and garbage near a house or a town should be methodically destroyed. Each female can lay 1,000 eggs, and thus, by

PLATE XXXII.

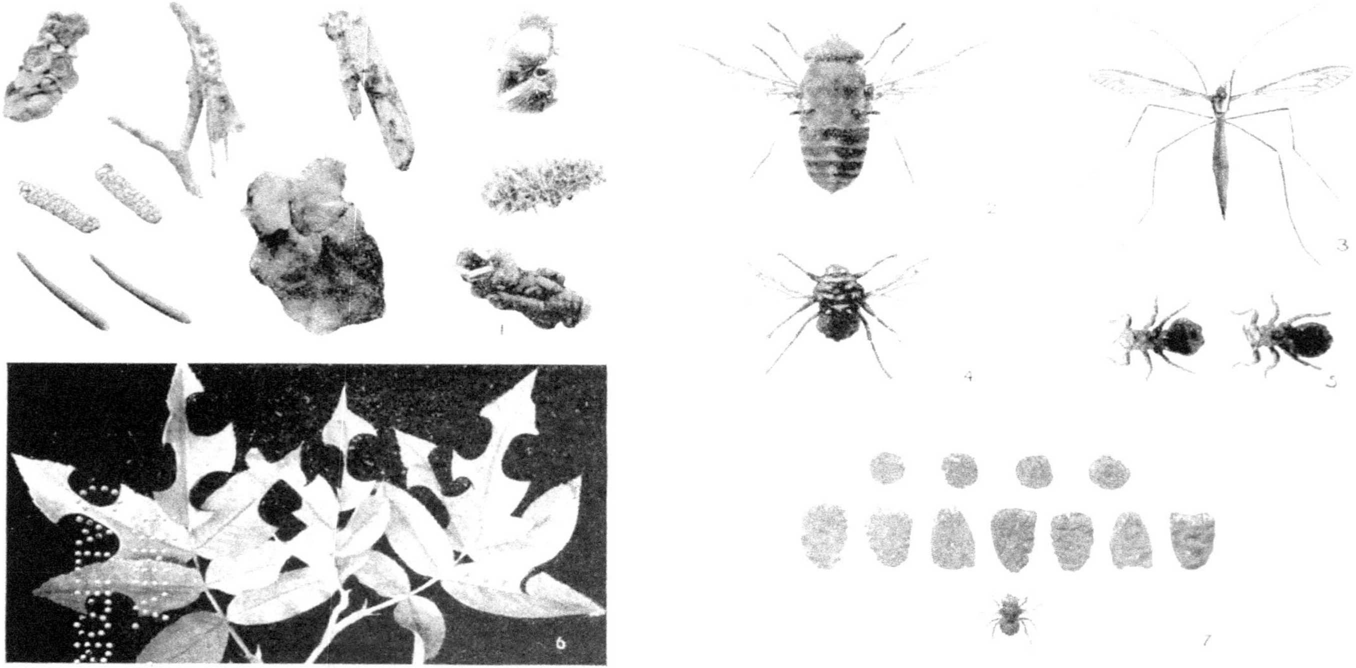

1. Protective Cases of Caddis-worms.   2. Great Ox-foot Bot.   3. Cow Bot.   4. Rabbit Louse [?].   5. Louse [?].   6. Sheep-tick, or "Ked."
6. Rose leaves mutilated by Leaf-cutting Bee.   7. Female Leaf-Cutting Bee, with eleven pieces of leaf, used to form a single cell.

" FLIES " 289

a simple calculation, it may be gathered that she may be the ancestor of 25,000,000 others in a single season.

The House-fly is distinguished from others by its ashy grey colour—the male with some ochreous colour—the thorax having four black cross lines. The eggs are laid in dung and decaying refuse, often hatching in one day, when the larva, a legless grub, begins to feed upon this putrid matter.

It should be remembered, however nauseous it may be, that before the fly begins to eat any fresh food, it first vomits up whatever is in its stomach.

The **Bluebottle**, or BLOW-FLY, also lives on decaying matter, and without doubt is useful as a scavenger; but on no account should it be allowed in the larder, or upon any human food. There is also a brighter-coloured fly known as the **Greenbottle Fly**, more frequently seen sunning itself on bushes and hedgerows.

The **Noonday Fly** is larger than the House-fly, shining black, the male having a bright yellow on the sides and under the head. Frequently seen at midday round and upon trees.

Other insects in this sub-order are the **Cabbage-root Flies**, very small and injurious insects. The **Sheep-ticks**, or KEDS, and the **Forest-fly** are viviparous, and suck the blood of mammals or birds. Others are parasites upon bats, and others, like the **Bee-louse**, live upon bees.

Order XVIII. SIPHONAPTERA.

This order consists of the **Fleas**, which are entirely wingless insects, with laterally flattened bodies, and with legs long and powerful, adapted for hopping. They are capable of leaping two hundred times their own length. The larvæ live in and feed upon dust.

Order XIX. HYMENOPTERA—

Saw-flies, Ichneumons, Ants, Wasps, and Bees—insects with two pairs of transparent wings. The name refers to a general characteristic which is of great interest: The wings on each side are joined during flight by a series of hooks on the margin of the hind-wing, which engage in a groove or fold in the fore-wing. This is easily seen if the wings (for example, of a bee) are examined under the microscope. The females have elaborate ovipositors, which in many cases have been modified into poison-stings.

Sub-order i. SYMPHYTA.

THE SAW-FLIES.

These insects have their ovipositor developed into a pair of saws, by which an incision can be made into a leaf or stem, in which the egg is laid. There are more than 2,000 species, many, such as the Currant Saw-fly and Pear Saw-fly, being pests of garden and orchard. Some are about $\frac{1}{2}$ inch across the wings; the Currant and Gooseberry Saw-flies being yellow, with black head, antennæ, and three short patches on the back. The larvæ have twenty legs. Many feed on leaves, others in galls. The pupa is in a silken cocoon, generally buried in the ground.

WOOD-WASPS

(which, though like in general colouring, are not to be confused with the true wasps) are represented in Great Britain by two species, not very common. The Giant Wood-wasp (*Sirex gigas*) looks a very formidable insect, with its long and strong ovipositor, by which it inserts its eggs in the wood of trees, in and on which the larvæ feed. This wood-wasp is yellow, with two black bands. The female is at once distinguished from the male by its egg-laying instrument. It is quite harmless, as it possesses no sting.

The Steel-blue Wasp (*S. juvencus*) is not so large, and the female has a purple-blue abdomen, that of the male being yellow with a black apex. The male has black antennæ, and thus may be distinguished from the male of the preceding, which has yellow antennæ.

The Gall-flies, of which we have three hundred species, are responsible for the "oak-apples" and "bedeguars" and other strange excrescences upon our trees. The female pierces the leaf or twig, and lays her egg within the incision. This irritates and inflames the vegetable tissue, so that a swelling takes place, forming the gall in which the larva lives.

Sub-order ii. APOCRITA.

The larva of all insects in this group is a white, legless grub, dependent on provision made by its parent.

ICHNEUMON FLIES.

There are probably two thousand species at least in Great Britain. Some lay their eggs in the bodies of caterpillars, upon which the larvæ feed, in this case performing a very useful task, for they destroy in this manner countless numbers of butterflies and moths.

Others attack wood-burrowing grubs, such as those of the Giant-tailed Wasp, in which case they have a very long ovipositor, capable of boring through the wood and reaching the grub below. The full-fed larvæ leave the body of their victim and spin cocoons, in which they pupate.

The Ichneumon which preys upon the Giant-tailed Wasp is almost as large an insect, black, with red legs, and two white spots on each segment of the abdomen. Other species are very small. The typical Ichneumon is about 1 inch across the wings, generally yellow or black in colour. There are some species which are aquatic.

Ruby Wasps, or RUBY-TAILED FLIES (*Chrysididæ*), have brilliant blue, green, and red colours; sometimes called CUCKOO-WASPS. The females lay their eggs in the nests of other hymenopterous insects, where the larvæ feed on the food of the rightful owner. They are known to roll themselves into a ball when attacked.

ANTS (*Formicidæ*).

There are more than thirty known species in this country. The following is a list of the more common species :—

Family i. *Formicidæ*.

These are Stingless Ants, whose pupæ are always cased in cocoons (the latter being the so-called "ants' eggs," used for feeding goldfish and various birds).

Genus : *Formica*.

1. *Formica rufa*.—This is the Common Wood Ant, whose large hillocks of pine needles may be found in many fir woods in all parts of the country. When disturbed, this species ejects formic acid, and if one's face happens to be sufficiently near, the strong smell of this volatile fluid is quite plainly discernible ; in fact, I have before now found my eyes stinging and watering from its effects. Occasionally bits of yellow resin, known as "ant-amber," are found in the nests. A great number of other animals are found living in friendship with this species—more than twenty species of beetles, also spiders and wood-lice. Its general colour is brown ; the queens have a shining black bead-like abdomen. A closely allied ant is *F. congerens*, with hairy eyes, but this is rare.

2. *F. sanguinea*.—The Blood-red Robber Ant. Famous for the fact that it makes slaves, raiding the nests of *F. fusca*, and carrying off the pupæ, which it brings up at home. Generally found on heaths and commons, where the nest is chiefly subterranean, covered with short-cut grass. It is very active, and brighter than *F. rufa ;* fairly widely distributed. Nine species of beetles have been found in the nests.

3. *F. exsecta*.—A much smaller species, yellowish red ; makes distinct nests of cut grass, etc., about the size of a man's head, on the edges of fir woods. Found round Bournemouth and the New Forest.

4. *F. fusca*.—This is the "Slave" Ant: very nervous and shy ; black in colour. Found under stones, in banks, and amongst roots of trees. Quite common. Six species of beetles and other insects have been found with it, including *Atemeles emarginatus*. It is very quick and active, and of graceful shape ; larger than the Common Black Ant.

Genus: *Lasius.*

5. *Lasius fuliginosus.*—Sometimes called the **Jet Ant**, because of its shining black colour, the tips of legs and antennæ being paler and reddish. It has a peculiar aromatic scent, like that of the Musk Beetle. Makes its nest in trees, old posts, and sometimes underground. It moves slowly. Local and rare.

6. *L. umbratus* is of a yellow or mahogany colour, nesting under stones. Widely distributed, but uncommon.

7. *L. flavus* is the **Common Yellow Ant**, whose mounds are familiar in meadows and on embankments. Seven species of beetles have been found with it. It is one of the easiest to keep in an " ant-case " or formicarium.

8. *L. niger.*—The **Little Black Ant**, perhaps the most common of all. Found everywhere.

Genus: *Tapinoma.*

9. *Tapinoma erratica.*—A small black ant, very much like the preceding, but it has some grey pubescence. Found on heaths. Moves actively in sunlight, but disappears when the sun is clouded.

Family ii. *Poneridæ.*

These have well-developed stings, and the pupæ are always in cocoons. Generally speaking, they are long and narrow in shape.

10. *Ponera contracta.*—Polished red-brown. Nests found on chalky hillsides, under moss and stones. Widely distributed, but not common.

11. *P. punctatissima.*—Rare; probably introduced from abroad.

Family iii. *Myrmicidæ.*

These also possess stings, but the pupæ are always naked—that is, without cocoons.

12. *Formicoxenus nitidulus.*—A small species found in the nests of *F. rufa.*

13. *Myrmecina latreillei.*—Distinct black, with red legs. Rare. Found under stones, generally in South of England.

14. *Tetramorium cæspitum.*—Common on the sea coast. Dark brown.

15. *Leptothorax acervorum.*—A small red-headed species; abdomen very dark; sparsely covered with whitish hairs. Common and widely distributed. Nests in old stumps, under bark, and in company with *F. rufa.*

16. *L. nylanderi.*—Pale reddish yellow; *female* banded with brown. Sometimes in nests of *F. rufa;* under bark and in old stumps.

17. *L. unifasciatus.*—A still smaller species, but very similar; the club of the antennæ dark brown. Rare.

PLATE XXXIII.

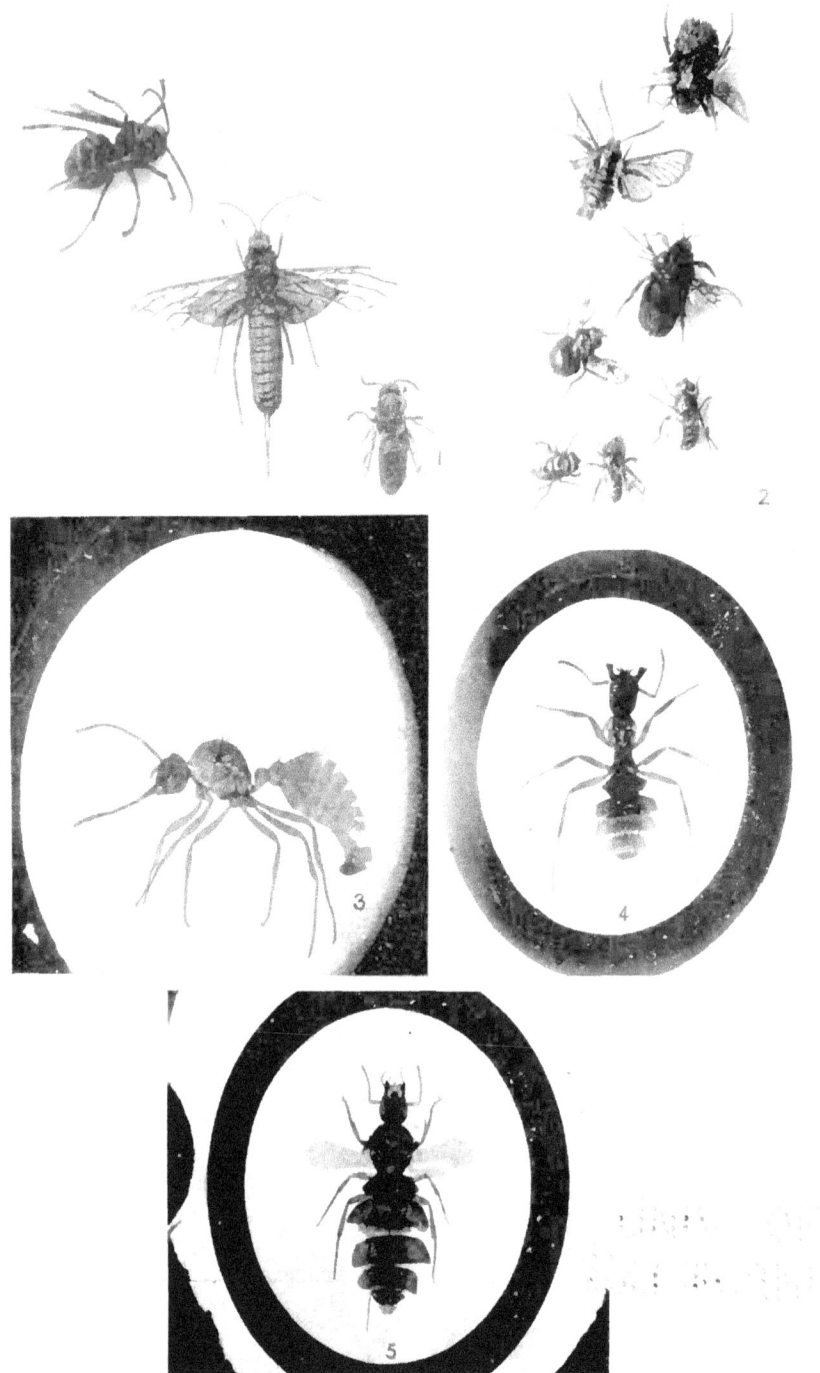

1. Hornet, Giant-tailed Wasp, and Common Wasp.   2. Humble Bees and their mimics.   3. Male Winged Ant.   4. Wood Ant (Worker).   5. Meadow Ant (Queen newly emerged, with wings still folded).

ANTS

18. *Myrmica ruginodis.*—Common and widely distributed; under stones, in decayed wood.

19. *M. lævinodis.*—Antennæ not so long in *male.*

20. *M. scabrinodis.*—Pale rust-red. Scape of antennæ distinctly elbowed. Very common under stones. Covered with bright yellowish hairs.

21. *M. sulcinodis.*—Deep rust-red colour; makes mounds like *F. flava.*

22. *M. lobicornis.*—Similar to above, but smaller; with a lobe or spine on the side of the antennæ. Not common.

23. *Solenopsis fugax.*—The Little Yellow Robber Ant. Hairy. Found in the nests of larger ants; but rare.

In addition to these, there are some twenty other species to be found, many of which have been introduced in flowers, bulbs, and plants from abroad. The hot-houses at Kew are a well-known hunting ground for most of these.

Having given a list of the principal species of ants to be found in this country, it remains to give a brief account of their life-history and manners.

Of all the dumb creatures that live a community life, there can be none more interesting than the ants. They possess remarkable intelligence, having, as the size of their heads shows, a very large brain in comparison to the body; and they appear to display something more than automatic loyalty to the society to which they belong. There are three sets of ants to be found in every nest: Workers, which are sterile females, capable of laying eggs if the community is perishing from the lack of a queen; males, which, like the drones in a hive, do no work; and females, or queens, which are always much larger than the rest, and spend their time in laying eggs.

The eggs are very minute (the so-called " ants' eggs " are really the pupæ, and generally pupæ of females or queens)—so small, in fact, that the workers, whose duty it is to look after them, carry them in clusters. During the day the eggs are brought up from the deeper parts of the nest to the surface, to get the advantage of the sun's heat.

In a few days they hatch into minute grubs, which are fed and cleaned by the workers, and carried up and down the nest galleries to the various chambers. They are sorted into sizes or ages by the workers, and grouped together. The care and attention bestowed upon these helpless larvæ are most remarkable. If a nest should be opened, the workers on duty as nurses immediately seize their charges and attempt to carry them into safety. A larva appears to be able to show its desire for food by assuming a curved or bent position. When lying straight, it is a sign that it is " full." The workers feed the babes from their own mouths, and frequently caress them with their antennæ.

Other workers go out and bring home food—sometimes honey, nectar, or other sweet liquid; or food obtained from caterpillars which they kill, or from some dead animal. This food they give to the others in the nest by transferring it from mouth to mouth, the queens themselves (of which there may be several in one nest) receiving their nourishment in the same way. Other workers act as guards, some being on duty at the entrances of the nest, ready to challenge any intruder and to fight to the death if necessary. They appear to know their own " fellow-citizens "—some kind of exchange of sign, done by touching antennæ, passing between them. I have introduced into one of my artificial nests, some weeks after it had been first made and filled, fresh workers from the original nest, and have seen the whole small community indulge in a sort of ecstatic dance, showing as plainly as can be both recognition and affection.

The queen, let me add, is constantly guarded and caressed by a crowd of workers, who act as royal attendants and devote themselves to her. I have elsewhere told the story of how I saw them try to restore to life a dead queen which I had removed from the nest, and do their best to drag her back into it.

They are very strong and active insects, capable of moving masses many times their weight and size. The Wood Ants may be seen moving their pine needles, as a workman might (if he could) carry scaffold poles; whilst their industry is seen in the case of the Meadow Ant, which, grain by grain, makes the mounds, so familiar a sight in fields and on banks; tunnels innumerable passages; makes chambers and rooms; and cements into a solid mass the deepest portions of the nest.

The larvæ grow rapidly, and at last change into pupæ, when they require no more feeding; but they are carried up to the surface chambers as regularly as ever by day, and removed to the deeper nurseries at night.

In the pupal form two distinct characteristics are to be noted. Those ants that have *stings* rear pupæ that are naked—that is, not enclosed in any cocoon. It almost seems as if Nature, having provided the workers with such defensive instruments, deemed it unnecessary to protect the infants further; but those species which have *no* stings rear pupæ that are enclosed in silken cocoons. When the time comes for these to emerge, the workers neatly bite off the top of the cocoon and help the inmate out. It is for a short while very helpless and limp. In the case of males and queens the wings are crumpled and folded. It is the duty of the workers to caress and "massage" them: to unfold and stretch the wings.

The virgin queens and the males are then shepherded by the workers towards the entrances of the nest, and on some warm evening in July or August these go on their honeymoon flight in thousands. The worker pupæ, be it said, have no wings.

When the queens drop to earth again, they either pull off their own wings or workers do so for them, since they will be needed no more; and these royal ladies become the mothers of the nests, living for some years, and each laying thousands of eggs.

All kinds of other insects and animals are to be found in the ants' nests. A remarkable minute white wood-louse, known as *Platyarthrus hoffmanseggii*, is kept as a sort of scavenger. It is quite blind, has two continually moving

PLATE XXXIV.

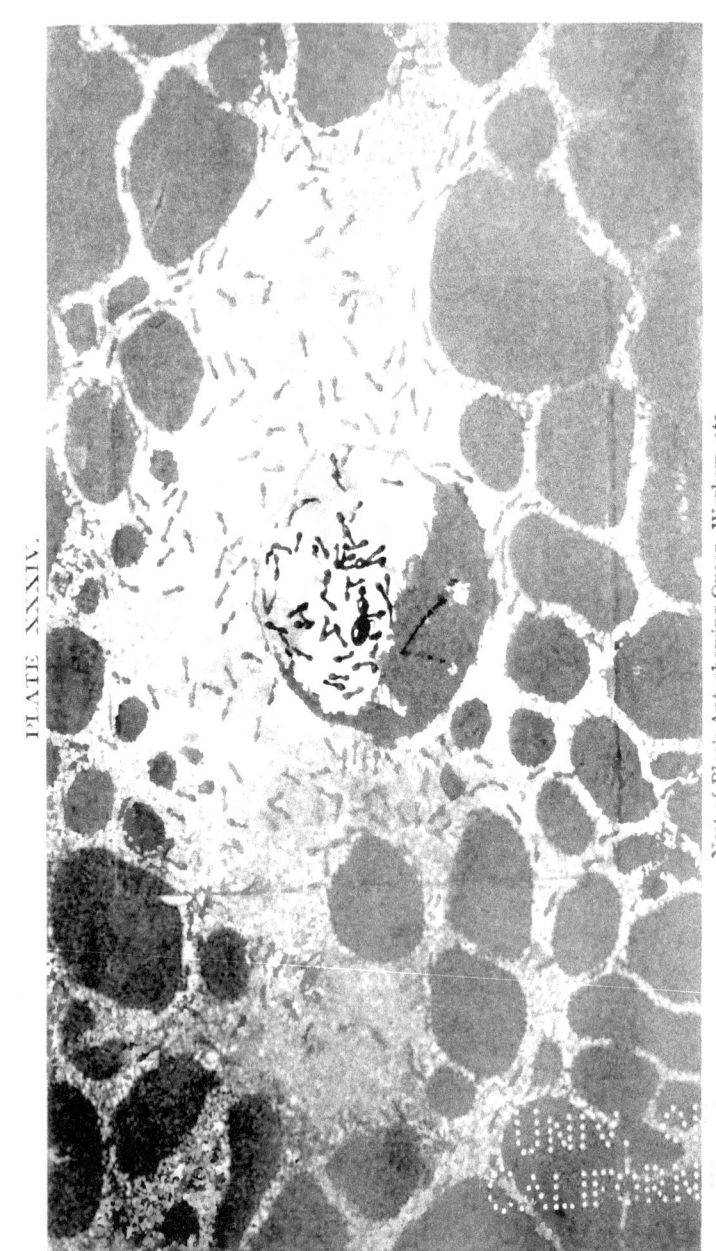

Nest of Black Ant, showing Queen, Workers, etc.

antennæ like horns, and is allowed free access to any part of the nest. Reference is made to the rare beetles often to be found amongst ants; and most interesting of all, perhaps, is the *aphis*. The ants " milk " aphides by touching the two " teats " on their backs, which exude the sweet fluid known as "honey-dew." In the winter aphides are actually kept in the nests, feeding upon the roots of grass; but during spring and summer they are taken out and placed on brambles or roses. The ants seen so frequently climbing roses are in reality engaged in seeking for aphides in order to " milk " them.

At least one British species, *Formica sanguinea*, keeps slaves. For this purpose it raids the nests of *F. fusca*, and carries off the pupæ, which it tends and cares for, and from which the workers on emerging take their place as servants in the robbers' nests.

This very brief and inadequate sketch must suffice; but the way to realize for oneself the extraordinary sagacity and intelligence of these insects is to keep them in artificial nests. These are easily made. Two pieces of glass, about 10 to 12 inches square, form the top and bottom of such a nest, while the sides consist of thin slips of the same glued between them. One side should have an opening of an inch or so, through which a spoonful of water can be occasionally poured to keep the inside moist. A drop or two of honey for food should be placed on a tuft of cotton wool, which is then used to plug the opening and serve as a " cork," as ants are unable to get through it.

The interior is filled with sifted earth or sand, and all that remains is to dig up an ants' nest, find one of the queens—known at once by her large size—and to bring her and some workers home. It is as well also to get some of the little white wood-lice referred to above, to act as scavengers in your glass nest. The simplest way to get the ants into the nest is to lay the nest on a board slightly larger, and place it in a basin of water so that it forms an island. Then pour your captured ants, soil and all, on the top, and leave them. In a few hours they will have found their way into the glass case.

Ants may be kept for many months in these cases, and require no attention but a little water to keep the earth within damp, and a little honey once or twice a week for food.

The Wood Ant requires a case at least 1 inch thick, in which pine needles may be placed; but the other species must be in cases which are no thicker than their own size. The slips of glass used for the sides should be about $\frac{1}{10}$ of an inch thick on this account. Keep the cases covered from light, except when used for observation purposes.

HORNETS, WASPS, AND BEES.

HORNETS AND WASPS.

Before we come to the true Wasps, the barest mention must be made of three families known as " Digger Wasps." One species, belonging to the *Scoliidæ*, burrows into the ground, and lays its eggs upon the larvæ of beetles.

The *Pompilidæ* make nests in banks, provisioning them with spiders which they have paralyzed; while the females of the *Sphegidæ*, which are solitary insects, hollow out long passages, at the end of which are three or four chambers, in each of which an egg is laid and a store of food deposited. The food consists of larvæ, sometimes of crickets, beetles, and flies. These are first paralyzed by stinging, and then patiently dragged to the nest. Here, outside, the helpless insect is left, while the Sphex enters to reconnoitre. If all is well, she takes her prey inside, four insects being placed in each chamber, which is then sealed up.

The true wasps (*Vespidæ*) are recognized by the longitudinally folded wings when at rest.

The Solitary Wasps (sub-family, *Eumeninæ*), generally smaller and darker than the Social wasps, have long narrow mandibles, and the tarsal claws are toothed. They usually build single cells of clay or sand in a hole, which they store with captured larvæ and other insects. The Wall Wasp (*Odynerus parietum*) is a well-known representative.

The Hornet (*Vespa crabro*) is the largest of our British wasps, about 1 inch long, brown or brownish red, with some yellow on head, abdomen, and legs. It feeds on the sap of trees, fruit, honey (which it steals from hives, etc.), though at times it is carnivorous as well, taking flies and other insects. The nest is often in a hole in a tree, or a crevice in a wall, and is built of paper, made by the insect from wood and bark. This is chewed into pulp by the wasp, and spread out in thin layers to dry.

There are males, females, and workers in a hornets' nest, some 200 in all, of which the females and workers do all the work, being provided with powerful stings. Several females or queens live in a nest. In winter all die except the females, each of which begins her own nest in the spring.

The Common Wasp (*V. vulgaris*) builds in the ground, but the Wood Wasp (*V. media*) hangs her ball-shaped nest from a branch of a tree. The nests of both vary very much in size. They feed on the juices of plants, fruits, nectar, etc., as well as on insects and spiders, and even dead bodies.

The community in each case starts with one female, which has survived the winter. She makes a very small nest, with two or three cells, in which eggs are laid. The larvæ from these are fed by the mother wasp till they are full-grown, when they act as workers and lighten her labours.

It is quite possible to keep these insects under observation, and if a small nest is found in spring and put into a box or case, it can be watched in detail. I have had such a case suspended from the side of a shed, with a glass panel at the back, so that it could be watched from the inside.

As autumn approaches, females, and finally males, are hatched. These leave the nest on a honeymoon flight, while the workers left at home, as winter draws near, turn out the remaining larvæ, and then gradually die themselves. The queens each find some sheltered cranny or crevice where they hibernate till next spring.

PLATE XXXV.

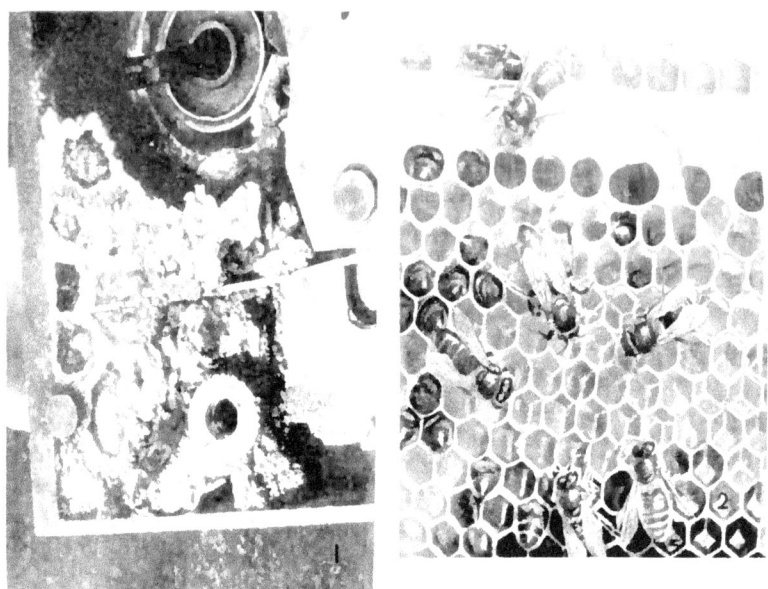

1. Mason Bee's Nest in a Door Lock.
2. Hive Worker Bees with Queen.
3. First Stage of Wasp Nest.
4. Humble Bee's Nest.

It is worth while remembering that if wasps do considerable damage to fruit, they render some service by destroying harmful grubs, larvæ, and insects.

BEES.

Over 200 species of Bees are found in this country, though most people would divide them into two, Honey Bees and Humble Bees! There are a large number of Solitary Bees, the life-history of which is very interesting. The genus *Colletes* resembles the familiar Honey Bee, though the males are smaller than the drones of a hive. These do not live a community life, although they often build their cells side by side, forming a small colony. They may be found in loose soil, or in the soft mortar of walls. I have seen them frequently by the side of graves in a churchyard. Each cell is beautifully lined with a delicate membrane like goldbeaters' skin. Another Solitary bee is *Prosopis*, to be seen from June to August, which makes its cells in the pith of bramble sticks. This bee when handled gives off a fragrant scent.

There are more than sixty British species of the genus *Andrena*, which appear very early in the spring, often on a sunny day in March. They burrow long tunnels in the earth, from which other passages lead to single cells, in which first a mass of pollen is placed and then an egg is laid. The larva when full grown hibernates till the following spring.

Halictus is another large genus of bees with similar habits, which use a *common* burrow, like families in a model dwelling, having their own apartments; while the *Nomada*, or **Wasp Bees**, are the most handsome of all our native species. These are known to enter the hives of other bees, and like *Prosopis* they emit a pleasant odour when handled.

The Mason Bees (*Osmia*), of which there are several species, make single cells of a kind of mortar or cement, made from earth mixed with saliva. In each single cell, when completed, a mass of honey and pollen is placed, an egg laid, and the top sealed. When eight or nine such cells have been made, the bee covers them with cement and minute stones.

There are also **Wood-boring Bees** (for example, *Xylocopa*), and **Leaf-cutting Bees** (*Megachile*), the latter a large genus, which excavate tunnels in the ground, or in decayed wood, and line them with circular discs cut from flowers and leaves. They are responsible for the neatly cut holes seen on leaves in the garden during the summer. At least eleven pieces are used to make one single cell. (The **Cuckoo Humble Bees** of the genus *Psithyrus*, or *Apathus*, having no means of gathering pollen, live in other humble bees' nests, and closely resemble their hosts, who bring up their guests' larvæ as well as their own.)

Humble Bees.—Of these there are some forty different species in Great Britain, many of which are familiar on account of their great size and loud humming, from which they get their name of "Humble" or "Bumble" Bee. Their nests are found in various situations. The **Moss Bee** (*Bombus muscorum*) builds its nest in moss or grass, on the surface of the ground; frequently in a bank or a hedgerow. I have often found them on the side of graves in a churchyard. The queens, which hibernate through the cold weather, may be seen in early spring seeking for a site for the nest. When found, the queen collects a quantity of dried moss and fragments of grass, in which she deposits a mass of pollen and honey; on this she lays a few eggs, covering them with more pollen, on which the larvæ feed till full grown. They then spin cocoons, from which they duly emerge as perfect insects, though not at first able to do active work. As soon, however, as they are mature, they (being " worker-bees ") undertake the duty of maintaining the small community, the queen restricting herself to the duty of laying eggs. Later on, drones are hatched, and the last brood of all each season consists of females, which after hibernating become the mothers of the next season's nests. These nests may be kept under observation in small glass cases, or indeed any kind of receptacle, provided it is placed on the ground in suitable surroundings. I have several times conducted the experiment with success. It will be noticed that the cells built are oval in shape. Some are left open, and appear to serve as store cells for honey. Between fifty and a hundred eggs—a comparatively small number—are laid by each queen, each laid in a brand-new cell, and not in any previously used. The drones on leaving the nest do not return, obtaining their food from the flowers they visit. Humble Bees, it should be remembered, play a most important part in fertilizing plants which other insects cannot approach effectively—such as the red clover, white dead-nettle, yellow iris, and especially the foxglove. All Humble Bees have stings (except the drones), but they do not use them so readily as Hive Bees, and generally a nest may be examined or taken with impunity.

Other Humble Bees (*Bombus pratorum*, and *B. elegans*, for example) make similar nests on the surface. The **Common Humble Bee** (*B. terrestris*) makes a nest in the ground, often using a mouse hole for the purpose. Others (*B. lapidarius*, the **Red-backed Bee**, *B. subterraneus*, and *B. virginalis*) build in similar situations—*B. lapidarius*, the most courageous of all and therefore the one most likely to sting, gets its name from making its nest in heaps of stones. *B. terrestris* is black and yellow-banded, with a tawny tail, and a large nest may contain 300 or 400 members in the autumn. The surface-nesting bees' nests contain considerably fewer individuals.

"**Carder**" **Bees** are bees (*B. agrorum*) which weave grass or moss into a kind of thatch above their nests. I have found them several times in deserted birds' nests, particularly those of the Golden-crested Wren.

The **Hive, or Honey, Bee** (*Apis mellifica*), consisting of some nine or ten species in all, only two or three of which are known in this country, is so important an insect that it would require a book to itself to do it justice. Only the merest outline of its story can be given here. There are three kinds in each hive—workers, drones, and females. Of the last named, one only is permitted to live in the same hive as queen: her sole duty that of laying eggs—between 2,000 and 3,000

PLATE XXXVI.

1. Dragon-fly. 2. Ichneumon Fly, emerged from Pupa of Swallow-tail Butterfly. 3. Pupa of Dragon-fly. 4. Glow-worms. 5. Ichneumon Flies, emerged from Magpie Moth Pupæ.

a day for several weeks together, and therefore, in her life of three or four years, more than one and a half millions. The "workers" outnumber the drones by at least twelve to one. The wax used for constructing the remarkable cells is secreted by the bees. The honey is made from the nectar of flowers, under a process of digestion in the "honey-bag" of the bee. The young bees (larvæ) are fed on compressed pollen.

The eggs which produce female bees are laid in a long and specially prepared cell, generally attached to the edge of the comb, with its mouth downwards. The larva is fed on special food, called "royal jelly," made by the nurse bees from honey and pollen mixed with saliva.

When a female is mature, the old queen leaves the hive, taking with her part of the community to form a new colony, while the young princess reigns at home in her stead.

The so-called "**English Hive Bee**," which is black, is a very hardy and strong species, but is generally regarded as bad-tempered. A great many beekeepers therefore import *Italian queens*, the little insects arriving safely from abroad in small special "cages." They are introduced into hives, the result being a very gentle, hard-working community of golden-coloured bees.

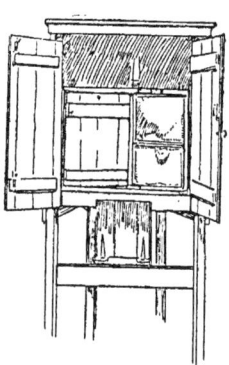

Observing hive.

The best way of observing the remarkable habits of Hive Bees is to set up an observing hive. The sketch represents, perhaps, the best sort in England. It is founded on one planned by Mr. Tickner-Edwards, but I have so adapted it that the bees can live in it all the year round. Beneath is a drawer containing a few frames, where the bees live in the winter; but above is a special arrangement of revolving glass cases, three in all, containing two bar-frames each, which are reached by the bees through a central passage. These may be turned and examined at any time quite freely, and without any danger of being "stung." For further information I would like to commend warmly the excellent book, *Bees, shown to the Children*, by Ellison Hawks, published by Messrs. Jack. Though written for children, it will be found of fascinating interest to adults as well, and it is beautifully illustrated.

CHAPTER XI.
Mollusca ("Shellfish").

MOLLUSCA (Latin *mollis*, "soft") means "soft-bodied," and the name is applied to a group of backboneless animals, numbering at least 50,000 species, the vast majority of which have no internal skeleton whatever. Instead, the body is enclosed in a hard shell, which serves the purpose of an external skeleton, and acts principally as a protection for the body.

Most of the molluscs belong to the sea, but a considerable number inhabit fresh water, and some, like the snail and slug, live upon the land.

They possess no limbs in the ordinary sense of the word, but their soft bodies are covered with a loose, thick skin, overlapping the sides and usually very slimy, called the *mantle*, and by its means the animal secretes the lime from which the shell is made. Another characteristic structure is the "foot," a muscular protrusion of the surface of the belly, by which the creature usually moves.

There are also remarkable sense-organs—tentacles like those of the octopus and cuttle-fish and the horns of the snail; eyes, such as the well-developed eyes of the cuttle-fish; a pair of hearing organs, called ear-sacs, situated in front of the foot; and also a smelling organ, or scent-patch, at the base of the gills.

Many of the molluscs have in the mouth region a toothed ribbon, tongue, or palate, like a file, by means of which they rasp the plants, etc., on which they feed.

Their blood is colourless, or with a light blue or greenish tinge.

They move, for the most part, slowly—as the word "sluggish" implies—though some are capable of travelling at considerable speed, especially those which, like the cuttle-fish, are free swimmers.

As to their food, some, such as the Bivalves, feed on microscopic animals and debris; others feed on plants and seaweeds; while others are flesh-eaters.

Mollusca are classified in two main divisions—

I. Those with a well-developed head (CEPHALOUS) and a rasping tongue.

II. Those without a distinct head (ACEPHALOUS) and without a rasping tongue.

They are sub-divided as follows:—

Class 1. *Cephalopods* (literally "head-footed"), in which the head has eight or ten long arms, or tentacles, which are covered with suckers, and by their means the creature can creep about at the bottom of the sea. These have

MOLLUSCA

no outside shell. This includes the Pearly Nautilus, the Octopus, and Cuttlefish, and forms the highest class of molluscs, and, indeed, of Invertebrates generally.

Class 2. *Gasteropods* (literally, " belly-footed "), which have, for the most part, single shells (Univalves), as compared with the double shells (Bivalves) of Class 4. Most of them have a " foot," for purposes of locomotion, and are marine animals, though others are found in fresh water, and, like the snail, on land.

There is a distinct sub-class known as *Pteropods* (" wing-footed "), sometimes called a separate class. They have two lobes of the foot, divided into " wings," or wing-like fins, by which they swim. They live in immense shoals in the open sea, and are the prey of many fishes, birds, and cetaceans.

Class 3. *The Scaphopoda.* This is a very small class, and need not be dealt with here. The Tooth or Tusk shellfish (so-named from the resemblance of the shell to a very small elephant's tusk)—*Dentalium entale*—is probably the only member whose shell is likely to be found by young people off the British coast. It is very smooth and white. The Grooved-tusk (*D. tarentinum*) is delicately grooved at the larger end, and has a pinkish tinge.

Class 4. *Acephalous* Molluscs—the *Lamelli branchiata*, or Bivalves—such as Mussels, Oysters, and many others, which have two shells hinged together. It should be borne in mind that these have no toothed-ribbons or rasps.

It is worth while to spend a few moments in observing the formation of shells and how they grow, as hereby we shall grasp the reason for some of the peculiarities we meet with in making a collection of shells. If you examine an Oyster, Mussel, or other bivalve, you will see first of all in opening it that there are two thin flaps, almost transparent, which enclose the animal. These are the " mantle." On the other hand, the mantle of a snail or a periwinkle is a single piece, out of which the head emerges as from a sort of tube ; from which also the animal pushes its " foot," and the horny lid (*operculum*) which closes the shell when the animal is at rest. (Not all univalves, however, possess this curious lid or door ; and therefore it is of importance in making a collection that the species which do possess it should be preserved with the operculum intact.)

Notice, next, that many bivalves have shells of unequal size and depth, the deeper one being in all cases the lower—the cradle, as it were, of its occupant ; the shallower one serves as a lid.

When very young these shellfish are minute, and the shell is like a glassy bead. As the animal grows this shell must, of course, increase in size proportionately. The animal extends its mantle till it reaches over the edge of the shell, and exudes a very thin fluid, which, being very limy, forms a new layer, and, in fact, a new rim to the shell. This process is repeated when necessary, and so the shell grows.

In many cases it is not difficult to trace the " lines of growth." The Garden Snail, for example, shows them very plainly on its shell.

THE BRITISH NATURE BOOK

It will be obvious now that bivalves—that is, molluscs having their mantles in two parts—produce two shells, one with each half of the mantle, while those molluscs that have the mantle in one piece produce one shell only, and thus are called Univalves.

Cuttle-fish.—These belong to the Cephalopods, the most highly developed of all the molluscs, and have a distinct head, and two large, cruel-looking eyes. The beak (or jaws) is an exceedingly powerful organ, very much like that of a parrot, and there is a thick fleshy tongue, covered with hooks, for rasping or tearing flesh.

The Common Cuttle, or SEPIA (*Sepia officinalis*), is most familiar to us from the so-called "bones" which are found on the beach, and are sold by bird dealers for cage birds, and, I believe, are also used by chemists for producing tooth powder.

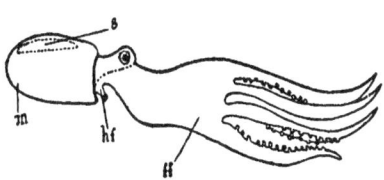

Side view of a Cuttle-fish swimming, as an example of the division of Mollusca called *Cephalopoda*: *ff*, fore-foot, produced into arms bearing suckers; *hf*, hind-foot or funnel—the dotted line shows upper edge of foot; *m*, mantle; *s*, concealed shell.

The animal itself is from 6 to 10 inches long, with a flattened body, shaped rather like a shield with a pointed end, and pale grey or brown in colour. It is not very likely to be found close to the shore, though sometimes it may be seen in a rock pool or caught in a net. None the less, it is an occupant usually of shallow waters. Enclosing the body is the mantle, a tough and muscular sac, expanding along the sides into a narrow fin. *Inside* the body, just under the skin of the back, is the "cuttle-bone," an internal shell (*sepiostaire*), which acts as a shield, and also as a float. Protruding from the front of the head are ten arms, eight of which are covered with tremendously powerful suckers, four rows on each arm; the remaining pair are "tentacles," twice as long as the others, swollen at the ends into a kind of club, covered with similar suckers. They can be entirely withdrawn into pockets below the eyes when not engaged in seizing upon their prey. When disturbed, the Sepia discharges a deep brown fluid from an "ink bag," which darkens the water around effectually; from this the paint known as sepia is prepared.

These animals are free swimmers, moving by means of their fins, but in addition they possess a means of discharging water through an organ known as a siphon, and by the recoil send themselves backwards at great pace through the water.

One other most interesting feature may be recorded : they can change colour with great rapidity. The cells under the skin contain various minute grains of pigment, and by expanding or contracting these cells the colour is concentrated or diffused, so that there is frequently a remarkable play of colour over the whole body, and the animal can match its surroundings with ease.

The Sepia's eggs, by-the-bye, are like clusters of grapes, and are frequently found on the shore cast up by storms.

MOLLUSCA

The Octopus (*Octopus vulgaris*) belongs to deeper water, and only small specimens are found round our shores. It has much the same habits as the Sepia, but does not discharge its ink so readily. Its principal food is small crabs, lobsters, and similar marine creatures, for which it hunts after dark. It has no internal " shell," like the Sepia, but two short rods of shelly matter in the mantle. The body is like a round bag; and the arms, eight in number, with two rows of suckers on each, are connected at their base by a web. The two eyes are fixed and staring. The arms of the Octopus are much longer than those of the other Cuttle-fish, and by their means the animal not only seizes and retains its prey, but is able to walk over smooth, perpendicular, and even overhanging surfaces. There are some fifty species known to scientists, some of which reach enormous sizes. Even the common species has been found with arms 8 feet long, though fortunately specimens of that size do not inhabit British waters, but other species have been found with bodies 8 or 9 feet long, and with arms 30 feet long.

As a rule it may be said that they are by nature timid animals, and the romantic stories of their attacking human beings are the work of pure imagination.

The Squid (*Loligo vulgaris*) is another member of the Cuttle-fish tribe, sometimes called the CALAMARY. It is longer and narrower than the Sepia, which it resembles, having the same eight short arms (studded with only two rows of suckers), and two longer tentacles. The mantle is also extended into two short angular " fins " at the lower end of the body, which ends in a sharp point. In place of the internal shell of the Sepia the Squid has a curious horny pen, with a long shaft in front of it.

It can both swim and crawl about head downwards. This species is often used for bait, as also for human food. It is pinkish or yellowish white in colour, with purplish brown spots, and is usually a foot or a foot and a half in length.

I have occasionally found the LITTLE CUTTLE (*Sepia rondeletii*) upon the shore (for example, in Guernsey and Jersey). This is a very small species, only some 2 inches in length, with rounded side-fins. It is easily identified.

Snails and Slugs.—These are land molluscs, though they have near relatives both in fresh and salt water. Here, however, we deal entirely with those two familiar slimy creatures which spoil our gardens.

The largest and commonest species is the Garden Snail (*Helix aspersa*), which hides in crevices of walls, heaps of stones, roots of plants, etc., and appears to go back after feeding to the same hiding-place time after time. Its brown shell with white tip is, unfortunately, well known to all garden lovers, and shows the lines of growth referred to above very plainly. It should be noted that the shell is in the form of a right-handed spiral, such shells being known as " dextral." Some of our land snails (for example, *Clausilia*) have shells which twist to the left, and are known as "sinistral." This applies to many seashells as well.

As is well known, snails can extend a large part of their bodies outside their shells at will; to see the under part in action, place a snail on a sheet of glass, and look through it as the snail moves.

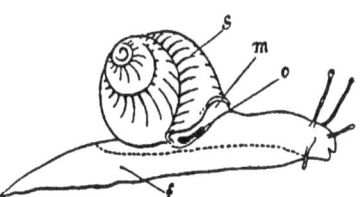

Side view of a living Snail, as an example of the division of Mollusca called *Gasteropoda*: *f*, foot—the dotted line shows the upper limit of the muscular portion; *m*, mantle; *o*, opening between mantle and body; *s*, shell.

Notice, first of all, the head, which has a very business-like mouth and lips; on the top are the "horns"—in reality two pairs of tentacles, the back and larger pair carrying at their tips a black spot, which is the eye. The other pair are sensitive organs of touch, and possibly of smell as well. These tentacles are easily withdrawn into the body, and the action is very curious. If you tied a string to the tip of one of the fingers of a glove, *on the inside*, and pulled, you would produce the same movement which in the snail's anatomy is produced by a muscle running up the hollow tentacle and fastened to the summit.

The ventral part of the snail is known as the "foot" and has powerful muscles, which may be seen in rippling movement on the glass. The part of the body which supports the shell is known as the "collar," and is cream coloured. In its right side may be seen a large hole opening and closing in a rhythmic manner. This is the breathing organ and leads to the lung cavity.

The slime which a snail leaves behind it comes chiefly from a special opening just under the mouth, but it is also continually exuding from the whole of the skin.

But as the snail feeds it leaves behind it very frequently another track, made by the rasping tongue or *radula*. Most snails are vegetable feeders, although some slugs are carnivorous. *Testacella*, for instance, devours earthworms. But in all cases the food is eaten by means of the remarkable rasp, a horny ribbon covered with thousands of teeth, set backwards, the whole worked to and fro against its hard horny upper jaw. This can be beautifully seen in water snails, if kept in an aquarium, when they browse upon the green algæ growing on the glass. Similar rasps are found in the sea "snails" or univalves. In the Garden Snail the tongue has 135 rows of 105 teeth—14,175 in all. Small wonder that it can do such damage!

All snails are hermaphrodite—that is, have both male and female organs, but the eggs are not fertilized except by mating. Before that act the snail discharges a remarkable dagger or spear-shaped dart of chalky substance into the body of its companion. That of the Garden Snail is exactly like a poniard, handle and all, and as the forms vary in different species, these darts form means of identification.

The eggs are laid in batches of thirty or more, deposited in moist places, each egg being in a round leathery shell, and hatching in about a month.

In winter the snail retires to some sheltered spot, or buries itself in the earth,

SLUGS AND SNAILS

closing up the mouth of the shell with a lid of slime and limy matter, which sets hard but remains porous.

Slugs are popularly supposed to be snails that have lost or not grown any shells; but this is not exactly true. In some species—for example, the Yellow Cellar Slug (*Limax flavus*) and the large grey species, with black spots, known as *Limax maximus*—there is a small shell under the skin. The Large Black Slug (*Arion ater*) has certain calcareous crystals in the same part of its body, and *Testacella* has a tiny visible shell, like a skullcap, on the hinder end of its body.

Slugs are more active than snails. It has been calculated that a slug would travel a mile in eight days, whilst a snail would take a fortnight to do so.

The British slugs form two classes (*Arionidæ* and *Limacidæ*), the largest and commonest being the Black Slug (*Arion ater*), which feeds not only on vegetable food but also on flesh, the excrement of other creatures, and even its own kith and kin. The young are yellowish white in colour.

Together with *Arion minimus*, this slug possesses the power of contracting its body into a round lump when alarmed. *A. minimus* has bands of colour on its sides which distinguish it from *A. ater*.

The Cellar Slugs (*Limax maximus* and *L. flavus*) are frequently found in cellars, it is true, but they also inhabit many other places. The former is usually grey, the latter yellow, with blue tentacles. The Tree Slug (*L. arborum* or *marginatus*) can lower itself from a branch to the ground by a cord of slime, and return by the same means. Altogether, we have nineteen species in the British islands.

To return to the snails, sufficient has been said about the Common Garden Snail; but there are many other species in these islands, some seventy in all, twenty-two belonging to the genus *Helix*. Others are very small, requiring a pocket lens to see them well: among these we may mention the BEAUTIFUL SNAIL (*H. pulchella*), the ROCK SNAIL, the PRICKLY SNAIL, the PLATED SNAIL, etc.

The Edible Snail (*H. pomatia*), sometimes called the ROMAN SNAIL, because it is said to have been introduced by the Romans, is the largest of all, and found still in certain parts of the country—Kent, Surrey, and Hants. The Common Snail also is eaten as a delicacy in some country districts, especially in the North.

The Striped Snail (*H. nemoralis*) is smaller than *H. aspersa*, and of red or yellow colour, striped with one to five spiral brown bands. This varies very much both in banding and colour. The rim or lip of the shell is dark brown; in *H. hortensis*, which is otherwise very similar, it is white.

The Hairy Snail (*H. hispida*) is a small brown species found in hedges, with minute hairs on the shell.

H. virgata, about $\frac{1}{2}$ inch in diameter, abounds on chalky downs near the sea. White, with one or more brown bands.

Hyalina crystallina is a member of a genus of small snails with smooth, glistening shells, some smelling distinctly of garlic. This particular species is white.

The genus *Pupa* contains species with minute brown shells, like seeds.

At this point we may as well deal with a few curious members of the *Gasteropoda*, which for want of a better name we may well call " Sea Slugs."

They resemble to some degree our land slugs, but they are not by any means closely related ; and as they carry their breathing apparatus exposed on the back and sides, they are called *Nudi-branchiata*, or Naked-gilled molluscs.

They may be looked for especially on rocky coasts, and if placed in clear water the beauty of their tentacles and the branchial plumes which form their lungs will be seen.

A common example is the **Sea Hare** (*Aplysia depilans*), which when contracted appears a rounded mass of brown jelly, but when expanded has a head and tentacles like the head and ears of a hare. It is some 3 inches long, and possesses the power of exuding a purple fluid, once considered to be deadly poison. It is, however, entirely harmless.

The **Sea Lemon** (*Doris tuberculata*) is about the same length, resembling the half of a cut lemon, both in its colour and warty surface. It has eight gills or branchiæ, feathery, and like the petals of a flower when expanded. There are several hundred species, of which *Doris johnstoni*, the **Sponge Slug**, is creamy in colour, spotted brown, like a sponge in appearance and touch, and feeds on sponges.

The **Crowned Eolis** (*Eolis coronata*), found under stones, is the most beautiful, having rows of scarlet and blue gills crossing the back. It devours sea anemones and zoophytes.

Fresh-water Molluscs.

It will be more convenient to group together the various shells to be found in fresh water. Both in rivers and ponds certain molluscs are to be found which are closely allied to the more familiar marine species. Four species of fresh-water mussel belong to the British Isles, three belonging to the genus *Unio*, the fourth to *Anodonta*. The *Unios* have the two valves of the shell united by strongly marked hinge teeth, but *Anodonta*, as its name implies (Greek *an*, " without ; " *odontes*, " teeth "), has none. Another characteristic feature which helps to distinguish the two classes lies in the fact that all *Unios* have thick shells, while *Anodonta* possess very thin ones.

The **Swan Mussel** (*Anodonta cygnea*) is 4 to 6 inches long, greenish brown in colour, though often with many white patches, where the surface layer has been removed. There are plainly marked lines running parallel with the margin, and these, be it again noted, are the " lines of growth."

The **Painter's Mussel** (*Unio pictorum*) is so called because once its shells were used for holding water-colour paints.

The **Pearl Mussel** (*Unio margaritifer*) is the fresh-water mussel which produced the pearls (and still does so in Scotland, Wales, and Ireland), for which,

"SHELLS"

in old days, there was considerable trade among the ancient Britons. Of univalves a considerable number of species occur in British waters, the commonest being *Limnæa stagnalis*, to be found in every stagnant pool or ditch. It has a thin shell, spirally coiled, conical in shape, $1\frac{1}{2}$ to 2 inches long. It is frequently seen travelling, shell downwards, along the under surface of the water. If kept in an aquarium, its eggs will often be seen in small gelatinous masses attached to weeds, or even to the glass.

The **Fresh-water Limpet** (*Anchylus fluviatilis*) is no near relative to the marine limpets, but gets its name from its similarity of appearance. It is very small, the shell seldom more than $\frac{1}{4}$ inch in length. It is found in streams. A similar species, but smaller still (*A. locustris*), is found in still water.

The **Pond Snail**, RAM'S HORN, or TRUMPET SNAIL (*Planorbis corneus*), has a large flat spirally coiled shell. It is quite common. When disturbed it discharges a purple-coloured fluid, probably as a means of defence as the Cuttlefish eject their ink. It is a vegetable feeder.

Paludina vivipara is common in the South of England. It belongs to a species which breathes by means of gills. Its name (*vivipara*) reminds us that it retains its eggs inside the body until they are hatched. The shell is over an inch long and nearly as wide, and has an *operculum*.

Bithynia is a genus having shells $\frac{1}{4}$ to $\frac{1}{2}$ inch long, provided with *opercula*. *B. tentaculus*, the commonest, has a shell of about six coils. Frequent in canals and ditches.

Marine Shells.

. Probably every visitor to the seaside has begun as a child to collect the shells to be found on every shore. My space is becoming limited, and I must confine myself to a brief description of some of the commoner species.

UNIVALVES.

1. **The Common Whelk** (*Buccinum undatum*).—This species is responsible for the clusters of yellowish white eggs found on the seashore, and often called "sponges," varying in size from a small to a large cricket ball, and of a parchment-like texture. When first laid they are very small, no bigger than a pin's head, but they rapidly swell as soon as water reaches the inside. This species, though common enough, is only apparent on the beach in the shape of its large empty shells, for its habitat is from low-water mark to a hundred fathoms.

2. **The Netted Dog-whelk** (*Nassa reticulata*) is much smaller. The shell is coloured brownish yellow outside, pinkish white within, and is covered with broad grooves, crossed by fine lines at right angles, producing a netted appearance. It is both a vegetarian and a carnivorous feeder. It possesses a toothribbon of nearly 1,000 teeth.

3. **The Sting Winkle** (*Murex erinaceus*) is white or yellowish white, about $1\frac{1}{2}$ inch long, with several high notched ridges. It has no "sting," but it

preys upon other shellfish, drilling a hole in its victim's shell, and then, thrusting its toothed tongue through the orifice, devours it at leisure.

4. **The Red Whelk** (*Fusus antiquus*) is larger than *Buccinum*, is iron-red in colour, and is often sold for food.

5. **The Cowry** (*Cyprœa europea*).—The *living* Cowry presents a very different appearance from the shells so plentiful on our shores, for its mantle almost entirely enwraps the shell, on the upper part of which you may see a pale streak showing where the edges of the mantle met in the days when it was alive. The shell is slightly flesh tinted above (sometimes with three chocolate blotches), and ornamented by fine transverse ribs.

6. **The Smooth Margin Shell** (*Erato lœvis*) is smaller and has the lip curved outward (instead of inward, like the Cowry), forming a distinct margin. It is white and smooth.

7. **The Periwinkle** (*Littorina littorea*) needs no description, being familiar both to sight and taste, for this is the species so often used for food.

8. **The Dog Periwinkle** (*L. rudis*), which is slightly larger and has a stouter shell, and a deep purplish colour, though almost as common, is not edible, for the reason that it retains its eggs inside its shell until hatched, and this makes it very gritty.

The small red or yellow shells found amongst the periwinkles belong to a variety of the same species (*L. littorea*).

9. **The Purpura** (*Purpura lapillus*), or PURPLE, is a form of Limpet, but its shell is not unlike the Dog Periwinkle in shape; indeed it is often known as " DOG WINKLE." It has an operculum, unlike the limpets, and when disturbed exudes a purple liquid, from which the famous Roman purple dye was obtained. This is contained in a small sac, and is at first white, but changes colour rapidly on exposure to light.

The shell is white, with two or three bands of yellowish brown. The eggs are fastened down to stones or little stalks. The Purple drills holes in other shells and devours the inmates.

10. **The Wentletrap** (*Scalaria communis*) is sometimes called the " STAIRCASE SHELL," the ridges that run round it being not unlike a circular staircase. It has a beautiful white colour.

11. **The Common Limpet** (*Patella vulgata*) needs no description, but is of great interest from various points of view. It can recess the rock on which it rests so as to form a shallow pit in which the edge of the shell fits neatly. This it does by scraping away the rock with its tongue (radula), armed with its 2,000 teeth ; and the sound of the scraping can actually be *heard* on a still day, when the rocks are out of water. After grazing on its vegetarian diet at night it returns to the same spot for the day, settling itself down, so to speak, upon its bedplate!

It has a broad foot, which exudes a thick glue, by which it literally sticks itself to the rock (and *not* by suction, as is so often imagined).

12. **The Key-hole Limpet** (*Fissurella grœca*) belongs to deep water, but

PLATE XXXVII.

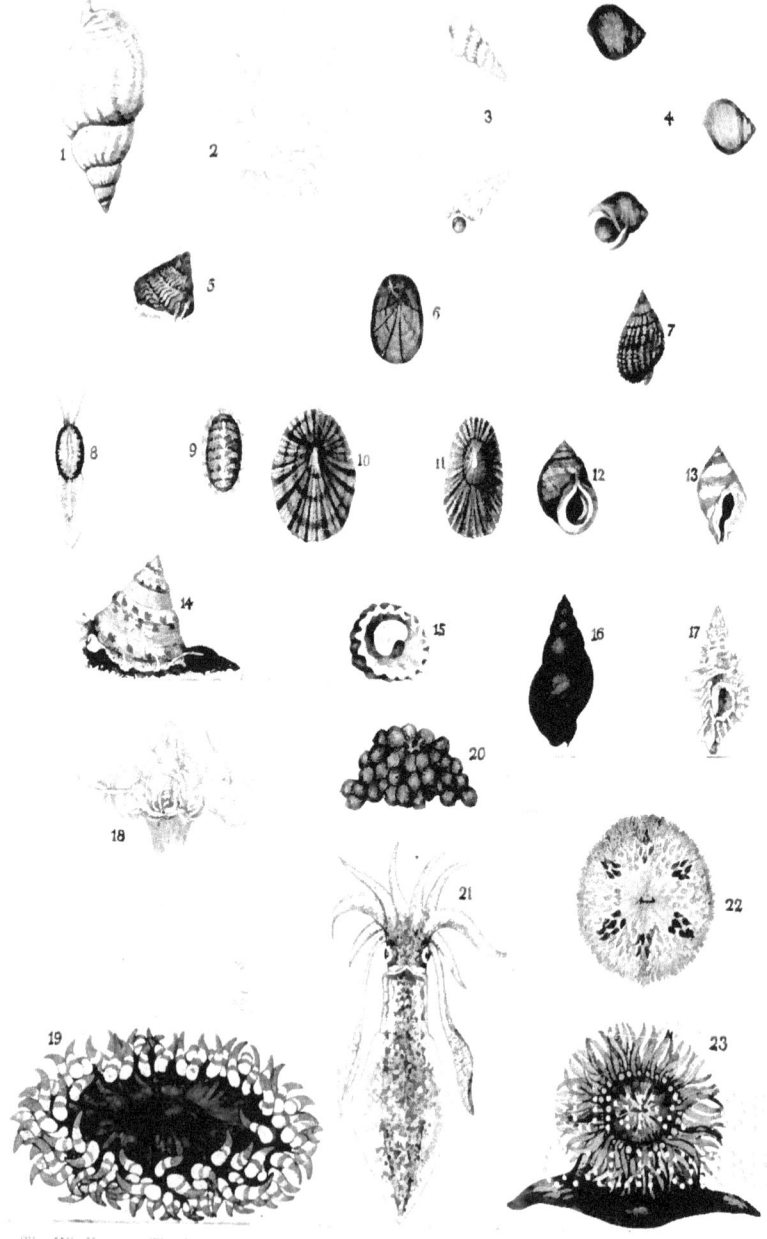

1. The Whelk. 2. The Eggs of Whelk. 3. The Wentletrap. 4. The Sea Snail. 5. The Grey Top. 6. The Smooth Limpet. 7. The Dog Whelk. 8. The Cowry. 9. The Chiton. 10. The Limpet. 11. The Key-hole Limpet. 12. The Periwinkle. 13. The Purpura. 14. The Painted Top. 15. The Cup-and-Saucer Limpet. 16. The Dog Periwinkle. 17. The Sting Winkle. 18. The Snake-locked Anemone. 19. The Thick-armed Anemone. 20. The Eggs of Cuttle. 21. The Cuttle. 22. The Daisy Anemone. 23. The Smooth Anemone.

may sometimes be found at spring tides at extreme tide limit. Its shell is ridged from the peak to the margin, and at the top is a hole shaped like a keyhole. Through this the water, passing over the gills, is squirted out by the mollusc.

13. **The Smooth Limpet** (*Patella pellucida*) is much smaller than the common species, and has a thin delicate shell, pale brown, with eight or nine narrow blue lines running down it. It will be found at extreme low-tide limit, where it feeds on the Great Oar-weed.

14. **The Cup-and-Saucer Limpet** is a South Coast mollusc, to be identified by its internal appearance. Inside the shell is a curved plate like a cup, the shell itself forming the saucer. To make it complete, at the end of its tooth-ribbon is an organ like a teaspoon!

15. **The Painted Top** (*Trochus magus*).—One of a number of cone-shaped shells, coming to a sharp point, usually beautifully coloured. This species has many streaks, dots, and patches of scarlet, pink, blue, white, and other colours, though the colouring is often damaged. The ridges of the shell are bold and plain. It is, like the rest, a vegetable feeder. All have opercula.

16. **The Grey Top** (*T. cinereus*) is smaller, yellowish grey, with dark zigzag marks.

17. **The Common Top** (*T. zizyphinus*) is not so plentiful, but may be identified by its reddish zigzag lines.

18. **The Chiton**, or MAIL SHELL (*Chiton cinereus*), has a remarkable shell, not unlike in appearance that of a tortoise. It consists of a number of plates (eight altogether), slightly overlapping, and, like the Wood-louse, it can roll itself up into a ball. It is ashy grey and is found on rocks. Length about $\frac{1}{2}$ inch.

19. **The Bristly Mail Shell** (*C. fascicularis*) has small bunches of bristles along the shell border opposite each plate.

20. **The Smooth Mail Shell** (*C. lævis*) is known by its reddish colour and glossy smoothness, and by the possession of a central ridge.

21. **The Marbled Mail Shell** (*C. marmoreus*) is the largest of the Chitons ($1-1\frac{1}{4}$ inch). The colour is a general marbling of brown and yellow.

22. **The Necklace Natica** (*Natica monilifera*) is a very familiar species, rounded, smooth, and glossy (having an operculum), with three lines of arrow-heads upon it. It gets its English name from its eggs, which are glued together into a broad spiral band not unlike a necklace. When alive, the mantle nearly covers the shell.

23. **The Turret Shell** (*Turitella communis*) is spiral in form, with ridges running from apex to mouth. It is fairly large.

24. **The Ruddy Pyramid** (*Chemnitsia rufescens*) is smaller, and the ridges run crosswise instead of down.

25. **The Horn Shell** (*Cerithium reticulatum*) is spiral also, and marked by rows of regular dots.

26. **The Pelican's Foot** (*Aporrhais pes-pelicani*), about 1½ inch long and very thick, has its shell expanded into a sort of lip or lobe, giving a fancied resemblance to the webbed foot of a water fowl.

27. **Pheasant Shell** (*Phasianella pullus*) is very small (¼ inch), and must be sought for carefully, but is quite common. It is smooth, white, or pale yellow, thickly covered with fine crimson lines.

28. **The Hungarian Cap** (*Pileopsis hungaricus*) is a brownish or whitish shell, which has a kind of curved beak, or horn, giving the appearance of a "Cap of Liberty." It is found frequently on the South Coast.

29. **The Tusk,** or TOOTH SHELLS (*Dentalium*), have already been referred to.

BIVALVES.

1. **The Oyster** (*Ostrea edulis*) has two unequal valves, as the shells are technically called, upon the left of which, being larger and more hollow, it always lies. It is only to be found in places where the bottom is muddy, because upon a sandy bed the oyster would be in danger of getting sand into the hinges of the shells, and thus be unable to close them, in which case it would quickly die of suffocation. Hence estuaries are a very favourite site for an oyster bed.

There are about a hundred different species found all over the world, most of them being edible.

The oyster spawns in May or June—the "spat" or spawn resembling fine slaty dust. A single oyster lays nearly 1,000,000 eggs, and she keeps them in her *gills* (known more popularly as the "beard") until they are hatched—that is, from May to July—during which time oysters are "out of season." Then she opens her shells, and squirts out the young ones in a cloud not unlike a puff of smoke. Each young one is provided with swimming organs (*cilia*), like fine eyelashes. Later on they sink down and fasten themselves to a rock or stone, and thenceforward they never move again. They reach their full size from the fifth to the seventh year.

They obtain their food in the following way: The *mouth* is under the "beard" or gills, and these organs not only suck out the air (which is in the water), but they filter out every minute particle of decaying matter upon which the oyster can feed, and thus pass it on to the mouth.

In many places oysters are cultivated—that is, grown under protection—for example, at the mouth of the Thames, at Whitstable, and elsewhere. When protected thus they attain their full size in four years.

It scarcely need be said that the spawn is greedily eaten by fishes, but it is not so well known that the Five-fingered Starfish is the greatest enemy of the largest oysters. It grasps the oyster firmly, and, when the shell opens slightly, sucks out the inmate!

The inner lining of the shell is known as *Mother-of-pearl*, and if a grain of sand or other foreign substance should get inside between the animal and the shell, the oyster covers it with the same material (called *Nacre*), and this forms a *pearl*.

2. **The Saddle Oyster** (*Anomia ephippium*).—Very often mistaken for a young oyster of the edible species. This species attaches itself to a rock by a muscular plug, which passes through an oval hole in the under shell near the hinge and sticks like a sucker to the rock. It may often be found attached to other molluscs, and hence derives its name of " SADDLE " OYSTER.

As it grows older it has the habit of altering its form, to adapt itself to the object on which it rests.

3. **The Cockle** (*Cardium edule*).—One of the commonest objects of the seashore, with its shells marked with bold ridges. The cockle gains its name of *Cardium* (Greek *kardia*, " heart ") from the heart-shaped appearance of the shells when viewed end on. It lies buried underneath the sand, and I have no doubt many of my readers have seen the spouts of water rising from the sand at low tide, the sign of the cockles buried below. It needs skill to dig them up, for the cockle possesses a powerful " foot," and can often burrow faster than a man can dig.

4. **The Spiny Cockle**, or RED NOSE (*Cardium aculeatum*), has a " foot " of a bright red colour. It is much larger than *C. edule*, has spines or prickles on its shells, and is much sought after for food.

5. **The Mussel** (*Mytilus edulis*).—Found often on the submerged piles of piers and breakwaters, where it has fastened itself down firmly, in clusters, by means of a bundle of threads known as *byssus*. So strong is this thread that mussels are valuable on many parts of the coast in keeping structures from being damaged or disturbed by the force of the water. The story of the bridge across the Torridge River is too well known to be repeated here as an illustration.

6. **The Horse Mussel** (*Modiola modiolus*), 5 or 6 inches long, is found occasionally on the beach. It is a burrowing mollusc, and weaves its byssus into an enormous tangled mass with sand or gravel. It is not used for food.

7. **The Variable Scallop**, or PECTEN (*Pecten varius*).—Scallops are familiar to us, if only by means of the fishmonger's shop, where the largest British species, the **Common Scallop**, QUIN, or PECTEN (*Pecten opercularis*), is sold for food. This is a deep-sea species, occurring in beds. It is not fixed like the oyster, but can swim in a curious way by opening and shutting its shell quickly, thus expelling the water and shooting itself to some distance. (The young, however, can attach themselves to rocks by means of byssus.) As it moves through the water it waves up and down a fringe of graceful feelers, by which it obtains its food. At their base is a row of black dots, said to be eyes. All scallops have a peculiarity in the pair of *ears* at the hinge of the shells; these ears are never of equal size.

The Variable Pecten is so called because it varies so much in colour— crimson, pink, yellow, or white, with dark red blotches. It has twenty-eight ridges, each of them having a row of small spikes.

THE BRITISH NATURE BOOK

8. **The Radiated Scallop** (*P. radiatus*) is rather rare, but may be known by the six or seven ridges running down it. It is also a variable species, generally reddish brown spotted with white.

9. **The Hunchback Scallop** has one of its valves so much deeper than the other that it has a hunch-backed appearance. It changes its shape very much as it grows, so that its shells might often be taken to be injured specimens. It is white, with reddish mottles.

10. **The Sunset Shell** (*Psammobia ferroensis*).—Very common in some localities, but entirely absent in others. Its name is given on account of the beautiful colouring of the inside—rosy pink, orange-yellow, or crimson-streaked, suggesting a sunset sky. The outside is white. There are four British species.

11. **The Wedge Shells** (*Donax*) are very similar, but the hinder end is wedge-shaped or pointed instead of round. They are similarly but not so strongly coloured. The **Common Wedge** (*Donax anatinus*) is the most familiar.

12. **The Gaper** (*Mya arenaria*).—So called because the shells are open at the top, through which the siphon tubes project. In some parts of the country it is used for food, the popular name being "OLD MAID."

13. **The Piddock** (*Pholas dactylus*) is 3 to 5 inches long, with a white shell, thin and delicate, covered in front with rasp-like ridges; the two valves not united by a hinge. There are, besides, three small additional valves to be seen on living specimens.

14. **The Little Piddock**, RED-NOSED BORER (*Saxicava rugosa*), has a shell much distorted and varied in shape. In an early stage it is symmetrical, having two minute teeth on each valve; but these are absent in older specimens. The shell is covered with ridges and wrinkles. The ends of the siphon are crimson, and may be seen sometimes protruding from a cliff face in which the borers have lodged themselves.

[The empty shells of these two species (Nos. 13 and 14), and of other allied ones, may be found near limestone or chalk cliffs, and if you examine the rocks at low tide you will find them perforated by large or small oval holes, several in close proximity, the work of these extraordinary shellfish. How they do it is uncertain—probably by taking a firm purchase with their foot and twisting the shell half-way in one direction, and then reversing the motion. When the burrow is choked with material thus excavated, the Pholas clears it with a jet of water from its siphon. In this way this mollusc is doubtless responsible for a considerable share in the undermining of our sea cliffs, and may even have helped in bygone ages to cut the neck of land that joined this country to France, thus making Great Britain an island.]

15. **The Ship Worm** (*Teredo navalis*) is in reality a mollusc and a bivalve, though it looks like a worm, about as long and as thick as a pencil. The two valves are very small, and at the head end of the body; they used to be considered jaws. It bores into timber, and can do much harm to wooden hulls and pier piles, in which it burrows its chamber, lining it with a shelly coating.

16. **The Razor** (*Solen siliqua*).—These are very familiar and need no de-

PLATE XXXVIII.

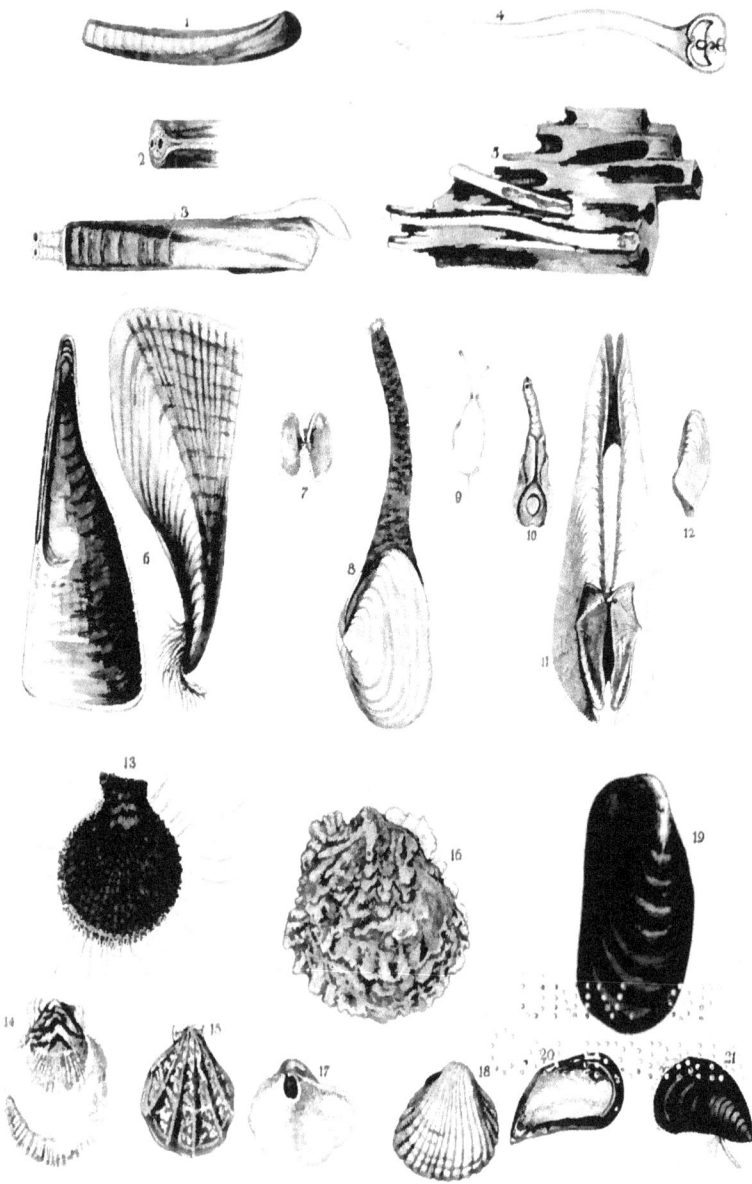

1. The Razor.   2. Top of Razor (from front).   3. The Sabre Razor.   4. The Ship-worm.
5. Wood bored by Ship-worms.   6. The Pinna.   7. Inside of Sunset Shell.   8. The Gaper.
9. The Sunset Shell.   10. The Little Piddock.   11. The Piddock.   12. The Little Piddock.
13. Variable Scallop.   14. Radiated Scallop.   15. Hunchback Scallop.   16. Oyster.   17. Saddle
Oyster.   18. Cockle.   19. Horse Mussel.   20. Horse Mussel (inside).   21. The Mussel.

scription. The mollusc lies buried in sand, and never leaves its burrow except on compulsion by a pinch of salt or the spade of a bait-seeking fisherman. The species with straight edges is the **Pod Razor** (*S. siliqua*).

17. **The Sabre Razor** (*S. ensis*) has a curved outline and is smaller.

18. **The Smooth Venus** (*Cytherea chione*).—There are a number of species belonging to the Venus shells, but they are deep-sea inhabitants. This species, however, is large enough to attract attention when it is washed up after a storm on our southern or western coasts. It is 3 or $3\frac{1}{2}$ inches across, white inside, pale brown with a touch of pink outside, with lines of lighter colour and darker radiating bands.

19. **The Smooth Artemis** (*Artemis lincta*) and (20) the **Rayed Artemis** (*Artemis exoleta*) are round shells with a slight indentation at the beak, thick and heavy, the latter with fine concentric ridges and rays of pinky brown, the former smaller and smooth, frequently washed up in winter.

21. **The Tapes**, or CARPET SHELLS, have usually beautiful patterns suggesting tapestry or carpets.

The **Cross-cut Carpet Shell** (*Tapes decussata*) is drab-coloured, with ridges radiating from the beak, *cross-cut* by fine lines.

22. **The Golden Carpet Shell** (*Tapes aurea*) is smaller, with shallow concentric lines, of a yellow or golden hue.

23. **The Comb Shell** (*Pectunculus glycimeris*) is fairly common, and has thick round valves about 2 inches long, smooth to the touch, but under the pocket lens showing many fine lines from beak to rim. The colour is reddish, set off by long sharp white wedges; very variable. On the under side is a broad flange with twenty-two teeth in two rows—the comb, in fact, which gives the shell its name.

24. **The Trough Shells** are plentiful, and must be briefly typed by the **Rayed Trough Shell** (*Mactra stultorum*), smooth, shaded brown, with a number of white radiations.

25. **The Unrayed Trough Shell** (*M. luteola*), as its name indicates, is similar, but without the rays.

26. **The Otter Shells** (*Lutraria*) are the largest British bivalves, some 5 inches long, not unlike Razor Shells, especially in their inability to close the *end* of their shells. They live in mud, the commonest being *L. elliptica*.

27. **The Tellen Shells** (*Tellina*) are delicate, flattened specimens, finely grooved and with broad bands of pink.

The **Thick Tellen** (*T. crassa*) is thick only in name, and has the pink bands radiating from the beak, the interior being tinted pink or orange. All the members of the genus burrow in sandy mud.

CHAPTER XII.

Echinodermata.

THIS name is applied to a sub-kingdom of invertebrate animals which belong -entirely to the sea, having no fresh-water or terrestrial representatives. It means "prickly-skinned," and is given to them because the skin is often furnished with prickles or spikes or horny bosses.

At the present day five kinds occur in our seas, four of which we can find near the shore—namely, Sea Urchins, Starfishes, Brittle-stars, and Sea Cucumbers. The fifth is the Sea Lily, found only in deep water.

One remarkable feature characterizes all the Echinodermata—"everything is governed by the number five." In most cases there are five rays or a multiple of five, the teeth or jaws are five, the boundaries of the plates, and so forth.

The most familiar creatures belonging to this group are the Starfish, so we will begin with them.

The Common Five-fingered Starfish (*Uraster rubens*).—To be found in shallow pools, or cast up on the shore. On the under side of its five rays are the hundreds of "legs" by which it moves. Place a live starfish upside down in some water, and the "legs"—which are in reality remarkable suckers, worked by hydraulic power—will soon be protruded and be seen madly waving and kicking in all directions. Through a pocket lens these suckers will be found to be tipped with a little cup—the sucker proper—and the starfish advances by taking hold of the ground with the suckers on its foremost rays and pulling up the hinder ones; then, holding on by their suckers, it pushes forward the other rays, and so moves in a manner not unlike that of a caterpillar.

As you observe the under side, notice the deep groove along each ray. This is characteristic of the true starfish, the sand-stars and brittle-stars not possessing this feature. At the tip of each ray is a red spot called the "eye," which is sensitive to light. The mouth is in the middle of the under side, and opens straight into the stomach, which branches off into each of the rays.

On the upper side, close to the centre, is a small round stony knob, which is a minute filter, technically known as the "madreporiform plate." Through this the water is taken in to work by pressure the sucker feet, either forcing them out and distending them, or, when the pressure is relaxed, leaving them

STARFISH

empty and limp. A wonderful system of pipes conveys the water through each ray to the sucker feet.

Amongst these sucker feet may be found many tiny stalks, ending, not in suckers, but in three claws, continually opening and shutting. These are "pedicels," and their business is to take hold of objects in lieu of the sucker feet, as also to keep the latter free from dirt and other clogging matter.

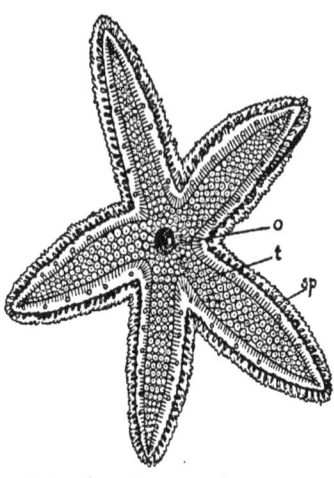

Under view of common Starfish, as an example of Echinodermata: o, mouth; sp, spines; t, tube-feet.

The upper side is always rough to the touch, being covered with limy plates and bosses, in patterns which help to distinguish the different species.

Starfishes feed on molluscs, often wreaking considerable havoc in oyster and mussel beds, and an extraordinary characteristic is seen in their manner of feeding. The mouth being small, few, if any, shellfish could be swallowed; but the starfish protrudes its stomach through its mouth, surrounds the shellfish, reduces it to a fluid condition by its gastric juice, and thus takes it back through the mouth to its "inside."

Another strange fact is that if a starfish loses a ray it can soon grow a new one; and if the creature is cut in two, each half begins to throw out new rays, and thus it can "multiply by division," if occasion arises.

The female lays her eggs in a little heap, and, bending her rays over them, stands as it were on tiptoe guarding them. The larva is a peculiar free-swimming creature with two ciliated bands about an inch long, long known as *Bipinnaria asterigera*, and classed among jelly-fish until its true relationship was established, about seventy years ago. Inside it the adult form of the starfish is developed.

The **Spiny Star** (*Uraster glacialis*) is not so common as the preceding, but is much larger. The bosses on the upper side are much more spiny, and the colour, instead of being red, is greenish.

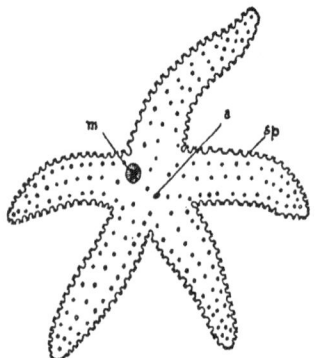

Upper view of common Starfish, as an example of Echinodermata: a, anus; m, madreporite; sp, spines.

The **Eyed Cribella** (*Cribella oculata*) is purple, and quite smooth to the touch.

The Sun Star (*Solaster papposa*) is recognized by its red colour, blotched with white, and its twelve or fifteen rays.

The Gibbous Starlet, or CUSHION STAR (*Asterina gibbosa*), is like a little cushion, the space between the rays being filled up.

The Bird's-foot Starfish (*A. ornithopus*) has its rays joined together by a membrane, much like the toes of a duck's foot, and is thus immediately recognized.

The Feather Stars are beautiful animals, living in deep water. The Rosy Feather Star (*Comatula rosacea*) has five rays, each forking into two, and feathered with egg-holding appendages. It is tinted bright rose-red.

The Brittle-stars have five active arms, which, being jointed, move freely in all directions. They readily snap off their arms when alarmed. They are to be sought for under stones at low-water mark.

One of them (*Ophiocoma neglecta*) is very minute, and although common is, seldom seen, on account of its size; but it is a most interesting object in an aquarium.

The Red Brittle-star (*Ophiothrix rosula*) is quite common, and one of the handsomest and most variable in colour; but it is very seldom taken whole, as it sheds its arms at the slightest touch. Parts of it are found often enough among the debris in a fisherman's boat.

The Sea Cucumber (*Cucumaria pentactes*) at first sight would not appear to have any relationship with starfish or sea urchins, but it is in reality closely allied. The body has no spines or plates, and is much more like that of a slug; but there are ten rays round the head, and the body has five distinct angles, and there are other internal points of resemblance.

It is greyish white in colour, and is found in dark rock pools. When alarmed it throws off portions of its *inside* organs—its teeth, throat lining, etc.—becoming almost a mere skin, but it speedily recovers and grows new organs.

SEA URCHINS.

These are very unlike starfish in outward appearance, but closer study reveals their near relationship. The fact is that if you were to take a starfish and double up its rays until the tips touch, and then petrify it, you would have a sea urchin, for this latter has a limy shell consisting of five segments, covered with spines in place of the starfish's bosses of lime, and with two rows of small holes on each segment, through which the feet are protruded when required. There is also the same hydraulic system of tubes and pipes as in the starfish. At the meeting-place of the five segments are five " ocular plates," each bearing an eye-spot. The spines of starfish are movable, and when a section of one is seen under the microscope it presents a most exquisite patterned appearance.

There is a large mouth, and five teeth, with enamel-pointed tips—the whole forming an elaborate masticating structure still known as the " Lantern of

PLATE XXXIX.

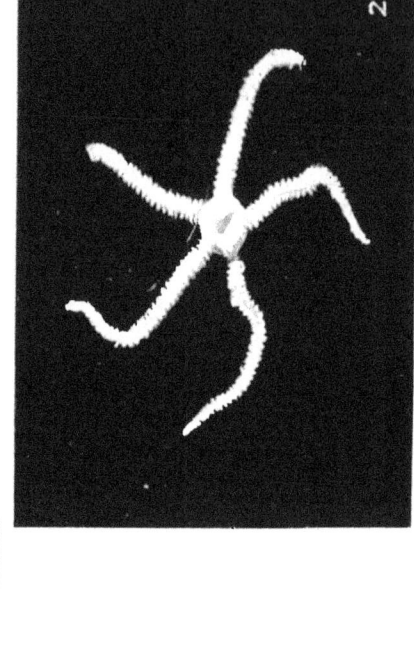
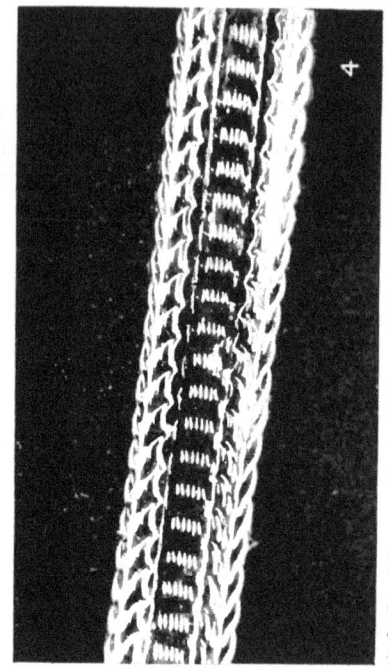
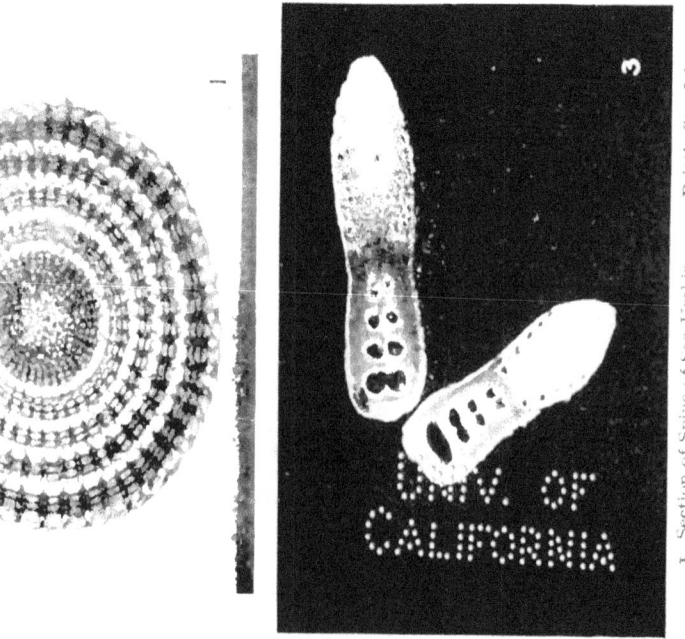

1. Section of Spine of Sea Urchin.   2. Brittle Starfish.   3. Jaws of Brittle Starfish.   4. Part of Palate of Whelk, showing "Teeth."

Aristotle," because the philosopher so named first likened it to a lantern. The test or shell of the sea urchin is composed of some 600 five-sided plates of lime.

The Common Sea Urchin (*Echinus esculentus*) is nowhere frequent in the shore pools, but must be sought for just below low-tide mark. Its Latin name shows us that it can be used for food.

The Purple-tipped Sea Urchin (*E. miliaris*) is much smaller and commoner. It has its spines tipped with purple. This urchin has a habit of covering itself with fragments of weed, shell, etc., for the purpose of concealing itself, so that very often it escapes observation.

Although the most familiar sea urchins are those which are covered like a hedgehog with spines, there are others which are almost bare, or covered with fine downy hairs. Among these are the very light and fragile Heart- or Shield-shaped Urchins often found on the seashore. They are mud-loving species, to which a thick array of spines would be most inconvenient; so it comes about that the spines have vanished or been modified in the scanty flattened golden down. They are sluggish movers, feeding on seaweeds and organisms in the mud. The Heart-shaped Smooth Urchins belong to the genus *Spatangus*; the Shield-shaped, to *Clypeaster*.

CHAPTER XIII.
Polyzoa—Annelida—Platyhelminthes.

Polyzoa.

THIS is a small group of animals which, with one exception, form colonies and live a kind of communal life. Imagine a solitary individual settling down and building a house, and then producing other individuals which occupy separate rooms in this ever-increasing block of tenements, so that at last there is an enormous colony living in the one house, and you have a picture of the complex life of the Polyzoa. The separate members of the colony are exceedingly minute, and must be examined under the microscope.

Some of them are found in fresh water—for example, *Cristatella, Lophopus*, and *Plumatella* (illustrated in *The Young People's Microscope Book*); but the more familiar forms are marine, and are known as Sea Mats, Sea Moss, Bird's-head Coralline, etc.

The Sea Mat (*Flustra foliacea*) is perhaps the most usually observed, for, though it is a deep-sea form, it is thrown up on the beach in large quantities, looking like seaweed—hemp-coloured, papery in texture, and built up in fronds much like *Fucus serratus*. Examined with a strong lens, the fronds are seen to be covered with a network of chambers or cells, in each of which one of the colony lives; and the chamber is lined with a horny substance secreted by its inmate, the *Polypite*, showing its connection with the Molluscs in their shell-building characteristics. Through a small opening the polypite thrusts its head and fringe of tentacles, thus obtaining food and air.

Each chamber of the Sea Mat is thus occupied by a complete individual living an independent life, in this way differing entirely from the Zoophytes (among the Hydrozoa), which have a common living base, known as the *cœnosarc* (" common flesh "). In the case of the Polyzoa the separate individuals live in a common house. Each can multiply by budding, and eggs also are laid, from which a free-swimming larva is hatched, which in time settles down on a rock and, developing its horny chamber, becomes the founder of another colony.

One of the most curious facts of such colonies is that not all the individual members are alike—some have heads like birds' beaks with snapping bills; others end in a whip-like lash. It appears that these must act in some way for the benefit of the community—perhaps as scavengers, soldiers, or police!

WORMS

There are several varieties of Sea Mats (*Flustra*), which will be found among the debris on the shore.

Many other species of Polyzoa will be found attached to seaweeds, matting the surfaces of the larger fronds or encrusting the others. Foliaceous Coralline (*Membranipora pilosa*) is one such species, looking like narrow strings of velvet. The Creeping Coralline (*Scrupocellaria reptans*) is another of the 250 species to be found round our coasts. *Lepralia* is seen as a sort of stony scurf covering seaweeds. *Alcyonidium gelatinosum* is not unlike a stick of barley sugar.

Annelida.

To this group belong the Segmented Worms and the Leeches, etc. Almost all the former have minute bristles (*setæ*) concealed in the skin, which act as feet for purposes of locomotion, and for this reason they are known as *Bristle Worms*.

The Common Earthworm (*Lumbricus communis*) is the most familiar, yet few people realize the immense importance of these lowly animals. " It may be doubted," says Darwin, " whether there are many other creatures which have played so important a part in the history of the world."

The part they play in opening and renewing the soil can be realized when Darwin's figures are mentioned. He states that there are over 53,000 worms in an acre of garden, which pass some ten tons of soil per year through their bodies, and bring up mould from below at the rate of 3 inches in thickness in fifteen years!

Points to be noted in examining the Earthworm are the ringed body, with its iridescent skin and curious swollen girdle, and especially the four double rows of minute bristles, eight in each segment, by means of which it moves. It feeds on vegetable matter in the soil. It lays eggs in a cocoon formed by secretions from the skin. This cocoon is gradually stripped off from the body, and, when free, the ends close.

We have some twenty different species of Earthworms, amongst which the Lob-worm and the Brand-worm are the most brightly coloured, and are very active.

The Marine Bristle-worms form two divisions: (1) Those which move about freely like the Earthworm; (2) those which live in a tube or case.

The Lug-worm (*Arenicola piscatorum*), which burrows in the sand, lining the walls of its tunnel with a sticky substance, is at first sight a repulsive animal; but if put into clear water it becomes more attractive, its bristles and the thirteen pairs of red gills lending beauty to its appearance.

The Sabella (*Sabella alveolaria*) lives in tubes built up of grains of sand stuck together, and is found in numbers at low-water mark. The Sabellæ move up and down these tubes by means of their bristles, and can leave them entirely at will. Placed in an aquarium, they will soon start making new tubes, choosing the grains of sand and placing them in position in a remarkable manner by means of their trowel-like antennæ. The Sabellæ breathe by means of a beautiful plume of feathered gills protruding from their sand-tubes.

The Serpula makes the limy white tubes often found on stones and old shells, and has an exquisite plume of red or scarlet gills, to be seen if the stone is placed in a glass of salt water. It also possesses tufts of bristles, by which it moves up and down its tube; but it can vanish within with a suddenness which is almost startling. This is due to a row of hooked teeth on its back, 13,000 odd in number.

Notice the curious stopper-like organ (a modified tentacle) by which the Serpula blocks the entrance to its home. There are several species to be found.

The Spirorbis is very like the Serpula, but coils its tube in a flat spiral. It is exceedingly common on stones and weeds.

The Terebella (*Terebella figulus*) is some 4 inches long, and makes a tube covered with grains of sand of a tough and almost leathery consistency. The Shellbinder (*T. littoralis*) uses particles of broken shells instead of sand.

The Nemertes, or LONG-WORM (*Nemertes borlasii*, now known as *Lineus marinus*), is a most curious creature, found beneath stones, and looking like a twisted bootlace coiled and tangled and of remarkable length. It can stretch itself also like a piece of elastic—a trick which it plays in capturing its prey, which it holds with its sucker-like mouth and interior beak. It then proceeds to "play" its victim as a fly-fisher plays a trout, stretching itself out and then retracting its length until the victim is exhausted.

The Nereis (LEAF-WORM) is a common seaside worm, some species being of great length. It is a favourite worm for bait, and may be found under stones and in muddy sand. Its head is conical, with several antennæ; its colour brown, with a red line down the back, and in sunlight a blue iridescence plays over the skin. The under side is pink. It has well-developed feet—400 pairs!

Of such are the Wilfry (*Nereis pelagica*), fleshy fawn-coloured (6–8 inches); the Pearly Nereis (*Nephthys margaritacea*), much smaller; the Rainbow Nereis (*Phyllodoce lamelligera*).

The Sea Mouse (*Aphrodita aculeata*), 3 or 4 inches long, is like a slug covered with matted bristles, and usually very dirty; but when washed in clear water it is a beautiful object, glowing with many iridescent colours. The bristles act as a sort of filter, purifying the water that enters the gills. In addition, they have barbed tips and saw-like edges, and so serve as a means of defence. The bristles, however, are too weak to pierce the hands.

Leeches.—These worm-like animals have no bristles or feet, but ringed and extensile bodies, with a sucker at the tail and a strong sucking mouth. Several varieties inhabit both salt and fresh water, the marine species being found on fish.

The Medicinal Leech (*Hirudo medicinalis*) was once far more largely used than it is to-day in blood-letting. It has a greenish black body, 2 or 3 inches long, and broken yellow bands and spots on the back. It possesses

PLATE XL.

1. The Green Laver. 2. The Purple Laver. 3. The Bladder Wrack. 4. The Oarweed. 5. Coralline.
6. Dulse. 7. Carrageen Moss. 8. The Grass Wrack. 9. The Sea Grass. 10. The Sabella. 11. The
Sea Mouse. 12. The Nemertes. 13. The Nereis. 14. The Serpula. 15. Serpulæ in Tubes.
16. The Terebella. 17. The Lug worm.

ten distinct eye-spots. In the mouth are three semicircular saws, each with eighty or ninety teeth, with which it makes its bite; then, clinging with its suctorial mouth, it fills itself with blood until it is gorged, after which hearty meal it can fast and digest for a year.

The **Horse Leech** (*Hæmopsis sanguisuga*) is the commonest British species, about $4\frac{1}{2}$ inches long, feeding largely on worms. It has much blunter teeth, and is to be found in many ponds and ditches.

Platyhelminthes.

Flatworms.—A group which includes the Cestoid Worms, which live inside other creatures. There are more than 500 species in the world, among them the **Tapeworm** (*Tænia*), the **Bladder-worm**, and the **Flukes**, of which little need be said here.

CHAPTER XIV.
Cœlenterata.

THIS group of very low forms of life contains the Jelly-fish, Sea Anemones, and Corals.

Jelly-fish.—Most people have some passing acquaintance with these strange creatures, if only from the sight of their shapeless masses on the seashore; but they possess many remarkable features, and in their native element are beautiful objects, while their life-history is in itself of very great interest.

The **Marigold** (*Aurelia aurita*) is one of the commonest of the British species, and may be known by the four crimson rings on its body. If one is examined carefully in water, the disc will be seen to be divided into eight divisions, marked off by eight tubes, each ending at the margin in a little notch, where there is a very sensitive organ, possibly acting as nose and eye. It swims by contracting and expanding its body. The four crimson rings are ovaries, in which the eggs are produced. The young, when "hatched," swim away as minute flat objects, propelled by *cilia*. They settle down on a rock and change in form, hanging downwards, producing tentacles, and becoming mere tubes of jelly, known as *Hydra tuba*, $\frac{1}{8}$ inch long. Later on this develops into a form likened to a pile of saucers with serrated edges, and these float off one by one, turn over, and become jelly-fish proper. Under the bell-shaped disc there are a group of pendent organs, known as the *manubrium* or handle, in the centre of which are four dangling, ribbon-like lobes surrounding the mouth.

The **Sea Nettle** (*Cyanea chrysaora*) is a large species found on the North and East Coasts, with a disc marked by fine radiating brown lines.

The **Hairy Stinger** (*C. capillata*) has a bulging disc, tawny coloured, and with the foregoing species can " sting "—that is to say, the long yellow threads dangling from its body act like nettles, containing minute darts, answering to the nettle's. These fringes of threads are in reality the fishing-lines by which Jelly-fish catch their prey—the fry of fishes, the zoëas of shrimps and prawns, etc. Each thread contains hundreds of cells, in each of which is a tiny dart, coiled up like a spring, and these spring out at a touch, embedding themselves in the body of their victim. Obviously persons with sensitive skins should avoid contact with these species.

JELLY-FISH

The *Thaumantia* is an exceedingly common form, with a four-section bell-shaped disc.

Turris digitalis is a brightly coloured, cone-shaped species, very much smaller in size.

The **Tube-mouthed Sarsia** (*Sarsia tubulosa*) is a very small species, about ½ inch in height, with a stomach like a bell-clapper, twice as long.

Off the Devon and Cornish coasts there is frequently found a very beautiful glass-like species, tinted blue, and with curved lines of crimson, known as *Æquorea forbesiana*, about 4 inches across.

The **Sea Acorn**, SEA GOOSEBERRY, or BERÖE (*Pleurobrachia pileus*) is quite common, yet seldom seen, being almost transparent and very small.

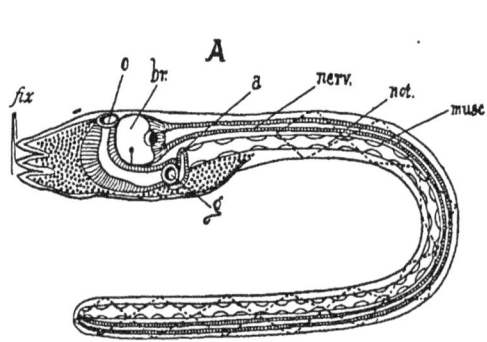

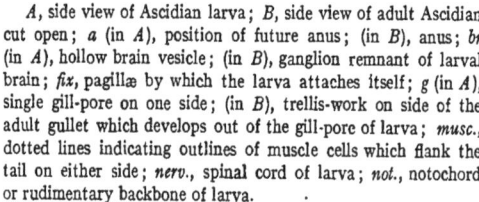

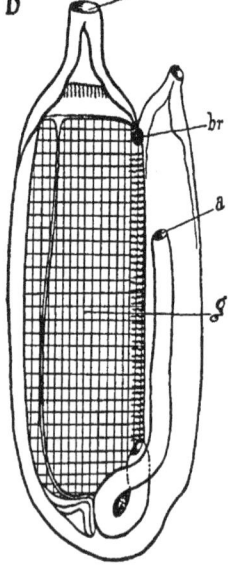

A, side view of Ascidian larva; *B*, side view of adult Ascidian cut open; *a* (in *A*), position of future anus; (in *B*), anus; *br* (in *A*), hollow brain vesicle; (in *B*), ganglion remnant of larval brain; *fix*, pagillæ by which the larva attaches itself; *g* (in *A*), single gill-pore on one side; (in *B*), trellis-work on side of the adult gullet which develops out of the gill-pore of larva; *musc.*, dotted lines indicating outlines of muscle cells which flank the tail on either side; *nerv.*, spinal cord of larva; *not.*, notochord or rudimentary backbone of larva.

Round its oval body are eight narrow bands, on which are the many " paddles " by which it moves itself through the water, giving remarkable flashes of coloured light, with prismatic effects.

At this point, although entirely out of place, mention may be made of some other curious marine creatures, one of which at least is not infrequently mistaken for some sort of jelly-fish. I refer to the **Ascidians** or **Tunicates**.

These are really a class of " survivals of ancestral vertebrates " that have degenerated in the course of time. When young they are active swimmers, have a brain, a spinal cord, and a rudimentary backbone; but they attach themselves to rocks, and soon lose these parts, becoming no more than living " filters " for the rest of their existence. Some are known as **Sea Squirts**, and are pear-shaped, jelly-like masses, quite firm to the touch, planted firmly

THE BRITISH NATURE BOOK

on a rock or stone, and are given their name of Ascidian (Greek *askos*, a "leathern bottle") from their similarity to a bottle with two mouths, through one of which water enters, and through the other it emerges. The outer coat is of a tough, leathery consistency.

Some of them will be found at low water, but many are deep-sea inhabitants. One of the most curious is *Botryllus violaceus*, which is found on stones, and looks like a flattened jelly-fish ornamented with starry patterns. As a matter of fact, it is a colony of Ascidians, and not just one single individual, living in a compound mass of jelly.

The commonest is *Ascidia mentula*, often found in the debris from a trawler's nets; but there are some twenty species in British waters. The **Currant Squirter** (*Styela grossularia*) is, when retracted, like a red currant, and is often found on old shells.

Sea Anemones.—There are more than seventy British species of these animated "flowers" of the sea. Their bodies consist of a double bag, forming a kind of water jacket; the tentacles, which spread out like the petals of a flower, are tubes connected with this water jacket, and are expanded by forcing the water into them. The lower part of the body is the "foot"— a powerful sucker by which the animal clings to its base of rock or stone; but the anemone can also crawl slowly, and on occasion will float upside down on the surface of the water.

These animals multiply sometimes by dividing into two, sometimes by producing a bud, but usually by development of eggs, which they cast out from their mouths in batches. Their food consists of shrimps, crabs, sand-hoppers, and other small creatures, which they paralyze with poison lassoes, similar to the jelly-fishes' darts, and hold down with their tentacles to digest at leisure.

The **Smooth Anemone**, or BEADLET (*Actinia equina*), is the commonest of all. Its colour varies very greatly—brown, olive-green, or dark crimson. When the tentacles are expanded, a ring of bead-like objects is revealed of a bright blue colour, from which its name is derived; probably these are eye-spots.

The **Daisy Anemone** (*Cereus pedunculatus*) is greyish yellow in colour, with fine red lines radiating from the mouth and four hundred odd tentacles, and can alter its height and shape very greatly. Its tentacles are marked with grey and white specks and rings.

The **Rose Anemone** (*Sagartia rosea*) has rosy tentacles and an olive disc on a brown-coloured base. It must be found at low-water mark amongst the rocks when the spring tides ebb. It belongs to the rock pools at low-tide limit.

The **Snowy Anemone** (*S. nivea*) is a pale olive-brown, with white tentacles and mouth.

The **Scarlet-fringed Anemone** (*S. miniata*) has the outer row of tentacles scarlet or orange-coloured, the others being brown, with darker rings.

SEA-ANEMONES

The Snake-locked Anemone (*Cyliata venusta*) has a slender body about two inches high, with a bunch of almost thread-like, grey, writhing tentacles. When compressed (in day time), it is no more than a nondescript yellowish button.

The Dahlia Wartlet, or THICK-ARMED ANEMONE (*Urticina felina*), resembles, when expanded, a cactus Dahlia, its short thick tentacles being banded with scarlet and white. It is found on rock, partially covered with sand and fragments of broken shells.

The Opelet (*Anemonia sulcata*) is one of a group which cannot retract the tentacles, and is often found in great numbers. I well remember a rock pool in Guernsey filled with them, looking, with their long flaccid tentacles, like olive-green seaweed.

Several anemones are parasitic in their habit of attaching themselves to the shells inhabited by hermit-crabs. I have found both the "Parasite" (*Cribrina effœta*)—pale brown, with whitish tentacles—on the shell of *Eupagurus bernhardus*, and also the Cloaklet Anemone (*Adamsia palliata*) on the shell of another species. They exhibit a remarkable illustration of "partnership"—commensalism—in nature, for thus the anemone gets the advantage of locomotion, and a share in the crab's booty; whilst the crab sits secure from marauders under the anemone's shelter, for no fish will touch any of the actinia, and doubtless finds its rider's paralyzing powers useful in numbing its prey.

The Pimplets are a fairly large group, covered with "pimples."

The Gem Pimplet (*Bunodes verrucosa*) is usually partially buried in sand in its rock pool.

The Globe-horn (*Corynactis viridis*) is very small, about $\frac{1}{4}$ of an inch, and grows in colonies, its tentacles having minute knobs instead of coming to a point.

The Plumose Anemone (*Metridium senilis*) is recognized at once by its feathered tentacles and tall column.

The Cave Anemone (*Sagartia troglodytes*) is common, very variable in colour, but identified by a mark like the letter B on the tentacles.

Corals.—These are closely related to anemones, being, in fact, sea anemones with calcareous skeletons. Few, however, belong to our British waters, though off Devonshire you may find the Common Madrepore, which, when its tentacles are outspread, you would take for an anemone until you touched it, when you would discover it to withdraw into a flinty little tower of lime. Occasionally also you will find the so-called "Dead Man's Fingers," a soft, pinkish, fleshy object, which is a closely allied animal or rather colony of animals living together.

Hydroid Zoophytes, or POLYPS.*—In this section we come to a freshwater representative, the Common Hydra, which bears some resemblance to the Sea Anemone, in its power to contract into a tiny round lump of jelly,

* Technically, this includes most of the jelly-fish, etc., which have been dealt with above, and which are, as a matter of fact, transitional phases of the fixed Hydroid Polyp.

or to extend into a long stalk or column, tipped with a few slender tentacles. This is one of the objects for study with your pocket lens or microscope, and is to be found on duckweed in many a ditch or shallow pool. It is very minute, remember, and will have to be looked for, but is very common. There are three kinds—orange-coloured, brown, and green. Their tentacles are studded with suckers capable of paralyzing the water-fleas and other minute creatures on which they live. They multiply by putting out buds, which separate from the parent and start an independent existence of their own. As I have written at some length on these fascinating creatures in *The Young People's Microscope Book*, I must refer interested readers to its pages.

But most of the Zoophytes (to use the familiar term—literally, "animal-plant") are marine, and are frequently mistaken for some kind of seaweed from their outward appearance. They are, however, colonies of minute animals (polyps or polypites), living not separate lives, but held together by a common "body" known as the *cœnosarc*—generally a living tube of thin flesh, which acts as a trunk or support for the community. Yet though not independent, each polyp is distinct, and each chamber or cup of the whole zoophyte is occupied by one member of the colony.

Usually the outer wall of the cœnosarc is hard, being composed of *chitin*—the same substance that forms the outside skeletons of insects, and forms a sheath known as the polypary.

The food caught and eaten by one polyp nourishes the others as well as itself; for this purpose each has a number of tentacles, in the centre of which is the mouth.

At certain seasons of the year special polypites are formed, whose business is not to catch food but to produce eggs, which they discharge at last by bursting. Others detach themselves from the parent colony and float away, resembling minute jelly-fish; but others, it must be added, attain an enormous size, as jelly-fish, so that it is almost impossible to credit their having had so lowly an origin. To repeat a well-used illustration, the jelly-fish *Cyanea artica*, which has been found with a disc 7 feet in diameter and tentacles 50 feet long, is produced from a tiny zoophyte not $\frac{1}{2}$ an inch high.

Many are to be found living on seaweeds; and it must be remembered that they are very small. The **Sea Oak Coralline** (*Sertularia pumila*) is found quite commonly on the serrated wrack. It looks like a miniature leafless tree about $\frac{1}{2}$ an inch in height. Under the microscope it is seen to have minute cells, in each of which one of the polypites lives. There are some twenty species of these Sertularians in our British seas.

The **Sea Fir** (*Sertularia abietina*) is an abundant species, often found on old oyster shells, and much resembling a fir tree. Another, even more common, is the **Sea Hair Coralline** (*S. operculata*), frequently growing on seaweeds, and from 3 to 6 inches long. It grows in tufts not unlike bunches of hair. The **Squirrel's-tail Coralline** (*S. argentea*) is very small, with stiff erect branches, and is the most common of all.

CHAPTER XV.
Porifera and Protozoa.
Porifera.

Sponges.—Accustomed to the familiar form of the bathroom sponge, people are usually surprised to learn that there are any other varieties, and that in our own home waters many species (three hundred at least) abound, two at least in *fresh* water.

Naturally they are entirely unlike the "Turkey sponge" in form; many of them appear to be little more than masses of slime on the rocks—in fact, the red, orange, yellow, or green colourings on the sides of the rocks at low water are some of the Porifera.

Their life-story is a fascinating one. A sponge is to all intents and purposes a sort of city, traversed in every direction by streets and lanes, or, more properly, canals. The surface is covered with small openings or pores, which communicate with the main canals, the outer ends of which are seen in the fewer but much larger holes in the sponge (*oscula*).

The whole city is a living colony of animals joined together in a common mass, to which the sponge is really the skeleton or framework, covered with a slimy flesh, and divided internally into myriads of cells. The minute organisms which inhabit these are like glass flasks, each with a long whip or lash protruding from it, by which they thrash the water in unison, thus producing a current which flows through the main canals and out at the *oscula*, continuously fed by other water entering through the little pores. This water bears with it all sorts of other microscopic creatures to provide the sponge's food.

Some of the cells when full grown split into portions, which increase the size of the sponge; others develop into eggs, which are swept out along the current into the open sea, and settle down upon a rock to grow, by division and subdivision, into a new colony.

Another remarkable fact to be noted is that the substance of these sponges consists of a horny fibre, together with innumerable quantities of flinty spicules of the most beautiful shape. These can only be examined under the microscope, which shows them to be of most diverse forms—rods, grapnels, anchors, arrows, crosses, etc., generally entangled together—forming the skeleton of the colony. Over all this mass of spicules and embedding them is the sarcode, or living matter of the sponge, like a thin jelly.

328 THE BRITISH NATURE BOOK

The shapes of the spicules help in many cases to differentiate the species.

This is only the barest and most general outline, and can only give a very rough idea of the wonderful nature of these simple animals.

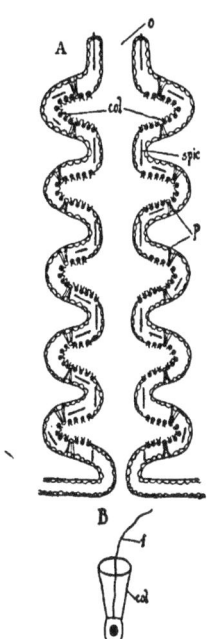

A, diagrammatic longitudinal section of a simple Sponge. The collar-cells and spicules are represented in black; B, a single collar-cell enlarged; *col* (in A), collar-cell; (in B), collar-cell; *o*, osculum; *p*, pore; *spic*, spicule.

The two fresh-water Sponges referred to above are the River Sponge, found in the Thames and other rivers and canals, as a dirty, yellowish slime on wood and stone, and the Pond Sponge, which is dark green, and found in rounded masses.

During the winter these die away, leaving certain cells which develop winter eggs and give rise to male and female forms.

Among the Marine forms the "Mermaid's Gloves" (*Chalina oculata*) may often be picked up, and recognized by its branching, tree-like shape, sometimes not unlike fingers. It may be from 6 to 10 inches long. It is a deep-water sponge, and is only thrown up ashore after a storm.

Another common form is the Crumb-of-Bread Sponge (*Halichondria panicea*), found on large weeds and covering rocks, looking when dry like a piece of the crumb of brown bread.

Amongst those that encrust the rocks and give them their colour patches is the crimson-coloured *Grantia coriacea*, a thick soft substance, $\frac{1}{4}$–1 inch in diameter. Another is *Microciona carnosa*—pale red, growing in thick narrow bands.

Many oyster and scallop shells are found perforated and bored with many small holes. These are the home of *Cliona celata*, a sponge with a yellowish tinge, which it is supposed—though the question is still unsettled—has performed the work of drilling the holes, or dissolving them away.

Protozoa.

These are the lowest forms of living animals, and are known popularly as Animalcules. They can only be studied under the microscope. They exist in countless myriads, and would require a whole volume to themselves. They consist of single cells, and are so minute that hundreds can live in a drop of water.

Many of them can be seen through the microscope described in the chapter on Apparatus, and I know of no more entrancing study than that of the contents of a drop of water thus inhabited. A delightful book on the subject

ANIMALCULES

is *Pond Life* (1s.), No. 65 of "The People's Books" (Jack), which deals with many of them, and also with other microscopic water creatures.

Any one can produce these Protozoa by leaving a little hay in water for a few days, or allowing flowers to remain in water till dead.

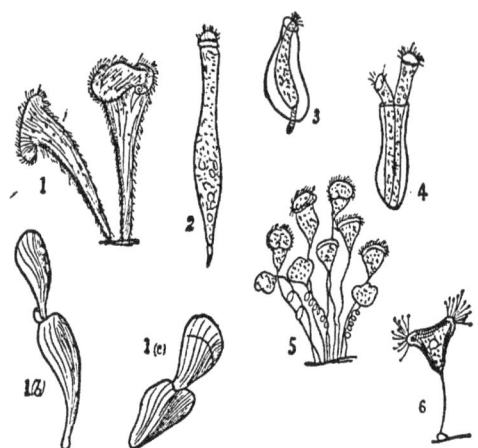

BELL ANIMALCULES.—1. *Stentor polymorphus*. 1 (*b*) and (*c*). Free swimming and multiplying. 2. *Ophrydium versatile*. 3. *Corthurnia imberis*. 4. *Vaginicola*. 5. *Vorticella*. SUCTORIA.—6. *Acineta*.

Naturally the sea is the home of untold millions. The phosphorescence often visible in the sea is due to one species, *Noctiluca miliaris*.

Fresh, or drinking water, contains only small numbers, but any stagnant water is found to be full. So the rain-water barrel, the wayside ditch, or the duck pond will yield a host of "finds" to the hunter with his microscope. The simplest form is the naked lump of jelly which appears to move by flowing along, known as Amœba. It obtains its food by literally surrounding it, and it multiplies by breaking itself into two.

The Slipper Animalcule (*Paramecium*), so called from its shape, swims actively by means of cilia or lashes.

The Swan Animalcule (*Trachclocera olor*) has a swan-like neck, which it can stretch or contract at will. Frequently there may be noticed on duckweed a whitish filmy mass, which under the microscope is seen to consist of hundreds of exquisite bells, each on a slender stalk. This is Vorticella, a larger and more trumpet-shaped animal, generally green in colour; and fastened to a stem or leaf is Stentor.

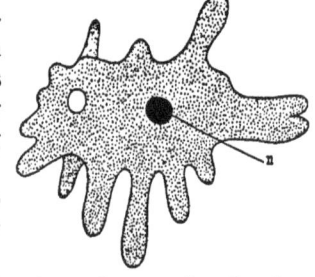

An *Amœba* progressing. The direction of movement is towards the right; *n*, the nucleus.

THE BRITISH NATURE BOOK

The **Foraminifera** are found to possess minute calcareous shells of most beautiful form. Many exquisitely shaped species have been dredged up from the ooze of the ocean bed; some may be found in the sand from a new-bought sponge; others are obtained by taking up the whitest-looking sand left in the ripples by the outgoing tide.

Side by side with these are the **Radiolaria**, the flinty skeletons of which,

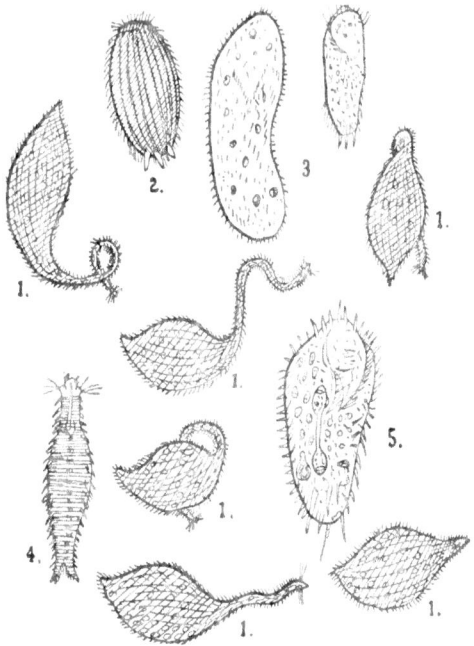

INFUSORIA.—1. Swan-necked Animalcule. 2. *Coleps hirtus*, or Barrel Animalcule. 3. *Paramecium*. 4. *Choetonotus larus*. 5. *Stylonychia mytilus*.

like beautiful carved and fretted ivory, make some of the most wonderful exhibits under the microscope. But the merest mention must suffice. All that can be added is that these almost invisible things, whether in a drop of water or a pinch of sand, fill the thinking mind with a sense of wonder, which is but an instinctive and unconscious act of praise to that Great Creator whom we call God.

PART II.
THE VEGETABLE WORLD.

SECTION I.
INTRODUCTORY.

THOSE who study any of the preceding sections of this book will realize that some knowledge of plants is absolutely necessary. For example, to breed butterflies, it is essential to know the plant upon which to feed the larvæ; or to collect beetles, it is of equal importance to know something of the trees or low plants whereon some species are to be found.

In order to make this book of all-round usefulness to the Nature student, therefore, it must contain some reference to the Vegetable World.

Yet the subject is too vast for more than a very condensed amount of matter.

It is chiefly, however, with flowering plants and trees that we have to deal, because these are of first-rate importance to the study of bird and insect life.

The Vegetable Kingdom is divided into four sub-kingdoms :—

1. The *Thallophyta*, to which seaweeds and fungi belong.
2. The *Bryophyta*, or mosses and liverworts.
3. The *Pteridophyta*, including ferns, horse-tails, and club-mosses.
4. The *Phanerogamia*, or *Spermaphyta*, in which are the flowering, seed-bearing plants.

For the purposes of this book we deal principally with the fourth group. The student will find a list of more than 600 British plants, arranged in a special order and after a special method, in order that he may recognize very quickly almost any of the wild flowers or trees which he is likely to come across. There are more than 1,200 species of British flowering plants; but many of them are very rare, or confined to a few localities; the majority with which most students will come into touch are to be found in the subjoined list.

As in other sections of the book, I suggest that the student should obtain *Wild Flowers* (1s. 3d.), No. 117 of "The People's Books" (Jack), and use it as a basis. It is an excellent work, and with a little adaptation can be supplemented by the descriptions given in the following pages.

It should be interleaved, and when a flower is discovered and identified which is not mentioned in that book, it should be inserted in its appropriate place. It would also be most excellent practice to *paint* the illustrations, from actual specimens.

In order to identify plants, it is necessary to know something of their structure, etc.; for which purpose a magnifying-glass or pocket-lens is necessary. If a collection is to be made, a tin box should be carried in which the plants can be placed and kept fresh; but I am not in favour of digging up plants, unless they are common ones. For the purpose of most collectors, it is sufficient to carry home a piece of the plant bearing leaves and flowers.

I most strongly urge that the would-be student should *draw* his flowers. The pen-and-ink illustrations in this book make excellent examples, and it does not require a great amount of skill or knowledge to learn to make similar drawings of other plants. There is no doubt whatever that if you take the trouble to draw a plant carefully, you will never afterwards forget it.

Those who can use a camera will find an equal fascination in photographing their finds, whether *in situ* or at home.

How to Dry Plants.

There is a special kind of absorbent paper sold for this purpose, but sheets of thick blotting-paper, and even ordinary newspaper, will serve. The plant specimen should be arranged on a sheet, the topmost of some half-dozen sheets, and should be carefully covered with another piece. Upon this several other sheets are placed; then another specimen, and so on, till the pile is complete. Then the whole should be pressed between two boards, with some weight on the top; in which condition the pile should be left for twenty-four hours. Then the papers should be changed; the plants arranged, each on a new sheet, and the pile again pressed. · This process should be continued until the plants are thoroughly dry. They may then be mounted on sheets of stiff white paper, stuck down with strips of gummed paper, and the names, Latin and English, locality, and date of finding, duly written in one corner.

The General Structure of Plants.

There are four distinct parts of every flowering plant, each of which has its work to do in the life and growth of the whole. These are the *Root*, the *Stem*, the *Leaf*, and the *Flower*.

About the Root.—It is only in a few cases that the root is of any use as a means of identifying the plant—for example, the fibrous entangled root of the Bird's-nest Orchis.

About the Stem.—This should be carefully inspected, as in many cases it bears some characteristic feature. Notice, first, whether it is branched or simple (that is, without branches). Then its shape: it may be round, or angled, or flattened; also, hollow or solid; smooth, rough, or hairy. It may be stiff and erect, or " prostrate," lying on the ground; or it may support itself by climbing or rambling.

About the Leaf.—This is of great importance as a means of identification,

LEAVES

and various leaves should be examined in any special plant, especially those at the root, as well as those on the stem or near the flower. There are many different shapes. As far as possible, in the following list, the fewest technical terms have been employed.

ALTERNATE means that the leaves are set one above the other on opposite sides of the stem.

OPPOSITE means that they are in pairs, starting from the same point, but on opposite sides of the stem.

RADICAL means that the leaves are found close to the root, on or near the ground.

SESSILE means that the leaves have no stalk, but "sit" close to the stem or the root.

SIMPLE means that each leaf is in one piece, having no distinct or separate divisions.

ACUTE leaves come to a point at their tips.

CRENATE means that the margins of the leaf are indented or rounded, smoothly and regularly, instead of being toothed sharply.

CORDATE means "heart-shaped." Frequently a leaf is heart-shaped at the base alone.

ENTIRE means that the margin of the leaf is free from indentation.

ELLIPTICAL is "egg-shaped"—refers to leaves of long oval form.

LANCEOLATE means "lance-like"—leaves three or four times as long as broad, tapering to a point.

LINEAR leaves are very long and narrow.

LOBED means that the leaves are deeply indented or divided.

LYRATE leaves are deeply-lobed, with the end lobe largest of all.

OBOVATE leaves are those which are broadest near the apex.

OVATE leaves are broadest near the base.

PALMATE means that the leaf is five-lobed, the midrib of each lobe meeting at the base.

PELTATE leaves have the stalk near their centre (as in the Common Nasturtium). They are generally roundish in shape.

PINNATIFID leaves are simple leaves with the segments or lobes arranged like the leaflets in a pinnate leaf (see below), but the lobes are not cut so deeply as to be removed without destroying the leaf-blade structure.

BIPINNATIFID means that the leaf is pinnatifid, and each lobe or segment pinnatifid too.

SERRATE means "toothed," the margins of such leaves being toothed like a saw.

WHORLED leaves start from the same point, being set regularly round the stem.

COMPOUND leaves have distinct leaflets, each starting from the leaf-stalk.

PINNATE leaves are composed of leaflets situated on opposite sides of the leaf-stalk. The rose leaf is an example.

THE BRITISH NATURE BOOK

BIPINNATE leaves are pinnate leaves the divisions of which are pinnate also (see illustration).

TRIPINNATE means "three times pinnate."

TERNATE applies to leaves consisting of three leaflets starting from the same point on a common stalk—for example, the Trefoils.

GLAUCOUS refers to the blue-grey waxy bloom with which certain leaves are covered—for example, the Sea Holly.

About the Flower.—If we dissect a simple flower, such as the buttercup, we find it built up of four different organs. First, a whorl or circle of greenish scales—SEPALS—which, counted together, make up the CALYX (cup), a name suggestive of its purpose—namely, of containing or supporting the rest of the flower. Then comes a second whorl or circle of PETALS, usually large and brightly coloured. These together form the COROLLA, or crown.

Inside the corolla is a large number of STAMENS, little stalks, on the end of each being an ANTHER, or head, from which the pollen is produced. Finally, in the centre is the PISTIL, which usually consists of three parts. The lower part is known as the OVARY, containing minute "eggs" or OVULES, which after fertilization become seeds. Upon the top of the ovary is one or more slender stalks called the STYLE, the tip of which in some cases becomes flattened or rounded. This latter is the STIGMA. Its function is to receive on its sticky surface the ripened pollen grains from the anthers. In some cases (for example, the poppy) the stigma is set directly upon the ovary, without the intervention of a style. The pollen grains germinate by pushing a slender tube down the style into the ovary, where they reach the "ovules"; and these change into seed, the ovary becoming the SEED VESSEL. The style, stigma, and ovary together form the CARPEL or CARPELS.

The calyx and corolla together are called the PERIANTH.

Some flowers have no pistil or ovary, others no stamens; while some have no sepals, others no petals, and a few neither sepals nor petals. In addition, it should be noted that simple flowers are of different shapes and structures.

Many flowers—for example, the Primrose—have their petals so joined as to form a corolla in one piece—"MONOPETALOUS." In such cases it is sometimes possible to count the number of petals composing the corolla; in the Primrose it is five, but in many other species the shape of the corolla prevents any separation into distinct petals.

Certain flowers are "lipped"—for example, White Dead-nettle and Snapdragon.

Flowers may occur singly, on stalks, or in the AXILS ("Armpits") of the leaves—that is, in the angle between the leaf and the stem; but more often they are grouped in characteristic "INFLORESCENCES." An UMBEL is a flat flower-cluster, in which several flower-stalks (PEDICELS) appear to start from the same point on the main stalk, so that the flowers all occupy one level, forming a flat or convex group (for example, Hemlock). In a SIMPLE UMBEL each flower-stalk carries a single flower; in a COMPOUND UMBEL each branch

Diagram illustrating the technical terms used.

THE BRITISH NATURE BOOK

or stalk bears a smaller umbel. A SPIKE is an elongated mass of flowers, without separate stalks, fixed close along the main stem.

A RACEME is an elongated cluster of stalked flowers, like the Mignonette.

A PANICLE is a branched cluster of flowers, mostly on side branches growing along the main stalk.

A CORYMB is similar to a raceme, but the lower flower-stalks are longer, bringing all the flowers nearer to a level, as in the Wallflower.

A CYME is the name given to a flower-cluster when the topmost or central flower opens first.

COMPOSITE flowers consist generally of numbers of small stalkless flowers crowded tightly together in a head. The Dandelion or Daisy serves as a type. In the Dandelion each yellow ray is a flower complete in itself, with pistils and stamens; in the Daisy the yellow "eye" part is made up of many tube-shaped flowers or florets, and each white petalous-looking ray is also a floret.

BRACTS are small leaves generally to be found below the flower. In the Dandelion, for instance, there is a ring of green bracts, called an INVOLUCRE, underneath the flower-head.

This short description is all that need be mastered in order to make use of the list of flowers and the description given.

There are many other simplified methods for identifying British wild flowers in existence, many of them dependent, as this one is, primarily upon the colours of flowers, that characteristic being the one which is invariably noted first of all by the would-be student.

But after trying them all, and making many further experiments, I believe that the following arrangement is the best, and that by its means the 684 species named may be identified with little difficulty, and without recourse to any scientific knowledge.

Explanation of the Lists.

First of all, note that the flowers are divided into groups according to their colours. The divisions are as follows :—

White—Nos. 1–127.
Whitish—Nos. 128–143.
White or Whitish, with some other tint—Nos. 144–181.
Creamy White—Nos. 182–192.
Pale Yellow—Nos. 193–209.
Yellow—Nos. 210–321.
Yellow or Yellowish, with some other tint—Nos. 322–350.
Red, Rose, or Pink—Nos. 351–401.
Crimson and Scarlet—Nos. 402, 403.
Reddish, or Purplish, or Red-purple, or with some other tint—Nos. 404–453.

FLOWERS

Lilac or Pale Purple—Nos. 454–495.
Blue or Bluish—Nos. 496–534.
Violet, Purple, or Bluish Purple—Nos. 535–563.
Brown or Brownish, or with some other tint—Nos. 564–591.
Blackish, with White or Brown—No. 592.
Green or Greenish—Nos. 593–652.
Green or Greenish, with some other tint—Nos. 653–684.

Each of these groups is divided into two classes—POLYPETALOUS and MONOPETALOUS.

Polypetalous refers to plants with corolla composed entirely of separate petals.

Monopetalous strictly refers to plants with corolla two or more lobed, composed of petals more or less joined together. But, *for the purposes of this book only*, there are added under this division also (1) plants with either corolla, calyx, or both absent, and (2) a few special flowers (belonging scientifically to the Class *Monocotyledon*), such as the orchids, irises, garlics, rushes, etc., which are too few to place by themselves, but are easily identified by some specially marked characteristic.

Each of these classes (polypetalous and monopetalous) is subdivided into groups according to the size of the flower. In each case the diameter of the flower is given approximately.

LARGE includes flowers 1 inch or more in diameter.
MEDIUM includes flowers $\frac{1}{2}$ to 1 inch in diameter.
SMALL includes flowers less than $\frac{1}{2}$ inch in diameter.

In cases where there is a specially large number, there may be a still further division of VERY SMALL, consisting of flowers of from $\frac{1}{8}$ to $\frac{1}{4}$ inch in diameter.

Each plant is given its English and Latin names, and a brief description of flower, number of sepals, petals, stamens, etc., leaf, habitat, months when in flower, etc.

Under the heading "Months" figures will be found, standing for the months corresponding numerically—for example, 7–9 means July to September; 3–5 means March to May.

$C.$ = Common, $L.$ = Local, $R.$ = Rare.

To Use the Lists.

First, note the colour of your flower.
Second, whether it is polypetalous or not.
Third, its approximate diameter.

These points decided, you can place it at once in the group or division corresponding; and then you should note its leaves, its locality, and the month in which you have found it. A few moments' rapid glancing through the lists will enable you, I trust, to name the flower.

A WORKING ILLUSTRATION.

I find a small red flower in August. On examination I find that its petals are joined: I shall therefore place it among the "Monopetalous, Red or Pink" class. Its size is between $\frac{1}{4}$ and $\frac{3}{8}$ inch: I shall therefore expect it to be in the Group "Small." I decide that its leaves are "ovate and sessile": it must be one of ten species in that division, and its name is soon discovered—"Scarlet Pimpernel."

SECTION II.

PHANEROGAMIA.

Flowering and Seed-bearing Plants.

English Name.	Latin Name.	Description of Flower.	Petals, Sepals, Stamens, etc.	
LARGE.				
Wood Anemone.	*Anemone nemorosa.*	1¼ in. Flowers solitary.	Petals, 6. Stamens, many.	1.
Evening Campion.	*Lychnis vespertina.*	1¼ in. Opening at night.	Petals, 5, two-cleft. Calyx, five-toothed. Stamens, 10.	2.
White Water Lily.	*Nymphæa alba.*	4 in. Not scented.	Petals, many. Sepals, 4. Stamens, many.	3.
Blackberry or Bramble.	*Rubus fruticosus.*	1⅛ in. Sometimes pink.	Petals, 5. Sepals, 5. Stamens, many.	4.
Mountain Avens.	*Dryas octopetala.*	1 in. Large, handsome.	Petals, usually 8.	5.
MEDIUM.				
Snowdrop.	*Galanthus nivalis.*	¾ in. Solitary, hanging.	Petals, 3. Sepals, 3. Stamens, 6.	6.
Broad-leaved Garlic	*Allium ursinum.*	¾ in. In flat umbel.	Petals, 6. Stamens, 6.	7.
Greater Stitchwort.	*Stellaria holostea.*	¾ in. Satiny white.	Petals, 5, deeply two-cleft. Sepals, 5. Stamens, 10.	8.
Wood Sorrel.	*Oxalis acetosella.*	⅝ in. Solitary, bell-shaped.	Petals, 5. Sepals, 5. Stamens, 10.	9.
Wild Cherry.	*Prunus avium.*	⅝ in. In umbels.	Petals, 5. Sepals, 5. Stamens, many.	10.
Wild Service Tree.	*Pyrus torminalis.*	⅝ in. In corymbs.	Petals, 5 Sepals, 5. Stamens, many.	11.
Field Mouse-ear Chickweed.	*Cerastium arvense.*	½ in.	Petals, 5, cloven. Sepals, 5. Stamens, 10.	12.
Strawberry-leaved Cinquefoil.	*Potentilla fragariastrum.*	¾ in. Prostrate stems.	Sepals, 10. Petals, 5, notched. Stamens, many.	13.
Wood Strawberry.	*Fragaria vesca.*	⅝ in. Erect flower stalks.	Petals, 5. Calyx, ten-cleft. Stamens, many.	14.
Hawthorn or May.	*Cratægus oxyacantha.*	½ in. In clusters.	Petals, 5. Sepals, 5. Stamens, many.	15.
White Beam.	*Pyrus aria.*	½ in. Clustered.	Petals, 5. Stamens, many.	16.
Glaucus Marsh Stitchwort.	*Stellaria palustris.*	½ in. Stem, four-angled.	Petals, 5, deeply cloven. Sepals, 5. Stamens, 10.	17.
Sea Campion.	*Silene maritima.*	1 in. Few on stem, or solitary.	Petals, 5. Calyx, inflated, five-toothed. Stamens, 10.	18.
Bladder Campion.	*Silene inflata.*	⅝ in. Often tinged purple.	Calyx, five-cleft; inflated with network of veins.	19.
Dewberry.	*Rubus cæsius.*	1 in. Stem prostrate: whitish.	Petals, 5. Sepals, 5. Stamens, many.	20.
Frog-bit.	*Hydrocharis morsus-ranæ.*	⅞ in. Flowers, two to three.	Petals, 3. Sepals, 3. Stamens and pistil on different plants.	21.
SMALL.				
Blackthorn or Sloe.	*Prunus spinosa.*	½ in. Flowers usually appear before leaves.	Petals, 5. Sepals, 5. Stamens, many.	22.
Scurvy Grass.	*Cochlearia officinalis.*	$\frac{5}{16}$ in. Flowers clustered.	Petals, 4. Sepals, 4. Stamens, 6.	23.
Common Mouse-ear Chickweed.	*Cerastium triviale.*	¼ in. Flowers in panicles.	Petals, 5, cloven. Sepals, 5. Stamens, 10.	24.
Garlic Mustard.	*Alliaria officinalis.*	$\frac{5}{16}$ in.	Petals, 4. Sepals, 4. Stamens, 6.	25.
Lesser Stitchwort.	*Stellaria graminea.*	¼ in. In forked panicles.	Petals, 5, deeply cleft. Sepals, 5. Stamens, 10. Styles, 3.	26.
English Scurvy Grass.	*Cochlearia anglica.*	⅜ in. Clustered.	Petals, 4. Sepals, 4. Stamens, 6.	27.
Water-cress.	*Nasturtium officinale.*	$\frac{5}{16}$ in. Clustered.	Petals, 4. Sepals, 4. Stamens, 6.	28.

WHITE. Polypetalous.

Leaves.	Months.	Habitat.	Remarks.
			LARGE.
three divisions.	3–5	Woods.	What appear to be petals are really sepals. (*V. C.*)
	5–8	Waste places.	1–2 ft. Plant hairy and sticky. *Lychnis* = "lamp," referring to cottony down of leaf used for lamp-wick. Fragrant in evening. (*C.*)
floating.	7	Ponds.	3–10 ft. Flowers rise above water in morning and expand only in sunshine. In evening they close and sink. (*C.*)
more leaflets.	7–8	Hedges.	2–10 ft. Stem angular. Many species. (*V.C.*)
white, woolly beneath.	6–7	Mountains.	*Rare.*
			MEDIUM.
	1–3	Woods.	*Common.*
ose of Lily of	5–6	Woods.	15–30 in. Plant strongly scented of onion. (*V. C.*)
tapering.	4–6	Hedges.	Stem angular, rough-edged. (*V. C.*)
se of Clover.	4–6	Woods and hedges.	Supposed by many to be the true Shamrock. (*C.*)
? pointed.	4	Woods.	Fruit black or red. Leaves turn scarlet in autumn. (*C.*)
lobed.	4	Woods and hedges.	Fruit a brown spotted berry. (*L.*)
nceolate.	All summer.	Everywhere.	5–8 in. Downy, generally sticky. (*C.*)
three obovate	1–5	Banks and hedges.	Distinguished from Wild Strawberry by its notched petals. (*V. C.*)
iflets.	4–7	Woods.	Strawberry, from custom of laying straw between rows. (*C.*)
haped, deeply	5–6	Hedges.	*Very Common.*
ind silky be- ; serrate.	6	Woods.	*Local.*
row ; sessile.	6–8	Marshy places	6–12 in.
tapering.	6–8	Seashore.	3–6 in. Resembling Bladder Campion, but larger flowers. (*L.*)
	All summer.	Pastures.	1–2 ft. Well marked by bladder-like calyx. (*V. C.*)
iflets.	6–8	Thickets.	1–4 ft. A Bramble. Fruit half enclosed in calyx, covered with grey bloom. (*C.*)
heart-shaped.		Pools.	3–6 in. A floating plant. (*L.*)
			SMALL.
	3–5	Hedges.	3–8 ft. The fruit is used to make sloe gin. (*V. C.*)
heart-shaped,	4–8	Muddy seashore.	4–15 in. (*L.*)
te.	All summer.	Dry places.	6–10 in. A common weed, downy, and generally sticky. (*V. C.*)
heart-shaped, hick veins.	4–6	Hedges.	2–3 ft. An early hedge plant; when bruised smelling strongly of garlic. (*V. C.*)
row.	6–7	Roadsides.	1–2 ft. Distinguished from Greater Stitchwort by very deeply divided petals. (*V. C.*)
fleshy.	4–8	River banks and seashore.	10–18 in. Leaves more entire, and flowers larger than in common Scurvy Grass. (*L.*)
end leaflet and large.	6–8	Brooks.	1–2 ft. (*C.*)

Polypetalous.   **WHITE.**

English Name.	Latin Name.	Description of Flower.	Petals, Sepals, Stamens, etc.	
SMALL (contd.).				
Ivy-leaved Crowfoot.	Ranunculus hederaceus.	$\frac{5}{16}$ in. Rayed.	Petals, 5, narrow. Sepals, 5. Stamens, many.	29.
Wild Cornel or Dogwood.	Cornus sanguinea.	$\frac{1}{2}$ in. In clusters.	Petals, 4. Sepals, 4. Stamens, 4.	30.
Sea Kale.	Crambe maritima.	$\frac{1}{2}$ in. In clusters.	Petals, 4. Sepals, 4. Stamens, 6.	31.
Cow Parsnip, or Hogweed.	Heracleum sphondylium.	$\frac{3}{8}$ in. In compound umbels.	Petals, 5, two or more lobed. Sepals, 5. Stamens, 5.	32.
Corn Spurrey.	Spergula arvensis.	$\frac{6}{16}$ in. Panicled, bent down when seeding.	Petals, 5. Sepals, 5. Stamens, 5–10. Styles, 5.	33.
English Stonecrop.	Sedum anglicum.	$\frac{5}{16}$ in. Starlike.	Petals, 5. Sepals, 5. Stamens, 10.	34.
Water Stitchwort.	Stellaria aquatica.	$\frac{1}{2}$ in.	Petals, narrow, deeply cleft. Sepals, 5. Stamens, 10.	35.
White Stonecrop.	Sedum album.	$\frac{1}{4}$ in.	Petals, 5, spreading. Sepals, 5, green. Stamens, 10.	36.
Great Sundew.	Drosera anglica.	$\frac{1}{2}$ in.	Petals, 5. Sepals, 5. Stamens, 5.	37.
Knotted Pearlwort.	Sagina nodosa.	$\frac{1}{4}$ in. Erect, two to three together.	Petals, 5. Sepals, 5. Stamens, 10. Styles, 5.	38.
Bitter Candy-tuft.	Iberis amara.	$\frac{1}{4}$ in. In flat head.	Petals, 4, two outer longest. Sepals, 4. Stamens, 6.	39.
Wood Vetch.	Vicia sylvatica.	$\frac{1}{2}$ in. With blue veins numerous; stalks long; tendrils branched.	Petals, 5. Sepals, 5.	40.
VERY SMALL.				
Shepherd's Purse.	Capsella bursa-pastoris.	$\frac{1}{8}$ in. Clustered.	Petals, 4. Sepals, 4. Stamens, 4 long and 2 short.	41.
Little Mouse-ear Chickweed.	Cerastium semidecandrum.	$\frac{1}{8}$ in. Few flowered.	Petals, 5, notched. Sepals, 5, longer than petals. Stamens, 10.	42.
Common Whitlow Grass.	Draba verna.	$\frac{1}{8}$ in.	Petals, 4, deeply cleft. Sepals, 4. Stamens, 4 long, 2 short.	43.
Hairy Bitter Cress.	Cardamine hirsuta.	$\frac{1}{8}$ in. Clustered.	Petals, 4. Sepals, 4. Stamens, 4 or 6.	44.
Rock Hutchinsia.	Hutchinsia petræa.	$\frac{1}{12}$ in. Clustered, minute.	Petals, 4. Sepals, 4.	45.
Broad-leaved Mouse-ear Chickweed.	Cerastium glomeratum.	$\frac{1}{12}$ in. In panicles.	Petals, 5, notched. Sepals, 5, hairy tipped, with glands.	46.
Four-cleft Mouse-ear Chickweed.	Cerastium tetrandrum.	$\frac{1}{4}$ in.	Petals, 4, notched. Sepals, 4, sticky. Stamens, 4.	47.
Rue-leaved Saxifrage.	Saxifraga tridactylites.	$\frac{1}{8}$ in. Terminal, on separate stalks.	Petals, 5, rounded. Sepals, 5. united.	48.
Common Burnet Saxifrage.	Pimpinella saxifraga.	$\frac{1}{10}$ in. In small umbels.	Petals, 5. Sepals, 5.	49.
Wild Beaked Parsley.	Anthriscus sylvestris.	$\frac{1}{8}$ in. Terminal umbels on long stalks.	Petals, 5. Stamens, 5.	50.
Spreading Hedge Parsley.	Torilis infesta.	$\frac{1}{12}$ in. Umbels stalked.	Petals, 5. Sepals, 5.	51.
Upright Hedge Parsley.	Torilis anthriscus.	$\frac{1}{4}$ in. In compound umbels.	Petals, 5. Sepals, 5.	52.
Common Beaked Parsley.	Anthriscus vulgaris.	$\frac{1}{8}$ in. Umbels on side of stem.	Petals, 5. Sepals, 5.	53.
Parsley Water Dropwort.	Œnanthe pimpinelloides.	$\frac{1}{12}$ in. In compound, flat umbels.	Petals, 5. Sepals, 5.	54.

WHITE. Polypetalous.

Leaves.	Months.	Habitat.	Remarks.
l and lobed.	All summer.	Muddy places.	SMALL (*contd.*). 4–8 in. (*C.*)
>ed, pointed.	6	Hedges.	5–7 ft. A bushy shrub. If the young leaves are pulled into pieces the spiral veins are plainly seen. (*V. C.*)
vaved, toothed.	6	Sea coast.	1–2 ft. Does not differ from garden species. (*L.*)
:ly cut, rough,	7	Fields.	2–5 ft. A tall stout plant, with channelled hairy stem. Sometimes mistaken for Hemlock. (*V. C.*)
:al, in whorls.	All summer.	Cornfields.	6–12 in. Plant hairy. (*C.*)
>ed, fleshy,	6–7	Rocky places.	2–3 in. Leaves often tinged with red. Petals spotted with red. Anthers purple. (*C.*)
essile.	7–8	Wet places.	1–2 ft. (*L.*)
:al, fleshy.	7–8	Rocks and old walls.	3–5 in. Found on Malvern Hills. Not uncommon as a garden escape. (*L.*)
narrow, on mooth stalks.	7–8	Bogs.	4–8 in. Leaves with sticky, shining hairs. (*R.*)
rowing in knots.	Summer.	Wet places.	3–4 in. A pretty plant, with conspicuous flowers. (*C.*)
lanceolate.	7	Chalkfields.	6–9 in. Similar to garden plant. (*L.*)
leaflets with >oints.	6–8	Mountain woods.	2–5 ft. Climbing. (*L.*)
ves cut; those m oblong, araped at base. >ed.	All the year.	Everywhere.	VERY SMALL. 4–18 in. Whole plant rough and hairy. (*V. C.*)
	1–8	Seashore.	1–6 in. (*C.*)
al, in a rosette.	2–5	Walls and banks.	1–6 in. (*C.*)
leaflets stalked.	All summer.	Everywhere.	3–12 in. Long seed pods, the valves of which when touched curl rapidly and scatter seed. (*V. C.*)
	3–4	Rocks.	2–5 in. (*L.*)
	4–9	Dry places.	6–10 in. Plant hairy and sticky. (*C.*)
ves long, egg- l.	5–7	Sandy places.	6–12 in. (*L.*)
aped.	5–6	Walls.	2–5 in. Whole plant sticky and reddish. (*C.*)
leaflets in four t pairs, serrate.	7–9	Dry pastures.	1–2 ft. Stem round. (*V. C.*)
	4–6	Waysides.	1–4 ft. An early spring flower, distinguished when in bud by drooping umbels. (*V. C.*)
inate; leaflets , sharply cut.	7–8	Hedges.	4–12 in. Seeds with hooked bristles. (*C.*)
inate; leaflets ', sharp cut,	7–8	Hedges.	2–3 ft. A slender plant, with solid rough stem. Seeds covered with incurved bristles. (*V. C.*)
innate, blunt, / hairy beneath.	5	Waysides.	2–3 ft. Distinguished by smooth polished stem and delicate green leaves. Seed bristly. (*V. C.*)
ves twice pin- stem leaves ?.	6–8	Meadows and marshes.	1–3 ft. (*L.*)

253. Agrimony.　　1. Wood Anemone.　　158. Angelica.　　162. Arrow-head.

246. Common Avens.　　412. Water Avens.　　124. Hedge Bedstraw.　　121. Heath Bedstraw.

318. Yellow Bedstraw.　　545. Giant Bell-flower.　　444. Betony.　　159. Bindweed.

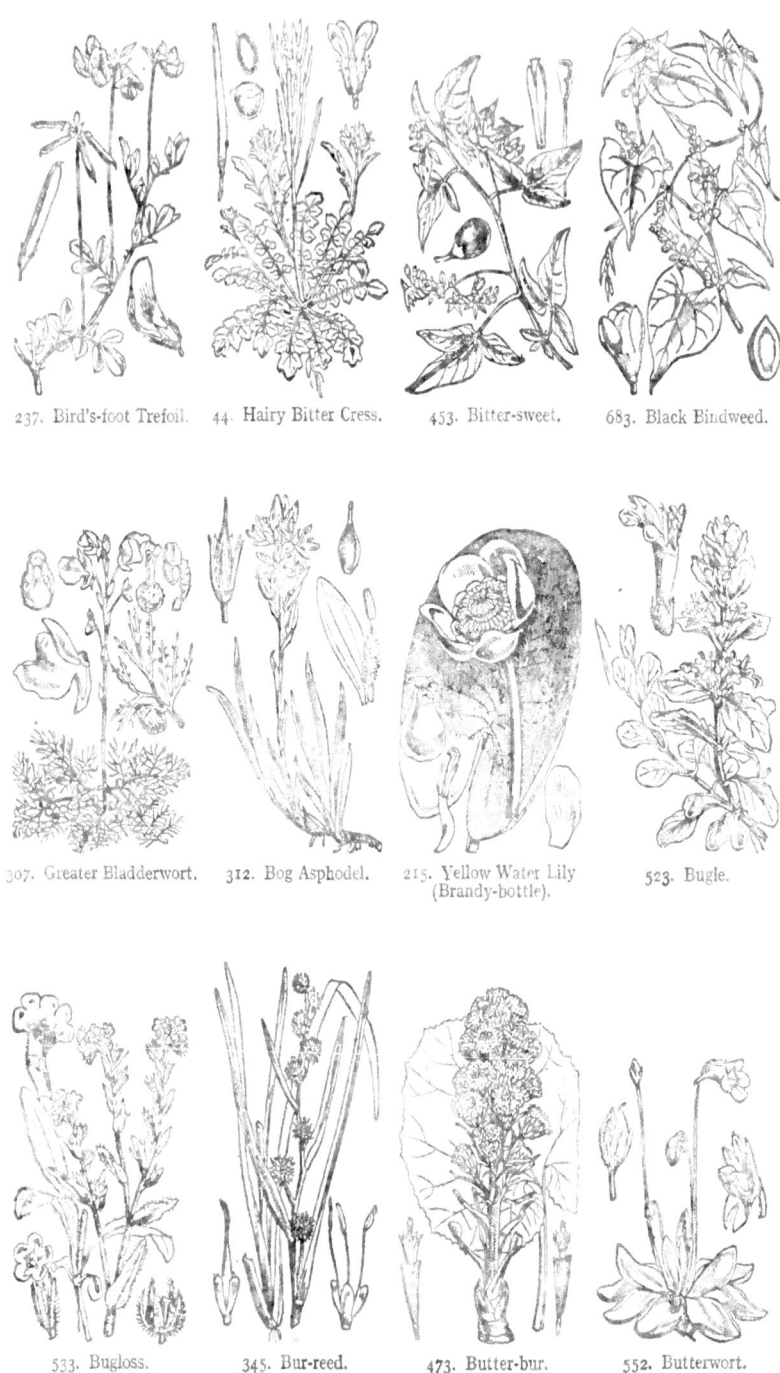

237. Bird's-foot Trefoil. 44. Hairy Bitter Cress. 453. Bitter-sweet. 683. Black Bindweed.

307. Greater Bladderwort. 312. Bog Asphodel. 215. Yellow Water Lily (Brandy-bottle). 523. Bugle.

533. Bugloss. 345. Bur-reed. 473. Butter-bur. 552. Butterwort.

Polypetalous.   **WHITE.**

English Name.	Latin Name.	Description of Flower.	Petals, Sepals, Stamens, etc.	
VERY SMALL (*contd.*).				
Hemlock Water Dropwort.	*Œnanthe crocata.*	$\frac{1}{18}$ in. In large compound umbels.	Petals, 5. Sepals, 5.	55.
River Water Dropwort.	*Œnanthe fluviatilis.*	$\frac{1}{8}$ in. In compound umbels.	Petals, 5.	56.
Field Pepperwort.	*Lepidium campestre.*	$\frac{1}{12}$ in. Minute.	Petals, 4. Sepals, 4. Stamens, 6. Anthers yellow.	57.
Smooth Field Pepperwort.	*Lepidium smithii.*	$\frac{1}{8}$ in.	Petals, 4. Sepals, 4. Stamens, 6. Anthers violet.	58.
Broad-leaved Pepperwort	*Lepidium latifolium.*	$\frac{1}{8}$ in. In leafy clusters.	Petals, 4. Sepals, 4. Stamens, 6.	59.
Narrow-leaved Pepperwort.	*Lepidium ruderale.*	$\frac{1}{8}$ in.	No petals. Sepals, 4. Stamens, 2.	60.
Naked-stalked Teesdalia.	*Teesdalia nudicaulis.*	$\frac{1}{8}$ in. In small racemes.	Petals, 4. Sepals, 4. Stamens, 4 or 6.	61.
Field Penny Cress.	*Thlaspi arvense.*	$\frac{1}{8}$ in.	Petals, 4. Sepals, 4. Stamens, 6.	62.
Perfoliate Penny Cress.	*Thlaspi perfoliatum*	$\frac{1}{8}$ in.	Petals, 4. Sepals, 4. Stamens, 6.	63.
Alpine Penny Cress.	*Thlaspi alpestre.*	$\frac{1}{8}$ in.	Petals, 4. Sepals, 4. Stamens, 6.	64.
Hairy Rock Cress.	*Arabis hirsuta.*	$\frac{1}{16}$ in.	Petals, 4. Sepals, 4. Stamens, 6.	65.
Thale Rock Cress.	*Arabis thaliana.*	$\frac{1}{8}$ in.	Petals, 4. Sepals, 4. Stamens, 6.	66.
Common Wart Cress.	*Senebiera coronopus.*	$\frac{1}{8}$ in.	Petals, 4. Sepals, 4. Stamens, 2, 4, or 6. Style prominent.	67.
Upright Mœnchia.	*Mœnchia erecta.*	$\frac{1}{4}$ in.	Petals, 4. Sepals, 4, sharp. Stamens, 4. Styles, 4.	68.
Horse-radish.	*Cochlearia armoracia.*	$\frac{1}{4}$ in.	Petals, 4. Sepals, 4. Stamens, 6.	69.
Three-nerved Sandwort.	*Arenaria trinervis.*	$\frac{1}{8}$ in. Solitary.	Petals, 5. Sepals, 5, three-nerved. Stamens, 10.	70.
Fine-leaved Sandwort.	*Arenaria tenuifolia.*	$\frac{1}{8}$ in.	Petals, 5. Sepals, 5, twice as long as petals. Stamens, 10.	71.
Thyme-leaved Sandwort.	*Arenaria serpyllifolia.*	$\frac{1}{9}$ in.	Petals, 5. Sepals, 5. Stamens, 10.	72.
Common Milkwort.	*Polygala vulgaris.*	$\frac{5}{16}$ in. Often blue or red in a raceme.	Petals, 3. Sepals, 3 small green and 2 coloured. Stamens, 8.	73.
Bog Stitchwort.	*Stellaria uliginosa.*	$\frac{1}{4}$ in. In a panicle.	Petals, 5, deeply cloven. Sepals, 5. Stamens, 10.	74.
Spiked Water Milfoil.	*Myriophyllum spicatum.*	$\frac{1}{16}$ in. Greenish white, whorled.	Petals, 2 or 4. Sepals, 4. Stamens, 8.	75.
Whorled Water Milfoil	*Myriophyllum verticillatum.*	$\frac{1}{8}$ in.	Petals, 2 or 4. Sepals, 4. Stamens, 8.	76.
Broad-leaved Water Parsnip.	*Sium latifolium.*	$\frac{1}{4}$ in. In umbels.	Petals, 5. Stamens, 5.	77.
Round-leaved Sundew.	*Drosera rotundifolia.*	$\frac{1}{16}$ in. All on same side of stalk.	Petals, 5. Sepals, 5. Stamens, 5.	78.
Long-leaved Sundew.	*Drosera longifolia.*	Similar to above.	Petals, 5. Sepals, 5. Stamens, 5.	79.
Fine-leaved Water Dropwort.	*Œnanthe phellandrium.*	$\frac{1}{8}$ in. In compound umbels.	Petals, 5. Stamens, 5.	80.

WHITE. Polypetalous.

Leaves.	Months.	Habitat.	Remarks.
			VERY SMALL (*contd.*).
innate leaflets, -shaped, pol- cut.	7	Marshes.	2–5 ft. Leaves somewhat like those of Dahlia. A poisonous plant. (*C.*)
pinnate, sub- d.	7	Streams.	1–4 ft. Stem floating, very stout. (*L.*)
upper ones shaped at base.	7–8	Fields.	10–12 in. (*C.*)
upper ones - shaped at	4–8	Fields.	6–12 in. This and the preceding are common hedge plants—*L. campestre*, an annual with single stem; *L. smithii*, a perennial with several stems. (*C.*)
ᴐed, pointed, h.	7	Salt marshes and sea coast.	2–4 ft. The largest British species. (*R.*)
lower, cut; linear, entire.	6	Salt marshes.	6–12 in. (*L.*)
radical.	4	Dry banks.	2–4 in. Central stem always leafless. (*R.*)
arrow-shaped ase, toothed, h.	All summer.	Fields.	1–2 ft. Name derived from likeness of seed-vessels to silver pennies. (*C.*)
eaves oblong, shaped at base, ig stem.	4–5	Limestone pastures and rocks.	4–6 in. Oxfordshire and Gloucestershire. (*R.*)
ᴐaves narrow, ig stem.	6–7	Pastures.	6–10 in. Mountain pastures in North of England. (*R.*)
hairy, stem clasping stem.	6–7	Walls and banks.	8–20 in. Root leaves in rosette, dark green. (*C.*)
ives few; root spreading, ob- oothed.	All summer.	Walls and banks.	6–10 in. (*C.*)
innate, leaflets	All summer.	Waysides.	3–10 in. Common wayside weed, with trailing stems and disagreeable smell. (*C.*)
stiff.	6	Waysides.	2–6 in. Flowers expand only in sunshine. (*L.*)
leaves broad, late.	6–8	Waste places.	2–3 ft. Really a garden plant, but wild in places. (*R.*)
cute, lower one d.	5–6	Wet places.	5–12 in. Similar to Chickweed, but distinguished from it by undivided petals. (*C.*)
ᴐed.	4–8	Sandy fields in East of England.	4–6 in. Stem slender, much forked. (*L.*)
ovate, pointed, sessile.	6–8	Waysides and walls.	2–6 in. A shrubby plant.
lanceolate.	6–8	Heaths and dry pastures.	2–10 in. The blue form is the commonest. (*C.*)
lanceolate, with ᴐiut, smooth.	5–6	Bogs.	6–12 in.
in a whorl, ry.	7–8	Ponds.	1–3 ft. Whole plant submerged except leafless flower stems. Stamens and pistils on different flowers, but on same plant. (*C.*) Differs from above in having flowers in whorls at base of leaves. (*C.*)
large; leaflets ᴐ six, toothed.	7–8	Watery places.	3–4 ft. Stem furrowed. (*C.*)
al, covered with h hairs.	7–8	Bogs.	2–6 in. Well marked by hairs on leaves, with drop of sticky fluid on each. (*C.*)
	7–8	Bogs.	Differing from above in shape of leaves, which are longer, broad at end, and tapering towards base. (*L.*)
into very fine nts; lower, sub- d.	7–9	Wet places.	1–4 ft. Stem very stout at base. (*C.*)

Polypetalous. **WHITE.**

English Name.	Latin Name.	Description of Flower.	Petals, Sepals, Stamens, etc.	
VERY SMALL (*contd.*).				
Burnet Saxifrage.	*Pimpinella saxifraga.*	$\frac{1}{16}$ in. In compound umbels.	Petals, 5. Stamens, 5.	81.
Greater Burnet Saxifrage.	*Pimpinella magna.*	$\frac{1}{8}$ in. In compound umbels.	Petals, 5. Stamens, 5.	82.
Sweet Cicely.	*Myrrhis odorata.*	$\frac{1}{8}$ in. In downy umbels.		83.
Perfoliate Claytonia.	*Claytonia perfoliata.*	$\frac{1}{8}$ in.	Petals, 5. Sepals, 2. Stamens, 5.	84.
Common Earth-nut or Pig-nut.	*Conopodium denudatum.*	$\frac{1}{8}$ in. In umbels.	Petals, 5. Stamens, 5.	85.
Common Caraway.	*Carum carui.*	$\frac{1}{8}$ in. In compound umbels, with one bract at base of main umbel.	Petals, 5. Stamens, 5.	86.
Hemlock.	*Conium maculatum.*	$\frac{1}{16}$ in. In compound umbels.	Petals, 5. Stamens, 5.	87.
Rough Chervil.	*Chærophyllum temulentum.*	$\frac{1}{8}$ in. In compound umbels, drooping in bud.	Petals, 5. Stamens, 5.	88.
Fool's Parsley.	*Æthusa cynapium.*	$\frac{1}{16}$ in. In compound umbels.	Petals, 5. Stamens, 5.	89.
Cowbane or Water Hemlock.	*Cicuta virosa.*	$\frac{1}{16}$ in. In compound umbels.	Petals, 5. Stamens, 5.	90.
Narrow-leaved Water Parsnip.	*Sium angustifolium.*	$\frac{1}{12}$ in. In compound umbels, opposite leaves.	Petals, 5. Stamens, 5.	91.
Corn Parsley.	*Petroselinum segetum.*	$\frac{1}{16}$ in. In compound umbels.	Petals, 5. Stamens, 5.	92.
Procumbent Marshwort.	*Helosciadium nodiflorum.*	$\frac{1}{8}$ in. In compound umbels.	Petals, 5. Stamens, 5.	93.
Least Marshwort.	*Helosciadium inundatum.*	$\frac{1}{16}$ in. In compound umbels; small umbels only two-rayed.	Petals, 5. Stamens, 5.	94.
Honewort.	*Trinia glaberrima.*	$\frac{1}{12}$ in. In compound umbels.	Stamens and pistils on different plants.	95.
Shepherd's Needle or Venus' Comb.	*Scandix pecten.*	$\frac{1}{8}$ in. Few rayed simple umbels.	Petals, 5. Stamens, 5.	96.
Sweet Alyssum.	*Alyssum maritimum.*	$\frac{1}{4}$ in. Sweet-scented.	Petals, 4. Sepals, 4. Stamens, 6.	97.
Water Awlwort.	*Subularia aquatica.*	$\frac{1}{8}$ in. Few.	Petals, 4. Sepals, 4, spreading. Stamens, 6.	98.
Thyme-leaved Flax Seed, or All Seed.	*Radiola millegrana.*	$\frac{1}{8}$ in. A large number.	Petals, 4. Stamens, 4. Styles, 4.	99.
Autumnal Lady's Tresses.	*Spiranthes autumnalis.*	$\frac{1}{5}$ in. A spike. Flowers in single row, arranged spirally round stalk.	Petals, 3. Sepals, 3.	100.
Water Blinks.	*Montia fontana.*	$\frac{1}{12}$ in.	Petals, 5, 3 smaller than others. Calyx, two-cleft.	101.
Monopetalous.				
LARGE.				
Great Bindweed.	*Calystegia sepium.*	2 in. Bell-shaped, solitary, on square stalks.	Petals, five-lobed. Sepals, 5. Stamens, 5.	102.
Great White Ox-eye Daisy.	*Chrysanthemum leucanthemum.*	2 in. Ray florets white, disc yellow.		103.
Corn Chamomile.	*Anthemis arvensis.*	1 in. Ray florets white, disc yellow.		104.
Scentless Mayweed.	*Matricaria inodora.*	1¼ in. Ray florets white, disc greenish yellow, very convex.		105.

WHITE. Polypetalous.

	Leaves.	Months.	Habitat.	Remarks.
				VERY SMALL (*contd.*).
81.	Root leaves pinnate, leaflets four to eight pairs; stem leaves bipinnate.	7–8	Dry pastures.	1–2 ft. Stem round, smooth. (*V. C.*)
82.	All leaves pinnate.	7–8	Shady places.	2–4 ft. Stem angular. (*L.*)
83.	Large, tripinnate, downy, bright pale green.	5–6	Mountain pastures.	2–3 ft. Stem furrowed hollow. Plant sweet-scented. (*L.*)
84.	Roundish.	4–7	Waste places.	3–10 in. Of North American origin. (*R.*)
85.	Finely divided, segments hair-like.	5–6	Fields.	8–20 in. The root a tuber which is eatable by pigs. A slender plant, smooth. (*V. C.*)
86.	Bipinnate, leaflets cut into narrow segments.	6	Waste places.	1–2 ft. Produces the well-known scented caraway seeds. (*L.*)
87.	Tripinnate.	6–7	Waysides.	2–4 ft. Distinguished by hollow, smooth stem, spotted with red. (*C.*)
88.	Bipinnate, deeply lobed, hairy, purple in autumn.	6–7	Woods and waysides.	2–3 ft. Stem slender, rough, hairy, spotted with purple, and swollen beneath joints. (*C.*)
89.	Bipinnate.	7–8	Waste places.	1 ft. Common garden weed. Distinguished by having no bracts at base of main umbel, but three long narrow bracts at base of partial umbel. Poisonous. (*V. C.*)
90.	Lower, bipinnate; upper, twice ternate.	7–8	Ditches.	3–4 ft. Stem hollow, very stout. Poisonous. (*R.*)
91.	Pinnate; leaflets unequally cut, oval.	8	Ditches.	1–3 ft. General and partial bracts, reflexed, often cut. (*C.*)
92.	Small, pinnate.	8–9	Waste places.	1–2 ft. Distinguished by slender, branched stem, which is very tough and wiry. (*L.*)
93.	Pinnate; leaflets egg-shaped, serrate.	7–8	Brooks.	1–3 ft. Often mistaken for Water-cress, with which it grows; distinguished by serrated leaves and hollow stems. (*V. C.*)
94.	Upper, pinnate; lower, submerged, with hair-like segments.	6–7	Ponds.	3–12 in. Flowers and upper leaves only parts above water. (*C.*)
95.	Thrice pinnate, shiny; leaflets very narrow.		Limestone.	3–8 in. In Somerset and at Barry Head, Devon. (*R.*)
96.	Tripinnate.	6–9	Cornfields.	4–12 in. Long beaked seed-vessels. (*C.*)
97.	Linear.	All summer.	Coasts.	4–8 in. A garden escape. (*L.*)
98.	Radical, awl-shaped.	7	Side of lakes.	3–4 in. Plant often entirely submerged. (*R.*)
99.	Minute, opposite, sessile, ovate.	7–8	Damp heaths.	1–3 in. One of the smallest British plants. (*C.*)
100.	Ovate, appearing after flowers.	9–10	Pastures.	4–8 in. Flowers fragrant in evening. (*L.*)
101.	Opposite, spoon-shaped.	5–8	Wet places.	1–4 in. (*C.*)

Monopetalous.

LARGE.

102.	Arrow-shaped.	7–9	Hedges.	3–8 ft. A mischievous climbing weed. (*C.*)
103.	Lower leaves stalked; upper, sessile.	6–7	Meadows.	1–2 ft. (*V. C.*)
104.	Deeply cut, white with down.	6–7	Cornfields.	1–2 ft. Erect, branched. (*C.*)
105.	Sessile, hair-like segments.	7–10	Waste places.	6–18 in. Stem branched. (*V. C.*)

359. Red Campion.   280. Cat's-ear.   167. Cat's-foot (Mountain Everlasting).   224. Greater Celandine.

219. Lesser Celandine.   384. Centaury.   230. Charlock.   88. Wild Chervil.

24. Chickweed.   111. European Chickweed.   505. Chicory (Succory).   149. Purple Clover.

Monopetalous. **WHITE.**

English Name.	Latin Name.	Description of Flower.	Petals, Sepals, Stamens, etc.	
MEDIUM.				
Common Daisy.	Bellis perennis.	¾ in. Ray florets white; disc yellow.		106.
Stinking Chamomile.	Anthemis cotula.	1 in. Ray florets white; disc yellow.		107.
Wild Chamomile.	Matricaria chamomilla.	½ in. Ray florets white, short; disc yellow.		108.
Common Chamomile.	Anthemis nobilis.	1 in. Ray florets white; disc yellow. Drooping in bud.		109.
Common Feverfew.	Matricaria parthenium.	½ in. Ray florets white; disc yellow, nearly flat.		110.
European Chickweed or Wintergreen.	Trientalis europæa.	½ in. On slender stalks, few drooping.	Petals, 5. Sepals, 5. Stamens, 7-9.	111.
Guelder Rose.	Viburnum opulus.	⅝ in. (outer flowers), inner smaller. Flat cymes, 3 in. diameter.		112.
White Dead-nettle.	Lamium album.	⅝ in. Irregular, two-lipped.	Petals in tube. Stamens, 4, black.	113.
SMALL.				
Lily of the Valley.	Convallaria majalis.	⅜ in. Bell-shaped; drooping, in one-sided raceme.	Perianth, six-lobed. Stamens, 6.	114.
Black Nightshade.	Solanum nigrum.	¼ in. In drooping umbels.	Petals, 5, spreading. Stamens, 5. Anthers yellow.	115.
Yarrow or Milfoil.	Achillea millefolium.	⅛ in. In flat-topped clusters. Rays white, sometimes pink; disc yellow.		116.
Privet.	Ligustrum vulgare.	⅜ in. Panicles of sickly-smelling flowers.	Petals, 4. Sepals, 4. Stamens, 2.	117.
Intermediate Wintergreen.	Pyrola media.	¼ in. In racemes, drooping, roundish.	Petals, 5. Sepals, 5. Stamens, 10. Style straight, longer than stamens.	118.
Creeping Goodyera.	Goodyera repens.	¼ in. Lipped, narrow, spiral spike.	Petals, 3. Sepals, 3.	119.
VERY SMALL.				
Sweet Woodruff.	Asperula odorata.	¼ in. In terminal panicles.	Petals, 4. Stamens, 4.	120.
Heath Bedstraw.	Galium saxatile.	⅛ in. In clusters.	Petals, 4. Stamens, 4.	121.
Corn Bedstraw.	Galium tricorne.	⅛ in. In axillary cluster.		122.
Rough Water Bedstraw.	Galium uliginosum.	⅛ in. In few flowering cymes.	Petals, 4. Stamens, 4.	123.
Hedge Bedstraw.	Galium mollugo.	⅛ in. In loose panicles.	Petals, 4. Stamens, 4.	124.
Water Bedstraw.	Galium palustre.	⅛ in. In loose, spreading panicles.	Petals, 4. Stamens, 4.	125.
Goose-grass or Cleavers.	Galium aparine.	⅛ in. Two to three together.	Petals, 4. Stamens, 4.	126.
White Horehound.	Marrubium vulgare.	¼ in. In dense whorls.	Two-lipped. Stamens, 4. Calyx teeth sharp, hooked.	127.

WHITE. Monopetalous.

Leaves.	Months.	Habitat.		Remarks.
				MEDIUM.
obovate.	All the year.	Everywhere.	2–8 in.	(V. C.)
t, with hair-like ats.	7–8	Waste places.	8–16 in.	Has a disagreeable smell. (V. C.)
innatifid, very v segments.	6–8	Waysides.	12–18 in.	(C.)
t into hair-like ats; slightly '.	8	Heaths.	6–12 in.	Has a pleasant apple-like smell. Hence its name Chamomile, signifying in Greek "ground apple." (L.)
e, stalked.	7–8	Waste places.	1–2 ft.	Name Feverfew is a corruption of Febrifuge, from its medicinal properties. Whole plant has a strong odour. (C.)
ound, smooth; ' at top of stems.	6		4–6 in.	Scottish Highlands and North of England. (R.)
bed, serrate.	6–7	Woods and hedges.	6–8 ft.	Outer flowers have no stamens or pistils. In the garden variety the cyme is in globular form. (C.)
aped, toothed.	All summer.	Waysides.	6–18 in.	Similar to common nettle, but distinguished by square stalk and white flowers. (V. C.)
				SMALL.
adical.	4	Woods.	5–8 in.	Berries scarlet. (L.)
ped, wavy.	7–9	Waste places.	1–2 ft.	Berries round, black. Plant has disagreeable smell. (C.)
e; twice pinna- lightly downy; s in hair-like nts.	6–9	Waste places.	6–18 in.	Has a strong smell. (V. C.)
', narrow, oval, een.	5–6	Hedges.	4–10 ft.	A bush much used for hedges. Berries black. (C.)
h oval.	7–8	Woods.	8–12 in.	Distinguished by protruding style. North of England. (L.)
cute.	Late summer.	Fir woods.	4–8 in.	In Cumberland and Scotland. (R.)
				VERY SMALL.
a whorl, slightly at edges.	5	Woods.	6–10 in.	Flowers fragrant. When dry, plant smells like new-mown hay. (C.)
six in a whorl, v, pointed.	6–8	Heaths.	4–10 in.	Stem four-angled, smooth, prostrate. (V. C.)
six to eight in rl.	6–10	Fields.	1–3 ft.	Stem rough. Seed with hooked bristles. (L.)
ght in a whorl; bristly at edges.	7–8	Wet places.	2–5 ft.	Angles of stem rough. (C.)
ght in a whorl; ;, tapering, at edges.	7–8	Hedges.	1–4 ft.	Stem four-angled, rough. (C.)
six in a whorl; r, blunt, taper- base.	7–8	Wet places.	1–3 ft.	Stem weak; rather rough. (C.)
ght in a whorl; ough, with short d bristles.	6–8	Hedges.	1–5 ft.	Leaves and stem cling to fingers when touched. Seeds dispersed by attaching themselves to coats of animals. Hence name of Cleavers. (V. C.)
rrinkled.	8	Waste places.	12–18 in.	Stems woolly. A bushy plant. (C.)

Polypetalous.

WHITISH.

English Name.	Latin Name.	Description of Flower.	Petals, Sepals, Stamens, etc.	
MEDIUM. Large - flowered Bitter Cress.	*Cardamine amara.*	$\frac{1}{2}$ in.	Petals, 4. Sepals, 4. Stamens, 6. Anthers purple.	128.
White Bryony.	*Bryonia dioica.*	$\frac{5}{8}$ in. In bunches with green veins.	Petals, 5. Sepals, 5. Stamens, 3.	129.
Grass of Parnassus.	*Parnassia palustris.*	$\frac{7}{8}$ in. Solitary, veined.	Petals, 5. Sepals, 5. Stamens, 5.	130.
VERY SMALL. Hedge Stone Parsley.	*Sison amomum.*	$\frac{1}{8}$ in. General umbels with about four rays. Partial umbels with four bracts at base. Cream-coloured.	Petals, 5. Stamens, 5.	131.
Glabrous Rock Cress or Tower Mustard.	*Arabis perfoliata.*	$\frac{1}{4}$ in. Yellowish white.	Petals, 4. Sepals, 4. Stamens, 6.	132.
Underground Trefoil.	*Trifolium subterraneum.*	$\frac{1}{8}$ in. About four in cluster.	Petals, 5. Sepals, 5. Stamens, 10.	133.
Rigid Trefoil.	*Trifolium scabrum.*	$\frac{1}{16}$ in. Dense prickly heads.	Petals, 5. Sepals, 5. Calyx prickly.	134.
Sea Samphire.	*Crithmum maritimum.*	$\frac{1}{16}$ in. Yellowish white, in compound umbels.	Petals, 5. Stamens, 5.	135.
Mossy Tillæa.	*Tillæa muscosa.*	$\frac{1}{16}$ in. Greenish white, tipped with red.	Petals, 3. Sepals, 3. Stamens, 3.	136.
Wood Sanicle.	*Sanicula europæa.*	$\frac{1}{16}$ in. In compound umbels, dull white.	Petals, 5.	137.

Monopetalous.

English Name.	Latin Name.	Description of Flower.	Petals, Sepals, Stamens, etc.	
SMALL. Common Comfrey.	*Symphytum officinale.*	$\frac{5}{8}$ in. White, pink, or purple; tubular, in two forked clusters.	Petals, 5.	138.
Canadian Fleabane.	*Erigeron canadensis.*	$\frac{1}{4}$ in. Ray florets whitish, tinged red; disc pale yellow. Many heads.		139.
Butcher's Broom.	*Ruscus aculeatus.*	$\frac{1}{4}$ in. Greenish white, growing from centre of leaves.	Petals, 6, joined. Sepals, 0. Stamens, 3.	140.
VERY SMALL. Common Solomon's Seal.	*Polygonatum multiflorum.*	$\frac{1}{4}$ in. In small clusters, tipped with green, opposite to leaves.	Petals, 6. Sepals, 6. Stamens, 6.	141.
Wayfaring Tree.	*Viburnum lantana.*	$\frac{1}{4}$ in. In terminal cymes.	Petals, 5. Stamens, 5.	142.
Corn Gromwell.	*Lithospermum arvense.*	$\frac{3}{16}$ in.	Petals, 5. Calyx deeply five-cleft. Stamens, 5.	143.

WHITISH. Polypetalous.

Leaves.	Months.	Habitat.	Remarks.
aves pinnate, d. Root leaf undish.	4-5	Wet places.	MEDIUM. 9-20 in. By banks of rivers. (L.)
d, rough.	4-8	Hedges.	1-3 ft. Stem angled. Stamens and pistils on different flowers. A climbing plant, with tendrils. (C.)
, cordate, ses-	8-10	Bogs.	8-10 in. Stem angular. (L.)
cut. Upper very narrow.	8	Waysides.	VERY SMALL. 2-3 ft. Plant has unpleasant smell. (C.)
aves clasping smooth. Root rather hairy.		Banks.	2-3 ft. (L.)
three.	5-6	Pastures.	4-18 in. Flower stems erect, in seed bending down and sending out fibres which penetrate ground. (R.)
three.	6-7	Fields.	3-10 in. Especially found near sea. (C.)
inear.	7-8	Sea rocks.	6-10 in. Plant has strong smell. (L.)
, blunt, thick	6-7	Sandy places.	1-2 in. South and East of England. (L.)
glossy, three--lobed, cut.	6-7	Woods.	6-12 in. Slender, smooth plant. Seeds covered with hooked prickles. (C.)

Monopetalous.

tapering toward and running stem.	4-8	Wet places.	SMALL. 2-3 ft. Stem winged above. (C.)
	8-9	Waste places.	1-2 ft. Somewhat resembling groundsel. (L.)
iny.	4-5	Bushy places.	1-4 ft. Not uncommon in South of England. (L.)
turned opposi-ly to flowers.	6	Woods.	VERY SMALL. 1-2 ft. Stems arched. (L.)
Heart-shaped e; downy be-; serrate.	5-6	Woods.	5-20 ft. A large shrub. Leaves turn purple in autumn. (L.)
tapering, hairy.	5-7	Cornfields.	10-16 in. Stem branched below. Calyx lengthening in seed. (C.)

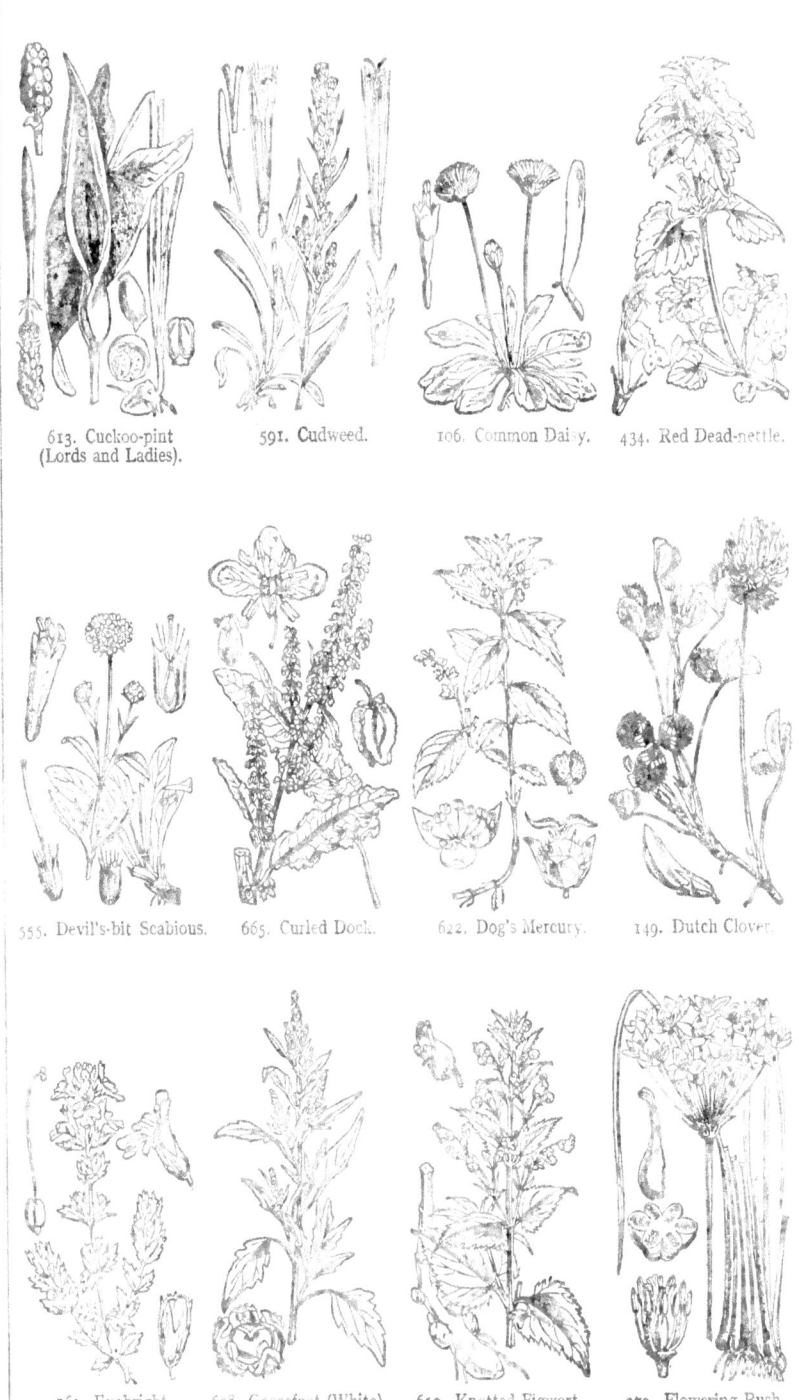

613. Cuckoo-pint (Lords and Ladies).   591. Cudweed.   106. Common Daisy.   434. Red Dead-nettle.

555. Devil's-bit Scabious.   665. Curled Dock.   622. Dog's Mercury.   149. Dutch Clover.

163. Eyebright.   638. Goosefoot (White).   650. Knotted Figwort.   379. Flowering Rush.

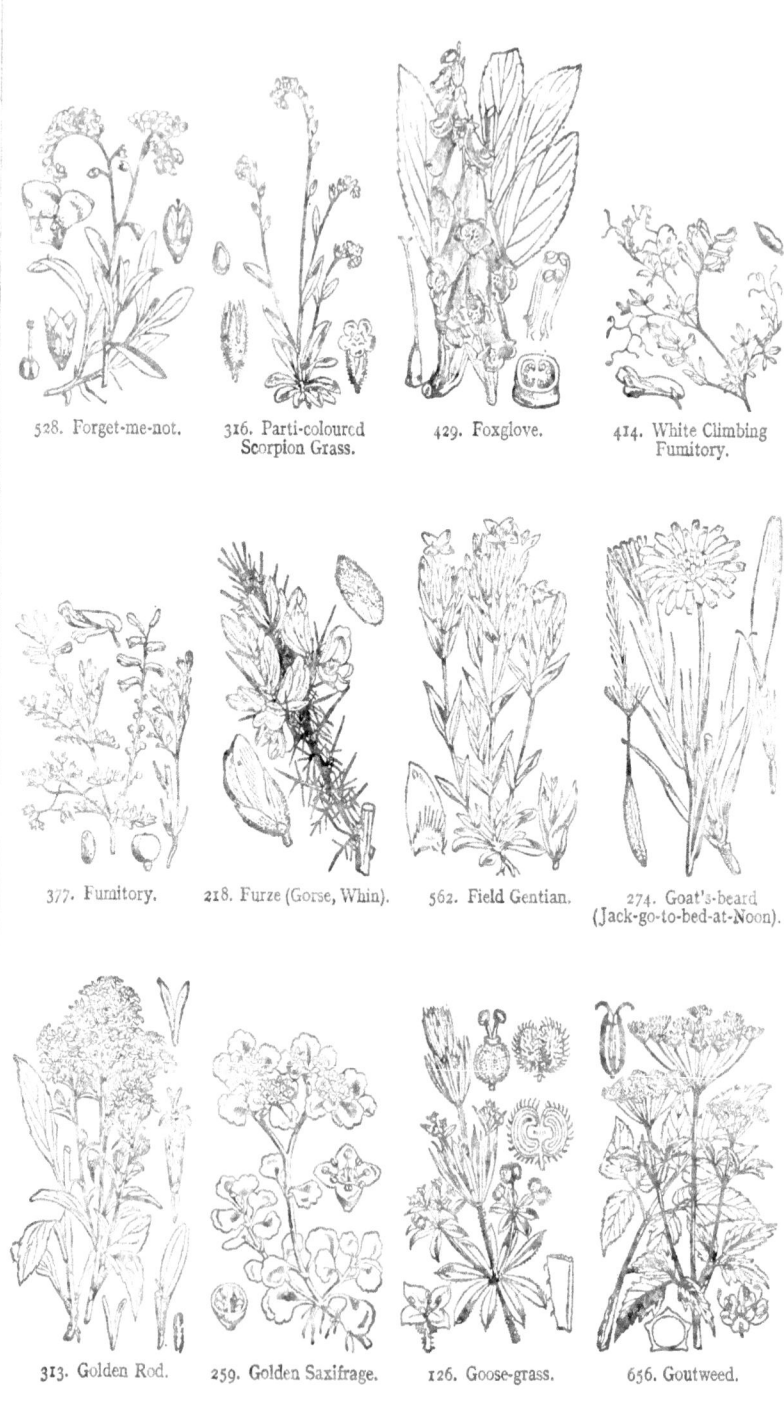

528. Forget-me-not.   316. Parti-coloured Scorpion Grass.   429. Foxglove.   414. White Climbing Fumitory.

377. Fumitory.   218. Furze (Gorse, Whin).   562. Field Gentian.   274. Goat's-beard (Jack-go-to-bed-at-Noon).

313. Golden Rod.   259. Golden Saxifrage.   126. Goose-grass.   656. Goutweed.

Polypetalous.   WHITE OR WHITISH,

English Name.	Latin Name.	Description of Flower.	Petals, Sepals, Stamens, etc.	
LARGE. Burnet Rose.	Rosa spinosissima.	1¼ in. Creamy; pinkish in bud.	Petals, 5. Sepals, 5. Stamens, many.	144.
Water Crowfoot.	Ranunculus aquatilis.	1 in. White, with yellow centre.	Petals, 5, yellow at base. Sepals, 5. Stamens, many.	145.
Cloudberry.	Rubus chamæmorus.	1 in. White, with rose tint. Solitary.	Petals, 5. Sepals, 5. Stamens, many.	146.
White Opium Poppy.	Papaver somniferum.	1 in. White, with purple tint at base.	Petals, 4. Sepals, 2. Stamens, many.	147.
MEDIUM. Wild Radish.	Raphanus raphanistrum.	¾ in. Straw-coloured, with purple veins.	Petals, 4. Sepals, 4. Stamens, 6.	148.
SMALL. White or Dutch Clover.	Trifolium repens.	⁵⁄₁₆ in. In roundish heads; pinkish tint, fading brown.	Petals, 5. Sepals, 5. Stamens, 10.	149.
Common Bird's-foot.	Ornithopus perpusillus.	¹⁄₁₆ in. Cream-coloured, with crimson veins.	Petals, 5. Sepals, 5.	150.
London Pride.	Saxifraga umbrosa.	¼ in. White, with pink spots.	Petals, 5. Sepals, 5. Stamens, 10.	151.
Enchanter's Nightshade.	Circæa lutetiana.	⅛ in. Pinkish white.	Petals, 2, cleft. Sepals, 2, bent back. Stamens, 2, pink.	152.
Wild Carrot.	Daucus carota.	⅛ in. White; central flower red. In umbels.		153.
Fenugreek.	Trigonella ornithopodioides.	⅛ in. Whitish or pink. One to three together in axils of leaves.	Petals, 5. Sepals, 5.	154.
Hairy Stonecrop.	Sedum villosum.	⅛ in. Pinkish white.	Petals, 5. Sepals, 5. Stamens, 10.	155.
English Catchfly.	Silene anglica.	⁵⁄₁₆ in. In one-sided spikes, pinkish white.	Petals, 5, slightly cleft. Stamens, 10.	156.
Alpine Enchanter's Nightshade.	Circæa alpina.	⅛ in. In racemes, pinkish white.	Petals, 2. Sepals, 2. Stamens, 2.	157.
Wild Angelica.	Angelica sylvestris.	⅛ in. In compound umbels, tinged with pink.	Petals, 5. Stamens, 5.	158.

Monopetalous.

LARGE. Field Bindweed.	Convolvulus arvensis.	1¼ in. Bell-shaped; five-angled. One to three together.	Petals, 5. Sepals, 5. Stamens, 5.	159.
MEDIUM. Buckbean or Marsh Trefoil.	Menyanthes trifoliata.	½ in. Bright rose in bud. In clusters, opposite to leaves.	Petals, 5, covered with white hairs. Sepals, 5. Stamens, 5.	160.
Bastard or Wild Balm.	Melittis melissophyllum.	⅞ in. Lipped, blotched with rose.	Calyx two- to three-lobed. Stamens, 4.	161.
Arrow-head.	Sagittaria sagittifolia.	¾ in. In whorls.		162.
SMALL. Eyebright.	Euphrasia officinalis.	⅜ in. White, with yellow spot and purple lines.	Lipped. Sepals, 4. Stamens, 4.	163.
Dwarf Orchis.	Orchis ustulata.	¹⁄₁₆ in. In dense spike, purple in bud.	Petals, 2. Sepals, 3.	164.
Star-fruit.	Actinocarpus damasonium.	⅝ in. White, with yellow spot at base of petals.	Petals, 3. Sepals, 3. Stamens, 6.	165.
Black Bearberry.	Arctostaphylos uva-ursi.	⅛ in. White, purplish tinge. Berries black.	Petals, 5. Sepals, 5. Stamens, 10.	166.

WITH SOME OTHER TINT. Polypetalous.

	Leaves.	Months.	Habitat.	Remarks.
				LARGE.
144.	Seven to nine small leaflets, serrate, smooth.	5-6	Waste places.	1-4 ft. Found especially near sea. Many straight prickles. (L.)
145.	Leaves above water, roundish; submerged, in hair-like segments.	5-7	Ponds and rivers.	1-10 ft. (C.)
146.	Simple, five- to seven-lobed, serrate.	6-7	Mountains.	6-10 in. Stamens and pistils on different plants. North of England, Scotland, Ireland. (L.)
147.	Clasping stem, waved or toothed.	7-8	Waste ground.	2 ft. (L.)
				MEDIUM.
148.	Root leaves rough, lyre-shaped.	All summer.	Fields.	1-2 ft. Distinguished in seed by jointed one-celled pods. (L.)
				SMALL.
149.	Three ovate leaflets, toothed, sometimes with mark in centre.	All summer.	Fields.	3-12 in. A common pasture plant. (V. C.)
150.	Downy, six to twelve pairs, set close.	7-8	Sandy heaths.	6-18 in. Seeds jointed, curved, resembling a bird's foot. (C.)
151.	Fleshy, in a rosette.	6	Mountains.	6-15 in. More often a garden plant. (L.)
152.	Egg-shaped, toothed.	7-8	Damp places.	1-2 ft. Stem hairy. Seeds with hooked bristles. (C.)
153.	Tripinnate, much cut.	7-8	Pastures.	1-3 ft. Distinguished by red central flower. (C.)
154.	Leaflets, three.	6-8	Sandy places.	2-8 in. Seed pods curved, twice as long as calyx. (L.)
155.	Fleshy.	6-7	North of England.	3-4 in. Leaves and stems sticky. (L.)
156.	Narrow.	All summer.	Sandy fields.	1-2 ft. Whole plant hairy and sticky. (L.)
157.	Very thin, ovate, toothed, glossy.	7-8	Mountain woods.	1-2 ft. Leaves when dry almost transparent. North of England. (L.)
158.	Twice pinnate; leaflets ovate, serrate.	7	Wet places.	2-6 ft. Stem hollow, furrowed, purplish, rather downy in upper part. (C.)

Monopetalous.

	Leaves.	Months.	Habitat.	Remarks.
				LARGE.
159.	Arrow-shaped.	6-7	Waysides.	6-24 in. Flowers open only in sunshine. (V. C.)
				MEDIUM.
160.	Three leaflets, thick.	6-7	Bogs.	1-2 ft. (R.)
161.	Heart-shaped, hairy, serrate.	6-7	Woods.	1-2 ft. Leaves when fresh have unpleasant smell. (R.)
162.	Arrow-shaped.		Ponds and ditches.	6-8 in. out of water. Easily distinguished by distinctly arrow-shaped leaves. (C.)
				SMALL.
163.	Sessile, deeply cut.	6-9	Heaths and dry places.	2-10 in. An infusion of plant supposed good for eyes. (V. C.)
164.	Narrow, pointed; not spotted.		Chalk pastures.	4-5 in. (L.)
165.	Floating, oblong.	6-7	Ditches.	4-6 in. Mostly found in Midland counties. (R.)
166.	Wrinkled, serrate.		Mountains.	3-4 in. North of Scotland. (L.)

Monopetalous. **WHITE OR WHITISH,**

English Name.	Latin Name.	Description of Flower.	Petals, Sepals, Stamers, etc.	
SMALL (contd.). Mountain Everlasting.	Antennaria dioica.	$\frac{1}{12}$ in. Pinkish white; in small heads, not rayed.		167.
Lesser Wintergreen.	Pyrola minor.	$\frac{1}{4}$ in. In racemes; drooping, globular, with large stigma.	Petals, 5. Sepals, 5. Stamens, 10.	168.
Clover Dodder.	Cuscuta trifolii.	$\frac{1}{8}$ in. With pinkish tint, reddish stems.	Petals, 4–5. Sepals, 4–5. Stamens, 4–5.	169.
Dwarf Elder or Danewort.	Sambucus ebulus.	$\frac{1}{6}$ in. In clusters with three main branches. Pink-tipped; fragrant.	Petals, 5. Sepals, 5. Stamens, 5.	170.
Lesser Water Plantain.	Alisma ranunculoides.	$\frac{3}{8}$ in. In whorled umbels.	Petals, 3. Sepals, 3. Stamens, 6.	171.
VERY SMALL. Red Whortleberry or Cowberry.	Vaccinium vitis-idæa.	$\frac{1}{8}$ in. Pinkish, drooping, bell-shaped.	Petals, 4. Sepals, 4. Stamens, 8.	172.
Viviparous Bistort.	Polygonum viviparum.	$\frac{1}{8}$ in. Few in spike; pinkish.	Petals, 0. Sepals, 5. coloured. Stamens, 5.	173.
Great Wild Valerian.	Valeriana officinalis.	$\frac{1}{8}$ in. Pinkish, in corymb. Corolla swollen at base.	Petals, 5. Stamens, 3.	174.
Common Bistort or Snake-weed.	Polygonum bistorta.	$\frac{1}{8}$ in. Flesh-coloured; in spike.	Petals, 0. Sepals, 5. coloured. Stamens, 5.	175.
Common Mudwort.	Limosella aquatica.	$\frac{1}{8}$ in. Rose-tinted or white; overtopped by leaves.	Petals, 5. Sepals, 5. Stamens, 4.	176.
Cornish Moneywort.	Sibthorpia europæa.	$\frac{1}{16}$ in. Pinkish or yellow.	Petals, 5. Sepals, 5. Stamens, 4.	177.
Chaffweed or Bastard Pimpernel.	Centunculus minimus.	$\frac{1}{12}$ in. Numerous. Very like Pimpernel. Sessile.	Petals, 4. Sepals, 4. Stamens, 4.	178.
Toothed Corn Salad.	Fedia dentata.	$\frac{1}{8}$ in. In corymbs, with one sessile flower in fork of stem.	Petals, 5. Stamens, 3.	179.
Gipsy-wort.	Lycopus europæus.	$\frac{1}{8}$ in. Flesh-coloured. Sessile, in crowded whorls.	Petals, 5. Sepals, 5. Stamens, 2.	180.
Cat Mint.	Nepeta cataria.	$\frac{1}{2}$ in. Dotted with crimson; in dense whorls.	Sepals, 5. Stamens, 4.	181.

Polypetalous. **CREAMY WHITE.**

English Name.	Latin Name.	Description of Flower.	Petals, Sepals, Stamens, etc.	
LARGE. Trailing Dog Rose.	Rosa arvensis.	2 in. Scentless.	Petals, 5. Sepals, 5. Stamens, many.	182.
MEDIUM. Dropwort.	Spiræa filipendula.	$\frac{3}{4}$ in. Pink outside in bud. Scentless. In cyme.	Petals, 5. Sepals, 5. Stamens, many.	183.
Meadow-sweet.	Spiræa ulmaria.	$\frac{1}{16}$ in. Fragrant. Clustered in plumes.	Petals, 5. Sepals, 5. Stamens, many.	184.
Traveller's Joy or Clematis.	Clematis vitalba.	$\frac{3}{4}$ in. In loose panicles. Fragrant.	Petals, 0. Sepals, 4. Stamens, many.	185.

WITH SOME OTHER TINT.   Monopetalous.

	Leaves.	Months.	Habitat.		Remarks.
					SMALL (contd.).
167.	Downy beneath, broader at ends.	7–8	Mountains.	3–8 in.	(C.)
168.	Roundish.	7–8	Woods.	8–12 in.	Chiefly in North of England. (C.)
169.	None.	7–8	On clover.	1–2 ft.	A parasitic plant. Stems thread-like. (L.)
170.	Pinnate; seven to eleven narrow segments, and two serrate leaves at base of stalk.	7–8	Copses.	2–4 ft.	Supposed to have been introduced by Danes. (C.)
171.	All radical; narrow, tapering at both ends.	6–8	Ditches.	6–18 in.	(C.)
					VERY SMALL.
172.	Resembling those of Box. Dotted beneath, edges turned back.	5–6	Heaths.	6–18 in.	North of England. (C.)
173.	Very narrow; edges turned back.	6–7	Pastures.	4–8 in.	Scottish Highlands and North of England. (L.)
174.	Pinnate; segments narrow, toothed; rather hairy beneath.	6–7	Wet places.	2–5 ft.	(V. C.)
175.	Ovate. Radical leaves on long stalks.	6	Wet meadows.	12–18 in.	Chiefly in North of England. (C.)
176.	Radical, on long stalks.	7–8	Wet places.	1–4 in.	(L.)
177.	Small, round, downy.	6–9	River banks.	6–12 in.	Cornwall and some southern counties. (L.)
178.	Egg-shaped, smooth.	6–8	Damp places.	1–3 in.	Found especially where water has been standing. (C.)
179.	Narrow, toothed at base.	6–7	Cornfields.	6–12 in.	(C.)
180.	Lanceolate, deeply cut.	7–8	Ditches.	1–3 ft.	Stem four-angled. (C.)
181.	Serrate, whitish beneath.	7–8	Waste places.	2–3 ft.	(L.)

CREAMY WHITE.   Polypetalous.

	Leaves.	Months.	Habitat.		Remarks.
					LARGE.
182.	Smooth.	6–8	Hedges.	2–6 ft.	Distinguished by slender, trailing stems. Common in South of England. (C.)
					MEDIUM.
183.	Pinnate; alternate leaflets smaller; serrated segments.	7–9	Downs.	12–18 in.	(C.)
184.	Pinnate; alternate leaflets smaller; downy beneath.	7–8	Wet meadows.	2–4 ft.	The terminal leaflet is large and three-lobed. (V. C.)
185.	Three to five leaflets.	5–6	Hedges.	3–10 ft.	Common in limestone or chalk soil. Conspicuous in autumn. Feathery seed-vessels; commonly called "Old Man's Beard." (C.)

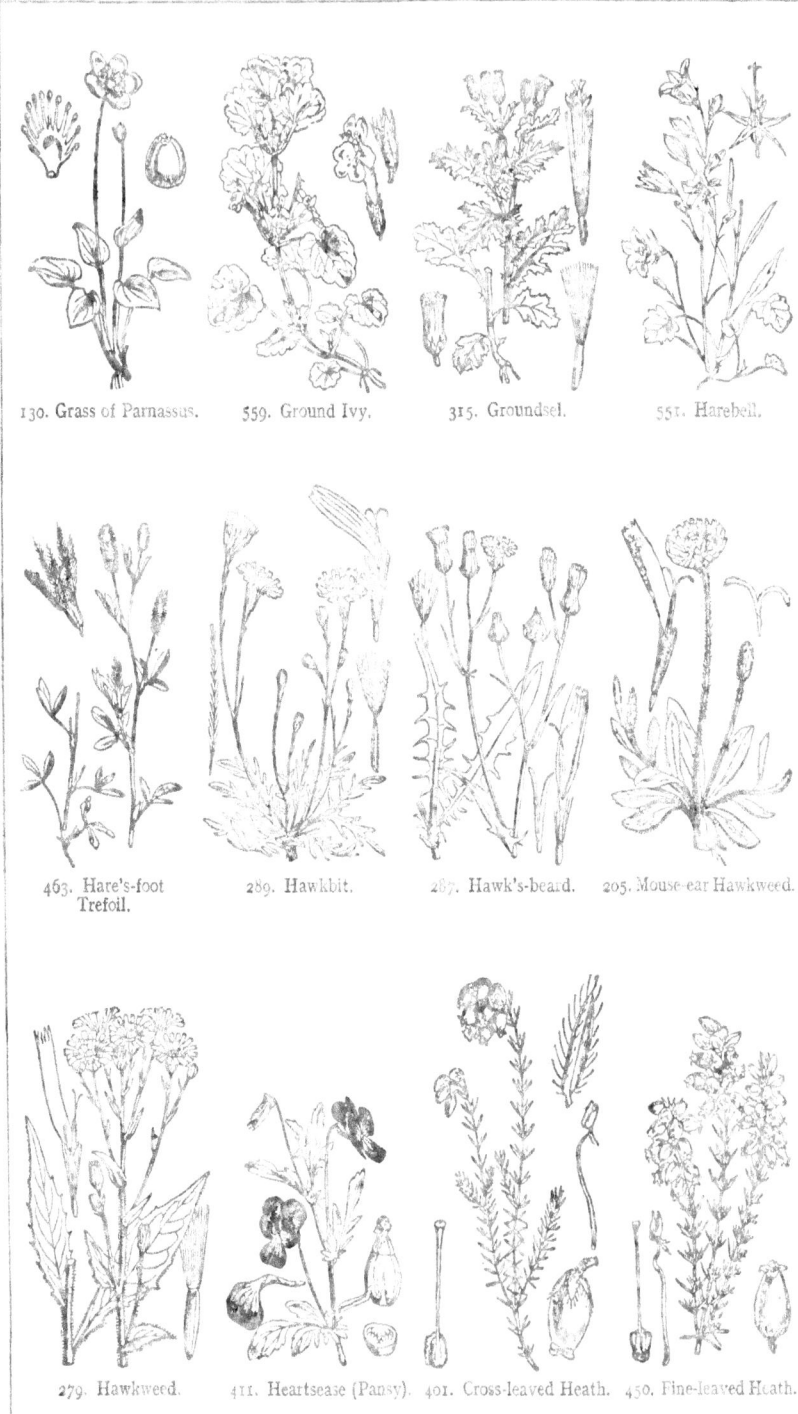

130. Grass of Parnassus. 559. Ground Ivy. 315. Groundsel. 551. Harebell.

463. Hare's-foot Trefoil. 289. Hawkbit. 287. Hawk's-beard. 205. Mouse-ear Hawkweed.

279. Hawkweed. 411. Heartsease (Pansy). 401. Cross-leaved Heath. 450. Fine-leaved Heath.

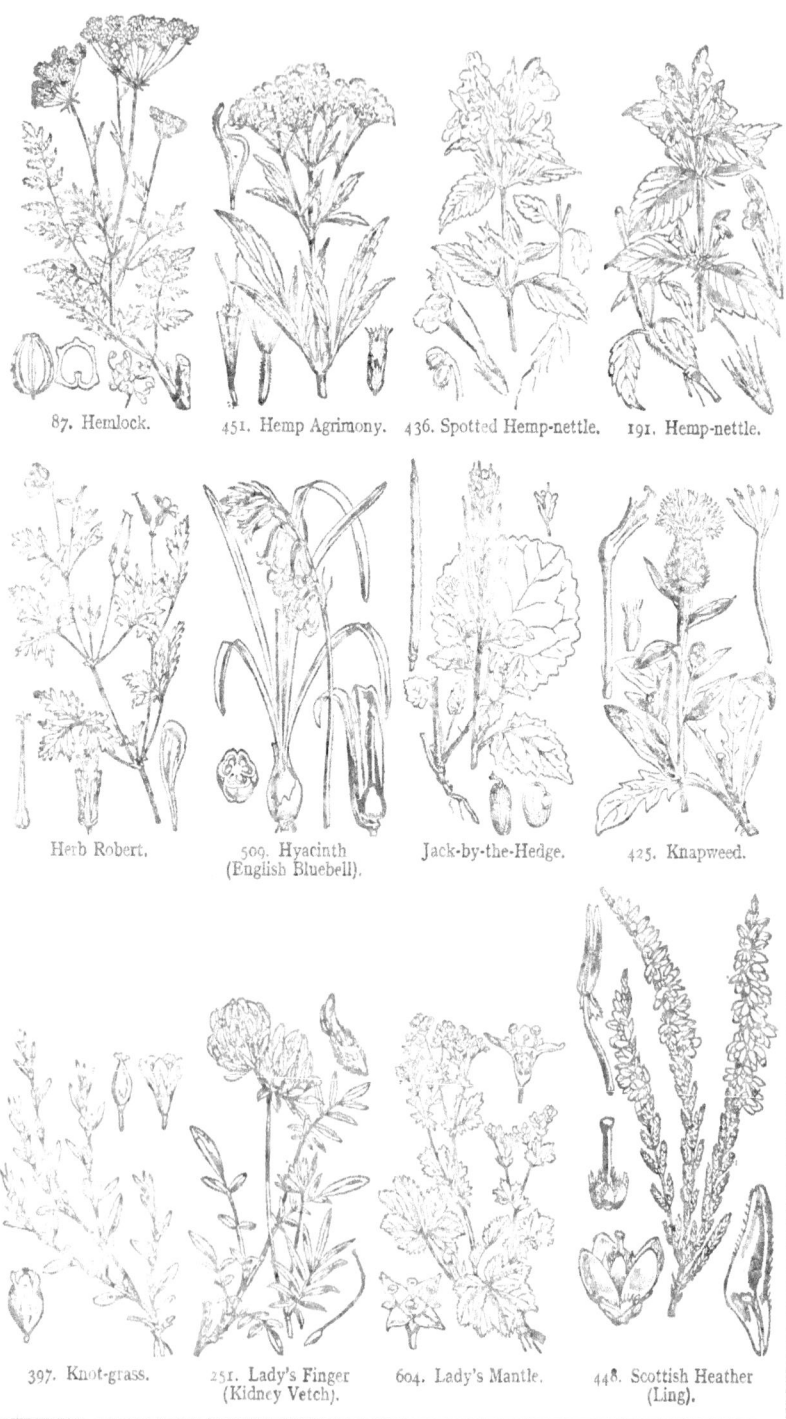

87. Hemlock. 451. Hemp Agrimony. 436. Spotted Hemp-nettle. 191. Hemp-nettle.

Herb Robert. 509. Hyacinth (English Bluebell). Jack-by-the-Hedge. 425. Knapweed.

397. Knot-grass. 251. Lady's Finger (Kidney Vetch). 604. Lady's Mantle. 448. Scottish Heather (Ling).

Polypetalous.   **CREAMY WHITE.**

English Name.	Latin Name.	Description of Flower.	Petals, Sepals, Stamens, etc.	
SMALL.				
Starry Clover.	Trifolium stellatum.	1/6 in. In round heads.	Petals, 5. Sepals, 5. Calyx spreading, star-like.	186.
Climbing Corydalis.	Corydalis claviculata.	1/3 in. In small clusters.	Petals, 4. Sepals, 2. Stamens, 6.	187.
White Melilot.	Melilotus alba.	1/8 in. In one-sided clusters.	Petals, 5, unequal. Sepals, 5. Stamens, 10.	188.
Alpine Meadow Rue.	Thalictrum alpinum.	1/8 in. In terminal clusters, point drooping.	Petals, 0. Sepals, 4, purplish white. Stamens, many.	189.
Monopetalous.				
LARGE.				
Honeysuckle or Woodbine.	Lonicera periclymenum.	1 in. Outside reddish.	Petals, 5. Sepals, 5. Stamens, 5.	190.
SMALL.				
Common Hempnettle.	Galeopsis tetrahit.	3/8 in. Two-lipped; in whorls. Variegated purple and yellow.	Sepals, 5, prickly. Stamens, 4.	191.
Common Comfrey.	Symphytum officinale.	3/8 in. Pinkish creamy or purple.	Petals, 5.	192.

Polypetalous.   **PALE YELLOW.**

English Name.	Latin Name.	Description of Flower.	Petals, Sepals, Stamens, etc.	
LARGE.				
Yellow Balsam.	Impatiens noli-me-tangere.	1 in. Spotted with orange.	Petals, 3. Sepals, 3-5. Stamens, 5.	193.
MEDIUM.				
Yellow Mountain Pansy.	Viola lutea.	1/2 in.	Petals, 5, unequal. Sepals, 5. Stamens, 5.	194.
Wild or Sea Cabbage.	Brassica oleracea.	3/4 in. Lemon-coloured.	Petals, 4. Sepals, 4. Stamens, 6.	195.
Isle of Man Cabbage.	Brassica monensis.	1/2 in. Lemon-coloured, veined with purple.	Petals, 4. Sepals, 4. Stamens, 6.	196.
Yellow Meadow Rue.	Thalictrum flavum.	1/8 in. Crowded, erect.	Petals, 0. Sepals, 4-5. Stamens, many, long.	197.
Marsh St. John's Wort.	Hypericum elodes.	1/2 in. Few, open for short time.	Petals, 5. Sepals, 5, with reddish glands. Stamens in three bundles of fifteen.	198.
SMALL.				
Celery-leaved Crowfoot.	Ranunculus sceleratus.	1/3 in.	Petals, 5. Sepals, 5. Stamens, many.	199.
Corn Crowfoot.	Ranunculus arvensis.	3/8 in.	Petals, 5. Sepals, 5. Stamens, many.	200.
Barberry.	Berberis vulgaris.	3/8 in. In drooping clusters.	Petals, 6. Sepals, 6. Stamens, 6.	201.
VERY SMALL.				
Treacle Mustard or Wormseed.	Erysimum cheiranthoides.	3/8 in. Cross-shaped.	Petals, 4. Sepals, 4, whitish. Stamens, 6.	202.
Common Hare's-ear or Thoroughwax.	Bupleurum rotundifolium.	1/10 in.	Petals, 5. Stamens, 5.	203.
Pepper Saxifrage.	Silaus pratensis.	1/8 in. In terminal umbels.	Petals, 5. Stamens, 5.	204

CREAMY WHITE. Polypetalous.

Leaves.	Months.	Habitat.	Remarks.
flets.	6–7	Shores.	SMALL. 4–12 in. Found only on coast at Shoreham, Sussex. (L.)
ending in red tendrils.	6–8	Woods and hedges.	6–24 in. Stem slender, climbing. (C.)
flets, toothed.		Waste places.	9–24 in. (C.)
rnate.	6–7	Bogs.	4–6 in. Scottish mountains, and North of England and Wales. (L.)

Monopetalous.

			LARGE.
iry.	7	Hedges.	6–15 ft. (V. C.)
bristly.	7–9	Cornfields.	SMALL. 1–2 ft. Stem square, swollen at joints. (V. C.)
pering towards and running stem.	4–8	Wet places.	2–3 ft. Stem winged above. (C.)

PALE YELLOW. Polypetalous.

Leaves.	Months.	Habitat.	Remarks.
ed, serrate.	7–8	River banks and woods.	LARGE. 1–2 ft. Chiefly in North of England. Stem swollen at joints. (L.)
crenate.	6–7	Mountain pastures.	MEDIUM. 4–10 in. North of England and Scotland. Leafy, deeply cut stipules. (C.)
lobed, wavy, us.	5–8	Sea coast.	1–2 ft. Original of garden cabbage. (L.)
d, upper leaves	Summer.	Seashores.	6–20 in. West of Britain. (L.)
nnate.	6–7	River banks.	3–4 ft. (L.)
h, clasping covered with	7–8	Bogs.	3–12 in. West of England. (C.)
cut into three v segments.	6–8	Ditches.	SMALL. 1–2 ft. (C.)
ut.	6–8	Cornfields.	6–24 in. A common weed in cornfields. (C.)
, serrate.	6	Hedges.	4–6 ft. Distinguished by forked spines, and yellow colour under bark. (L.)
roughish, pale	6	Waysides.	VERY SMALL. 1–2 ft. (L.)
ed, stem passthrough leaves, us.	7	Cornfields.	1–2 ft. Distinguished by perfoliate leaves. (L.)
innate, leaflets v.	7–9	Damp meadows.	1–3 ft. Smell unpleasant when bruised. (C.)

Monopetalous. PALE YELLOW.

English Name.	Latin Name.	Description of Flower.	Petals, Sepals, Stamens, etc.	
LARGE.				
Mouse-ear Hawk-weed.	*Hieracium pilosella.*	1 in. Under side reddish, no disc, solitary.		205.
MEDIUM.				
Henbane.	*Hyoscyamus niger.*	⅞ in. With purple veins and dark eye. Bell-shaped, on one side of stem.	Petals, 5. Sepals, 5. Stamens, 5.	206.
SMALL.				
Common Gromwell.	*Lithospermum officinale.*	$\frac{3}{16}$ in.	Petals, 5. Sepals, 5. Stamens, 5.	207.
Spiked Rampion.	*Phyteuma spicatum.*	⅛ in. In terminal head, which lengthens with age.	Petals, 5. Sepals, 5. Stamens, 5.	208.
Wood Sage or Wood Germander.	*Teucrium scorodonia.*	$\frac{5}{16}$ in. Greenish yellow, in one-sided racemes.	Two-lipped, upper lip very small. Stamens, 4.	209.

Polypetalous. YELLOW.

English Name.	Latin Name.	Description of Flower.	Petals, Sepals, Stamens, etc.	
LARGE.				
Marsh Marigold.	*Caltha palustris.*	1½ in. Like large buttercup.	Petals, 0. Sepals, 5. Stamens, many.	210.
Globe Flower.	*Trollius europæus.*	1½ in. Flower composed of coloured sepals.	Petals, minute. Sepals, 10. Stamens, many.	211.
Bulbous Crowfoot.	*Ranunculus bulbosus.*	1⅛ in. Flower stalk furrowed.	Petals, 5. Sepals, 5. Stamens, many.	212.
Welsh Poppy.	*Meconopsis cambrica.*	2¼ in.	Petals, 4. Sepals, 2. Stamens, many.	213.
Yellow Horned Poppy.	*Glaucium luteum.*	2 in.	Petals, 4. Sepals, 2. Stamens, many.	214.
Yellow Water Lily.	*Nuphar lutea.*	2 in. Globular.	Petals, 18–20. Sepals, 5. Stamens, many.	215.
Great Spearwort.	*Ranunculus lingua.*	1¼ in. Like buttercup.	Petals, 5. Sepals, 5. Stamens, many.	216.
Silver Weed or Goose-grass.	*Potentilla anserina.*	1 in. Solitary.	Petals, 5. Sepals, 10. Stamens, many.	217.
MEDIUM.				
Gorse or Furze.	*Ulex europæus.*	⅝ in. Shaped like pea flower.	Sepals, 5–8, yellow. Stamens, many.	218.
Lesser Celandine.	*Ranunculus ficaria.*	1 in. Like buttercup.	Petals, 8 or 9. Sepals, 3. Stamens, many.	219.
Meadow Crowfoot or Common Buttercup.	*Ranunculus acris.*	⅞ in. Flower stalks round.	Petals, 5. Sepals, 5. Stamens, many.	220.
Creeping Buttercup.	*Ranunculus repens.*	⅞ in. Flower stalks furrowed.	Petals, 5. Sepals, 5. Stamens, many.	221.
Pale Hairy Buttercup.	*Ranunculus hirsutus.*	⅞ in.	Petals, 5. Sepals, 5, reflexed. Stamens, many.	222.
Lesser Spearwort.	*Ranunculus flammula.*	½ in. Like buttercup.	Petals, 5. Sepals, 5. Stamens, many.	223.
Greater Celandine.	*Chelidonium majus.*	¾ in. In stalked umbels.	Petals, 4. Sepals, 2. Stamens, many.	224.
Tutsan.	*Hypericum androsæmum.*	⅞ in. In clusters.	Petals, 5. Sepals, 5, unequal. Stamens in five bundles.	225.
Imperforate St. John's Wort.	*Hypericum dubium.*	⅞ in.	Petals, 5. Sepals, 5, reflexed. Stamens in three bundles.	226.

PALE YELLOW. Monopetalous.

	Leaves.	Months.	Habitat.	Remarks.
				LARGE.
205.	Radical; small, oblong or lanceolate, entire; long hairs above, hoary beneath.	5–7	Banks.	2–10 in. (*V. C.*)
				MEDIUM.
206.	Oblong, toothed, clasping stem, sticky.	6–7	Waste places.	2–3 ft. Found especially near sea. A poisonous plant with unpleasant smell. (*C.*)
				SMALL.
207.	Narrow, tapering, half clasping stem; bristly above, hairy beneath.	6–7	Dry places.	2–3 ft. Stems erect, much branched at top; several from same root. (*C.*)
208.		5–7	Only in Sussex.	2–3 ft. (*R.*)
209.	Heart-shaped; wrinkled, like garden sage.	6–8	Hedges and woods.	1–2 ft. (*V. C.*)

YELLOW. Polypetalous.

	Leaves.	Months.	Habitat.	Remarks.
				LARGE.
210.	Kidney-shaped, glossy.	3	Marshy places.	6–18 in. (*V. C.*)
211.	Lower, with fine-cut lobes.	6–7	Woods.	6–18 in. Scotland, Wales, and North of England. (*R.*)
212.	In three parts.	5–6	Meadows.	8–15 in. Root bulbous. (*V. C.*)
213.	Pinnate.	6–7	Rocky places.	1–2 ft. Wales, Devonshire, and Westmorland. Distinguished by yellow juice, and from Horned Poppy by green, not glaucous, leaves. (*L.*)
214.	Clasping stem; rough, wavy, glaucous.	6–8	Seashores.	1–2 ft. Seed pods very long. (*L.*)
215.	Roundish, floating.	7	Ponds.	2–6 ft. Flowers smell like brandy. (*L.*)
216.	Narrow, sessile.	6–7	Watery places.	2–3 ft. The largest of buttercup tribe. (*C.*)
217.	Sharply cut, silvery.	6–7	Waysides.	3–9 in. Distinguished by silky leaves. (*V.C.*)
				MEDIUM.
218.	Leafless, except as seedling.	2–6	Commons.	2–10 ft. (*V. C.*)
219.	Heart-shaped.	3–5	Banks.	3–8 in. One of earliest spring flowers. (*V. C.*)
220.	Three-lobed. Each lobe trifid.	6–7	Meadows.	1–3 ft. (*V. C.*)
221.	Three-parted. Each part trifid.	6–8	Meadows.	6–12 in. A common weed, with creeping stems which root at each leaf. (*V. C.*)
222.	Three-parted.	6–10	Meadows.	6–12 in. Sepals and stem hairy. (*C.*)
223.	Narrow, tapering.	6	Wet places.	4–15 in. (*V. C.*)
224.	Pinnate.	5–8	Waste places.	1–2 ft. Distinguished by yellow juice. (*L.*)
225.	Ovate.	7	Woods and thickets.	2–3 ft. A shrubby plant, found in South and West of England. Stem two-edged. (*L.*)
226.	Ovate, broad.	7–8	Mountainous places.	1–2 ft. Stem four-sided, with raised angles. (*C.*)

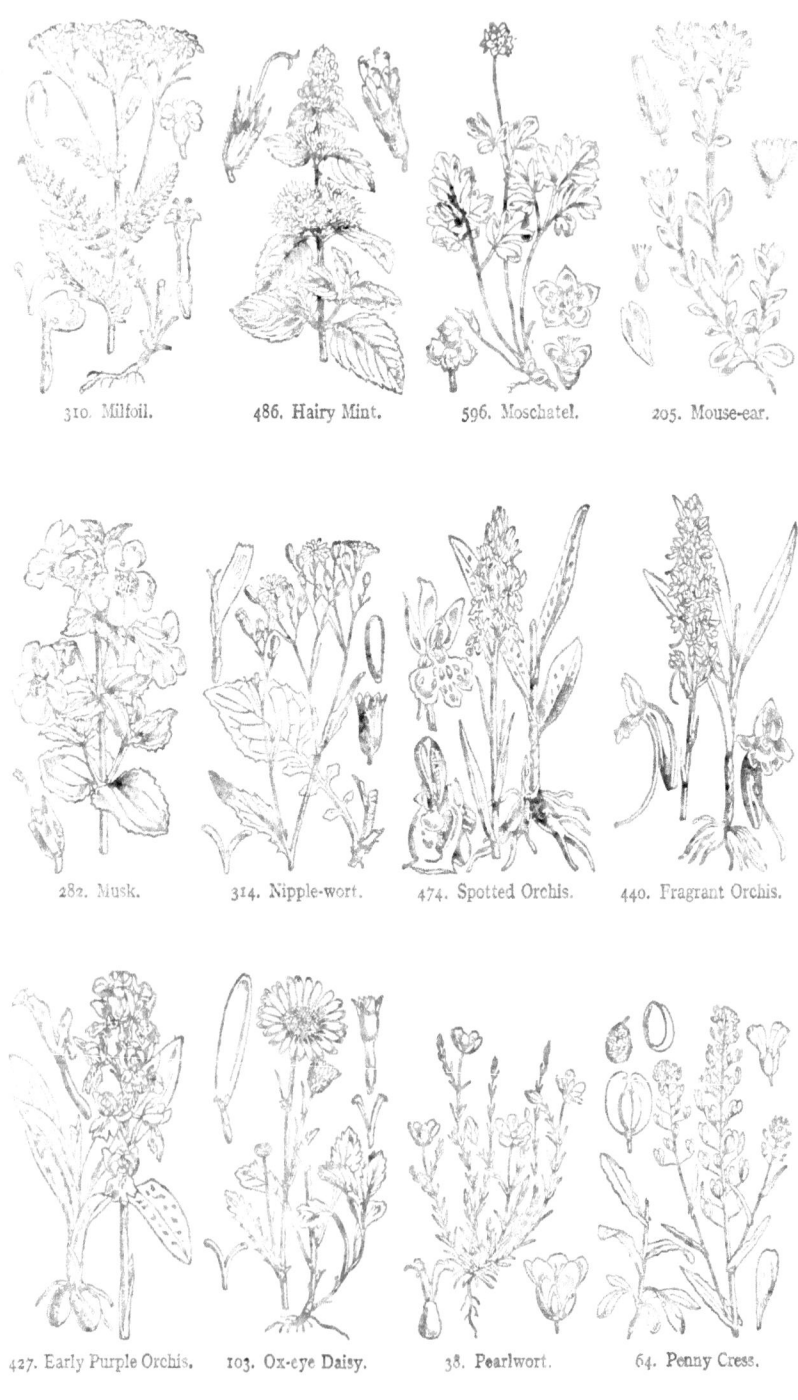

310. Milfoil.   486. Hairy Mint.   596. Moschatel.   205. Mouse-ear.

282. Musk.   314. Nipple-wort.   474. Spotted Orchis.   440. Fragrant Orchis.

427. Early Purple Orchis.   103. Ox-eye Daisy.   38. Pearlwort.   64. Penny Cress.

English Name.	Latin Name.	Description of Flower.	Petals, Sepals, Stamens, etc.	
MEDIUM (*contd.*).				
Mountain St. John's Wort.	*Hypericum montanum.*	3/4 in.	Petals, 5. Sepals, 5. Stamens in three bundles.	227.
Perforated St. John's Wort.	*Hypericum perforatum.*	3/4 in.	Petals, 5. Sepals, 5. Stamens in three bundles.	228.
Hairy St. John's Wort.	*Hypericum hirsutum.*	3/4 in.	Petals, 5. Sepals, 5. Stamens in three bundles.	229.
Charlock or Wild Mustard.	*Brassica sinapis.*	1/2 in.	Petals, 4. Sepals, 4. Stamens, 6.	230.
Sea Radish.	*Raphanus maritimus.*	5/8 in.	Petals, 4. Sepals, 4. Stamens, 6.	231.
Wall Rocket.	*Diplotaxis tenuifolia.*	5/8 in.	Petals, 4. Sepals, 4. Stamens, 6.	232.
Broom.	*Sarothamnus scoparius.*	7/8 in. Like pea flower.	Petals, 5, unequal. Sepals, 5. Stamens, 10.	233.
Dyer's Greenweed.	*Genista tinctoria.*	5/8 in. In racemes.	Petals, 5, unequal. Sepals, 5. Stamens, 10.	234.
Common Rock Rose.	*Helianthemum vulgare.*	1 in. In racemes.	Petals, 5. Sepals, 3. Stamens, many.	235.
Creeping Cinquefoil.	*Potentilla reptans.*	7/8 in. Solitary, on long stalks.	Petals, 5. Sepals, 10. Stamens, many.	236.
Bird's-foot Trefoil.	*Lotus corniculatus.*	5/8 in. Orange red in bud. In umbels of five to ten.	Petals, 5. Sepals, 5. Stamens, 10.	237.
Yellow Marsh Saxifrage.	*Saxifraga hirculus.*	1 in. Solitary.	Petals, 5, dotted at base. Sepals, 5. Stamens, 10.	238.
SMALL.				
Yellow Alpine Whitlow Grass.	*Draba azoides.*	1/4 in. In clusters.	Petals, 4, notched. Sepals, 4. Stamens, 6.	239.
Needle Greenweed or Petty Whin.	*Genista anglica.*	3/8 in. Solitary, turning green when dry.	Petals, 5, unequal. Sepals, 5. Stamens, 10.	240.
Common Winter Cress.	*Barbarea vulgaris.*	5/16 in.	Petals, 4. Sepals, 4. Stamens, 6.	241.
Tufted Horseshoe Vetch.	*Hippocrepis comosa.*	5/16 in. Six to ten in cluster.	Petals, 5, unequal. Sepals, 5.	242.
Tormentil.	*Potentilla tormentilla.*	5/16 in.	Petals, 4. Sepals, 8. Stamens, many.	243.
Yellow Corydalis.	*Corydalis lutea.*	1/4 in.	Petals, 4. Sepals, 2.	244.
Slender St. John's Wort.	*Hypericum pulchrum.*	1/2 in. Tipped with red; in clusters.	Petals, 5. Sepals, 5. Stamens in three bundles.	245.
Common Avens or Herb Bennet.	*Geum urbanum.*	1/2 in. Erect.	Petals, 5, short. Sepals, 10, 5 long. Stamens, many.	246.
Meadow Vetchling.	*Lathyrus pratense.*	1/2 in. Pea-shaped, all one side of stalk.	Petals, 5, unequal. Sepals, 5. Stamens 10.	247.
Biting Stonecrop.	*Sedum acre.*	1/2 in. Star-like.	Petals, 5. Sepals, 5. Stamens, 10.	248.
Black Mustard.	*Brassica nigra.*	1/3 in.	Petals, 4. Sepals, 4. Stamens, 6.	249.
White Mustard.	*Brassica alba.*	3/8 in.	Petals, 4. Sepals, 4. Stamens, 6.	250.
Kidney Vetch or Lady's Finger.	*Anthyllis vulneraria.*	1/4 in. In crowded heads, woolly; two heads at end of each stalk.	Petals, 5. Sepals, 5. Stamens, 10.	251.
Wild Navew.	*Brassica campestris.*	1/2 in. Often mistaken for Charlock.	Petals, 4. Sepals, 4. Stamens, 6.	252.

YELLOW. Polypetalous.

Leaves.	Months.	Habitat.	Remarks.
			MEDIUM (*contd.*).
with black dots e of outer side.	7	Hills.	1–2 ft. Distinguished by black edge of sepals. (*L.*)
perforated with arent dots.	7–8	Woods and hedges.	1–2 ft. (*V. C.*)
wny beneath.	7	Woods.	1–3 ft. Stem round, downy. (*C.*)
oothed.	Summer.	Fields.	1–2 ft. A troublesome weed. (*V. C.*)
d small leaflets, ed alternately.	6	Sea coast.	1–3 ft. Sometimes white. (*L.*)
arrow, pinnataucous.	7–9	Old walls.	1–3 ft. Leaves have unpleasant smell when crushed. (*L.*)
leaflets.	6	Commons and woods.	2–10 ft. Branches angled.
acute, smooth.	7–8	Heaths.	1–2 ft. A shrubby plant, bright, without spines. (*C.*)
nged stipules; above, hoary h.	7–8	Dry places.	3–10 in. If stamens are touched, they sink down. (*C.*)
segments, ser-	6–8	Roadsides.	6–18 in. (*C.*)
bovate.	7–8	Banks.	4–12 in. (*V. C.*)
ves in rosette.	6–9	Wet moors.	4–8 in. North of England, Scotland, and Ireland. (*R.*)
			SMALL.
1 rosette; narpointed.	3–4	Walls.	2–5 in. Found near Swansea. (*R.*)
smooth.	5–6	Heaths.	1–2 ft. Stems with sharp thorns, upper branches thornless. (*C.*)
ives lyrate, end pundish, upper e toothed.	5–8	Damp places.	1–2 ft. A smooth, shiny plant. Stem furrowed. (*C.*)
six to twelve	5–8	Pastures.	6–18 in. Seed pods shaped like series of horseshoe. (*C.*)
ves, with three stalked leaflets.	Summer.	Heaths and waysides.	3–10 in. (*V. C.*)
s narrow, cut. inate and lobed.	5	Old walls.	6–10 in. Without tendrils. Stems angled. (*R.*)
aped, clasping	7–8	Banks.	1–2 ft. Leaves marked with transparent dots. (*V. C.*)
aves pinnate, maller leaflets e; stem leaves r.	6–8	Banks.	1–2 ft. Seeds hooked. (*C.*)
row leaflets.	7–8	Meadows.	1–3 ft. Stem angled. (*V. C.*)
fleshy, sessile, spurs at base; d.	6–7	Walls.	3–6 in. (*V. C.*)
aves pinnate, ounded lobe at upper entire, l.	6–7	Fields.	1–2 ft. Seeds produce table mustard. (*C.*)
ut, lobed.	6–7	Cornfields.	1–2 ft. Stem furrowed. Pods bristly. Branches spreading. (*C.*)
end leaflet ; two to six	6–8	Pastures.	6–18 in. (*V. C.*)
aves pinnate, toothed; stem smooth, heart-	6–7	Fields.	1–2 ft. (*V. C.*)

Polypetalous.   YELLOW.

English Name.	Latin Name.	Description of Flower.	Petals, Sepals, Stamens, etc.	
SMALL (contd.).				
Agrimony.	Agrimonia eupatoria.	⅜ in. In long spikes.	Petals, 5. Sepals, 5. Stamens, 15.	253
Hoary Cinquefoil.	Potentilla argentea.	⅜ in. Several in heads.	Petals, 4. Sepals, 10. Stamens, many.	254.
Dwarf Furze.	Ulex nanus.	½ in.	Petals, 5, unequal. Sepals, 2, yellow, hairy, toothed. Stamens, 10.	255.
Square-stalked St. John's Wort.	Hypericum quadrangulum.	½ in.	Petals, 5. Sepals, 5. Stamens in three bundles.	256.
Trailing St. John's Wort.	Hypericum humifusum.	⅜ in. Small.	Petals, 5. Sepals, 5. Stamens in three bundles.	257.
Dyer's Rocket.	Reseda luteola.	¼ in. In spikes.	Petals, 3–5, unequal. Sepals, 4. Stamens, many. Conspicuous.	258.
VERY SMALL.				
Common Golden Saxifrage.	Chrysosplenium oppositifolium.	¼ in. In clusters, yellow and green.	Petals, 0. Sepals, 4. Stamens, 8.	259.
Spotted Medick.	Medicago maculata.	1/16 in. Two to four together.	Petals, 5, unequal. Sepals, 5.	260.
Black Medick or Nonsuch.	Medicago lupulina.	1/16 in. In dense oblong heads.	Petals, 5, unequal. Sepals, 5.	261.
Common Melilot.	Melilotus officinalis.	⅛ in. One-sided on stalk, in long racemes.	Petals, 5. Sepals, 5. Stamens, 10.	262.
Lesser Yellow Trefoil.	Trifolium minus.	⅛ in.	Petals, 5. Sepals, 5. Stamens, 10.	263.
Marsh Yellow Cress.	Nasturtium palustre.	⅛ in.	Petals, 4. Sepals, 4. Stamens, 6.	264.
Common Hedge Mustard.	Sisymbrium officinale.	⅛ in.	Petals, 4. Sepals, 4. Stamens, 6.	265.
Fennel.	Fœniculum vulgare.	⅛ in. In compound umbels.	Petals, 5.	266.
Wild Parsnip.	Pastinaca sativa.	⅛ in. In compound umbels.	Petals, 5. Stamens, 5.	267.

Monopetalous.

LARGE.				
Dandelion.	Leontodon taraxacum.	1¼ in. Rayed, solitary.		268.
Daffodil or Lent Lily.	Narcissus pseudonarcissus.	2 in. In a tube.	Petals, 6. Sepals, 6. Stamens, 6.	269.
Primrose.	Primula vulgaris.	1¼ in.	Petals, 5. Sepals, 5. Stamens, 5.	270.
Yellow Iris or Flag.	Iris pseud-acorus.	3 in.	Petals, 3. Sepals, 3. Stigmas, 3. Stamens, 3.	271.
Marsh Ragwort.	Senecio aquaticus.	1 in. In a loose corymb. Disc florets five-cleft.		272
Common Ragwort.	Senecio jacobaea.	1 in. Rayed. Florets five-cleft.		273.
Yellow Goat's-beard.	Tragopogon pratensis.	1½ in. All rayed. Closes at noon.		274.
Corn Marigold.	Chrysanthemum segetum.	1½ in. Disc yellow. Florets five-cleft.		275.
Rough Hawkbit.	Apargia hispida.	1¼ in. All rayed, drooping in bud.		276.
Autumnal Hawkbit.	Apargia autumnalis.	1 in. All rayed.		277.

YELLOW. Polypetalous.

Leaves.	Months.	Habitat.	Remarks.
			SMALL (*contd.*).
alternate leaf- aller, all cut.	7–8	Waysides.	1–2 ft. Plant hairy, scented when bruised. (*V. C.*)
leaflets cut, beneath, edges back.	6	Roadsides.	6–15 in. (*L.*)
	8–11	Heaths.	1–2 ft. Distinguished from common gorse by being smaller throughout. (*L.*)
ed, with trans- dots.	7–8	Wet places.	1–2 ft. Distinguished by square stalk. (*V. C.*)
with trans- dots.	7–8	Commons.	4–10 in. Stem trailing. (*C.*)
tire, shining.	Summer.	Waste places.	1–2 ft. Especially on chalk or limestone. (*C.*)
			VERY SMALL.
; heart-shaped, green.	4–5	Wet places.	2–6 in. (*C.*)
with a purple	6–9	Pastures.	6–20 in. (*C.*)
finely toothed.	6–8	Waysides.	6–24 in. Seed pods black. (*C.*)
three, narrow, d.	6–8	Fields.	2–3 ft. (*C.*)
three, toothed.	6	Pastures.	10–20 in. Stem. (*C.*)
end lobe large.	6–11	Watery places.	1–2 ft. (*C.*)
lobed, points d backward; be large.	6–7	Roadsides.	1–2 ft. (*V. C.*)
ided, segments air-like.	7–8	Waste places.	3–5 ft. Found especially near sea. (*L.*)
downy be- end leaflet obed.	7–8	Waste places.	2–3 ft. (*C.*)

Monopetalous.

LARGE.

Leaves.	Months.	Habitat.	Remarks.
deeply cut, arp lobes turn- ckwards.	All the year.	Waysides.	6–12 in. Flower stalks hollow, milky. Name derived from French *Dent de Lion*—"Lion's Tooth." (*V. C.*)
	3–4	Woods.	10–18 in. Flower stalks hollow and two-edged. (*L.*)
l, radical.	3	Woods.	4–8 in. A white variety sometimes found. (*V. C.*)
aped.	6–7	Wet places.	2–4 ft. (*C.*)
leaves entire, d; upper with bes at base.	7–9	Wet places.	1–4 ft. (*C.*)
t, with smaller it base.	7–9	Fields.	1–4 ft. (*V. C.*)
; broad at tapering, chan-	6–7	Meadows.	1–2 ft. Distinguished by feathery pappus of seed. (*V. C.*)
stem; toothed, us, shiny.	6–7	Cornfields.	12–18 in. (*C.*)
pinnatifid, hairy. Lobes ig backwards.	6–9	Pastures.	6–18 in. (*V. C.*)
narrow, cut, on veins be-	8	Pastures.	6–18 in. Stalk swollen beneath flowers. (*V. C.*)

460. Marsh Pennywort. 57. Pepperwort. 399. Spotted Persicaria. 398. Amphibious Persicaria.

240. Petty Whin. 301. Yellow Pimpernel. 388. Scarlet Pimpernel (Poor Man's Weather-glass). 351. Poppy (Corn Rose).

270. Primrose. 354. Ragged Robin. 273. Ragwort. 7. Wild Garlic.

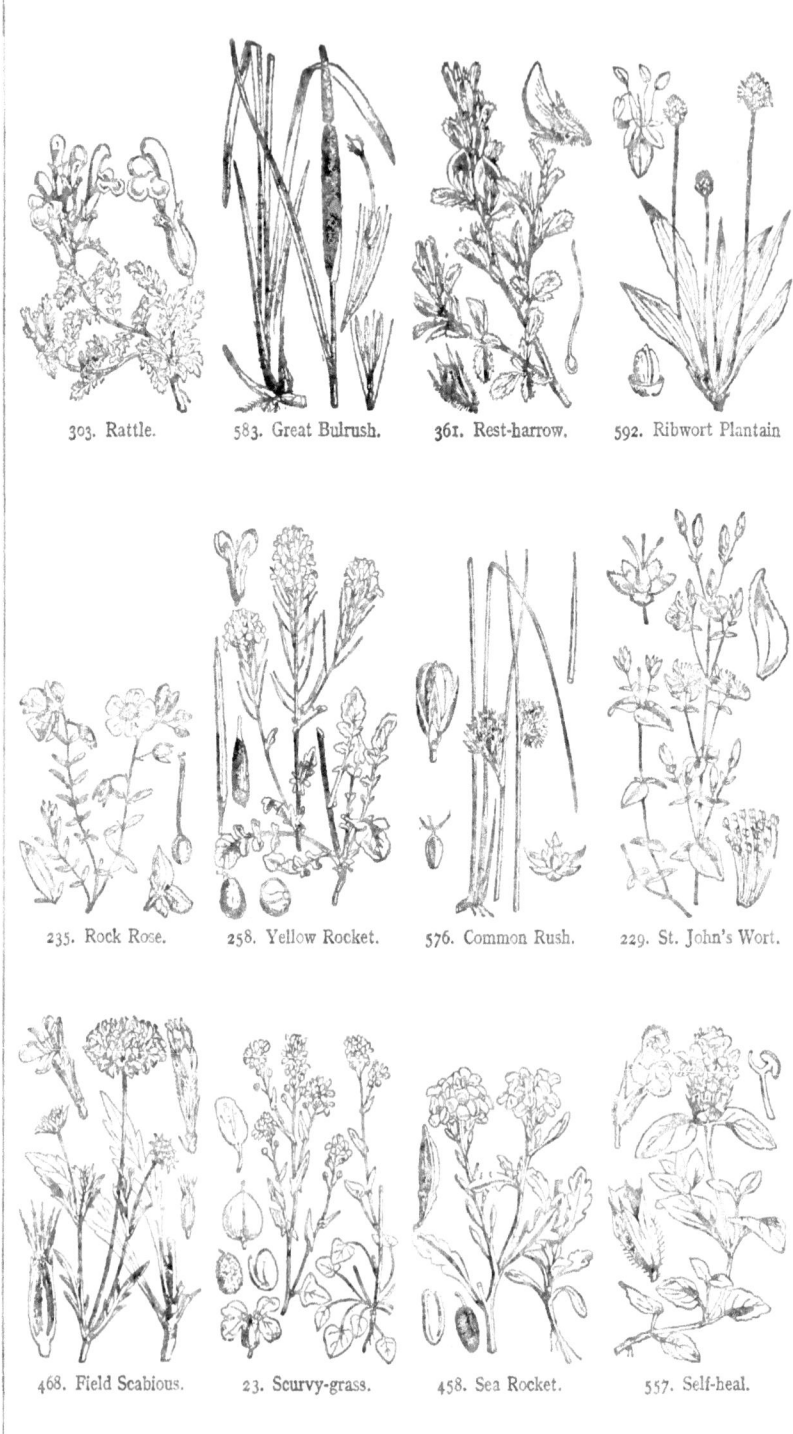

303. Rattle. 583. Great Bulrush. 361. Rest-harrow. 592. Ribwort Plantain

235. Rock Rose. 258. Yellow Rocket. 576. Common Rush. 229. St. John's Wort.

468. Field Scabious. 23. Scurvy-grass. 458. Sea Rocket. 557. Self-heal.

Monopetalous. YELLOW.

English Name.	Latin Name.	Description of Flower.	Petals, Sepals, Stamens, etc.	
LARGE (contd.).				
Hawkweed Picris.	Picris hieracioides.	1 in. All rayed.		278.
Wood Hawkweed.	Hieracium sylvaticum.	1 in. All rayed.	Calyx hoary.	279.
Long-rooted Cat's-ear.	Hypochæris radicata.	1¼ in. All rayed.		280.
Corn Sow-thistle.	Sonchus arvensis.	2 in. In loose corymb.		281.
Yellow Musk or Monkey Flower.	Mimulus luteus.	1 in. Often marked inside with reddish spots.	Petals, two-lipped. Sepals, 5. Stamens, 4.	282.
MEDIUM.				
Coltsfoot.	Tussilago farfara.	1 in. Solitary, rayed, appearing before leaves.		283.
Wall Hawkweed.	Hieracium murorum.	⅞ in. Branched, with three to four flowers.		284.
Bristly Ox-tongue.	Helminthia echioides.	⅞ in. All rayed. Much branched.		285.
Common Sow-thistle.	Sonchus oleraceus.	⅞ in. All rayed.		286.
Marsh Hawk's-beard.	Crepis paludosa.	⅞ in All rayed, few.		287.
Narrow-leaved Hawkweed.	Hieracium umbellatum.	⅞ in. All rayed; many-flowered in tuft.		288.
Hairy Hawkbit.	Apargia hirta.	¾ in. All rayed, solitary.		289.
Hoary Ragwort.	Senecio tenuifolius.	¼ in. With rays and disc in corymb.		290.
Oxlip.	Primula elatior.	⅝ in. In umbels.	Petals, 5. Sepals, 5. Stamens, 5.	291.
Cowslip.	Primula veris.	½ in. In umbels.	Petals, 5. Sepals, 5. Stamens, 5.	292.
Moth Mullein.	Verbascum blattaria.	1 in. In a spike.	Petals, 5. Sepals, 5. Stamens, 5, with purple hairs.	293.
Great Mullein.	Verbascum thapsus.	⅞ in. In a spike.	Petals, 5. Sepals, 5. Stamens, 5, with white hairs.	294.
Money-wort.	Lysimachia nummularia.	⅞ in. Solitary, axillary.	Petals, 5. Sepals, 5. Stamens, 5.	295.
Great Yellow Loosestrife.	Lysimachia vulgaris.	½ in. Many.	Petals, 5. Sepals, 5. Stamens, 5.	296.
Smooth Cat's-ear.	Hypochæris glabra.	½ in. All rayed.		297.
Common Fleabane.	Pulicaria dysenterica.	1 in. Rayed, with disc.		298.
Perfoliate Yellow-wort.	Chlora perfoliata.	⅝ in. Opening only in sunshine.	Petals, 8. Sepals, 8. Stamens, 8.	299.
SMALL.				
Wood Spurge.	Euphorbia amygdaloides.	⅜ in. In cluster, containing several barren flowers and one fertile.	Stamens, many. One pistil enclosed in calyx-like bract.	300.
Yellow Pimpernel or Wood Loosestrife.	Lysimachia nemorum.	½ in. Solitary, springing from axils.	Petals, 5. Sepals, 5. Stamens, 5.	301.
Yellow Cow-wheat.	Melampyrum pratense.	¼ in. Corolla four times as long as calyx. In pairs, turning one way.	Two-lipped. Sepals, 4.	302.
Yellow Rattle or Cockscomb.	Rhinanthus cristagalli.	¼ in. In loose spike.	Two-lipped. Sepals, 4. Calyx swollen.	303.
Bushy Yellow Rattle.	Rhinanthus major.	¼ in. Purple spot on tip of upper lip. In crowded spike.		304.

YELLOW. Monopetalous.

Leaves.	Months.	Habitat.	Remarks.
			LARGE (contd.).
rough, toothed,	7–9	Waste places.	2–3 ft. Stems rough, with hooked bristles. (C.)
toothed; teeth 1g upwards.	8–9	Woods.	1–2 ft. Stem with five to six leaves. (C.)
cut, bristly.	7–8	Waysides.	8–18 in. Flower stalks branched, smooth. Stem swollen under flowers. (V. C.)
toothed, wavy, prickly.	6–9	Fields.	2–4 ft. Stem hollow. (C.)
othed, smooth.	6–9	River banks.	6–18 in. A naturalized plant from North America. (L.)
			MEDIUM.
1, heart-shaped; y beneath, cob- above.	3–4	Fields.	4–10 in. A troublesome weed. Stalks covered with scaly bracts. (V. C.)
radical; usu- 1e on stem.	7–8	Walls and rocks.	12–18 in. (C.)
aves cordate.	6–7	Waste places.	2–3 ft. Distinguished by numerous prickles, each springing from raised white spot. (C.)
prickly, clasp- m.	6–9	Waysides.	1–4 ft. Juice milky. (V. C.)
lower, pinnati- th lobes turned contracting to- stalk. Upper, 7, clasping stem. toothed, sessile.	7–9	Moist mead- ows.	1–3 ft. Stem furrowed. (C.)
	8–9	Woods.	1–4 ft. (C.)
at lobed, with hairs.	7–9	Heaths.	4–8 in. (C.)
d; segments 7; downy be-	7–8	Dry banks.	1–4 ft. (C.)
becoming r above middle.	4–5	Woods.	4–12 in. Like a large cowslip. (L.)
	4–5	Fields.	6–12 in. (V. C.)
talked; upper, or clasping stem.	7–8	Banks.	1–4 ft. Found especially in South-west of England. (L.)
oval, running stem.	7–8	Banks.	2–5 ft. (C.)
1, short stalks, te, shiny.	6–7	Damp places.	1–2 ft. Stem trailing. (C.)
or in a whorl, 1g.	7	River banks.	2–3 ft. (C.)
lobed.	6–8	Dry places.	3–10 in. (L.)
aped at base, 1g stem, woolly.	8	Wet places.	6–15 in. (C.)
; joined at vith stem pass- rough them.	6–9	Pastures.	6–18 in. (L.)
			SMALL.
green, narrow, aped, hairy be-	3–4	Woods.	8–20 in. Juice milky. (C.)
ed, on short acute.	6–8	Woods.	2–12 in. (C.)
, narrow, taper- 100th.	6–8	Woods.	6–15 in. (C.)
tapering, ser-	6	Fields.	4–18 in. When ripe the seeds rattle in pod. (V. C.)
serrate.	4	Cornfields.	1–2 ft. At base of each flower is a yellow bract. (L.)

Monopetalous. **YELLOW.**

English Name.	Latin Name.	Description of Flower.	Petal , Sepals, Stamens, etc.	
SMALL (*contd.*).				
Dark Mullein.	*Verbascum nigrum.*	$\frac{1}{2}$ in. A long, crowded spike.	Petals, 5. Sepals, 5. Stamens, 5, covered with purple hairs.	305.
Ivy-leaved Lettuce.	*Lactuca muralis.*	$\frac{3}{8}$ in. With five florets, all rayed.		306.
Common Bladder-wort.	*Utricularia vulgaris.*	$\frac{3}{8}$ in. In clusters, six to eight.	Two-lipped. Sepals, 2. Stamens, 2.	307.
Common Tansy.	*Tanacetum vulgare.*	$\frac{3}{8}$ in. All disc, like buttons.		308.
Seaside Cotton-weed.	*Diotis maritima.*	$\frac{3}{8}$ in. All disc, in small heads.		309.
Common Yellow Milfoil.	*Achillea millefolium.*	$\frac{1}{4}$ in. With ray and disc, in clustered heads.		310.
Smooth Hawk's-beard.	*Crepis virens.*	$\frac{1}{2}$ in. All rayed, many.		311.
Bog Asphodel.	*Narthecium ossifragum.*	$\frac{1}{2}$ in. Spike of star-like flowers.	Stamens, 6, red.	312.
Golden Rod.	*Solidago virgaurea.*	$\frac{1}{2}$ in. Rayed, in clusters, rays five-cleft.		313.
Nipple-wort.	*Lapsana communis.*	$\frac{3}{8}$ in. All rayed, many.		314.
VERY SMALL.				
Groundsel.	*Senecio vulgaris.*	$\frac{3}{16}$ in. Not rayed.		315.
Parti-coloured Scorpion-grass.	*Myosotis versicolor.*	$\frac{1}{8}$ in. In cluster on long leafless stalk; yellow when opening, turning to blue.	Petals, 5. Sepals, 5. Stamens, 5.	316.
Crosswort Bedstraw.	*Galium cruciata.*	$\frac{1}{8}$ in. In clusters of six to eight. Upper ones have pistils only; lower, stamens only.	Petals, 4. Sepals, 4. Stamens, 4.	317.
Yellow Bedstraw.	*Galium verum.*	$\frac{1}{8}$ in. Many in panicle.	Petals, 4. Stamens, 4.	318.
Least Filago.	*Filago minima.*	$\frac{1}{8}$ in. In clusters of three to six; all disc.		319.
Common Wormwood.	*Artemisia absinthium.*	$\frac{3}{16}$ in. Not rayed; small roundish heads.		320.
Mountain Groundsel.	*Senecio sylvaticus.*	$\frac{1}{8}$ in. Rays rolled back.		321.

Polypetalous. **YELLOW OR YELLOWISH,**

English Name.	Latin Name.	Description of Flower.	Petals, Sepals, Stamens, etc.	
SMALL.				
Mousetail.	*Myosurus minimus.*	$\frac{3}{16}$ in. in diameter; 1 in. in length.	Petals, 5. Sepals, 5. Stamens few.	322.
Alexanders.	*Smyrnium olusatrum.*	$\frac{1}{8}$ in. Greenish yellow; many large umbels.	Petals, 5. Sepals, 0. Stamens, 5.	323.
Common Lime (tree).	*Tilia intermedia (vulgaris).*	$\frac{3}{8}$ in. Growing from large, leaf-like bract.	Petals, 5. Sepals, 5. Stamens, many.	324.
Broad-leaved Lime (tree).	*Tilia platyphyllos (grandifolia).*	$\frac{3}{8}$ in. Growing from large, leaf-like bract.	Petals, 5. Sepals, 5. Stamens, many.	325
Wild Mignonette.	*Reseda lutea.*	$\frac{1}{8}$ in. In short, broad spikes.	Petals, 6, very unequal. Sepals, 6. Stamens, 16–18.	326

YELLOW. Monopetalous.

	Leaves.	Months.	Habitat.	Remarks.
				SMALL (contd.).
305.	Upper, small, sessile; lower, oblong, cordate.	7-9	Banks.	2-3 ft. (L.)
306.	Cut, end lobe resembling ivy leaf.	7-9	Woods and walls.	1-2 ft. (C.)
307.	Finely divided, and bearing small air bladders.	6-7	Pools (submerged except flower).	After flowering the bladders fill with water, and the plant sinks. (L.)
308.	Much cut, segments narrow.	8	Waste places.	2-3 ft. Stem angled. Has a nauseous smell. (C.)
309.	Blunt.	8-9	Sandy shores.	6-12 in. Whole plant covered with cottony down. (L.)
310.	Woolly, in lobes, each lobe two-to three-cleft.	6-9	Waste places.	6-8 in. (L.)
311.	Smooth; pinnatifid, lobes turned back. Upper, narrow, clasping stem; lower, stalked.	7-9	Waste places.	1-2 ft. Stem furrowed. (V. C.)
312.	Narrow, stiff.	7-9	Bogs.	5-10 in. Fruit triangular, red. (L.)
313.	Serrated, narrow.	7-9	Woods.	2-3 ft. Stem angular. (C.)
314.	Toothed, heart-shaped at base.	7-8	Waste places.	1-2 ft. Plant milky. (V. C.)
				VERY SMALL.
315.	Deeply lobed.	All the year.	Waste places.	5-18 in. (V. C.)
316.	Linear-oblong.	4-6	Fields.	3-10 in. (V. C.)
317.	In whorls of four, downy.	5-6	Waysides.	6-18 in. (V. C.)
318.	In whorls of six to eight.	7-8	Dry banks.	1-2 ft. (V. C.)
319.	Narrow, close to stem.	7-8	Dry places.	4-6 in. (C.)
320.	Much cut, silky.	7-9	Waste places.	1-2 ft. Distinguished by silky stems and leaves. Has strong smell when crushed. (C.)
321.	Pinnatifid, toothed.	7-9	Stony places.	1-2 ft. Distinguished from Common Groundsel by larger size. (C.)

WITH SOME OTHER TINT. Polypetalous.

	Leaves.	Months.	Habitat.	Remarks.
				SMALL.
322.	Fleshy, long, radical.	4-6	Cornfields.	1-5 in. high. Recognized by the resemblance of its arrangement of carpels to a mouse's tail. (L.)
323.	Broad, glossy.	4-6	Wastes, especially near sea.	2-4 ft. Stout. Stem furrowed and hollow. Fruit nearly black. Formerly cultivated, the shoots being used for food. (L.)
324.	Thin, cordate, serrate.	6-7	Plantations, parks.	20-60 ft.
325.	Thin, cordate, serrate; downy beneath.	6-7	Old woods in West.	30-90 ft. Young shoots hairy. (L.)
326.	Three-cleft; lower, pinnatifid.	6-8	Fields, chalky districts.	1-2 ft. Bushy. (Reseda, "I calm." Supposed to possess sedative properties.) (C.)

41. Shepherd's Purse.   217. Silver Weed.   679. Sneezewort.   664. Sheep's Sorrel.

286. Sow-thistle.   223. Lesser Spearwort.   517. Germander Speedwell.   340. Petty Spurge.

33. Spurrey.   554. Sea Starwort.   8. Greater Stitchwort.   Stork's-bill.

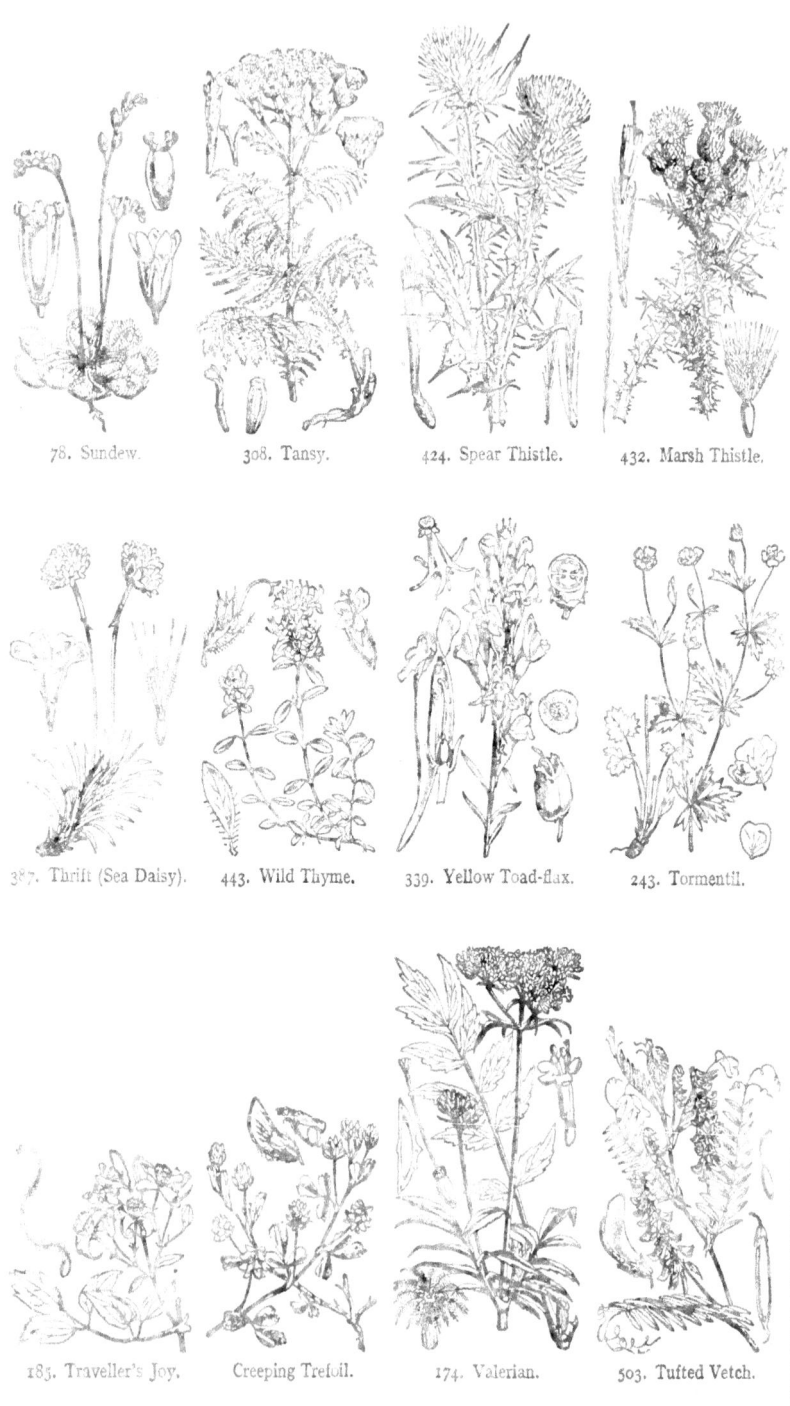

78. Sundew.   308. Tansy.   424. Spear Thistle.   432. Marsh Thistle.

387. Thrift (Sea Daisy).   443. Wild Thyme.   339. Yellow Toad-flax.   243. Tormentil.

183. Traveller's Joy.   Creeping Trefoil.   174. Valerian.   503. Tufted Vetch.

Polypetalous. YELLOW OR YELLOWISH,

English Name.	Latin Name.	Description of Flower.	Petals, Sepals, Stamens, etc.	
SMALL (contd.). Dyer's Weed (Dyer's Rocket).	Reseda luteola.	1/16 in. In long spike-like racemes.	Petals, 3-5. Sepals, 4. Stamens, many.	327.
Spignel, Mea, or Bald Money.	Meum athamanticum.	1/4 in. In umbels.	Petals, 5. Stamens, 5.	328.
Flixweed.	Sisymbrium sophia.	1/10 in. Greenish yellow.	Petals, 4. Sepals, 4. Stamens, 6.	329.
Small-leaved Lime (tree).	Tilia cordata (parvifolia).	3/8 in. Greenish yellow, growing from leaf-like bract in clusters.	Petals, 5. Sepals, 5. Stamens, many.	330.
Lesser Meadow Rue.	Thalictrum minus.	1/4 in. Drooping.	Petals, 0. Sepals, 4. Stamens, many.	331.
Ivy.	Hedera helix.	3/8 in. Yellowish green, in panicled umbels.	Petals, 5. Sepals, 5. Stamens, 5.	332.
Rose-root Stonecrop.	Sedum rhodiola (roseum).	1/4 in. Greenish yellow; compact, terminal cymes.	Petals, 4. Sepals, 4. Stamens, 8.	333.

Monopetalous.

English Name.	Latin Name.	Description of Flower.	Petals, Sepals, Stamens, etc.	
MEDIUM. Nodding Bur-marigold.	Bidens cernua.	7/8 in. All disc. Heads drooping; brownish yellow, roundish.		334.
Trifid Bur-marigold.	Bidens tripartita.	1/2 in. All disc. Heads erect.		335.
SMALL. Sun Spurge.	Euphorbia helioscopia.	1/4 in. In umbels, with five rays golden-green.	Stamens and pistils on different flowers.	336.
Common Hop.	Humulus lupulus.	Greenish yellow.	Male flowers in racemes 4 in. long. Female in heads and catkins.	337.
Viscid Groundsel.	Senecio viscosus.	3/8 in. In rays, about twelve turned back.		338.
Yellow Toad-flax.	Linaria vulgaris.	3/4 in. In dense spikes, spurred.	Sepals, 5. Stamens, 4.	339.
VERY SMALL. Petty Spurge.	Euphorbia peplus.	1/16 in. Pale yellow, in umbels of three forked rays.		340.
Dwarf Spurge.	Euphorbia exigua.	1/8 in. About four forked rays.		341.
Sea Spurge.	Euphorbia paralias.	3/16 in. Greenish yellow.		342.
Good King Henry.	Chenopodium bonus-henricus.	1/8 in. In leafless spikes.	Petals, 0. Sepals, 5. Stamens, 5.	343.
Great Nettle.	Urtica dioica.	1/8 in.	Stamens and pistils on different flowers.	344.
Branched Bur-reed.	Sparganium ramosum.	1/16 in. Heads globular, only lower ones fertile.	Stamens, 3.	345.
Small Nettle.	Urtica urens.	1/8 in. In short clusters.	Stamens and pistils in different flowers.	346.
Unbranched Bur-reed.	Sparganium simplex.	1/8 in. Heads globular.	Stamens and pistils in different flower head.	347.
Sharp-leaved Fluellen.	Linaria elatine.	1/4 in. Solitary; upper lip purple; lower yellow, spurred.	Sepals, 5. Stamens, 4.	348.
Great Dodder.	Cuscuta europæa.	1/8 in. Globular, dense sessile heads.		349.
Lesser Dodder.	Cuscuta epithymum.	1/8 in. In dense sessile flower heads, flesh-coloured.		350.

WITH SOME OTHER TINT. Polypetalous.

	Leaves.	Months.	Habitat.	Remarks.
				SMALL (*contd.*).
327.	Long, linear, undivided, shiny.	6-8	Wastes, chalky fields.	2-3 ft. Once used for dyeing purposes.
328.	Bipinnate, cut into bristly segments.	6-7	Dry mountainous pastures.	1-1½ ft. Strong aromatic smell. Root eaten by Highlanders. Found in Scotland; also Wales to Yorkshire. (*L.*)
329.	Much cut and divided.	6-8	Waste places.	1-2 ft. Downy. Fruit pods narrow, pinched. Not uncommon. Much used by old herbalists for wounds.
330.	Thick, leathery, pointed; heart-shaped, but oblique.	7-8	Woods.	20-40 ft. Probably the only indigenous lime. (*L.*)
331.	Like maidenhair fern, but stiff.	7-8	Fields and pastures.	½-4 ft. Stiff, often zigzag stem. (*L.*)
332.	Variable, lower with five lobes.	9-11	Walls, rocks, etc.	6-40 ft. Berries black. (*V. C.*)
333.	Thick, fleshy, pointed; closely set.	5-8	Mountains and sea-cliffs, chiefly in North.	6-12 in. high, unbranched. Root is rose-scented.
				Monopetalous.
				MEDIUM.
334.	Narrow, serrated.	7-9	Wet places.	1-2 ft. Fruit with barbed bristles. (*C.*)
335.	Three-cleft, opposite, serrated.	7-9	Wet places.	1-2 ft. Fruit with 3-5 bristles. (*C.*)
				SMALL.
336.	Alternate; upper, serrated.	7-8	Waste places.	6-18 in. Sap milky. (*C.*)
337.	Upper, opposite, ovate; lower, lobed.	7	Hedges.	10-20 ft. (*L.*)
338.	Cut, sticky, hairy.	7-9	Waste places.	1-2 ft. (*L.*)
339.	Narrow.	7-9	Hedges.	1-2 ft. Like small Snapdragon. (*C.*)
				VERY SMALL.
340.	Alternate, entire.	7	Waste places.	3-9 in. A common garden weed. Sap milky. (*C.*)
341.	Narrow, glaucous.	6-9	Cornfields.	2-8 in. (*C.*)
342.	Glaucous, leathery.	8-10	Sandy shores.	1-2 ft. A shrubby plant. (*L.*)
343.	Triangular, arrow-shaped.	5-8	Waysides.	1-3 ft. Stem stout, angled. (*C.*)
344.	Heart-shaped at base, stinging.	All the year.	Waysides.	1-4 ft. The Common Stinging Nettle. (*V. C.*)
345.	Sword-shaped; triangular at base, with concave sides.	7-8	Ditches.	2-4 ft. Stem branched. (*C.*)
346.	Elliptical, serrate.	7-9	Waste places.	1-2 ft. Resembling Great Nettle but smaller. (*C.*)
347.	Sword-shaped; triangular at base, with flat sides.	7-8	Ditches.	1-2 ft. Distinguished from Branched Burreed by flat sides of leaves and unbranched stem. (*C.*)
348.	Downy; lower ovate; upper two, pointed at base.	7-9	Cornfields.	6-18 in. (*C.*)
349.	None.	8-9		1-2 ft. A parasitical plant, growing on nettles, vetches, and other plants. Stems thread-like, tangled. (*L.*)
350.	None.	8-9		1-2 ft. A parasite, chiefly on furze. (*C.*)

Polypetalous. **RED OR PINK.**

English Name.	Latin Name.	Description of Flower.	Petals, Sepals, Stamens, etc.	
LARGE.				
Common Red Poppy.	*Papaver rhœas.*	2½ in. Scarlet, often black at base.	Petals, 4. Sepals, 2. Stamens, many.	351.
Long Smooth-headed Poppy.	*Papaver dubium.*	2 in.	Petals, 4. Sepals, 2. Stamens, many.	352.
Long Rough-headed Poppy.	*Papaver argemone.*	1¼ in. Light scarlet, black at base.	Petals, 4. Sepals, 2. Stamens, many.	353.
Ragged Robin.	*Lychnis flos-cuculi.*	1½ in. Rose-coloured.	Petals, 5, four-cleft. Sepals, 5.	354.
Great Hairy Willow-herb.	*Epilobium hirsutum.*	1 in. Rose-coloured.	Petals, 4. Sepals, 4. Stamens, 8.	355.
Marsh Mallow.	*Althæa officinalis.*	1½ in. Pink.	Petals, 5. Sepals, 5. Stamens, many.	356.
Dog Rose.	*Rosa canina.*	2 in. Colour variable, white to pink.	Petals, 5. Sepals, 5. Stamens, many.	357.
Sweet Briar.	*Rosa rubiginosa.*	1¾ in.	Petals, 5. Sepals, 5. Stamens, many.	358.
MEDIUM.				
Red Campion.	*Lychnis diurna.*	1 in. Rose-coloured.	Petals, 5, two-cleft. Sepals, 5, hairy. Stamens, 10, on different flowers.	359.
Soapwort.	*Saponaria officinalis.*	1 in. Pale pink.	Petals, 5. Sepals, 5. Stamens, 10.	360.
Common Rest-harrow.	*Ononis arvensis.*	⅝ in. Rose-coloured. Pea-shaped.	Petals, 5. Sepals, 5. Stamens, 10.	361.
Spiny Rest-harrow.	*Ononis spinosa.*	⅝ in. Striped. Pea-shaped.	Petals, 5. Sepals, 5. Stamens, 10.	362.
SMALL.				
Long-stalked Cranesbill.	*Geranium columbinum.*	½ in. Two-flowered; flower stalks long.	Petals, 5. Sepals, 5. Stamens, 10.	363.
Round-leaved Cranesbill.	*Geranium rotundifolium.*	½ in.	Petals, 5, entire. Sepals, 5. Stamens, 10.	364.
Small-flowered Cranesbill.	*Geranium pusillum.*	¼ in.	Petals, 5, notched. Sepals, 5. Stamens, 10.	365.
Saintfoin.	*Onobrychis sativa.*	½ in. In raceme; clover-like, with darker veins.	Petals, 5, unequal. Sepals, 5. Stamens, 10.	366.
Teasel-headed Trefoil.	*Trifolium maritimum.*	½ in. In roundish head; small, clover-like.	Petals, 5, unequal. Sepals, 5. Stamens, 10.	367.
Soft-knotted Trefoil.	*Trifolium striatum.*	½ in. Light purple, in downy heads, clover-like.	Petals, 5, unequal. Sepals, 5. Stamens, 10.	368.
Broad Smooth-leaved Willow-herb.	*Epilobium montanum.*	⅜ in. Rose-coloured. Buds drooping.	Petals, 4. Sepals, 4. Stamens, 8.	369.
Dove's-foot Cranesbill.	*Geranium molle.*	⅜ in. Light purple.	Petals, 5, notched. Sepals, 5. Stamens, 10.	370.
Shining Cranesbill.	*Geranium lucidum.*	¼ in.	Petals, 5, entire. Sepals, 5. Stameus, 10.	371.
Jagged-leaved Cranesbill.	*Geranium dissectum.*	⅜ in. Purple.	Petals, 5, notched. Sepals, 5, with long points. Stamens, 10.	372.
Tuberous Bitter Vetch.	*Lathyrus macrorrhizus.*	⅜ in. Crimson, fading to blue. Pea-shaped.	Petals, 5.	373.
Square-stalked Willow-herb.	*Epilobium tetragonum.*	⅜ in. Small, pink.	Petals, 4. Sepals, 4. Stamens, 8.	374.
Pale Smooth-leaved Willow-herb.	*Epilobium roseum.*	¼ in. Many; small, rose-coloured.	Petals, 4. Sepals, 4. Stamens, 8.	375.
Narrow-leaved Willow-herb.	*Epilobium palustre.*	¼ in. Buds drooping.	Petals, 4. Sepals, 4. Stamens, 8.	376.
Common Fumitory.	*Fumaria officinalis.*	¼ in. Rose-coloured, tipped purple. Tubular.	Petals, 4. Sepals, 2. Stamens, 6.	377.

RED OR PINK.   Polypetalous.

Leaves.	Months.	Habitat.	Remarks.
			LARGE.
d.	6–7	Cornfields.	1–2 ft. Flower stalk with spreading hairs. (V. C.)
nnatifid.	6–7	Cornfields.	1–2 ft. Flower stalk with closely pressed hairs. (C.)
nnatifid.	6–7	Cornfields.	6–10 in. (C.)
	5	Wet places.	1–2 ft. Stem angular, lower part bristly, upper sticky. (V. C.)
stem, serrate, r.	7–8	River sides.	4–6 ft. Stems and leaves downy. (C.)
to five-lobed; d, downy both	8–9	Sea marshes.	1–3 ft. (L.)
five to seven.	6–7	Hedges.	3–8 ft. The common Hedge Rose. (V. C.)
errated, hairy, scented.	6–7	Bushy places.	3–6 ft. Found specially on chalk. (L.)
			MEDIUM.
sessile, downy.	All summer.	Hedges.	1–2 ft. (V. C.)
three-ribbed.	8–9	Waste places.	2–4 ft. Generally found near cultivated land. (L.)
three, sticky.	All summer.	Waysides.	1–2 ft. Stem shrubby, without spines. (C.)
three, sticky.	6	Heaths.	6–12 in. Stem shrubby, hairy. (C.)
			SMALL.
d; lobes cut long narrow its.	6–8	Waste places.	1–2 ft. (C.)
l, lobed.	6–8	Waste places.	6–12 in. Plant downy. (C.)
l, lobed.	All summer.	Waste places.	6–18 in. Plant downy. (C.)
in eight to pairs.	6–7	Chalk and limestone.	1–2 ft. (L.)
three.	6–7	Salt marshes.	6–18 in. (L.)
three.	6–7	Barren places.	4–12 in. Found especially near sea. Plant spreading, with soft hairs. (C.)
nooth, toothed.	7–8	Waste places.	1–2 ft. Stem downy; seeds cottony. (V.C.)
obed, cut.	All summer.	Waste places.	6–15 in. Downy; distinguished by prostrate growth. (C.)
hiny.	All summer.	Walls and rocks.	6–12 in. Stems and leaves shiny, generally tinged with red. (C.)
; divided in segments.	All summer.	Waysides.	1–2 ft. Distinguished by deeply cut hairy leaves. (C.)
two to four	5–6	Heaths.	6–12 in. Distinguished by absence of tendrils. (C.)
sessile, toothed.	7–8	Wet places.	1–2 ft. Stem square. (C.)
alked, ovate, l.	7–8	Damp places.	1–2 ft. Mostly in South. Stem squarish. (L.)
sessile.	7–8	Wet places.	6–18 in. (C.)
divided, light	All the year.	Waste places.	3–12 in. (C.)

539. Bush Vetch.   247. Meadow Vetchling.   Tuberous Vetchling.   456. Marsh Violet.

498. Sweet Violet.   499. Dog Violet.   533. Viper's Bugloss.   248. Wall Pepper (Biting Stonecrop).

28. Water Cress.   3. Water Lily.   698. Water Milfoil.   171. Water Plantain.

 606. Water Starwort.
 684. Water Thyme.
 43. Spring Whitlow-grass.

 369. Willow-herb.
 111. Wintergreen.
 120. Woodruff.
 574. Great Wood-rush.

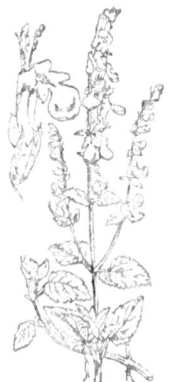 209. Wood Sage.
 9. Wood Sorrel.
 438. Hedge Woundwort.
 303. Yellow Rattle.

Monopetalous. **RED OR PINK.**

English Name.	Latin Name.	Description of Flower.	Petals, Sepals, Stamens, etc.	
LARGE.				
Small Bindweed.	*Convolvulus arvensis.*	$1\frac{1}{8}$ in. One to three together; rose-coloured, sometimes white, opening only in sunshine.	Petals, 5. Sepals, 5. Stamens, 5.	378.
Flowering Rush.	*Butomus umbellatus.*	1 in. Many in umbel, on tall round stalk.	Petals, 6. Sepals, 0. Stamens, 9.	379.
MEDIUM.				
Marsh Lousewort.	*Pedicularis palustris.*	$\frac{5}{8}$ in. Lipped, dull pink.	Calyx ribbed, cut in two lobes, hairy. Stamens, 4.	380.
Field Lousewort.	*Pedicularis sylvatica.*	$\frac{5}{8}$ in. Lipped, rose-coloured.	Calyx smooth, with five leaf-like lobes, angled. Stamens, 4.	381.
Bee Orchis.	*Ophrys apifera.*	$\frac{3}{4}$ in. Pink, with brown lip.	Petals, 3. Sepals, 3, pink.	382.
Buck-bean or Marsh Trefoil.	*Menyanthes trifoliata.*	$\frac{3}{4}$ in. Pink in bud; inner surface covered with white hairs.	Petals, 5. Sepals, 5. Stamens, 5.	383.
SMALL.				
Common Centaury.	*Erythræa centaurium.*	$\frac{3}{8}$ in. Bright pink.	Petals, 5. Sepals, 5. Stamens, 5.	384.
Sea Milkwort.	*Glaux maritima.*	$\frac{1}{4}$ in. Pink, dotted crimson	Petals, 0. Sepals, 5. Stamens, 5.	385.
Squinancy-wort.	*Asperula cynanchica.*	$\frac{3}{16}$ in. Flesh-coloured, purplish without.		386.
Thrift or Sea Pink.	*Armeria maritima.*	$\frac{3}{8}$ in. In roundish heads.	Petals, 5. Sepals, 5. Stamens, 5.	387.
Scarlet Pimpernel.	*Anagallis arvensis.*	$\frac{3}{8}$ in. Scarlet, opening only in sunshine.	Petals, 5. Sepals, 5. Stamens, 5.	388.
Red Spur Valerian.	*Centranthus ruber.*	$\frac{3}{16}$ in. Varying from crimson to white.	Corolla spurred. Stamen, 1.	389.
Pyramidal Orchis.	*Orchis pyramidalis.*	$\frac{5}{16}$ in. Deep rose; in tapering spike.	Petals, 3; lower one lipped and three-lobed, spurred.	390.
Bog Pimpernel.	*Anagallis tenella.*	$\frac{3}{8}$ in. Rose-coloured.	Petals, 5. Sepals, 5. Stamens, 5.	391.
Marsh Speedwell.	*Veronica scutellata.*	$\frac{3}{8}$ in. Pale pink; in alternate racemes.	Petals, 4. Sepals, 4. Stamens, 2.	392.
Mountain Cudweed.	*Antennaria dioica.*	$\frac{5}{16}$ in. Not rayed. Pinkish white; in heads, four to six together.		393.
VERY SMALL.				
Common Sorrel.	*Rumex acetosa.*	$\frac{1}{8}$ in. Reddish green.	Petals, 6. Stamens, 6.	394.
Red Bearberry.	*Arctostaphylos uva ursi.*	$\frac{1}{8}$ in. Rose-coloured; in clusters.	Petals, 5. Calyx five-cleft. Stamens, 10.	395.
Small Marsh Valerian.	*Valeriana dioica.*	$\frac{3}{8}$ in. Pink, lighter inside. Male flowers largest.	Stamens and pistils in different flowers. Stamens, 3.	396.
Knot-grass.	*Polygonum aviculare.*	$\frac{3}{16}$ in. In axillary clusters flesh-coloured or greenish white.	Stamens, 8. Styles, 3.	397.
Amphibious Persicaria.	*Polygonum amphibium.*	$\frac{3}{16}$ in. In oblong spike.	Petals, 0. Sepals, 5. Stamens, 5.	398.
Spotted Persicaria.	*Polygonum persicaria.*	$\frac{1}{8}$ in. In spikes; pinkish.	Petals, 0. Sepals, 5. Stamens, 5–8.	399.
Water Pepper or Biting Persicaria.	*Polygonum hydropiper.*	$\frac{1}{8}$ in. In slender racemes, drooping.	Sepals, 5, green and rose. Stamens, 6.	400.
Cross-leaved Heath.	*Erica tetralix.*	$\frac{1}{4}$ in. Bell-shaped, five-toothed; sometimes white.	Sepals, 4. Stamens, 8.	401.

RED OR PINK.   Monopetalous.

Leaves.	Months.	Habitat.	Remarks.
...aped.	6–7	Banks.	6–24 in. (C.) **LARGE.**
linear.	6–7	Ponds and ditches.	3–4 ft. (C.)
	6–9	Marshes.	6–18 in. (C.) **MEDIUM.**
	6–8	Pastures.	3–10 in. (V. C.)
parallel-veined.	6–7	Pastures.	6–12 in. Especially on chalk or limestone. (L.)
...ee leaflets.	6–7	Bogs.	3–9 in. (L.)
...with parallel ...smooth.	6	Pastures.	5–18 in. (C.) **SMALL.**
...vate, glaucous.	6–8	Seashores.	3–6 in. (L.)
...our in a whorl.	6–7	Downs.	6–10 in. Stem four-angled. Used as a remedy for quinsy. (L.)
...adical, crowded.	7–8	Seashores.	3–10 in. (C.)
sessile, dotted ...h.	6–9	Waysides.	3–12 in. Sometimes called "Poor Man's Weather-glass." (V. C.)
...nooth, glaucous.	6–9	Walls, railway banks.	1–2 ft. (L.)
...te; veins par-	7	Pastures.	6–18 in. Chiefly on chalk or limestone. (C.)
...opposite pairs.	6–8	Bogs.	4–6 in. Stems slender, four-angled. (L.)
lightly toothed.	6–8	Ditches.	6–12 in. A straggling plant. (C.)
broader at tips; ...y beneath.	7–8	Mountains.	3–8 in. (C.)
slightly arrow-...l.	6–7	Meadows.	**VERY SMALL.** 1–2 ft. Stems and leaves have acid taste. (V. C.)
...v egg-shaped; ...een, turning autumn.	5	Mountains.	4–6 in. A shrubby plant with trailing stems. (L.)
...aves ovate; leaves pinnati-...ith large ter-lobe.	4	Marshes.	3–8 in. (L.)
...small.	All summer.	Waste places.	1–2 ft. Growth prostrate. A common weed. (V. C.)
...te; smooth in rough on land.	7	Waste or wet places.	2–3 ft. (C.)
...tapering, usu-ith dark spot.	7–8	Waste places.	1–2 ft. (V. C.)
...tapering.	8–9	Wet places.	1–3 ft. Stem creeping and rooting. (C.)
a whorl, cross-	7–8	Heaths.	6–18 in. (C.)

Polypetalous. CRIMSON AND SCARLET.

English Name.	Latin Name.	Description of Flower.	Petals, Sepals, Stamens, etc.	
SMALL.				
Pheasant's-eye.	*Adonis autumnalis.*	$\frac{1}{2}$ in. Bright scarlet, dark at base.	Petals, 5–8. Sepals, 5.	402.
Scarlet Pimpernel.	*Anagallis arvensis.*	$\frac{3}{8}$ in. Opening only in sunshine.	Petals, 5, joined. Sepals, 5. Stamens, 5.	403.

Polypetalous. REDDISH OR PURPLISH, OR

English Name.	Latin Name.	Description of Flower.	Petals, Sepals, Stamens, etc.	
LARGE.				
Common Mallow.	*Malva sylvestris.*	$1\frac{1}{2}$ in.	Petals, 5. Calyx — outer, three-leaved inner, five-cleft. Stamens, many, in a column.	404.
Corn Cockle.	*Lychnis githago.*	1 in. Solitary.	Petals, 5. Calyx with five long teeth. Stamens, 10. Stigmas, 5.	405.
MEDIUM.				
Common Vetch.	*Vicia sativa.*	$\frac{1}{2}$ in. In pairs, short stalks.	Petals, 5, unequal. Calyx five-toothed.	406.
Purple Marsh Cinquefoil.	*Potentilla palustris.*	$\frac{3}{4}$ in. Few, brownish purple.	Petals, 5. Calyx ten-cleft. Stamens, many.	407.
Everlasting Pea.	*Lathyrus sylvestris.*	$\frac{3}{4}$ in. Greenish purple.	Petals, 5, unequal. Sepals, 5. Stamens, 5.	408.
Purple Loosestrife.	*Lythrum salicaria.*	$\frac{5}{8}$ in. In tall spikes, flowers whorled.	Petals, 6. Calyx twelve-ribbed. Stamens, 6 long and 6 short.	409.
House-leek.	*Sempervivum tectorum.*	$\frac{3}{4}$ in. Purple.	Petals, 12, fringed. Sepals, 12. Stamens, 12.	410.
Pansy.	*Viola tricolor.*	$\frac{3}{4}$ in. Purple and yellow.	Petals, 5. Sepals, 5. Stamens, 5.	411.
Water Avens.	*Geum rivale.*	$\frac{1}{2}$ in. Bell-shaped, drooping; purplish, tinged yellow.	Petals, 5. Sepals, 10—5 large, 5 small—tinged purple. Stamens, many.	412.
SMALL.				
Common Fumitory.	*Fumaria officinalis.*	$\frac{3}{16}$ in. Tubular. Rose, tipped purple.	Petals, 4. Sepals, 2. Stamens, 6.	413.
Ramping Fumitory.	*Fumaria capreolata.*	$\frac{3}{16}$ in. Pink or cream, tipped purple; spurred.	Petals, 4. Sepals, 2.	414.
Zigzag Clover.	*Trifolium medium.*	$\frac{1}{4}$ in. Red-purple; in roundish heads.	Petals, 5, unequal. Calyx five-toothed.	415.
Small-flowered Willow-herb.	*Epilobium parviflorum.*	$\frac{5}{16}$ in. Pinkish purple.	Petals, 4. Sepals, 4. Stamens, 8. Stigma four-cleft.	416.
Great Burnet.	*Sanguisorba officinalis.*	$\frac{1}{4}$ in. Purple-brown; oblong heads, long stalks.	Petals, 0. Flower calyx four-lobed. Stamens, 4.	417.
Strawberry-headed Trefoil.	*Trifolium fragiferum.*	$\frac{1}{16}$ in. Light purple; on long stalks.	Petals, 5, unequal. Calyx five-toothed. Stamens, 10.	418.

CRIMSON AND SCARLET. Polypetalous.

Leaves.	Months.	Habitat.	Remarks.
...at.	9-10	Cornfields.	SMALL. 6-10 in. (R.)
sessile, dotted h.	6-9	Waysides.	3-12 in. Popularly known as "Poor Man's Weather-glass." (V. C.) [Really Monopetalous (see No. 388), but repeated here on ground of colour.]

H SOME OTHER TINT. Polypetalous.

Leaves.	Months.	Habitat.	Remarks.
...o seven-lobed, downy.	6-8	Roadsides.	LARGE. 1-3 ft. Petals twisted in bud. (C.)
	6-7	Cornfields.	1-2 ft. A common weed in cornfields. (C.)
...o six pairs.	6-7	Fields.	MEDIUM. 1-2 ft. Grown for fodder. (C.)
five to seven ...; pale beneath.		Marshes.	6-18 in. (C.)
... leaflets.	7-8	Woods.	3-6 ft. Stems winged. (L.)
, long, narrow.	7-8	River banks.	2-4 ft. (C.)
...shy, fringed.	7	Cottage roofs.	Local.
crenate.	All summer.	Waysides.	4-10 in. Stem angular. (V. C.)
aves pinnate, ...ate leaflets stem leaves	6-7	Damp places.	6-18 in. (C.)
en, much cut.	All year.	Cornfields.	SMALL. 3-12 in. (C.)
green; twice ...	4-8	Cornfields.	1-2 ft. Climbing by twisted leaf-stalks. (C.)
three.	7-8	Meadows.	6-18 in. Stems straggling zigzag. (C.)
arrow, toothed.	7-8	Wet places.	1-2 ft. Stem downy. (C.)
in three to five l leaflets.	6-9	Meadows.	2-3 ft. (V. C.)
three.	7-8	Fields.	6-12 in. Calyx inflated, tinged with pink; somewhat resembling a Strawberry fruit. (C.)

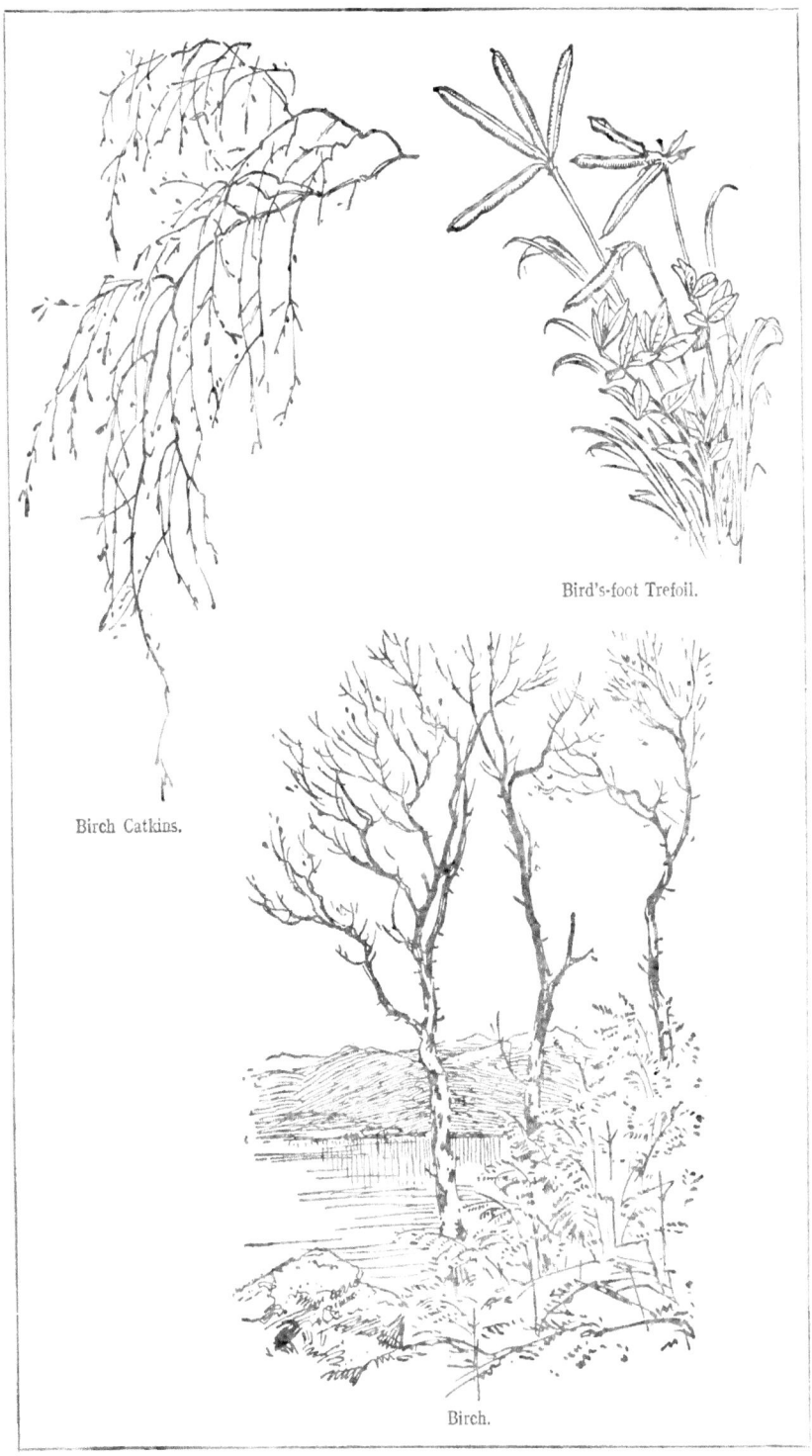

Bird's-foot Trefoil.

Birch Catkins.

Birch.

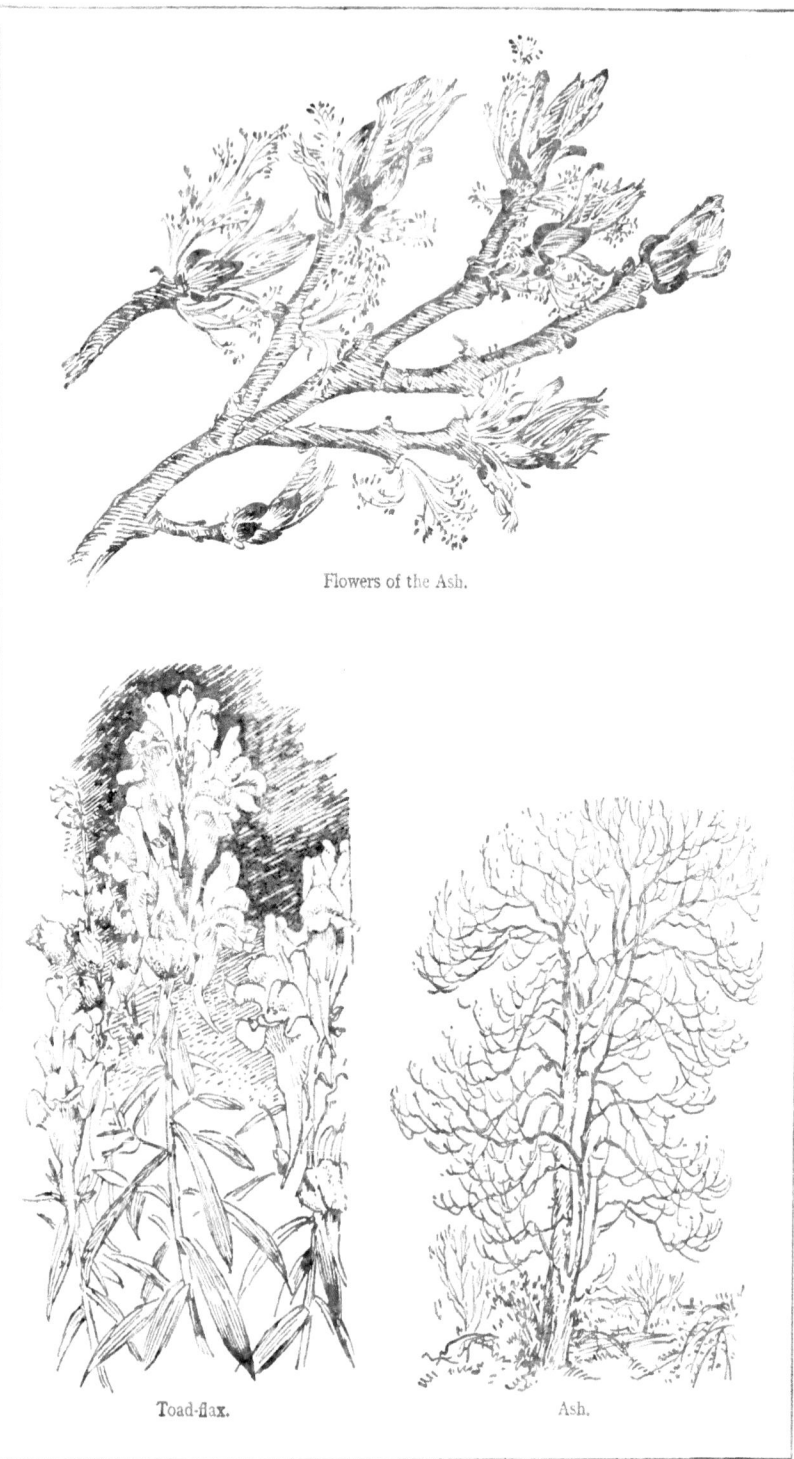

Flowers of the Ash.

Toad-flax.

Ash.

Monopetalous.   REDDISH OR PURPLE, OR

English Name.	Latin Name.	Description of Flower.	Petals, Sepals, Stamens, etc.	
LARGE.				
Nodding or Musk Thistle.	*Carduus nutans.*	1¾ in. Solitary heads drooping, with strong scent.		419.
Meadow Plume Thistle.	*Carduus pratensis.*	1¼ in. Heads mostly solitary.		420.
Melancholy Thistle.	*Carduus heterophyllus.*	1¾ in. Head solitary.		421.
Cotton Thistle.	*Onopordon acanthium.*	1¼ in. Slightly clustered, or solitary; large.		422.
Dwarf Plume Thistle.	*Carduus acaulis.*	1½ in. Heads solitary, almost stemless.		423.
Spear Plume Thistle.	*Cnicus lanceolatus.*	1½ in. Sometimes two or three heads, mostly solitary.		424.
Great Knapweed.	*Centaurea scabiosa.*	2 in. In florets, tubular, with five lobes.	Stamens, 5.	425.
Black Knapweed.	*Centaurea nigra.*	1¼ in. Dull purple, with brown scales.		426.
MEDIUM.				
Early Purple Orchis.	*Orchis mascula.*	⅝ in. Purple, marked with lighter and darker shades. Spurred.	Ovary twisted.	427.
Marsh Orchis.	*Orchis latifolia.*	⅜ in. In spike, rose-coloured, lip spotted.		428.
Foxglove.	*Digitalis purpurea.*	⅞ in. Bell-shaped, spotted inside.	Calyx five-lobed. Stamens, 4.	429.
Welted Thistle.	*Carduus acanthoides (crispus).*	⅜ in. Clustered, round.		430.
Creeping Thistle.	*Carduus arvensis.*	⅜ in. Many heads. Light purple.		431.
Marsh Thistle.	*Carduus palustris.*	⅜ in. Clustered, egg-shaped. Light purple.		432.
Burdock.	*Arctium lappa.*	⅞ in. Resembling Thistle. Dull purple.		433.
SMALL.				
Red Dead-nettle.	*Lamium purpureum.*	½ in. In whorls; two-lipped.	Sepals, 5, united. Stamens, 4.	434.
Henbit Dead-nettle.	*Lamium amplexicaule.*	½ in. In from one to three whorls. Lipped; rose-purple.	Calyx five-toothed, hairy. Stamens, 4.	435.
Red Hemp-nettle.	*Galeopsis ladanum.*	⁷⁄₁₆ in. Two-lipped, hairy. Purple, spotted crimson.	Sepals, 5. Stamens, 4.	436.
Corn Woundwort.	*Stachys arvensis.*	¼ in. Light purple, marked with white. Lipped.	Corolla scarcely longer than calyx.	437.
Hedge Woundwort.	*Stachys sylvatica.*	⅜ in. Dull purple, marked white. Two-lipped; whorled.	Sepals, 5. Stamens, 4.	438.
Slender-flowered Thistle.	*Carduus tenuiflorus.*	½ in. Pale purple-pink. Heads small, sessile, oblong, many.		439.
Fragrant Orchis.	*Gymnadenia conopsea.*	⅝ in. Rose-purple, not spotted; spur slender. Fragrant.	Petals, 2, with three-lobed lip. Sepals, 3.	440.
Black Horehound.	*Ballota nigra.*	¼ in. Purple, whorled.	Corolla two-lipped. Sepals, 5. Stamens, 4.	441.
Common Hound's-tongue.	*Cynoglossum officinale.*	¼ in. Lurid purple.	Corolla five-cleft. Sepals, 5. Stamens, 4.	442.
Wild Thyme.	*Thymus serpyllum.*	⅛ in. Purple, whorled, many heads.	Lower lip three-lobed. Sepals, 5, purplish. Stamens, 4.	443.
Wood Betony.	*Stachys betonica.*	⅜ in. Reddish purple; in short spike, whorled.	Corolla two-lipped, hairy. Sepals, 5.	444.

WITH SOME OTHER TINT.   Monopetalous.

	Leaves.	Months.	Habitat.	Remarks.
				LARGE.
419.	Deeply cut, thorny.	6-8	Waste places.	2 ft. Stem winged, furrowed, cottony. Scales on heads stiff pointed, lower ones bent back. (C.)
420.	Few; soft, wavy, toothed.	7	Wet meadows.	12-18 in. Stem cottony. (L.)
421.	Large, soft, sessile.	7	Mountain pastures.	2-3 ft. Not prickly. Stem not winged. (C.)
422.	Pinnatifid, spiny, cottony.	7-8	Waste places.	4-6 ft. Stem winged. (C.)
423.	Few, thorny.	7-8	Downs.	1-10 in. (L.)
424.	Pinnatifid, spiny, downy.	7-9	Waste places.	3-5 ft. Stem winged. (V. C.)
425.	Pinnatifid.	7-8	Dry places.	1-3 ft. Stem stout. (C.)
426.	Entire, roughish.	6-8	Meadows.	1-2 ft. Stem tough. (V. C.)
				MEDIUM.
427.	Oblong, clasping stem, usually spotted.	5-6	Pastures.	6-12 in. Plant has an unpleasant smell. (C.)
428.	Erect, sometimes spotted, lanceolate.	6-7	Wet pastures.	1-2 ft. Bracts longer than flowers, tapering. (L.)
429.	Downy.	6-7	Hedges and woods.	2-4 ft. (V. C.)
430.	Thorny, winging the stem.	6-7	Waste places.	1-3 ft. Scales of head lined; thorny, spreading. (C.)
431.	Cut, thorny, wavy.	7	Waysides.	2-4 ft. Scales of head close pressed. Stem not winged. (V. C.)
432.	Hairy, thorny.	7-8	Marshy places.	2-4 ft. Scales of head close pressed. Stem winged. (C.)
433.	Large, cordate, stalked.	7-8	Waste places.	3-5 ft. Scales of heads with clinging hooks. (V. C.)
				SMALL.
434.	Heart-shaped, crenate; tinted purple.	All summer.	Waysides.	6-12 in. (V. C.)
435.	Round, deeply crenate.	All year.	Fields.	4-10 in. Stem four-angled. (C.)
436.	Lanceolate, serrate; downy.	8-9	Sandy fields.	10-12 in. Stem square, not swollen at joints. (L.)
437.	Heart-shaped.	7-9	Fields.	6-8 in. Stem square, trailing. (C.)
438.	Heart-shaped, crenate.	7-8	Woods and hedges.	2-4 ft. Stem four-sided. Plant has strong, unpleasant smell. (V. C.)
439.	Cut, prickly; cottony beneath.	6-7	Waste places.	1-3 ft. Especially near sea. Stem winged. (C.)
440.	Lanceolate.	6-7	Heaths.	8-18 in. (C.)
441.	Heart-shaped, downy, wrinkled, crenate; dull green.	7-9	Waste places.	2-3 ft. Whole plant has offensive smell. (C.)
442.	Large, dull, downy.	6-8	Waste places.	1-2 ft. Plant has disagreeable smell. (C.)
443.	Small, oblong, fringed.	6-8	Downs and heaths.	2-8 in. Stems woody. Plant fragrant. (V. C.)
444.	In pairs; oblong, crenate.	7-8	Woods and hedges.	1-2 ft. (V. C.)

Monopetalous. REDDISH OR PURPLE, OR

English Name.	Latin Name.	Description of Flower.	Petals, Sepals, Stamens, etc.	
SMALL (*contd.*).				
Wild Basil.	*Calamintha clinopodium.*	3/8 in. Purplish; in dense whorls.	Corolla two-lipped, hairy. Sepals, 5. Stamens, 4.	445.
Red Bartsia.	*Bartsia odontites.*	1/4 in. Purple-pink; tip usually drooping.	Corolla two-lipped. Sepals, 4. Stamens, 4.	446.
Marjoram.	*Origanum vulgare.*	1/4 in. Purplish. In crowded heads.		447.
VERY SMALL.				
Ling or Heather.	*Calluna vulgaris.*	3/16 in. Purple-pink. Many, drooping; bell-shaped.	Sepals, 4. Stamens, 8. Calyx rose-coloured.	448.
Ivy-leaved Toad-flax.	*Linaria cymbalaria.*	5/16 in. Lipped, spurred. Purple and yellow.	Sepals, 5. Stamens, 4.	449.
Fine-leaved Heath.	*Erica cinerea.*	1/5 in. Egg-shaped, in irregular whorled clusters. Crimson-purple.	Sepals, 4. Stamens, 8.	450.
Hemp Agrimony.	*Eupatorium cannabinum.*	1/8 in. Red-purple; in terminal corymbs.	Styles deeply cloven.	451.
Saw-wort.	*Serratula tinctoria.*	[illegible] in. Florets tubular, with five lobes.		452.
Woody Nightshade or Bitter-sweet.	*Solanum dulcamara.*	3/8 in. Purple, with yellow centre. Drooping.	Petals, 5. Sepals, 5. Stamens, 5.	453.

Polypetalous. LILAC OR PALE PURPLE.

English Name.	Latin Name.	Description of Flower.	Petals, Sepals, Stamens, etc.	
LARGE.				
Musk Mallow.	*Malva moschata.*	1 5/8 in. Handsome, crowded at end of stem.	Sepals, 5. Petals, 5. Stamens, many.	454.
MEDIUM.				
Cuckoo Flower (Lady's Smock).	*Cardamine pratensis.*	1/2–3/4 in. Flowers lilac; cross-shaped.	Petals, 4. Sepals, 4. Stamens, 6.	455.
Marsh Violet.	*Viola palustris.*	1/2–5/8 in. Lilac with darker veins.	Sepals, 5. Petals, 5, unequal. Stamens, 5.	456.
Dwarf Mallow.	*Malva rotundifolia.*	1/2–5/8 in. Pale purple.	Sepals, 3 outer, 5 inner. Petals, 5. Stamens, many.	457.
Purple Sea Rocket.	*Cakile maritima.*	1/2 in. In corymbs.	Sepals, 4. Petals, 4. Stamens, 6.	458.
Night-flowering Catchfly.	*Silene noctiflora.*	[illegible] in. Reddish white calyx, with ten ribs.	Petals, 5, deeply notched. Stamens, 10.	459.
SMALL.				
Marsh Pennywort (White Rot).	*Hydrocotyle vulgaris.*	1/16 in. Few, never rising above leaves. In simple umbels.	Petals, 5.	460.
Knotted Hedge Parsley.	*Torilis (caucalis) nodosa.*	1/16 in. In small sessile nearly globular umbels; fruit covered with bristles.		461.
English Tamarisk.	*Tamarix anglica (gallica).*	1/4 in. In short spikes or clusters; pale pinkish.	Sepals, 5. Petals, 5. Stamens, 4–10.	462.
Hare's-foot Trefoil.	*Trifolium arvense.*	3/16 in. diameter. In terminal cylindric heads 1 in. long.	Calyx with long russet hairs. Petals, 5. Stamens, 10.	463.
Spring Vetch.	*Vicia lathyroides.*	1/2 in. Pea-flower shaped. Bright lilac-purple; solitary, sessile.	Sepals, 5. Petals, 5, unequal. Stamens, 10.	464.
Hemlock Stork's-bill.	*Erodium cicutarium.*	1/4–1/2 in. Rosy and white stalks, many-flowered.	Sepals, 5. Petals, 5. Stamens, 10.	465.

WITH SOME OTHER TINT. Monopetalous.

	Leaves.	Months.	Habitat.		Remarks.
445.	Ovate, distant.	7-8	Dry places.	10-18 in.	SMALL (contd.). Fragrant. (C.)
446.	Narrow, serrate, sessile; dingy green.	7-9	Cornfields.	6-18 in.	(C.)
447.	Egg-shaped; downy.	7-8	Dry places.	1-2 ft.	Especially on chalk. (C.)
448.	Linear, three-sided.	7-8	Heaths and moors.	1-3 ft.	VERY SMALL. (V. C.)
449.	Kidney-shaped, five-lobed.	5	Walls.	Creeping.	(C.)
450.	In threes; narrow, smooth.	7-8	Heaths.	6-12 in.	(C.)
451.	Opposite, downy, palmately divided; in three to five leaflets.	7-8	Wet places.	2-5 ft.	(C.)
452.	Deeply cut, serrate.	8	Pastures.	1-2 ft.	Stem angular, slender. (C.)
453.	Heart-shaped; upper ones eared at base.	6-7	Hedges.	8-10 ft.	(C.)

LILAC OR PALE PURPLE. Polypetalous.

	Leaves.	Months.	Habitat.		Remarks.
454.	Long-stalked; five- to seven-lobed, pinnatifid.	7-8	Banks and hedges.	1½-3 ft.	LARGE. Leaves when rubbed emit slight musky smell. (C.)
455.	Pinnate, narrow.	4-6	Damp meadows.	1 ft.	MEDIUM. Familiar spring flower. (V. C.)
456.	Heart- or kidney-shaped; smooth.	4-7	Marshy land.	Up to 6 in.	Creeping. (C.)
457.	Roundish, heart-shaped, with five shallow lobes.	6-9	Waste land.	6-12 in.	Prostrate stem. (C.)
458.	Fleshy, glaucous, variously cut.	6-9	Sandy shores.	1-2 ft.	Bushy, zigzag stems; curious seed vessels. (C.)
459.	Opposite; oblong-lanceolate.	7-8	Sandy fields.	1-2 ft.	Stem hairy and sticky, frequently forked; flowers open and fragrant at night. (L.)
460.	Round, smooth, shining, crenate; stalks hairy.	4-8	Marshes.		SMALL. Small creeping plant. (C.)
461.	Fern-like.	5-7	Waysides.	6-18 in.	Stem prostrate. (C.)
462.	Small, awl-shaped, scale-like.	7-9	Seasides.	5-10 ft.	Evergreen shrub, reddish branches. (L.)
463.	Leaflets, linear-ovate.	7-9	Roadsides, sandy places.	6-12 in.	Softly hairy, branched; distinct species. (C.)
464.	Leaflets, two to six; pinnate.	4-6	Dry pastures.	6 in.	Prostrate. (L.)
465.	Pinnate and pinnatifid.	All summer.	Waste places.	6-12 in.	Stems prostrate and hairy; fruit beaked. (C.)

Beech Mast.
Elms.

Walnut.

Wych Elm.

Polypetalous. **LILAC OR PALE PURPLE.**

English Name.	Latin Name.	Description of Flower.	Petals, Sepals, Stamens, etc.	
SMALL (*contd.*).				
Field Sandwort-spurrey.	*Buda* (*Spergularia*) *rubra.*	⅜ in. Pale pinkish.	Sepals, 5. Petals, 5. Stamens, 5 or 10.	466.
Seaside Sandwort-spurrey.	*Buda* (*Spergularia*) *marina.*	¼–⅜ in. Pink, with white base.	Sepals, 5. Petals, 5, shorter than sepals. Stamens, 5 or 10.	467.
Monopetalous.				
LARGE.				
Field Scabious.	*Scabiosa arvensis.*	1⅜ in. heads. Outer flowers large; calyces bristly; corolla bluish lilac, four-lobed.	Stamens, 4.	468.
Small Scabious.	*Scabiosa columbaria.*	1–1⅜ in. Florets five-lobed.	Stamens, 4, long. Calyx of four or five bristles.	469.
Sea Bindweed.	*Convolvulus* (*Volvulus*) *soldanella.*	1⅜ in. Pale rose, with red or yellow stripes; bell-shaped.	Two large bracts, close to flower. Stamens, 5.	470.
Wild Teasel.	*Dipsacus sylvestris.*	2 in. Oval-oblong prickly heads 2¼ in. in length.	Florets with four-lobed corolla. Stamens, 4.	471.
MEDIUM.				
Water Violet.	*Hottonia palustris.*	¾ in. Lilac or pale pinkish, with yellow eye.	Calyx five-cleft. Petals, 5, joined. Stamens, 5.	472.
Butter-bur.	*Petasites vulgaris* (*officinalis*).	⅜ in. heads. Dull lilac; many on a long, thick stalk; actual flowers minute.	Stamens, 5, whitish.	473.
Spotted Orchis.	*Orchis maculata.*	½ in. Lilac or whitish, with dark lines and spots; in an oblong spike.	Sepals, 3. Petals, 3, deeply three-lobed.	474.
SMALL.				
Common Calamint.	*Calamintha officinalis.*	¼–⅜ in. Light purple; in forked, few-flowered cymes.	Calyx two-lipped. Sepals, 5. Stamens, 4.	475.
Common Hemp Nettle.				476.
Field Madder.	*Sherardia arvensis.*	⅛ in. Close set, cross-shaped.	Petals, 4, joined. Stamens, 4. Sepals, 4–6.	477.
Lamb's Lettuce or Corn Salad.	*Valerianella olitoria.*	$\frac{1}{16}$ in. In dense heads; pale lilac.	Corolla five-lobed.	478.
Pale Butterwort.	*Pinguicula lusitanica.*	⅜ in. diameter. Pale lilac-yellow throat; spurred.	Sepals, 5. Stamens, 2.	479.
Blue Fleabane.	*Erigeron acre.*	Heads $\frac{4}{16}$ in. Disc flowers yellowish; others dull bluish lilac.	Disc florets five-cleft. Stamens, 5.	480.
Water Speedwell.	*Veronica anagallis.*	¼ in. Pale pink; in opposite racemes.	Sepals, 4. Corolla four-cleft. Stamens, 2.	481.
Common Sea-lavender.	*Statice limonium.*	$\frac{3}{16}$ in. On leafless stalk, branching at top into many spike-like clusters.	Sepals, 5. Petals, 5. Stamens, 5.	482.
Remote Sea-lavender.	*Statice rariflora.*			483.
Vervain.	*Verbena officinalis.*	⅛ in. On slender terminal spikes.	Corolla five-lobed. Stamens, 4.	484.
Marsh Whorled Mint.	*Mentha sativa.*	⅛ in. In dense separate whorls.	Sepals, 5. Corolla four-cleft. Stamens, 4.	485.
Hairy Mint (Capitate Mint, Water Mint).	*Mentha hirsuta* (*aquatica*).	⅛ in. Pale lavender; in axillary and terminal rounded heads.	Calyx with five teeth. Corolla four-lobed. Stamens, 4.	486.

LILAC OR PALE PURPLE. Polypetalous.

Leaves.	Months.	Habitat.	Remarks.
lat, pointed.	6–9	Sandy places, shores.	SMALL (contd.). 6–12 in. Small, creeping, pubescent. (C.)
)lunt.	6–9	Seashores.	6–12 in. Creeping. (L.)
			Monopetalous.
			LARGE.
Root leaves g-lanceolate; leaves pinnati-	6–9	Fields, waysides.	2–3 ft. Tall, bristly plant; stout, hairy stem. (V. C.)
d; lighter than those of ing.	6–9	Fields, chalky pastures.	1–1½ ft. (Name Scabiosa from "Scabies," leprosy, for which in old days some species were supposed to be a remedy.) (C.)
idney-shaped.	6–8	Seashores.	6–12 in. Not climbing; shows often half buried in sand. (C.)
, narrow, form- p round stem.	7–9	Wastes.	3–6 ft. A stout plant with prickly stem; leaves prickly beneath. (C.)
			MEDIUM.
finely divided water.	5–6	Pools and ditches.	Floating. The only British species. (L.)
rge, Rhubarb- 1–3 ft. wide;	1–3	River banks.	1–4 ft. Leaves appear after flowers. A pernicious weed where found. (C.)
- lanceolate, d brown.	5–7	Commons and heaths.	6–18 in. Stem long and solid. (V. C.)
			SMALL.
lightly serrate, gish stalks.	7–8	Dry wastes.	1–2 ft. Erect, bushy plant; downy stem, four-angled. (C.)
			Creamy white, with pinkish or lilac tinge. (See No. 191.)
pointed, four in a whorl.	4–10	Cornfields.	3–12 in. A small, branched, spreading plant. (C.)
iarrow, upper lasping stem.	5–6	Waysides.	4–12 in. Small, forked plant, once used as a salad. (C.)
white, veined,	6–8	Bogs.	2–4 in. Chiefly in the South-west of England, the West of Scotland, and in Ireland. (R.)
aves obovate- late; others ', half-clasping.	7–8	Dry places, walls.	1–2 ft. Much branched; hairy, rough to the touch. (L.)
anceolate, ser-	6–8	Stagnant water.	1–2 ft. Stout, succulent, erect; stem hollow. (C.)
lked, oblong,)bed, smooth.	7–11	Muddy shores.	4–12 in. (L.)
			Very similar to above, but more erect branches and fewer flowers. Not so frequent a plant.
', rough, three-	7–9	Waste land.	1–2 ft. Slender, tough-stemmed. The only British species. (C.)
, stalked, ovate, :; green, hairy h sides.	7–9	Wet places.	2–5 ft. Very like the following, but note the description. (C.)
ovate, serrate, downy on both	7–9	Banks of rivers and ditches.	1–4 ft. (see above). The commonest of the Mints, strong-smelling. (V. C.)

Monopetalous. LILAC OR PALE PURPLE.

English Name.	Latin Name.	Description of Flower.	Petals, Sepals, Stamens, etc.	
SMALL (*contd.*). Pennyroyal.	*Mentha pulegium.*	$\frac{1}{8}$ in. Reddish; in distant axillary whorls.	Corolla four-cleft. Stamens, 4. Calyx downy.	487.
Spathulate Sea-lavender.	*Statice auriculæfolia.*	$\frac{1}{8}$ in. Flower stalks branched into several erect tufts of lilac flowers.	Sepals, 5. Petals, 5. Stamens, 5.	488.
Matted Sea-lavender.	*Statice reticulata.*	$\frac{1}{8}$ in.		489.
Small-flowered Gentian (Common Autumn Gentian).	*Gentiana amarella.*	$\frac{3}{8}$ in. Purplish blue corolla.	Calyx five-lobed. Corolla four- to five-lobed. Stamens, 4–5.	490.
Peppermint.	*Mentha piperita.*	$\frac{1}{8}$ in. Calyx five-toothed, often red.	Corolla short, four-lobed. Stamens, 4.	491.
Corn Mint.	*Mentha arvensis.*	$\frac{1}{8}$ in. Lilac clusters; in dense, distant whorls.	Calyx five-toothed, hairy. Corolla four-lobed. Stamens, 4.	492.
Round-leaved Mint.	*Mentha rotundifolia.*	$\frac{1}{8}$ in. Lilac or white; in dense, interrupted spikes.	Calyx five-toothed, hairy. Corolla four-lobed. Stamens, 4.	493.
Horse Mint.	*Mentha longifolia.*	$\frac{1}{16}$–$\frac{1}{8}$ in. Lilac; in a dense, uninterrupted spike.	Corolla hairy.	494.
Spearmint.	*Mentha viridis.*	$\frac{1}{16}$–$\frac{1}{8}$ in. Flowers in whorls on slender spikes.	Corolla without hairs.	495.

Polypetalous. BLUE OR BLUISH.

English Name.	Latin Name.	Description of Flower.	Petals, Sepals, Stamens, etc.	
LARGE. Meadow Cranesbill (Blue).	*Geranium pratense.*	$1\frac{1}{2}$ in. Blue-purple.	Sepals, 5. Petals, 5, veined. Stamens, 10.	496.
MEDIUM. Common Flax.	*Linum usitatissimum.*	1 in. Petals notched. Sepals ovate, three-veined, and pointed.	Sepals, 5. Petals, 5. Stamens, 5.	497.
Sweet Violet.	*Viola odorata.*	$\frac{1}{2}$–$\frac{3}{4}$ in. Scented; on long stalks. Variable in colour.	Sepals, 5. Petals, 5. Stamens, 5.	498.
Dog Violet.	*Viola ericetorum (canina).*	$\frac{1}{2}$–$\frac{3}{4}$ in. Not scented; on long stalks.	Sepals, 5. Petals, 5. Stamens, 5.	499.
Hairy Violet.	*Viola hirta.*	$\frac{1}{2}$–$\frac{5}{8}$ in. Not scented.	Sepals, 5. Petals, 5.	500.
Field Larkspur.	*Delphinium ajacis.*	1 in. Four to sixteen flowers in a raceme.	Sepals, 5 (petal-like, with spur). Petals, 2. Stamens, many.	501.
SMALL. Narrow-leaved Flax.	*Linum angustifolium.*	$\frac{3}{8}$ in. Light blue.	Sepals, 5, sharp-pointed, elliptical. Petals, 5. Stamens, 5.	502.
Tufted Vetch.	*Vicia cracca.*	$\frac{1}{2}$ in. Flowers ten to thirty in racemes, blue and purple.	Sepals, 5. Petals, 5. Stamens, 10.	503.
Hairy Tare.	*Vicia hirsuta.*	$\frac{1}{8}$ in. One to six flowers together, pale blue, on long stalks.	Sepals, 5. Petals, 5. Stamens, 10.	504.

LILAC OR PALE PURPLE. Monopetalous.

Leaves.	Months.	Habitat.	Remarks.
			SMALL (contd.).
short-stalked, oblong.	7–9	Wet heaths.	2–10 in. An old remedy for colds. (C.)
at base, wider (spathulate).	7–8	Rocky shores	4–10 in. (L.)
		Salt marshes.	4–8 in. Like preceding, but leaves blunt, one-ribbed, short-stalked, few, 1 in. (R.)
, sessile, ovate-	7–8	Dry, chalky land.	6–12 in. Remarkably erect. Stem square, much branched. (C.)
ovate-lanceo- cute, serrate.	7–8	Wet places.	1–1½ ft. (L.)
ovate, serrate, acute or blunt.	7–9	Cornfields.	6–18 in. Branched, downy plant. (C.)
ovate, blunt, ed, smooth	8–9	Waste, wet land.	1–3 ft. A viscid plant; stem rather woody, much branched usually. (L.)
essile; oblong- late, acute, ser- silky white h.	8–9	Waste, wet land.	2–3 ft. Generally in masses; strongly and sweetly scented. (C.)
oblong-lanceo-	8–9	Wet places.	1–2 ft. More pungent in smell than the other Mints. Cultivated as the pot-herb. (L.)

BLUE OR BLUISH. Polypetalous.

Leaves.	Months.	Habitat.	Remarks.
			LARGE.
seven-lobed, errated.	6–9	Moist meadows.	2–4 ft. Erect, downy. (C.)
			MEDIUM.
nceolate, broad, te.	6–7	Cornfields.	12–18 in. Escape from cultivation. Stems mostly solitary. (L.)
slightly downy.	3–4	Banks, hedgerows.	3–6 in. (C.)
smooth, small- an those of ing.	4–5	Heaths and sandy places.	3–6 in. All the Violets have unequal petals, one spurred. (V. C.)
rough, hairy. many narrow	4–6 6–7	Chalky soils. Sandy or chalky cornfields.	3–6 in. Without runners. (L.) 1 ft. (L.)
			SMALL.
pointed, alter-	5–9	Dry pastures.	1–2 ft. Frequent in Southern and Western Counties. (L.)
with about narrow leaf- lky.	6–8	Hedges.	2–6 ft. Climbing, stem angled; branched tendrils. (V. C.)
six to eight	5–8	Fields and hedges.	1–2 ft. Slender, much branched, hairy. (V. C.)

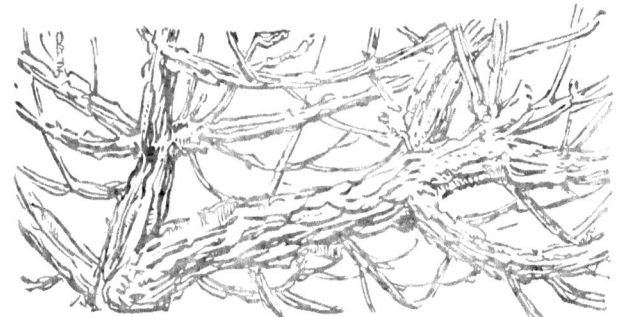

Corky bark of the Hedge Maple.

Black Poplar.

Purple Loosestrife and Water Mint. Devil's-bit Scabious.

BLUE OR BLUISH.

English Name.	Latin Name.	Description of Flower.	Petals, Sepals, Stamens, etc.	
LARGE.				
Chicory or Succory.	*Cichorium intybus.*	1½ in. Delicate blue heads.	Florets strap-shaped, distinctly five-toothed.	505.
Cornflower or Corn Bluebottle.	*Centaurea cyanus.*	1¼ in. Ray florets bright blue; disc florets with some dark purple.	Florets tubular, five-lobed.	506.
MEDIUM.				
Water Lobelia.	*Lobelia dortmanna.*	½ in. Drooping, pale blue.	Sepals, 5. Stamens, 5. Corolla two-lipped.	507.
Lesser Periwinkle.	*Vinca minor.*	¾ in. Wheel-shape, with a long tube.	Sepals, 5. Petals, 5, joined. Stamens, 5.	508.
Bluebell or Hyacinth.	*Hyacinthus non-scriptus (Scilla festalis).*	½ in. Five to twenty in a raceme. Bell-shaped.	Petals or Sepals, 6. Stamens, 6.	509.
Borage.	*Borago officinalis.*	¾–1 in. In terminal drooping clusters.	Sepals, 5. Petals, 5. Stamens, 5, in a black cone.	510.
Annual Sheep's Bit (Sheep's Scabious).	*Jasione montana.*	⅝–⅞ in. Lilac-blue heads. Florets five-cleft, calyx five-lobed.	Stamens, 5, united.	511.
SMALL.				
Ivy-leaved Speedwell.	*Veronica hederæfolia.*	¼ in. Pale blue, one in each leaf axil.	Sepals, 4. Petals, 4, joined. Stamens, 2.	512.
Green Field Speedwell.	*Veronica agrestis.*	⅓ in. Pale blue, with white lower lobe; solitary, in leaf axil.	Sepals, 5. Petals, 4, joined. Stamens, 2.	513.
Buxbaum's Speedwell.	*Veronica buxbaumii.*	½ in. Solitary, axillary; bright blue, on long stalks.	Sepals, 4. Petals, 4, joined. Stamens, 2.	514.
Wall Speedwell.	*Veronica arvensis.*	1/16 in. Inconspicuous, in terminal spikes or clusters.	Sepals, 4. Corolla, four-lobed. Stamens, 2.	515.
Grey Field-speedwell.	*Veronica polita.*	3/16 in. Solitary, axillary.	Sepals, 4. Petals, 4, joined. Stamens, 2.	516.
Germander Speedwell.	*Veronica chamædrys.*	½ in. Long axillary clusters.	Sepals, 4. Petals, 4, unequal. Stamens, 2.	517.
Brooklime.	*Veronica beccabunga.*	⅓ in. Deep blue, in axillary racemes.	Sepals, 4. Petals, 4. Stamens, 2.	518.
Water Speedwell.	(See No. 481.)			
Mountain Speedwell.	*Veronica montana.*	¼ in. Light blue; in short raceme with few flowers.	Sepals, 4. Petals, 4. Stamens, 2.	519.
Thyme-leaved Speedwell.	*Veronica serpyllifolia.*	¼ in. Many-flowered racemes; light blue, with darker veins.	Sepals, 4. Petals, 4. Stamens, 2.	520.
Common Speedwell.	*Veronica officinalis.*	¼ in. Pale blue; many-flowered spikes or racemes.	Sepals, 4. Petals, 4. Stamens, 2.	521.
Spring Squill.	*Scilla verna.*	½ in. Fragrant; bright blue, starlike, clustered.	Sepals with Petals, 6. Stamens, 6.	522.
Common Bugle.	*Ajuga reptans.*	⅝ in. Blue, with veins in whorls, forming a spike.	Sepals, 5. Stamens, 4.	523.
Early Field Scorpion Grass.	*Myosotis collina.*	⅛ in. In clusters, almost concealed.	Sepals, 5. Petals, 5, joined. Stamens, 5.	524.
Field Scorpion Grass.	*Myosotis arvensis.*	3/16 in. Pale blue on long slender stalks.	Calyx five-cleft, with hooked bristles. Corolla five-lobed. Stamens, 5.	525.
Wood Scorpion Grass.	*Myosotis sylvatica.*	⅜ in. In clusters.	Petals, 5, joined. Sepals, 5, hairy. Stamens, 5.	526.
Tufted Water Scorpion Grass.	*Myosotis cæspitosa.*	⅙ in. Sky blue, with yellow disc; short stalked, in long slender racemes.	Petals, 5. Calyx five-lobed. Stamens, 5.	527.

BLUE OR BLUISH. Monopetalous.

Leaves.	Months.	Habitat.	Remarks.
			LARGE.
aves like Dan-; upper clasp-	7–10	Wastes, especially chalky.	1–3 ft. Stem angled, grooved and strong; milky. (L.)
linear-lanceo- lower ones d.	7–8	Cornfields.	1–2 ft. Stem and plant slightly cottony. (C.)
			MEDIUM.
al, submerged.	7–8	Lakes.	1–2 ft. Aquatic, with a matted base. (L.)
)ssy, evergreen.	3–6	Woods.	3–12 in. Trailing, rooting stem. (L.)
ong.	5–6	Woods.	6–18 in. (V. C.)
essile, waved.	6–7	Wastes.	1–2 ft. Stems and leaves covered with bristles; juice smells like Cucumber. (L.)
blunt, hairy.	6–9	Dry heaths.	1 ft. Disagreeable smell when bruised. (C.)
			SMALL.
cordate, five- en-lobed.	3–8	Walls, etc.	6–18 in. (C.)
cordate, ser-	4–8	Fields, waste places.	4–8 in. (V. C.)
or ovate-cor-		Wastes.	6–12 in. (L.)
)rdate, crenate.	4–10	Walls, and dry places.	4–18 in. Downy, often covered in dust. (C.)
)rdate, irregu- errate.	3–7	Waste land.	4–12 in. (C.)
)rdate, sessile, serrate, hairy.	4–6	Banks.	8–20 in. Stem with two lines of hairs, shifting at each pair of leaves. (V. C.)
)lunt, slightly e.	5–9	Brooks and ditches.	1–2 ft. (V. C.)
			(See No. 481.)
ovate-cordate.	5–9	Moist woods.	1–2 ft. Stem hairy all round. (L.)
liptic, slightly e, leathery.	5–7	Waste land.	3–10 in. Downy stems. (V. C.)
errated, short- d.	5–7	Dry fields.	3–10 in. Hairy and rough; stems stiffish. (V. C.)
irrow.	4–5	Sea coast in West and North.	4–6 in. (L.)
leaves oblong, ; tinged with	5–6	Moist meadows and woods.	6–12 in. Solitary; erect stem, smooth, square. (V. C.)
blong.	4–7	Dry banks.	3–10 in. A slender plant; flowers bright blue. (C.)
blong.	6–8	Waste places.	6–18 in. Roughish, with spreading bristles or hairs. (V. C.)
anceolate.	5–9	Dry woods.	1–2 ft. Erect, no runners, spreading hairs. (C.)
id blunt.	5–9	Wet places.	6–18 in. Downy stem. (C.)

Monopetalous. **BLUE OR BLUISH.**

English Name.	Latin Name.	Description of Flower.	Petals, Sepals, Stamens, etc.	
SMALL (contd.). Forget-me-not (Water Scorpion Grass).	Myosotis palustris.	Nearly ¼ in. Pale blue, yellow eye; in leafless, one-sided clusters.	Calyx five-lobed. Corolla five-lobed. Stamens, 5.	528.
Creeping Water Scorpion Grass.	Myosotis repens.	⅛ in. Pale blue; in leafless, one-sided clusters.	Calyx five-lobed, with hooked hairs. Corolla, five-lobed. Stamens, 5.	529.
Scarlet Pimpernel.				530.
Common Milkwort.				531.
Corn Bell-flower.	Campanula hybrida.	1/10 in. Terminal, sessile; blue inside, lilac outside.	Calyx five-lobed, much longer than corolla, five-cleft. Stamens, 5.	532.
Common Viper's Bugloss.	Echium vulgare.	½ in. Curved lateral spikes; at first rose-coloured, then becoming bright blue.	Sepals, 5. Stamens, 5. Corolla five-lobed.	533.
Small Bugloss.	Lycopsis (Anchusa) arvensis.	¼ in. Clusters of funnel-shaped bent flowers.	Sepals, 5. Corolla five-lobed. Stamens, 5.	534.

Polypetalous. **VIOLET-PURPLE OR**

English Name.	Latin Name.	Description of Flower.	Petals, Sepals, Stamens, etc.	
LARGE. Columbine.	Aquilegia vulgaris.	1½ in. Flowers hanging; each petal has an incurved spur.	Petals, 5. Sepals, 5. Stamens, many.	535.
Hoary Shrubby Stock.	Mathiola incana.	1–2 in. Purple.	Petals, 4. Sepals, 4. Stamens, 6.	536.
Wood Cranesbill.	Geranium sylvaticum.	1 in. In purplish blue or rose colour.	Sepals, 5. Petals, 5. Stamens, 10.	537.
MEDIUM. Monkshood (Wolfsbane).	Aconitum napellus.	About 1 in. Purplish blue.	Sepals, 5; upper one hooded, containing two spurred petals.	538.
SMALL. Bush Vetch.	Vicia sepium.	½ in. Dull pale purple; four to six in axillary clusters.	Sepals, 5. Petals, 5. Stamens, 10.	539.
Lucerne or Purple Medick.	Medicago sativa.	¼ in. Short, close racemes.	Sepals, 5. Petals, 5. Stamens, 10.	540.
Slender Tare.	Vicia tetrasperma (gracilis).	⅓ in. Flowers one to four together. Pale purple-blue.	Sepals, 5. Petals, 5. Stamens, 10.	541.
Sea Holly.	Eryngium maritimum.	⅛ in. Sessile, in dense heads; grey-blue.	Recognized by its general resemblance to Thistle.	542.
Field Sea Holly.	Eryngium campestre.			543.

Monopetalous.

| LARGE. Gladdon or Stinking Iris. | Iris fœtidissima. | 2½ in. Dull leaden hue | Perianth, 6—three outer larger, three inner erect. Three stigmas, petal-like. Stamens, 3. | 544. |

BLUE OR BLUISH. Monopetalous.

Leaves.	Months.	Habitat.	Remarks.
			SMALL (contd.).
sessile; bright	5–8	Wet places.	9–18 in. Stem, with spreading hairs. (V.C.)
near-oblong.	6–8	Wet places.	6–18 in. With leafy runners above ground; stem with spreading hairs. (V. C.)
rough, wavy.	6–9	Cornfields, chiefly South.	Blue variety. (See Nos. 388, 403.) Often blue or red. (See under WHITE, No. 73.) 4–12 in. Rough, wiry, erect stem. (L.)
tapering.	6–8	Dry ground.	2–3 ft. Bristly stems and leaves. Once considered an antidote against viper's bite. (C.)
wavy, sessile.	6–7	Waste land.	6–18 in. Branched, prickly. (C.)

SH PURPLE. Polypetalous.

Leaves.	Months.	Habitat.	Remarks.
			LARGE.
; two to three,	5–7	Woods and heaths.	1–3 ft. (L.)
te, hoary, with	5–6	Sea cliffs, Hastings to Isle of Wight.	1–2 ft. Shrubby, erect, branched. The "Queen Stock" of gardens. (L.)
alked, deeply obed, serrate t.	6–7	Woods.	1–2 ft. Tall, hairy, erect plant, chiefly found in the North. (L.)
; cut into five a toothed lobes.	6–9	Damp, shady places.	MEDIUM. 1–2 ft. Very poisonous. Once used to poison bait in wolf traps. (L.)
twelve to six-vate, obtuse.	5–8	Hedges.	SMALL. 1–3 ft. (V. C.)
oblong, toothed, e.	6–7	Fields and coasts.	1–2 ft. Erect; stem hollow. (L.)
eight leaflets, , with tendril.	5–8	Wastes, chiefly in South.	1–2 ft. Slender stem. (C.)
like those of Glaucous.	7–8	Sandy sea-shores.	1–2 ft. Stout, stiff, prickly, thistle-like. (L.) A taller and slenderer plant, less glaucous; also found on seashores, wastes, and ballast heaps. (R.)
			Monopetalous.
			LARGE.
vord-shaped.	6–8	Copses.	2 ft. Stem has one sharp edge. Plant smells badly. (L.)

Some Common Grasses.

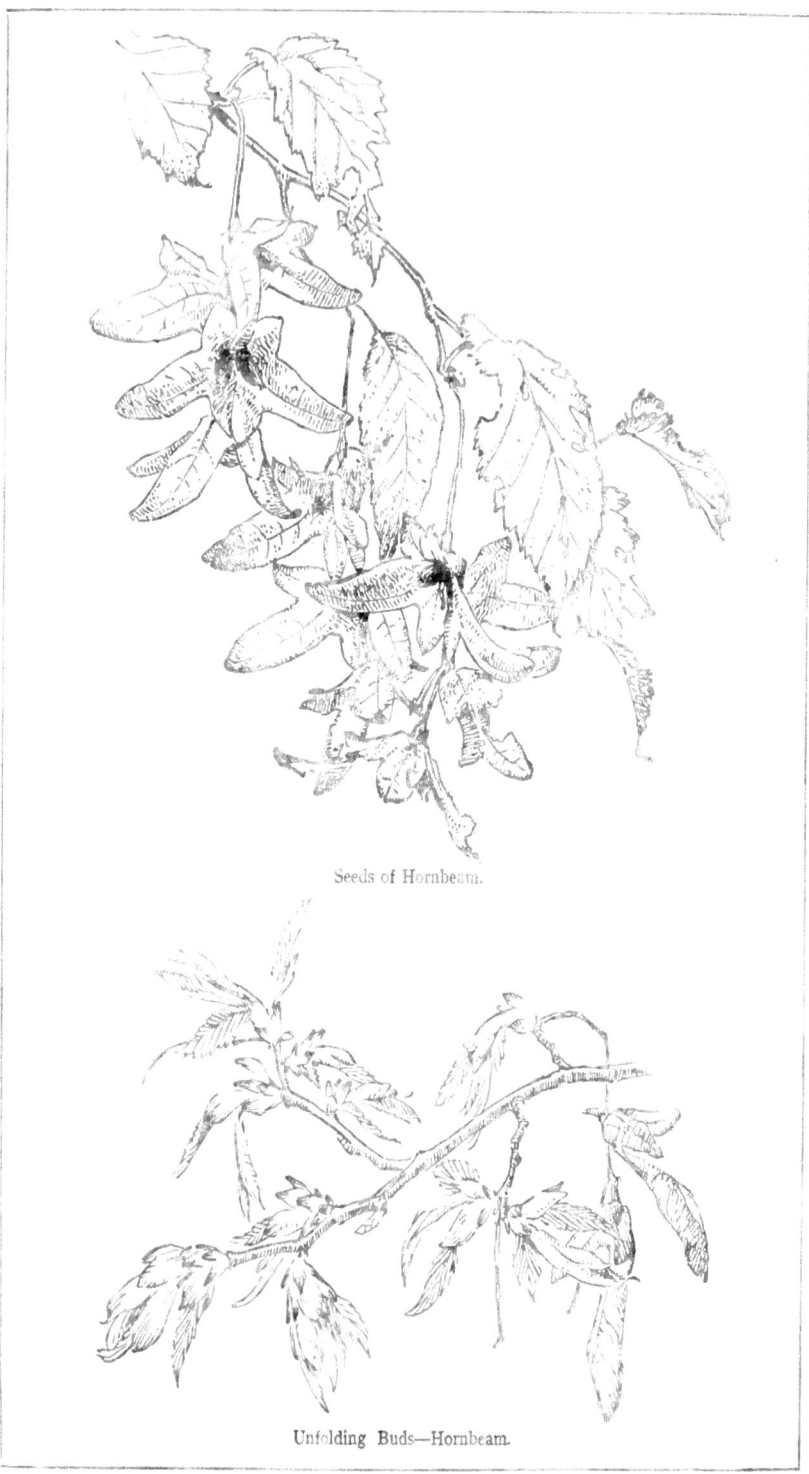

Seeds of Hornbeam.

Unfolding Buds—Hornbeam.

Monopetalous. VIOLET-PURPLE OR

English Name.	Latin Name.	Description of Flower.	Petals, Sepals, Stamens, etc.	
LARGE (contd.)				
Giant Bell-flower.	Campanula latifolia.	1½ in. Bell-shaped, deep blue or white, hairy inside.	Sepals, 5. Corolla five-lobed.	545
Spreading Bell-flower.	Campanula patula.	1 in. and more. Panicles of wide, cup-shaped flowers.	Sepals, 5. Stamens, 5, awl-shaped.	546
Nettle-leaved Bell-flower (Wild CanterburyBells).	Campanula trachelium.	¾-1 in. Axillary clusters of two or three; blue-purple, bell-shaped.	Sepals, 5, rough and hairy. Stamens, 5.	547
Creeping Bell-flower.	Campanula rapunculoides.	1 in. On long raceme, drooping, all one side.	Sepals, 5. Corolla five-lobed. Stamens, 5.	548
MEDIUM.				
Rampion Bell-flower.	Campanula rapunculus.	½ in. Clustered panicles of erect flowers.	Sepals, 5. Corolla five-lobed, cup-shaped. Stamens, 5, awl-shaped.	549
Clustered Bell-flower.	Campanula glomerata.	½-¾ in. Nearly sessile, funnel-shaped flowers.	Sepals, 5, short. Corolla five-lobed. Stamens, 5.	550
Harebell.	Campanula rotundifolia.	½-¾ in. Drooping, in a raceme.	Sepals, 5, long and narrow. Corolla bell-shaped, five-toothed. Stamens, 5.	551
Common Butterwort.	Pinguicula vulgaris.	½ in. Long, violet, nodding.	Sepals, 5. Corolla two-lipped, spurred. Stamens, 2.	552
Deadly Nightshade (Dwale).	Atropa belladonna.	½-¾ in. Solitary, drooping, bell-shaped, lurid purple.	Sepals, 5. Corolla five-lobed. Stamens, 5.	553
Sea Starwort.	Aster tripolium.	Heads ⅔ in. Inner florets yellow; outer, purple.	Stamens, 5.	554
Devil's-bit Scabious (Premorse).	Scabiosa succisa.	Heads ¾ in., round-topped. Florets four-cleft.	Calyx of four or five bristles. Stamens, 4, long.	555
SMALL.				
Common Skull-cap.	Scutellaria galericulata.	½ in. Axillary, in pairs.	Sepals, 5. Corolla two-lipped, white inside, longer than calyx. Stamens, 4.	556
Self-heal.	Prunella vulgaris.	¼ in. Dull violet; in cylindrical head, with two purple - edged bracts.	Sepals, 5. Corolla two-lipped. Stamens, 4.	557
Common Basil (Basil Thyme).	Calamintha acinos (arvensis).	¼ in. In whorls of five or six.	Calyx five-toothed, two-lipped, lower one bulging. Corolla spotted with white.	558
Ground Ivy (Alehoof).	Nepeta glechoma.	¼ in. Three or four flowers in axils of leaf.	Calyx five-cleft. Stamens, 4.	559
Tea-plant (Duke of Argyll's).	Lycium barbarum.	⅜ in. Flowers purplish, funnel-shaped, turning yellow.	Corolla five-cleft. Stamens, 5.	560
Wild Sage or Clary.	Salvia verbenaca.	¼ in. In whorls of six, on long, hairy spikes.	Sepals, 5. Stamens, 2. Corolla two-lipped.	561
Field Gentian.	Gentiana campestris.	⅜ in. Numerous, in groups at top of stem.	Sepals, 4, two outer much larger than inner. Corolla four-cleft.	562
Ivy-leaved Bell-flower.	Campanula (Wahlenbergia) hederacea.	¼ in. Solitary, on long, very thin stalks.	Sepals, 5. Corolla five-cleft. Stamens, 5.	563

BLUISH PURPLE. Monopetalous.

Leaves.	Months.	Habitat.	Remarks.
			LARGE (contd.).
Ovate-lanceolate, doubly serrate, hairy.	7–8	Woods and copses.	3–4 ft. Stem furrowed. More common in Scotland. (L.)
Stem leaves narrow.	7–8	Hedges and copses.	1–3 ft. Stem rough. Chiefly in the West. (L.)
Like Nettle.	7–10	Woods and hedges.	2–3 ft. Very rough plant. Stem angular. Frequent, but Local.
Stem leaves ovate; root leaves cordate.	7–8	Woods and hedges.	1–2 ft. Downy, with runners. (L.)
			MEDIUM.
Stem leaves narrow, sessile; root leaves ovate, long-stalked.	7–8	Hedges and copses.	2–3 ft. Chiefly in the West. (L.)
Ovate, serrate; upper, sessile.	7–10	Dry pastures.	3–18 in. Stiff, erect plant. Roughish, leafy, hairy stem. (L.)
Linear mostly.	7–9	Heaths and dry ground.	6–24 in. (C.)
Oblong, sticky, in a rosette.	5–7	Bogs and wet heaths, principally in North.	2–8 in. A beautiful plant, with fibrous root. (C.)
Ovate, pointed.	6–8	Waste places.	3–4 ft. Stout, erect, herbaceous, with runners. Most dangerous poisonous plant in England, owing to its attractive black berries. (L.)
Lanceolate, smooth, fleshy.	7–8	Salt marshes.	1–3 ft. Stout, succulent. (L.)
Mostly entire, oblong.	7–10	Heaths and pastures.	1–2 ft. "The Devil bit away parte of ye roote, and thereof came the name *succisa*." (C.)
			SMALL.
Opposite, narrow; base leaves cordate.	7–9	River and pond banks.	1–1½ ft. Stem four-angled. (C.)
Opposite, ovate-oblong.	7–9	Waste ground, roadsides.	4–10 in. Stem four-angled. (V. C.)
Hairy, ovate, serrate, acute.	7–8	Dry places.	6–8 in. Small, bushy plant.
Kidney-shaped, crenate, roughish.	3–6	Waysides.	6–24 in. Stem trailing. Aromatic odour; once used in brewing; leaves sometimes dried and made into tea. (C.)
Narrow, lanceolate.	6–8	Specially near sea.	6–12 ft. An African shrub, naturalized in many places. (L.)
Oblong, much wrinkled.	5–9	Dry pastures.	1–2 ft. Aromatic, herbaceous. (C.)
Stem leaves ovate-oblong; root leaves obovate.	7–10	Dry pastures.	6–12 in. Erect, square, leafy stem. (C.)
Stalked; like those of Ivy.	7–10	Wet, peaty places, especially in South.	4–6 in. Straggling, thread-like stems.

(No Polypetalæ under this Colour.)

English Name.	Latin Name.	Description of Flower.	Petals, Sepals, Stamens, etc.	
LARGE.				
Alder (tree).	*Alnus glutinosa.*	Catkins, 2 in. long.	Flower with 4 stamens. Pistillate catkins separate, woody.	564.
Aspen (tree).	*Populus tremula.*	Catkins, 2 in. long.	Stamens, 4–12 in each flower. Stigmas two- to four-lobed.	565.
Black Poplar.	*Populus nigra.*	Catkins, 2–3 in.	Stamens, 12–20, red-purple. Stigmas, two, roundish.	566.
Grey Poplar.	*Populus canescens.*	Catkins, 2 in.	Stamens, 6–10.	567.
White Poplar (Abele).	*Populus alba.*	Catkins, 2 in.	Stamens, 6–10. Stigmas yellow, in two parts.	568.
SMALL.				
Wych Elm.	*Ulmus montana.*	In clusters, about $\frac{1}{2}$ in.; flowers $\frac{1}{8}$ in.; on bare twigs.	Sepals or petals, 4 or 5. Stamens, 5.	569.
Common Elm.	*Ulmus campestris.*	In clusters, about $\frac{1}{2}$ in.; flowers $\frac{1}{8}$ in.; on bare twigs.	Sepals or petals, 4 or 5. Stamens, 5.	570.
Field Wood-rush.	*Luzula campestris.*	$\frac{1}{8}$ in. In dense clusters of dark brown, almost black, flowers.	Sepals with petals, 6. Stamens, 6.	571.
Broad-leaved Hairy Wood-rush.	*Luzula pilosa.*	$\frac{1}{4}$ in. Flowers one to three together, chestnut-brown.	Sepals with petals, 6. Stamens, 6.	572.
Narrow - leaved Hairy Wood-rush.	*Luzula forsteri.*	$\frac{1}{4}$ in. On one-flowered erect foot-stalks.	Sepals with petals, 6. Stamens, 6.	573.
Great Hairy Wood-rush.	*Luzula sylvatica.*	$\frac{1}{4}$ in. Many, in large cyme.	Sepals with petals, 6. Stamens, 6.	574.
Many - flowered Wood-rush.	*Luzula erectum.*	$\frac{1}{4}$ in. In many-flowered clusters, sometimes pale brown.	Sepals with petals, 6. Stamens, 6.	575.
Common Rush.	*Juncus communis.*	$\frac{1}{8}$ in. In branched or rounded cluster half-way up stem.	Perianth, 6. Stamens, 3.	576.
Heath Rush.	*Juncus squarrosus.*	$\frac{1}{4}$ in. Two to three together, terminal.	Perianth chaffy. Stamens, 6.	577.
Lesser Sea Rush.	*Juncus maritimus.*	$\frac{1}{4}$ in. In lateral clusters, very light brown.	Perianth lanceolate.	578.
Sharp - flowered Jointed Rush.	*Juncus acutiflorus.*	$\frac{1}{16}$ in. Dark chestnut-brown; in dense clusters, three to twelve in terminal panicle.	Stamens, 6.	579.
Hard Rush.	*Juncus glaucus.*	$\frac{1}{8}$ in. In loose, much-branched, erect panicle, below the end of stem.	Perianth, 6. Stamens, 6.	580.
Shining - fruited Jointed Rush.	*Juncus lamprocarpus.*	$\frac{1}{8}$ in. In clusters, in much-forked terminal panicle.	Perianth, 6. Stamens, 6.	581.
Toad Rush.	*Juncus bufonius.*	$\frac{1}{8}$ in. Solitary, sessile, green-brown flowers.	Perianth, 6, unequal. Stamens, 3 or 6.	582.
Great Bulrush.	*Typha latifolia.*	$\frac{1}{16}$ in. In club-like spike of pistillate flowers, with staminate flowers above it.		583.
Lesser Bulrush.	*Typha angustifolia.*	$\frac{1}{16}$ in. In club-like spike of pistillate flowers, with staminate flowers above it.		584.
Ash (tree).	*Fraxinus excelsior.*	Each flower $\frac{1}{8}$ in. In clusters, purplish at first.	Sepals and petals, 0. Stamens, 2.	585.
Bird's-nest Orchis.	*Neottia nidus-avis.*	$\frac{3}{8}$–$\frac{1}{2}$ in. With lip; in dense spike.	Sepals, 3. Petals, 3, one being lipped.	586.
Sweet Gale (Bog Myrtle).	*Myrica gale.*	$\frac{1}{8}$ in. Catkins, sessile.	Stamen flowers with 4–8 stamens.	587.

WITH SOME OTHER TINT. Monopetalous.

	Leaves.	Months.	Habitat.	Remarks.
				LARGE.
564.	Obovate, 2-4 in.; short-stalked, wavy.	3-4	Wet places.	20-40 ft. Greyish black bark. (C.)
565.	Nearly round, acute, serrate.	3-4	Woods.	20-80 ft. Grey bark; many downy suckers. (C.)
566.	Rhomboid, serrate.	3-4	River banks.	40-60 ft. Grey bark; no suckers. (L.)
567.	Not lobed.	3-4	Damp woods.	50-100 ft. (L.)
568.	Cottony and white beneath; ovate-cordate.	3-4	Damp woods.	50-100 ft. Smooth grey bark; many suckers. (L.)
				SMALL.
569.	Ovate-oblong, doubly serrate.	3-4	Woods.	30-100 ft. Furrowed bark; downy twigs; no suckers. (C.)
570.	Leaves not so serrate.	3-4	Woods.	30-100 ft. Furrowed bark; many suckers. (C.)
571.	Hairy, grass-like.	3-5	Pastures.	4-10 in. "Good Friday Grass"; "Chimney Sweeps." (C.)
572.	Slightly hairy, about ¼ in. broad.	4-6	Woods.	6-12 in. (C.)
573.	About ½ in. broad.	3-6	Woods, chiefly in South.	About 1 ft. Slender. (R.)
574.	About 8 in. long; channelled, shining, hairy-edged.	4-6	Woodlands.	1-2 ft. (C.)
575.	Grass-like, hairy.	6	Heaths and damp ground.	8-20 in. (C.)
576.	None.	7	Wet places.	1-3 ft. Stem soft, with continuous pith. (V. C.)
577.	All radical, triangular.	6-7	Moors and heaths.	4-12 in. Rigid, stiff stems and leaves. (C.)
578.	Sheath-like, solid, linear.	7-8	Salt marshes.	1-3 ft. Stem smooth, stout, wiry. (C.)
579.	Linear, slightly compressed.	6	Boggy places.	1-2 ft. Stem with internal joints, hollow. (C.)
580.	None.	7-8	Wet places.	12-18 in. Rigid, deeply furrowed, glaucous stem. (C.)
581.	Compressed, with internal divisions.	7-8	Boggy places.	1-2 ft. Leafy, compressed stem. (C.)
582.	Narrow, bristle-like.	6-8	Wet places.	2-8 in. Very small species. Stem hollow, repeatedly forked. (C.)
583.	Flat, linear, glaucous.	7-8	Ponds.	4-8 ft. Known as "Cat's-tail." (C.)
584.	Narrow, grooved below; not glaucous.	7-8	Ponds.	1-3 ft. (L.)
585.	Pinnate.	4-5	Woods.	20-60 ft. Smooth, light, ash-coloured bark. (C.)
586.	Reddish brown sheathing scales.	6-7	Shady woods.	About 1 ft. Name alludes to fibrous root. (L.)
587.	Obovate - lanceolate; fragrant when bruised.	5-7	Moors and bogs.	2-4 ft. Bushy, resinous shrub.

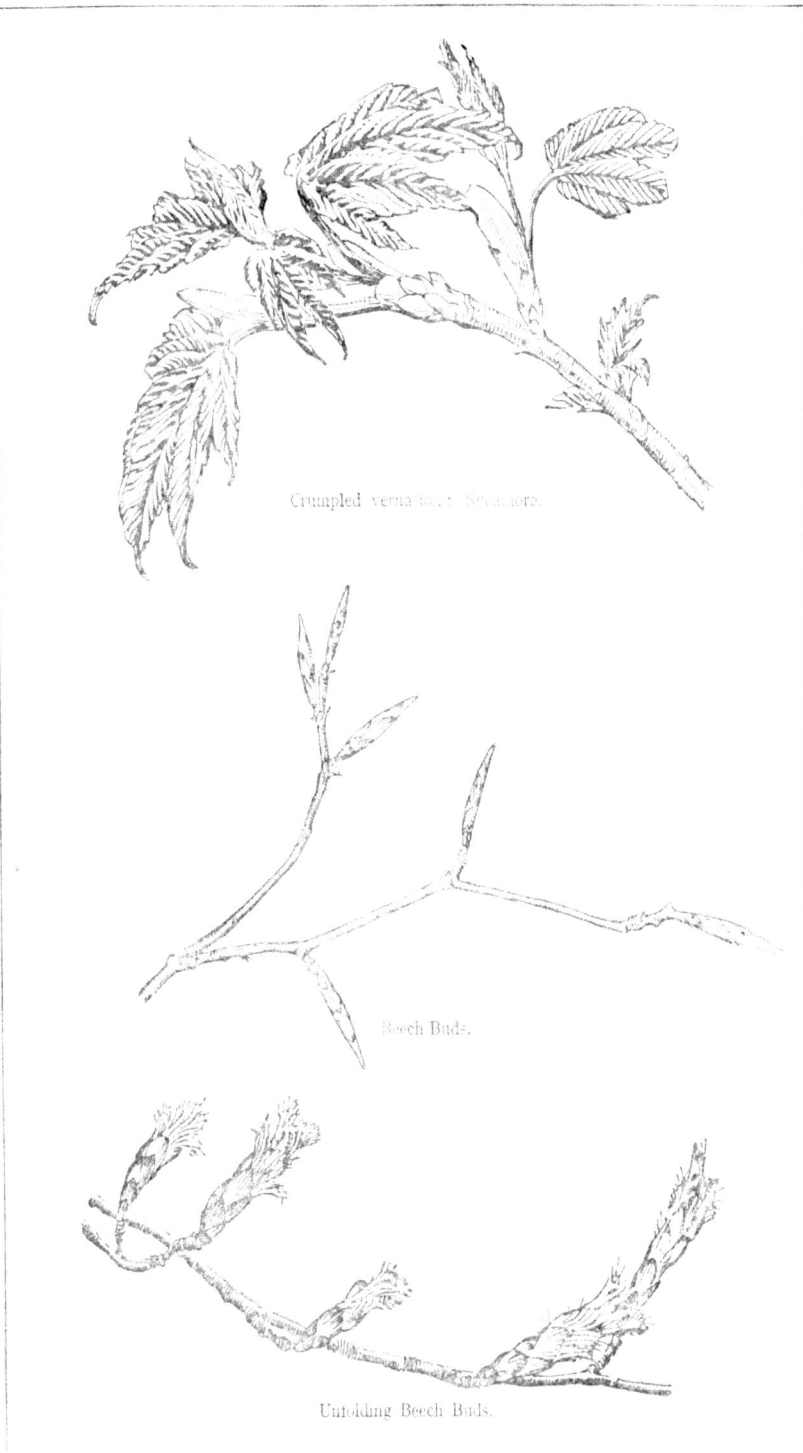

Crumpled vernation: Sycamore.

Beech Buds.

Unfolding Beech Buds.

Sycamore.

Sycamore Seeds.

Horse Chestnut.

Monopetalous. BROWN OR BROWNISH, OR

English Name.	Latin Name.	Description of Flower.	Petals, Sepals, Stamens, etc.	
SMALL (*contd.*).				
Marsh Cudweed.	*Gnaphalium uliginosum.*	Heads, $\frac{1}{8}$–$\frac{1}{6}$ in. diameter. Crowded terminal tufts.	Florets all disc, five-cleft.	588.
Wood Cudweed.	*Gnaphalium sylvaticum.*	Narrow leafy spike of yellowish brown heads.		589.
Mugwort.	*Artemisia vulgaris.*	Heads, $\frac{1}{8}$ in. diameter. Many in woolly spike, reddish or brownish yellow.	Disc florets, five-cleft.	590.
Common Filago (Cudweed).	*Filago germanica.*	Heads, $\frac{1}{8}$ in. diameter. Terminal rounded clusters of twenty.	[Two or more branches spring from base of heads.]	591.

Monopetalous (Only). BLACKISH, WITH

English Name.	Latin Name.	Description of Flower.	Petals, Sepals, Stamens, etc.	
SMALL.				
Ribwort Plantain.	*Plantago lanceolata.*	$\frac{1}{8}$ in. In oval spikes about $\frac{5}{8}$ in. wide; on long, five-ribbed stalk.	Sepals, 4. Petals, 4. Stamens, 4, very long and whitish.	592.

Polypetalous. GREEN OR GREENISH.

English Name.	Latin Name.	Description of Flower.	Petals, Sepals, Stamens, etc.	
LARGE.				
Green Hellebore.	*Helleborus viridis.*	$1\frac{1}{2}$-2 in. Pale green, rayed.	Sepals, 5. Petals, 9-12 (minute). Stamens, many.	593.
MEDIUM.				
Stinking Hellebore.	*Helleborus fœtidus.*	1 in. Drooping, cup-shaped. Sepals have a purplish hue.	Sepals, 5. Petals, small. Stamens, many.	594.
SMALL.				
Common Mare's-tail.	*Hippuris vulgaris.*	$\frac{1}{8}$ in. Inconspicuous; sessile in axils of upper leaves.	Sepals, 0. Petals, 0. Stamen, 1.	595.
Moschatel.	*Adoxa moschatellina.*	$\frac{1}{8}$ in. Each of the five-clustered flowers about $\frac{1}{4}$ in. in diameter.	Sepals, 3. Petals, 4 or 5. Stamens, 8–10.	596.
Mistletoe.	*Viscum album.*	$\frac{3}{16}$ in. Clustered, without stalk.	Petals, 4. Stamens on different plants from pistils.	597.
Wild Gooseberry.	*Ribes grossularia.*	$\frac{1}{4}$–$\frac{3}{8}$ in. In hanging racemes.	Sepals, 5. Petals, 5. Stamens, 5.	598.
Spindle Tree.	*Euonymus europæus.*	Creamy green; loose clusters.	Sepals, 4. Petals, 4. Stamens, 4.	599.
Common Maple (tree).	*Acer campestre.*	$\frac{1}{4}$ in. Erect racemes.	Sepals, 5. Petals, 5. Stamens, 8.	600.
Sycamore (tree).	*Acer pseudoplatanus.*	$\frac{1}{4}$ in. Hanging racemes.	Sepals, 5. Petals, 5. Stamens, 8.	601.
Common Buckthorn.	*Rhamnus catharticus.*	$\frac{1}{4}$ in. Crowded axillary racemes.	Sepals, 4. Petals, 4. Stamens, 4.	602.
Alder Buckthorn.	*Rhamnus frangula.*	$\frac{1}{4}$ in. Greenish white.	Sepals, 5. Petals, 5. Stamens, 5.	603.

WITH SOME OTHER TINT.   Monopetalous.

	Leaves.	Months.	Habitat.	Remarks.
				SMALL (contd.).
588.	Linear-lanceolate; downy, ¾ in.	7–9	Wet places.	3–6 in. Much branched; woolly, white. (C.)
589.	Long, narrow, acute.	7–9	Woods and heaths.	1 ft. White, cottony plant; unbranched. (C.)
590.	Pinnatifid; green above, white below.	7–9	Hedges and waste places.	3–4 ft. "Tea" said to be good for rheumatism. (C.)
591.	Linear, acute, wavy.	7–8	Dry, gravelly places.	4–12 in. Greyish. Erect, cottony stem. (C.)

WHITE OR BROWN.   Monopetalous.

	Leaves.	Months.	Habitat.	Remarks.
				SMALL.
592.	Narrow, tapering, ribbed.	5–10	Waste land.	4–12 in. ("Cocks and hens.") (V.C.)

GREEN OR GREENISH.   Polypetalous.

	Leaves.	Months.	Habitat.	Remarks.
				LARGE.
593.	Digitate, with five to seven long, narrow, serrate leaflets.	3–4	Woods.	1 ft. (L.)
				MEDIUM.
594.	Palmate, with five to seven long leaflets.	2–4	Woods.	1–2 ft. (L.)
				SMALL.
595.	Whorls of six to ten; narrow, with hard tips.	6–7	Ponds.	6–18 in. Erect, unbranched, jointed stem (not to be confused with Equisetum, Horse-tail). (C.)
596.	Root leaves triangular-ovate; cut in three-lobed leaflets.	4–7	Hedgerows.	4–6 in. Stem four-angled. Musk-like scent. (C.)
597.	Oblong, thick, leathery.	3–5	Apple and other trees.	1–3 ft. Berries waxen white. (L.)
598.	Roundish, three- to five-lobed.	4–5	Hedges.	2–4 ft. Distinguished by its spines under leaf buds. (C.)
599.	Glossy, ovate-lanceolate; minutely serrated.	5–6	Woods.	5–20 ft. Smooth, green, angular branches. Rose-coloured and orange fruit. (L.)
600.	Five blunt lobes (2–4 in. across).	5–6	Hedges and woods.	10–20 ft. Rugged, corky bark. (C.)
601.	Five lobes, unequally serrate.	5–6	Woods.	30–50 ft. (C.)
602.	Ovate, serrate.	5–7	Woods.	5–10 ft. Much branched, thorny. (C.)
603.	Obovate, entire.	5–6	Woods.	6–10 ft. Not thorny. (C.)

Polypetalous. GREEN OR GREENISH.

English Name.	Latin Name.	Description of Flower.	Petals, Sepals, Stamens, etc.	
SMALL (contd.). Common Lady's Mantle.	Alchemilla vulgaris.	1/16 in. In dense clusters, yellowish green.	Petals, 0. Calyx eight-cleft, in two rows.	604.
Field Lady's Mantle (Parsley Piert).	Alchemilla arvensis.	1/14 in. In sessile heads.	Petals, 0. Calyx eight-cleft. Stamens, 1–4.	605.
Spring Water Starwort.	Callitriche verna.	1/8 in. In axils of leaves.	No sepals or petals. Stamen, 1.	606.
Alternate-flowered Water Milfoil.	Myriophyllum alterniflorum.	1/5 in. In whorls, forming a slender spike.	Petals, 4. Sepals, 4. Stamens, 8.	607.
Spiked Water Milfoil.	Myriophyllum spicatum.	1/10 in. Greenish white; in spike, 1–4 in. above water.	Stamen flowers: Sepals, 4; petals, 2 or 4; stamens, 8. Pistil flowers: Sepals, 4; petals, small or 0; styles, 4.	608.
Wall Pennywort.	Cotyledon umbilicus.	1/4 in. Hanging in raceme on erect stem.	Sepals, 5. Corolla bell-shaped, five-toothed. Stamens, 10.	609.
Annual Knawel.	Scleranthus annuus.	1/8 in. In clusters in the axels, or terminals.	Sepals, 5. Petals, 0. Stamens, 1, 2, 5, or 10.	610.
Common Hornwort.	Ceratophyllum demersum.	1/16 in. Minute, axillary.	Sepals, many. Petals, 0. Stamens, 12–20.	611.
Salad Burnet.	Poterium sanguisorba.	Each flower 1/8 in. Heads 1/2 in. on long, bending stalks; upper flowers have crimson stigmas.	Sepals, 4. Petals, 0. Stamens, many, pendulous.	612.

Monopetalous.

English Name.	Latin Name.	Description of Flower.	Petals, Sepals, Stamens, etc.	
LARGE. Cuckoo-pint (Lords and Ladies).	Arum maculatum.	Length of green spathe (or sheath), 5 or 6 in.	Flowers form a purple club or spike, inside the spathe.	613.
Spanish Chestnut (tree).	Castanea vulgaris.	1/4 in. Catkins, 4–6 in. long.	[Fruit large and prickly.]	614.
Common Hornbeam (tree).	Carpinus betulus.	1/8 in. Catkins, 2–3 in. long.		615.
Herb Paris (True Love-knot).	Paris quadrifolia.	1 1/2 in.	Sepals, 4, long, narrow, green. Petals, 4, linear, yellow. Stamens, 8.	616.
MEDIUM. Common Birch (tree).	Betula alba.	Staminate catkins, 1 in., hanging; pistillate, 1/2 in., almost erect.	Stamens, 2.	617.
Beech (tree).	Fagus sylvatica.	Diameter of heads, 1/2 in.	Stamens, many. Styles, 3, linear.	618.
Oak (tree).	Quercus robur.	Staminate catkins, 1 1/2 in., each flower, 1/8 in.	Stamens, 10.	619.
SMALL. Spurge Laurel.	Daphne laureola.	1/4 in. In drooping, axillary clusters.	Petals, 4, joined. Stamens, 8.	620.
Caper Spurge.	Euphorbia lathyris.	1/4 in. In umbel of three or four unequal rays.	Stamens, many.	621.
Dog's Mercury.	Mercurialis perennis.	1/8 in. On footstalks in axils of upper leaves; in racemes and spikes.	Sepals, 3. Stamens, 8–20.	622.
Yew (tree).	Taxus baccata.	1/8 in. Stamen flowers in very small catkins.	Flowers under branches.	623.
Common Juniper (tree).	Juniperus communis.	1/8 in. Stamen flowers in roundish catkins.		624.
Common Twayblade.	Listera ovata.	Yellowish green; a long, loose spike or raceme.	Flowers with a two-lobed lip.	625.
Heart-leaved Twayblade.	Listera cordata.	1/14 in. Few, in a narrow, loose raceme.	Sepals, 3. Petals, 2, brownish green; lip petal yellowish green.	626.

GREEN OR GREENISH. Polypetalous.

Leaves.	Months.	Habitat.	Remarks.
idney-shaped; to nine-lobed, ed, fan-like.	6–8	Pastures.	SMALL (contd.). 1 ft. (C.)
bed, and cut.	5–8	Dry places.	3–8 in. Inconspicuous, hairy weed. (C.)
joined at base.	4–10	Ditches and ponds (floating).	Floating in star-like rosette, stamens only above water. (C.)
ivided, four in d.	5–8	Ponds.	Stem 2–6 ft., much branched. Floating. (L.)
rls of four; ery, under	6–8	Ponds.	1–3 ft. (C.)
peltate, fleshy.	6–8	Walls, rocks, chiefly in West.	6–18 in. Succulent, glabrous. (C.)
wl-shaped.	6–11	Fields.	2–8 in. Numerous, much-branched, tangled stems. (C.)
cked; in a horn-ike, bristle-like.		Streams.	1–3 ft. Entirely under water. (C.)
innate; leaflets d.	6–8	Heaths.	8–12 in. Smells and tastes of cucumber. (C.)

Monopetalous.

LARGE.

Leaves.	Months.	Habitat.	Remarks.
shaped, often d.	4–5	Woods and hedges.	8–12 in. (C.)
-lanceolate; y serrated.	5	Parks, etc.	50–100 ft.
ovate; doubly te, hairy be-	5	Woods.	20–60 ft. Smooth grey bark. (L.)
large, ovate,	5–6	Woods.	1 ft. (L.)

MEDIUM.

Leaves.	Months.	Habitat.	Remarks.
ovate, pointed; , 2 in.	4–5	Woods.	20–50 ft. (C.)
ovate, folded e.	4–5	Woods.	20–100 ft. Thin, smooth, olive-grey bark. (C.)
obovate; wavy	4–5	Woods.	40–100 ft. Deeply furrowed, rugged bark. (C.)

SMALL.

Leaves.	Months.	Habitat.	Remarks.
n, lanceolate.	1–4	Woods.	2–3 ft. Smooth, erect stems; bare except at summit. (L.)
, sessile; 2–6 op-like.	6–7	Woods and thickets.	2–3 ft. Succulent, milky juice; tinged with purple. (L.)
g-lanceolate; hairy.	4–5	Woods.	1 ft. Stem solitary, erect. (V. C.)
narrow, ever-	3–4	Woods and hillsides.	10–50 ft. (L.)
pointed, in of three.	5–6	Hills and downs.	1–5 ft. Red-brown flaky bark. (L.)
vate, opposite,	5–7	Woods and orchards.	1–2 ft. (L.)
ordate, sessile,	6–9	Moors.	4–8 in. Stem angled. (L.)

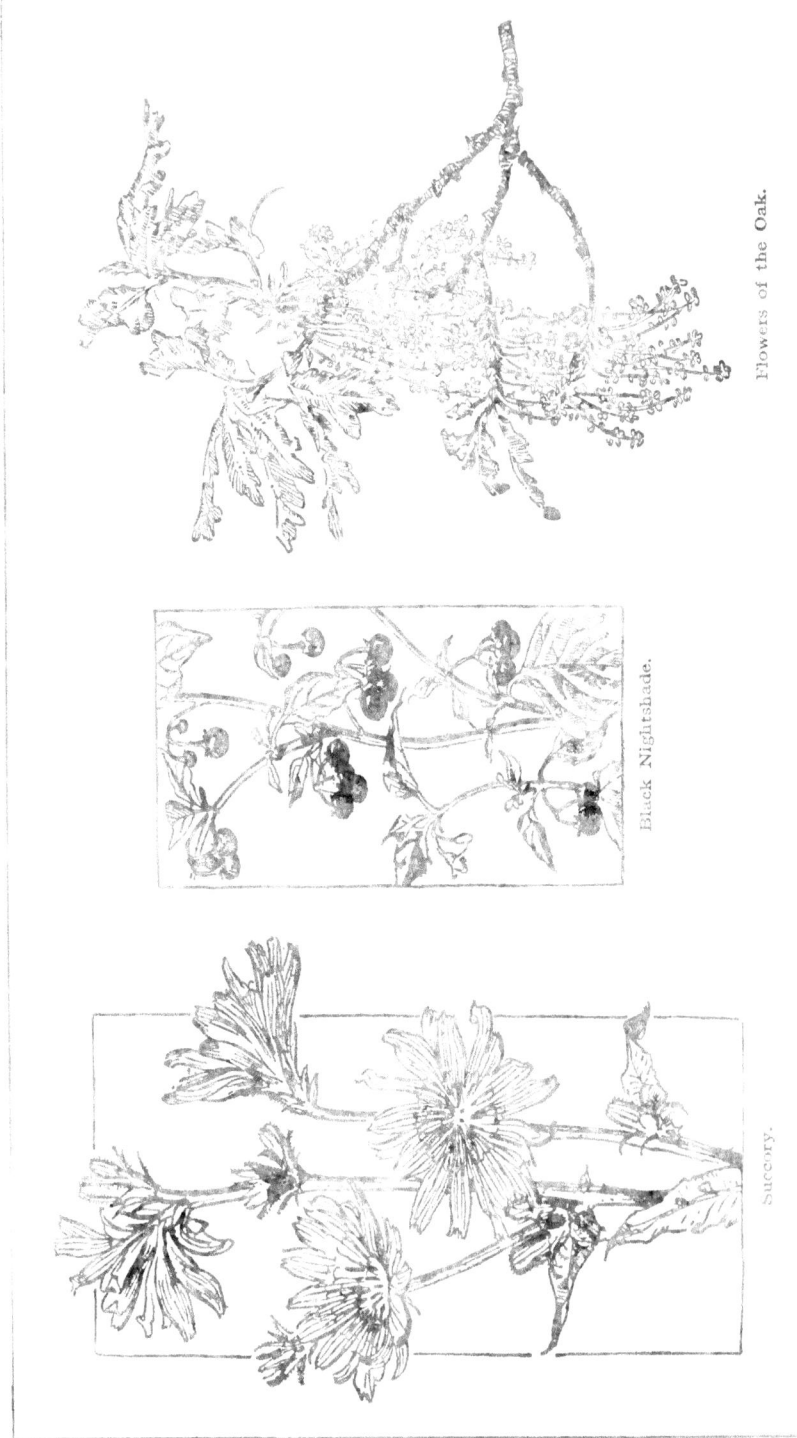

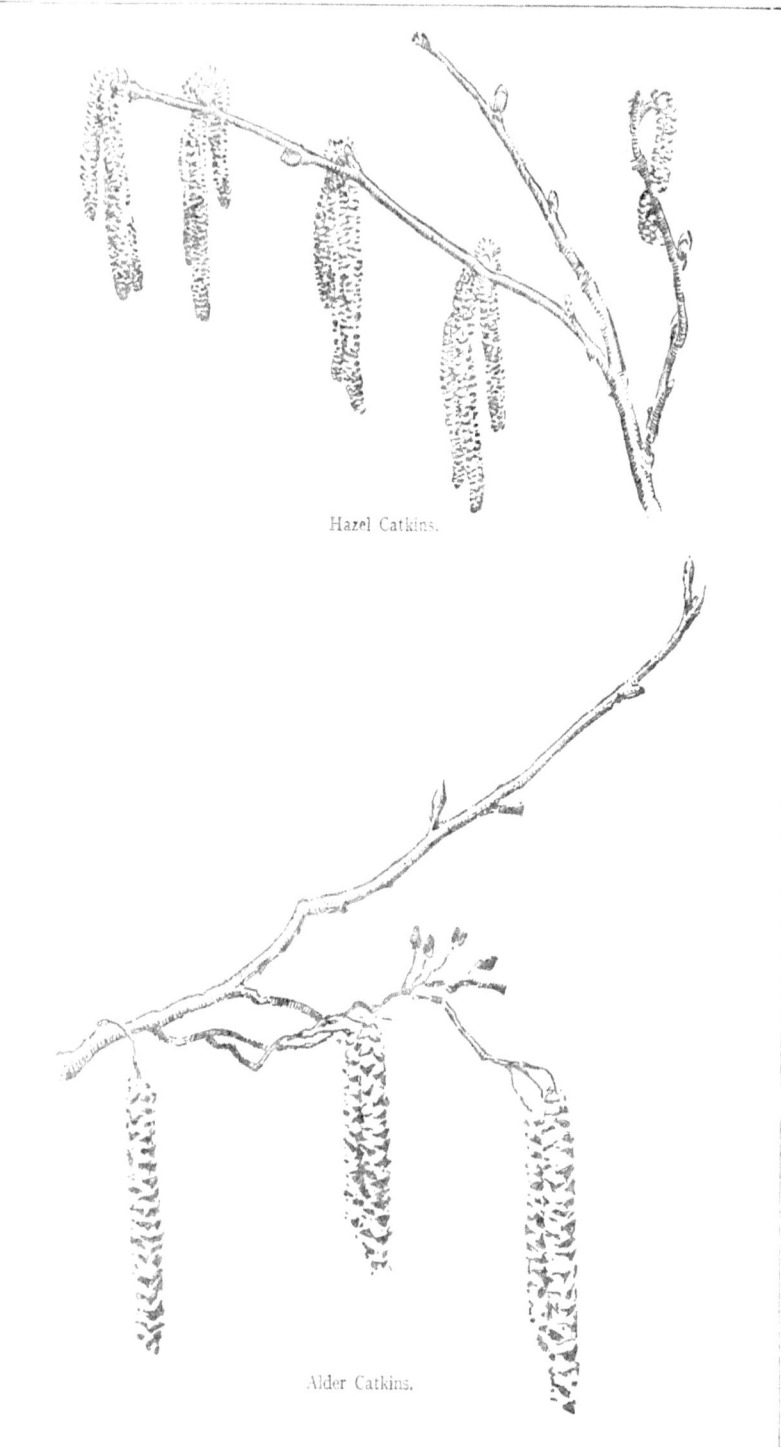

Hazel Catkins.

Alder Catkins.

Monopetalous. **GREEN OR GREENISH.**

English Name.	Latin Name.	Description of Flower.	Petals, Sepals, Stamens, etc.	
SMALL (contd.). Black Bryony.	Tamus communis.	$\frac{1}{4}$ in. Perianth bell-shaped.	Stigmas two-lobed. Stamens, 6.	627.
Seaside Arrow-grass.	Triglochin maritimum.	$\frac{1}{8}$ in. On a loose raceme or spike.	Perianth six-cleft. Stamens, 6.	628.
Marsh Arrow-grass.	Triglochin palustre.	$\frac{1}{8}$ in. On a loose raceme.	Sepals with petals, 6. Stamens, 6.	629.
Sea (Wild) Beet.	Beta maritima.	$\frac{1}{8}$ in. Long, loose, leafy spikes.	Perianth five-cleft. Stamens, 5.	630.
Seaside Plantain.	Plantago maritima.	$\frac{1}{8}$ in. (each flower). On a cylindrical spike, $1\frac{1}{2}$–2 in.	Sepals, 4. Petals, 4. Stamens, 4.	631.
Buck's-horn Plantain.	Plantago coronopus.	$\frac{1}{10}$ in. On a slender spike (stamens yellow).	Sepals, 4. Petals, 4. Stamens, 4.	632.
Frosted Sea Orache.	Atriplex arenaria (laciniata).	$\frac{1}{16}$ in. Clustered in spikes.	Stamen flowers: Sepals and stamens, 3–5. Pistil flowers: Sepals, 2; styles, 2.	633.
Spreading-fruited (or Rose-coloured) Orache.	Atriplex babingtonii.	$\frac{1}{8}$ in. In loose, leafy spikes.	Stamen flowers: Sepals and stamens, 3–5. Pistil flowers: Sepals, 2; styles, 2.	634.
Grass-leaved Orache.	Atriplex littoralis.	$\frac{1}{16}$ in. In narrow spikes.	Stamen flowers: Sepals and stamens, 3–5. Pistil flowers: Sepals, 2; styles, 2.	635.
Prickly Saltwort.	Salsola kali.	$\frac{1}{8}$ in. Solitary; axillary.	Perianth deeply five-cleft. Stamens, 3–5.	636.
Great Water Dock.	Rumex hydrolapathum.	$\frac{1}{4}$ in. In crowded whorls, forming almost leafless panicles.	Perianth, 6. Stamens, 6. Styles, 3.	637.
White Goosefoot (Fat Hen).	Chenopodium album.	$\frac{1}{8}$ in. In dense, clustering spikes.	Perianth, 5. Stamens, 5.	638.
Maple-leaved Goosefoot.	Chenopodium hybridum.	$\frac{1}{8}$ in. In large axillary clusters.	Sepals, 5. Stamens, 5.	639.
Upright Goosefoot.	Chenopodium urbicum.	$\frac{1}{8}$ in. In dense, erect spike.	Sepals, 5. Stamens, 5.	640.
Stinking Goosefoot.	Chenopodium vulvaria (olidum).	$\frac{1}{12}$ in. In small spikes.	Sepals, 5. Stamens, 5.	641.
Many-seeded Goosefoot.	Chenopodium polyspermum.	$\frac{1}{12}$ in. In branched, slender spikes.	Sepals, 5. Stamens, 5.	642.
Nettle-leaved Goosefoot (Sow-bane).	Chenopodium murale.	$\frac{1}{12}$ in. In short, dense spikes.	Sepals, 5. Stamens, 5.	643.
Red Goosefoot.	Chenopodium rubrum.	$\frac{1}{12}$ in. In short spikes, in leafy panicles.	End flowers: Sepals, 5; stamens, 5. Side flowers: Sepals, 3; stamens, 3.	644.
Annual Sea-blite.	Suæda maritima.	$\frac{1}{18}$ in. One to five together.	Perianth five-cleft. Stamens, 5.	645.
Sea Wormwood.	Artemisia maritima.	Heads $\frac{1}{8}$ in. diameter. In racemes (reddish).	All florets tubular, five-cleft.	646.
Jointed Glasswort (Marsh Samphire).	Salicornia herbacea.	$\frac{1}{8}$ in. Three together on each side of a node.	Perianth three- to four-lobed. Stamens, 2.	647.
Frog Orchis.	Habenaria viridis.	$\frac{3}{8}$ in. In short, brownish green spike.	Sepals, 3, forming hood. Petals, 3, lower one lipped, spurred, cleft.	648.
Water Figwort.	Scrophularia aquatica.	$\frac{1}{4}$ in. Greenish tipped, chocolate-coloured, almost globular, in close panicles.	Sepals, 5. Corolla two-lipped, five-lobed. Stamens, 4.	649.
Knotted Figwort.	Scrophularia nodosa.	$\frac{1}{4}$ in. Greenish and purplish.	Sepals, 5. Corolla two-lipped, five-lobed. Stamens, 4.	650.
Floating Pondweed (Broad-leaved).	Potamogeton natans.	$\frac{1}{18}$ in. In a spike $1\frac{1}{4}$ in., protruding from water.	Perianth, 4. Stamens, 4.	651.
Wall Pellitory.	Parietaria officinalis.	$\frac{1}{16}$ in. Hairy, in axillary clusters.	Perianth, 4. Stamens, 4.	652.

GREEN OR GREENISH. Monopetalous.

Leaves.	Months.	Habitat.	Remarks.
ordate, acute.	5–6	Hedgerows.	SMALL (contd.). 3–10 ft. Climbing among bushes (oblong scarlet berries). (C.)
linear, fleshy.	5–9	Salt marshes.	10–12 in. (C.)
linear, fleshy.	6–8	Marshy places.	6–18 in. Grass-like. (C.)
glossy, stalked,	6–10	Seashores.	2 ft. Angular, striped stems. (C.)
near, grooved, three- to five-; woolly at base.	6–10	Shores and hills.	3–10 in. (C.)
usually pinna-*livided*; downy.	6–8	Dry places.	3–8 in. (C.)
ar, toothed, ; 1 in.	7–10	Shores.	4–10 in. Covered with silvery scales, giving a whitish hue. (L.)
pposite; ovate-ular.	7–10	Shores.	1–2 ft. Stem striped with red. (C.)
entire; some-toothed.	7–10	Salt marshes.	1–2 ft. Mealy plant. Stem striped with red, resinous lines. (L.)
t, awl-shaped, in sharp spine.	7–8	Seashores.	About 1 ft. Stiff, glaucous, hairy plant. Striped, angular stem. (L.)
nceolate, acute, :al.	7–8	River banks.	3–6 ft. (C.)
gg-shaped; base ular; bluntly d.	7–9	Waste places.	1–3 ft. Covered with whitish powder. (V. C.)
rdate, pointed, wo to four large m each side.	8–9	Waste places, chiefly South.	1–3 ft. Stem stout. Plant has a strong smell. (L.)
iangular, acute, d.	8–10	Waste places, chiefly South.	6–30 in. Stem stout. (L.)
angular-ovate.	8–9	Waste places.	6–18 in. Covered with fishy-smelling, greasy meal. (L.)
nearly sessile; elliptic.	8–10	Waste places.	4–18 in. Tinged with red. (L.)
iangular-ovate, ally serrate.	8–9	Waste places.	6–18 in. Fœtid. (L.)
ar-ovate, vari-	8–9	Waste places and salt marshes.	1–3 ft. Smooth, shining species. (C.)
shy, half-cylin- pointed.	7–9	Muddy sea-shores.	6–18 in. Straggling, slender, smooth. (C.)
wice pinnatifid, on both sides.	7–9	Salt marshes.	10–18 in. (C.)
	7–8	Salt marshes.	4–8 in. Stem fleshy, branched, jointed, each joint fitting into one below. (Formerly used in manufacture of glass, and still used as a pickle—"Samphire.") (C.)
blunt, narrow.	6–8	Pastures.	3–8 in. (C.)
lanceolate, ser-	7–9	Stream sides, marshy places.	2–5 ft. Square, winged stem. Strong-smelling. (C.)
ordate, serrate.	6–7	Stream sides, marshy places.	2–3 ft. Square, winged stem. Strong-smelling. (V. C.)
nostly floating; g-oval, leathery.	6–9	Pools.	1–5 ft. (V. C.)
iairy, reddish.	6–10	Walls.	3–12 in. Bushy, reddish; brittle stems. (Once a favourite medicine.) (C.)

English Name.	Latin Name.	Description of Flower.	Petals, Sepals, Stamens, etc.	
MEDIUM.				
Narrow - leaved Everlasting Pea.	*Lathyrus sylvestris.*	$\frac{3}{4}$ in. Three to ten in loose raceme; rose-coloured standard, greenish yellow wings, with purple tinge.	Sepals, 5. Petals, 5, unequal. Stamens, 10.	653.
Wild Raspberry.	*Rubus idæus.*	$\frac{1}{2}$ in. Drooping; greenish white.	Sepals, 5. Petals, 5, short. Stamens, many.	654.
Stone Bramble.	*Rubus saxatilis.*	$\frac{3}{8}$ in. Few, clustered; green and white.	Petals, 5, whitish. Sepals, 5, spreading. Stamens, many.	655.
Goutweed (Bishop's Weed, Herb Gerard).	*Ægopodium podagraria.*	$\frac{1}{8}$ in. In umbels; greenish white.	Petals, 5. Stamens, 5.	656.
Wild Celery (Smallage).	*Apium graveolens.*	$\frac{1}{16}$ in. Greenish white; in umbels.	Petals, 5. Stamens, 5. Bracts, 0.	657.
Common Water Dropwort.	*Œnanthe fistulosa.*	$\frac{3}{16}$ in. In small, few-rayed umbels.	Greenish white.	658.
Lesser Wart Cress.	*Coronopus didyma.*	$\frac{1}{8}$ in. Greenish white.	Sepals, 4. Petals, 4.	659.
Water Purslane.	*Peplis portula.*	$\frac{1}{16}$ in. Solitary axillary flowers; purplish green.	Calyx twelve-toothed. Petals, 6 or 0. Stamens, 6.	660.
Monopetalous.				
MEDIUM.				
Lesser Butterfly Orchis.	*Habenaria bifolia.*	$\frac{5}{8}$ in. Greenish white; fragrant in evening.	Sepals with petals, 6, one-lipped and spurred; sepals spreading.	661.
Great Butterfly Orchis.	*Habenaria chlorantha.*	$\frac{3}{4}$ in. Larger, greener flowers than above.	Spur stouter, bending downwards.	662.
SMALL.				
Greater or Broad-leaved Plantain (Way-bread).	*Plantago major.*	$\frac{1}{8}$ in. In spike, 4–8 in. long; brownish green.	Sepals, 4. Petals, 4. Stamens, 4.	663.
Sheep's Sorrel.	*Rumex acetosella.*	$\frac{1}{8}$ in. Reddish green; many hanging flowers.	Sepals, 6. Petals, 0. Stamens, 6.	664.
Curled Dock.	*Rumex crispus.*	$\frac{1}{8}$ in. Reddish green; in crowded whorls, forming panicle.	Sepals, 6, in two rows, inner larger. Petals, 0. Stamens, 6.	665.
Sharp Dock.	*Rumex conglomeratus.*	$\frac{1}{8}$ in. Reddish green.	Sepals, 6, in two rows, inner larger. Petals, 0. Stamens, 6. Each inner sepal bears a large oblong wart.	666.
Fiddle Dock.	*Rumex pulcher.*	$\frac{1}{8}$ in. Reddish green.	Sepals, 6, in two rows; inner three larger; oblong and deeply toothed, with network of veins.	667.
Broad-leaved Dock.	*Rumex obtusifolius.*	$\frac{1}{8}$ in. Reddish green.	Sepals, 6. Petals, 0. Stamens, 6. Inner sepals triangular, toothed.	668.
Grainless Water Dock.	*Rumex aquaticus.*	$\frac{1}{8}$ in. Reddish green; in whorls.	Sepals, 6, inner three larger. Petals, 0. Stamens, 6. Inner sepals entire, cordate, without any wart.	669.
Alpine Dock (Monk's Rhubarb).	*Rumex alpinus.*	$\frac{1}{8}$ in. Reddish green.	Sepals, 6. Petals, 0. Stamens, 6.	670.

WITH SOME OTHER TINT. Polypetalous.

Leaves.	Months.	Habitat.	Remarks.
Leaflets sword-shaped.	6-9	Thickets.	MEDIUM. 2-6 ft. Clambering, glaucous. Stem winged. (*C.*)
Leaves of three to five ovate leaflets, white beneath.	5-8	Woods.	2-5 ft. Round, prickly stem. (*C.*)
Leaves of three roundish leaflets.	6-8	Copses.	1-2 ft. Stem rooting, with few scattered bristles. (*C.*)
Root leaves; two to three ternate leaflets, oblique, serrate.	5-7	Shrubberies and damp places.	1-2 ft. Creeping white, pungent, aromatic root. Stem hollow, furrowed. (*C.*)
Shining, pinnate; lobes cut.	6-8	Moist places near sea.	1-2 ft. Stem furrowed and branched. Plant identified by its strong smell. (*L.*)
Lower leaves submerged; two- and three-pinnate. Upper leaves hollow, tube-like.	7-9	Ditches and marshes.	1-3 ft. Stem with racemes, hollow. (*C.*)
Once or twice pinnatifid; lobes small, obovate.	7-9	Waste places in Southwest.	2-6 in. Creeping. Strong smell and disagreeable taste. (*L.*)
Obovate, ½-¾ in.; opposite.	7-8	Wet places.	4-8 in. Aquatic, rooted, and creeping in mud; stems four-angled; plant tinged with red. (*C.*)

Monopetalous.

			MEDIUM.
Two broad, glossy leaves at root.	6-7	Meadows.	1 ft. Stem slender, angular. (*C.*)
Usually two, elliptical.	7-8	Moist meadows.	10-18 in. (*C.*)
			SMALL.
Radical, 2-9 in.; broadly ovate, ribbed.	5-9	Waysides.	8-20 in. (Seeds favourite food for cage birds.) (*C.*)
Hastate, 1-2 in.; two spreading lobes at base, stalked.	5-8	Pastures.	3-12 in. (*C.*)
Oblong-lanceolate, 6-10 in.; pointed, curled edges.	6-10	Waste land.	1-3 ft. The commonest of all Docks. (*C.*)
Oblong-lanceolate.	6-8	Moist places.	1-3 ft. (*C.*)
Lower leaves fiddle-shaped; upper, lanceolate, acute.	6-10	Waysides.	6-8 in. (*L.*)
8 in.; oblong-ovate, cordate, not pointed.	7-9	Waste land.	2-3 ft. (*C.*)
Long, 3 in. wide; lanceolate, oval, wavy.	6-8	Marshes.	1-3 ft. (*L.*)
10-20 in.; broadly ovate-cordate; long, stout leaf stalks.	7-8	Roadsides.	1-3 ft. Slightly downy. (Once cultivated as a pot herb.) (*L.*)

Woody Nightshade.

Deadly Nightshade.

Musk Mallow.

Monopetalous. GREEN OR GREENISH,

English Name.	Latin Name.	Description of Flower.	Petals, Sepals, Stamens, etc.	
SMALL (contd.). Bloody-veined Dock.	Rumex sanguineus.	$\frac{1}{8}$ in. Reddish green.	Sepals, 6. Petals, o. Stamens, 6.	671.
Bilberry (Whortleberry, Whinberry).	Vaccinium myrtillus.	$\frac{1}{8}$ in. Reddish green; bell-shaped, drooping, solitary.	Calyx four-toothed. Corolla four-toothed. Stamens, 8.	672.
Pale-flowered Polygonum (Persicaria).	Polygonum lapathifolium.	$\frac{1}{8}$ in. Reddish green; in cylindrical spikes.	Sepals, 5. Petals, o. Stamens, 5-6.	673.
Spreading Orache.	Atriplex patula.	$\frac{1}{16}$ in. In simple interrupted spikes; reddish green.	Stamen flowers: Sepals, 3-5; stamens, 3-5. Pistil flowers: Sepals, 2.	674.
Halberd-leaved Orache.	Atriplex hastata.	$\frac{1}{16}$ in. In simple, interrupted spikes; reddish green.		675.
Knot-grass or Knotweed.	Polygonum aviculare.	$\frac{1}{8}$ in. Greenish white and pink; in short-stalked, axillary clusters.	Perianth, 5. Stamens, 8.	676.
Common Elder.	Sambucus nigra.	$\frac{1}{4}$ in. Greenish white; in flat-topped umbel-looking heads, five main branches.	Calyx five-cleft. Corolla five-lobed. Stamens, 5.	677.
Hoary Plantain (Lamb's-tongue).	Plantago media.	$\frac{1}{4}$ in. each flower. Spikes 2-4 in.; greenish white.	Sepals, 4. Petals, 4. Stamens, 4, very long and noticeable.	678.
Sneezewort.	Achillea ptarmica.	Heads $\frac{1}{2}$ in. In corymbs. Greenish white; hairy, stiff bracts.	Ray florets, 8-12; white disc florets tubular, five-toothed, creamy.	679.
Marsh Helleborine.	Epipactis palustris.	$\frac{3}{4}$ in. Few in a spike; greenish, with a lip petal white, striped with red; sepals green striped with red.		680.
Broad-leaved Helleborine.	Epipactis latifolia.	$\frac{1}{2}$ in. Green; red-lipped, short-stalked, drooping, in a long, loose raceme.	Sepals, 3, broadly ovate. Petals, 2, ovate-lanceolate, and a third with hollow lip.	681.
Plantain Shoreweed.	Littorella lacustris.	$\frac{1}{4}$ in. Greenish white. Stamen flowers solitary, on long stalks; pistil flowers sessile.	Stamen flowers: Sepals, 4. Petals, 4. Stamens, 4.	682.
Black Bindweed (Climbing Bistort).	Polygonum convolvulus.	$\frac{1}{8}$ in. In slender racemes; greenish white; four- to ten-flowered clusters.	Sepals, 5, with white edges. Petals, o. Stamens, 8.	683.
Canadian Waterweed (Water Thyme).	Elodea canadensis.	Pistil flowers, $\frac{1}{8}$ in. Purplish green; floating on water, 4-8 in. long.	Sepals, 3. Petals, 3. Stamens, 3 (useless).	684.

WITH SOME OTHER TINT. Monopetalous.

	Leaves.	Months.	Habitat.	Remarks.
				SMALL (contd.).
671.	Ovate-lanceolate, 7-8 in.; base cordate, veins crimson.	6-8	Roadsides.	1-4 ft. (C.)
672.	Egg-shaped, serrate, ¾ in.	4-6	Heaths.	6-18 in. Acute angular stem. (L.)
673.	5 in.; oblong-ovate.	7-9	Waste places.	1-4 ft. Stem much branched. Sometimes red or spotted, swollen at nodes. (C.)
674.	Lower leaves opposite, triangular, with two lobes spreading upwards, toothed. Upper leaves lanceolate, entire.	7-10	Waste places, seashores, etc.	1-3 ft. Mealy, often tinged with red. Stem with reddish stripes. (C.)
675.	Lower leaves triangular or hastate; lobed at the base.			1-3 ft. Dark green, mealy. (C.)
676.	¼ in.; narrow, elliptical, nearly sessile.	5-10	Waste places.	1-3 ft. Stem branched, prostrate. (V. C.)
677.	Pinnate; leaflets ovate, serrate.	6	Woods, etc.	10-20 ft. Corky bark; leaves with strong smell. (C.)
678.	Radical, broad, oval, ribbed, 2-4 in.	6-10	Meadows, etc.	6-18 in. (C.)
679.	2 in.; sessile, narrow, with stiff teeth.	7-8	Meadows, heaths, etc.	1-2 ft. Erect. (C.)
680.	Lanceolate, acute.	7-8	Marshes.	12-18 in. Downy stem. (C.)
681.	Broadly ovate, ribbed.	8	Woods.	1-3 ft. Solitary; downy stem. (C.)
682.	Radical, linear, fleshy.	6-9	Lake shores.	2-6 in. (C.)
683.	Cordate-arrow-shaped.	7-9	Fields.	1-3 ft. Climbing. (C.)
684.	¾ in.; sessile, oblong, in whorls of three.		Streams.	1-4 ft. Submerged; dark green. Introduced from America. (C.)

Meadow Crane's-bill.

Corn Marigold.

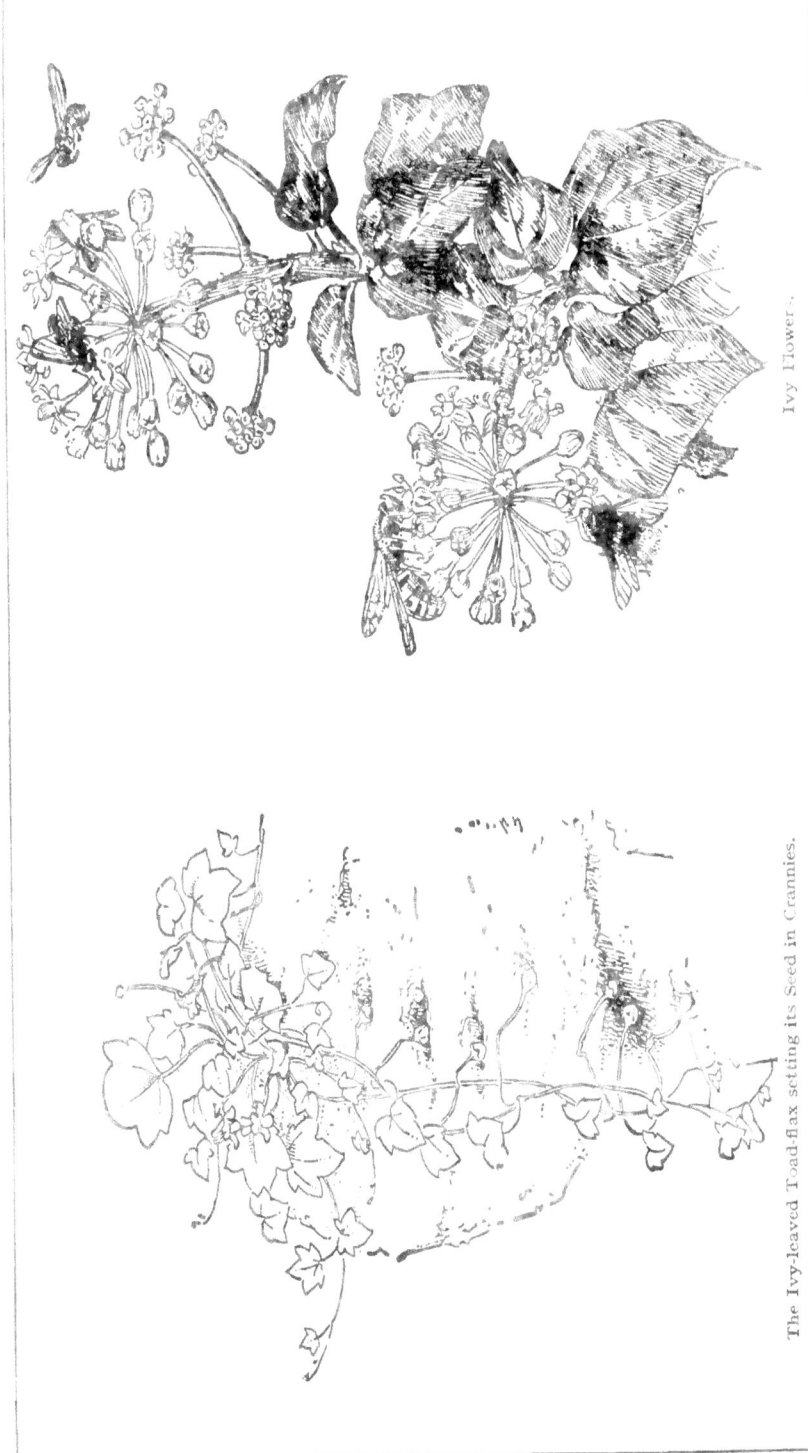

Ivy Flower.

The Ivy-leaved Toad-flax setting its Seed in Crannies.

ALPHABETICAL LIST OF FLOWERS:
ENGLISH.

Abele, 568.
Agrimony, 253.
Agrimony, Hemp, 451.
Alder, 561.
Ale-hoof, 559.
Alexanders, 323.
Allseed, 99.
Alyssum, Sweet, 97.
Anemone, Wood, 1.
Angelica, Wild, 158.
Arrow-grass. See GRASS.
Arrow-head, 162.
Arum, Wild, 613.
Ash, 585.
Aspen, 565.
Asphodel, Bog, 312.
Avens, Common, 246.
Avens, Mountain, 5.
Avens, Water, 412.
Awlwort, Water, 98.

Balm, Wild, 161.
Balsam, Yellow, 193.
Barberry, 201.
Bartsia, Red, 446.
Basil, Common, 558.
Basil, Wild, 445.
Bastard, 161.
Bearberry, Black, 166.
Bearberry, Red, 395.
Bedstraw, Corn, 122.
Bedstraw, Crosswort, 317.
Bedstraw, Heath, 121.
Bedstraw, Hedge, 124.
Bedstraw, Rough Water, 123.
Bedstraw, Water, 125.
Bedstraw, Yellow, 318.
Beech, 618.
Beet, Sea (Wild), 630.
Bell-flower, Clustered, 550.
Bell-flower, Corn, 532.
Bell-flower, Creeping, 548.
Bell-flower, Giant, 545.
Bell-flower, Ivy-leaved, 563.

Bell-flower, Nettle-leaved, 547.
Bell-flower, Rampion, 549.
Bell-flower, Spreading, 546.
Betony, Wood, 444.
Bilberry, 672.
Bindweed, Black, 683.
Bindweed, Field, 159.
Bindweed, Great, 102.
Bindweed, Sea, 470.
Bindweed, Small, 378.
Birch, Common, 617.
Bird's-foot, Common, 150.
Bistort, Climbing, 679.
Bistort, Common, 175.
Bistort, Viviparous, 173.
Bitter-sweet, 453.
Bitter Vetch, Tuberous, 374.
Blackberry, 4.
Blackthorn, 22.
Bladderwort, Common, 307.
Blinks, Water, 101.
Bluebell, 509.
Bluebottle, Corn, 506.
Borage, 510.
Bramble, 4.
Bramble, Stone, 655.
Briar, Sweet, 358.
Brooklime, 518.
Broom, 233.
Broom, Butcher's, 140.
Bryony, Black, 627.
Bryony, White, 129.
Buckbean, 160, 383.
Buckthorn, Alder, 603.
Buckthorn, Common, 602.
Bugle, Common, 523.
Bugloss, Common Viper's, 533.
Bugloss, Small, 534.
Bulrush, Great, 583.
Bulrush, Lesser, 584.
Burdock, 433.
Bur-marigold, Nodding, 334.
Bur-marigold, Trifid, 335.
Burnet, Great, 417.

Burnet, Salad, 612.
Bur-reed, Branched, 345.
Bur-reed, Unbranched, 347.
Butter-bur, 473.
Buttercup, Common, 220.
Buttercup, Creeping, 221.
Buttercup, Pale Hairy, 222.
Butterwort, Common, 552.
Butterwort, Pale, 479.

Cabbage, Isle of Man, 196.
Cabbage, Wild or Sea, 195.
Calamint, Common, 475.
Campion, Bladder, 19.
Campion, Evening, 2.
Campion, Red, 359.
Campion, Sea, 18.
Candytuft, Bitter, 39.
Canterbury Bell, Wild, 547.
Caraway, Common, 86.
Carrot, Wild, 153.
Catchfly, English, 156.
Catchfly, Night-flowering, 459.
Cat Mint, 181.
Cat's-ear, Long-rooted, 280.
Cat's-ear, Smooth, 297.
Celandine, Greater, 224.
Celandine, Lesser, 219.
Celery, Wild, 657.
Centaury, Common, 384.
Chaffweed, 178.
Chamomile, Common, 109.
Chamomile, Corn, 104.
Chamomile, Stinking, 107.
Chamomile, Wild, 108.
Charlock, 230.
Cherry, Wild, 10.
Chervil, Rough, 88.
Chestnut, Spanish, 614.
Chickweed, Broad-leaved Mouse-ear, 46.
Chickweed, Common Mouse-ear, 24.
Chickweed, European, 111.

438 THE BRITISH NATURE BOOK

Chickweed, Field Mouse-ear, 12.
Chickweed, Four-cleft Mouse-ear, 47.
Chickweed, Little Mouse-ear, 42.
Chicory, 505.
Cicely, Sweet, 83.
Cinquefoil, Creeping, 236.
Cinquefoil, Hoary, 254.
Cinquefoil, Purple Marsh, 407.
Cinquefoil, Strawberry-leaved, 13.
Clary, 561.
Claytonia, Perfoliate, 84.
Cleavers, 126.
Clematis, 185.
Cloudberry, 146.
Clover, Starry, 186.
Clover, White or Dutch, 149.
Clover, Zigzag, 415.
Cockle, Corn, 405.
Cockscomb, 303.
Coltsfoot, 283.
Columbine, 535.
Comb, Venus', 96.
Comfrey, Common, 138, 192.
Cornel, Wild, 30.
Cornflower, 506.
Corn Salad, Toothed, 179.
Corydalis, Climbing, 187.
Corydalis, Yellow, 244.
Cotton-weed, Seaside, 309.
Cowbane, 90.
Cowberry, 172.
Cowslip, 292.
Cow-wheat, Yellow, 302.
Cranesbill (Blue), Meadow, 496.
Cranesbill, Dove's-foot, 370.
Cranesbill, Jagged-leaved, 372.
Cranesbill, Long-stalked, 363.
Cranesbill, Round-leaved, 364.
Cranesbill, Shining, 371.
Cranesbill, Small-flowered, 365.
Cranesbill, Wood, 537.
Cress, Alpine Penny, 64.
Cress, Common Wart, 67.
Cress, Common Winter, 241.
Cress, Field Penny, 62.
Cress, Glabrous Rock, 132.
Cress, Hairy Bitter, 44.
Cress, Hairy Rock, 65.
Cress, Large-flowered Bitter, 128.
Cress, Lesser Wart, 659.
Cress, Marsh Yellow, 264.
Cress, Perfoliate Penny, 63.
Cress, Thale Rock, 66.
Cress, Water, 28.
Crowfoot, Bulbous, 212.

Crowfoot, Celery-leaved, 199.
Crowfoot, Corn, 200.
Crowfoot, Ivy-leaved, 29.
Crowfoot, Meadow, 220.
Crowfoot, Water, 145.
Cuckoo Flower, 455.
Cuckoo-pint, 613.
Cudweed (Filago), 591.
Cudweed, Marsh, 588.
Cudweed, Mountain, 393.
Cudweed, Wood, 589.

Daffodil, 269.
Daisy, Common, 106.
Daisy, Great White Ox-eye, 103.
Dandelion, 268.
Danewort, 170.
Dewberry, 20.
Dock, Alpine, 670.
Dock, Bloody-veined, 671.
Dock, Broad-leaved, 668.
Dock, Curled, 665.
Dock, Fiddle, 667.
Dock, Grainless Water, 669.
Dock, Great Water, 637.
Dock, Sharp, 666.
Dodder, Clover, 169.
Dodder, Great, 349.
Dodder, Lesser, 350.
Dog's Mercury, 622.
Dogwood, 30.
Dropwort, 183.
Dropwort, Common Water, 658.
Dropwort, Fine-leaved Water, 80.
Dropwort, Hemlock Water, 55.
Dropwort, Parsley Water, 54.
Dropwort, River Water, 56.
Dwale, 553.
Dyer's Greenweed, 234.
Dyer's Weed, 327.

Earth-nut, Common, 85.
Elder, Common, 677.
Elder, Dwarf, 170.
Elm, Common, 570.
Elm, Wych, 569.
Everlasting, Mountain, 167.
Eyebright, 163.

Fennel, 266.
Fenugreek, 154.
Feverfew, Common, 110.
Figwort, Knotted, 650.
Figwort, Water, 649.
Filago, Common, 591.
Filago, Least, 319.
Flag, 271.
Flax, Common, 497.

Flax, Narrow-leaved, 502.
Flax Seed, Thyme-leaved, 99.
Fleabane, Blue, 480.
Fleabane, Canadian, 139.
Fleabane, Common, 298.
Flixweed, 329.
Fluellen, Sharp-leaved, 348.
Forget-me-not, 528.
Foxglove, 429.
Frog-bit, 21.
Fumitory, Common, 377, 413.
Fumitory, Ramping, 414.
Furze, 218.
Furze, Dwarf, 255.

Gale, Sweet. *See* SWEET GALE.
Garlic, Broad-leaved, 7.
Gentian, Common Autumn, 493.
Gentian, Field, 562.
Gentian, Small-flowered, 490.
Germander, Wood, 209.
Gipsy-wort, 180.
Gladdon, 544.
Glasswort, Jointed, 647.
Globe Flower, 211.
Goat's-beard, Yellow, 274.
Golden Rod, 313.
Good King Henry, 343.
Goodyera, Creeping, 40, 119.
Gooseberry, Wild, 598.
Goosefoot, Many-seeded, 642.
Goosefoot, Maple-leaved, 639.
Goosefoot, Nettle-leaved, 643.
Goosefoot, Red, 644.
Goosefoot, Stinking, 641.
Goosefoot, Upright, 640.
Goosefoot, White, 638.
Goose Grass, 126, 217.
Gorse, 218.
Goutweed, 656.
Grass, Common Whitlow, 43.
Grass, Creeping Water Scorpion, 529.
Grass, English Scurvy, 27.
Grass, Field Scorpion, 525.
Grass, Goose, 126, 217.
Grass, Knot, 397, 676.
Grass, Marsh Arrow, 629.
Grass of Parnassus, 130.
Grass, Scorpion, Early Field, 524.
Grass, Scorpion, Parti-coloured, 316.
Grass, Scurvy, 23.
Grass, Seaside Arrow, 628.
Grass, Tufted Water Scorpion. 527.

FLOWERS

Grass, Water Scorpion, 528.
Grass, Wood Scorpion, 526.
Grass, Yellow Alpine Whitlow, 239.
Greenweed, Dyer's, 234.
Greenweed, Needle, 240.
Gromwell, Common, 207.
Gromwell, Corn, 143.
Ground Ivy. *See* Ivy.
Groundsel, 315.
Groundsel, Mountain, 321.
Groundsel, Viscid, 338.

Harebell, 551.
Hare's-ear, Common, 203.
Hawkbit, Autumnal, 277.
Hawkbit, Hairy, 289.
Hawkbit, Rough, 276.
Hawk's-beard, Marsh, 287.
Hawk's-beard, Smooth, 311.
Hawkweed, Mouse-ear, 205.
Hawkweed, Narrow-leaved, 288.
Hawkweed, Wall, 284.
Hawkweed, Wood, 279.
Hawthorn, 15.
Heath, Cross-leaved, 401.
Heath, Fine-leaved, 450.
Heather, 448.
Hedge Mustard, Common, 265.
Hellebore, Green, 593.
Hellebore, Stinking, 594.
Helleborine, Broad-leaved, 681.
Helleborine, Marsh, 680.
Hemlock, 87.
Hemlock, Water, 90.
Hemp Nettle, Common, 191, 476.
Henbane, 206.
Herb Bennet, 246.
Herb Gerard, 656.
Herb Paris, 616.
Hogweed, 32.
Holly, Field Sea, 543.
Holly, Sea, 542.
Honewort, 95.
Honeysuckle, 190.
Hop, Common, 337.
Horehound, Black, 441.
Horehound, White, 127.
Hornbeam, Common, 615.
Hornwort, Common, 611.
Hound's-tongue, 442.
House-leek, 410.
Hutchinsia, Rock, 45.
Hyacinth, 509.

Iris, Stinking, 544.
Iris, Yellow, 271.
Ivy, 332.

Ivy, Ground, 559.

Joy, Traveller's, 164.
Juniper, Common, 624.

Kale, Sea, 31.
Knapweed, Black, 426.
Knapweed, Great, 425.
Knawel, Annual, 610.
Knot Grass, 397, 676.
Knotweed, 676.

Lady's Finger, 251.
Lady's Mantle, Common, 604.
Lady's Mantle, Field, 605.
Lady's Smock, 455.
Lamb's Lettuce, 478.
Lamb's-tongue, 678.
Larkspur, Field, 501.
Lavender, Common Sea-, 482.
Lavender, Matted Sea-, 489.
Lavender, Remote Sea-, 483.
Lavender, Spathulate Sea-, 488.
Leek, House-, 411.
Lettuce, Ivy-leaved, 306.
Lily, Lent, 269.
Lily of the Valley, 114.
Lily, White Water, 3.
Lily, Yellow Water, 215.
Lime, Broad-leaved, 325.
Lime, Common, 324.
Lime, Small-leaved, 330.
Ling, 448.
Lobelia, Water, 507.
London Pride, 151.
Loosestrife, Great Yellow, 296.
Loosestrife, Purple, 409.
Loosestrife, Wood, 301.
"Lords and Ladies," 613.
Lousewort, Field, 381.
Lousewort, Marsh, 380.
Lucerne, 540.

Madder, Field, 477.
Mallow, Common, 404.
Mallow, Dwarf, 457.
Mallow, Marsh, 356.
Mallow, Musk, 454.
Maple, Common, 600.
Mare's-tail, Common, 595.
Marigold, Corn, 275.
Marigold, Marsh, 210.
Marjoram, 447.
Marshwort, Least, 94.
Marshwort, Procumbent, 93.
May, 15.
Mayweed, Scentless, 105.
Mea, 328.

Meadow Rue, Alpine, 189.
Meadow Rue, Lesser, 331.
Meadow Rue, Yellow, 197.
Meadow-sweet, 184.
Medick, Black, 261.
Medick, Purple, 540.
Medick, Spotted, 260.
Melilot, Common, 262.
Melilot, White, 188.
Mercury, Dog's, 622.
Mignonette, Wild, 326.
Milfoil, 116.
Milfoil, Alternate - flowered Water, 607.
Milfoil, Common Yellow, 310.
Milfoil, Spiked Water, 75, 608.
Milfoil, Whorled Water, 76.
Milkwort, Common, 73, 531.
Milkwort, Sea, 385.
Mint, Corn, 492.
Mint, Hairy, 486.
Mint, Horse, 494.
Mint, Marsh Whorled, 485.
Mint, Pepper, 491.
Mint, Round-leaved, 493.
Mint, Spear, 495.
Mint, Water, 486.
Mistletoe, 597.
Mœnchia, Upright, 68.
Money-wort, 295.
Money-wort, Cornish, 177.
Monkey Flower, 282.
Monkshood, 538.
Moschatel, 596.
Mousetail, 322.
Mudwort, Common, 176.
Mugwort, 590.
Mullein, Dark, 305.
Mullein, Great, 294.
Mullein, Moth, 293.
Musk, Yellow, 282.
Mustard, Black, 249.
Mustard, Common Hedge, 265.
Mustard, Garlic, 25.
Mustard, Tower, 132.
Mustard, Treacle, 202.
Mustard, White, 250.
Mustard, Wild, 230.
Myrtle, Bog, 581.

Navew, Wild, 252.
Needle, Shepherd's, 96.
Nettle, Great, 344.
Nettle, Henbit Dead, 435.
Nettle, Red Dead, 434.
Nettle, Red Hemp, 436.
Nettle, Small, 346.
Nettle, White Dead, 113.

440 THE BRITISH NATURE BOOK

Nightshade, Alpine Enchanter's, 157.
Nightshade, Black, 115.
Nightshade, Deadly, 553.
Nightshade, Enchanter's, 152.
Nightshade, Woody, 453.
Nipple-wort, 314.
Nonsuch, 261.
Oak, 619.
Orache, Frosted Sea, 633.
Orache, Grass-leaved, 635.
Orache, Halberd-leaved, 675.
Orache, Rose-coloured, 631.
Orache, Spreading, 674.
Orache, Spreading-fruited, 634.
Orchis, Bee, 382.
Orchis, Bird's-nest, 586.
Orchis, Dwarf, 164.
Orchis, Early Purple, 427.
Orchis, Fragrant, 440.
Orchis, Frog, 648.
Orchis, Great Butterfly, 662.
Orchis, Lesser Butterfly, 661.
Orchis, Marsh, 428.
Orchis, Pyramidal, 390.
Orchis, Spotted, 474.
Oxlip, 291.
Ox-tongue, Bristly, 285.

Pansy, 411.
Pansy, Yellow Mountain, 194.
Parsley, Common Beaked, 53.
Parsley, Corn, 92.
Parsley, Fool's, 89.
Parsley, Hedge Stone, 131.
Parsley, Knotted Hedge, 461.
Parsley, Narrow-leaved Water, 91.
Parsley, Spreading Hedge, 51.
Parsley, Upright Hedge, 52.
Parsley, Wild Beaked, 50.
Parsnip, Broad-leaved Water, 77.
Parsnip, Cow, 32.
Parsnip, Wild, 267.
Pea, Everlasting, 408.
Pea, Narrow-leaved Everlasting, 653.
Pearlwort, Knotted, 38.
Pellitory, Wall, 652.
Pennyroyal, 487.
Pennywort, Marsh, 460.
Pennywort, Wall, 609.
Peppermint. *See* MINT.
Pepper, Water, 403.
Pepperwort, Broad-leaved, 59.
Pepperwort, Field, 57.
Pepperwort, Narrow-leaved, 60.
Pepperwort, Smooth Field, 58.

Periwinkle, Lesser, 508.
Persicaria, Amphibious, 398.
Persicaria, Biting, 400.
Persicaria, Pale-flowered, 673.
Persicaria, Spotted, 399.
Petty Whin, 240.
Pheasant's-eye, 402.
Picris, Hawkweed, 278.
Pig-nut, 85.
Pimpernel, Bastard, 178.
Pimpernel, Bog, 391.
Pimpernel, Scarlet, 388, 403, 530.
Pimpernel, Yellow, 301.
Pink, Sea, 387.
Plantain, Buck's-horn, 632.
Plantain, Great or Broad-leaved, 663.
Plantain, Hoary, 678.
Plantain, Lesser Water, 171.
Plantain, Ribwort, 592.
Plantain, Seaside, 631.
Polygonum, Pale-flowered, 673.
Pondweed, Broad-leaved, 647.
Pondweed, Floating, 651.
Poplar, Black, 566.
Poplar, Grey, 567.
Poplar, White, 568.
Poppy, Common Red, 351.
Poppy, Long Rough-headed, 353.
Poppy, Long Smooth-headed, 352.
Poppy, Welsh, 213.
Poppy, White Opium, 147.
Poppy, Yellow Horned, 214.
Pride, London, 153.
Primrose, 270.
Privet, 117.
Purse, Shepherd's, 41.
Purslane, Water, 660.

Radish, Horse, 69.
Radish, Sea, 231.
Radish, Wild, 148.
Ragged Robin, 354.
Ragwort, Common, 273.
Ragwort, Hoary, 290.
Ragwort, Marsh, 272.
Rampion, Spiked, 208.
Raspberry, Wild, 63.
Rattle, Yellow, 303.
Rattle, Yellow, Bushy, 304.
Rest-harrow, Common, 361.
Rest-harrow, Spiny, 362.
Rhubarb, Monk's, 661.
Rocket, Dyer's, 258, 327.
Rocket, Purple Sea, 458.
Rocket, Wall, 232.
Rose, Burnet, 144.

Rose, Common Rock, 235.
Rose, Dog, 357.
Rose, Guelder, 112.
Rose, Trailing Dog, 182.
Rush, Common, 576.
Rush, Flowering, 379.
Rush, Hard, 580.
Rush, Heath, 577.
Rush, Lesser Sea, 578.
Rush, Sharp-flowered Jointed, 579.
Rush, Shining-fruited Jointed, 581.
Rush, Toad, 582.
Rush, Wood-. *See* WOOD-RUSH.

Sage, Wild, 561.
Sage, Wood, 209.
Saintfoin, 366.
St. John's Wort, Hairy, 229.
St. John's Wort, Imperforate, 226.
St. John's Wort, Marsh, 198.
St. John's Wort, Mountain, 227.
St. John's Wort, Perforated, 228.
St. John's Wort, Slender, 245.
St. John's Wort, Square-stalked, 256.
St. John's Wort, Trailing, 257.
Salad, Corn, 478.
Salad, Toothed Corn, 179.
Saltwort, Prickly, 636.
Samphire, Marsh, 647.
Samphire, Sea, 135.
Sandwort, Fine-leaved, 71.
Sandwort-spurrey, Field, 466.
Sandwort-spurrey, Seaside, 467.
Sandwort, Three-nerved, 70.
Sandwort, Thyme-leaved, 72.
Sanicle, Wood, 137.
Saw-wort, 452.
Saxifrage, Burnet, 81.
Saxifrage, Common Burnet, 49.
Saxifrage, Common Golden, 259.
Saxifrage, Greater Burnet, 82.
Saxifrage, Pepper, 204.
Saxifrage, Rue-leaved, 48.
Saxifrage, Yellow Marsh, 238.
Scabious, Devil's-bit, 555.
Scabious, Field, 468.
Scabious, Sheep's, 511.
Scabious, Small, 469.
Scorpion Grass. *See* GRASS.
Scorpion Grass, Parti-coloured, 316.
Sea Blite, Annual, 645.
Sea-lavender. *See* LAVENDER.
Seed, Thyme-leaved Flax, 99.

FLOWERS

Self-heal, 557.
Service Tree, Wild, 11.
Sheep's Bit, Annual, 511.
Shoreweed, Plantain, 682.
Silver Weed, 217.
Skullcap, Common, 556.
Sloe, 22.
Smallage, 657.
Snake-weed, 175.
Sneezewort, 679.
Snowdrop, 6.
Soapwort, 360.
Solomon's Seal, Common, 141.
Sorrel, Common, 394.
Sorrel, Sheep's, 664.
Sorrel, Wood, 9.
Sow-thistle, Common, 286.
Sow-thistle, Corn, 281.
Spearwort, Great, 216.
Spearwort, Lesser, 223.
Speedwell, Buxbaum's, 514.
Speedwell, Common, 521.
Speedwell, Germander, 517.
Speedwell, Green Field, 513.
Speedwell, Grey Field, 516.
Speedwell, Ivy-leaved, 512.
Speedwell, Marsh, 392.
Speedwell, Mountain, 519.
Speedwell, Thyme-leaved, 520.
Speedwell, Wall, 515.
Speedwell, Water, 481.
Spignel, 328.
Spindle Tree, 599.
Spring Squill, 522.
Spurge, Caper, 621.
Spurge, Dwarf, 341.
Spurge, Laurel, 620.
Spurge, Petty, 340.
Spurge, Sea, 342.
Spurge, Sun, 336.
Spurge, Wood, 300.
Spurrey, Corn, 33.
Squinancy-wort, 386.
Star-fruit, 165.
Starwort, Sea, 554.
Starwort, Spring Water, 606.
Stitchwort, Bog, 74.
Stitchwort, Glaucous Marsh, 17.
Stitchwort, Greater, 8.
Stitchwort, Lesser, 26.
Stitchwort, Water, 35.
Stock, Hoary Shrubby, 536.
Stonecrop, Biting, 248.
Stonecrop, English, 34.
Stonecrop, Hairy, 155.
Stonecrop, Rose-root, 333.
Stonecrop, White, 36.
Stork's-bill, Hemlock, 465.

Strawberry, Wood, 14.
Succory, 505.
Sundew, Great, 37.
Sundew, Long-leaved, 79.
Sundew, Round-leaved, 78.
Sweet Briar, 358.
Sweet Gale, 587.
Sycamore, 601.

Tamarisk, English, 462.
Tansy, Common, 308.
Tare, Hairy, 504.
Tare, Slender, 541.
Tea-plant, 560.
Teasel, Wild, 471.
Teesdalia, Naked-stalked, 61.
Thistle, Cotton, 422.
Thistle, Creeping, 431.
Thistle, Dwarf Plume, 423.
Thistle, Marsh, 432.
Thistle, Meadow or Plume, 429.
Thistle, Melancholy, 421.
Thistle, Nodding or Musk, 419.
Thistle, Slender-flowered, 439.
Thistle, Spear Plume, 424.
Thistle, Welted, 430.
Thorough-wax, 203.
Thrift, 387.
Thyme, Basil, 558.
Thyme, Water, 680.
Thyme, Wild, 443.
Tillæa, Mossy, 136.
Toad-flax, Ivy-leaved, 449.
Toad-flax, Yellow, 339.
Tormentil, 243.
Traveller's Joy, 185.
Trefoil, Bird's-foot, 237.
Trefoil, Hare's-foot, 463.
Trefoil, Lesser Yellow, 263.
Trefoil, Marsh, 160, 383.
Trefoil, Rigid, 134.
Trefoil, Soft-knotted, 368.
Trefoil, Strawberry-headed, 418.
Trefoil, Teasel-headed, 367.
Trefoil, Underground, 133.
Tresses, Autumnal Lady's, 100.
Tutsan, 225.
Tway-blade, Common, 625.
Tway-blade, Heart-leaved, 626.

Valerian, Great Wild, 174.
Valerian, Redspur, 389.
Valerian, Small Marsh, 396.
Vervain, 484.
Vetch, Bitter, Tuberous, 373.
Vetch, Bush, 539.
Vetch, Common, 406.
Vetch. Kidney, 251.

Vetchling, Meadow, 247.
Vetch, Spring, 464.
Vetch, Tufted, 503.
Vetch, Tufted Horseshoe, 242.
Vetch, Wood, 40.
Violet, Dog, 499.
Violet, Hairy, 500.
Violet, Marsh, 456.
Violet, Sweet, 498.
Violet, Water, 472.

Wart Cress, Lesser, 659.
Water Milfoil. See MILFOIL.
Waterweed, Canadian, 684.
Wayfaring Tree, 142.
Whinberry, 672.
Whitebeam, 16.
Whitlow Grass, Yellow Alpine, 239.
Whortleberry, 672.
Whortleberry, Red, 172.
Willow-herb, Broad Smooth-leaved, 369.
Willow-herb, Great Hairy, 355.
Willow-herb, Narrow-leaved, 376.
Willow-herb, Pale Smooth-leaved, 375.
Willow-herb, Small-flowered, 416.
Willow-herb, Square-stalked, 374.
Winter Cress, Common, 241.
Wintergreen, 111.
Wintergreen, Intermediate, 118.
Wintergreen, Lesser, 168.
Woodbine, 190.
Woodruff, Sweet, 120.
Wood-rush, Broad-leaved Hairy, 572.
Wood-rush, Field, 571.
Wood-rush, Great Hairy, 574.
Wood-rush, Many-flowered, 575.
Wood-rush, Narrow-leaved Hairy, 573.
Wood Sage, 209.
Wood Spurge, 302.
Wormseed, 202.
Wormwood, Common, 320.
Wormwood, Sea, 646.
Woundwort, Corn, 437.
Woundwort, Hedge, 438.

Yarrow, 116.
Yellow Cress, Marsh, 266.
Yellow Rattle, 305.
Yellow Rattle, Bushy, 306.
Yellow-wort, Perfoliate, 299.
Yew, 623.

ALPHABETICAL LIST OF FLOWERS:

LATIN.

Acer campestre, 600.
Acer pseudoplatanus, 601.
Achillea millefolium, 116, 310.
Achillea ptarmica, 679.
Aconitum napellus, 538.
Actinocarpus damasonium, 165.
Adonis autumnalis, 402.
Adoxa moschatellina, 596.
Ægopodium podagraria, 656.
Æthusa cynapium, 89.
Agrimonia eupatoria, 253.
Ajuga reptans, 523.
Alchemilla arvensis, 605.
Alchemilla vulgaris, 604.
Alisma ranunculoides, 171.
Alliaria officinalis, 25.
Allium ursinum, 7.
Alnus glutinosa, 564.
Althæa officinalis, 356.
Alyssum maritimum, 97.
Anagallis arvensis, 388, 403.
Anagallis tenella, 391.
Anemone nemorosa, 1.
Angelica sylvestris, 158.
Antennaria dioica, 167, 399.
Anthemis arvensis, 104.
Anthemis cotula, 107.
Anthemis nobilis, 109.
Anthriscus sylvestris, 50.
Anthriscus vulgaris, 53.
Anthyllis vulneraria, 251.
Apargia autumnalis, 277.
Apargia hirta, 289.
Apargia hispida, 276.
Apium graveolens, 657.
Aquilegia vulgaris, 535.
Arabis hirsuta, 65.
Arabis perfoliata, 132.
Arabis thaliana, 66.
Arctium lappa, 433.
Arctostaphylos uva-ursi, 166, 395.
Arenaria serpyllifolia, 72.
Arenaria tenuifolia, 71.
Arenaria trinervis, 70.

Armeria maritima, 387.
Artemisia absinthium, 320.
Artemisia maritima, 646.
Artemisia vulgaris, 590.
Arum maculatum, 613.
Asperula cynanchica, 386.
Asperula odorata, 120.
Aster tripolium, 554.
Atriplex arenaria, 633.
Atriplex babingtonii, 634.
Atriplex hastata, 675.
Atriplex littoralis, 635.
Atriplex patula, 674.
Atropa belladonna, 553.

Ballota nigra, 441.
Barbarea vulgaris, 241.
Bartsia odontites, 446.
Bellis perennis, 106.
Berberis vulgaris, 201.
Beta maritima, 630.
Betula alba, 617.
Bidens cernua, 334.
Bidens tripartita, 335.
Borago officinalis, 510.
Brassica alba, 250.
Brassica campestris, 252.
Brassica monensis, 196.
Brassica nigra, 249.
Brassica oleracea, 195.
Brassica sinapis, 230.
Bryonia dioica, 129.
Buda marina, 467.
Buda rubra, 466.
Bupleurum rotundifolium, 203.
Butomus umbellatus, 379.

Cakile maritima, 458.
Calamintha acinos (arvensis), 558.
Calamintha clinopodium, 445.
Calamintha officinalis, 475.
Callitriche verna, 606.
Calluna vulgaris, 448.

Caltha palustris, 210.
Calystegia sepium, 102.
Campanula glomerata, 550.
Campanula hederacea, 563.
Campanula hybrida, 532.
Campanula latifolia, 545.
Campanula patula, 546.
Campanula rapunculoides, 548.
Campanula rapunculus, 549.
Campanula rotundifolia, 551.
Campanula trachelium, 547.
Capsella bursa-pastoris, 41.
Cardamine amara, 128.
Cardamine hirsuta, 44.
Cardamine pratensis, 455.
Carduus acanthoides (crispus), 430.
Carduus acaulis, 423.
Carduus arvensis, 431.
Carduus heterophyllus, 421.
Carduus nutans, 419.
Carduus palustris, 432.
Carduus pratensis, 420.
Carduus tenuiflorus, 439.
Carpinus betulus, 615.
Carum carui, 86.
Castanea vulgaris, 614.
Caucalis. See TORILIS.
Centaurea cyanus, 506.
Centaurea nigra, 426.
Centaurea scabiosa, 425.
Centranthus ruber, 389.
Centunculus minimus, 178.
Cerastium arvense, 12.
Cerastium glomeratum, 46.
Cerastium semidecandrum, 42.
Cerastium tetrandrum, 47.
Cerastium triviale, 24.
Ceratophyllum demersum, 611.
Chærophyllum temulentum, 88.
Chelidonium majus, 224.
Chenopodium album, 638.
Chenopodium bonus-henricus, 343.

FLOWERS 443

Chenopodium hybridum, 639.
Chenopodium murale, 643.
Chenopodium polyspermum, 642.
Chenopodium rubrum, 644.
Chenopodium urbicum, 640.
Chenopodium vulvaria (olidum), 641.
Chlora perfoliata, 299.
Chrysanthemum leucanthemum, 103.
Chrysanthemum segetum, 275.
Chrysosplenium oppositifolium, 259.
Cichorium intybus, 505.
Cicuta virosa, 90.
Circæa alpina, 157.
Circæa lutetiana, 152.
Claytonia perfoliata, 84.
Clematis vitalba, 185.
Cnicus lanceolatus, 424.
Cochlearia anglica, 27.
Cochlearia armoracia, 69.
Cochlearia officinalis, 23.
Conium maculatum, 87.
Conopodium denudatum, 85.
Convallaria majalis, 114.
Convolvulus arvensis, 159, 378.
Convolvulus soldanella, 470.
Cornus sanguinea, 30.
Coronopus didyma, 659.
Corydalis claviculata, 187.
Corydalis lutea, 244.
Cotyledon umbilicus, 609.
Crambe maritima, 31.
Cratægus oxyacantha, 15.
Crepis paludosa, 287.
Crepis virens, 311.
Crithmum maritimum, 135.
Cuscuta epithymum, 350.
Cuscuta europæa, 349.
Cuscuta trifolii, 169.
Cynoglossum officinale, 442.

Daphne laureola, 620.
Daucus carota, 153.
Delphinium ajacis, 501.
Digitalis purpurea, 429.
Diotis maritima, 309.
Diplotaxis tenuifolia, 232.
Dipsacus sylvestris, 471.
Draba azoides, 239.
Draba verna, 43.
Drosera anglica, 37.
Drosera longifolia, 79.
D osera rotundifolia, 78.
Dryas octopetala, 5.

Echium vulgare, 533.

Elodea canadensis, 684.
Epilobium hirsutum, 355.
Epilobium montanum, 369.
Epilobium palustre, 376.
Epilobium parviflorum, 416.
Epilobium roseum, 375.
Epilobium tetragonum, 374.
Epipactis latifolia, 681.
Epipactis palustris, 680.
Erica cinerea, 450.
Erica tetralix, 401.
Erigeron acre, 480.
Erigeron canadensis, 139.
Erodium cicutarium, 465.
Eryngium campestre, 543.
Eryngium maritimum, 542.
Erysimum cheiranthoides, 202.
Erythræa centaurium, 384.
Euonymus europæus, 599.
Eupatorium cannabinum, 451.
Euphorbia amygdaloides, 300.
Euphorbia exigua, 341.
Euphorbia helioscopia, 336.
Euphorbia lathyris, 621.
Euphorbia paralias, 342.
Euphorbia peplus, 340.
Euphrasia officinalis, 163.

Fagus sylvatica, 618.
Fedia dentata, 179.
Filago germanica, 591.
Filago minima, 319.
Fœniculum vulgare, 266.
Fragaria vesca, 14.
Fraxinus excelsior, 585.
Fumaria capreolata, 414.
Fumaria officinalis, 377, 413.

Galanthus nivalis, 6.
Galeopsis ladanum, 436.
Galeopsis tetrahit, 191.
Galium aparine, 126.
Galium cruciata, 317.
Galium mollugo, 124.
Galium palustre, 125.
Galium saxatile, 121.
Galium tricorne, 122.
Galium uliginosum, 123.
Galium verum, 318.
Genista anglica, 240.
Genista tinctoria, 234.
Gentiana amarella, 490.
Gentiana campestris, 562.
Geranium columbinum, 363.
Geranium dissectum, 372.
Geranium lucidum, 371.
Geranium molle, 370.
Geranium pratense, 496.

Geranium pusillum, 365.
Geranium rotundifolium, 364.
Geranium sylvaticum, 537.
Geum rivale, 412.
Geum urbanum, 246.
Glaucium luteum, 214.
Glaux maritima, 385.
Gnaphalium sylvaticum, 589.
Gnaphalium uliginosum, 588.
Goodyera repens, 40, 119.
Gymnadenia conopsea, 440.

Habenaria bifolia, 661.
Habenaria chlorantha, 662.
Habenaria viridis, 648.
Hedera helix, 332.
Helianthemum vulgare, 235.
Helleborus fœtidus, 594.
Helleborus viridis, 593.
Helminthia echioides, 285.
Helosciadium inundatum, 94.
Helosciadium nodiflorum, 93.
Heracleum sphondylium, 32.
Hieracium murorum, 284.
Hieracium pilosella, 205.
Hieracium sylvaticum, 279.
Hieracium umbellatum, 288.
Hippocrepis comosa, 242.
Hippuris vulgaris, 595.
Hottonia palustris, 472.
Humulus lupulus, 337.
Hutchinsia petræa, 45.
Hyacinthus nonscriptus, 509.
Hydrocharis morsus-ranæ, 21.
Hydrocotyle vulgaris, 430.
Hyoscyamus niger, 206.
Hypericum androsæmum, 225.
Hypericum dubium, 226.
Hypericum elodes, 198.
Hypericum hirsutum, 229.
Hypericum humifusum, 257.
Hypericum montanum, 227.
Hypericum perforatum, 228.
Hypericum pulchrum, 245.
Hypericum quadrangulum, 256.
Hypochæris glabra, 297.
Hypochæris radicata, 280.

Iberis amara, 39.
Impatiens noli-me-tangere, 193.
Iris fœtidissima, 544.
Iris pseud-acorus, 271.

Jasione montana, 511.
Juncus acutiflorus, 579.
Juncus bufonius, 582.
Juncus communis, 576.
Juncus glaucus, 582.
Juncus lamprocarpus, 581.

THE BRITISH NATURE BOOK

Juncus maritimus, 578.
Juncus squarrosus, 577.
Juniperus communis, 624.

Lactuca muralis, 306.
Lamium album, 113.
Lamium amplexicaule, 435.
Lamium purpureum, 434.
Lapsana communis, 314.
Lathyrus macrorrhizus, 373.
Lathyrus pratensis, 247.
Lathyrus sylvestris, 408, 653.
Leontodon taraxacum, 268.
Lepidium campestre, 57.
Lepidium latifolium, 59.
Lepidium ruderale, 60.
Lepidium smithii, 58.
Ligustrum vulgare, 117.
Limosella aquatica, 176.
Linaria cymbalaria, 449.
Linaria elatina, 348.
Linaria vulgaris, 339.
Linum angustifolium, 502.
Linum usitatissimum, 497.
Listera cordata, 626.
Listera ovata, 625.
Lithospermum arvense, 143.
Lithospermum officinale, 207.
Littorella lacustris, 682.
Lobelia dortmanna, 507.
Lonicera periclymenum, 190.
Lotus corniculatus, 237.
Luzula campestris, 571.
Luzula erectum, 575.
Luzula forsteri, 573.
Luzula pilosa, 572.
Luzula sylvatica, 574.
Lychnis diurna, 359.
Lychnis flos-cuculi, 354.
Lychnis githago, 405.
Lychnis vespertina, 2.
Lycium barbarum, 560.
Lycopsis arvensis, 534.
Lycopus europæus, 180.
Lysimachia nemorum, 301.
Lysimachia nummularia, 295.
Lysimachia vulgaris, 296.
Lythrum salicaria, 409.

Malva moschata, 454.
Malva rotundifolia, 457.
Malva sylvestris, 404.
Marrubium vulgare, 127.
Mathiola incana, 536.
Matricaria chamomilla, 108.
Matricaria inodora, 105.
Matricaria parthenium, 110.
Meconopsis cambrica, 213.

Medicago lupulina, 261.
Medicago maculata, 260.
Medicago sativa, 540.
Melampyrum pratense, 302.
Melilotus alba, 188.
Melilotus officinalis, 262.
Melittis melissophyllum, 161.
Mentha arvensis, 492.
Mentha hirsuta (aquatica), 486.
Mentha longifolia, 494.
Mentha piperita, 491.
Mentha pulegium, 487.
Mentha rotundifolia, 493.
Mentha sativa, 485.
Mentha viridis, 495.
Menyanthes trifoliata, 160, 383.
Mercurialis perennis, 622.
Meum athamanticum, 328.
Mimulus luteus, 282.
Mœnchia erecta, 68.
Montia fontana, 101.
Myosotis arvensis, 525.
Myosotis cæspitosa, 527.
Myosotis collina, 524.
Myosotis palustris, 528.
Myosotis repens, 529.
Myosotis sylvatica, 526.
Myosotis versicolor, 316.
Myosurus minimus, 322.
Myrica gale, 587.
Myriophyllum alterniflorum, 607.
Myriophyllum spicatum, 75, 608.
Myriophyllum verticillatum, 76.
Myrrhis odorata, 83.

Narcissus pseudo-narcissus, 269.
Narthecium ossifragum, 312.
Nasturtium officinale, 28.
Nasturtium palustre, 264.
Neottia nidus-avis, 586.
Nepeta cataria, 181.
Nepeta glechoma, 559.
Nuphar lutea, 215.
Nymphæa alba, 3.

Œnanthe crocata, 55.
Œnanthe fistulosa, 658.
Œnanthe fluviatilis, 56.
Œnanthe phellandrium, 80.
Œnanthe pimpinelloides, 54.
Onobrychis sativa, 366.
Ononis arvensis, 361.
Ononis spinosa, 362.
Onopordon accenthium, 422.
Ophrys apifera, 382.
Orchis latifolia, 428.
Orchis maculata, 474.
Orchis mascula, 427.

Orchis pyramidalis, 390.
Orchis ustulata, 164.
Origanum vulgare, 447.
Ornithopus purpusillus, 150.
Oxalis acetosella, 9.

Papaver argemone, 353.
Papaver dubium, 352.
Papaver rhœas, 351.
Papaver somniferum, 147.
Parietaria officinalis, 652.
Paris quadrifolia, 616.
Parnassia palustris, 130.
Pastinaca sativa, 267.
Pedicularis palustris, 380.
Pedicularis sylvatica, 381.
Peplis portula, 660.
Petasites vulgaris (officinalis), 473.
Petroselinum segetum, 92.
Phyteuma spicatum, 208.
Picris hieracioides, 278.
Pimpinella magna, 82.
Pimpinella saxifraga, 49, 81.
Pinguicula lusitanica, 479.
Pinguicula vulgaris, 552.
Plantago coronopus, 632.
Plantago lanceolata, 592.
Plantago major, 663.
Plantago maritima, 631.
Plantago media, 678.
Polygala vulgaris, 73.
Polygonatum multiflorum, 141.
Polygonum amphibium, 398.
Polygonum aviculare, 397, 676.
Polygonum bistorta, 175.
Polygonum convolvulus, 683.
Polygonum hydropiper, 400.
Polygonum lapathifolium, 673.
Polygonum persicaria, 399.
Polygonum viviparum, 173.
Populus alba, 568.
Populus canescens, 567.
Populus nigra, 566.
Populus tremula, 565.
Potamogeton natans, 651.
Potentilla anserina, 217.
Potentilla argentea, 254.
Potentilla fragariastrum, 13.
Potentilla palustris, 407.
Potentilla reptans, 236.
Potentilla tormentilla, 243.
Poterium sanguisorba, 612.
Primula elatior, 291.
Primula veris, 292.
Primula vulgaris, 270.
Prunella vulgaris, 557.
Prunus avium, 10.

FLOWERS

Prunus spinosa, 22.
Pulicaria dysenterica, 298.
Pyrola media, 118.
Pyrola minor, 168.
Pyrus aria, 16.
Pyrus torminalis, 11.

Quercus robur, 619.

Radiola millegrana, 99.
Ranunculus acris, 220.
Ranunculus aquatilis, 145.
Ranunculus arvensis, 200.
Ranunculus bulbosus, 212.
Ranunculus ficaria, 219.
Ranunculus flammula, 223.
Ranunculus hederaceus, 29.
Ranunculus hirsutus, 222.
Ranunculus lingua, 216.
Ranunculus repens, 221.
Ranunculus sceleratus, 199.
Raphanus maritimus, 231.
Raphanus raphanistrum, 148.
Reseda lutea, 326.
Reseda luteola, 258, 327.
Rhamnus catharticus, 602.
Rhamnus frangula, 603.
Rhinanthus crista-galli, 303.
Rhinanthus major, 304.
Ribes grossularia, 598.
Rosa arvensis, 182.
Rosa canina, 357.
Rosa rubiginosa, 358.
Rosa spinosissima, 144.
Rubus cæsius, 20.
Rubus chamæmorus, 146.
Rubus fruticosus, 4.
Rubus idæus, 654.
Rubus saxatilis, 655.
Rumex acetosa, 394.
Rumex acetosella, 664.
Rumex alpinus, 670.
Rumex aquaticus, 669.
Rumex conglomeratus, 666.
Rumex crispus, 665.
Rumex hydrolapathum, 637.
Rumex obtusifolius, 668.
Rumex pulcher, 667.
Rumex sanguineus, 671.
Ruscus aculeatus, 140.

Sagina nodosa, 38.
Sagittaria sagittifolia, 162.
Salicornia herbacea, 647.
Salsola kali, 636.
Salvia verbenaca, 561.
Sambucus ebulus, 170.
Sambucus nigra, 677.

Sanguisorba officinalis, 417.
Sanicula europæa, 137.
Saponaria officinalis, 360.
Sarothamnus scoparius, 233.
Saxifraga hirculus, 238.
Saxifraga tridactylites, 48.
Saxifraga umbrosa, 151.
Scabiosa arvensis, 468.
Scabiosa columbaria, 469.
Scabiosa succisa, 555.
Scandix pecten, 96.
Scilla verna, 522.
Scleranthus annuus, 610.
Scrophularia aquatica, 649.
Scrophularia nodosa, 650.
Scutellaria galericulata, 556.
Sedum acre, 248.
Sedum album, 36.
Sedum anglicum, 34.
Sedum rhodiola (*roseum*), 333.
Sedum villosum, 155.
Sempervivum tectorum, 410.
Senebiera coronopus, 67.
Senecio aquaticus, 272.
Senecio jacobæa, 273.
Senecio sylvaticus, 321.
Senecio tenuifolius, 290.
Senecio viscosus, 338.
Senecio vulgaris, 315.
Serratula tinctoria, 452.
Sherardia arvensis, 477.
Sibthorpia europæa, 177.
Silaus pratensis, 204.
Silene anglica, 156.
Silene inflata, 19.
Silene maritima, 18.
Silene noctiflora, 459.
Sison amomum, 131.
Sisymbrium officinale, 265.
Sisymbrium sophia, 329.
Sium angustifolium, 91.
Sium latifolium, 77.
Smyrnium olusatrum, 323.
Solanum dulcamara, 453.
Solanum nigrum, 115.
Solidago virgaurea, 313.
Sonchus arvensis, 281.
Sonchus oleraceus, 286.
Sparganium ramosum, 345.
Sparganium simplex, 347.
Spergula arvensis, 33.
Spergularia. See BUDA.
Spiræa filipendula, 183.
Spiræa ulmaria, 184.
Spiranthes autumnalis, 100.
Stachys arvensis, 437.
Stachys betonica, 444.
Stachys sylvatica, 438.

Statice auriculæfolia, 488.
Statice limonium, 482.
Statice rariflora, 483.
Statice reticulata, 489.
Stellaria aquatica, 35.
Stellaria graminea, 26.
Stellaria holostea, 8.
Stellaria palustris, 17.
Stellaria uliginosa, 74.
Suæda maritima, 645.
Subularia aquatica, 98.
Symphytum officinale, 138, 192.

Tamarix anglica (*gallica*), 462.
Tamus communis, 627.
Tanacetum vulgare, 308.
Taxus baccata, 623.
Teesdalia nudicaulis, 61.
Teucrium scorodonia, 209.
Thalictrum alpinum, 189.
Thalictrum flavum, 197.
Thalictrum minus, 331.
Thlaspi alpestre, 64.
Thlaspi arvense, 62.
Thlaspi perfoliatum, 63.
Thymus serpyllum, 443.
Tilia cordata (*parvifolia*), 330.
Tilia intermedia (*vulgaris*), 320.
Tilia platyphyllos (*grandifolia*), 325.
Tillæa muscosa, 136.
Torilis anthriscus, 52.
Torilis infesta, 51.
Torilis nodosa, 461.
Tragopogon pratensis, 274.
Trientalis europæa, 111.
Trifolium arvense, 463.
Trifolium fragiferum, 418.
Trifolium maritimum, 367.
Trifolium medium, 415.
Trifolium minus, 263.
Trifolium repens, 149.
Trifolium scabrum, 134.
Trifolium stellatum, 186.
Trifolium striatum, 368.
Trifolium subterraneum, 133.
Triglochin maritimum, 628.
Triglochin palustre, 629.
Trigonella ornithopodioides, 154.
Trinia glaberrima, 95.
Trollius europæus, 211.
Tussilago farfara, 283.
Typha angustifolia, 584.
Typha latifolia, 583.

Ulex europæus, 218.
Ulex nanus, 255.

Ulmus campestris, 570.
Ulmus montana, 569.
Urtica dioica, 344.
Urtica urens, 346.
Utricularia vulgaris, 307.

Vaccinium myrtillus, 672.
Vaccinium vitis-idæa, 172.
Valeriana dioica, 396.
Valeriana officinalis, 174.
Valerianella olitoria, 175.
Verbascum blattaria, 293.
Verbascum nigrum, 395.
Verbascum thapsus, 294.
Verbena officinalis, 484.

Veronica agrestis, 513.
Veronica anagallis, 481.
Veronica arvensis, 515.
Veronica beccabunga, 518.
Veronica buxbaumii, 514.
Veronica chamædrys, 517.
Veronica hederæfolia, 512.
Veronica montana, 519.
Veronica officinalis, 521.
Veronica polita, 516.
Veronica scutellata, 302.
Veronica serpyllifolia, 520.
Viburnum lantana, 142.
Viburnum opulus, 112.
Vicia cracca, 503.

Vicia hirsuta, 504.
Vicia lathyroides, 464.
Vicia sativa, 406.
Vicia sepium, 539.
Vicia sylvatica, 40.
Vicia tetrasperma (*gracilis*), 541.
Vinca minor, 508.
Viola arvorum (*canina*), 492.
Viola hirta, 500.
Viola lutea, 194.
Viola odorata, 493.
Viola palustris, 456.
Viola tricolor, 411.
Viscum album, 597.

SECTION III.
PTERIDOPHYTA.
Ferns.

Ferns belong to the third subdivision of the Vegetable Kingdom—the *Pteridophyta*—which also includes the Horse-tails and Club-mosses—plants which have no flowers, in the ordinary sense of the word, and therefore no seeds, but are reproduced from *spores*.

These spores are contained in small cases on the edges and under side of the *fronds*, the latter being the name given to that part of the fern which, in flowering plants, we should call the leaf.

This distinction of name serves to call attention to other characteristics of these plants.

Ferns have roots and stems, but not the whole of the plant which we find beneath the ground is *root*. The true roots are always fibres which naturally grow downwards into the soil; the stem (*rhizome*) is frequently underground, or prostrate upon it, and consists of a thick mass of tissue from which the stalks of the fronds grow upwards, as the roots grow downwards. When above the surface they are covered with scales and hairs, and appear very shaggy. In the Common Bracken, however, the stem rises erect like that of a flowering plant. This stem is worth examination. If you cut it through transversely, you will find it to consist of cellular tissue, through which distinct bundles of woody fibres run, generally darker in colour. Those of the bracken form a rough horseshoe shape. This is one of the subjects which should be examined in the microscope.

The fronds vary very much in form, but all consist of a stalk (*stipes*) and blade. In some cases—as, for instance, the Hart's Tongue—the blade is undivided, *entire;* others are deeply divided. When the indentations do not reach the midrib, the frond is said to be *pinnatifid*; when they do reach the midrib, thus forming a series of little leaflets, *pinnae*. These leaflets, if cut again, are called *bipinnate;* if a third time, *tripinnate;* if still more, *decompound*.

The fronds are veined in various ways; the arrangement may be almost straight and parallel, or forked.

Another point of interest is that when the fronds are first formed in the bud they are rolled up upon themselves, and each leaflet (*pinna*) is also rolled up upon itself. This is called *circinate*, and is characteristic of all the British ferns except the Adder's Tongue and Moonwort.

But the characteristic which is most noticeable and interesting is that connected with the organs of fructification.

If you examine the under side of a mature fern, you will notice a number of minute brown patches, grouped either along the sides of the veins (*dorsal*), or along the edge of the frond (*marginal*).

These patches are called *sori*, and are in reality clusters of minute spores. In a very few cases, however, such as the *Osmunda regalis* and the Adder's Tongue, a whole frond becomes the receptacle and, in popular parlance, becomes a *flower*.

These spore-cases should be examined with your pocket lens or microscope. They are surrounded by a ring, fixed at one end to the frond. When the spores are ripe, the case bursts across, and the spores are scattered. In the case of three species, *Osmunda*, Adder's Tongue, and Moonwort, the spore-cases are not ringed, but consist of two valves.

Notice that in many cases the sori are covered at first by a thin, skin-like membrane, or scale, known as the *indusium*, which is cast off as the spores become ripe. The presence or absence of the indusium is a means of identification.

The after history of the spore is very interesting. It does not immediately become a fern, but expands on the earth or rock to which it is attached, in the form of a green, minute, leaf-like body, known as the *prothallus*, and in time two sets of organs grow out, from which in due course the young fern is produced.

Keeping these points in mind, it is not a difficult matter to identify the common ferns of this country. Notice first of all the method of fructification.

(*a*) If it is in a *terminal spike or panicle*, it will be either *Osmunda* (the Royal or Flowering Fern), *Ophioglossum* (Adder's Tongue), or *Botrychium* (Moonwort).

(*b*) If it is in a *tiny cup at the edge* of the frond, the species is *Hymenophyllum* or *Trichomanes* (the latter to be found only in Ireland).

(*c*) If it is *on the back or under side* of some or all the fronds, then it belongs to one of the remaining species, and a further means of identification must be used : you must now notice the shape of the frond, the shape and position of the sori, and the presence or absence of the indusium.

The following notes give some of the main distinctions of the genera of British ferns :—

1. POLYPODIACEÆ.—Sori round, without indusium.

(*a*) If the sori are dorsal, circular, and exposed—*Polypodium*.

(*b*) If the sori are dorsal, roundish, and running together beneath the margins of the frond—*Allosorus*.

2. GYMNOGRAMMEÆ.—Sori linear, without an indusium.

Sori are dorsal, linear, forked, and naked—*Gymnogramma*.

FERNS

3. ASPIDIEÆ.—Sori covered with a circular or roundish indusium, springing from the back of the veins.

(a) If the sori are dorsal, with round, target, or kidney-shaped indusia—*Aspidium*.

(b) If sori are round, with kidney-shaped indusium—*Nephrodium*.

4. ASPLENIEÆ.—Sori covered with an oblong or elongated indusium springing from the sides of the veins.

(a) If the indusium is straight and elongated—*Asplenium*.

(b) If sori are elongated and in parallel pairs, with indusium opening along the centre—*Scolopendrium*.

(c) If the sori are hidden amongst rusty, chaffy scales, with indusium invisible—*Ceterach*.

5. BLECHNEÆ.—The sori have indusia, and form longitudinal lines between the midrib and the margins of the pinnæ, or leaflets.

Sori, which are dorsal, are covered by a linear indusium—*Blechnum*.

6. PTERIDEÆ.—The sori are on the margins of the fronds, and are covered by a special indusium.

Sori in a continuous line at the edge of the frond—*Pteris*.

7. ADIANTEÆ.—Here the margins of the fronds are *turned back*, forming indusia, which have the sori underneath.

Sori in patches, under the reflexed indusium—*Adiantium*.

8. CYSTOPTERIDEÆ.—The sori have a special ovate indusium attached behind, and bent over them like a hood—*Cystopteris*.

9. WOODSIEÆ.—The sori have a circular indusium springing from the back of the veins, and attached beneath them—*Woodsia*.

10. HYMENOPHYLLEÆ.—The sori are at the end of the veins, and project from the margin, being surrounded by urn-shaped and two-valved membranes. When urn-shaped—*Trichomanes*; when two-valved—*Hymenophyllum*.

11. OSMUNDACEÆ.—Sori have no ring, but burst vertically by two regular valves. Fronds circinate—*Osmunda*.

12. OPHIOGLOSSACEÆ.—Sori without ring, and two-valved; young fronds folded up straight.

(a) Sori in irregularly branched clusters on a separate branch of the frond—*Botrychium*.

(b) Sori sessile, in two-ranked simple spikes on a separate frond—*Ophioglossum*.

Many of our British ferns are very rare, and the majority of them are local; but the following notes on some of the commoner varieties will be of use to the student:—

1. **The Common Polypody** (*Polypodium vulgare*).—Roots thick, woody, creeping. Fronds 6 to 12 inches, broadly oblong, lanceolate. Fructification conspicuous, generally at upper part of frond; golden circular patches. Found on old trees, roofs, walls, and rocks. Once a remedy for colds and coughs.

2. **Oak Fern** (*Polypodium dryopteris*).—Roots a dense matted mass. Stem

slender, purple, longer than frond. Fronds delicate, three-branch pinnate; pinnæ segmented. Sori on margins of the segments. Found in mountainous localities and wet woods in North. Local.

3. **Beech Fern** (*Polypodium phegopteris*).—Fronds 6 to 12 inches; pinnate at base, more or less hairy on under side. Sori small close to margins of the lobes. Mountains, wet woods, and waterfalls in South, West, and North. Local.

4. **Parsley Fern** (*Allosorus crispus*).—Fronds 6 inches, like parsley. The fertile fronds have reflexed ends covering the indusium. Stem slender and brittle. Local in North-west and North on stones and rocks—for example, round Snowdon.

5. **Common Prickly-shield Fern** (*Aspidium aculeatum*).—Fronds tufted, 1 to 2 feet, lanceolate, twice-pinnate, stout, rigid. Stalk shaggy, with brown scales. Root large, woody. Veins alternately branched. Common in hedgerows.

6. **Broad Prickly-toothed or Crested Fern** (*Nephrodium dilatatum*).—Stem-like root, often rising 6 to 12 inches above soil. Fronds pinnate; frond-stalk covered with long pointed scales. Common in woods and hedgerows.

7. **Male Buckler Fern** (*Nephrodium filix-mas*).—Fronds 2 to 3 feet, in circular clumps, five to ten in number. Sori with kidney-shaped indusium. Very common. A well-known remedy for tapeworm.

8. **Broad Prickly Buckler Fern** (*Nephrodium spinulosum*).—Closely allied with preceding, but not so tall, and much broader. Fronds 1 to 2 feet; bipinnate; segments of the pinnæ deeply toothed. Equally common.

9. **Marsh Buckler Fern** (*Nephrodium thelypteris*).—Fronds single, not tufted; bipinnate. Fertile fronds 2 to 3 feet, barren fronds shorter. Indusium soon lost. Found in marshy districts.

10. **Black Spleenwort, or** BLACK MAIDENHAIR (*Asplenium adiantum-nigrum*). —6 to 12 inches. Stalk long, purple or black. Fronds bipinnate. Sori at first distinct near midrib, becoming massed as plant grows. Found on old walls, rocks, and hedgebanks. Local.

11. **Lady Fern** (*Asplenium filix-femina*).—One of the most beautiful varieties. Tufted. Fronds lanceolate, bipinnate, lobes sharply toothed. Very fragile. Found in sheltered woods chiefly. Very common in Ireland.

12. **Lanceolate Spleenwort** (*Asplenium lanceolatum*).—Tufted. Fronds bipinnate, lanceolate, 3 to 6 inches. Sori two to four on each segment, uniting when old. Very local, chiefly on sea coast. Abundant in Cornwall and Jersey.

13. **Sea Spleenwort** (*Asplenium marinum*).—Fronds 6 to 12 inches, pinnate, tufted, narrow, lanceolate. Sori on midrib, linear, large. Common on all coasts except East.

14. **Wall Rue** (*Asplenium Ruta-muraria*).—A little fern, densely tufted. Fronds thick, dark green; 2 to 3 inches. Pinnæ often wedge-shaped. Found on old walls and rocks.

15. **Common Wall Spleenwort, or** MAIDENHAIR SPLEENWORT (*Asplenium*

trichomanes).—2 to 6 inches. Stalk slender, hairlike, black. Ovate pinnæ. Abundant on shaded rocks, old walls, and buildings.

16. **Common Hart's Tongue** (*Scolopendrium vulgare*).—Fronds 6 to 18 inches; oblong, strap-shaped, simple. Sori at short intervals on upper portion. Common on shady banks and rock clefts.

17. **Hard Fern** (*Blechnum spicant*).—Fronds simple, pinnate, tufted. Fertile 12 to 18 inches, with narrow acute segments. Under side covered with sori. Barren fronds deeply pinnatifid. Found in moist boggy land, and heaths and woods.

18. **Brakes**, or BRACKEN (EAGLE FERN) (*Pteris aquilina*).—Very common, sometimes attaining a height of 6 to 10 feet. Continuous lines of sori on the margins. Fronds compound bipinnate.

19. **True Maidenhair** (*Adiantium capillus-veneris*).—The only British species, recognized by its fan-shaped leaflets and wiry black stalks. 9 to 15 inches. Very local in Cornwall and Devon.

20. **Brittle Bladder Fern** (*Cystopteris fragilis*).—Fronds 5 to 6 inches, growing in tufts. Lanceolate and bipinnate. Veining in fronds very distinct. Almost every vein terminates in a group of roundish capsules, becoming confluent as fern grows. Widely distributed; moist mountainous districts.

21. **Tunbridge Hymenophile** (FILMY FERN) (*Hymenophyllum tunbridgense*).— The smallest of our British ferns (2 to 3 inches); pinnate, lanceolate; olive-brown. Veins very strongly marked, the leafy part being slight and membranous. Roots thread-like, matted. Found in many mountainous districts among moss.

22. **Royal or Flowering Fern** (*Osmunda regalis*).—Noted for its flowery panicle, sometimes 3 to 4 feet above the other fronds. In old plants the stem looks like a trunk, the leafy bipinnate fronds depending from its crown. Found in marshy districts, but local.

23. **Moonwort** (*Botrychium lunaria*).—In its early stages hardly like a fern, consisting of an upright simple stem, in reality a bud, enclosing a fertile and barren frond. The pinnæ are obliquely fan-shaped or half-moon, thick and entire. Found on dry open moors; chiefly in Staffordshire, Surrey, and Yorkshire; also Isle of Wight. Name derived from the crescent shape of the pinnæ.

24. **Common Adder's Tongue** (*Ophioglossum vulgatum*).—Resembling in its growth the Cuckoo-pint (*Arum maculatum*). 3 to 9 inches. One frond, barren, enclosing an upright spike, in which are two lines of spore-cases. When ripe, the spike opens, the pollen is discharged, leaving behind a double row of round empty cells. Generally distributed.

Club-mosses and Horse-tails.

Of the **Club-mosses** and **Horse-tails** but little need be said. There are six species of the former in Britain, of which the commonest is the **Wolf's Claw** (*Lycopodium clavatum*).

THE BRITISH NATURE BOOK

It is found on hills and moors, its roots so interlaced as to form a sort of carpet. The narrow leaves turn inwards and overlap each other, clinging closely to the stem; and the branches spring up in tufts, bearing one, two, or three cones, covered with bracts, in the axils of which are the capsules which contain the "seed."

There are some nine species of British Horse-tails—*Equisetaceæ* (*equus*, "horse," and *seta*, "hair" or "bristle")—leafless plants, the survivors of prehistoric plants which in those bygone ages flourished as trees. The commonest species is the **Field Horse-tail** (*Equisetum arvense*)—a plague to the farmer or allotment holder, owing to its long underground roots and stems. The fructification is in capsules, arranged in cones. The outer skin of the stems abounds in flinty particles, placed in rows or ridges; and on this account the stems were, and still are, used in many parts of the country for scouring brass and wooden vessels, "Dutch rushes" being the old name for them.

SECTION IV.

BRYOPHYTA.

Mosses.

The Mosses, of which there are more than six hundred British species (excluding varieties and the *Sphagnaceæ*), belong to the sub-kingdom *Bryophyta*, together with the Liverworts, and though so minute and apparently insignificant, play quite an important part in the economy of Nature. It has been said that at least a quarter of the vegetation covering the surface of Great Britain is formed by one genus of moss alone. In any case, the mosses are the first things to grow on any virgin soil, whether it be new-turned earth or a new-built wall; and by their decay the first fragments of soil are formed upon which other and higher plants can germinate. Peat is the accumulated debris of countless successions of moss plants. Many a mighty tree has begun its life in the shady moisture of a moss bed, and in after years has repaid its debt by offering to other mosses a habitation on its trunk and branches.

Much of the work of the student of mosses can be done in the winter season, for it is in winter and in early spring—at least in low-lying districts—that they appear in their greatest beauty in " flower " and " fruit."

The moss plant is a very minute thing, and needs a lens to make out its characteristics. It consists of a stem, single or branching, with tiny leaves clustering closely about it, sometimes bright green, yellow, red, purple, or brown. The leaves are stalkless, and may be simple, thickened, or toothed, with a single or forked midrib, in some cases projecting like a bristle from the tip of the leaf.

Under the microscope the leaves are seen to be made up of a single layer of cells, in definite patterns, varying in the different species, and these form important means of identification, the character being known as "areolation."

Mosses have little or no roots, although in some species a few slender fibres may be found; in others a compact woolly mass of them, which are probably not roots but anchors holding the plant securely to its resting-place. But this is a vexed question.

They are usually considered as flowerless plants, but they have organs which closely resemble flowers and may be found sometimes at the end of slender, graceful stalks, in the form of little stars, or like buds, concealed in the axils of the leaves.

The fruits consist of capsules containing a number of spores, but many species bear no fruit, and are reproduced from little threads growing on the leaves and in other ways. As in the case of ferns, the spores do not produce the plants immediately, but certain minute green threads like the *Confervæ* of stagnant pools, and from these the mature plant is derived.

The capsules, which every observer must have noticed on their stalks springing upwards from the midst of the plant on an old wall or elsewhere, and giving even at a distance a touch of golden or other colour, are most remarkable in their mechanism and beauty.

Under the microscope the capsule, which often is bright red or gold in colour, is found to have a minute cap (*calyptra*). When this is removed a second lid is found below (the *operculum*), closely fitting, and in some cases having a projecting tip or handle! When this is taken away there is disclosed a fringe of fairy-like fingers or teeth folded over the cup, and known as the *peristome*. If breathed upon, this organ only contracts still more tightly, and the only way to open it is to put it aside in a dry place, where, in a little while, the teeth will open, spread out like rays, and reveal below the golden spores which they have protected. This is a marvellous provision of Nature. It does not exist, it is true, in all species, but is found in one form or another in a large number. Its sensitiveness to damp causes it to close the cup whenever the air is moist; but when fine, dry weather comes, it opens, and allows the spores to escape and be carried away by the wind.

The form of the peristome varies: it may be absent or rudimentary, or, on the other hand, highly complex. The fringes or teeth are, however, always four, or in a multiple of four, up to sixty-four.

In one genus (*Tortula*) the fringes are thread-like and twisted together like the strands of a rope. In another (*Polytrichum*) they are fixed to a central disc, leaving openings in the side for the spores to escape. In the genus *Andreæa* the whole capsule splits vertically into four, scattering its spores by the violence of its opening.

It is impossible to describe many of the species in simple words, for they need expert dissection and examination; but a few notes on some of the commoner ones may start a student on this fascinating branch of Nature study.

The POLYTRICHACEÆ, the highest developed of all the mosses, possess certain peculiarities which enable them to be fairly easily identified. The leaves have a stiff, bristly appearance, and the capsule is most distinctive.

Polytrichum commune (the Common Hair Moss) is found on wet moors and peaty bogs, growing sometimes as high as 18 inches. The capsules at first are covered with fine hairs; the operculum is pointed: it can be removed with the point of a needle after being placed in boiling water, and underneath will be found a disc, attached to the tips of the teeth of the peristome, which grows from the capsule wall.

P. commune has sixty-four teeth; *P. aloides*, thirty-two; and several other species only sixteen.

The male plants of *P. commune* have the star-shaped heads to which reference has been made.

The spore-cases of this species ripen in June and July; those of *P. aloides* in winter.

Catharinea undulata (another member of the *Polytrichaceæ*) is not so bristly in appearance; the capsule is longer, and the lid is as long as the capsule. It is found on clayey or sandy soil, and ripens in autumn and winter.

Tetraphis pellucida, about $\frac{1}{2}$ inch high, found on turfy banks and rotten tree stumps, has a four-toothed capsule. Some of the leaves at the end of the stems form a minute cup containing a green, dust-like mass of gemmæ.

Dicranum scoparium (**Broom Fork Moss**) is one of the largest species, found on shady banks, heaths, and in woods. The capsule is yellow or reddish brown, and the peristome bright red. The cells of the young leaves contain, besides chlorophyll, certain round oil globules, two or three in a cell; these are a means of identification.

Ceratodon purpureus, $\frac{1}{2}$ to 3 inches in height, is recognized under the microscope by the colour of its teeth—dark purple at the base, gradually changing through red, orange, and yellow to a pearly transparency at the tip.

Tortula muralis is a typical species of the TORTULACEÆ, found on brick walls, generally on the cement. It has a twisted peristome, hence its name —**Wall Screw Moss**. The central rib of the leaf projects into a fine bristle-like hair. Most of the species have long, corrugated capsules, dark purple in colour, and pink peristomes of twisted teeth.

Funaria hygrometrica (**Common Cord Moss**) has fruit-stalks which twist up when dry; when breathed upon, they uncurl. It is frequently found growing on patches of ground which have been burnt.

In *Mnium hornum*, which is very common, the capsules are to be found in May and June: orange or reddish brown, with bright red mouths. There is only one capsule to each plant; but in *Mnium undulatum* ten, and sometimes eleven and twelve capsules, even more brightly coloured, will be found growing from each stem.

The SPLACHNACEÆ are recognized by their habit of growing on decayed animal matter or dung; the BARTRAMIACEÆ, by their rounded capsules.

SECTION V.
THALLOPHYTA.
Fungi.

Fungi and Seaweeds form the first of the sub-kingdoms of the Vegetable World —the *Thallophyta*. In olden days the former were considered to be mere "sports"—*lusus naturæ*—and to have no connection with the vegetable world at all; and as some of them were poisonous, and all of them seemed to have something uncanny and mysterious about them, they were regarded as definitely evil both in origin and effect. Their bad name still clings to them. Yet the fact remains that the *majority* of them are non-poisonous— some fifty species may be eaten safely—and it is only a few that are harmful.

It is, however, of the greatest importance that the would-be eater of fungi should be able to distinguish between these different kinds, and I cannot emphasize too strongly the fact that *there is no rough-and-ready way*. The country folks' idea that if the skin peels off readily the specimen is edible is as false as the statement that the poisonous sorts tarnish a silver spoon.

A most valuable book, containing very fine coloured illustrations, is that published by the Board of Agriculture and Fisheries (price 1s.), to which I pay my acknowledgments, not only for details in this section, but also for more than one meal in which "toadstools" have added their share to my enjoyment.

Let the **Mushroom** serve as an object lesson on the general structure of these curious vegetables.

First, notice the thick, fleshy stem or stalk, on the top of which is the cap (*pileus*). Under this cap are a number of thin, skin-like plates, which are called gills; and if these be examined with your lens you will find on their surfaces a number of little bodies on short stalks. These are the *spores* of the mushroom. Leave a mushroom upright on a sheet of paper, and in a few hours' time there will be a purplish dust beneath the gills, a deposit of spores.

These spores, falling on moist ground, grow into an interlacing mass of threads, known as the *mycelium*, or, in popular parlance, the *spawn*, and from this the mushrooms are produced in the following autumn.

Fungi are very largely common objects of the country in the autumn, especially in the six weeks from the middle of October to the end of November; and a walk for an hour or two in any damp wood will enable us to find a number

FUNGI 457

of different specimens. The **Inky Mushroom**, for example (*Coprinus atramentarius*), with its bell-shaped cap of dark shiny grey, will be seen at the foot of an old tree trunk; while in a glade hard by appears the **Shaggy Cap** (*Coprinus comatus*), some 4 to 6 inches in height, unmistakable by its name,

The "Fairy Ring."

and with white gills that turn to pink and black, dissolving into "ink" in two or three days.

Horse Mushrooms (*Agaricus arvensis*) are common on marshy ground; they have soft, smooth caps, yellowish in colour, and often full of grubs.

In some wooded dell or copse we perceive another well-known fungus, not by the eye at first, but the *nose*: it is the **Stinkhorn** (*Phallus impudicus*), with its vile smell. Probably when you find it you will see that it is covered with bluebottles and other flies, which are frequently intoxicated by its juices.

On many decayed trees may be found the **Common Polyporus** (*Polyporus versicolor*), the upper side marked with green and brown concentric lines, and velvety to the touch; while the **Common Puff-ball** (*Lycoperdon perlatum*), at first so white and solid, but later filled with brown spores and bursting at the touch, is to be found on the grass of meadows and roadsides.

Deflated Puff-balls.

Later in the autumn **Liberty Caps** (*Agaricus semilanceatus*) take their place in the meadows, and are very poisonous. The cap is conical, and about $\frac{1}{2}$ inch wide, brownish white, with a white stem.

Such are a few of the fungi to be found in a walk such as I have described, and it will show how varied are the sites and localities in which the fungi are to be found—open meadows, shady spots, decaying stumps, living trees.

Some turn pink when bruised (*Rubescens*); others discharge a milky juice (*Lactarius*). The AGARICS, to which the Mushroom belongs, include also the "Toadstools and Frogstools," and are the only fungi which possess *gills*. The POLYPOREI hold their spores in little pores opening underneath the cap.

Magpie Mushroom.

But not all the fungi resemble these familiar forms. The **Witches' Butter** (*Exidia*), found on dead trees, is a dark patch of jelly, with a rough crape-like surface below, and little projections on the top; and a large number are microscopic, such as the **Bunt**, which appears on wheat; and the **Mould** or **Mildew**, which is to be found on so many materials left in the open air—even bread and jam. These latter growths belong to the **Thread Fungi** (*Hyphomycetes*), the **Dust Fungi** (*Coniomycetes*), and other kinds, which cannot be studied without the microscope.

The following is a brief description of some of the EDIBLE varieties:—

1. **Common Mushroom** (*Agaricus campestris*).—Has a cap which is white in colour.

The *Flesh*—Thick and white, changing to brownish when broken.

The *Gills*—Crowded; rosy at first, becoming dark brown.

The *Stem*—Stout, white, with a ring or frill near the cap.

2. **Horse Mushroom** (*A. arvensis*).—White, changing to primrose-yellow; 4-6 inches in diameter, sometimes more.

The *Flesh*—White, does not change colour.

The *Gills*—Brown, remaining *dry* when old (whereas those of the Mushroom deliquesce).

The *Stem*—Stout, white, with a broad frill.

Sometimes found in large fairy rings, in pastures, and under trees.

3. **Tufted Mushroom** (*A. elvensis*).—Grows in tufts or clusters.

Cap—Hemispherical, whitish, covered with large brown scales; margin warted; diameter, 4-6 inches.

Flesh—Thick, turning reddish brown when cut.

Gills—Brownish flesh-coloured; remain dry.

Stem—4-6 inches; rather swollen in middle, bearing a large ring; warted beneath.

On ground under trees, especially oak.

4. **Bleeding Agaric** (*A. hæmorrhoidarius*).

Cap—Globose; brownish when expanded; scaly; tinged with red or purple at centre; 3-5 inches diameter.

Common Mushroom.

The Common Morel.

Horse Mushroom.

Tufted Mushroom.

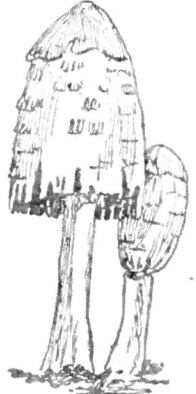
Shaggy Cap.

Edible Boletus.

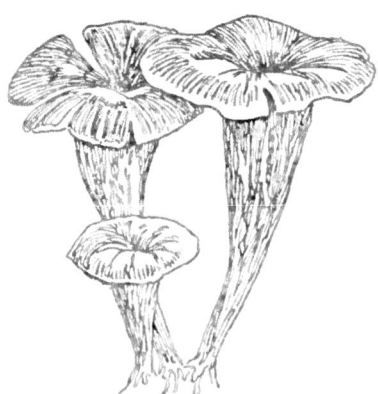
Horn of Plenty.

Sheathed Agaric.

EDIBLE FUNGI.

Gills—Rosy, then purplish umber.
Both stem and flesh *become instantly red when cut*, hence the name.
In pine woods in autumn.

5. **Shaggy Cap** (*Coprinus comatus*).

Cap—Cylindrical, covered with dull yellow crust, which becomes broken into shaggy scales, showing white flesh beneath ; 4–7 inches high.

Gills—First white, then pinkish, then black, close packed.

Stem—White ; 6–9 inches long ; thickish at bottom.

When mature, cap splits, turning upwards ; gills deliquesce. Amongst grass or on waste land.

6. **Warty Cap** (*Amanita rubescens*).

Cap—At first globose, then nearly flat; brick-red or dingy rusty brown, covered with whitish patches, easily rubbed off; 3–5 inches diameter.

Flesh—White, changing quickly to reddish brown when cut.

Gills—White, becoming blotched with brown.

Stem—White, changing to brown, with a large ring.

Under trees, etc.

Note.—To be distinguished from poisonous species by the fact that its flesh changes colour quickly when broken.

7. **Parasol Mushroom** (*Lepiota procera*).

Cap—Globose when young; expanding to 5–9 inches diameter, and flattening, with a boss in centre; whitish, covered with brown scales.

Gills—White, unchanging.

Stem—6–8 inches, thick at base, with a broad, loose ring; whitish, with brown markings.

In glades, on heaps of leaves, etc.

8. **Sheathed Agaric** (*Amanitopsis vaginata*).

Cap—Bell-shaped, becoming flat, with slight boss at centre. Edge grooved ; lead-grey ; 3–5 inches diameter.

Gills—White, unchanging.

Stem—Long, slender, whitish ; base surrounded by loose sheath or cup.

Note.—To be distinguished from harmful species by the fact that the gills remain persistently white.

9. **Scaly Agaric** (*Lepiota rachodes*).—Very similar to Parasol Mushroom, except that there is no boss in centre of cap, and the stem is shorter and white.

Flesh—Changes instantly from white to reddish brown when broken.

On ground in woods.

10. **Blewits** (*Tricholoma personatum*).

Cap—3–4 inches diameter ; convex at first. When expanded, the edge is still incurved ; smooth and polished, dingy white or pale yellow.

Flesh—Thick and white, tinged with lilac.

Gills—Crowded ; deeply white.

Stem—Stout, bright lilac colour.

On open grassy places.

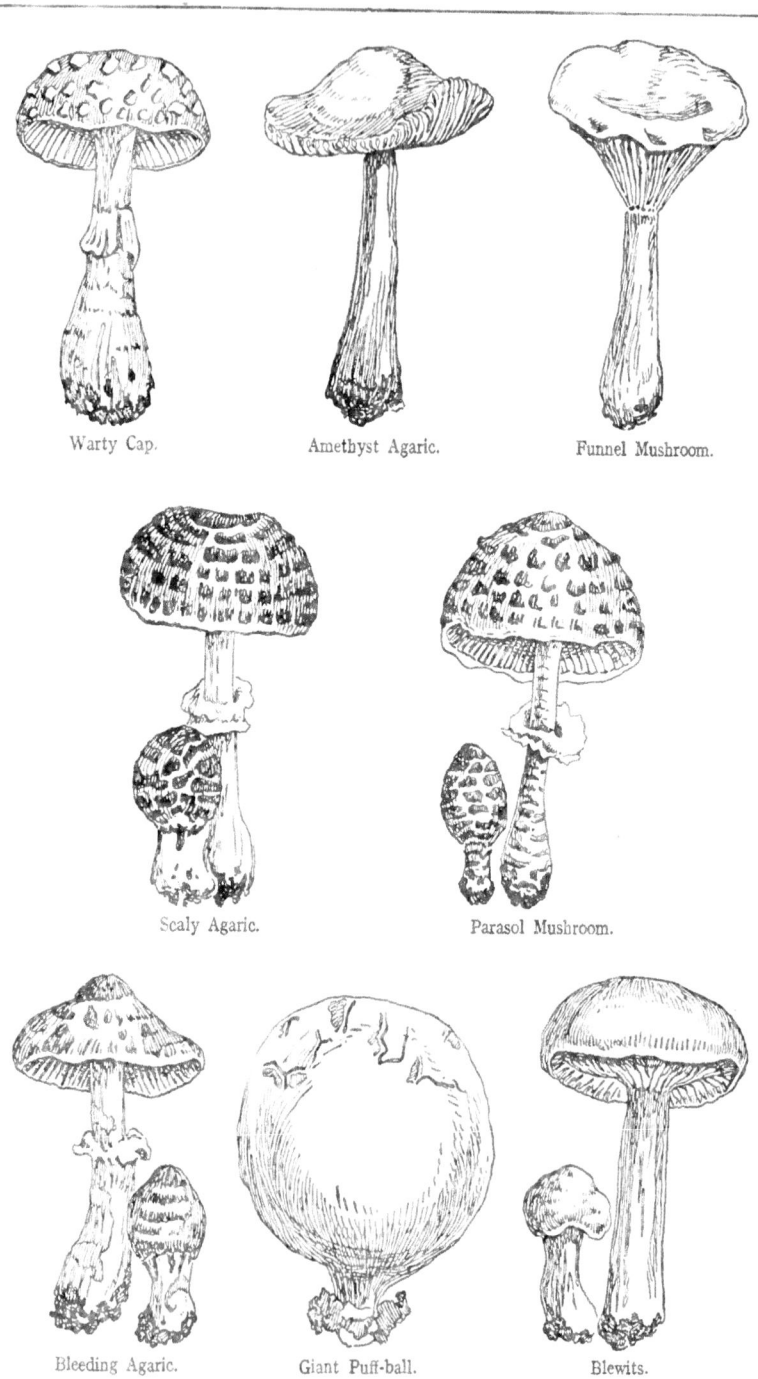

EDIBLE FUNGI.

Note.—To be distinguished from poisonous species by the fact that the gills *remain white when full grown.*

11. **Funnel Mushroom** (*Clitocybe maxima*).

Cap—Funnel-shaped, with incurved margin; bright yellow, though sometimes paler or deeper coloured; 5–9 inches diameter, and about 4 inches deep.

Gills—Narrow, crowded, whitish.

Stem—2–3 inches; stout; same colour as cap.

Under trees in autumn.

Note.—Distinguish this species from a similar but harmful species which is white, and exudes white milky liquid when broken.

12. **Amethyst Agaric** (*Tricholoma nudum*).—Deep violet or amethyst all over, fading when old.

Cap—3–4 inches diameter, smooth, shining, often wavy.

Gills—Narrow, crowded.

Stem—3–4 inches; slender.

Generally in clusters, amongst leaves, under trees.

Note.—Distinguish this species from other violet-coloured fungi by the gills. In the *inedible* species these are *rust-coloured.*

13. **Horn of Plenty** (*Craterellus cornucopioides*).—Unmistakable in shape, like a long, narrow funnel, with an edge turned back and more or less wavy; thin and pliant in substance.

Inside—Dark brown, with olive shading.

Outside—Dull leaden, with scattered depressions or pits.

Stem—Hollow, blackish, tapering to base.

Grows in tufts in woods.

14. **Great Puff-ball** (*Lycoperdon giganteum*).—Unmistakable by its large size and persistently pale colour; ball-shaped; pure white at first; when old, tinged with yellow.

Flesh—At first white, changing to primrose-yellow. To be eaten only while flesh is perfectly white.

Found in fields and meadows.

15. **Edible Boletus** (*Boletus edulis*).

Cap—Like a penny bun in size and colour; 4–6 inches diameter; flesh white, unchanging.

Under Surface—Not gills, but compact mass of tubes, giving appearance of crowded pin-holes.

Stem—Stout; 3–4 inches.

On ground in woods.

Remove *tubes* before cooking.

16. **Common Morel** (*Morchella esculenta*).—Unmistakable in appearance.

Cap and *stem*—Hollow; surface of cap covered with ridges, forming a network. (Only the STINKHORN has similar network, and this has a long stem and a foul smell.)

Found in early spring and summer.

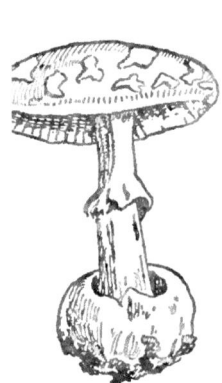
Bulbous Agaric.

Shield Agaric.

Purple Agaric.

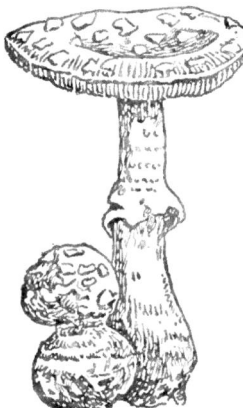
Fly Agaric.

The Death Cap.

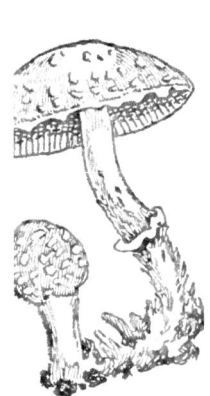
Verdigris Agaric.

Glutinous Agaric.

Warted Agaric.

POISONOUS FUNGI.

464   THE BRITISH NATURE BOOK

The following notes refer to some common POISONOUS varieties :—

1. **Bulbous Agaric** (*Amanita mappa*).
Cap—At first convex, then flat; smooth, dry, whitish or yellowish, with a few irregular patches, easily rubbed off; 3–4 inches diameter.
Gills—Crowded; white.
Stem—White; cylindrical, with a torn ring; bulbous base, with remains of a sheath or cup.
Has unpleasant smell; very poisonous.

2. **Warted Agaric** (*A. pantherina*).
Cap—3–4 inches diameter; convex, edge grooved; rusty brown or reddish yellow.
Flesh—White, unchanging.
Gills—White, unchanging.
Stem—Whitish, with a ring; base bulbous, with a sheath attached.
Note.—The SHEATHED AGARIC (No. 8 in preceding list) has no ring, and stem is not bulbous.
The WARTY CAP (No. 6 in preceding list) has flesh changing to reddish brown when cut.

3. **The Death Cap** (*A. phalloides*).—The most deadly of all.
Cap—Slimy when moist; pale yellow or green; 3–4 inches diameter.
Gills—White, unchanging.
Stem—White and smooth; base bulbous, with a large sheath or cup.
The *ring* is large and pendent.
Usually in woods.
Distinguishing marks—The colour, pale yellow or greenish; *the ring and sheath; the unchanging white gills.*

4. **Fly Agaric** (*A. muscaria*).
Cap—Globose when young, becoming flat; 4–7 inches diameter; bright scarlet, with white patches.
Stem—White, swollen below, with a ring or frill.
In woods, especially under birches and firs.

5. **Shield Agaric** (*Lepiota clypeolaria*).
Cap—2–3½ inches diameter; at first cylindrical, smooth, brown; expands flat, when the whole surface, except central boss, breaks into scales.
Gills—White.
Stem—Covered with *small spreading scales* below ring—a distinguishing feature.

6. **Glutinous Agaric** (*Volvaria gloiocephala*).
Cap—3–5 inches diameter; becoming almost flat, with central boss; dark grey; very glutinous.
Gills—Broad; salmon colour.
Stem—Long, whitish, with a sheath or cup round base.
Distinguished from SHEATHED AGARIC by its glutinous cap and salmon-coloured gills.

SEAWEEDS

7. **Verdigris Agaric** (*Stropharia æruginosa*).—In vigorous specimens the whole fungus is of a bright green colour, but in the open the *cap* (2–3 inches diameter) bleaches to a pale dingy yellow. Very glutinous.
Stem—Scaly below ring.
Gills—Becoming purple.

8. **Purple Agaric** (*Cortinarius purpurascens*).—Distinguish this species from BLEWITS and AMETHYST AGARIC. In the poisonous species the *stem* has a bulb at the base, and the *gills* are rusty-coloured when mature.
Cap—Very glutinous.
Flesh—Rather thick, clear blue.

[For the above notes I am indebted to the pamphlet mentioned previously, published by the Board of Agriculture and Fisheries.]

Seaweeds.

The **Seaweeds**, the remaining members of the sub-kingdom *Thallophyta*, are classified according to their *colour*.

That portion of the sea which forms the shore-belt has been divided into four zones, in each of which, generally speaking, seaweeds of one of four colours are found living.

1. At and above high-water mark, they are chiefly thread-like and encrusting species, which under the microscope appear bluish green—CYANOPHYCEÆ.

2. From high-water mark to a line about half-tide level, they are chiefly of a bright green colour—CHLOROPHYCEÆ.

3. From half-tide level to low-tide mark, they are chiefly olive-brown—PHÆOPHYCEÆ.

4. From low-tide mark to deep water, they are red—RHODOPHYCEÆ.

In all cases the green colour (chlorophyll) commonly associated with land plants is present, but in the olive-brown and red varieties it is masked by these other pigments, which serve to protect it against injurious rays of light.

The green seaweeds found about high-water mark are able to bear the same amount of light as land plants; but the brown weeds, from their position between high and low water mark, are exposed twice each day to great changes of light, and therefore need more protection, while the red varieties, growing only in deep water, find their red pigment (like the photographer's red glass window) a special safeguard against the injurious blue rays of light which penetrate to their depth.

Seaweeds are useful for many purposes, edible, agricultural, and commercial. Some species may be made into a jelly, others can be treated as a vegetable dish. Some are used by the farmer as manure upon his land, while the larger and coarser species were formerly used to produce Kelp, an impure carbonate of soda. All marine Algæ contain iodine, and some are occasionally used in special forms in medicine, while it is from the ashes of the Rockweeds that the chief supply of this important element is obtained.

All seaweeds, except the **Grass-wrack** (*Zostera maritima*), belong to the flowerless division of plant life, being made up of cells, without woody or other tissues. They have no roots, that portion in the larger species which looks like a root being really a sucker, by means of which the plant adheres firmly to the rock.

Turning to the *Chlorospermeæ*—those with green spores—it should be borne in mind that whilst usually light green, the plant is sometimes olive or purple.

Every one who visits the seaside knows the thin, flat, transparent fronds of the **Sea-lettuce** or GREEN LAVER (*Ulva latissima*), with its crisped, folded margins—a valuable plant for the marine aquarium, as its leaves give off a plentiful supply of oxygen. A companion is the **Purple Laver**, known in Ireland as "SLOKE," and often boiled down into a jelly for food, as is also the case with the Green.

Confervæ—masses of green hairy threads—may be found in any tidal pool, and correspond to those found in fresh water; while another common green weed is **Sea-grass** (*Enteromorpha compressa*), which forms a narrow tube of rugged shape, occasionally found inflated with oxygen gas.

The *Zostera*, or **Grass-wrack**, is not really a seaweed, but a flowering plant which somehow has taken to living in the sea. It may be found thrown up on the shore after a storm, or growing in the deeper pools just above low-water mark. Its leaves are less than ½ inch wide, and may be 3 or 4 feet long, and it has real flowers which grow in a sheath, springing from one of the shorter leaves. Below low-water mark it abounds in large stretches, the abode of all sorts of sea animals.

Bryopsis plumosa is another green weed, fairly common, found in rock pools, and with fronds like fine feathers.

Cladophora rupestris and *C. arcta* are two other common green seaweeds, the former coarse and horsehair-like, growing in thick tufts, 4 or 5 inches long, the latter a brighter green, and growing in a radiating manner from a broad disc.

The **Brown Seaweeds** (*Melanospermeæ*), always of an olive colour, include our gigantic oarweeds and tangles, and afford a great variety of forms. The most striking on account of their size and abundance are the *Fucaceæ*.

The **Channelled Wrack** (*Fucus canaliculatus*) is a small leathery plant, growing abundantly on rocks. It looks so dry and shrivelled that most people consider it to be dead, but it softens when the water reaches it. It is much branched, and the edges of the fronds turn in so much as to give the appearance of being channelled or furrowed. The receptacles containing the spores are pod-like organs, dark orange in colour, found at the end of some of the fronds.

The **Knotted Wrack** (*F. nodosus*) may be as much as 6 feet long, and has

SEAWEEDS

solitary bladders in the centre of the fronds, above which the frond divides. These bladders, as in other species, give the plant that buoyancy and support needed under water.

The **Bladder Wrack** (*F. vesiculosus*) is very similar, but has a broader frond with a distinct midrib, and the bladders are in groups, frequently pairs, on each side of the midrib. It is common wherever there are rocks, and is much used by farmers for manure.

The **Saw-edged Wrack** * (*F. serratus*) is named from the sharply toothed edges of its broad fronds. It has no bladders.

Another brown seaweed, which is almost as common, is the **Sea-oak** or POD-WEED (*Halidrys siliquosa*), which is identified at once by its long, pod-like air-chambers, each divided into several compartments. Other pods contain the element from which the spores are produced, and these have perforated surfaces.

On the South Coast, specially, is a tufted weed which under water shines with a beautiful iridescence, and is many branched, the branches being full of little air-bladders. This is *Cystoseira ericoides*, known sometimes as the **Rainbow Bladder-weed**.

The **Oarweed** (*Laminaria digitata*) is a deep-water plant, reaching a height of 10 or 12 feet. It is often flung ashore after storms, when it may be recognized by its huge round stems, terminating in claw-like " roots," as most people insist on calling the suckers. The leafy portion is broad and slit into sections, so that the whole frond bears a rude resemblance to the fingers of a hand. The stem is so tough that it can be used for making handles to knives and other tools. When fresh, the tang of a knife can be thrust into it and in a few months it is dry and fast, having contracted so as to fix the blade immovably.

Amongst the *Laminariæ* is to be found the **Sea-rope** (*Chorda filum*), attaining a length of many feet. Its name is apt, for it consists of a long, tubular frond, slimy to the touch, and covered, as your lens will show, with dense fine hairs.

Another familiar species is the **Sugar Tangle** (*Laminaria saccharina*). This derives its name from the fact that when dry it is covered with a hoar-frost-like powder, sweet to the taste, called *mannite* or manna. This species is generally chosen by visitors to the sea to take back home as a weather gauge, as it is a ready absorbent of moisture; but the stem can be used as a handle for forks and knives, like that of the Oarweed. The fronds are undivided and glossy.

L. bulbosa, **Sea Furbelows**, is recognized by the large hollow bulb from which it springs, and which, being perforated, becomes a refuge for all sorts of small creatures. It will be found on the shore after a storm, like so many of the other seaweeds.

* The word "wrack" is from the French *varec* = seaweed, and is still common in Jersey patois as *vraic*.

THE BRITISH NATURE BOOK

The **Peacock's Tail** (*Padina pavonia*) derives its name from its shape, and is only 2 or 3 inches in height. Though really a species of the tropics, it is to be found on our South Coasts, and is identified by its shape, and by the concentric lines and bands, which are magnificently iridescent in water. It is to be found quite commonly at Weymouth.

The **Net-weed** (*Dictyota dichotoma*) is a delicate-looking seaweed, having each frond cut in two at the top; the surface, if examined closely, will be found to exhibit a network of square or oblong meshes. It is light olive in colour, and is found growing in tufts on stones and other weeds in our rock pools.

Some of the seaweeds in this group are mere tufts of brown shaggy threads growing on other weeds. Among them is *Ectocarpus siliculosus*, its name implying that it has external fruit, in little pod-like bodies on the branches; but these must be examined with your pocket lens. *Ectocarpus granulosus* is a similar minute plant without the pods, but with square-shaped cells showing plainly through the magnifier.

The **Red Seaweeds** (*Rhodospermæ*) include some of the most graceful and attractive of all, although they are very small. There are, for example, more than twenty species of *Callithamnion* (Gr. "beautiful shrub"), some attaining a length of 6 inches, but the majority very minute, looking almost like red velvet. The different kinds of *Ceramium* are sure to be noticed by any collector. The **Common Red** has forked threads with tips turned towards one another. *Ceramium diaphanum* has soft silky tufts, and white stems with red joints.

Plocamium coccineum, **Braided Hair**, has flat, crimson, hair-like branches, serrated on one side like a finely toothed comb, much branched, but without ribs or veins. This is one of the commonest species.

Ptilota plumosa has feather-like fronds varying from 3 to 10 inches, and can be identified by them, while *Griffithsia setacea* has stiffer, more bristle-like fronds, which, when placed in fresh water, burst, shooting out the red colouring matter within.

Nitophyllum punctatum is a delicate plant, 6 to 10 inches in length and breadth, rather like the Red Dock Leaf—a large lettuce-like frond, crisped and wavy at the edges, which are cut into lobes, those at the top being forked. It has no midrib, and is thus distinguished from *Wormskoldia* and *Delesseria*.

The *Wormskoldia sanguinea*, **Red Dock Leaf** or ASH-LEAVED SEAWEED, is magnificently scarlet-coloured, with fronds 5 to 6 inches long, extraordinarily like those of a Dock, and very transparent. It has a strong midrib and branching nervures, and is much folded or waved. It is at its best in June and July, becoming ragged later on.

Delesseria hypoglossum is a small plant, with fronds about ¼ inch in length, found on almost every coast.

Delesseria alata is found growing in thick tufts on the stems of other weeds— for example, *Laminaria digitata*; it possesses a slight midrib, on the edges of which is the narrow membranous frond, the "wings" referred to in its technical name.

Polysiphonia urceolata is a plant of dense, thread-like, rather stiff fronds, growing either on rocks or *Laminaria*. On cutting through one of the stems, it will be noticed that it is composed of six tubes round a central aperture: the branches are jointed. There are more than twenty British species of this genus. It possesses pitcher-like fruits, to be examined through the microscope for their beauty.

Chylocladia articulata (parvula) is a remarkable seaweed, its name signifying "jointed juice-branch." It is some 8 to 10 inches in length, jointed, each cactus-like joint being filled with red gelatinous juice.

Iridæa edulis is a striking seaweed, with fronds 9 or 10 inches long and 4 or 5 inches wide, shaped rather like a racquet. Under the water it is beautifully iridescent.

The Carrageen, or Irish Moss (*Chondrus crispus*) is a very common species, growing on rocks. Its shape is like a stag's antlers, but it varies much in colour, from greenish white and yellow to a dull purple. It was once used for food, boiled down to a jelly, and considered very beneficial to invalids; also to make a size for calico manufacturers, and as a fattening food for calves. I have noticed it specially abundant in estuaries and the mouths of tidal rivers.

The common *Gigartina mamillosa* is very similar, but has broader and grooved fronds, rough to the touch, and with little tubercles or warts like grape stones.

Dulse (DILLISK or DILLOSK) (*Rhodymenia palmata*) is still eaten in Scotland, Ireland, and on the West Coast of England. It is very common, dark red in colour, with fronds about 2 inches long and $\frac{1}{4}$ inch wide, roughly fan-shaped.

Rhodymenia jubata is more slender, and ragged, in some parts deeply lobed.

The Coralline (*Corallina officinalis*) is found everywhere, and is identified by its chalky, stony-coated little joints. For many years it was a question whether this was a seaweed or a kind of coral, but it is now known to be a vegetable. Other Algæ also have a similar power of secreting lime—*Jania*, for example, with its much shorter and slenderer branches, and *Melobesia*, which grows in thin horizontal plates and masses.

APPENDIX.

Some Wild Pets I have known.

No. 1. PADDY, THE OTTER.

I HAVE known two or three tame otters, including one which was caught in Surrey, two miles away from a river, in a poultry shed, where, night after night, chickens were found dead. As it was obvious that neither fox, nor rat, nor stoat, was responsible for the murders, a trap was specially made to catch the culprit alive, and one fine morning the young otter was inside.

The thief must have had a very perverted taste, for he had come from a river, two miles across the fields, in which there were plenty of trout. Strange to say, though half-grown, he became very tame in captivity.

But the tamest of all is Paddy, whose photograph is on Plate II. Paddy and his brothers were found last spring close to a river, in a bed of reeds and rushes. I fear that in all probability their mother had been shot or trapped, for the river is closely preserved, and it was said that considerable damage had been done among the fish. Personally, I don't believe it; and even if it were true that otters kill more fish than they can possibly eat, they are amongst the few surviving British mammals, and it would be a thousand pities if they were exterminated.

Paddy and a brother, however, fell into the hands of a kind mistress, who attempted to bring them up on the bottle. The brother died, but Paddy survived and grew into a playful and affectionate pet, as tricksome and wilful and a good deal more intelligent than a puppy. He was allowed to wander all over the house, and was as much at ease in the drawing-room as in the kitchen. At night, however, he was put into a large outdoor aviary.

As a tiny baby—some 14 inches long, quite blind and helpless—he was fed with milk; he soon began to recognize the kind hands that fed him and fondled him, and would give a low whine of comfort when stroked; whilst, like many another baby, he uttered screaming whistles when hungry.

So fond was he of the bottle that, when he grew older, it was with difficulty that he could be "weaned," and at first juicy pieces of pike had to be forced into his mouth before he could be got to appreciate solid food.

A fortnight after his arrival he was eating fish and drinking from a saucer; every day he had a warm bath, with some Condy's fluid added, and wouldn't he cry if it was not warm enough! He would follow his mistress wherever she went, get under her dress to hide, roll like a puppy on the rug in front of the fire, and love to be rubbed and romped with.

He must be full grown, or nearly, now, but he is as tame as ever. He sleeps in the aviary; but when any one comes to the door he sits up and puts his hands together, exactly as if he were praying, and moves them up and down with an unmistakable meaning. The moment the door is opened out he bolts, and disappears for a run in the shrubbery or rushes to his mistress to seize her dress and worry it like a dog. He gets a pound of cod every day for his staple diet, and as much more of any other sort of fish as he can get. He loves eels ; but his tit-bit is the roe of a jack.

In the house he is a delightful pet, always ready for a romp, but curiously silent in all his movements ; in fact, whether indoors or out, when free his silence is a noticeable characteristic. Yet he possesses three distinct cries. When hungry or lonely (the latter when he thinks he has got lost in the grounds of his mistress's home) he utters a plaintive whistle ; when perfectly happy and at ease he coos—in fact, when thus speaking he most perfectly fulfils Bottom's intentions and " roars you as gently as any sucking dove " ; and, thirdly, when he is angry or in pain, my word ! he yowls like a tomcat on a roof.

His delight indoors is to indulge in a wild game round the furniture—the rougher it is the better. You cannot hurt him; his skin and skull are too thick to suffer from the knocks and concussions gained by falling over stools and colliding with table legs, or being violently thwarted when he makes a ferocious assault upon you. And all this " rough and tumble " exercise is indulged in without a sound.

Out of doors, almost every day, he accompanies his mistress down to the river. A long flight of steps leads downhill to the water, but Paddy takes care not to descend by them. He prefers the smooth grassy bank by their side. And he likes to toboggan down the slope on his tummy, his hind-legs stretched out behind him. This is a very interesting feat, for on certain rivers with high banks there are often noticeable " slides " to be found, down which it is said the wild otters slip into the water.

Paddy loves the river, although at first in his younger days he was strangely afraid of it. He slips into it, noiselessly and smoothly—no splashing or disturbance. As he dives he puts his ears back close against his head, and so wonderfully arranged is the inner mechanism that the action of laying back the ear closes an internal flap, which entirely prevents water from entering.

It is a wonderful sight to see him in the water. There is nothing to trace him by, and you wonder where he has got to until you catch sight of his smooth sleek head silently but actively examining into the contents of a mass of floating weed and driftage. Watch him swimming under water, a dark brown streak, moving with almost incredible swiftness, and you think at once of a living submarine, so straight is his body and so relentless his speed.

You can see him investigating at the bottom of the river amidst the roots of the waterweed until he needs to take a breath, when up he comes to the surface, plunging in and out exactly as you may see a porpoise alongside a steamer in the Channel.

Then he hunts the banks, head alone out of the water, searching for a possible frog or rat ; or he will fetch a stick or a ball thrown into the water by his mistress and retrieve it.

It is not often that he gets a fish from the river, but he knows of a pond hard by where, if he can outdistance his keeper, he may get a meal. Like another otter I knew, he dodges his mistress, and will play a regular game of peep-bo in the effort to slip round her to the pond he seeks.

He plays with a live fish as a cat with a mouse, and is quite capable of holding two at a time, one in his mouth and the other between his forepaws and his chest. On days when he cannot get to the river he is content with a tank which is nearer home; and here, as the photograph shows, he enjoys himself under the tap or indulging in make-believe fishing with a ball.

Then, when the bath is over, he accompanies us for a walk. Generally he keeps quite close to his mistress, paddling along at a good trotting pace on his short legs ; but occasionally he dives into the bushes or under the laurels for a momentary hunt.

He is wonderfully obedient, and comes readily at call ; he hates coming home, and yet, when the door is opened, it is but seldom that he has to be picked up and placed inside his cage ; with that silence which is his marked feature, though at this moment wistful and pathetic, he looks at his mistress, finds her adamant, and quietly leaps the threshold to his prison for the night.

He has wonderful fur, very thick and very loose—you may pick him up anywhere by it and find him, as it were, loose inside. When he emerges from the water he looks very wet and draggled, but within a few minutes the fur is perfectly dry again. He has no objection to being handled, though he may pretend to bite ; in fact, his tail makes a convenient handle, and he offers no objection to being swung by it.

So far he has shown no signs of desiring to return to the wild, but we wonder sometimes whether the day will come when Paddy will hear that irresistible call of Nature, and dive into the river, never to come back.

No. 2. VICKY, THE FOX.

I confess that to me the most eerie and weird of all the sounds of wild life in England is the cry of the fox at night. The owls' voices are creepy enough in the distance, and horribly disturbing if close to, and the " churr " of the nightjar is strange and bewildering; but these are birds, not beasts; and of the latter the fox is practically the only wild animal to be heard at night, and he only raises his voice during the spring. I shall never forget the thrill that passed deliciously through me when, as a town-bred boy, I went to stay at a farm in the country, and the very first night, as we stood in the dark at the door, there came to us across the hills the solitary barking of a fox. Akin, in imagination, to the howls of wolves or hyenas in foreign lands, the sound never ceases to bring home to me the joyous thought that in spite of modern civilization there is still some real wild life left in this old England of ours.

I notice that books say that the fox does not howl, and beyond a subdued whine, has no other note but the short bark ; but I have heard a fox howl at close quarters in much the same manner as a chained dog at night. The fox was my quondam friend Vicky.

Vicky's mother had the effrontery to enlarge a rabbit burrow in a private ground close to the garden, not a hundred yards away from the house. The result was inevitable. The burrow was opened and four tiny cubs were found. Three of them were sent to other parts of the country to be turned down there, when old enough ; but Vicky was begged from the owner for a pet.

I do not know how old he was when he became a member of the household, but certainly not more than a few days; for he was still blind, and fox cubs do not open their eyes till the tenth day. For two or three weeks he had to be fed with

VICKY, THE FOX

milk, for he would have been suckled in the ordinary way for that time. Then gradually, and with some difficulty, he had to be introduced to his regular diet, which came to consist at last of rabbits as his chief article of food, though he did not draw the line at other flesh when he came across it. Rats and mice, frogs, even beetles and grubs, never came amiss, and what he would have enjoyed more than anything, had he been allowed, was a nice ripe piece of carrion!

Vicky speedily became very tame, though he always preferred the society of ladies to that of gentlemen. As a cub he was a delightful ball of greyish-brown fur, with no particular markings; but as he grew up the fur darkened to a warmer tint—from yellow-brown to red on his back and sides, shading off to white beneath. Black nose, black feet, black ears, and a tail tipped with white made up his full grown-up costume.

He often uttered a curious little whine when a baby, but at play gave vent to a series of little sharp barks like a puppy. He was absolutely bursting with life and energy, and gloried in the maddest, most frolicsome games with his two-legged friends.

He had the run of the house, and used to play hide-and-seek in and out of the rooms, through the hall, to the umbrella stand, where he would hide himself behind the thick undergrowth of "mushes" and sticks. When hunted out of that, he would dash back, perhaps to the drawing-room, where he would take flying leaps over chairs and stools and occasional tables. By the side of the fireplace there used to be a foot-warmer made of the skin of a fox, and to Vicky this was a hateful rival and a deadly foe. Sometimes he would stalk it from the shelter of the fender, and then leap upon it with what answers in baby-fox language for a ferocious roar; at other times he would worry it savagely, shaking it as a terrier does a rat until its weight overbalanced him and he toppled headlong into it.

Unfortunately, though he was kept spotlessly clean, it was impossible to keep him free from smell! That scent gland, which he possessed in common with so many of his family, was so often in evidence, especially when he was excited, that he had to be kept out of doors on a light chain, and only allowed within as a special treat.

So tame was he, however, that whenever he could sneak indoors unobserved he did so. He had plenty of exercise in the grounds of his owner's house, where he would enjoy a mad rush from tree to tree and back again, in accordance with the laws of young foxes' sport, which is to make a track between two chosen points and have innumerable races and chases to and fro. He hunted a ball with intense enjoyment, but his favourite toy was a highly smelly rabbit skin, which he would mouth and shake and toss madly in the air.

His special treat was to be taken to a neighbouring warren and let go. Here he simply revelled in diving as far as he could into one hole after another, chasing imaginary rabbits and very occasionally real ones. Of this recreation he never tired; if one hole appeared empty, he would emerge backwards, shake himself and plunge into the next one. Then he would check himself, and sit up, contracting the pupil of the eye until it was a mere slit. Coming to the conclusion that it really was a rabbit he saw concealed in a distant tuft of grass, he would break into a headlong gallop for it, and repeat this manœuvre until he was so hot that his tongue would be lolling from his mouth.

Such was Vicky, the fox, when loose. When he was picked up and petted, he would cock his head on one side with ears erect, and a most knowing air, and playfully snap at the tickling fingers. He grew in twelve months into a large and handsome creature, in the best of condition; but when the following spring came round, though he was as tame as ever, there were signs of increasing restlessness. At night, in his big caged-in kennel, he would sit with ears erect, listening, listening, listening, with low wistful whines, breaking into a sharp " Yep, yep, yip," repeated again and again. If you listened attentively, you might hear far off an answering or challenging reply. The sequel is inevitable. One morning, put out on a long chain for exercise on the lawn, the yearning for the Wild proved too much for him. The length of his chain was found, the link close to his collar snapped. He was hunted for and called in vain. A report reached the searchers that a handsome fox had been seen careering through a garden half a mile away, on the way to the open country.

That was the last time Vicky was seen and recognized. Doubtless he found his way to the woods, whence the call of the siren had come. Doubtless he found his mate. May they long escape the hounds!

No. 3. JOEEE, THE STARLING.

I have written more than one article from time to time about starlings; but this time my pen is to tell the story of one with whom (I refuse to write " which," for he had a personality that was rich and varied) I was on most intimate terms a year or two ago.

Next to the sparrow, the starling ranks as the most ubiquitous and mischievous of garden birds. He is often an alien, too, who arrives in company with thousands of his fellows every year; but a large number remain in England all the year round. There is, and I must add deservedly, no close season for him in the garden, where he is a wastrel and a robber. He belongs to the " submerged tenth," except that he will not stay submerged. The gardener wages incessant war upon him; he is an Ishmael, or ought to be, and yet he is one of the most lovable of birds, and I do not hesitate to say that of many birds which I have kept as pets I know none for which I have a tenderer memory than for Joeee.

I would rather, I think, lose a good many other of our British birds than the starling; for whilst others sing for the few months of spring, the starling is ready to give his celebrated performance as a mimic all through the winter, so long as he has a chimney top to stand on and a gleam of sunlight to show off the gloss upon his wings. A happy-go-lucky, good-for-nothing, care-for-nobody sort of tramp, he holds his own against everybody (except Jack Sparrow, who easily beats him when it is a case of securing a building site), and he is, with all his ups and downs, the most cheerful of knaves. He will eat anything he can get; he pokes his beak into every hole and corner he comes across; he will place his untidy nest with the utmost impudence wherever he pleases. In this neighbourhood he sticks it in under the rooks' nests—a blatant piece of insolence, when you remember the dignity of the bird in black. He bathes in any sort of a bath he can find. My pigeons have their drinking bowl just outside my study window, but they do not get a drink until the starlings have been in it. A patch of water on my lawn unfortunately shows itself every spring, and the starlings make such a prodigious mess of it that there is a bare patch all the summer.

The starling is a dreadfully cheap bird, too; you can buy one for a few pence,

JOEEE, THE STARLING

freshly caught alas, and at a terrible reduction if you will buy a dozen. It is surprising to me that so few people know how whimsical and delightful a pet the starling makes in captivity. But I would rather have a starling any day than the finest blackbird or thrush, though I would not keep either of the latter in a cage at all. I am not suggesting that any reader should go and buy one of these wild-caught starlings, which is a miserably cruel thing to do; but if you get such a chance as I did to adopt a bird, take it, and you will agree that I have not exaggerated his points as a pet.

Joeee—so called because that is how he pronounced his own name, and if you don't know how to pronounce your own name, who does?—was born on the establishment in the early spring.

His parents were, for their class, a respectable couple, who came over from Russia and settled down in my garden. They speedily made acquaintance with my bird table, and soon learnt the trick of avoiding the black thread which was stretched round it and across it to keep off the sparrows.

I give them a good character, but their manners at table " was horrid." The moment the breakfast appeared they would plunge down and wolf as much as they could and spill the rest. They certainly dropped over the edge of the table quite as much as they ate. The sparrows quickly discovered this vulgar habit and scored off me, for the moment the starlings appeared on the table a plague of sparrows would fly down underneath it, knowing that in a minute or two those aliens up above, whom they despised, would scatter as much food as they wanted over the edge, and so provide them with a meal easily, in spite of my precautions with black thread.

They were the first inhabitants of " Starling Castle," which hangs just in reach of my bedroom window. The sparrows did their best to oust them afterwards, but in vain. The starlings took possession of it with their usual disregard of its nearness to a human being's room, whilst the sparrows shrank from such proximity. It was not until the starlings were well established, and had begun building, that the sparrows came to the conclusion that the castle was safe enough, or that I was tame enough, and made determined efforts, night after night, to eject the Russians !

My only way of retaining the starlings was to fight their battles for them, but I draw a veil over the proceedings. Suffice it to say the starlings settled down, and made themselves perfectly at home. Morning after morning I heard the gentleman singing, shouting, whistling, calling, going through all the varied items of his repertoire, from the cry of the plover, which every starling seems to pick up, down to a note or two of the canaries, which are in an outdoor aviary close by.

During the very early days of their courtship at least one rival lover turned up ; this usually happened about five o'clock in the morning, when I was awakened by the awful ructions taking place outside. A small perch served as approach to the castle door, and the gentlemen threw one another off the step repeatedly, until one of them tired of the game and went off till evening, when he generally returned for another bout. However, I presume that victory went to the strongest, the course of true love eventually ran smooth, the eggs were laid and duly hatched.

It was then that fate stepped in and secured me my pet. Hunger, not unmixed with greed, may have been the reason why one of the children toppled head foremost out of the door. I rather incline, however, to think that an owl had something to do with it, for it is an interesting fact, which I have noted often, that the owls of the neighbourhood come hunting round my starlings' boxes regularly at night. Whatever the cause, there was Joeee, a mass of quills and temper (not unmixed with fear), on the ground before breakfast. And a broken leg; which was a sufficiently good reason for some one to play the part of good Samaritan and take him in, though he cost me a good deal more than twopence. After sulking for a day, he got accustomed to being fed on fine chopped meat, powdered dog biscuit, egg, and bread crumbs. His chief taste was for mealworms; and the number he could eat at a time was astonishing. At 1s. 6d. a thousand, they added to his bulk and his expense. But there was no denying him; the moment I entered the room he screamed for mealworms, and when he grew well enough to fly he would make a dash for the pickle bottle in which they were kept and dive in head foremost amongst them. He had to be pulled out backwards, swearing and kicking, with his mouth full.

He grew into a fine bird, in exquisite plumage, with a gorgeous metallic sheen. He started practising his programme of imitations very early, and learnt to say " Joeee " plainly enough, though I had no leisure to teach him any other words.

He lived in a large cage in my study; and when I was at work at my typewriter he would sing his loudest and imitate the clicking as best he could, with a curious little chuckle for the bell at the end of each line. He was most exceeding alert, noticing every strange sound; the clock striking always set him off, and if a stranger knocked at the hall door or spoke outside, he would give an alarm at once, exactly like a watch dog, but without the bark.

Every morning he came out of his cage, took a flight round the room, and settled for a song on exactly the same book in the same corner of the bookshelf. Whether the width of it fitted his feet I don't know, but he never used any other book as his perch.

He would, at his own convenience, jump down on to my desk, poke about my papers, raising them by opening his beak; occasionally he found a mealworm amongst them. Then he would have a furious fight with my typewriter, pecking at the carriage as it travelled its length, backing away from it as it advanced, and then charging after it as I drew it back at the end of a line.

Tired of that, he would jump on my head and part my hair with his beak, exactly as you may see his relations doing to the grass. It was a most ticklish sensation, but nothing to compare with his thrusting his bill into one's ear or down one's collar.

The only way to get him back to his cage was to put a mealworm there. He would watch slyly and pretend he didn't care; he would stick to his seat on the bookshelf and sing lightheartedly to show his indifference, but all the same he could not resist the bait for long. He had uneasy fears about that mealworm getting into a crack or under the board in the cage. He would endure the torture for a moment, and at last with a scream would bolt home, gobble the mealworm, and try to get out again before he was shut in.

He had a bath every morning in a developing dish in front of the window, when he soaked himself to the skin, and became the most bedraggled rake of a bird you ever saw. At first, too drenched to be able to fly, he would sit in helplessness on the mat, then jump to my desk as a stepping-stone to his favourite book, leaving a smear of wet over my papers, added to by a vigorous shake, and then he would reach his perch and finish drying and preening himself there.

He was a merry scoundrel, full of tricks, and he would answer back as long as you cared to pretend to scold him. He thoroughly disliked any other persons in

MR. SPINES, THE HEDGEHOG 477

the room, but his master he regarded as an inexhaustible supplier of endless mealworms. He occasionally went out-of-doors on his master's hand or head. So long as mealworms—excuse the repetition of the word, it is unavoidable in this connection—were obtainable, he never wanted to fly away. In fact, I never gave him the chance. He would call to me when I came home from work—" Joeee-Joeee-Joeee," and would not be silenced until he got the inevitable larva of *Tenebris molitor* (avoided it that time !).

So the years passed in uncommonly happy companionship until one morning, without any warning, I found him dead in his cage. It certainly wasn't old age; it wasn't fat. I couldn't account for it. Perhaps it was those m-lw-ms after all !

No. 4. MR. SPINES, THE HEDGEHOG.

I wonder how Shakespeare knew that hedgehogs whine ? He certainly was correct in saying so, when he puts into the mouth of one of his witches in *Macbeth* the words " Thrice and once the hedgepig whined." But I expect that only a very few out of the thousands of people who have seen hedgehogs alive have ever heard them utter a sound. The fact is that the few wild mammals which we possess are almost all of them nocturnal in their habits, and therefore very silent creatures. But the hedgehogs which I have kept as pets have made themselves audible when necessary, and have shown that they can not only whine, but also utter a hoarser cry, more like a squeak than a whine ; whilst they could also emit a much softer and lower note when they were happy and comfortable. I am told that they squeal loudly when in pain, as for instance when caught in a trap ; but I am glad to say I have never heard one under such circumstances.

They make rather interesting pets, and have a droll dignity which is all their own. They can travel at a much faster pace than would be supposed ; but their habit of seeking protection, not in flight but in rolling themselves up into a ball, and playing " possum," lends colour to the impression that they are but slow walkers.

Spines, my hedgehog friend of whom I write, took a long time to uncurl himself, and a still longer time to set off on his travels round my room ; but when he was thoroughly at ease he certainly " trotted."

What is more, he could climb. I kept him first in a large open box, with sides at least two feet high ; but he was outside the box the next morning, and asleep under my bookcase in a dark corner. I put him back, and later on in his career I saw him climb out. He stood up on his hind-legs at the corner, and, with a little jerk, clung to the roughnesses of the wood. He slipped back two or three times before he managed to get a front paw on the top edge ; but once there, he was quickly over.

Spines came to me one springtime, when the boys of the village were constantly bringing me things to photograph. He came in a fish basket, and I promised to take his picture. The boy left him, basket and all, on my study table, and I went out of the room to get my camera and plates. I did not want to keep the creature, and thought it best to fulfil my promise as soon as possible, and turn the hedgehog loose. However, I was longer about my task than I expected, and when I returned to the room the basket was on the floor, and Spines was seated on the hearthrug in front of the fire, perfectly at his ease, and enjoying the warmth. There had been two other creatures in that fortunate position—my dog and a cat. Spines had evidently ousted them both, or had pushed his way between them with such prickly persuasiveness that they had left him in peace. At any rate, there he was, and the cat's dignity was badly hurt, whilst Tiny (the dog) was furious.

I put Spines back in the basket on the table, and sat down to watch what would happen. In a minute or two the basket began to wobble and contort itself, and finally turned over and fell to the floor. Spines emerged with slow and jerky steps, rolled across the room, and sat down on the rug again.

After that I thought he showed such character, to say nothing of a real appreciation of home comforts, that I decided to keep him, and he was duly introduced to the household by his name of Mr. Spines.

He lived with me quite a long time, and became perfectly tame. I cannot say that he was a very cleanly pet; as a matter of fact he had no manners; but if you must keep such creatures about your study you must take the consequences.

He was also infested with vermin, as most hedgehogs are; but I took care that he should be kept decently clean, and should have his bath regularly. It was not difficult to rid him of his numerous undesirable guests, and I believe Spines came to appreciate the water on that account. At least he enjoyed sitting in his bath and letting "the water free curl through the twisted roots." He did not like the water too deep, though he could swim remarkably well if he had to, when he looked very much like a water-rat, lying strangely flat upon the water, with little but his snout out—very different from his usual hump-backed appearance on dry ground.

I did not allow Spines to find his own meals by eating all the black beetles—that is, cockroaches—he could catch in my kitchen; but I have, before now, heard of people who thought that this was all that was necessary in providing for their little scavenger. Some years ago I was actually asked why a domestic hedgehog had died. I had to point out that a kitchen full of cockroaches was hardly a nourishing diet for *Erinaceus europæus* (you must talk learnedly with some people!), and that their specimen had died simply of starvation.

Mr. Spines shared his meals with us, for he had an omnivorous appetite, and ate anything in the way of scraps and cooked vegetables. He was not therefore a difficult pet to keep, and I added a saucer of bread and milk, to which he was very partial. When I brought the saucer into the room after breakfast and tapped upon the edge, Spines would emerge from his corner—always the same corner, under the bookcase (I never knew him give that up, except on the night when my badger—but that is another story)—and would drink out of the saucer whilst I held it. Sometimes he would rear himself up on his short hind-legs, looking not unlike a thorny cat, and put his front feet in the milk (he was an untidy feeder).

He would also eat any kind of insect, spiders, snails, and worms. I have no doubt that he would have tackled frogs; but I did not provide him with any nor with eggs, though in a wild state hedgehogs are said to be fond of them.

It was rather horrible to see him eat a worm, for it took some time, and was slowly crunched from one end to the other before being chewed and swallowed.

I had read some interesting accounts of the way in which the hedgehog is said to attack adders and kill them, much after the way of the immortal Rikki-tikki-tavi, and when a dead grass snake came into my possession I tried it on Spines. At first he took no notice; but when I pretended to make it dart at him he rolled himself up in a ball, and then, waiting till the supposed living snake was still, made a startling, sudden spring upon it. After that I saw him play with it, almost as a cat does with a mouse, darting upon it, retiring, playing possum, seizing it again in his teeth, until he tired of it and went rolling back to his bed.

Spines enjoyed being stroked. It may seem a rather difficult task to stroke a hedgehog without painful results; but I used a small stick, and Spines would stretch himself out to get the full enjoyment of my rasping; or he would ask to be rubbed with one's boot, and I have often sat in front of the fire with the funny creature stretched out in front of me, enjoying the warmth on one side and the toe of my boot on the other. He had also a taste for blacking, and occasionally would come out whilst I was at work at my desk and lick my boots.

He would amble off into the garden, when allowed, and lose himself; but I generally found him easily the next morning by means of my saucer, for he would come out of his hiding-place at the sound of its clicking.

The next-door neighbour's dog met him in the early stages of our acquaintance and did his best to kill him. Spines rolled himself up and didn't budge. I heard a most fearful commotion and went out to see what was the matter. Spines had lost a great many of his prickles, and the dog had a *cheval-de-frise* all round his nose and mouth, and was very considerably astonished.

As my hedgehog got more familiar, he used to go down into a little conservatory and bask there in the heat. And Plate I. shows him in that attitude. I fancy this must be almost a unique picture of a living hedgehog, lying on his side, with eyes half shut, and little paws almost pathetically held out. But in that attitude he would lie for a long time, and allow himself to be tickled underneath. He was an "amusin' little cuss," as Artemus Ward puts it, and I was very sorry when some stupid person left my garden door open one day and Spines did not respond to the chinking of his saucer.

One thing I learnt from him which I shall not forget. He could bite, upon occasion !

No. 5. " YOUNG WISDOM," THE LITTLE OWL.

The little owl (*Athene noctua noctua*) has been reintroduced into this country of recent years, and has settled down with a vengeance ; for already complaints have been heard of its depredations amongst young pheasants and partridges on one hand, and many of the smaller birds on the other. The bird must, however, do an immense amount of good in its way, as generally its food consists of grasshoppers, chafers, and other insects. I have dissected a good many of its castings, and found large quantities of the wing-cases of beetles predominating.

An enterprising Nature student in my neighbourhood introduced two pairs of these birds some years ago, and I have no doubt that it was in consequence of his action that one spring morning a breathless boy arrived at my door with news of a strange " crittur with glittering eyes," that had been heard in an empty house not a hundred yards away, and was now " looking out o' the winder."

Needless to say, I followed him to the scene, and found, sure enough, a tiny heap staring out of a bedroom window. We went round the house, and I played successfully the part of a burglar, and forced a window (I hope the landlord won't see this). It was thus that I found Wisdom, a diminutive bird, 9 inches long when full grown, with pale yellow eyes. If Truth gets to the bottom of the well,

Wisdom had evidently come down the chimney, for he was uncommonly sooty and rather cross.

We called him Young Wisdom, because first, he was only just able to fly, and second, he was so small that even when full grown he looked a babe compared with the old barn-owl which was also residing with me at the time. The name, however, was not so far-fetched, for I believe this was the owl that was the sacred bird of the ancient Greeks, and was engraved on their coins as the emblem of Pallas Athene. Not that he showed any preternatural wisdom or even the semblance of it which the larger owls attain to in the gravity of their demeanour. But he made a very amusing pet, and grew quite tame. It is not every owl which you could carry through the street on your finger to the nearest photographer to be photographed in his studio. There I got the photographer to rig up a perch for him, but he refused to sit on it, and insisted on flying to my shoulder or hand. He lived in a fair-sized aviary out-of-doors, and it was noteworthy that he was much more awake by day than his neighbour. The little owl hunts regularly in the daylight, and is much less nocturnal than his bigger cousins. He learnt to associate my approach with the gift of beetles—chiefly the result of those mealworms to which a previous article alludes—and when I arrived he would begin " bobbing " in the most absurd way until he had been satisfied. He did not object to the most unsavoury of beetles of other species, and if it was a very large one would hold it in his claw and enjoy it in pieces. In addition, he lived on mice, and when the supply failed, on small pieces of raw meat.

He had a large basin of water within reach, and though I never saw him I am sure he used to bathe ; and on one occasion I put some minnows into it, in the hope that he would repeat the antics of another owl I once had, which would go in head first after fish. However, Young Wisdom would not enter the water in my presence ; but in my absence the minnows disappeared.

Circumstances made it necessary after a year for me to decrease my outdoor pets, and I turned the little owl out. Judge of my surprise when I found him perched on the top of the aviary two days afterwards waiting to be let in ! Naturally he got his way, and I kept him another month or so. Then I was forced to bid him farewell again, and this time I took him five miles away to a big wood and let him go there. He flew to the low branch of the nearest tree, " bobbed " at me, uttered his usual cry " Cu-cu-cu," and went off into the deeper part of the wood. This time he did not return.

INDEX.

N.B.—An asterisk prefixed to a page denotes that an illustration will be found on that page.

For Flowers see the Alphabetical Lists: English, pp. 437-441; Latin, 442-446.

ACORN BARNACLE, 166.
Acorn Shell, 166.
Adder, 145, Pl. XIII. 3.
Æsop Prawn, 167.
Agarics, 458-65.
Alder-flies, 189, 190.
   Common, 190.
Alevin, 156.
American Cockroach, 183.
Amœba, *329.
Amphibians, 147-9.
   Characteristics, 147.
   In captivity, 149.
Anchovy, 161.
Angular Crab, 170, Pl. XIV. 3.
Animal, definition, 21.
Animalcula, 164, 328, *329, *330.
Animalcule, Barrel, *330.
   Slipper, 329.
   Swan, 329, *330.
Animal Kingdom, 4.
Annelida, 164, 319-21, Pl. XL.
Antlers, Deer's, 47-9.
Ants, 291-5, Pl. XXXIII., XXXIV.
   Artificial Nests, 295.
   Life-history, 293-5.
   Nests, 291-5, Pl. XXXIV.
   Black, 291, Pl. XXXIV.
   Blood-red Robber, 291.
   Common Wood, 291, 295, Pl. XXXIII. 4.
   Common Yellow, 292.
   Jet, 292.
   Little Black, 292.
   Little Yellow Robber, 293.
   Meadow, 294, Pl. XXXIII. 5.
   "Slave," 291.
   Stingless, 291.
   White, 185.

Aphides, 188, 189, 295, Pl. XIX. 4.
Apparatus, 6-17.
Arctic Skua, *131, 138.
Arctic Tern, *117, 124.
Aristotle, Lantern of, 317.
Artemis, Rayed, 313.
   Smooth, 313.
Arthropoda, 164-299, Pl. XIII.-XXXVI.
Ascidians, *323, 324.
Auk, Little, 68.

Badger, Common, 35, Pl. III. 3.
Baggits, female Salmon, 156.
Ballard, 157.
Barbel, 151.
Bark-louse, 189.
Barnacle, Acorn, 166.
   Goose, 167.
Barnacle Goose, *131, 132.
Barn Owl, *115, 120.
Bar-tailed Godwit, 114.
Bass, 153, 157.
Basse, 157.
Bat, Barbastelle, 30, 32.
   Bechstein's, 31.
   Common, 31.
   Daubenton's, 31.
   Great, 31.
   Greater Horseshoe, 32.
   Hairy-armed, 31.
   Lesser Horseshoe, 32.
   Long-eared, 32, Pl. II. 2.
   Noctule, 31.
   Pipistrelle, 31.
   Reddish Grey, 31.
   Serotine, 31.
   Short-eared, Pl. IV. 1.
   Whiskered, 32.

Bats, 30-2, Pl. II. 2, IV. 1, 2.
Beam Bird, 75.
Bean Goose, 132.
Bearded Reedling, 89.
Bearded Tit, 89.
Beavers, 40.
Bed-bug, 187.
Bees, 297-9, Pl. XXXII., XXXIII., XXXV.
   Observing hive, *299.
   Bumble, 297.
   Carder, 298.
   Common Humble, 298.
   Cuckoo Humble, 297.
   "English Hive Bee," 299.
   Hive Bee, 298, Pl. XXXV. 2.
   Honey Bee, 298.
   Humble, 297, 298, Pl. XXXIII. 2, XXXV. 4.
   Leaf-cutting, 297, Pl. XXXII. 6, 7.
   Mason, 297, Pl. XXXV. 1.
   Moss, 297.
   Red-backed, 298.
   Solitary, 297.
   Wasp, 297.
   Wood-boring, 297.
Bees, shown to the Children, 299.
Beetle, Black, 183.
Beetles, 191-217, Pl. XX.-XXIV., XXXVI. 4.
   Characteristics, 191-3.
   Classification, 192.
   Collecting, 191, 192.
   Diagram, *181.
   Life-history, 192.
Asparagus, 212.
Bacon, 205.
Black, 183.
Black Burying, 202.

INDEX

Beetles—*continued*.
Black Skipjack, 208.
Bloody-nosed, 212.
Bombardier, 196.
Burying, 202.
Carnivorous Ground, 193–7.
Carnivorous Water, 197, 198.
Chafers, 206.
Churchyard, 214.
Click, 208, 209.
Clock, 207.
Cockchafers, 207.
Cocktail, 200.
Common Cockchafer, 207.
Common Dor, 207.
Death Watches, 210.
Devil's Coach-horse, 200.
Dumbledor, 207.
Flea-beetles, 213.
Four-spot Carrion, 203.
Glow-worm, 193, 209, Pl. XXXVI. 4.
Great Water, 199.
Green Tiger, 193.
Ground, 193–7.
Lady-birds, 204.
Leaf-horned, 205.
May-bug, 207.
Mealworm, 214.
Musk, 211.
Oil, 214.
Pill, 205.
Pine Weevil, 216.
Plant-eaters, 211–13.
Reddish Skipjack, 209.
Red Rose, 200.
Rose, 208.
Rove, 200.
Sexton, 202.
Small Dung, 206.
Small Tiger, 193.
Soft-skinned, 209, 210.
"Soldiers and Sailors," 209, 210.
Stag, 192, 206, Pl. XX.
Tiger, 193.
Tortoise, 213.
Turnip-blossom, 203.
Two-spot Ladybird, 204.
Violet Ground, 194.
Violet Oil, 214.
Watchman, 207.
Weevils, 215–17.
Whirligig, 199.
Wood Tiger, 193.
Bell Animalcules, *329.
Beröe, 323.
Bewick, 138.

Bib, 158.
Bible, 1–5.
Genesis i., 1.
2 Kings xix., 46.
1 Samuel vi., 46.
Bird-lice, 185.
Birds, 50–142, Pl. VII.–IX.
About size of Blackbird, 67 *101, 99–112.
About size of Rook and larger, 67, *129, *131, 126–39.
About size of Sparrow, 66, *69, *71, *73, 68–98.
About size of Wood Pigeon, 67, *115, *117, 112–26.
Beaks and Bills, *53.
Characteristics, 51.
Classification, 55, 59–66.
Eggs, 51, 52, 140–2, Pl. X., XI.
Feeding, 139, 140.
Guide to identification, 59, 66, 67.
How to attract, 139.
How to skin, 54.
Irregular visitors, 58.
Latin names, 59–66.
Migration, 55–8.
Nests, 51, 52, 139–42, Pl. IX.
Observation, 58.
"Passers-by," 58.
Preservation, 54.
Residents, 56.
Summer visitors, 57.
Terms illustrated, *50.
Winter visitors, 57.
Bird table, 139.
Bittern, 135.
Little, 135.
Black-backed Gull, Great, 134.
Lesser, *129, 134.
Black Beetle, 183.
Blackbird, 99, Pl. IX. 3.
Blackcap, *68, *69.
Blackcock, 133.
Black Cormorant, 126.
Black Duck, 137.
Black Fish, 24.
Blackgame, 133.
Black Goby, 162.
Black Grouse, *129, 133.
Black Guillemot, 102.
Black-headed Gull, *117, 118.
Black-necked Grebe, 133.
Black Redstart, 84.
Black-tailed Godwit, 116.
Black Tern, 110.
Black-throated Diver, 127.
Blackwall on Spiders, 177.
Bladder-worm, 321.

Bleak, 153.
Blenny, Smooth, 162.
Blight, 188.
Blind-worm, 143, 144, Pl. XII. 3.
Blue Tit, 89.
Board of Agriculture and Fisheries book on Fungi, 456.
Bonxie, 138.
Book-lice, 185.
Bot-flies, 288.
Bottle-nose, 122.
Bottle Tit, 91.
Brambling, 68.
Brandlings, 156.
Brand-worm, 319.
Brassy, 158.
Bream, 153.
Sea, 157.
White, 153.
Brent Goose, *131, 132.
Brine Shrimp, 167.
Bristle-tails, 182.
Bristle Worms, 319, 320.
Marine, 319, 320, Pl. XL.
British Beetles, 217.
British Bird Book, 58, 66.
British Coal Tit, *71, 90.
British Spiders, 177.
Broad-claw Crab, 170.
Brown Linnet, 77.
Brown Owl, 121.
Brown Scale, 189.
Bryophyta, 333, 453–5.
Buffon's Skua, 138.
Bug, Harvest, 179.
Bugs, 186–8.
Bullfinch, 68, *69.
Bullhead, 154.
Bull Trout, 156.
Bunting, Cirl, 70.
Corn, *69, 70.
Reed, *69, 70.
Snow, 70.
Yellow, *69, 70.
Butcher Bird, 84.
Butter Fish, 162.
Butterflies, 218–37, Pl. XXV.–XXIX.
Breeding, 221, 222.
Caterpillar, 218, 219.
Characteristics, 218.
Collecting, 220, 221.
Eggs, 218.
Larvæ, 218–37, Pl. XXVII., XXVIII.
Pupæ, 219–37, Pl. XXVII.–XXIX.
Rearing cages, *222, 223.
Setting board, *221.

INDEX

Butterflies—*continued*.
Adonis Blue, 234.
Artaxerxes, 234.
Bath White, 225.
Bedford Blue, 235.
Black Hair-streak, 233, Pl. XXVII. 1, XXVIII. 2.
Black-veined White, 225.
Brimstone, 220, 226.
Brown Argus, 234, Pl. XXV. 11.
Brown Hair-streak, 232.
Camberwell Beauty, 228, Pl. XXVI. 2.
Chalk Hill Blue, 234, Pl. XXV. 15.
Chequered Skipper, 237.
Clifton Blue, Pl. XXV. 12.
Clouded Yellow, 226, Pl. XXV. 16.
Comma, 227.
Common Blue, 234.
Dark-green Fritillary, 229.
Dingy Skipper, 236, Pl. XXV. 20.
Duke of Burgundy Fritillary, 235.
Essex Skipper, 236.
Gatekeeper, 232.
Glanville Fritillary, 230.
Grayling, 231.
Green Hair-streak, 233, Pl. XXV. 10.
Green-veined White, 225.
Grizzled Skipper, 236, Pl. XXV. 21.
Heath Fritillary, 230.
High-brown Fritillary, 229.
Holly Blue, 234, Pl. XXIX. 1.
Large Blue, 235.
Large Copper, 218, 233.
Large Heath, 232, Pl. XXV. 6.
Large Skipper, 237, Pl. XXV. 18.
Large Tortoise-shell, 227.
Large White, 225.
Little Blue, 235, Pl. XXV. 14.
Long-tailed Blue, 233.
Lulworth Skipper, 236.
Marbled White, 230, Pl. XXV. 3.
Marsh Fritillary, 230.
Mazarine Blue, 235.
Meadow Brown, 231.
Milkweed, 230.
Monarch, 230.
Orange-tip, 225, Pl. XXV. 22, 23, XXIX. 3, 4.
Painted Lady, 228, Pl. XXV. 8.
Pale Clouded Yellow, 226, Pl. XXV. 17.

Butterflies—*continued*.
Peacock, 220, 228, Pl. XXVII. 3.
Pearl-bordered Fritillary, 229, Pl. XXV. 2.
Pearl-bordered Likeness, 230.
Purple Emperor, 227, Pl. XXVIII. 1.
Purple Hair-streak, 233, Pl. XXV. 9.
Queen of Spain Fritillary, 229.
Red Admiral, 228.
Ringlet, 232.
Scotch Argus, 231.
Short-tailed Blue, 234.
Silver-spotted Skipper, 237.
Silver-studded Blue, 234.
Silver-washed Fritillary, 228, Pl. XXV. 1.
Small Blue, 235.
Small Copper, 233.
Small Garden White, Pl. XXVI. 4.
Small Heath, 232, Pl. XXV. 7.
Small Mountain Ringlet, 231.
Small Pearl-bordered Fritillary, 230.
Small Skipper, 236, Pl. XXV. 19.
Small Tortoise-shell, 220, 228.
Small White, 225.
Speckled Wood, 231, Pl. XXV. 5.
Swallow-tail, 224, Pl. XXV. 13, XXVII. 4, XXXI. 3.
Wall Butterfly, 231, Pl. XXV. 4.
White Admiral, 227.
White Letter Hair-streak, 233.
Woodwhite, 226.
Butterflies, and how to identify Them, 224.
Butterflies and Moths of the United Kingdom, 239.
Buzzard, 126, Pl. VIII. 3.
Rough-legged, 126.

Cachalot, 25.
Caddis-flies, 217.
Caddis-worms, Pl. XXXII. 1.
Cadzow " herd," 49.
Calamary, 303.
Camera, A simple Nature, 12.
Construction (Figs. 9–18), 13–16.
Uses, 17, 51, 52, 59, 334.
Capercaillie, 126.
Carp, 151.
Crucian, 151.
Golden, 151.
Carpet Shells, 313.
Carrion Crow, 127, *131.
Cat, Wild, 38.

Caterpillars, 218, 219, *240, *244, *246, *248.
Cattle, Wild, 49.
Centipede, Red, 180.
Centipedes, 180.
Chad, 157.
Chafers, 206.
Chaffinch, *69, 72.
Charr, 156.
Chaucer, 41.
Cheese Mite, 179.
Chiffchaff, 72.
Chillingham Cattle, 49.
Chiton, 309, Pl. XXXVII. 9.
Chough, 112.
Chub, 152.
Cirl Bunting, 70.
Click Beetle, 180.
Cloaklet Anemone, 170.
Club-mosses, 451, 452.
Wolf's Claw, 451, 452.
Coal Tit, British, *71, 90.
Irish, 90.
Cobbler, Horny, 163.
Cockchafers, 207.
Cockle, 311, Pl. XXXVIII. 18.
Spiny, 311.
Cockroach, American, 183.
German, 183.
Cockroaches, 183, Pl. XIX. 1, 2, XX. 2.
Cod, 158.
Cœlenterata, 164, 322–6, Pl. XIV., XXXVII.
Comb Shell, 313.
Common Curlew, 127, *131, Pl. VII. 1.
Common Eel, 155.
Common Eider, 130, *131.
Common Frog, 147.
Common Gull, 118, 134.
Common Heron, *129, 134.
Common Limpet, 308.
Common Lizard, 143, Pl. XII. 1.
Common Lobster, 168.
Common Newt, 148.
Common Sandpiper, *101, 107.
Common Shelduck, *129.
Common Shore Crab, 169.
Common Skate, 161.
Common Snake, 145.
Common Snipe, 85, *86, *101, 108, Pl. VII. 2.
Common Sole, 160.
Common Tern, 124.
Common Toad, 148.
Common Trout, 156.
Conger Eel, 160.

INDEX

Coot, 112, *117.
Coralline, Creeping, 319.
  Foliaceous, 319.
  Sea Hair, 326.
  Sea Oak, 326.
  Squirrel's-tail, 326.
Corals, 325.
Corbie, 127.
Corixa, 187.
Cormorant, Black, 126.
  Great, 126.
  Green, 137.
Corn Bunting, *69, 70.
Corncrake, 99, *101.
Cornish Daw, 112.
Cornish Sucker, 163.
Corn Thrip, 186.
Cowry, 308, Pl. xxxvii. 8.
Crab, Angular, 170, Pl. xiv. 3.
  Broad-claw, 170.
  Common Shore, 169.
  Common Swimming, 169.
  Edible, 169.
  Four-horned Spider, 169.
  Green, 169.
  Hairy, 170.
  Hairy Porcelain, 170.
  Harbour, 169.
  Hermit, 170.
  Large Thorny Spider, 169.
  Masked, 169.
  Pea, 170.
  Slender Spider, 169.
  Velvet Fiddler, 169.
  Zebedee, 170.
Crabs, 168–70.
Crake, Spotted, 111.
Crane-flies, 287, Pl. xxxii. 3.
Crayfish, 166, Pl. xiii. 2.
Creation, Science and, 2–4.
Creeper, Tree-, 72, *73.
Crested Grebe, Great, *129, 133.
Crested Tit, 90.
Cricket, Field, 184.
  House, 184.
  Mole, 184.
  Wood, 184.
Crossbill, *69, 74.
Crow, Carrion, 127, *131.
  Hooded, 127, *129.
Crowned Eolis, 306.
Crucian Carp, 151.
Crustaceans, 164, *165–70, Pl. xiii. 2, xiv. 3.
Cuckoo, 112, *115.
Cuckoo's Mate, 98.
Cuckoo-spit Insect, 188, Pl. xix. 3.
Cuckoo-wasps, 291.

Cup-and-Saucer Limpet, 309, Pl. xxxvii. 15.
Curlew, Common, 127, *131, Pl. vii. 1.
Stone, 113, *117, Pl. viii. 1.
Currant Squirter, 324.
Cuttle-fish, *302, Pl. xiv. 4.
  Common, 302, Pl. xxxvii. 21.
  Eggs, 302, Pl. xxxvii. 20.
  Little, 303.
Cyclops, *165, 166.
Cypris, *165, 166.

Dab, 159.
Dabchick, *101, 102.
Dace, 152.
Daddy-longlegs, 287, Pl. xxxii. 3.
Dartford Warbler, *69, 92.
Darwin, C. R., 3, 319.
Daw, Cornish, 112.
  Red-legged, 112.
"Dead Man's Fingers," 325.
Deer, Fallow, *48, 49.
  Red, 47, Pl. vi. 2.
  Roe, 46, *47.
Demoiselle, 186.
Digger Wasps, 295, 296.
Dipper, *69, 74.
Diver, Black-throated, 127.
  Great Northern, 128, *129.
  Red-throated, 128.
Dog-fish, Lesser Spotted, 162.
  Picked, 161.
Dog Periwinkle, 308, Pl. xxxvii. 16.
Dolphin, Bottle-nosed, 25.
  Common, 24.
Dormouse, Common, *42.
Dotterel, 100.
Dove, Ring, 122.
  Rock, 114.
  Stock, 114.
  Turtle, 100, *101.
Drake, Green, 185.
  Grey, 185.
Dragon-flies, 185, 186.
Dragon-fly, Great, 186.
Duck, Black, 137.
  Long-tailed, 128, *129.
  Scaup, 128.
  Tufted, 114, *117.
  Wild, 128.
Dunlin, *69, 74.
Dunnock, 86.
Dutch rushes, 452.

Eagle, Golden, 130.
  White-tailed, 130.

Eared Grebe, 133.
Earthworm, 319.
Earwigs, 182.
Echinodermata, 164, 314–17, Pl. xxxix.
Edible Crab, 169.
Edible Frog, 148.
Eel, Common, 155.
  Conger, 160.
  Sand, 160.
Efts, 148.
Eggs, Amphibians', 147.
  Birds', 51, 52, 140–2, Pl. x., xi.
  How to blow, 52.
  Butterflies', 218.
  Cuttle's, 302, Pl. xxxvii. 20.
  Fishes', 150.
  Reptiles', 143.
  Sepia's, 302, Pl. xxxvii. 20.
  Whelk's, 307, Pl. xxxvii. 2.
Eider, Common, 130, *131.
Ellison Hawks, Bees, shown to the Children, 299.
Emmanuel College, Cambridge, fishponds, 151.
Eolis, Crowned, 306.
Eperlan, 161.
Ermine, 37.
Evolution, Creative, 5.
Evvats, 148.
Eyed Cribella, 315.

Falcon, Peregrine, 114, *115.
Father Lasher, 154, 163.
Fern-owl, 103.
Ferns, 447–51.
  Characteristics, 447, 448.
  Classification, 448, 449.
  Identification, 448, 449.
  Beech, 450.
  Black Maidenhair, 450.
  Black Spleenwort, 450.
  Bracken, 451.
  Brakes, 451.
  Brittle Bladder, 451.
  Broad Prickly Buckler, 450.
  Broad Prickly-toothed, 450.
  Common Adder's Tongue, 451.
  Common Hart's Tongue, 451.
  Common Polypody, 449.
  Common Prickly-shield, 450.
  Common Wall Spleenwort, 450, 451.
  Crested, 450.
  Eagle, 451.
  Filmy, 451.
  Flowering, 451.

INDEX

Ferns—*continued.*
Hard, 451.
Lady, 450.
Lanceolate Spleenwort, 450.
Maidenhair Spleenwort, 450.
Male Buckler, 450.
Marsh Buckler, 450.
Moonwort, 451.
Oak, 449.
Parsley, 450.
Royal, 451.
Sea Spleenwort, 450.
True Maidenhair, 451.
Tunbridge Hymenophile, 451.
Wall Rue, 450.
Ferret, 36.
Fiddler Velvet, 169.
Field-bugs, 187.
Fieldfare, *101, 102.
Fifteen-spined Stickleback, 154.
Fingerlings, 156.
Fireflare, 161.
Fire-tail, *83.
Fish, Coarse, 151.
Fishes, 150–163, Pl. XIII. 1.
 Characteristics, 150, 151.
 Spawn, 150.
Fish-insects, 182.
Fitzsimmons, Mr. F. W., on House-fly, 288.
Five-bearded Rockling, 163.
Flat-fish, 159.
Flatworms, 321.
Flea, Water, *165, 166, Pl. XVIII. 3.
Fleas, 289.
Flies, 287–9, Pl. XXXII.
 Bee-flies, 287.
 Bee-louse, 289.
 Blow-fly, 289.
 Bluebottle, 289.
 Cabbage-root Flies, 289.
 Common Gnat, 287.
 Crane-flies, 287, Pl. XXXII. 3.
 Daddy-longlegs, 287, Pl. XXXII. 3.
 Forest-fly, 289, Pl. XXXII. 4.
 Gadflies, 287, Pl. XXXII. 2.
 Greenbottle, 289.
 Grey Flesh-flies, 288.
 Horse-bot, 288.
 House-fly, 288, 289.
 Hover-flies, 288.
 Keds, 289, Pl. XXXII. 5.
 Midges, 287.
 Noonday Fly, 289.
 Ox-bot, 288.
 Robber-flies, 287.
 Sheep-bot, 288.
 Sheep-ticks, 289, Pl. XXXII. 5.

Flies—*continued.*
 Tachnid Flies, 288.
 Warble-fly, 288.
Flounder, 159.
Flowers, Alphabetical List of: English, 437–41.
 Alphabetical List of: Latin, 442–6.
Flukes, 321.
Flycatcher, Grey, 75.
 Pied, *69, 75.
 Spotted, *73, 75.
Foraminifera, 330, Pl. XIII. 4.
Forest-fly, 289, Pl. XXXII. 4.
Fork-tailed Petrel, Leach's, 80.
Foul Marten, 36.
Four-horned Spider Crab, 169.
Fowler, Mr. Warde, 94.
Fox, Common, *33, 34, 472–4, Pl. III. 2.
French Partridge, 121.
Fresh-water Limpet, 307.
Fresh-water Perch, 153.
Fresh-water Shrimp, 166.
Frog, Common, 147.
 Edible, 148.
Froghoppers, 188.
Fulmar, 130, *131.
Fungi, 456–65.
 Characteristics, 456–8.
 Deflated Puff-balls, *457.
 Edible, 458, *459, 460, *461, 462.
 "Fairy Ring," *457.
 Poisonous, *463, 464, 465.
 Amethyst Agaric, *461, 462, 465.
 Bleeding Agaric, 458, *461.
 Blewits, 460, *461, 465.
 Bulbous Agaric, *463, 464.
 Bunt, 458.
 Common Morel, *459, 462.
 Common Mushroom, 458, *459.
 Common Polyporus, 457.
 Common Puff-ball, *457.
 Death Cap, *463, 464.
 Dust, 458.
 Edible Boletus, *459, 462.
 Fly Agaric, *463, 464.
 Funnel Mushroom, *461, 462.
 Giant (Great) Puff-ball, *461, 462.
 Glutinous Agaric, *463, 464.
 Horn of Plenty, *459, 462.
 Horse Mushroom, 457, 458, *459.
 Inky Mushroom, 457.
 Liberty Caps, 457.

Fungi—*continued.*
 Magpie Mushroom, *458.
 Mildew, 458.
 Mould, 458.
 Parasol Mushroom, 460, *461.
 Purple Agaric, *463, 465.
 Scaly Agaric, 460, *461.
 Shaggy Cap, 457, *459, 460.
 Sheathed Agaric, *459, 460, 464.
 Shield Agaric, *463, 464.
 Stinkhorn, 457, *462.
 Thread, 458.
 Tufted Mushroom, 458, *459.
 Verdigris Agaric, *463, 465.
 Warted Agaric, *463, 464.
 Warty Cap, 460, *461, 464.
 Witches' Butter, 458.

Gadflies, 287, Pl. XXXII. 2.
Gall-flies, 290.
Gannet, *131, 132.
Gaper, 312, Pl. XXXVIII. 8.
Garden Spider, 171, 177, Pl. XV. 4, XVI. 1, 2.
Garden Warbler, 93.
Gedd, 157.
Genesis, Book of, 1, 2.
Geological epochs, 22 (note).
German Cockroach, 183.
Glaucous Gull, 133.
Glow-worm, 193, 209, Pl. XXXVI. 4.
Gnat, Common, 287.
Goatsucker, 103.
Goby, Black, 162.
 Little, 162.
 Rock, 162.
Godwit, Bar-tailed, 114.
 Black-tailed, 116.
Goldcrest, *69, 75.
Gold-crested Wren, 75.
Golden Carp, 151.
Golden Eagle, 130.
Golden-eye, 116, *117.
Golden Plover, *101, 105.
Goldfinch, *69, 76.
Goldfish, 151.
Goosander, 132.
Goose, Barnacle, *131, 132.
 Bean, 132.
 Brent, *131, 132.
 Greylag, 132.
 Pink-footed, 132.
 Solan, 132.
 White-fronted, 132.
Goose Barnacle, 167.
Gorcrow, 127.
Grampus, 24.

486 INDEX

Grasshopper, Common, 184.
Great Green, 184.
Grasshoppers, 183, 184.
Grasshopper Warbler, 93.
Grass Snake, 145, 146, Pl. XII. 4.
Grayling, 156.
Great Black-backed Gull, 134.
Great Cormorant, 126.
Great Crested Grebe, *129, 133.
Greater Pipe Fish, 163.
Greater Redpoll, 83.
Great Grey Shrike, 84.
Great Lake Trout, 156.
Great Northern Diver, 128, *129.
Great Prawn, 167.
Great Skua, 138.
Great Snipe, 109.
Great Spotted Woodpecker, 111.
Great Tit, *71, 90.
Great Water Newt, 148.
Grebe, Black-necked, 133.
　Eared, 133.
　Great Crested, *129, 133.
　Little, *101, 102.
　Red-necked, 133.
　Slavonian, 133.
Green Cormorant, 137.
Green Crab, 169.
Green Drake, 185.
Greenfinch, 76.
Green-fly, 188.
Green Linnet, 76.
Green Plover, *101, 105, Pl. VIII. 2.
Green Sandpiper, 108.
Greenshank, 102.
Green Woodpecker, *101, 112.
Grey Drake, 185.
Grey Flycatcher, *73, 75.
Greyhen, 133.
Greylag Goose, 132.
Grey Mullet, 158.
Grey Partridge, 105.
Greypates, 76.
Grey Plover, 106.
Grey Shrike, Great, 84.
Grey Top, 309, Pl. XXXVII. 5.
Grey Trout, 156.
Grey Wagtail, 92.
Grilse, 156.
Grosbeak, 77.
Grouse, Black, *129, 133.
　Red, *115, 116.
Gudgeon, 152.
Guillemot, 116, *117.
　Black, 102.
Gull, Black-headed, *117, 118.
　Common, 118, 134.
　Glaucous, 133.

Gull—continued.
　Great Black-backed, 134.
　Herring, 134.
　Iceland, 134.
　Lesser Black-backed, *129, 134.
Gunnel, Spotted, 162.

Haddock, 158.
Hairy Crab, 170.
Hairy Porcelain Crab, 170.
Hairy Stinger, 322.
Hake, 159.
Halibut, 159.
Hamilton, Mr. G. C. H. Barrett, 44.
Harbour Crab, 169.
Hare, Common, 40.
　Mountain, 40.
Harrier, Hen, 134.
　Marsh, 134.
　Montagu's, 134, *135.
Harvest Bug, 179.
Harvester, Pl. XVIII. 1.
Harvest Men, 179, Pl. XVIII. 1.
Hawfinch, *69, 76.
Hawk, Night, 103.
　Sparrow, *115, 118.
Hedgehog, Common, 26, 477–9, Pl. I. 1, 4.
Hedge Sparrow, 86.
Hen Harrier, 134.
Hermit Crabs, 170.
Heron, Common, *129, 134.
Herring, 160.
Herring Gull, 134.
Herring Hake, 159.
Hobby, 103.
Holiday Nature Book, 139.
Hooded Crow, 127, *129.
Hornet, 296.
Horns, Deer's, 47–9.
Horny Cobbler, 163.
Horse Stinger, 186.
Horse-tails, 452.
　Field, 452.
Hound, Rough, 162.
House Martin, *73, 78.
House Sparrow, 87.
House Spider, 172, 176, Pl. XVI. 3.
Humble Bees, 297, 298.
Hydra, 325, 326, Pl. XVIII. 2.
Hydroid Zoophytes, 325, 326.

Iceland Gull, 134.
Ichneumon Flies, 290, Pl. XXXVI. 2, 5.
Insects, 181–299, Pl. XV.–XXXVI.
　Characteristics, 181.

Insects—continued.
　Classification, 182.
　Diagram, *181.
　Invertebrates, 4.
Iodine, 465.
Irish Coal Tit, 90.

Jack, 157.
Jackdaw, *115, 119.
Jack Snipe, *71, 85, *86.
Jack Squealer, 89.
Jay, *115, 119.
Jelly-fish, 322, 323, 326.
Jenny Wren, *71, 97.
Johnston, Sir H., 39 (note), 40, 44, 49 (note).

Kearton, Mr. C., on emptying egg, 52.
Ked, 289, Pl. XXXII. 5.
Kelp, 465.
Kelts, 155.
Kentish Plover, 106.
Kestrel, *115, 119.
Key-hole Limpet, 308, Pl. XXXVII. 11.
Kingfisher, *71, 77.
Kippers, male Salmon, 155.
Kirby, Mr., *Butterflies and Moths of the United Kingdom*, 239.
Kirkman, Mr., on Birds, 58, 59 (note), 66.
Kite, 103.
Kittiwake, 119.
Knot, 103.

Labrax, 157.
Lacewing-flies, 190.
Lady-birds, 204.
　Two-spot, 204.
Landrail, 99.
Lantern-flies, 188.
Lapwing, *101, 105.
Lark, Scribbling, 72.
　Shore, 97.
　Sky, *71, 85.
　Wood, 97.
　Writing, 72.
Lasher, Father, 154, 163.
Launce, 160.
Leach's Fork-tailed Petrel, 80.
Leaf-worm, 320.
Leech, 320.
　Horse, 321.
　Medicinal, 320.
Lemon Sole, 160.
Lesser Black-backed Gull, *129, 134.

INDEX 487

Lesser Redpoll, 83.
Lesser Spotted Dog-fish, 162.
Lesser Spotted Woodpecker, 97.
Lesser Weever, 163.
Lesser Whitethroat, 96.
Lice, True, 189.
Lichenaria: larvæ feeding, Pl. xxvii. 2.
Lifford, Lord, and Little Owl, 104.
Limpet, Common, 308, Pl. xxxvii. 10.
   Cup-and-Saucer, 309, Pl. xxxvii. 15.
   Fresh-water, 307.
   Key-hole, 308, Pl. xxxvii. 11.
   Smooth, 309, Pl. xxxvii. 6.
Ling, 159.
Linnet, Brown, 77.
   Green, 76.
   Mountain, 91.
Little Auk, 68.
Little Bittern, 135.
Little Cuttle, 303.
Little Goby, 162.
Little Grebe, *101, 102.
Little Owl, 104.
Little Tern, *101, 110.
Liverworts, 453.
Lizard, Common, 143, Pl. xii. 1.
   Sand, 144.
Lizards in captivity, 144.
Loach, 153.
Lobster, Common, 168.
   Norway, 168.
   Scaly Squat, 168.
   Spanish, 168.
   Spinous Squat, 168.
   Spiny, 168.
Lob-worm, 319.
Lochleven Trout, 156.
Locusts, 184.
Long-eared Owl, *115, 120.
Long-nose, 158.
Long-tailed Duck, 128, *129.
Long-tailed Skua, 138.
Long-tailed Tit, *73, 91.
Long-worm, 320.
Louse, Water, *165, 166.
   Wood, 170.
Lug-worm, 319, Pl. xl. 17.
Lyre Bird, 123.
Lythe, 158.

Mackerel, 157.
Mackerel Cock, 123.
Mackerel Guide, 158.
Madrepore, 325.
Magpie, *117, 120.

Mallard, 128.
Mammals, British, 21-49, Pl. i.-vi.
   Characteristics, 21.
   Classification, 22-23 (note).
   Orders, 21, 22 (note).
Manx Puffin, 123.
Manx Shearwater, 123.
Marigold (Jelly-fish), 322.
Marsh Harrier, 134.
Marsh Tit, *73, 91.
Marsh Warbler, 93.
Marten, Foul, 36.
   Pine, 36.
Martin, House, *73, 78, 88.
   Sand, 79.
Masked Crab, 169.
May-bug, 207.
Mayflies, 185.
Meadow Pipit, 81.
Mealworms, 214.
Mealy Bugs, 189.
Megalopa, 168.
Merganser, Red-breasted, *129, 135.
Merlin, 103.
"Mermaid's Gloves," 328.
"Mermaid's purses," 162.
Microscope, Simple, 10.
   Condensers for (Figs. 7, 8), 12.
   Home-made stand (Fig. 6), 10.
   Uses, 165, 171, 179, 218, 219, 288, 289, 318, 326, 327, 328, 330, 453, 454, 458, 465.
Miller's Thumb, 154.
Millipede, Common Snake, 180.
Millipedes, 180, Pl. xviii. 4.
Minnow, 152, Pl. xiii. 1.
Mistle Thrush, 109.
Mite, Cheese, 179.
   Water, 179.
Mites and Ticks, 179.
Mole, 27, *28, 29, 208, Pl. i. 2.
Mollusca, 164, 300-13, Pl. xii.-xiv., xxxvii.-xxxix.
   Characteristics, 300.
   Classification, 300, 301.
   Formation of shells, 301.
Money-spinner, Pl. xviii. 1.
Montagu's Harrier, 134, *135.
Moorhen, 124.
Mosses, 453-5.
   Characteristics, 453, 454.
   Broom Fork, 455.
   Common Cord, 455.
   Common Hair, 454.
   Wall Screw, 455.

Mother Carey's Chicken, 80.
Mother-of-pearl, 310.
Moths, 218, 222-4, 237-86, Pl. xxvii.-xxxi.
   Antennæ, 237, *238.
   Breeding, 223, 239.
   Caterpillars, *240, *244, *246, *248.
   Characteristics, 218, 237-9.
   Classification, 237, 239-86.
   Collecting, 222-4.
   Diagram of wing, *238.
   Larvæ, 222, 223, 239-86.
   Pupæ, 223, 239-86.
   Rearing cages, 223.
   Setting, 224.
   Sugar mixture, 224.
Alder Kitten, 242.
Angle Shades, 261, Pl. xxxi. 12.
Antler, 259.
Archer's Dart, 254.
Ash Pug, 279.
August Thorn, 281.
Autumn Green Carpet, 275.
Barred Chestnut, 256.
Barred Hook-tip, 249.
Barred Red, 280.
Barred Rivulet, 277.
Barred Straw, 275.
Barred Umber, 280.
Barred Yellow, 275.
Beaded Chestnut, 265.
Beautiful Brocade, 258.
Beautiful Carpet, 277.
Beautiful Golden Y, 268.
Beautiful Hook-tip, 269.
Beautiful Snout, 270.
Beautiful Yellow Underwing, 267, Pl. xxxi. 2.
Beech Green Carpet, 276.
Bee Hawk, Pl. xxx. 23.
Bee-robber, 241.
Belle Moth, 273.
Bell Moths, 286.
Bindweed Hawk, 241.
Bird's Wing, 261.
Black Arches, 247.
Blossom Underwing, 264.
Blood Vein, 272,
Blotched Emerald, 271.
Blue-bordered Carpet, 277.
Bordered Beauty, 282.
Bordered Gothic, 259.
Bordered White, 284, Pl. xxxi. 3, 4.
Brick, 265.
Bright-line Brown-eye, 257.
Brimstone, 282, Pl. xxxi. 5.

INDEX

Moths—*continued.*
Brindled Beauty, 283.
Brindled Green, 259.
Broad-barred White, 258.
Broad-bordered Bee Hawk-moth, 242.
Broad-bordered Yellow Underwing, 256.
Broken-barred Carpet, 275.
Broom, 258.
Brown-line Bright-eye, 262.
Brown Rustic, 263.
Brown Scallop, 274.
Brown Silver-line, 284.
Brown-spot Pinion, 265.
Brown-tail, 246.
Buff Arches, 245.
Buff Ermine, 251.
Buff Footman, 253.
Buff Tip, *244, Pl. xxx. 22.
Bulrush Wainscot, 262.
Burnet Companion, 269.
Burnets, 284.
Burnished Brass, 268, Pl. xxxi.6.
Buttoned Snout, 270.
Cabbage Moth, 257.
Campion, 258.
Canary-shouldered Thorn, 281, Pl. xxxi. 8.
Chalk Carpet, 273.
Chamomile Shark, 267.
Chestnut, 266.
Chestnut-coloured Carpet, 275.
Chevron, 275.
Chimney Sweeper, 273.
Chinese Character, 249.
Chocolate Tip, 244.
Cinnabar, 252, Pl. xxx. 3.
Cistus Forester, 284.
Clay, 262.
Clay Triple Lines, 272.
Cloaked Minor, 260.
Clothes Moths, 286.
Clouded Border, 280.
Clouded Bordered Brindle, 260.
Clouded Brindle, 260.
Clouded Buff, 251.
Clouded Drab, 264.
Clouded Magpie, 280.
Clouded Silver, 280.
Coast Dart, 255.
Common Carpet, 276.
Common Emerald, 271.
Common Fan-foot, 269.
Common Footman, 253.
Common Heath, 284.
Common Magpie, 280, Pl. xxxi. 7.

Moths—*continued.*
Common Marbled Carpet, 275.
Common Pug, 279.
Common Quaker, 264.
Common Rustic, 260.
Common Swift, 286, Pl. xxx. 17.
Common Wainscot, 262.
Common Wave, 280.
Common White Wave, 280.
Common Yellow Underwing, 256.
Convolvulus Hawk-moth, 241.
Copper Underwing, 263.
Coronet, 254.
Coxcomb Prominent, 244.
Cream-bordered Green Pea, 250.
Cream-spot Tiger, 252.
Cream Wave, 272.
Crescent, 261.
Crescent Dart, 254.
Currant Clearwing, 285, Pl. xxx. 25.
Currant Pug, 278.
Dark Arches, 260.
Dark-barred Twin-spot Carpet, 276.
Dark Brocade, 259.
Dark Chestnut, 266.
Dark Crimson Underwing, 269.
Dark Dagger, 253.
Dark Marbled Carpet, 275.
Dark Spectacle, 269.
Dark Spinach, 280.
Dark Sword-grass, 254.
Dark Tussock, 246.
Dark Umber, 274.
Death's-head Hawk-moth, *240, Pl. xxix. 2.
December Moth, 247.
Dew Moth, 252.
Dingy Footman, 253.
Dingy Shears, 265.
Dingy Shell, 278.
Dismal Moth, 265.
Dog's Tooth, 258.
Dot, 257.
Dotted Border, 282.
Dotted Clay, 255.
Dotted Fan-foot, 269.
Dotted Footman, 253.
Double Dart, 255.
Double Square Spot, 255.
Drab Looper, 273.
Drinker, *248, Pl. xxx. 19.
Dun-bar, 264.
Dusky Brocade, 259.
Dusky-lemon Sallow, 266.
Dusky Sallow, 259.

Moths—*continued.*
Dusky Thorn, 281.
Dwarf Cream Wave, 271.
Ear Moth, 261.
Early Grey, 266.
Early Moth, 282.
Early Tooth-striped, 273.
Early Thorn, 281.
Eggars, 247, 248.
Elephant, 241, Pl. xxxi. 14.
Emperor Moth, 249, Pl. xxx. 4.
Engrailed, 283.
Ermine Moths, 251.
Eyed Hawk-moth, 240, Pl. xxx. 8.
False Mocha, 272.
Fan-foot, 269.
Feathered Gothic, 259.
Feathered Prominent, 244.
Feathered Thorn, 281.
Fen Wainscot, 262.
Festoon, 285.
Figure of Eight, 259, Pl. xxxi. 28.
Figure of Eighty, 245.
Five-plumed Moth, Pl. xxviii. 3.
Five-spot Burnet, 284.
Flame, 256.
Flame Carpet, 276.
Flame Shoulder, 255.
Flounced Rustic, 259, 265.
Footman Moths, 252, 253.
Forester, 284.
Four-dotted Footman, 252.
Four-spotted Footman, 252.
Foxglove Pug, 278.
Fox Moth, 248.
Frosted Green, 245.
Frosted Orange, 262.
Garden Carpet, 276, Pl. xxxi. 10.
Garden Dart, 255.
Garden Tiger, 251.
Geometers, 270–84.
Ghost Moth, 285, Pl. xxx. 15, 16.
Glaucous Shears, 258.
Goat Moth, 285.
Golden Plusia, 268.
Golden-rod Pug, 279.
Gold Spot, 268.
Gold-tail, 246, Pl. xxx. 21.
Gothic, 259, 261.
Grass Eggar, 248.
Grass Emerald, 270.
Grass Rivulet, 277.
Great Prominent, 243.
Green Arches, 257.

INDEX

Moths—*continued.*
Green Brindled Crescent, 261.
Green Carpet, 276.
Green Forester, 284, Pl. xxx. 2.
Green Pug, 279.
Green Silver-lines, 250.
Grey Arches, 257.
Grey Dagger, 253, Pl. xxxi. 23.
Grey Pine Carpet, 275.
Grey Pug, 279.
Grey Rustic, 255.
Grey Shoulder-knot, 266.
Ground Lackey, 247.
Hawk-moths, 239–42.
Heart and Club, 254.
Heart and Dart, 254.
Heath Rustic, 255.
Hebrew Character, 264.
Herald, 268.
Hook-tips, 249.
Hop-dog, 246.
Hornet Clearwing, Pl. xxx. 26.
Hornet Moth, 285.
Humming-bird, Hawk-moth, 241, Pl. xxx. 24.
Ingrailed Clay, 256.
Iron Prominent, 243.
Jersey Tiger, 252.
Juby High Flyer, 277.
Juniper Pug, 279.
Kent Black Arches, 250.
Kentish Glory, 249.
Knot-grass, 253.
Lace border, 272.
Lackey, 247, Pl. xxx. 11.
Lappet, 248.
Large Emerald, 271, Pl. xxxi. 24.
Large Footman, 252.
Large Marbled Tortrix, 250.
Large Nutmeg, 260.
Large Red-belted Clearwing, 285.
Large Wainscot, 262.
Large Yellow Underwing, 256.
Latticed Heath, 284.
Lead Belle, 273.
Least Black Arches, 250.
Least Yellow Underwing, 257.
Leopard Moth, 285.
Lesser Broad-bordered Yellow Underwing, 256.
Lesser Cream Wave, 272.
Lesser Lutestring, 245.
Lesser Satin Moth, 245.
Lesser Swallow Prominent, 243.
Lesser Yellow Underwing, 256.
Light Arches, 260.
Light Brocade, 257.

Moths—*continued.*
Light Crimson Underwing, 269.
Light Emerald, 281.
Light-feathered Rustic, 255.
Light Knot-grass, 254.
Light Orange Underwing, 270.
Lilac Beauty, 281.
Lime Hawk-moth, 239, Pl. xxx. 10.
Lime-speck Pug, 278.
Ling Pug, 279.
Little Emerald, 271.
Lobster, 243, Pl. xxxi. 11.
Lunar Hornet, 285.
Lunar Marbled Brown, 243.
Lunar Underwing, 265.
Lychnis, 258.
Magpie, 280, Pl. xxxi. 7.
Maiden's Blush, 272.
Mallow, 273.
Marbled Beauty, 254.
Marbled Brown, 243.
Marbled Coronet, 258.
Marbled Green, 254.
Marbled Minor, 260.
March Moth, 283.
May High Flyer, 278.
Merveille du Jour, 261.
Middle-barred Minor, 260.
Miller, 253.
Minor Shoulder-knot, 259.
Mocha, 272.
Mother Shipton, 269.
Mottled Beauty, 283.
Mottled Grey, 276.
Mottled Rustic, 263.
Mottled Umber, 283.
Mouse, 263.
Mullein, 267.
Mullein Wave, 272.
Muslin Footman, 252.
Muslin Tiger, 251.
Narrow-bordered Bee Hawk-moth, 242.
Narrow-bordered Five-spot Burnet, 284.
Narrow-winged Pug, 279.
Neglected Rustic, 255.
Netted Pug, 278.
Northern Footman, 253.
Northern Winter Moth, 274.
November Moth, 276.
Nutmeg, 258.
Nut-tree Tussock, 253.
Oak Beauty, 283.
Oak Eggar, 247, Pl. xxx. 18.
Oak Hook-tip, 249.
Oblique Striped, 273.

Moths—*continued.*
Old Lady, 261, Pl. xxxi. 26.
Olive, 265.
Orange Footman, 253.
Orange Moth, 281.
Orange Sallow, 266.
Orange Swift, 286.
Orange Underwing, 270, Pl. xxxi. 1.
Orange Upperwing, 266.
Pale Brindled Beauty, 283.
Pale Mottled Willow, 263.
Pale Oak Eggar, 247.
Pale Pinion, 266.
Pale Prominent, 244.
Pale Shining Brown, 257.
Pale-shouldered Brocade, 258.
Pale Tussock, *246, Pl. xxx. 20.
Peach Blossom, 245, Pl. xxxi. 27.
Pearly Underwing, 254.
Pebble Hook-tip, 249, Pl. xxxi. 18.
Pebble Prominent, 243.
Pepper and Salt, Pl. xxxi. 9.
Peppered Moth, 283.
Phœnix, 274.
Pine Beauty, 263, Pl. xxxi. 22.
Pine Carpet, 275.
Pine Hawk, 241.
Pinion-streaked Snout, 270.
Pink-barred Sallow, Pl. xxxi. 17.
Plain Golden Y, 268.
Plain Wave, 271.
Plumed Prominent, 244.
Plume Moths, 286, Pl. xxviii. 3.
Poplar Grey, 253.
Poplar Hawk, 240, Pl. xxx. 14.
Poplar Kitten, 242.
Poplar Lutestring, 245.
Powdered Quaker, 264.
Pretty Chalk Carpet, 277.
Privet Hawk, 241, Pl. xxviii. 4, xxx. 9.
Prominents, 242–4.
Purple Bar, 277.
Purple-bordered Gold, 271.
Purple Clay, 256.
Puss Moth, 243.
Red-belted Clearwing, 285.
Red Chestnut, 264.
Red-green Carpet, 275.
Red-line Quaker, 265.
Red-necked Footman, 252.
Red Sword Grass, 267.
Red Twin-spot Carpet, 276.
Red Underwing, 269.

INDEX

Moths—*continued.*
Riband Wave, 271.
Rivulet, 277.
Rosy Footman, 252.
Rosy Minor, 260.
Rosy Rustic, 262.
Round-winged Muslin, 252.
Ruby Tiger, 251.
Ruddy High Flyer, 278.
Rustic, 263.
Rustic Shoulder-knot, 260.
Sallow, 266.
Sallow Kitten, 242.
Sandy Carpet, 277.
Satellite, 266.
Satin Carpet, 245.
Satin Wave, 271.
Satyr Pug, 279.
Scalloped Hazel, 281.
Scalloped Hook-tip, 249.
Scalloped Oak, 281.
Scallop Shell, 274.
Scarce Black Arches, 250.
Scarce Burnished Grass, 268.
Scarce Footman, 253.
Scarce Silver-lines, 250.
Scarce Silver Y, 268.
Scarce Tissue, 274.
Scarce Umber, 282.
Scarce Vapourer, 246.
Scarlet Tiger, 252.
Scorched Carpet, 280.
Scorched Wing, 282.
September Thorn, 281.
Seraphim, 274.
Setaceous Hebrew Character, 255.
Shaded Broad-bar, 273.
Shark, 267.
Shears, 258.
Short-cloaked Moth, 250.
Shoulder Stripe, 278.
Shoulder-striped Wainscot, 262.
Shuttle-shaped Dart, 255.
Silver-ground Carpet, 276.
Silver Y, 268, Pl. XXXI. 16.
Silvery Arches, 257.
Single-dotted Wave, 271.
Six-spot Burnet, 284, Pl. XXX. 1.
Six-striped Rustic, 256.
Slender Pug, 279.
Small Angle Shades, 261.
Small Black Arches, 250.
Small Blood-vein, 272.
Small Chocolate Tip, 244.
Small Clouded Brindle, 260.
Small Dotted Buff, 263.
Small Dusty Wave, 271.

Moths—*continued.*
Small Eggar, 247.
Small Elephant, 241, Pl. XXXI. 15.
Small Emerald, 271.
Small Fan-foot, 269.
Small Fan-footed Wave, 271.
Small Mallow, 273.
Small Phœnix, 274.
Small Purple-barred, 267.
Small Quaker, 264.
Small Rivulet, 277.
Small Scallop, 272.
Small Seraphim, 274.
Small Square Spot, 256.
Small Wainscot, 262.
Small White Wave, 278.
Small Yellow Underwing, 267.
Small Yellow Wave, 278.
Smoky Wainscot, 262.
Smoky Wave, 272.
Snout, 269.
Speckled Yellow, 282.
Spectacle, 268.
Spinach, 275.
Sprawler, 261.
Spring Usher, 282, Pl. XXXI. 19.
Square-spot Rustic, 256.
Square-spotted Clay, 256.
Star-wort, 267.
Straw Dot, 267.
Straw Underwing, 259.
Streak, 273.
Streamer, 278.
Striped Wainscot, 262.
Swallow Prominent, 243.
Swallow-tailed Moth, 282, Pl. XXX. 7.
Swifts, 285, 286.
Sword Grass, 267.
Sycamore, 253.
Tawny-barred Angle, 282.
Tawny Pinion, 266.
Tawny Shears, 258.
Tiger Moths, 251, 252.
Tissue, 274.
Toadflax Pug, 278.
Treble Bar, 273.
Treble Lines, 263.
Turnip Moth, 254.
Tussock Moths, 246, 247.
Twenty-plume Moth, 286.
Twin-spot Carpet, 276.
Twin-spotted Quaker, 264.
Twin-spotted Wainscot, 262.
Uncertain, 263.
Unicorn, 241.

Moths—*continued.*
Vapourer, 246, Pl. XXVII. 1, XXX. 12, 13.
V Moth, 284.
V Pug, 279.
Water Carpet, 275.
Water Ermine, 251.
Waved Umber, 283.
White Colon, 257.
White Ermine, 251, Pl. XXX. 6.
White-line Dart, 255.
White-line Snout, 270.
White Prominent, 244.
White Satin, 247.
White-spotted Pinion, 264.
Willow Beauty, 283, Pl. XXXI. 25.
Winter Moth, 274, Pl. XXXI. 20, 21.
Wood Leopard, Pl. XXX. 5.
Wood Tiger, 251.
Wormwood Pug, 279.
Yellow Horned, 245.
Yellow-line Quaker, 265.
Yellow Shell, 277, Pl. XXXI. 13.
Yellow-tail, 246.
Moths of the British Isles, 239.
Moths of the Months, 223, 237.
Mountain Linnet, 91.
Mountain Sparrow, 87.
Mouse, Common, 43, Pl. IV. 3; V. 2, VI. 3.
Field, 45, Pl. V. 3.
Harvest, 45.
Long-tailed Field, *44.
Sea, 320, Pl. XL. 11.
Wood, *44.
Mullet, Grey, 158.
Red, 158.
Mushrooms, 456-62.
Mussel, 311, Pl. XXXVIII. 21.
Horse, 311, Pl. XXXVIII. 19, 20.
Painter's, 306.
Pearl, 306.
Swan, 306.
Mussel Scale, 189.
Mute Swan, 138.

Natterjack Toad, 148.
Nature's Nursery Tales, 155.
Nemertes, 320, Pl. XL. 12.
Nereïs, 320, Pl. XL. 13.
Pearly, 320.
Rainbow, 320.
Nests, Birds', 51, 52, 139-42, Pl. IX.
Sites, 141, 142.

INDEX

Netted Dog-whelk, 307, Pl. XXXVII. 7.
Nettle-creeper, 96.
Newt, Common, 148.
  Great Water, 148.
  Palmated, 149.
  Smooth, 148.
Newts, characteristics, 148.
  In an aquarium, 149.
Night-hawk, 103.
Nightingale, *73, 79.
Nightjar, *101, 103.
Nine-eyes, 163.
Nits, 189.
Norfolk Plover, 113.
Northern Diver, Great, 128, *129.
Norway Lobster, 168.
Nuthatch, *71, 80.

Octopus, 303.
Old Maid, 312.
Otter, Common, 34, 470–2, Pl. II. 1, 4.
Otter Shells, 313.
Ouzel, Ring, *101, 104.
  Water, *69, 74.
Owl, Barn, *115, 120.
  Brown, 121.
  Fern-, 103.
  Little, 104, 479, 480.
  Long-eared, *115, 120.
  Screech, 120.
  Short-eared, *115, 120.
  Tawny, *115, 121.
  White, 120.
Oyster, 310, Pl. XXXVIII. 16.
  Saddle, 311, Pl. XXXVIII. 17.
Oyster-catcher, *117, 121.

Painted Ray, 161.
Painted Top, 309, Pl. XXXVII. 14.
Palmated Newt, 149.
Parrs, 156.
Partridge, 105.
  French, 121.
  Grey, 105.
  Red-legged, 121.
Pea Crab, 170.
Pecten, 311.
Peewit, 105.
Peggy Whitethroat, 96.
Perch, Fresh-water, 153.
Peregrine Falcon, 114, *115.
Periwinkle, 308, Pl. XXXVII. 12.
  Dog, 308, Pl. XXXVII. 16.
Petrel, Leach's Fork-tailed, 80.
  Storm, *71, 80.
Phanerogamia, 333–446.

Pheasant, 135.
  Reed, 89.
Picked Dog-fish, 161.
Piddock, 312, Pl. XXXVIII. 11.
  Little, 312, Pl. XXXVIII. 10, 12.
Pied Flycatcher, *69, 75.
  Wagtail, *73, 92.
Pigeon, Wood, *115, 122, Pl. VII. 3.
Pike, 156.
Pilchard, 161.
Pine Marten, 36.
Pink-footed Goose, 132.
Pinks, 156.
Pinna, Pl. XXXVIII. 6.
Pintail, *131, 136.
Pipe Fish, Greater, 163.
  Worm, 163.
Pipit, Meadow, 81.
  Rock, 81.
  Tree, *71, 81, *82, Pl. VIII. 4.
Plaice, 159.
Plant-lice, 188, Pl. XIX. 4.
Plants, 333–446.
  Alphabetical List of Flowers: English, 437–41.
  Alphabetical List of Flowers: Latin, 442–6.
  Diagram of terms, *337.
  Flower, 336–40.
  General structure, 334.
  Groups according to colour of flowers, 338–9.
  Groups according to size of flowers, 339.
  How to dry, 334.
  Illustrations, 346–7, 352–3, 358–9, 364–5, 370–1, 376–7, 382–3, 388–9, 394–5, 400–1, 406–7, 412–13, 418–19, 424–5, 430–1, 434–6.
  Leaf, 334–6.
  Lists, 342–433.
    Explanation, 338–9.
    How to use, 339, 340.
  Root, 334.
  Stem, 334.
  Terms, 335–9.
Platyhelminthes, 164, 321.
Plover, Golden, *101, 105.
  Green, *101, 105, Pl. VIII. 2.
  Grey, 106.
  Kentish, 106.
  Norfolk, 113.
  Ringed, *101, 106.
Pochard, *129, 136.
Pod Razor, 313.
Polecat, Common, 36.
Pollack, 158.

Polyps, 325, 326.
Polyzoa, 164, 318, 319.
Pomathorine Skua, 138.
Pond Life, 329.
Pond Snail, 307.
Pope (bird), 122.
Pope (fish), 154.
Porcelain Crab, Hairy, 170.
Porifera, 164, 327, *328.
Porpoise, Common, 24.
Post Bird, 75.
Pout, 158.
  Whiting, 158.
Prawn, Æsop, 167.
  Great, 167.
  Protective coloration, 143, 159, 167, 302, 317.
Protozoa, 164, 328, *329, *330, Pl. XIII. 4.
Ptarmigan, 122.
Pteridophyta, 333, 447–52.
Puey, 83.
Puffin, *117, 122.
  Manx, 123.
Purple, 308.
Purple Sandpiper, 108.
Purpura, 308, Pl. XXXVII. 13.

Quail, 82.
Quin, 311.

Rabbit, Common, 39, Pl. III. 4, VI. 4.
Radiolaria, 330.
Rail, Spotted, 111.
  Water, 111.
Ram's Horn, 307.
Rat, Black, 43, Pl. IV. 4.
  Brown, 43, Pl. V. 1.
  White, 43.
Rattle-wings, 138.
Raven, *129, 136.
Ray, Painted, 161.
  Sharp-nosed, 161.
  Sting, 161.
Rayed Artemis, 313.
Ray's Wagtail, 92.
Razor, 312, Pl. XXXVIII. 1, 2.
  Pod, 313.
  Sabre, 313, Pl. XXXVIII. 3.
Razorbill, *117, 123.
Red-backed Shrike, *71, 84.
Redbreast, Robin, 83, Pl. IX. 4.
Red-breasted Merganser, *129, 135.
Red Centipede, 180.
Red Grouse, *115, 116.
Red-legged Daw, 112.

INDEX

Red-legged Partridge, 121.
Red Mullet, 158.
Red-necked Grebe, 133.
Red Nose, 311.
Red-nosed Borer, 312.
Redpoll, Greater, 83.
 Lesser, 83.
 Mealy, 83.
Redshank, 107.
Red Spider, 179.
Redstart, *71, *83.
 Black, 84.
Red-throated Diver, 128.
Red Whelk, 308.
Redwing, 107.
Reed Bunting, *69, 70.
Reed Pheasant, 89.
Reed Sparrow, 70.
Reed Warbler, 94.
Reedling, Bearded, 89.
Reeler, 93.
Reptiles, 143-6, Pl. XII. 1, 4.
 Characteristics, 143.
 Classes in Great Britain, 143.
 Eggs, 143.
Ring Dove, 122.
Ringed Plover, *101, 106.
Ringed Snake, 145.
Ring Ouzel, *101, 104.
Roach, 152.
Robin Redbreast, 83, Pl. IX. 4.
Rock Dove, 114.
Rock Goby, 162.
Rockling, Five-bearded, 163.
 Three-bearded, 163.
Rock Pipit, 81.
Rook, *129, 136.
Rorqual, Common, 25.
 Lesser, 26.
 Rudolphi's, 26.
 Sibbald's, 26.
Roseate, 110.
Rough Hound, 162.
Rough-legged Buzzard, 126.
Ruby-tailed Flies, 291.
Ruby Wasps, 291.
Rudd, 152.
Ruffe, 154.
Running Toad, 148.

Sabella, 319, Pl. XL. 10.
Sabre Razor, 313.
Saddle Oyster, 311, Pl. XXXVIII. 17.
Salmon, 155.
Salmon Trout, 156.
Samlets, 156.
Sand Eel, 160.

Sanderling, 107.
Sand-hopper, 167.
Sand Lizard, 144.
Sand Martin, 79.
Sandpiper, Common, *101, 107.
 Green, 108.
 Purple, 108.
 Wood, 108.
Sand-screw, 167.
Sand Sole, 160.
Sandwich Tern, *115, 124.
Sardines, 161.
Saw-flies, 289, 290.
 Currant, 290.
 Gooseberry, 290.
 Pear, 290.
Scale Insects, 189.
Scallop, Common, 311.
 Hunchback, 312, Pl. XXXVIII. 15.
 Radiated, 312, Pl. XXXVIII. 14.
 Variable, 311, XXXVIII. 13.
Scaly Squat Lobster, 168.
Scaup Duck, 128.
Scorpion, Water, 187.
Scorpion-fly, Common, 217.
Scoter, 137.
 Velvet, 137.
Scott, Sir W., and Seal, 39.
Screech Owl, 120.
Scribbling Lark, 72.
Sea Acorn, 323.
Sea Anemones, 324, 325, Pl. XXXVII.
 Beadlet, 324.
 Cave, 325.
 Cloaklet, 325.
 Dahlia Wartlet, 325.
 Daisy, 324, Pl. XXXVII. 22.
 Gem Pimplet, 325.
 Globe-horn, 325.
 Opelet, 325.
 Parasite, 325.
 Pimplets, 325.
 Plumose, 325.
 Rose, 324.
 Scarlet-fringed, 324.
 Smooth, 324, Pl. XXXVII. 23.
 Snake-locked, 325, Pl. XXXVII. 18.
 Snowy, 324.
 Thick-armed, 325, Pl. XXXVII. 19.
Sea Bream, 157.
Sea Cucumber, 316.
Sea Fir, 326.
Sea Gooseberry, 323.
Sea Hair Coralline, 326.

Sea Hare, 306.
Sea-horse, 163.
Seal, Common, 38.
 Grey, 39.
Sea Lemon, 306.
Sea Mat, 318, 319.
Sea Mouse, 320, Pl. XL. 11.
Sea Nettle, 322.
Sea Oak Coralline, 326.
Sea-pie, 121.
Sea-slater, 170.
Sea Snail, Pl. XXXVII. 4.
Sea Squirts, 323, 324.
Sea Trout, 156.
Sea Urchin, 316, 317, Pl. XXXIX. 1.
 Common, 317.
 Heart-shaped, 317.
 Purple-tipped, 317.
 Shield-shaped, 317.
Seaweeds, 465-9, Pl. XL.
 Characteristics, 465, 466.
 Classification, 465.
 Ash-leaved, 468.
 Bladder Wrack, 467, Pl. XL. 3.
 Braided Hair, 468.
 Brown, 466.
 Carrageen Moss, 469, Pl. XL. 7.
 Channelled Wrack, 466.
 Common Red, 468.
 Confervæ, 466.
 Coralline, 469, Pl. XL. 5.
 Dillisk, 469.
 Dillosk, 469.
 Dulse, 469, Pl. XL. 6.
 Grass-wrack, 466, Pl. XL. 8.
 Green Laver, 466, Pl. XL. 1.
 Irish Moss, 469.
 Knotted Wrack, 466.
 Net-weed, 468.
 Oarweed, 467, Pl. XL. 4.
 Peacock's Tail, 468.
 Pod-weed, 467.
 Purple Laver, 466, Pl. XL. 2.
 Rainbow Bladder-weed, 467.
 Red, 468.
 Red Dock Leaf, 468.
 Saw-edged Wrack, 467.
 Sea Furbelows, 467.
 Sea-grass, 466, Pl. XL. 9.
 Sea-lettuce, 466.
 Sea-oak, 467.
 Sea-rope, 467.
 Sloke, 466.
 Sugar Tangle, 467.
Sedge Warbler, *71, 94.
Selborne Society, 139.
Sepia, 302.
Serpula, 320, Pl. XL. 14, 15.

INDEX

Sewen, 156.
Shag, *131, 137.
Shakespeare: "cockshut" time, 126.
"Hedgepig," 27.
"Rere-mice," 30.
Shrew, 29.
Shannies, 162.
Sharp-nosed Ray, 161.
Shearwater, Manx, 123.
Shedders, female Salmon, 155.
Sheep, Wild, 49.
Sheep-tick, 289, Pl. XXXII. 5.
Shelduck, Common, *129, 137.
Shell, Acorn, 166.
Shellbinder, 320.
Shells, 300-13, Pl. XXXVII., XXXVIII.
  Bivalves, 310-13.
  Bristly Mail, 309.
  Carpet, 313.
  Chiton, 309, Pl. XXXVII. 9.
  Cockle, 311, Pl. XXXVIII. 18.
  Comb, 313.
  Common Limpet, 308, Pl. XXXVII. 10.
  Common Scallop, 311.
  Common Top, 309.
  Common Wedge, 312.
  Common Whelk, 307, Pl. XXXVII. 1, XXXIX. 4.
  Cowry, 308, Pl. XXXVII. 8.
  Cross-cut Carpet, 313.
  Cup-and-Saucer Limpet, 309, Pl. XXXVII. 15.
  Dog Periwinkle, 308, Pl. XXXVII. 16.
  Dog Winkle, 308.
  Fresh-water, 306, 307.
  Fresh-water Limpet, 307.
  Gaper, 312, Pl. XXXVIII. 8.
  Garden Snail, 303.
  Golden Carpet, 313.
  Grey Top, 309, Pl. XXXVII. 5.
  Hairy Snail, 305.
  Horn, 309.
  Horse Mussel, 311, Pl. XXXVIII. 19, 20.
  Hunchback Scallop, 312, Pl. XXXVIII. 15.
  Hungarian Cap, 310.
  Key-hole Limpet, 308, Pl. XXXVII. 11.
  Little Piddock, 312, Pl. XXXVIII. 10, 12.
  Mail, 309.
  Marbled Mail, 309.
  Marine, 307-13.

Shells—*continued*.
  Mussel, 311, Pl. XXXVIII. 21.
  Necklace Natica, 309.
  Netted Dog-whelk, 307, Pl. XXXVII. 7.
  Otter, 313.
  Oyster, 310, Pl. XXXVIII. 16.
  Painted Top, 309, Pl. XXXVII. 14.
  Painter's Mussel, 306.
  Pearl Mussel, 306.
  Pecten, 311.
  Pelican's Foot, 310.
  Periwinkle, 308, Pl. XXXVII. 12.
  Pheasant, 310.
  Piddock, 312, Pl. XXXVIII. 11.
  Pinna, Pl. XXXVIII. 6.
  Pod Razor, 313.
  Pond Snail, 307.
  Purple, 308.
  Purpura, 308, Pl. XXXVII. 13.
  Quin, 311.
  Radiated Scallop, 312, Pl. XXXVIII. 14.
  Ram's Horn, 307.
  Rayed Artemis, 313.
  Rayed Trough, 313.
  Razor, 312, Pl. XXXVIII. 1, 2.
  Red Nose, 311.
  Red-nosed Borer, 312.
  Red Whelk, 308.
  Ruddy Pyramid, 309.
  Sabre Razor, 313, Pl. XXXVIII. 3.
  Saddle Oyster, 311, Pl. XXXVIII. 17.
  Sea Snail, Pl. XXXVII. 4.
  Ship Worm, 312, Pl. XIV. 2, XXXVIII. 4, 5.
  Smooth Artemis, 313.
  Smooth Limpet, 309, Pl. XXXVII. 6.
  Smooth Mail, 309.
  Smooth Margin, 308.
  Smooth Venus, 313.
  Spiny Cockle, 311.
  Staircase, 308.
  Sting Winkle, 307, Pl. XXXVII. 17.
  Striped Snail, 305.
  Sunset, 312, Pl. XXXVIII. 7, 9.
  Swan Mussel, 306.
  Tapes, 313.
  Tellen, 313.
  Thick Tellen, 313.
  Tooth, 310.
  Trough, 313.
  Trumpet Snail, 307.

Shells—*continued*.
  Turret, 309.
  Tusk, 310.
  Univalves, 307-10.
  Unrayed Trough, 313.
  Variable Scallop, 311, Pl. XXXVIII. 13.
  Wedge, 312.
  Wentletrap, 308, Pl. XXXVII. 3.
  Whelp, 307, Pl. XXXVII. 1, XXXIX. 4.
Shield-bugs, 187.
Pentagonal, 187.
Ship Worm, 312, Pl. XIV. 2, XXXVIII. 4, 5.
Shore Lark, 97.
Short-eared Owl, *115, 120.
Shoveller, *129, 138.
Shrew, Common, 29, Pl. V. 4.
  Lesser, 29.
  Water, 29.
Shrike, Great Grey, 84.
  Red-backed, *71, 84.
  Woodchat, 85.
Shrimp, 167.
  Brine, 167.
  Fresh-water, 166.
Shuffle-wing, 87.
Silver-fish, 182.
Silver Lady, Pl. XX. 3.
Siskin, 85.
Skate, 161.
Skua, Arctic, *131, 138.
  Buffon's, 138.
  Great, 138.
  Long-tailed, 138.
  Pomathorine, 138.
Skylark, *71, 85.
Slavonian Grebe, 133.
Slow-worm, 144.
Slugs, 305.
  Black, 305.
  Cellar, 305.
  Sea, 306.
  Sponge, 306.
  Tree, 305.
Smelt, 161.
Smew, 132.
Smolts, 156.
Smooth Artemis, 313.
Smooth Blenny, 162.
Smooth Limpet, 309, Pl. XXXVII.6.
Smooth Newt, 148.
Smooth Snake, 146.
Smooth Venus, 313.
Snails, 303, *304, 305.
  Life-history, 304.
  Beautiful, 305.

Snails—continued.
　Edible, 305, Pl. XII. 2.
　Garden, 303–5.
　Hairy, 305.
　Plated, 305.
　Pond, 307.
　Prickly, 305.
　Rock, 305.
　Roman, 305.
　Sea, Pl. XXXVII. 4.
　Striped, 305.
　Trumpet, 307.
Snake, Common, 145.
　Grass, 145, 146, Pl. XII. 4.
　Ringed, 145.
　Smooth, 146.
Snake-flies, 190.
Snakes, 145, 146, Pl. XII. 4, XIII. 3.
　How to preserve, 146.
　In captivity, 146.
Snipe, Common, 85, *86, *101, 108, Pl. VII. 2.
　Great, 109.
　Jack, *71, 85, *86.
Snow Bunting, 70.
Solan Goose, 132.
Soldier, 154.
" Soldiers and sailors," 209, 210.
Sole, Common, 160.
　Lemon, 160.
　Sand, 160.
Song Thrush, *101, 110, Pl. VII. 4.
South, Mr., *The Moths of the British Isles*, 239.
Spanish Lobster, 168.
Sparling, 161.
Sparrow, Hedge, 55, 86.
　House, 87.
　Mountain, 87.
　Reed, 70.
　Tree, *69, 87.
Sparrow Hawk, *115, 118.
Spawn, 150, 155.
Spider, Garden, 171, 177, Pl. XV. 4, XVI. 1, 2.
　House, 172, 176, Pl. XVI. 3.
　Red, 179.
　Wolf, 172, Pl. XVI. 4.
Spider Crab, Four-horned, 169.
　Large Thorny, 169.
　Slender, 169.
Spiders, 171–9, Pl. XV.–XVII.
　Characteristics, 171.
　Eggs, 172.
　Eyes, *171, *173–*177.
　Families, 173.
　Gossamer, 172.
　In captivity, 172, 175, 178.

Spiders—continued.
　Notes on species, 173–8.
　Preservation, 172, 178.
　Study, 178.
　Webs, 171, 172, Pl. XV.
Spinous Squat Lobster, 168.
Spiny Cockle, 311.
Spiny Lobster, 168.
Spirorbis, 320.
Sponges, 327, *328.
　Life-story, 327.
　Crumb-of-Bread, 328.
　" Mermaid's Gloves," 328.
　Pond, 328.
　River, 328.
Spotted Crake, 111.
Spotted Dog-fish, Lesser, 162.
Spotted Flycatcher, *73, 75.
Spotted Gunnel, 162.
Spotted Rail, 111.
Spotted Woodpecker, Great, 111.
　Lesser, 97.
Sprat, 161.
Spring-tails, 182, Pl. XX. 1.
Squid, 303.
Squirrel, Common, 40, Pl. II. 3.
Squirrel's-tail Coralline, 326.
Starfish, 314, *315, 316, Pl. XXXIX.
　Bird's-foot, 316.
　Brittle-stars, 316, Pl. XXXIX. 2, 3.
　Common Five-fingered, 310, 314.
　Cushion Star, 316.
　Eyed Cribella, 315.
　Feather Stars, 316.
　Gibbous Starlet, 316.
　Red Brittle-star, 316.
　Rosy Feather Star, 316.
　Sea Cucumber, 316.
　Spiny Star, 315.
　Sun Star, 316.
Starling, *101, 109, 474–7, Pl. IX. 1, 2.
Staveley, E. F., *British Spiders*, 177.
Stentor, 329.
Stickleback, Fifteen-spined, 154.
　Ten-spined, 154.
　Three-spined, 154.
Sticklebacks, 154, Pl. XIII. 1.
Sting Fish, 163.
Sting Ray, 161.
Sting Winkle, 307, Pl. XXXVII. 17.
Stoat, 37, Pl. VI. 1.
Stock Dove, 114.
Stock-fish, 159.

Stonechat, *71, 87.
Stone Curlew, 113, *117, Pl. VIII. 1.
Stone-flies, 184.
Storm Petrel, *71, 80.
Sucker, Cornish, 163.
　Two-spotted, 163.
Sunset Shell, 312, Pl. XXXVIII. 7, 9.
Swallow, *73, 88.
Swan, Mute, 138.
Swift, *73, 89. .
Swimming Crab, Common, 169.

Tadpoles, 147.
Tangle Picker, 110.
Tapes, 313.
Tapeworm, 321.
Tawny Owl, *115, 121.
Teal, 123.
Teeth of Mammals, 23 (note).
Telescope, Pocket, 6.
　Diagram of (Fig. 1), 7.
　Fixed to a walking-stick (Fig. 5), 9.
　Objective (Fig. 2), 8.
　Placed on a camera stand (Fig. 4), 9.
　Used as microscope (Fig. 3), 8.
Tellen Shells, 313.
Tench, 153.
Ten-spined Stickleback, 154.
Terebella, 320, Pl. XL. 16.
Termite, 185.
Tern, Arctic, *117, 124.
　Black, 110.
　Common, 124.
　Little, *101, 110.
　Roseate, 110.
　Sandwich, *115, 124.
Thallophyta, 333, 456–69, Pl. XL.
Thick-knee, 113.
Thornback, 169.
Three-bearded Rockling, 163.
Three-spined Stickleback, 154.
Thrip, Corn, 186.
Thrips, 186.
Thrush, Mistle, 109.
　Song, *101, 110, Pl. VII. 4.
Tickner-Edwards, Mr., his observing hive, 299.
Ticks, 179, Pl. XXXII. 5.
Tit, Bearded, 89.
　Blue, 89.
　Bottle, 91.
　British Coal, *71, 90.
　Crested, 90.
　Great, *71, 90.
　Irish Coal, 90.
　Long-tailed, *73, 91.

INDEX

Tit—*continued.*
  Marsh, *73, 91.
  Willow, 91.
Titlark, 81.
Toad, Common, 148.
  Natterjack, 148.
  Running, 148.
Tree-creeper, 72, *73.
Tree Pipit, *71, 81, *82, Pl. VIII. 4.
Tree Sparrow, *69, 87.
Trough Shells, 313.
Trout, Bull, 156.
  Common, 156.
  Great Lake, 156.
  Grey, 156.
  Lochleven, 156.
  Salmon, 156.
  Sea, 156.
Trumpet Snail, 307.
Tube-mouthed Sarsia, 323.
Tufted Duck, 114, *117.
Tunicates, 323, 324.
Turbot, 159.
Turnstone, 110.
Turtle Dove, 100, *101.
Twite, 91.
Two-spotted Sucker, 163.

Vegetable Kingdom, 4, 333.
Velvet Fiddler, 169.
Velvet Scoter, 137.
Venus, Smooth, 313.
Vertebrates, 4, 21.
Viper, 145, 146.
Vole, Bank, 46.
  Short-tailed Field, 45.
  Water, 45, Pl. I. 3.
  Wood, 46.
Vorticella, 329.

Wagtail, Grey, 92.
  Pied, *73, 92.
  Ray's, 92.
  White, 92.
  Yellow, 92.
Warbler, Dartford, *69, 92.
  Garden, 93.
  Grasshopper, 93.
  Marsh, 93.
  Reed, 94.
  Sedge, *71, 94.
  Willow, *73, 94.
  Wood, 94.
Wasps, 295-7, Pl. XXXIII. 1, XXXV. 3.
  Common, 296, Pl. XXXIII. 1.

Wasps—*continued.*
  Cuckoo, 291.
  Digger, 295, 296.
  Giant-tailed, 290, Pl. XXXIII. 1.
  Hornet, 296, Pl. XXXIII. 1.
  Ruby, 291.
  Solitary, 296.
  Wall, 296.
  Wood, 290, 296.
Water-boatman, 187.
Water-bugs, 187.
Water-flea, *165, 166, Pl. XVIII. 3.
Waterhen, *117, 124.
Water-louse, *165, 166.
Water Mite, 179.
Water Newt, Great, 148.
Water Ouzel, *69, 74.
Water-rail, 111.
Water Scorpion, 187.
Water Vole, 45, Pl. I. 3.
Weasel, 37, Pl. III. 1.
Wedge Shells, 312.
Weever, Lesser, 163.
Weevils, 215-17.
Wentletrap, 308.
Whale, "Blue," 26.
  Bottle-nosed, 25.
  Common Beaked, 25.
  Common "Killer," 24.
  Greenland, 25.
  Hump-backed, 25.
  Lesser Killer, 24.
  Pike, 26.
  Pilot, 24.
  Right, 25.
  Southern Right, 25.
  Sowerby's, 25.
  Sperm, 25.
Whales and Porpoises, 22-6.
Wheatear, *73, 95.
Whelk, Common, 307, Pl. XXXVII. 1, 2, XXXIX. 4.
Netted Dog-, 307, Pl. XXXVII. 7.
  Red, 308.
Whimbrel, 125.
Whinchat, *71, *95.
White, Gilbert, on Nightjar, 104.
White Ant, 185.
Whitebait, 160.
White Bream, 153.
White-fronted Goose, 132.
White Owl, 120.
White-tailed Eagle, 130.
Whitethroat, *73, *96.
  Lesser, 96.
  Peggy, 96.

White Wagtail, 92.
Whiting, 158.
Whiting Pout, 158.
Whooper, 138.
Widgeon, 125.
Wild Cat, 38.
  Cattle, 49.
  Sheep, 49.
Wild Duck, 128.
Wild Flowers, 333.
Wilfry, 320.
Willow Tit, 91.
Willow Warbler, *73, 94.
Willow Wren, 94.
Winkle, Dog, 308.
  Sting, 307, Pl. XXXVII. 17.
Wire-worm, 180, 209.
Wolf's Claw, 451, 452.
Wolf Spider, 172, Pl. XVI. 4.
Woodchat Shrike, 85.
Woodcock, *115, 125.
Woodlark, 97.
Wood-louse, 170, 294.
Woodpecker, Great Spotted, 111, 112.
  Green, *101, 112.
  Lesser Spotted, 97.
Wood Pigeon, *115, 122, Pl. VII. 3.
Wood Sandpiper, 108.
Wood Warbler, 94.
Wood-wasps, 290.
  Giant, 290.
  Steel-blue Wasp, 290.
Wood Wren, 94.
Worm, Ship, 312, Pl. XIV. 2.
Worm Pipe, Fish, 163.
Wren, Gold-crested, 75.
  Jenny, *71, 97.
  Willow, *73, 94.
  Wood, 94.
Writing Lark, 72.
Wryneck, *71, 98.

Yaffle, 112.
Yellow Bunting, *69, 70.
Yellowhammer, *69, 70.
Yellow Wagtail, 92.
Young People's Microscope Book, 12, 17, 318, 326.
Young People's Nature Study Book, 6, 35, 223.

Zebedee, 170.
Zoëa, 168.
Zoophytes, 325, 326, Pl. XIV. 1.

PRINTED IN GREAT BRITAIN BY
THOMAS NELSON AND SONS, LTD.

THIS BOOK IS DUE ON THE LAST DATE
STAMPED BELOW

AN INITIAL FINE OF 25 CENTS
WILL BE ASSESSED FOR FAILURE TO RETURN
THIS BOOK ON THE DATE DUE. THE PENALTY
WILL INCREASE TO 50 CENTS ON THE FOURTH
DAY AND TO $1.00 ON THE SEVENTH DAY
OVERDUE.

MAY 12 1942

LD 21-100m-7,'39(402s)

UNIVERSITY OF CALIFORNIA LIBRARY

ImTheStory.com

Personalized Classic Books in many genre's

Unique gift for kids, partners, friends, colleagues

Customize:

- Character Names
- Upload your own front/back cover images (optional)
- Inscribe a personal message/dedication on the inside page (optional)

Customize many titles Including
- Alice in Wonderland
- Romeo and Juliet
- The Wizard of Oz
- A Christmas Carol
- Dracula
- Dr. Jekyll & Mr. Hyde
- And more...

CPSIA information can be obtained
at www.ICGtesting.com
Printed in the USA
BVHW07s1209030718
520735BV00013B/237/P